VADIM ZELAND

REALITY TRANSURFING

STEPS I–V

FOREWORD

DEAR LISTENER,

Everyone wants their life to be comfortable, abundant, free of illness and chaos, and yet we often find that life has its own plans, and can leave us feeling like a little paper boat spinning round on life's turbulent waters. You may have tried all sorts of popular methods aimed at achieving happiness but I wonder how effective you found them if they conformed to the traditional worldview.

This book introduces many strange and wonderful things. It is all so mind-blowing you might not want to believe it. But you will not have to believe. The methods introduced here invite you to test everything out for yourself and when you do, your current worldview will crumble.

Transurfing is a powerful technique aimed at giving you the power to create aspects of your life in a way that would ordinarily seem impossible; In particular, Transurfing will give you the power to control your own destiny as you see fit. I promise no miracles and yet something greater than a miracle awaits you. You will discover that the hidden quality of reality is more extraordinary than any mystic tradition.

There are many books available now on how to become successful, rich and happy. It is a tempting prospect, for who would not want these things? The problem is that when you start reading these self-help books you discover that in order for the technique to work you have to do certain exercises, embark on some serious soul searching, meditate, and straight away, your enthusiasm wanes. For most people life is busy and stressful enough without having to add to the workload by giving yourself any more to do.

The books will tell you that you are imperfect and that change will have to start with yourself otherwise there is no point in hoping for anything more. You might not be entirely satisfied with yourself but deep down you know that you do not really want to change and neither should you have to. Be careful of anyone who tells you that you are less than perfect, for how could anyone else possibly know how you are meant to be? If you are told that you must change yourself in order to achieve the things you want in life the solution is not where you were looking for it.

The main idea of Transurfing is based on the existence of the alternatives space which stores the scripts of all possible events. The number of alternatives is infinite just like the number of possible points on a coordinate graph is infinite. In the alternatives space is written everything that was, is, or ever will be. Under certain conditions, a person's thought energy can materialise a given sector of the alternatives space.

A potential alternative is embodied in physical reality like a reflection in the mirror of alternatives. The individual is capable of shaping their own reality as long as they observe certain rules. The mind tries unsuccessfully to influence the reflection. Instead you have to change the image that is being reflected.

In this book we are not going to do exercises, meditate or obsess with the self. Transurfing is not so much a new method of self-improvement as a fundamentally different way of thinking and behaving in order to get what you desire out of life. It implies exactly this–to get what you desire from life, rather than having to fight for it. The method of Transurfing is not aimed at changing the self. It offers a way of returning to self.

We all make mistakes in life and then think how wonderful it would be if we could turn back the clock and put everything right. I am not promising you a "train ticket back to your childhood", but mistakes can be put right and doing so is a bit like returning to the past, or even stepping 'forward into the past'. The meaning of these words will become clearer towards the end of the book. You will not have heard or read anywhere else the things I am going to tell you here, so be prepared for the unexpected as enjoyable as it is surprising.

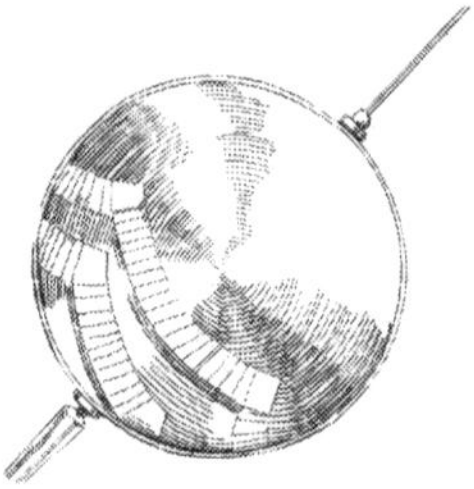

Chapter I. THE ALTERNATIVES MODEL

Dreams Don't Come True

The Rustle of the Morning Stars

I was woken by the neighbour's dog barking. The nasty animal was always waking me up. How I hated it! Why should I have to be woken up by the noise of someone else's pet? I decided to go out for a walk, calm down and distract myself from the intense desire to set fire to my neighbour's house. They say dogs are like their owners. This one was. There always seemed to be some idiot in my life trying to get me down. Feeling stressed I started to get dressed. My slippers had disappeared again. Where are you, you sneaky little buggers? When I find you I will chuck you out!

It was foggy and damp outside. I walked along the slippery path through the gloomy forest. Almost all the leaves had fallen, exposing the grey trunks of half-dead trees. Why do I live in the middle of this depressing bog? I reached for a cigarette. I didn't really want one, but old habits told me I needed one. Need? At what point had I become addicted to cigarettes? It's not very pleasant smoking in the morning on an empty stomach. I used to be a social smoker. It had been fashionable, a symbol of freedom and style. But the party ends and the grey, drizzle of everyday life sets in, bringing with it problems in patches like slimy puddles. You smoke each problem away several times as if saying to yourself: "I'll just have this quick smoke, catch my breath and then launch myself back into the dreaded routine."

The smoke got in my eyes making them sting, so I placed my hands over them for a minute like an upset child. I was so fed up of everything. As if reading my thoughts, a birch branch bent spitefully and hit me hard on the forehead. Bastard! In my outrage I broke the branch in half and threw it to one side. The branch got caught in a tree and bounced from side to side and sprang up and down like a jack in a box as if mocking my inability to change any aspect of my world. Feeling very low I pushed on.

Every time I tried to battle with the world it would at first yield, giving me false hope, only then to come back at me with a hard slap. It's only in films that the hero sets off towards his goal casting aside anything and everything that stands in the way. In reality, things are a bit different. Life is like a game of roulette. You win once, twice, even three times. You imagine yourself the prizewinner with the world at your feet but always end up with less than you started. You are just the turkey fattened up to be roasted and devoured to the sounds of happy music and laughter. You were fooling yourself. It's not your lucky day. You made a mistake...

Wallowing in dark thoughts I arrived at the beach. Sharp waves were biting viciously at the sandy shore. The cold, damp sea breeze blew at me bitterly. Fat sea gulls wandered the shoreline, lazily pecking at rotten waste. Their eyes carried a cold, black empty look as if reflecting the cold and antagonism of the world around me.

A tramp was collecting empty bottles on the beach. I wished he would disappear. I wanted to be alone but he was walking towards me, probably wanting to scrounge something. I decided to go home. Was there no peace anywhere? I was so tired. I realised that the feeling of tiredness never left me, even when I was relaxing. At some point I had started killing time as if sitting out a prison sentence. I was always waiting for things to change, for a new stage in my life to begin where I would be different and able to enjoy life, but that stage was always somewhere in the future. In the meantime it was the same old drudgery. I kept waiting but the better future remained as elusive as ever. I would return home and do the same thing I always did; eat a boring breakfast and then leave for my dull job, forcing myself to produce results which mattered to someone else but not to me. It would be just another day of the same tiresome, meaningless life.

I was woken by the rustle of the morning stars. What a sad dream. It was as if I had returned to a period in my past. Thank goodness it was only a dream. I stretched with relief just like my cat does. There he was lying lazily sprawled out–only his ears giving any sign that he was aware of my presence. Get up you whiskered thing. Are you coming with me for a walk? I had placed an order for a sunny day and so set off towards the sea.

The path led through the forest and the rustle of the morning stars gradually faded, giving way to the multi-voiced choir of the bird nation. Someone in the bushes was trying especially hard "Food! Food!" There he was the little wretch. However can such a little ball of fluff squawk so loudly? Only now did it occur to me that although every bird had a different voice, none were ever out of tune with the rest of the choir. They always managed to produce such a graceful symphony; no orchestra, however sophisticated could be favourably compared.

The sun stretched its rays between the trees, creating a magical backlighting that highlighted the voluminous depth and richness of the colours of the forest and transforming it into one miraculous hologram. The path led me diligently towards the sea. The emerald waves exchanged whisperings with the warm sea breeze. The shore seemed endless and empty but I felt comfortable and at peace as if the overpopulated world had created a secluded corner just for me. Some people believe the world is an illusion created by the mind but I could not imagine having such a high opinion of myself that I could think all this beauty was the product of my own consciousness.

Still feeling the effect of my oppressive dream I began to reminisce about my former life, which had actually been as dull and gloomy as my dream. Like a lot of people, I had often demanded that the world give me all I felt it owed me but in response it had turned its back on me in indifference. I was advised by others wiser and more experienced than myself not to give up because the world doesn't give up that easily either. "You have to fight for what you want". So I tried battling with the world but I didn't get anywhere and ended up exhausted. My advisers had a ready answer for this too. "You are the problem. Change yourself before you start demanding things of life". So, I battled with myself but this turned out to be even harder than battling with the world.

Then one day, I dreamed that I was in a nature reserve. In the dream I was surrounded by indescribable beauty. I was walking through the reserve and admiring the full wonder of it all when I came across an angry old man with a grey beard who, as far as I could make out, was the Guardian of the Reserve. He watched me in silence. I walked up to him but as soon as I opened my mouth to speak he cut across me. In a cold tone he said that he didn't want to hear a word; he was tired of noisy and capricious visitors who were constantly displeased, always making demands and left mountains of rubbish after themselves. I nodded in sympathy and walked on.

I was amazed by the unique beauty of the reserve and wondered why I hadn't visited it before. Enchanted, I continued to wander around taking in the magnificence on all sides. No words could fully describe the perfection of the landscape. My mind went blank in stunned admiration.

Soon the Guardian appeared before me again. The austere look on his face had softened and he beckoned for me to follow. We climbed to the top of a green hill and from there the spectacular view of a picturesque valley opened before us. I could make out some kind of village with toy houses decorated with plants and flowers like an illustration in a book of fairy-tales. Had the scene before me appeared more real I could have stood regarding it with delight for some time. As it was, I started to suspect that such fabulous beauty was the stuff of dreams and not real life. I turned to the Guardian with a questioning look but he just sneered into his beard as if to say: "We're only just getting started!"

As we descended into the valley below it began to dawn on me that I could not remember how I had arrived at the reserve. I was hoping the old man could give me an explanation. Then I must have made some clumsy remark about how it must feel pretty damn good to be one of the lucky ones who could afford to live in such a beautiful place, to which, openly displaying his irritation, the Guardian replied: "Who is stopping you from joining them?"

I started to go on about how not everyone was born rich and we don't choose our fate. The Guardian ignored my words and said: "That's the point. Everyone is free to choose *any* destiny they wish. The only freedom we truly have is the freedom of choice. You can choose anything you want."

His statement did not at all fit with my philosophy of life and I made to argue with him, but the Guardian would not listen: "Fool!" he said. "You have the right to choose, but you don't exercise it. You do not even understand what '*to choose*' really means." This is ridiculous, I thought. What does he mean by, "I can choose whatever I want"? Anyone would think that you could just conjure up anything you wanted. At that moment I suddenly realised that I was dreaming. The situation threw me and I did not know how to behave.

As far as I can recollect I hinted to the old man that he could choose to speak rubbish whether in a dream or in waking but there ended the extent of his freedom. My comment did not seem to bother the Guardian at all; in fact he laughed in response. Aware of how ridiculous the situation was (what was the point of getting into a debate with a figure from my own dream?) I was considering whether it would be better to wake myself up. As if reading my mind the old man said: "That's enough. We don't have much time. I hadn't expected them to send me a moron like you, but I must carry on with my mission nonetheless."

I was going to ask him what his 'mission' was, and who 'they' were but he ignored me, instead giving me a riddle, which at the time seemed quite absurd: *"Everyone can have the freedom to choose whatever they want; but here's a riddle for you: how do you acquire that freedom? When you guess the answer correctly your apples will fall to the sky."*

What apples? I was beginning to loose patience and said that I had no intention of solving any riddles. Miracles only happened in dreams and fairy-tales. In reality, apples generally fall to the ground, to which he replied: "That's enough! Let's go. There is something I must show you."

Regrettably, when I woke up I could not remember the end of the dream. However, I did have the distinct feeling that although I was unable to express it consciously, the Guardian had imparted some kind of information to me. Just one word seeped through into my mind but I had no idea what it meant: *Transurfing*. The thought I found going round my mind was that I did not have to totally furnish my world myself; that everything that was to be mine had been created long ago without my participation but for my own well-being. There was absolutely no point in battling with the world for a place under the sun, and no-one was stopping me from simply choosing the life I wanted to have.

At first the idea seemed absurd. I would probably have forgotten all about it if I had not to my amazement soon afterwards started having very clear recollections of what the Guardian meant by the word 'choose', and how to actually make a choice. The answer to the Guardian's riddle came to me of its own accord; as knowledge does sometimes seem to come from nowhere. Every day I learned something new and each time I felt huge surprise, sometimes bordering on fear. I can give no rational explanation of how this knowledge came to me but of one thing I am certain. I could never have made it up myself.

Ever since I discovered Transurfing (or rather, since I was given it to discover) my life has been filled with joyful meaning. Anyone who has ever been involved in some kind of creative work will know the happiness and fulfilment that comes with creating something with your own hands. Imagine then the feeling of creating your own destiny. Even the expression 'to create your own destiny' as it is interpreted in its usual sense, fails to describe what I mean here. Transurfing is a method that frees you to choose your own destiny, literally like you would choose something in a supermarket. I want to share this with you so that you can understand why 'apples fall to the sky', why the 'morning stars rustle', and many other curious things.

The Guardian's Riddle

There are different interpretations of the nature of fate. One interpretation is that fate is your lot in life, something predetermined and which however hard you try, you can never escape. This definition is rather limiting as it suggests that if a rough lot has befallen you in life there is no hope of anything ever getting any better. Despite this, there will always be those who willingly accept this definition of fate because it is convenient. They would rather life be reliable and the future more or less predictable than live with the fear of uncertainty.

Nonetheless, the total inevitability implied by this interpretation of fate leaves one feeling dissatisfied and even a little resentful. People who are deprived of good luck lament their fate and naturally question why life is so unfair. Why is it that some people have more than they could ever desire, while others never seem to have enough? Why is it that things come easily to some, while others never achieve results however hard they try? Some people are endowed with natural beauty, intellect and strength, while others seem to have an inferior goods label stuck to their forehead for their entire life as if paying for some kind of previously committed sin. Why does such inequality exist? Why does life in its endless diversity place limits on certain groups of people and where exactly did those less lucky go wrong?

People often feel hurt and indignant when they realize they are less fortunate than others and they search for an explanation for their circumstances. This is when many people turn to teachings that support ideas such as karma and retribution for sins committed in previous lives. One would think that all the Lord our God had to do with his time was discipline his naughty children and that despite his omnipotence he evidently struggles with the parenting side of things, putting off the punishment of retribution until a later date. One wonders what the point could be of punishing a person for something they do not actually remember doing.

Another popular explanation for inequality spreads the false hope that those who suffer and live their lives in need will later receive generous compensation, although it is not clear whether good fortune awaits them in heaven or in a future life. Whatever the arrangement, explanations like these can never leave one fully satisfied. Whether past and future lives exist or not is also of little significance. You can only be aware of the life you are living now and so in this sense, it is the only one you have.

If you believe that your fate is predetermined then the best remedy for the despondence you may feel is acceptance. There will always be people around to give you good advice like, "If you want to be happy just be happy! Be optimistic; be satisfied with what you have." There will always be someone to tell you that the cause of your unhappiness is your own constant complaining and unrealistic expectations of life and that you could be happy by definition if you would simply reconnect with your inner *joie de vivre*. You might half-heartedly agree whilst at the same time awkwardly acknowledging how uninspired you really feel about greeting your dull life with new-found joy. Surely we have the right to expect more. Why should we have to force ourselves to be happy when it is as futile as trying to force yourself to love someone?

Then there are the "enlightened" individuals preaching universal love and forgiveness. Their world is like a blanket of illusion that you can pull up over your head to protect yourself from encountering the severity of life head on, and everything does get a little easier as a result. Deep down however, it is still difficult to comprehend why you should forgive those you hate and love those you have no genuine feeling for. What good is happiness if it is faked? Surely happiness should come naturally rather than being squeezed from the soul like the last drop of toothpaste from a tube.

There are others who refuse to believe that life is boring and primitive enough to be reduced to predetermined fate. This type of person would rather be satisfied with what they have managed to achieve by their own abilities than accept the lot they have been dealt. This is a different perception of fate whereby you make your own luck and good luck has to be fought for. That is just how it is. Wise people will tell you that life is not given to anyone on a plate and that if you are not satisfied with what you have, you must dig your heels in and work hard to attain the happiness you want.

The history books describe brave heroes who fought and laboured day and night, overcoming unimaginable obstacles. The victors were rewarded with the laurels of success but only after suffering all the burdens and privations of battle. This take on fate is not very logical either. Millions of people battle and labour but true success comes to but a few. You can spend your entire life struggling desperately for a place under the sun and yet get nowhere. Why would life be so cruel and unyielding?

What a heavy burden it is to have to battle with the world to get what you want and if the world does not respond, to have to battle with yourself. How hard it is to believe that if you are poor, ill, ugly or unlucky it is your own fault; that you are flawed and so must change. These ideas suggest that you are an accumulation of various shortcomings and defects which must be worked on. Unless you are lucky enough to be born rich and happy, your lot in life is either to humbly bear your own cross or dedicate your entire life to fighting against it. It is somehow not a view of life that readily fills the heart with joy. Surely, there is a glimmer of hope among these dismal beliefs.

Fortunately, there is a glimmer of hope that comes from a totally different view of things. The solution is as simple as it is enjoyable in contrast to the other views described above. In Transurfing the concept of fate is based on an alternative model of the universe. Before you wave your hand in disappointment and decide that you are being fed yet another chimera, remember, that every known concept of fate originates from a specific worldview, which in turn, is based on a number of unproven principles.

For example, materialism is founded on the proposition that matter is primary and consciousness is secondary. Idealism claims the opposite. Neither of these philosophies has been proven, and yet models of the universe are constructed around both. Each model is convincing enough and has its loyal defenders. Both materialism and idealism explain the phenomenon of the world via philosophy, science and religion, and both are right and both are wrong in their own ways. Man will never be able to describe absolute truth with total accuracy because the notions used in our attempts to describe the truth are of themselves relative. There is a well known parable about three blind men who describe an elephant by studying it with their hands. The first blind man touches the elephant's trunk; the second touches the leg, and the third touches ear. Each draws conclusions about what kind of animal the elephant represents based on their own findings. It would be pointless to try and prove that only one description of the three is correct. What is important is that the description be relevant and applicable.

You have no doubt heard the idea expressed that reality is an illusion created by the mind, but no one has explained in detail where the illusion comes from.

Does it mean that we are all in a sense watching a film? Of course, it is highly unlikely that a concrete, rational substantiation of this idea will ever be upheld. Others hold the opposite opinion that the material world is simply a mechanism which functions according to its own immutable laws and cannot be governed by human consciousness. There is surely an irrefutable grain of truth in this idea.

The human mind likes to have its feet on solid ground free of ambiguity and so for centuries scholars have been tearing one theory to pieces in favour of another which is then placed high on a pedestal. After every fight on the intellectual battlefield for truth just one fact remains undefeated: *every theory represents a separate aspect of the phenomenon of a multi-faceted reality.*

Each theory that stands the test of time has its place for they all represent one aspect of reality. If you decide that fate is something predestined that you cannot personally change, then this is how it will be. In effect you are voluntarily giving yourself to the will of others, becoming like a small boat floating at the mercy of the waves. If however, you decide that you can create your own destiny then you will consciously take responsibility for everything that happens in your life, battling against the waves in an attempt to sail your little boat. You may have noticed that *whatever you choose is always manifested. What you choose is what you get.* Whatever worldview you choose to believe in, the truth of that worldview will always be on your side and others will argue with you because they too are right.

Any aspect of reality can be taken as a starting point and subsequently developed into a whole field of knowledge and it will have logical consistency and successfully reflect one manifestation of reality. An entire field of knowledge can be substantiated by just one fact which although not fully understood, has its place.

For example, quantum physics is based on a number of unproven truths and postulates which cannot be proven because they serve as the basic starting point for a given field of knowledge. In quantum physics a microcosm sometimes acts as a particle and sometimes as a wave. Unable to provide an unambiguous explanation for such dualism, scientists took the phenomenon to be an axiom. The postulates of quantum physics bring together different aspects of reality in all its diversity of form, just like the blind men in the parable in one case proclaimed that the elephant functions like a stump and in another, like a snake.

If in describing the microcosm one chooses to start with its particle quality as fundamental then one arrives at the model of the atom created by the famous physicist Neils Bohr. In the Bohr Model the electrons rotate around the nucleus like the planets in the solar system. If on the other hand, one takes the main quality to be the wave then the model of the atom will look like a blurry dot. Both models work reflecting different manifestations of reality. In this case too, one could say that the scientists *get what they choose.*

Any manifestation of reality can serve as a postulate, or the basis for an argument which will undoubtedly make sense and have its place. In search of truth people have always striven to understand the nature of the world, studying its individual parts. Bodies of scientific knowledge were created to describe and explain the various phenomenon of nature and often they contradict each other.

The nature of the world is one but it reveals itself to us in many guises. As soon as one face has been studied and explained another appears that does not fully correspond to the first. Scientists have attempted to overcome these contradictions by encompassing the diverse manifestations of reality in a single model of the universe, but this is no easy task. There is one irrefutable fact that unites and reconciles all branches of knowledge and that is the diverse and multifaceted nature of reality. *Variability is the world's most fundamental quality.*

For some reason, the defenders of different fields of knowledge disregard this fact in their attempts to describe individual phenomenon, despite the fact that there is so much that could be learned from it. Variability is a key reference point, just like zero is the main reference point on a coordinate grid. Any starting point for a particular area of knowledge is secondary in relation to this key reference point of variability and yet it is bypassed as if it held no information. Nonetheless, it does carry information and information of quite an extraordinary nature.

To solve the Guardian's riddle we will take the quality of variability as a starting point. In other words, we will take as a postulate the fact that *reality manifests itself in an infinite variety of forms*. Despite the very general nature of this postulate it reveals quite fascinating knowledge.

We start with the idea that all diverse manifestations of reality originate in a common source. The world manifests itself as movement of matter through time and space and this movement is subject to certain laws. As you know, points are plotted on a graph in accordance with mathematical formula. You could say that the function which determines how points are plotted on a graph is also a law. So where are the laws of the universe 'written'? Formulae like laws are but an abstract product of the human mind created for the convenience of expressing concepts. It is highly unlikely that the laws of nature are recorded anywhere.

Could a graph be created that marked the position of all points of matter? Of course, one could theoretically mark the coordinates of the infinite number of all existing points in the universe but the capacity of the human memory is too limited to cope with such a massive volume of data. Nature on the other hand has no difficulty with eternity. Nature has no need of a formula to generalize the position and movement of points on a graph. If the graph line were to be broken up into infinitely small points then every point could be seen as a cause and the next point as the consequent effect, whereby any movement of a point of matter through time and space could be perceived as an infinite chain of infinitesimal examples of cause and effect.

In science, we describe the movement of matter in terms of laws but in nature this movement exists in its natural form as the infinite flow of cause and effect. Generally speaking, information concerning all possible points along the path of moving matter is stored in an information field which we refer to here as the *alternatives space*. The field contains information about everything that ever has been, is, and ever will be.

The *alternatives space* is a material *information structure*. It is an infinite field containing information on all possible scenarios of any event that could ever possibly take place. One could say that the alternatives space contains absolutely everything. We can hardly guess the form this information takes and yet our purpose here does not require us to know this. The important thing is to establish that *the alternatives space serves as a template or coordinate grid for the movement of all matter in time and space.*

Every point in space contains its own version of a given event. For the ease of understanding let us say that each variation or version has a script and scenery. The scenery is the external form of a phenomenon, whereas the script is the path that matter moves along. For the sake of convenience the alternatives space can be said to have different sectors. The greater the distance between the sectors, the more the script and scenery will differ. A person's destiny also has numerous alternatives.

Theoretically speaking, there are no limits to the scripts and sceneries of human existence because the alternatives space is infinite. Any seemingly insignificant event can affect a twist of fate. A person's life, just like any other movement of matter represents a chain of cause and effect events. In the alternatives space the effect is always located in close proximity to its cause. One follows the other and so the sectors of a person's destiny create a *life line.* The scripts and settings of the sectors on one line are more or less uniform. A person's life flows evenly in one direction, until such time as an event occurs that changes the scripts and sceneries. When this happens destiny takes a turn and shifts to another life line.

Experiencing life lines placed very close together is like watching a play and then the next day going to the theatre again to see the same play but this time the stage scenery is different. If during the next theatre season you saw the play with the same actors but there had been significant changes to the script this would be like experiencing a life line situated slightly further away in the alternatives space. Finally, if you watched the same production in a different theatre you would see a totally different interpretation of the play and this would be like experiencing a life line that exists a significant distance from the first.

Reality has such diversity of form because the number of alternatives for its manifestation is limitless. Any starting point for one or another form of manifestation results in a chain of cause and effect relationships. One could say that reality unfolds through life depending on the selection of the original reference point and so ultimately, everyone gets what they choose. You have the right to choose precisely because an eternal number of alternatives already exist. No-one is preventing you from choosing the destiny you would feel comfortable having. Managing your own destiny comes down to one single thing – *making the choice.* Transurfing shows you how to make that choice.

So, an information structure exists that contains an infinite number of potential alternatives each with its own unique script and scenery. The process of transformation into physical reality corresponds to that laid down in the information structure. How matter moves through the alternatives space can be demonstrated by the following metaphor.

Imagine a water pipe with a cooling ring that moves slowly along the pipe causing the water inside it to freeze. The effect of the cooling ring makes it look as if a crystal of ice is moving through the water. Water molecules tend to remain in roughly the same place in a relatively free state. At the moment that the cooling ring passes through a given section of water the molecules inside the ring are solidified into a frozen crystal. As the ring moves further down the pipe, the frozen water in the area behind the ring melts again and the molecules are freed up. It is not the crystal itself that moves. In other words, it is not a single chunk of ice that floats through the water, but the potential to create the structure of ice, i.e. the frozen state.

The water in the pipe serves as an analogy for the alternatives space and the crystal of ice as an analogy for the material manifestation of a particular alternative. The water molecules are like people and their position in the crystal structure is like a manifestation in physical reality of one possible fate. There is no single answer to the question of what the cooling ring symbolises. In other words, how and why the information structure transforms into physical matter, no one can say. In a microcosm, matter can behave as a bundle of energy. We know that in a vacuum for example, micro particles undergo a continual process of birth and annihilation suggesting that matter is present and yet does not represent a physical substance. The one thing that is clear is that the things we can touch have an intangible energetic foundation to them.

I hope I have not overwhelmed the listener with too much physics, particularly as we are just at the very beginning of Transurfing. The things you learn in this book may come as a bit of a surprise, so naturally, I offer some theoretical substantiation just to help the mind keep a firm footing. Do be patient.

The wave is another analogy for the process of physical manifestation in which the sea is the alternatives space and the wave the material manifestation of a given alternative. Take a wave that forms in the sea after an earthquake. It looks like the wave moves across the surface of the sea in a hump, but in fact, the water remains in the same place. It is not a mass of water that is moving across the sea so much as the energetic potential for transformation into physical reality. It is only when the accumulation of water finally reaches the shore that it breaks on the ground. Any other wave behaves in the same manner.

Does this mean that material manifestation moves through time and space while the potential alternatives remain in one place for eternity in the space of everything that was, is, and will be? Why not? Time of itself is as static as space. The passing of time is only felt when it turns like film footage, one shot following another. If you unroll the film and look at all the frames put together, there is no time because all the frames exist simultaneously. Time is static until we start looking at each frame in sequence. It is the same in life, which is why the idea that everything comes and goes is so deeply rooted in our minds.

Everything that is recorded in the field of information has always been there and will always be there. Life lines exist like a reel of film. Things that have happened in the past do not just disappear and what has yet to be in the future is already present here in the now. The current section of a person's life is a material manifestation of the alternatives space in this section of their life line.

This idea might be slightly perturbing and you may be asking yourself how it is possible for countless alternatives of your own fate to exist simultaneously in stasis. Who is responsible for this, God or the laws of Nature perhaps? Imagine a point on a coordinate grid. In school we are taught that any point on the grid can have any *x and y* coordinate from minus to plus infinity and yet it does not occur to anyone to ask why a point can have absolutely any coordinate. Imagine if the point that moves along the function line were surprised and asked: "How can this be that the path I have travelled so far has always existed and always will and how can it be that the path I am about to travel has already been outlined in advance?" It would seem strange to the point but not to you because you are observing its path from above able to see things from a different perspective.

The alternatives space serves as a template that determines how physical reality can show itself. Imagine a person walking through a dark forest with a torch. In the dark the person holding the torch lights up a small area around themselves. The entire forest is like the alternatives space while the area which is lit up is like the physical manifestation of the alternative in that area. The question remains as to what provides the light; in other words, what 'ignites', i.e. materializes a particular alternative within the template.

To answer this question we need to take a different starting point. Nowadays most people agree that thoughts are material. There is also evidence that reality takes two forms: on the one hand material existence defines consciousness and on the other hand there is clear evidence to the contrary indicating that consciousness also defines physical existence. Therefore, thoughts not only provide the motivation for human action, they also have a direct influence on our reality. For example, our worst expectations generally tend to come true. Of course one could argue that this is not because our thoughts were materialized but rather that our thoughts were a premonition of impending misfortune that would have occurred anyway. There is undoubtedly much that is unclear and ambiguous about paranormal phenomena. However, that does not mean that one should ignore or negate the relationship between thought and the process of material realization. Much evidence exists to indicate the direct impact of thought on reality.

One way or another, individual consciousness shapes a person's destiny. This book focuses specifically on how this is possible. *Thought energy transforms possible alternatives into physical reality.* This statement is correct because reality can be manifested in any form defined by consciousness. Evidence of this hypothesis can be found not only in everyday life but also in the experiments of quantum physics. For our purposes, the specific mechanism by which thought energy interacts with the alternatives space is of no great consequence. It is not yet clear by what means the transfer of information takes place, whether on an energetic level or by some other means. For convenience sake we will simply work with the idea that thought energy 'lights up' a certain sector of the alternatives space, as a result of which, one alternative is transformed into physical reality. Waves of thought energy find the sector in the alternatives space that corresponds in quality. The alterative of that sector is then made manifest on the physical level, marking the process of how consciousness creates reality.

You should bear in mind that this is only one way of manifesting reality. Generally speaking it is not possible to create the reality you desire simply by sitting in one place and contemplating it. Although people do exist who are capable of materializing objects literally out of air, they are very few in number and as a rule do not advertise their abilities. Nonetheless, thoughts have as much impact on a person's destiny as concrete actions do. People are used to the idea that there is a visible and clearly comprehensible connection between their actions and the consequences of them. By contrast, the impact of one's thoughts manifests imperceptibly and so appears inexplicable and unpredictable. It might seem difficult to determine a causal relationship between one's thoughts and subsequent events, but soon you will see that the connection is quite direct. A person gets what they choose.

Some may conclude that I seem to be saying that the seas, mountains, planets and the galaxy are all just a product of their personal thought energy. This is because people have a tendency to consider themselves the centre of the universe, whereas in actual fact they are just a tiny dot in infinite space. The world is inhabited by millions of living organisms and *every single one of them contributes to the creation of reality*. Every living being has its own characteristic thought energy. If you are not comfortable viewing plants as capable of 'thought', then you can refer to the process differently; it does not change the nature of the phenomenon. Nobody can say with certainty that inert objects do not have a quality similar to the thought energy emanated by living beings, to say nothing of the One Spirit, permeating all things, which we call God. Every being has consciousness and forms the layer which makes up its own world. One could say that everything in this world carries a particle of God and this is how he governs the whole world.

We all live in the same world and yet every individual moves along their own life line. The qualities of the material world are the same for everybody; it is just that its concrete realization is unique within the context of a person's life. For example, imagine that you are a tourist walking around a beautiful city. You admire the sites and the architecture. You take in the flower beds, the fountains, the park avenues and the smiling faces of the city's prosperous inhabitants. Then as you pass by a rubbish bin you see a homeless person. He is in the same city as you, and the same dimension but he does not see what you see. He sees an empty bottle in the bin, a dirty wall, his competitor who wanted the bottle too and a policeman eyeing him with suspicion. You live on one life line and the homeless man on another. Your life lines intersected at a point in the alternatives space, bringing you together into the same world in the dimension of physical reality.

All manifestation of a material nature has an energetic foundation. The energy field is primary and all physical manifestation is secondary. Scientists attempt to unite different manifestations of energy within the context of a single theory and soon they will achieve good results. However, they will find that they have to keep adding many more things to the theory because reality takes an infinite number of forms. Without going into too much detail we will take energy to be an abstract force which is invisible but nonetheless exists. For our purposes it is enough to accept the fact that the energy of human thought is material. Thought energy does not just spin round inside a person's head; it flows out into the space beyond the head and interacts with the wider energy field around us. Few would dispute this fact now.

For convenience sake we can talk about the parameter of thought energy that is frequency, just as radio waves have a frequency. Whenever you think about something in particular the frequency of your thoughts becomes attuned to a certain area within the alternatives space. When the thought energy reaches the relevant sector in the alternatives space the potential reality held within that sector begins to materialize. Energy has a highly complex structure and permeates everything that exists in the world. When energy passes through the human body it is modified by that person's thoughts. By the time it exits the body it has acquired the same parameters as the thoughts. A radio transmitter works in the same way. Energy absorbs the characteristics of the thoughts of one's mind. When energy exits the human body it radiates outwards in a thought wave that in turn transforms the sector of the alternatives space into physical reality. Whenever you think about something be it negative or positive you are radiating thought energy in the alternatives space. Modified energy accumulates in a specific sector of the field and this has the effect of introducing corresponding changes into your life.

The circumstances of a person's life are not only created by their actions but also by the nature of their thoughts. If a person has a hostile attitude towards the world, they will find the world responds to them with the same. If a person constantly expresses dissatisfaction, they will find more and more reasons to be dissatisfied. If a person's attitude to life is predominantly negative, the world will show them the worst side of its nature. Conversely, having a positive attitude is the most natural way to change your life for the better. People get what they choose. Like it or not, that is how life works.

Whilst your thoughts are pretty much homogenous you will stay on the same life line. As soon as your relationship to reality changes in any way the parameters of thought energy take on new characteristics and the material manifestation of the layer of your world shifts to another line. On this new line events unfold according to a different script in accordance with the parameters of thought. If for some reason you dislike the new script you will struggle to change the situation. People tend to react negatively when they come up against obstacles, expressing their dissatisfaction or falling into despair. As a result, the thought energy they radiate refocuses to a line on which the number of obstacles is even greater making it seem as if their life is a slippery slope.

It might seem as if this process cannot be controlled but in fact the individual is in control and it is their own thoughts that are directing the path of material realization into problematic areas of the alternatives space. People think that obstacles can be overcome by action but in actual fact they ultimately experience whatever their dominant thoughts are. So if you choose to battle against the obstacles on your path you will experience an abundance of obstacles. If you are absorbed by thoughts about your own problems you will find that there are always problems in your life. Even if you take action to change the situation on your current life line on the material level it will not change the original script in the alternatives space. All you can effectively do is *choose a different script*. By trying to change parts of the script you do not like you inevitably get caught up thinking about what you do not like. Your thoughts are then successfully realised and *you end up getting what you do not want.*

You cannot change anything about the current life line just as in an art gallery you cannot take away or reconstruct exhibitions that are not to your taste as you are not the owner. However, no-one is to stop you from turning round and walking into the next room to look at something you can appreciate more. Of course, the shift to a life line in which everyone gets what they want on demand does not happen simply by wishing for it. Not all thoughts can be realized and not all desires are fulfilled. The reason for this is not the content of a person's thoughts so much as their quality. A dream or a wish does not qualify as a choice. *Dreams do not come true.* To create the reality you want you have to observe certain conditions which you will read about later in this book.

The alternatives space contains an infinite number of possible life lines for every individual. No-one should feel hard done by if they do not like their fate, because everyone has the right to *choose*. The problem is that we do not know how to choose. The world has such diversity of form one would think it was created to satisfy any need. Everyone can find whatever their heart desires. Even in the academic world life manifests the side of it we wish to see. For example, idealism holds that the world is an illusion, and life agrees. Materialism says the opposite, and again the world has nothing against that. People argue with each other, trying to force others to accept their relationship to the world, and yet the world shows that they are all right. Is that not wonderful? The alternatives space is the so-called illusion and material realization is what is meant by physical reality. We always get what we choose.

Those who are familiar with the principles of Islam will understand what is meant by "a person's fate is written in the Book". This means that fate is preordained and therefore cannot be changed or avoided. Similar statements can be found in other religions. In a sense, a person's destiny is indeed already preordained. The error of religion is in teaching that there is just one version of a person's fate when in fact there are endless alternatives. They say you cannot avoid your own fate and to some extent this is true because it is impossible to change the script within any given alternative of it. To battle with the world around you in the hope of changing your fate is a difficult and thankless task. It is not worth trying to change the script. It is far more effective to choose a different alternative more to your liking.

Of course, this is all quite strange and you may quite reasonably have your doubts. I do not expect anyone to accept the alternatives model just like that. I did not believe in it myself until I became convinced that it actually works and flawlessly at that. It makes no sense to give preference to one model of the universe over another just for the sake of some absolute truth. It is not the model itself that has meaning so much as what it can help you achieve. Different mathematical models can illustrate the same physical phenomenon in different ways. It would be hilarious if specialists in analytical geometry suddenly took up arms against mathematical analysis and tried to prove that geometry is the only true mathematical discipline. Mathematicians have been able to agree among themselves, but philosophers and religious leaders have not.

It is difficult to say where the alternatives space actually is. From the point of view of our three-dimensional reality one could say that it is everywhere and nowhere. Imagine an endless surface without beginning and without end inhabited by two-dimensional people. These people would not suspect that a third dimension exists. They would believe that the surface they live on is the only world that exists and could not imagine that anything else existed beyond it. We know though, that a third dimension should be added to this model, and that an infinite number of similar surfaces could be created. So there is no need to be concerned if you cannot visualize an infinite number of parallel worlds aside from our own. It is just a matter of perspective.

It is hard to believe in the existence of parallel worlds. Having said that, how easy is it to believe in the theory of relativity, which claims that an accelerating body increases its mass, reduces its size and slows down the time through which it moves? It is impossible to test the theory firsthand but that does not matter. It does not matter whether we understand a theory. What matters is the practical benefit that can be derived from it.

In the context of infinite space it is ridiculous and even petty to argue about the advantages of one model over another. Try to imagine the infinite in terms of increasing distance that never reaches a horizon. Oddly enough, infinity in terms of decreasing distance has no limit either. We can observe only a limited portion of the visible universe for telescopes and microscopes have their limits too. Nonetheless, infinity in the context of the microcosm is no different from infinity in terms of the macrocosm.

There is a theory that the visible universe emerged as a result of the 'Big Bang'. According to the theory the universe has been constantly expanding ever since. Celestial bodies move through the cosmos with phenomenal speed but when we take into account the huge distances involved it seems as if the expansion of the universe is taking place incredibly slowly.

It is also a well established fact that in a vacuum, at any given moment in time elementary particles are born out of nowhere and then immediately disappear. We do not yet know the exact structure of elementary particles but given the relativity of time and space there is nothing to stop us perceiving each particle as if it were a separate universe like our own. Physicists claim that they can appear either in the form of waves or in the form of particles. The further one goes into the microcosm the more relative distances appear huge, and for the internal observer time slows down. To an external observer our universe might appear to last for just one brief moment like a particle birthed and extinguished in a vacuum, whereas we, its internal observers, perceive the universe to have been in existence for billions of years.

The next time you take a mouthful of coffee ask yourself how many universes you have just swallowed. Infinity cannot be divided into parts and so if you think about it, every time you swallow a mouthful of coffee you are swallowing an infinite number of universes. Flying through a microcosm takes as long and seems as far as it does flying through the boundless expanse of outer space. Time like space goes on for infinity whether you look backwards or forwards. Intervals of time can be as infinitely large as they can be infinitely small. Any point within a time interval can be seen as a reference point–both sides of which extend into the infinity of time. Changing the reference point to another place within the time interval does not change the extent of infinity in either direction.

The infinity of worlds within worlds exists simultaneously. The centre of the universe is at the same time to be found in every point of matter because every point is surrounded by infinity on all sides. All events exist concurrently for the same reason that the centre of the universe is located in every point at the same time. This is difficult to imagine but so is it impossible to grasp infinity in one moment of contemplation. Even more convoluted theories have been designed which claim that the visible universe becomes a finite sphere in fourth-dimensional space, but that does not help particularly, because theoretically speaking, an infinite number of dimensions could exist. Unable to clearly imagine all of this, we have to content ourselves with a narrower perspective and at least pretend that we understand something of these theories.

There are many things about contemporary science that are impossible to explain or comprehend; however, this should not prevent us from benefiting from the fruits of scientific thinking. Applying the principles of Transurfing can lead to stunning results. The important thing is to decide from the very beginning not to torture yourself with questions of why and how exactly it all works which would be as productive as a child asking a physicist why different bodies attract. The scientist would reply: "Because of the law of gravity." The child then follows with the next question: "How does the law of gravity work? Why do bodies attract?" There is no answer to this question, so we will leave the thankless task of trying to explain these things, for it is not ours to know and understand everything. We will simply enjoy the results of the alternatives model.

From the alternatives model it follows that man can create his own destiny. In Transurfing the concept of fate differs from other more widely accepted interpretations. The difference is that in the context of Transurfing *a person can choose their happiness; they do not have to fight for it.* There is no need to accept or reject the alternatives model straight away. First ask yourself this question: Have you achieved much by battling with the world to find happiness? Each person will decide for themselves whether they wish to carry on in the same vein or whether they would prefer to try using a different method. A person can spend their entire life battling without achieving anything at all. Would it not be simpler to act in a way that encouraged life to meet you half way, for all life does is help manifest your personal choice.

Whatever you 'order', your choice is always granted unconditionally. Choice however, is different to desire. Wishes are only granted in fairy tales and most people just keep on wishing. It is no wonder that the belief is so ingrained in our minds that wishes are very difficult, if not impossible to fulfil. We have already taken the first small step towards solving the Guardian's riddle. Soon you will find out why wishes are not granted and dreams do not come true.

SUMMARY

Reality is manifest in an infinite variety of forms.

Variability is the world's most fundamental quality.

Any model of the universe represents just one manifestation of reality.

Any branch of knowledge bases itself on one chosen aspect of the manifestation of reality.

Your choice is always realized. You always receive what you choose.

The alternatives space is an information field recording all that was, is and ever will be.

The information field contains potential alternative scenarios to any event.

Each alternative has a script and scenery.

Space can be divided into sectors and each sector contains an alternative scenario of an event.

The greater the distance between sectors, the more the alternatives will differ.

Sectors with roughly uniform parameters are arranged in a life line.

Material realisation moves through space like a bundle of density.

The radiation of thought energy materializes an alternative.

Every organism contributes to the creation of material realization.

When the parameters of thought energy change, a shift occurs to a different life line.

You cannot change the fact that scenery exists, but you can choose a different type of scenery.

You do not have to fight for happiness. You simply have to choose an alternative reality that is more to your liking.

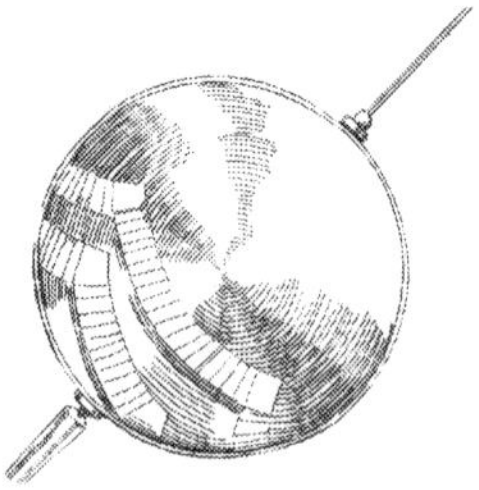

Chapter II. PENDULUMS

Rent Yourself Out

Destructive pendulums

We are taught from childhood to obey the will of others, to perform our duties, serve our country, our family, the company we work for, a political party, the state, or even an idea; to serve anyone except ourselves. To varying degrees, everyone has a sense of duty, responsibility, necessity and guilt. Everyone is ready to serve a group or organization in one way or another, be it family, a club, school, company, political party, the state and so on. All these *structures* emerge and develop when a separate group of people begin to think and act in the same way. Then, they are joined by others and the structure grows, gaining strength, forcing its members to follow the rules and eventually amassing the potential to gain control over large groups of society.

On the material level the structure consists of a group of people united by common goals and material objects, such as buildings, furniture, equipment, machinery, technology and so on. On an energetic level however, a structure appears when a group of people think in the same way, as a result of which, the parameters of their thought energy are identical. Their thought energy finally unites into a single current. When this happens, as if in the middle of an entire ocean of energy, a separate, independent energy-information structure is created which is referred to as an *energy pendulum*. Eventually this structure begins to live its own life and subjugate to its laws the very people who created it.

The structure is referred to as a pendulum because the more people–adherents–that feed it with their energy, the more powerfully it sways. Every pendulum has its own characteristic beat frequency. For example, if you want to get a swing moving you have to push it to a certain rhythm or frequency. This is called the resonant frequency. If the number of adherents decreases, the force of its swing is weakened. If it loses all its adherents the pendulum will stop moving completely, and thereby cease to exist as a separate identity. Examples of defunct pendulums are ancient pagan religions, stone tools, ancient weapons, out-dated trends of fashion and vinyl records; in other words, all that once existed but now no longer functions.

You might be surprised that all the things in this list qualify as pendulums. Any structure whose particular features were created by collective thought energy represents a pendulum. Generally speaking, all living beings capable of radiating energy at a particular vibration will sooner or later form an energy pendulum. Examples of pendulums in nature are bacterial colonies, populations of living creatures, schools of fish, herds of animals, forests, prairies, ant hills, etc., Essentially, any organised, homogenous structure made up of living organisms can be a pendulum.

Every living organism represents a single unit of energy and so can also be considered an elementary pendulum. When a group of individual pendulums begin to sway in unison, a group pendulum is created which looms over its followers like a superstructure. The group pendulum exists as an independent entity and sets rules for its adherents to follow, partly to keep them together but also to attract new ones. This type of entity is independent in the sense that it develops according to its own laws. Its adherents are unaware of the fact that they are acting in accordance with the laws of the pendulum, and not their own will. For example, a bureaucratic apparatus develops as an independent structure irrespective of the will of its individual officials. Of course, an influential official is free to make their own decisions but only to the extent that they do not contradict the laws of the system, otherwise that particular adherent will be rejected. Even people who represent individual pendulums are not always aware of their true motivations, energy vampires being one such example.

Any pendulum is by its nature inherently *destructive* because it consumes the energy of its adherents and establishes power over them. The pendulum's destructive quality is clearly demonstrated by the fact that it attributes no meaning to the fate of each individual adherent. The purpose of the pendulum is only to get energy from its adherents, whether it is to their personal benefit or not. When a person comes under the influence of a system, they are forced to build their lives in accordance with its laws; otherwise the system will chew them up and spit them out. Once under the influence of a destructive pendulum, you can easily end up ruining your entire life and as a rule it is difficult to break free without suffering losses.

If a person is lucky, they find their place within the system and feel at home there. The adherent gives their energy to the pendulum which in return provides the individual with an environment. If a follower rebels against the laws of the structure, the frequency of their thought energy ceases to be in harmony with the resonance frequency of the pendulum. Being deprived of essential energy the pendulum either drives the maverick adherent out of the system or destroys them.

If however, a person has ended up a long way away from a life line favourable to their growth, life inside the structure of an alien pendulum can be as soulless as hard labour or just turn into a very sad existence. In this case the pendulum is purely destructive to the adherent. Whether they like it or not, a person who falls under a pendulum's influence loses their freedom, being forced to live by imposed laws and becoming a small cog in a big machine.

That said, an individual can find themselves under the protectorship of a pendulum and achieve outstanding results. Napoleon, Hitler, Stalin and other similar figures were all *favourites* of destructive pendulums. This does not mean that the pendulum was actually concerned for their personal well-being for it exploited them to its own end. When Napoleon was asked whether he had ever been truly happy he could count just a few days over his entire life.

The pendulum uses sophisticated methods to lure new adherents, who fly to it like moths to a flame. How often people are deceived by the pendulum's advertising tricks and move far away from a potential happiness that was so close! Young men leave for the army and lose their lives. Students go to university learning in vain to master a profession that is not really for them. They find work that feels alien but is supposedly prestigious and end up drowning in a swamp of problems or they join their lives with a stranger only to regret it later.

The pendulum can hide its motives behind various well meaning masks and yet its activities can ruin the lives of its adherents. The greatest threat the pendulum poses to the individual is that it leads its victims away from other life lines where they would be able to find happiness. These are the characteristic features of a destructive pendulum:

A pendulum feeds on the energy of its adherents which increases the power of its sway.

- A pendulum strives to attract as many followers as possible to source as much energy as possible.
- A pendulum makes a contradistinction between its group of adherents and all other groups (we are good and they are bad, we are better than they are, etc).
- A pendulum acts aggressively towards anyone who refuses to follow it, attempting to win them over, neutralize their position or get rid of them.
- A pendulum hides behind masks and lofty ideas; it plays on people's feelings to justify its actions and attract as many adherents as possible.

The Battle of the Pendulums

The main feature of a destructive pendulum is its aggressive impulse to destroy other pendulums in order to win over potential adherents. With this purpose the pendulum works to turn its followers against the followers of other pendulums in the sense of: 'We are good and they are bad.' People who get involved in this type of argument end up losing their way and striving towards spurious goals which they mistakenly consider their own. This is the destructive nature of the pendulum. Fighting against the followers of other pendulums is totally futile and can destroy lives, one's own and the lives of others.

War is the most extreme manifestation of the battle between pendulums. Each pendulum uses various arguments to persuade its adherents to take up arms and the nature of the argument is specific to the historical epoch. The earliest, most primitive argument used was simply to order the followers to take something from the hands of others by force. As society became more civilized the arguments became slightly more refined. One nation declares itself supreme, progressive and the most developed with all the others less developed, somehow flawed. The lofty objective is to raise the underdeveloped nations to a higher level, using force if they resist. Metaphorically speaking, the contemporary conception of war is like a beehive hanging from a tree in the forest. The wild bees in the nest are busy making honey and raising their offspring, but then, a pendulum comes up to the nest and announces to its followers: "Look! Wild bees! They are very dangerous and must be destroyed or, at least, their hive must be destroyed. If you do not believe me, look!", and then the pendulum stirs up the nest by beating it with a stick. The bees fly out of the hive and start stinging the adherents. The pendulum then cries out triumphantly: "See how aggressive they are! They must be annihilated."

Whatever exculpatory slogans are used to justify war and revolution, in essence, the motivation is the same; the battle for adherents. The form the battle takes may differ but its one goal is to win over as many adherents as possible. New force is a vital necessity for the pendulum, for without it the pendulum's sway would stop entirely. The battle of the pendulums is an inevitable struggle for survival.

Once the wars and revolutions are over, other less aggressive but nonetheless tough forms of battle continue, such as the battle for market control, competition between political parties, all kinds of marketing, advertising campaigns, ideological propaganda, and so on. Human society is totally based on pendulums, so all fields of activity are gripped with competition. The rivalry goes on at all levels, from public debate to competition between club teams and individuals.

Things that are new, unusual or strange always have a hard time carving out their niche and not only because of inertia in people's thinking. The main reason for this is that it is not profitable for the old pendulums to support the appearance of a novice, who would distract its devotees. For example, internal combustion engines which so contaminate the atmosphere of our cities could have been relegated to the past a long time ago. After all, a number of alternative, ecologically friendly engine models have long been developed. The problem is that they threaten the downfall of the oil corporation pendulums, and for the time being these hold too strong a position to allow some inventor to wipe them from the stage. These monsters literally buy up the patents for new engine models and keep them secret at the same time declaring them to have low levels of efficiency.

Implementing its structure on a material level, the pendulum strengthens its position via financial means, facilities, equipment, and of course, human resources. The pendulum places its favourites at the top of the human pyramid. The favourites are made leaders at all levels, starting with low level managers and continuing up to heads of state and they are generally not required to have any particularly outstanding qualities. As a rule, those adherents become leaders whose qualities best fit with the structure of the pendulum. To the favourite it might appear that he has achieved impressive results in his life solely on individual merit. To some extent this may be true, but most of the work in promoting favourites is performed by the self-organizing structure of the pendulum. If a favourite's parameters fail to meet the requirements of the system, they will be ruthlessly eliminated.

The pendulum battle is destructive to its followers because they think they are acting on personal conviction when in fact they are following the will of another entity. In the majority of cases, the personal conviction of the devotees is taken over by the pendulum. As soon as a person attunes to the pendulum's frequency an interaction begins to take place between them on an energetic level. The frequency of the devotee's thought energy is stabilized and supported by the energy of the pendulum. A kind of lock-on takes place, and the adherent is trapped in a feed-back loop. The adherent radiates energy to the resonance frequency of the pendulum which in turn, feeds a little energy to the devotee thereby maintaining its influence over them.

On the material level this is an everyday standard scenario. For example, the pendulum of a political party conducts an election campaign, attracts a new devotee and gives them a little energy in the form of positive feelings like righteousness, satisfaction, dignity and importance. The adherent thinks they are in control of the situation and still able to choose their affiliation whereas, in truth, the devotee was chosen, and control established over them, not the other way around. The adherent only appears to be acting according to their own will when in fact it is the pendulum that is artificially and unnoticeably manipulating the will of the adherent. The adherent enters the pendulum's information field, socializes with like-minded others on important topics and establishes an energetic connection with them, and in this way becomes consistently attuned to a certain vibration. Later, the adherent may begin to feel that the pendulum has not lived up to their expectations and they begin to have doubts about their former idol. When this happens the frequency of the adherent's thought energy falls out of the pendulum's loop. The tightness of the pendulum's grip varies depending on its power. In some cases the devotee is simply allowed to leave. In other cases the heretic may pay with his freedom or even his life.

A pendulum gets a firm grip on the frequency of an adherent's thought energy by dominating it. It is like when you are humming a little tune to yourself but become aware of some other loud music being played nearby. The loud music dominates your senses, making it extremely difficult to stay focused on your own tune.

For the purposes of Transurfing it does not actually matter too much how interaction occurs on an energetic level between the pendulum and the devotee. We will examine the nature of the interaction using a simplified model. No-one can explain precisely how something *really* happens because at that level of questioning one has to ask what is meant by '*really*' and the questions and speculation continue with the infinite process of learning. This is not what we are interested in here so will make do with simplified models and metaphors that serve our purpose, satisfied with the fact that we are at least capable of understanding some things. Now we will look at how pendulums manipulate their adherents.

Puppet Strings

Pendulums are very good at coercing their adherents to give up energy voluntarily. A large, powerful pendulum, for example, can force its adherents to act according to a certain set of rules. Weaker pendulums go about things slightly differently. When an individual lacks the power to force another to do something they turn to other methods such as reasonable argument, persuasion and promises. These are feebler methods unique to a human society that has divorced itself from the forces of nature. Sometimes pendulums will use these techniques as well but they also have a much more powerful weapon at their disposal. Pendulums are energy-beings, and so they function in accordance with the immutable laws of the universe.

The individual gives their energy to the pendulum when their thought energy is radiating at the same resonance frequency.

A person does not have to be consciously sending thoughts to benefit the pendulum. As you know, most human thought and action originates in the realm of the unconscious. The pendulums make use of this feature of the human psyche. They manage to get energy not only from their adherents but also from their ardent opponents. You have probably already guessed how.

Imagine a group of old ladies sitting on a bench criticizing the government. They are obviously not adherents of the government pendulum. They hate it for a number of reasons. However, what happens is that the old ladies criticize the government for being so inept, corrupt, cynical and stupid and in so doing they emit intense thought energy at the frequency of the pendulum. It does not matter to the pendulum which side you rock it from. It can use both positive and negative energy just as long as that energy is resonant with its own.

The pendulum's main task is to engage people in any way possible in order to occupy their thoughts. With the advent of mass media the pendulums' techniques have become more sophisticated, and a person can become highly dependent. You have probably noticed that news programs are usually dominated by bad news evoking strong emotions: anxiety, fear, resentment, anger and hatred. The task of the journalists and correspondents is to attract attention. The media, being pendulums themselves, stand in service to yet more powerful pendulums. Their declared aim is free access to all information but their true singular goal is to attune people's thoughts in all ways possible to the desired frequency.

One of the pendulums' favourite ways of gaining access to your energy is to throw you off balance. Once you have lost a sense of your own equilibrium you start to 'wobble' at the same frequency of the pendulum, thereby enabling it to sway more strongly. Let us say, for example, that prices have risen. You react negatively, become resentful, complain, and exchange information with your friends. This is a natural and even proper response, but it is also exactly what the pendulum is expecting. You radiate negative energy into the world at the frequency of the pendulum. It receives the energy, swings harder, and the situation is aggravated.

The strongest string the pendulum can pull you with is fear, the most ancient and powerful of human emotions. It does not matter what exactly you are afraid of. If the fear is associated with any aspect of the pendulum it will receive your energy. Anxiety and worry are weaker emotions but still relatively effective puppet strings. These feelings are excellent at attuning thought energy to the frequency of a pendulum. If you are concerned about something you find it hard to focus on anything else.

The feeling of guilt is also one of the most extensive of channels through which the pendulum can pump your energy. Guilt is imposed on us from childhood and it is a convenient method of manipulation. "If you are guilty you must do what I say." Guilt is hard to live with and so people try to get rid of it either via punishment or righting the wrong they have done. Both imply submission, obedience and a certain thought pattern. A sense of duty is a special type of guilt. To owe something means that you are in some way guilty and therefore obliged to do something. As a result, the guilty–both the truly guilty and the falsely accused–wander around with their heads hung low, paying tribute to the pendulum in the form of energy. An induced, conditioned sense of guilt is the favourite weapon of any manipulator, and we will return to this theme later.

It is also worth mentioning the various psychological complexes people have. In the case of an inferiority complex the thoughts people have are: I'm not good-looking; I have no skills or talents; I'm not intelligent or sharp enough; I don't know how to communicate with people; I'm not worthy. In the case of a guilt complex the thoughts are: I have done something wrong; everyone is judging me; I must carry my cross. In the warrior complex the thoughts go along the line of: I have to be cool; I declare war on myself and all around me; I will fight for my place under the sun; I claim my power. The thoughts of someone with the truth-lover complex go along the lines of: I'll prove at any cost that I am right and prove to others that they are wrong. These and other complexes are the personal keys to the energy of different individuals. The pendulum strikes a chord and begins intensely draining that person's energy.

The list of strings the pendulum uses to control its puppets goes on: justice, pride, ambition, honour, love, hate, greed, generosity, curiosity, interest, hunger, and other feelings and needs. Feelings and interests allow a person's thoughts to be directed in a certain way. If a theme evokes neither interest nor emotion, then it is very difficult to focus on. Pendulums wound a person's feelings or play on their needs in order to capture a flow of thought energy.

As a rule, people react in uniform ways to external negative stimulus. Bad news evokes discontent. Worrying news evokes anxiety and fear. Insult evokes animosity, etc. Habits also serve as a trigger for the clamping mechanism such as the habit of getting irritated or anxious over nothing, responding to provocation and responding negatively to negative stimulus in general. A person can be aware of the fact that negative thoughts and actions lead to no good but continue to make the same old mistakes out of habit.

Habits often create problems and cause a person to act ineffectively and yet it is difficult to get rid of them. Old habits are an illusion of comfort. People have more trust in things that are long familiar. Everything that is new causes some concern. The old is familiar and has already been tested through experience. It is like the old chair in which you sit down to relax after work. Maybe a new one would be more convenient, but the old one is still more comfortable. Comfort is characterized by notions such as convenience, trust, positive experience and predictability. The new possess these qualities to a much lesser degree, so it takes time for a new habit to become an old habit.

So, we have looked at the methods pendulums use to influence people. The question arises as to whether a person can escape the influence of a pendulum and we will talk about ways of freeing oneself from the association with a pendulum later on. Sometimes a person will openly take a stand against a pendulum that has been controlling them but the individual is always defeated because their position is so isolated. No one individual can change anything. If a person has escaped the grip of obligation and entered into a battle with a pendulum they will only waste their energy, at best being thrown out of the system, and at worst being more aggressively squashed. An adherent that takes it upon themselves to break the rules established by a pendulum may find themselves beyond the law. On the surface of things it looks as if the former adherent is being punished for their protest but in actual fact punishment is delivered because the adherent is no longer submissive enough to continue being a source of energy.

We say that 'a fault confessed is half redressed' because a person who has acknowledged their guilt is willing to subjugate themselves to the power of the pendulum. The pendulum is not interested in the adherent's remorse for their actions. It is only interested in restoring lost control. A pendulum will instantly become kinder if you allow it to manipulate you. If the accused refuses to repent they can be got rid of because nothing more can be gained from them. If they do repent the pendulum's true motives are usually veiled behind moral principles saying that a person who has shown remorse cannot be such a villain after all. You can easily differentiate between true moral principles and the hidden interests of the system if you keep in mind what the pendulum really represents and what its true goals are.

You get what you do not want

As illustrated above, a pendulum can be powered both by its supporters and its opponents. Loss of energy on behalf of an adherent is just half the story. If a pendulum is sufficiently destructive it can damage a person's welfare and future.

Everyone is confronted with negative information or a challenging event at some time or another. Bad news and unfortunate events are provocation on the part of the pendulum. People obviously do not want to have this negativity in their lives, but generally speaking they always respond in one of two ways. If the information they receive is not too hurtful they let it go and it is quickly forgotten. If the provocative information is annoying or frightening, i.e. touches a chord in a person's soul, then their mental energy is captured in the pendulum's loop and the person is attuned to the resonance frequency.

Events then unfold fairly predictably. The person gets angry, worried and afraid, expresses their upset in an agitated fashion, and in general, actively radiates energy at the frequency of the destructive pendulum. Not all the negative energy is harvested by the pendulum. Some of it radiates out to sectors in the alternatives space that correspond to the quality of the person's thought energy which facilitates a shift to a life line where what the person would rather avoid is to be found in excess. If you remember, when a person's thought energy is attuned to a certain frequency, they shift to a corresponding life line. A pendulum ensnares a person's thought energy holding it at a certain frequency. This is what is so destructive about the role of a pendulum.

For example, generally we let information about accidents and disasters pass us by. If we are not directly affected, why upset ourselves unnecessarily? As a rule, when you hear the news, a disaster is taking place somewhere in the world but you are on a life line where you play the role of witness rather than victim. The line on which you are the victim is somewhere further away. Conversely, if you allow yourself to take on board information about disaster and misfortune and discuss it with friends, it is quite possible that you will soon shift to a life line where you may well end up in the role of the victim.

The stronger your desire to avoid something, the more likely it is that you will encounter it. To actively fight against what you do not want in your life is to make every effort to ensure that it is present in your life. You do not have to take any specific action to shift onto undesired life lines. It is enough to think negative thoughts and then fertilize them with emotion. When you do not want there to be bad weather you think about how much you dislike rain. Noisy neighbours wear you down and you end up arguing with them all the time or silently hating them. You are afraid of something and the fact greatly concerns you, or you have had enough of your present job and savour your dislike for it.

Everywhere you are pursued by exactly the very thing you do not want, that you fear, hate or despise. There may be other things that you would also like to avoid, but because you are not investing any negative emotion into them they do not appear in your life. Once you let the thing you do not want into your life, associate feelings of hostility with it, and indulge in those feelings, it will instantly become a physical reality within your life layer.

The only way to eliminate the things you do not want from your life is to break free from the influence of the pendulum that has seized your thought energy and from then on, avoid responding to its provocation or getting pulled into its game. You can free yourself from a pendulum's influence in two ways by *defeating* it or by *stopping* its sway. We will look more closely at how this can be done below.

Defeating the Pendulum

Trying to battle with a pendulum is futile. As was explained above, when you battle with a pendulum you just end up supplying it with energy. The first and most important condition for successfully defeating a pendulum is to *refuse to get into conflict* with it. Firstly, the more actively you try to fight off pendulums that get you down the more they will pressure you. You can repeat endlessly: "Leave me alone! Get away from me!" and think you are fighting them off, but actually, you are just providing them with energy making them cling to you even more.

Secondly, you do not have the right to judge or change anything. Everything you see and experience should be accepted as if they were paintings on display, whether you like them or not. There may be many paintings in an exhibition that are not to your taste but it would never occur to you to demand that they be removed from the exhibition room. Once you have recognized the pendulum's right to exist, you also have the right to leave it behind remaining free of its influence. The main thing is not fight it, judge it, get angry, or loose your self-control because by doing so you agree to play the game. The pendulum should be calmly taken for granted as a necessary evil and left at that. Any position of opposition supplies the pendulum with energy.

Before you can fully understand what it means *to choose*, you have to know how *to decline*. Most people have a vague idea of what they do want but know exactly what they do not want. In an effort to get rid of things or events that they do not want in their life, people act in a manner that has the opposite effect. To decline something you have to first accept its existence. The word "accept" in this context does not mean to embrace something and let it into your personal space. It means simply to recognize its right to existence and then pass by indifferently. To accept and let go of something means to consider the meaning of something and let it pass, waving goodbye as it leaves. This is much more effective than letting something into you personal space, becoming attached to something and then trying to oppose it.

When you think about the things you do not want, you attract them further into your life. Imagine a person who detests apples. Rather than simply paying them no attention it irritates the person that apples exist at all. On a material level they get annoyed every time they see an apple and openly express their disgust. On an energetic level the person may as well be hungrily pouncing on apples, stuffing their mouth and chomping loudly screaming about how much they hate apples, stuffing their pockets, only to be sick and once again complain about how they just cannot stomach apples. What the person does not realize is that they could simply delete apples from their experience of life.

It does not matter whether you love or hate. If your thoughts are latched onto the object of your emotions your thought energy will be attuned to a certain frequency and you will end up caught by a pendulum and transferred to a corresponding life line where the object of your fixation is present in abundance.

If you want to eradicate something from your life all you have to do is stop thinking about it, pass it by with indifference and it will disappear. *To eliminate something from your life, ignore it, do not avoid it.* There is a difference. When you avoid something it means you have let it into your personal space but are now actively trying to get rid of it. To 'ignore' something means not to react to it and consequently not to experience its presence in your space.

Imagine that you are a radio. If your day to day life is like waking up every day listening to a radio programme that you hate all you have to do is tune in to a different frequency!

You might think that you can protect yourself from unwanted pendulums by putting up iron boundaries between yourself and the world but this is an illusion. Putting on protective armour is like saying: "I am a blank wall. I see nothing; I hear nothing; I do not know anything. I won't talk to anyone. I am unavailable." It requires a huge amount of energy to support this kind of protective field.

A person who deliberately isolates themselves from the world will find themselves in a constant state of tension. Aside from that, the energy of their protective field will be vibrating at the same frequency as the pendulum against which their defence is directed. This is exactly what the pendulum wants. The pendulum does not care whether you provide it with your energy willingly or not. True protection from a pendulum is to be found in emptiness. If I am empty there is nothing for the pendulum to hook onto. There is no point in playing a game with a pendulum or trying to protect yourself from it if it can simply be ignored. When you can ignore the pendulum its energy will pass by you, dissipating into space without causing you any harm. You pendulum cannot push your buttons or upset you if you are empty in relationship to it.

The pendulum's principal objective is to attract as many adherents as possible and reap their energy. If you ignore the pendulum it will leave you alone and switch its focus to others who can be drawn into the game and attuned to the necessary resonance frequency.

A basic example of this would be a dog that starts following you and barking loudly. If you turn round to face the dog it will bark even louder and yet if you take it seriously and start trying to dodge it or fight it the dog will follow you for a long time just because it wants someone to lock horns with. If you ignore the dog from the outset it will simply switch its attention to someone else and will not be at all offended that you paid it no attention. The dog is too absorbed in its goal of sourcing energy to think about anything else. The dog is a metaphor. It could be a person or trouble maker of some kind. The principle is the same.

If someone is getting to you, see whether the model of the destructive pendulum fits that person. It will probably be a perfect match. If you cannot deal with the situation choose not to react to provocation. Ignore the person totally because whilst they are getting your energy they will not leave you alone. When you get into a conflict with someone or hate them in passive silence you are directly giving them your energy. To stop giving away your energy means to stop thinking about them altogether; to erase them from your mind. When you can say to yourself: "They're not worth it!", and really mean it that person will disappear from your life.

We often come across situations, however, where it is not that easy to ignore the pendulum. For example, if your boss demands something from you, an outright refusal or open defense of yourself would entail a loss of energy because both approaches amount to fighting the pendulum. You can however, act as if you are willing to play the pendulum's game as long as you remain aware of the fact that you are just pretending.

Imagine a heavily built burly man was to come at you with a sledgehammer and take a blow at you. If you react as if you are totally unperturbed, neither going to defend yourself nor to attack him you could calmly step aside and observe the man take his sledgehammer and hack down into the empty space beside you. When you behave in this calm and unperturbed manner the pendulum cannot hook into you and instead falls past you into empty space.

The same principle is central to certain martial arts like aikido. In aikido when one player makes an attack the opponent defends by taking the other player by the arm and moving in the direction of the attack as if casually seeing them on their way. Without having to exert any force the defending player sends their opponent flying in the direction of the original attack. The secret lies in not trying to block the attack. The players learn to accept the momentum of the attack and to move with the other player in this direction for a while before letting go. The energy of the attack is spent in empty space, because there is nothing to catch hold of.

The technique of the gentle dodge lies in responding with acceptance when the pendulum makes its first blow and then diplomatically stepping back, or subtly directing the movement in the direction that suits you. For example, imagine your boss is stressed and heaps a pile of work on you demanding it be done exactly in the way he thinks best. You know that the work would be better done differently, or maybe the work does not ordinarily come within your responsibilities. If you object, argue or defend yourself your boss will simply demand that you accept his authority and do what he says; after all, he has made a decision and you are defying him. Do the opposite; listen carefully and agree with everything he says. This allows the pendulum to discharge its first impulsive surge of energy. Then, start carefully discussing the details of the job. By now, you will have accepted your boss's energy and be radiating at his frequency. Because it has not met with any opposition the energy of your boss's initial approach will gradually subside. It is not advisable to tell your boss that you know better how the job should be done. Neither is it advisable to refuse to do the job or to get into an argument. It is much more diplomatic to ask for his advice on how he thinks the job could be done most efficiently or how perhaps another employee could do it more effectively. By doing this, you are swinging along with the pendulum, but you are doing it consciously, from the position of the observer without being caught up in the game. The pendulum on the other hand continues to swing completely absorbed by its own game. In the game the pendulum is the one who makes the decisions. The others agree with it or consult it for advice. If you try out this approach you will see that energy which was previously directed at you will be redirected towards a colleague or other potential solution to a problem. For you personally, the pendulum will have been defeated.

Stopping a Pendulum

There are some situations where the pendulum cannot be defeated which means it cannot be ignored or escaped. I had a friend once, who was a really nice, kind-hearted guy as well as being gifted with incredible physical strength. Late one evening we were travelling in a tram and spotted a group of bullies looking for trouble; in other words, a really destructive pendulum. There were quite a few of them and they were feeding each other with negative energy convinced of their own invulnerability. As a rule, this type of group needs to be constantly bullying someone who will react to their provocation in order to increase their energy level.

The men in the group started picking on my friend, probably because the kind and peaceful expression on his face suggested he was easy prey. They tried in any way they could to pick a fight by insulting and taunting him; however, my friend remained silent and refused to be provoked. In other words, he was trying to defeat the pendulum. I decided not to get involved because I knew he had nothing to fear whereas the thugs were really risking it. Finally, my friend could not take it any longer and got up from his seat and headed for the exit. The most brazen adherent blocked his way. Then my friend, who was by now totally cornered, grabbed the punk by the scruff of the neck and delivered a powerful blow to his head.

The victim's face was smashed to a pulp. The remaining toughies froze with fear and amazement. My friend turned to grab the next one, who in a trembling voice mumbled: "That's enough, man…stop!" The energy of the pendulum had been instantly dispersed and its adherents, who were very taken aback, edged slowly away from him, finally tumbling out of the tram.

Of course, people like my friend who can stand up for themselves are lucky but what do you do if you are not like that? If there is nowhere to retreat to you can stop the pendulum's swing by doing something extraordinary that no one would ever expect.

Somebody told me a story once about a man who was cornered by a pack of "fearless" street gang members. He was about to get beaten up when he turned to the gang leader with an insane stare and said, "What would you like me to break first: your jaw or your nose?" The question clearly did not fit with the usual script and the gang leader was taken aback for a moment. Then with unhealthy enthusiasm the man cried: "Or maybe I'll just tear your ear off!" and with that he grabbed the gang leader by the ear, who let out an agonizing cry. The entire scenario that the gang was used to playing out had gone awry. The gang leader was no longer thinking about beating anybody up. His only concern was how to save his ear from the madman's grip. The gang let the man go, assuming he was a psychiatric patient, and he escaped a fatal beating.

If you ever find yourself in a situation that you know will unfold according to a set script, do something surprising. It does not matter what you do as long as it is something that does not fit with the standard script. This will stop the pendulum's swing. As long as you are acting out a prepared script you are effectively agreeing to play by the pendulum's rules and give away your energy at the resonance frequency. If however, the vibrational frequency of your energy differs significantly from that of the pendulum, dissonance will be created which will disturb the pendulum's beat.

At the same time, it is not worth looking for trouble if you are dealing with a pendulum that has nothing to lose. If you are mugged by a person who is desperate for money it is better to hand over your wallet right away. Some people even carry a ten pound note with them just in case they end up in a similar situation. If the robber is a drug addict or mentally ill, even a martial arts expert could end up losing their life. Obviously, it is better to have no contact at all with types like this, just as you would avoid a rabid dog. If things were to suddenly go wrong it could end in a tragic and yet absurd death.

A sense of humor and strong imagination can be very helpful if you want to stop a pendulum's swing because they can help you transform your irritation into a game. For example, imagine that you are being tormented by the crush of a crowd of people on the street or in public transport. Everyone is rushing in the opposite direction, making it difficult for you to make your way. Now imagine that you are in Antarctica and that all the people around you are actually penguins, waddling, fussing and pottering about in their own funny way. Imagine that you are a penguin too. Holding this image in your mind, the people who had seemed so irritating just a few moments ago, will appear more pleasant, even evoking your curiosity.

Of course, it is difficult to control yourself at moments when what you really want to do is vent your anger and have a good rant. At these times it is hardest of all to *remember* that a pendulum is behind it all, trying to incite a response so that it can draw on your energy. Do not respond to provocation. The pendulum is like a vampire that exploits the anaesthetic of your habit of responding negatively. Even now, despite having just read these lines you could express your irritation if you were distracted by an unwanted telephone call. If you set yourself the goal of *remembering* until it becomes habit, you will gradually work up immunity to the provocation of pendulums.

You will probably have noticed how when you respond to a disappointing situation with irritation, displeasure or other negative emotion the situation escalates in the same spirit or other things start to go wrong too. This is the pendulum swinging higher and higher. If you react, you end up being the one to push it higher. It is more effective to act in the opposite manner: either not reacting at all or reacting in an abnormal way. For example, if when you find yourself in an unpleasant situation you respond with false enthusiasm or wacky delight the pendulum's swing will be brought to rest and you will see that the provocation stops with it.

Earlier we said that the habit of reacting negatively to unpleasant circumstances triggers the pendulum's mechanism for capturing thought energy. This habit will fade if you decide to play your own game in which you deliberately substitute negative emotion with positive emotion: confidence for fear, enthusiasm for gloom, indifference for resentment; joy for irritation. Try reacting "inappropriately" to small nuisances. You have nothing to lose. It might seem a silly game to play but the pendulum will have no chance. The game style only seems silly because pendulums have trained us to exclusively play the games that are of benefit to them. You can experiment with forcing the pendulum to play your game. You will enjoy it and be surprised to discover what a powerful technique it is. The working principle is this: when you radiate thought energy at a different frequency to the pendulum's resonance frequency you are in dissonance with the pendulum. The dissonance stills the pendulum's sway in relationship to your personal energy; the result being that the pendulum leaves you in peace.

There is another interesting method aimed at gently bringing a pendulum to rest. If someone is getting to you or causing you a problem, try and work out what that person is missing and what they need. It could be health, confidence or peace of mind. If you think about it these are the three things we all need to feel fulfilled. Ask yourself what the person you are finding so challenging might really need at that moment.

For example, if your boss shouts at you, maybe they are tired or having problems at home and what they really need is a little peace of mind. Imagine your boss relaxing in a comfortable armchair watching the television, sitting beside an open fire, fishing by a river or having a beer with friends. Perhaps you know of something else your boss likes to do. It may be that your boss is being pressured to take on more responsibility and is afraid of doing so. Perhaps what he needs is confidence. Imagine your boss skiing confidently, driving around in a sports car or being the centre of attention at a party. Your boss might be in some kind of pain. Imagine him feeling happy and fresh, swimming in the sea, riding a bicycle or playing football. Of course, it is better to imagine them doing what they specifically like to do in their free time but you do not have to guess. It is enough to simply imagine the person feeling content and happy.

What is really happening in a situation like this where your boss suddenly appears on the scene with a problem (or it could be someone else like a mugger)? Try to instantly distract yourself from whatever the problem is. That way, you avoid putting your head into the noose that locks your thoughts into a certain frequency from the very outset. Now imagine this person receiving exactly what they need. (What does a robber need; to eat; drink; get high?) Visualize an image of the person's fulfillment. If you are successful you can consider the problem solved. After all, the pendulum does not swing randomly. Something specific shifts it out of balance, causing it to start swaying. Consciously or unconsciously the pendulum is seeking for the one thing that will restore its balance. The energy of your thoughts set to a certain positive frequency will do that, at least indirectly, and the pendulum will instantly substitute its aggression with goodwill as a result. If this is hard to believe, test out the technique for yourself.

A pendulum-person approaches you with a problem which you solve, not in an obvious way, but on an energetic level. The technique is based on the principle that stops a pendulum. You give the pendulum your energy, but only a tiny piece of it in comparison to the amount of energy you could have lost had you been drawn into the pendulum's game. Besides that, you have also done a good deed by helping someone in need, if only for a short time. The interesting thing is that this person will adopt a friendlier attitude towards you even though they may never guess why they feel so comfortable in your company. That can be your secret.

The same technique can be successfully applied in cases where you need something from someone who is absorbed in their own problems and not in the mood to collaborate. If for example you need an official's signature on a document and you suspect they might be ill-disposed towards you, try treating them to a healthy dose of visualization and you will find that they will be quite amenable.

The last question is where all the energy goes when a pendulum is brought to rest. The answer is that the energy comes to you. Having coped with the problem once, you become stronger. The next time you try to solve a problem using this technique it will not be as difficult. Is this not always the way? Fighting a problem head-on only leads to a loss of energy which is absorbed by the pendulum that created it.

Psychologists and psychotherapists are well acquainted with equivalent practices of defeating or stopping a pendulum. In this sense the techniques described here are nothing new. However, they will be of value to anyone unfamiliar with practical psychology and give a clear understanding of how and why psychological protection is so effective.

Simple Solutions to Complex Problems

Another practical value of these techniques for defeating or stopping a pendulum is acquiring the ability to solve all kinds of problems: complicated situations in your personal life, conflict, unfavorable circumstances or simply a set task. There are always simple solutions to complex problems. The key to solving a problem always lies somewhere on the surface, the question is how to spot it. The pendulum that creates the problem obscures your vision, making it harder to find the key.

The goal of a destructive pendulum is always to feed on your energy. To do this it has to attune the vibration of your thought energy to the frequency of the problem and keep it there. This is easy to do if you are convinced that the problem is complex. If you accept the game rules, the pendulum will take you by the hand and lead you into an intricate labyrinth. Only later will you look back in hindsight and see how easily the mystery could have been solved.

If you play on someone's complexes by scaring, worrying or confusing them, they will take the bait and readily agree how complicated the problem really is. You do not even have to scare a person to achieve the same effect. Most people will agree that there are no easy solutions to the majority of their problems. We are all constantly confronted with difficulties of some kind over the course of our lives, especially when we face something new or unfamiliar. Approaching problems with anxiety or even a reverential fear is for most people a deeply rooted habit. When weighing up their ability to deal with a problem most people verge on the side of self-doubt. Consequently, all this anxiety is an excellent puppet string.

A pendulum can act via its adherents, i.e. people who are connected with a particular problem as well as non-living objects. The pendulum holds a person's thought energy at a certain frequency, sucking their energy whilst they carry the burden of the problem. You might think that focusing on the problem would help you to concentrate on finding a solution to it, and yet the opposite happens; it actually hinders you from finding a solution.

The pendulum focuses our thinking on a very narrow sector of the informational field. As a result, a person thinks and acts within the limits of a narrow corridor, unable to see the bigger picture or perceive the solution which may well lie outside that sector of the information field. Unusual or intuitive solutions often present themselves when you free yourself from the pendulum and are able to think in a different way. The secret of genius lies in remaining free from the influence of pendulums. While the thought energy of most people is held at certain frequencies by pendulums, the thought energy of a genius is free to attune itself to different frequencies and move into unexplored areas of the information field.

The way to avoid getting caught in the pendulum's snare is to keep whatever problem you are dealing with in perspective and remain aware of the pendulum's intent to trick you into playing its game. *Rent yourself out–be detached.* Try looking at the situation as if you had no emotional attachment to it. Act as you normally would but *remain observant,* don't *play the game.* Remember that the pendulum wants to take you by the hand and lead you into a complex labyrinth. Do not let the problem get a hold on you, scare, worry, or confuse you. Just remember that there is always a straightforward solution to every problem. Do not accept the "complicated" interpretation projected by the pendulum.

If you are confronted with a problem or tricky situation, be aware of your attitude towards it. Even though the problem may stir up feelings of confusion, fear, resentment, despair and so on, it is important to change your initial attitude to the exact opposite because then the problem will either disappear by itself or you will quickly find a simple solution to it. Despite the stereotypes and habits you have already adopted, try to regard any problems you encounter as just another part of the road you are walking along, like any other aspect of it, rather than as obstacles that must be overcome. Do not take the problem onboard so that it occupies your inner space. Be empty to the problem.

If you have to solve a challenging problem remember that you do not have to rely solely on logical reasoning. Your subconscious is directly linked to the information field where the solution to any potential problem already exists. Relax; release any fear or anxiety you may have been experiencing in connection with the issue, confident in the knowledge that the solution already exists. Let go. Quiet the chatter of the mind and contemplate the nature of emptiness. It is very likely that the solution will come to you instantly, and it will probably be very simple. If this does not work, do not give up returning immediately to the rational thinking process. Try the exercise again. You will probably find that it works the second time. This exercise develops the ability to obtain knowledge intuitively. You just have to make it a habit.

This method really does work if you are able to stay detached and free yourself from the pendulum. This is not always easy but later in the book you will discover new methods for dealing with pendulums. For now we are just at the beginning of the Transurfing technique. Are you feeling as if I have taken you by the hand and am leading you into a labyrinth? Stay free, even of those who preach to you of freedom.

The Suspended State

When you have disentangled yourself from the influence of destructive pendulums you acquire a newfound freedom but if you do not have a goal to focus on you can find yourself hanging in a *suspended state.* If you have neglected your goals being because of a preoccupation with defeating the pendulums around you or stopping their sway, you may end up in a vacuum. On the one hand, conflicts and concerns that previously haunted you, fade; arguments occur less frequently; anxiety and worry gradually disappear from your life and all without you really noticing it, like a storm that gradually calms and passes.

This is all very positive but you may discover a downside to this new state. Events that before had you at the centre of things now carry on without you. You are no longer as important to other people around as you used to be and so they pay you less attention. You have fewer worries, but as yet no new desires have arisen to replace them. There is less pressure from the outside world but that does not seem to be bringing you any dividends. You have fewer problems, but have not necessarily made any new achievements either. Why is that?

The human environment is built entirely on pendulums. Therefore, when a person isolates themselves from these structures they begin to find themselves in a kind of desert. The suspended state is therefore, not much better than being dependent on pendulums. It is a bit like when children who have everything they could possibly want whine about the fact that there is nothing more to want. They are genuinely unhappy and drive everyone around them up the wall with their whining because it is human nature to need something to strive for.

Your freedom lies in being free from the pendulums of others. There are pendulums however, that can be of use to you and *these are your personal pendulums.* It is essential to recognize the goals you have been conditioned to chase after, which in fact lead you further away from your life line of happiness. The task is then to remain free and choose those life lines on which true success and happiness await you.

Pendulums do not necessarily have to represent something detrimental as long as a person is self-aware. It is never possible to be completely free of pendulums. The question is how to avoid being oppressed by a pendulum's influence so that you can consciously work them in favour of your own purpose. Transurfing offers the specific tools needed to achieve this. Even though it is not possible to free yourself from the phenomenon of pendulums completely, it is not entirely necessary that you do so. On the contrary, at the end of the day, it is pendulums that turn dreams into reality.

SUMMARY

A pendulum is created by the energy of a group of people thinking in the same way.

A pendulum is an energy based information structure.

A pendulum maintains the thought energy of the adherent at its own vibrational frequency.

A harsh battle for adherents takes place between the pendulums.

A destructive pendulum forces goals onto its adherents that are not of their own making.

A pendulum plays on human emotion, thereby catching the individual in their web.

If there is something that you really do not want it will appear in your life.

To free oneself from a pendulum means to give it no place in your life.

To give something no place in your life does not mean to try and avoid it; it means to ignore it.

To bring a pendulum to rest you have to change the established game script.

Positive visualization will gently bring the swing of a human pendulum to rest.

The energy of a stilled pendulum becomes available to you.

Problems are solved by defeating or stopping the pendulum that created them.

To solve a problem, rent yourself out.

To avoid getting stuck in a suspended state, find your own pendulums.

It is essential to acquire the habit of remembering what you know.

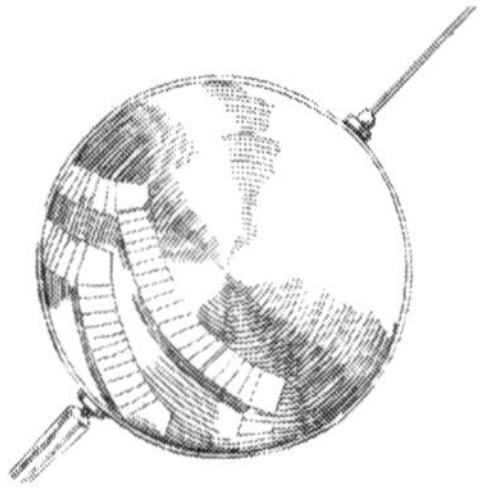

Chapter III. THE WAVE OF FORTUNE

Your thoughts return to you like a boomerang

Antipode to the Pendulum

Now we can look at the task I set you earlier of determining which type of pendulums could be described as constructive. The answer is none. It sounds paradoxical but it is true and I hope I have not offended the listener by asking a trick question. *All pendulums* have one and the same goal, which is to receive energy from their adherents. If the energy supply is cut off then the pendulum's swing stops.

A pendulum is constructive only in relationship to itself, never in relationship to an adherent. What could possibly be constructive or creative about the fact that your energy is being taken? Of course, different pendulums are destructive and aggressive to different degrees. It is difficult to imagine a beach volleyball club ganging up against the winter swimming club, and membership to the beach volleyball club is hardly likely to ruin your life. Of course these types of pendulums still need to feed on the energy of their adherents; if the members became bored of playing volleyball the life of the club would die and the pendulum along with it. However, this is nothing compared to the membership of a criminal gang, where one could lose one's freedom or even one's life.

One might ask how a person can be giving their energy to the pendulum of the gym where they train if whilst they are there they are completely focused on getting fit. You are focused entirely upon yourself whilst you are training but you are still obliged to observe a certain set of rules. At home you can do whatever you like but at the gym, all its members are required to act in relatively the same way; to follow the established rules of the system and in this way, make their energy available to the pendulum. If all the club's members suddenly leave, the pendulum will no longer receive its source of energy and therefore stop swinging.

The question can be put in a different way: Do energetic structures exist that do not require your energy? It turns out that they do. One is the *wave of fortune*, or set of circumstances that are favourable to you personally. Every individual has their own wave of fortune. Sometimes you are lucky with something and then a whole cascade of other pleasant events unfold unexpectedly as if the sun had really chosen to shine on you. A cascade of pleasant events may not always follow the first, but if the first sign of good fortune pleased you and lifted your spirits then a cascade of the same will definitely follow.

The 'wheel of fortune' and 'bluebird of happiness' are not simply abstract metaphors. The wave of fortune is really a set of life lines that are auspicious for you personally. The alternatives space contains everything, including lines like golden veins than run through the information field. If you have found the outer line of a golden vein and catch onto a piece of good luck, you can slide by inertia on to other life lines where events of a similar nature are accumulated and a new set of fortuitous circumstances awaits you. If however, the first piece of good luck is followed by a streak of bad luck, it means that a destructive pendulum has managed to hook into you and draw you away from the golden vein.

The wave of good fortune brings happiness without taking your energy. It can be compared to a sea wave that carries an exhausted swimmer onto the shore. The wave of fortune will carry you onto happy life lines. Like the pendulum, the wave has no interest in your fate, but it has no need of your personal energy either. If you want to, you can float with the wave and let it carry you but if you do not want go with the wave it will pass you by with no regret. The wave of fortune is a temporary formation. It does not feed on the energy of other beings and so eventually fades like sea waves break upon the shore.

The wave of fortune sometimes touches your life in the form of good news. The wave of good fortune brings in information from other life lines. In comparison with your current life line, the resonance of the information is perceived as good news. The task is to grab hold of the rope and pull yourself onto the line that the information originated from, for there you will find not just good news but fortuitous circumstances also.

It seems as if the wave comes and goes, whereas in actual fact the wave of fortune does not move, increase in strength or weaken. In this model we have used the term 'wave' as a metaphor but as has already been mentioned, the wave of fortune is stationary in the alternatives space existing in the form of more rewarding life lines. In fact it is the discontinuity created by moving among different life lines that creates the impression of the wave as you either take hold of a from stroke of luck, embracing the blessing and inviting it into your life, or distance yourself from it, distracted by other pendulums.

Because the wave has no interest in you personally it is easy to lose sight of. The wave will pass you by and set off on its own way. This is why people are inclined to believe that the bluebird of happiness is hard to catch. You do not actually have to make a huge effort to saddle a wave of good luck. It is a question of choice. If you accept the wave of fortune into your life it will stay with you. If you allow yourself to be influenced by a destructive pendulum and become immersed in its negative energy you will be distanced from the wave of good fortune. As they say: "Finders keepers, losers weepers". The bluebird will happily peck grains from your hand. You do not have to catch the bird, but neither must you drive it away.

This is one of the most paradoxical aspects of the *freedom of choice*. People really can choose happiness and success for themselves and yet at the same time remain restricted by pendulums that lead them away from the wave of fortune. Here we return to a theme we discussed earlier; to claim freedom of choice you must *be independent*. You have the right to be free of the influence of other people's pendulums. Now we will clarify how you can *claim this right*.

The Boomerang

Most people's minds are filled with constant chatter. If the chatter is not controlled negative thoughts begin to dominate very often. As people we are most concerned with what we fear, with what oppresses or displeases us. The human psyche has developed over a period of thousands of years under the influence of destructive pendulums, which have kept people in a condition of fear so that they can be manipulated. As a result, people tend to have a very clear idea of what they do not want and yet have a very vague idea of what they do want.

To align your will with a negative thought machine means to play the game of a destructive pendulum and radiate energy at its resonance frequency. This is a very detrimental habit. It is entirely in your interests to replace it with the habit of consciously controlling your thoughts. Whenever your mind is unoccupied, when you are travelling, going for a walk or doing work that does not require deep concentration, make sure that you programme yourself to think positive thoughts. Do not think about what you have been unable to achieve. Think about what you want to achieve, and you will achieve it.

If for example, you do not like the house you are living in you will probably say to yourself: "I'm sick and tired of this house. Everything about it irritates me. I'll be so happy when I move to a new place. I can't help it, I just hate it!" With thoughts such as these there is no way that you could possibly receive what you want. Even if you are definitely moving to a new home you can be sure that huge disappointments await you.

'Ok', you say, but I am still leaving this old shed and moving into a luxurious mansion! What disappointments could possibly await me? The greater your enmity for the home you currently live in, the more unpleasant surprises you can expect to experience in your new palace. You can expect all sorts of problems: a leaking tap, peeling paint, crumbling walls, pestering neighbours; in short, anything that maintains the parameters of your current negativity. It makes no difference whether you are living in the old house or the new one. You may find a life path equipped with all the mod cons, but you will be as dissatisfied as you were before. The alternatives space has no shortage of luxurious houses where you will feel like you are living in hell.

If you have nowhere else to move to you are all the more likely to stay living in a space you cannot bear because your thoughts are unlikely to be attuned to the frequency of a life line on which you are successful in finding the house of your dreams. You are currently thinking about the things you do not like and consequently radiating negative energy which matches the life line you are on now. Until you change the vibration of your energy you will just have to keep putting up with the same line. Changing your vibration, however, is not that difficult to do.

First of all, accept the current situation and let go of feelings of dissatisfaction and resentment. If you try you can find little causes for joy in any situation. Even if you do not like your house, be grateful to it for having taken you in and looked after you. There may be wind and rain outside but the house takes it all for you keeping you warm and safe. Surely the house at least deserves some recognition? If in this moment you are thankful for what you have and feel love for all the things that are helping you to survive you will radiate positive energy. Then, if you so desire, you can quite realistically expect an improvement in your circumstances.

When you finally do move, make a point of thanking everything that surrounded you in your previous home. Even the things you plan to throw away deserve your gratitude. In these moments you are transmitting positive energy into the environment which will return to you later.

Secondly, start thinking about the house you would like to have. This is a little harder to do than simply being irritated by the things that surround you right now but the goal is worth it. What is better, to react to every external irritation like an oyster in a shell or to make a little effort and change your habits? Look through estate agency advertisements with photographs of houses, go window shopping in search of furniture and decorations and live the thoughts of what you want to have. We always end up getting the things and situations which our thoughts are most strongly attached to. *Our thoughts always come back to us like a boomerang.*

There are so many examples that illustrate how a negative attitude can ruin your life. Imagine that you are getting ready to go on holiday in the south where it is hot but the weather where you live is terrible. You walk outside cringing from the cold wind and getting soaked in the rain. Naturally, it is difficult to derive much pleasure from this type of weather but you can at least take a neutral standpoint and ignore the potentially destructive pendulum associated with it. If you openly express your displeasure you are accepting the pendulum and pushing it to make it swing higher.

You say to yourself: "Soon I will be in the south, enjoying the sunshine and warm sea–so sod this dump!" This kind of attitude is hardly likely to attune you to a life line filled with heavenly pleasures. You just will not ever get there. Do not be lulled into a false sense of security simply because you have already bought your ticket. You could easily arrive to find more bad weather or some other issue. Everything will turn out fine as long as you stay positive.

It is not enough to make sure you are not *taking in* negative energy from without. You have to make sure that you are not *putting out* negative energy too. If you shout at someone because you are irritated by something they have done, you can be certain that soon afterwards something will go wrong or some kind of annoyance or problem will arise. The parameters of the negative energy you are transmitting correspond to life lines where you experience irritation and so you are inevitably carried in the direction of life lines where the density of disappointments and misfortune is higher than average. Do not fall into the trap of self-justification with the thought that the particular irritation could not have been avoided. I have nothing to prove in writing this. Simply observe for yourself how every time you react negatively, something else regrettable follows.

One very clear conclusion can be drawn from all that has been said above. You are always on a life line that represents the quality of your energetic vibration. If you take in negative energy you will experience disappointments in your life and if you give out negative energy it will return to you like a boomerang in the form of disappointment.

Transmission

Instead of playing the game of a destructive pendulum, seek out pendulums that benefit you in some way by their game. Acquire the habit of giving your attention to all that is positive and good. As soon as you see, read or hear something pleasing or encouraging hold it in your thoughts and let it lift your spirits. Imagine that you are walking through a forest where there are beautiful flowers as well as poisonous thorns. Which would you choose? If you pick a bunch of elderberry flowers and put them in a vase in your home you will soon get a headache. What would be the point of that? It is the same thing as reacting to destructive pendulums. It is better to pick a jasmine flower, admire its beauty, and savour its aroma. Let in the things that are positive and you will be greeted on your path by ever more good news and auspicious opportunity.

Once you have experienced a brief moment of inspiration or joy it is easy to get pulled back into the stresses of your daily routine. The feeling of elation is forgotten and the working day takes over. To keep the festive feeling in your life, first and foremost you have to remember it. Habit makes us jump head first back into the monotony of everyday life. The negative pendulums make us forget whatever the good thing was that happened and we loose a sense of the pleasure it gave us.

You have to support the little flame of enthusiasm and nourish the feeling it gives you inside. Observe how life is moving in a better direction, take hold of any straw of happiness you are offered and look for good signs in everything. At the very least it will keep you from being bored. It is essential to remember that in every minute you give to the Transurfing practice, you are consciously moving towards your dream, setting the course of your own destiny. This in itself imparts a feeling of calm, confidence and happiness that helps you to stay positive. Once this feeling becomes a habit you will be constantly riding the crest of the wave of good fortune.

Be happy for all that you have in this given moment. Being happy by definition is no empty invocation. Sometimes circumstances unfold in such a way that it is genuinely difficult to be content, but nonetheless, from a practical point of view, expressing your dissatisfaction is highly disadvantageous. You want to get to the life lines that inspire you but you cannot make that shift if your energy field is filled with the vibration of dissatisfaction. Good life lines differ in that the circumstances you encounter fill your thoughts with happiness and contentment.

Good news is quickly forgotten because it gives us no cause for concern. In contrast, bad news evokes an active response because it poses a potential threat. If you do not let bad news into your heart, you will not allow it into your life. Close yourself off to bad news and remain open to good news. It is important to note and carefully nourish any positive change in your life for these are the messengers of the wave of fortune. As soon as you hear any even slightly encouraging news, rather than forgetting the information immediately afterwards, as you would have done previously, savour, discuss and track it. Think the news over from all points of view. Take pleasure in it. Make predictions and expect further improvement. In this way the vibration of your thoughts will remain at the frequency of the wave of good fortune and you will be attuning yourself to its parameters. The good news will increase and life will get better. To filter information in this way is neither a practice of mysticism nor is it a particular quality of the human psyche. It is the nature of reality. The pessimist looks at the world through black tinted glasses and the optimist through rose-tinted glasses. Either way, you shift to different life lines according to the quality of your thoughts.

When you are in the right relationship with yourself and your environment, you *transmit* harmonious energy into the world around you. You create an area of harmonious vibration around yourself in which everything unfolds successfully. A positive attitude always leads to success and creativity.

Negativity by contrast is always destructive and aimed at disruption. There is a certain category of individual who prefer to *look for problems rather than their solution.* This type of person is always happy to discuss their difficulties and seek out new obstacles. People like this usually have trouble offering a practical way out of a situation because they are programmed to search for difficulties rather than solutions. A determination to focus on problems will bring them to you in abundance, leaving you stuck with the situation that is causing you grief. Criticism and targeting the negative side of a situation will always bring fruits of a corresponding nature. This does plenty of harm and not much good. Look around and you will find people like this in your circle of friends and acquaintances. This is not to say that they are 'good' or 'bad'; they are firmly hooked up by a destructive pendulum.

The majority of people respond antagonistically to any undesirable event that occurs in their lives. As a rule, any event which does not follow the original script is claimed undesirable. The opposite is also true. We can only perceive success in forms that correspond to the expectations of our original script. A person might be terribly upset about being late for a plane which then crashes.

The opposite can also happen where a person lets a unique opportunity pass them by because it did not fit into their plans.

The more negative your thoughts about life, the worse your life will become. The more a person worries about failure the more readily new failures will appear in their life. As the saying goes: "As the call, so the echo". A person who chooses this way of being practices the opposite of Transurfing on a daily basis; they are sliding down a life line that can only lead to their personal hell. Take the exact opposite position; be joyful in the face of failure, and deliberately look for even the slightest blessing. You can always find something. Maintain the perspective that the glass is half full. The rather banal saying that: 'everything happens for a reason", always stands true if you decide to make it your tenet. You have to firmly hold your course in the direction of all that is good, letting go of the old habit of getting upset and downhearted at any minor obstacle.

If a person is strong, every failure they experience is taken to be a useful lesson, making them tougher and more experienced. Find joy in all parts of your world and you will transform it into paradise. This is of course a very unusual way of behaving but it fits the unusual goal of becoming your own genie and making all your wishes come true. Unusual goals require unusual methods.

It is difficult to practice this type of behaviour at first because the old habit of reacting negatively to anything that disappoints us is so deeply entrenched. The most important thing to *remember* when you suffer a setback is that the setback has been created by a pendulum that is trying to get its hook into you. Once you remember this fact, you can make a conscious choice as to whether you would rather vent your negative emotions and give energy to the pendulum, or gain victory over the pendulum by leaving it without a scrap of your emotional energy.

Once you can *remember* this, it is not that difficult to defeat a pendulum or still its sway. As has already been said, pendulums pull on your emotional strings, and your habits are the trigger for the mechanism that captures your thoughts. Even though you have just read this chapter and have set yourself the goal of not responding to any bitter pill, you might still fall into the old pattern of expressing a negative reaction. However, you will become conscious of the fact that you *forgot* and responded out of habit instead. As soon as you can *remember in time*–the situation will be under your control. You will laugh to yourself: "Aha! So, it's you again, you old pendulum! You won't hook me so easily this time!" You will be free to accept of reject the pendulum consciously. You will no longer be the puppet.

If you practice this technique consistently, with time you will succeed in replacing the old habit with a new one. Until that happens, pendulums will try to provoke you in all kinds of ways. You will notice how as soon as you start behaving differently you are bombarded with unpleasant news and circumstances as if someone was deliberately trying to thwart you. Do not give up. On the whole these will be small frustrations rather than anything more serious. If you do not give up and learn to *remember* the victory will be quite impressive. Mind my words!

Another possible result is that the next time you meet with the wave of fortune, pendulums will not succeed in distracting you from it and the bird of happiness will remain in your hand. In order to fully embrace the bird you have to surround yourself with positive energy. You have to become a transmitter of positive energy as well as a receiver of exclusively positive energy. If you can do this the world around you will very quickly change for the better and you will easily slide onto more successful life lines. In the end, the wave of fortune will greet you, lift you up and rush forward carrying you on to success. Transurfing does not end with learning to ride the wave of good fortune. This is just the first step. As you read on you will see that there are many more surprising discoveries to be found.

Magic Rituals

To conclude this chapter I want to share an example of how the technique of attuning to the wave of success works. There are various situations in which people automatically make attempts to attune to this frequency even though they may not be aware of what they are doing on an energetic level. For example, at the beginning of the day, traders often give their first buyer a significant reduction. Intuitively they feel that their first buyer is very important and so they give a good deal to the first buyer to secure the day's trade. In the language of Transurfing they are attuning to the vibration of successful trading. It is difficult to simply hold the idea of a good day's trade in mind, whereas the first sale instils the trader with real hope and faith as a result of which the attunement takes place of its own accord. Through action, the trader has mounted the wave of successful trading by radiating thought energy with corresponding parameters. The trader believes that their wares will sell quickly and buyers are immediately 'gripped' by the vibration of this thought and obediently make a purchase when the trader hints at the idea, convinced that they have found a bargain.

Another curious magic ritual is used by market traders who brush paper money across their wares. Of course, of itself this action has no impact and in essence there is no magic in this ritual. However, if the trader believes in the power of the ritual it will help them to attune to the frequency of the life line of successful trading. The attunement takes place on a subconscious level. The person performing the ritual is only aware of the superficial, visual side of the ritual but nonetheless, for whatever reason, it works. The ritual works as a theatrical requisite rather than as a power unto itself. The key power involved is the thought energy of the person carrying out the ritual.

People in different professions invent their own 'magical' rituals which they conduct to help them in various situations. People believe in them and apply them in order to attune to a successful life line and mount the wave of good fortune. As you already know, it is not the form the ritual takes that matters but the result it produces.

SUMMARY

The wave of good fortune is an accumulation of favourable life lines in the alternatives space.

A cascade of good luck follows only if you have let yourself become imbued with the joyful energy evoked by the first stroke of luck.

Destructive pendulums will try to coax you away from the wave of fortune.

When you overcome dependence on pendulums you win your freedom.

By taking on and transmitting negative energy you create your own hell.

By accepting and transmitting positive energy you create your own heaven.

Your thoughts always return to you like a boomerang.

Pendulums cannot throw you off the wave of fortune once remembering has become a habit.

The habit of remembering is developed through consistent practice.

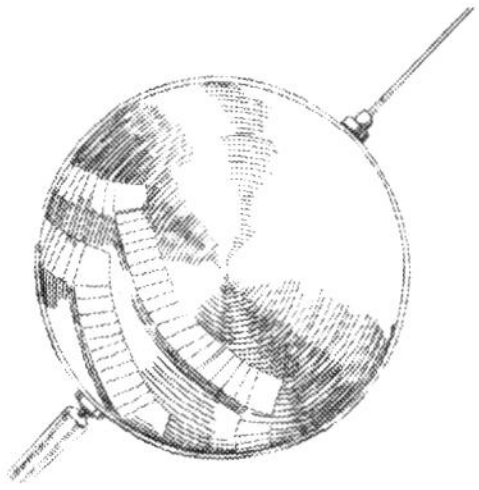

Chapter IV. BALANCE

Taking care without worrying

Excess Potential

Everything in nature strives towards balance. Changes in air temperature are balanced by wind. Differences in temperature are compensated by thermal exchange. Wherever there is excess potential of any energy form, balanced forces emerge to correct the imbalance. We are so accustomed to such statements on the nature of things that we fail to ask ourselves why it must necessarily be so, or how exactly the law of balance works.

Laws do not actually explain anything. They are just statements of fact. All laws of nature are secondary and derived from the law of balance. The law of balance is primary (at least it appears to be), and it is impossible to explain why equilibrium should exist in nature in the first place or more specifically, where balanced forces originate from and why indeed they exist at all. The fact that we have become accustomed to something doesn't mean it is the way things necessarily are. One can only imagine what the world would be like were it not for the law of balance; an atmospheric jelly or an aggressive furnace perhaps? However, the unsightliness of such a world is hardly a reason to support the existence of the law of balance and so we are left to accept it as fact and to wonder in admiration at the perfection of the world, nonetheless, puzzling over the question of what governs it all.

We are used to the fact that there are good and bad spells in life and that success is followed by defeat, for this is all a manifestation of the law of balance. Success, like misfortune, destroys the balance. Complete balance is when nothing happens. Absolute balance doesn't exist, or at least no-one has yet managed to observe it. Oscillation is observed everywhere in the world: night and day, incoming and outgoing tides, birth and death, etc. Even in a vacuum, elementary particles are involved in a process of continual birth and dematerialization.

The entire world can be seen in the form of pendulums that oscillate, fade and interact with one another. Every pendulum receives a jolt from its neighbours and in turn gives out its own. One of the main laws governing this complex system is the law of balance. Ultimately, everything strives towards balance. You are also a kind of pendulum. If you take it into your head to destroy the balance and sway sharply in a particular direction, you will brush against the neighbouring pendulums creating commotion all around which will then turn against you.

Balance can be destroyed by actions and also by thoughts and not only because thought is followed by action. As you know, thoughts radiate energy. In the world of material realization everything has an energetic foundation. Everything that occurs on an invisible level is reflected in the world of visible material objects. It might seem as if the energy of our thoughts is not powerful enough to have an impact on the world around us and if that were the case, everything would be a lot simpler.

However, let's not make guesses about what's happening on an energetic level; otherwise we could get entangled in a knot of conjecture. For our purposes it is enough to accept the simplified model of balance: where excess potential appears, balanced forces emerge to eliminate it.

Excess potential is created by mental energy when too much importance is given to a particular object. For example, let's compare two situations: in one situation you are standing on the floor in your house and in the other you are standing at the edge of a precipice. In the first case the situation causes you no concern. In the second case the situation is of grave significance–one careless movement and the mistake is irreparable. On an energetic level however, the fact of simply standing is of equal significance in both cases.

Standing above a precipice, your fear heightens intensity and creates inhomogeneity in the energy field. At this point, balanced forces emerge aimed at neutralizing the excess potential. You can even feel their influence: on the one hand an inexplicable force seems to pull you downwards and on the other, another force draws you to step away from the edge. To eliminate the excess potential of your fear the balanced forces are required either to drag you away from the edge or to cast you downwards and be done with it. It is the impact of the balanced forces that you are experiencing.

On an energetic level all material objects are of equal significance. It is we that attribute specific qualities to them such as good, bad, cheerful, sad, attractive, repulsive, kind, wicked, simple, complex, etc. Everything in this world is subject to our assessment. The assessment itself does not create inhomogeneity in the energy field. Sitting in an armchair at home you can make the assessment that sitting there is safe, but standing at the edge of a precipice is dangerous. At the moment of making the assessment, the situation you are considering does not worry you and so balance is in no way disturbed. *Excess potential only appears in cases where the level of importance attributed to the assessment is excessive.*

The amount of potential is increased if the assessment which is attributed huge value also greatly distorts reality. Generally speaking, if an object is very important to us we are incapable of objectively assessing its quality. For example, an object of worship is always attributed excess worth and an object of hate, excess detriment; an object of fear, terrifying qualities. Thought energy strives to artificially produce a certain quality there, where in fact it is not present. As a result, excess potential is created which summons the wind of balanced forces.

The bias of the assessment, which is a distortion of reality, is two-fold: The object in question is excessively attributed either negative or positive qualities. However, of itself, an error of assessment plays no role in the matter. Note that the bias in assessment generates excess potential only if it is attributed great meaning. It is only the *importance* that the assessment has for you personally that enables your energy to be transmitted to it.

Excess potential is invisible and intangible and yet it plays a significant and even insidious role in people's lives. When balanced forces eliminate excess potential they can generate myriad problems. Paradoxically, the end result is often the exact opposite of the original intention and people do not understand why this happens. It is this phenomenon that sometimes makes us feel as if some inexplicable dark force had a grip on our lives, like 'sod's law'. We touched on this when we were discussing why people get what they do not want rather than what they do want. Here is another example of how what we desire slips away from us.

Some people believe that if you devote yourself fully to your work you will achieve excellent results. If you look at this position from the point of view of scales and balance, it is obvious that immersing yourself so heavily in work is like placing your work on one dish of the scales and absolutely everything else in the other dish. Naturally, balance is destroyed and the consequences become visible all too soon. The result of prioritising work to this extent will be the exact opposite of what you expected.

If working harder means earning more money or improving your qualifications then of course a little extra effort will do no harm. Like everything in life, there should be good measure and proportionality. If however, you are constantly exhausted and have become your own slave driver then it would be better to slow down a little or even look for a different type of job. Either way, the point is that any effort made beyond measure will inevitably lead to negative consequences.

This is what happens on an energetic level. Aside from work, everyone has their own set of values, be it: home, family, leisure pursuits etc. If you juxtapose all your other values with the one value of work you create strong potential. Everything in nature strives towards equilibrium, which means that aside from your own will, other forces would come into play to mitigate the consequences of the excess potential you are creating. Balanced forces can work in all sorts of different ways. You may become ill, in which case there could be no question of working any harder. You may start suffering from depression which would not be altogether surprising because you would have been so hard on yourself. The voice of the rational mind shouts: "Come on! You must earn more money" while the soul or subconscious objects: "Surely this is not what I came into the world for, to suffer and torture myself? Why bring this on myself?" Eventually, you would become chronically tired and any plans to be more productive would have to be forgotten. You would probably end up feeling that you were banging your head against a brick wall; getting nowhere fast.

When people do overly prioritise their work there always seem to be someone else around who achieves more whilst making considerably less effort. Once a person achieves a certain level in their job there can be a tendency to place massive importance on their work, but unfortunately, the more disproportionately important it becomes, the more likely it is that problems will arise. People assume it quite natural for there to be problems, but in reality, the number of problems a person experiences is reduced significantly when they lower their expectations and relax their attachment.

The only conclusion that can be drawn from this is that you have to consciously re-evaluate your relationship to your work if you want to avoid creating excess potential. It is essential to have free time in which you can do the things you enjoy. People who do not know how to switch off and relax do not know how to work well either. When you arrive at work, *detach yourself*. Give of your head and hands, but do not give away your heart. The work pendulum wants all the energy you can give it, but you did not come into the world simply to work for a pendulum. Your efficiency at work will be noticeably increased when you stop creating excess potential and free yourself from destructive pendulums.

Match detachment with integrity. Be careful not to make small errors or faux pas, which would enable others to accuse you of being irresponsible or negligent. It is important to carry out your responsibilities with integrity. Detaching yourself from a situation does not mean behaving carelessly in a slack or slip shod manner. It means to act with a cold mind, without creating excess potential at the same time as fulfilling the tasks required of you. This approach protects you from being drawn into unpleasant situations. There will always be people you know or colleagues who continue to immerse themselves head first in their work. On a subconscious level they will sense that, although you act with impeccability, you are sufficiently emotionally detached not to put yourself on the line completely. These conscientious individuals will instinctively feel the urge to trip their competitor up on some oversight. As soon as you make a mistake they will be there to criticize you. The sad thing is that the mistake is likely to be something quite mundane and harmless. You might just be a little late for work or have forgotten something fairly minor. If you had sunk your head in the work-sand, as they do, no-one would make anything of it, however once you change your attitude to your work, little things give people the opportunity to accuse you of slacking or lacking in dedication.

Situations like these can also arise at home and among your friends so it is important in any situation where you are detaching yourself to fulfil your responsibilities attentively, thereby not giving anyone the opportunity to reproach you. It is the inner witness, the *Guardian that* enables you to act with integrity at the same time as holding back from throwing yourself headfirst into the race. The notion of the inner Guardian has nothing to do with a split personality. It is the part of yourself that stands in the background and observes what you are doing and how you are doing it. We will return to this theme in forthcoming chapters.

Some might say that throwing yourself completely into your work is on the contrary, a wonderful thing. Of course, it depends what your work is. Total immersion in your work is only justified from the point of view of balance if it is connected to your personal goal. The personal goal is also a theme we will look at more closely a little later. If you love your work because it coincides with your personal goal then it can serve as the tunnel that leads to success. This kind of work nourishes your energy, bringing joy, inspiration and fulfilment. If you are one of the lucky ones who can confidently say that they feel this way about their work then you have nothing to worry about.

Exactly the same goes for study. Later in this chapter we will look at other situations in life, where excess potential is created, and the impact of balanced forces.

Resentment and Judgement

We will begin with resentment of self. This feeling arises when a person is unfulfilled by their personal achievements and qualities, and finds it hard to accept their own weaknesses. It is quite possible to be conscious of your own shortcomings without inflating them into a complex. If you are intensely focused on your own foibles, excess potential will be created. Balanced forces immediately get to work to eliminate the potential. Their action can be focused either on developing certain new qualities or on battling with the original weakness. People have a tendency to work with one or the other depending on their nature. Most often a person chooses to battle with the less attractive parts of themselves and their position turns against them. There is no point in trying to hide weaknesses, and overcoming them can be tricky. Trying to hide them only creates the opposite effect which makes the situation even worse. For example, when a shy person makes an effort to hide their shyness they can come across as very held back or, on the contrary, excessively cheeky.

If a person is dissatisfied with their achievements to the degree that it serves as motivation for self-improvement then balance is not disturbed. The outside world is not affected and the inner shift towards balance is established via positive action. If a person starts upsetting themselves, beating themselves up, or even worse, punishing themselves, then a destructive dialogue between heart and mind is created. The heart is self-sufficient, perfect and does not deserve to be treated so harshly. All shortcomings that a person acquires are shortcomings of the mind, not the soul. You could write a whole book on just the connection between the heart and mind. Suffice to say, that conflict between the heart and the mind is greatly undermining. If reason dominates and the soul closes in on itself life can become chaotic. To avoid having to turn to a psychotherapist further down the road, let yourself go and forgive yourself for your perceived imperfections. Even if you have not yet learned to love yourself, you can at least refrain from fuelling the inner battle of self-criticism and accept yourself the way you are. Only then can the heart be the mind's ally, and what a powerful ally it is.

"Ok", you say, "if I let go and leave all my imperfections in peace how then will I acquire the better qualities I wish to have? I do not want to stop developing". This is not about having to give up the striving to embody whatever qualities you admire. It is about giving up the war with self over your perceived imperfections. When you wage war on yourself with constant criticism you waste energy by supporting something which is not so much futile as harmful because of the excess potential it creates. When you finally stop battling, energy is freed up that can be channelled into self-development.

Although this may all sound incredibly simple many people do in fact use up a colossal amount of energy battling against themselves, trying to hide their shortcomings. They are like titans committing themselves to a lifetime of carrying a heavy load. All they have to do is lay down the heavy burden, be themselves, and then life would become noticeably easier and simpler. Energy could then be transferred from battling with imperfection to developing more worthy qualities and the quality of this new energy would correspond to life lines where positive characteristics outweigh weaknesses. Think about it. How can you shift to a life line where your body is in good shape if all your thoughts centre on your physical shortcomings? You end up getting what you decisively do not want.

When you are dissatisfied with yourself you enter into conflict with your soul. When you are dissatisfied with the world around you, you end up entering into conflict with a large number of pendulums. As you know, there is absolutely nothing to be gained from succumbing to their influence, and waging war on them does not even bare thinking about.

Dissatisfaction represents an energetic vibration, whose frequency matches life lines where the thing you are dissatisfied with is ever more clearly present. Being pulled to these life lines makes you become even more dissatisfied and the vicious circle continues until you reach a life line where you are old and ill, incapable of changing anything for the better, with comfort only to be found in grumbling at the world together with others who are the same and sharing memories of how much better things used to be in the good old days.

Every generation is certain that life is worse today than it used to be, but the truth of the matter is, that life has only become worse for one generation, or more specifically, for those among that generation who wallow in their own discontentment. If life were gradually getting worse with every generation, there would come a point at which humanity would be doomed to living hell. A sorry image, is it not? Wallowing is one aspect of discontentment that makes life appear as if it is gradually getting worse.

The other side to the harmful habit of expressing intolerance is that it disturbs the balance. Lack of acceptance creates excess potential in a person's energy space irrespective of whether the response is justified or not. Excess potential generates balanced forces that strive to restore equilibrium. It would be wonderful if the impact of these forces changed every situation for the better. Unfortunately, it is often the other way around. Balanced forces besiege you so that your complaints about life will have as little weight as possible. This is much simpler than changing all the things about life that you are dissatisfied with. Imagine what would happen if a leader fervently expressed their displeasure at everything taking place in their country. It would not matter whether the leader's intentions were good or bad. History is filled with examples of political leaders who have behaved in such a way and have either been removed from government or physically annihilated as a result.

Generally speaking, when a person creates excess potential the impact of balanced forces is aimed at reducing their influence on the world. This can easily be achieved in many ways such as via social status, work, income, home, family, health, etc. Now you can see why the older generation lives the life it does.

If you take pleasure in life it might seem logical after what has been said above, that balanced forces would be motivated to ruin everything or push you away but this is not how things work, unless of course, joyfulness has been reduced to foolish rapture or wide-eyed enthusiasm. Firstly, a happy person transmits creative energy which shifts them onto positive life lines, and secondly, creative energy does not create the destructive potential that balanced forces strive to eliminate. It is no coincidence that different philosophies and religions have pronounced love in the universal meaning of the word to be the force that created the world. Balanced forces are a product of that same creative force. They simply strive to maintain order and are not capable of turning against the very energy that created them.

From the point of view of Transurfing, the habit of expressing displeasure at little things is harmful and undermining, whereas the habit of taking pleasure in tiny details is empowering. For this reason the technique is aimed at *substituting* the former habit with the latter.

The technique is very simple. However banal it sounds, every cloud has a silver lining. If you set yourself the task of looking for the positive in every negative situation you encounter, you will find that it is not actually that difficult to do. It can even be a kind of game. If you play the game consistently, the old habit will be replaced by the new one, which will be of great benefit to you personally but a nightmare for destructive pendulums!

If something terrible happens which it would be unnatural to see positively, follow the example of King Solomon. King Solomon wore a ring with the inscription "This too shall pass" on the inside edge of the ring so that no-one else would see it. When the king suffered misfortune or came up against a complex problem he would turn the ring over and read the words of the inscription.

The habit of expressing disapproval has developed under the influence of destructive pendulums that feed on negative energy. Once looking for the positive in life has become a habit you will generate positive energy which will build up into a powerful flow carrying you on to positive life lines.

If you are inspired by the prospect and consistently practice the technique of substituting one focus with another, from time to time you will notice that it is taking less conscious effort and as the habit becomes more deeply rooted you will eventually forget altogether that you once had a habit you wanted to change. As soon as you weaken, a pendulum will find a reason to upset you and you will observe that once again you have given it your energy. Do not be disappointed if this happens. If your intention is strong you will get there and eventually destructive pendulums will leave you alone. All you have to do is keep *reminding* yourself of your original intention.

We are all guests in this world and no-one has the right to judge that which they did not create. This statement should particularly be taken in the light of relationships with pendulums. As has already been said, you only make things worse for yourself if you start fighting a destructive pendulum that is causing you resentment. You do not have to play the obedient sheep but neither should you enter into open confrontation with the world around you. If a pendulum conflicts with you personally you can apply the methods of defeating or stilling it. When the pendulum tries to draw you into a fight with another pendulum try to remain self-aware and ask yourself, whether doing so would be of any personal benefit.

Returning to the metaphor of visiting an exhibition with pictures that you do not like, the saying "Make yourself at home, but don't forget you are a guest" is very fitting. No-one has the right to judge but everyone has freedom of choice. If you fervently express your discontent the pendulum benefits, but if you quietly walk away and visit a different exhibit, you will benefit. I hear you ask: "But what if there is nowhere else to go? That there is no alternative is a misconception instilled by the pendulum and this book is dedicated to the task of ridding the listener of this false limiting belief.

Dependent Relationships

Idealising the world is the reverse side of the coin of dissatisfaction. When you idealise the world things take on a rose-coloured tint and much appears better than it really is. As you know, when a person sees something that is not really there excess potential is created.

To idealise something means to overestimate it, to place it on a pedestal, to worship it, or create an idol to it. The love which creates and rules the world is very different to idealization. However paradoxical it may sound, love is in essence dispassionate and unemotional. *Unconditional love* is admiration without worship or the need to possess. In other words, it does not create interdependent relationships between the one doing the loving and the object of their love. This simple truth helps to determine where love ends and idealization begins.

Imagine walking through a mountain valley, filled with greenery and flowers. You are thrilled by the incredible landscape. You breathe in the fresh air and aromas and your soul is filled with happiness and tranquillity. This is love.

Then you begin to pick the flowers, gripping them in your hands, forgetting that they are alive, and the flowers slowly start to die. Later it occurs to you that you could make perfume and cosmetics from the flowers, sell them, or even create a flower faith, and worship them like icons. This would also represent a form of idealization because, either way, dependency would be created between yourself and the object of your love; in this case the flowers. At this stage there is no trace left of the love that existed in that moment of simply enjoying the vision of the flower-filled valley. Can you see the difference?

Love generates positive energy which carries you onto corresponding life lines. Idealization on the other hand creates excess potential, generating balanced forces intent on mitigating its impact. The effect of balanced forces is different depending on the situation but the result is always the same. In general terms it can be described that balanced forces 'debunk myths'. Depending on the object and level of idealization involved, the debunking may be stronger or weaker in effect, but balance is always restored.

When love changes into a dependent relationship it is inevitable that excess potential will be created because the desire to possess something creates an energetic 'drop in pressure'. Dependent relationships are determined by a statement of conditions such as: "if you ...this, then I ...that". There are endless examples of the conditions peoples place on relationships: "If you loved me you would drop everything and come with me to the end of the world. If you won't marry me it means you don't love me. If you praise me I will go out with you. If you don't give me your spade, I'll drive you out of the sandpit", etc.

As soon as one thing is compared to another, or juxtaposed with another, balance is destroyed. We often hear that "we are like this and they are like that!" as an expression of national pride, but in comparison to which nations, and where does this feeling of insecurity come from? Whenever contrast is made, be it positive or negative, balanced forces will eliminate the excess potential it creates. The impact of balanced forces will primarily work against the person creating the potential. Their actions are either aimed at pulling the parties involved apart or at uniting them, which in turn leads to a clash, or to mutual agreement.

All conflicts are based on contrast and contradistinction. An initial statement is made such as: "They are different to us". Then the statement is developed further. "They have more than we do. Let's take some of theirs". "They have less than we do. We must give them some of ours". "They are worse than we are. We must change them". "They are better than we are. We must fight them". "They don't behave like we do. Something will have to be done about it." All these comparisons in their various guises lead to conflict. They originate with feelings of discomfort within one individual and end in war and revolution. Balanced forces can eliminate contradictions via confrontation and via acceptance but given the fact that pendulums can feed on aggressive energy more often than not, pendulums often nudge the situation towards confrontation.

Below are several examples of the consequences of various types of idealization.

Idealization and Overvaluation

Overvaluation is when a person is imagined to have qualities they do not in fact embody. On one level the illusions of the mind are quite harmless. On the energetic level however, they generate excess potential because potential is created wherever there is a flux in quantity or quality. Overvaluation is a projection and concentration of qualities there where they are not present in reality. There are two types of idealization. In the first type an individual is portrayed as having qualities which are in fact totally uncharacteristic. In order to eliminate the resulting inhomogeneity in the energy field, balanced forces have to create some kind of counter force.

For example, a dreamy and romantic young man creates a mental image of his beloved, portraying her as an angel of pure beauty. In reality it turns out that the young women in question is a grounded individual, who loves having a good time and shows no interest in sharing the dreams of the love-struck young man. Whatever the circumstances, when a person creates an idol of another and places them on a pedestal, the myth will sooner or later be debunked and the necessary disillusionment follows.

In this context the story of the writer Karl May is quite remarkable. May was the author of some popular adventure novels set in the American Old West and best known for the characters of Winnetou and Old Shatterhand. May's novels were written in the style of first person narrator, creating the impression that he had personally participated in the events portrayed in his books, thereby earning great admiration. May's works are as vivid and rich as a film and so the reader could well assume that the story was a factual account. May's plots were so exciting that he was dubbed 'the German Dumas'.

Numerous Karl May fans identified the writer with the famous cowboy Old Shatterhand. His admirers could hardly have considered any different; after all, they had found an object of admiration and imitation, and one who lived close by, making his persona even more powerful. Imagine their surprise when it was announced that Karl May had never even visited America, and some of the works had been written during his time in prison. The myth was debunked, the illusion dispelled, and the writer's former fans became his execrators. Who was to blame? After all, the readers created the idol themselves and along with it, a dependent relationship: "Yes, you are our hero, but only if the book is a real life story".

In the second type of idealization, a person's attention is focused not on a person with illusory qualities but on rose-tinted dreams and castles in the air. The dreamer lives with their head in the clouds as a way of escaping the ugliness of the reality of life. Obviously, excess potential is created in this situation. To tear down the castles in the air, balanced forces make the romantic individual face harsh reality. Even if the person in question is capable of distracting hundreds with their idea, thereby creating a separate pendulum, the utopia will be flawed because it is based on the bias of excess potential. Sooner or later balanced forces will stop the pendulum's sway.

Here is another example of how an overvalued object exists as an ideal. A woman is imagining what her ideal husband would look like. The more she convinces herself that her future husband must be of a certain type the stronger the excess potential that is created. The excess potential can only be neutralized by a person who embodies qualities which are the exact opposite of what the women wanted to find in her partner. When she meets someone and later discovers what they are really like, the woman asks herself how she "could have been so blind". The opposite can also occur. If a woman focuses on how much she hates drunkenness and rudeness in a man she may fall into the trap of building a relationship with an alcoholic or a man who bad mouths her. Often people find they have to deal with the things they find totally unacceptable because in addition to creating excess potential their thought energy radiates at the frequency of their non-acceptance. Life often brings people together who are very different and who would appear to be totally incompatible. Balanced forces bring people together who have opposite qualities of potential, in that way striving to neutralize the imbalance created by one or the other.

The influence of balanced forces can be seen especially clearly in children because children tend to be more sensitive to energy than adults and behave more naturally. If a child is praised too much they will start being deliberately naughty. Children lose respect for and even end up despising adults that let the child twist them around their little finger. If a parent does all they can to turn their little boy into a well brought up goody-two-shoes, the child will probably end up breaking out and getting involved with some kind of street gang. If a parent tries to create a wunderkind out of their child the likelihood is that they will loose all interest in their studies. The more the parent burdens the child with after school clubs, activities and private lessons, the more likely the child is to grow up with a dull personality.

The best principle in bringing up children is to behave towards the child (and not only towards children) as if they were guests, i.e., giving them attention, respect and freedom of choice, without creating excess potential and without letting them run the show or make your life a misery. The relationship should be constructed on the analogy that you too are no more than a guest in this world. If you accept the rules of the game without going to extremes, you will be free to choose from all that exists in this world.

Healthy relationships are as common as unhealthy relationships and there is a certain balance in the existence of both. Hate exists and so does love. A quality of a healthy balanced relationship is that it does not produce excess potential. Potential emerges when there is a noticeable bias in an assessment with regards to the nominal value. Evaluations are relative. On the scale of distortion, zero can be considered unconditional love. As you know, unconditional love does not support dependent relationships, nor does it create excess potential. This kind of love however, is extremely rare. Normally, possession, dependence and overvaluation are mixed into love's vessel. It is difficult to resist feelings of possessiveness and quite natural that one should want to know that you have the person you love, as long as things do not go to one of two extremes.

The first extreme is the desire to possess the object of your love if that person is only vaguely associated with you and might not even suspect your desires (of course, you understand that I am not only talking about the physical aspect of possession). This is what happens in the classical case of unrequited love which always leads to much suffering. However, the mechanism at play here is not quite as simple as you might think. Remember the flower metaphor. You love to wander among the flowers, admiring their beauty and you may have wondered whether they love you too. Now try to imagine what the flowers think of you. All sorts of strange ideas will enter your mind such as fear, anxiety, dislike, indifference. You may wonder what reason the flowers could have to love you. Perhaps you desperately want to hold them in your hand but you cannot because they are growing in a flowerbed or are for sale but are very expensive. What one experiences at this stage is no longer love but dependency and with that, negative emotions begin to creep in.

So, you are in one place and the object of your love is in another and you would like to have the object of your love with you, i.e., you are creating energetic potential. One might think that excess potential would draw the desired object to you like air mass that shifts from an area of high to low pressure but that is not how things work at all. It makes no difference to balanced forces what method is used to re-establish equilibrium, and so they may place the object of your love at an either further distance from you thereby neutralizing the excess potential and breaking your heart at the same time. If, at the slightest sign of disappointment in love, a person is inclined to dramatise the situation even more with thoughts that the person of their dreams does not love them they will be pulled towards life lines where reciprocated love is a rare phenomenon.

The stronger your desire to have something or to experience reciprocated love the stronger the action taken by balanced forces will be. Of course, if they choose a path that brings you and your loved one closer together then the story will have a happy ending. The direction balanced forces will ultimately take can easily be determined at the very outset. If you are preoccupied or obsessed with the need for your feelings to be mutual and yet nothing seems to be going right, you need to change your tactics. Try loving without expectation of reward. If you do this the unstable vibrations of balanced forces can be drawn closer and made to work for you; otherwise the situation may go snowballing out of control until it is practically impossible to change anything.

There is only one solution in a situation like this. If you want your love to be mutual you have to love simply without thought of whether you are loved or not. Firstly, in taking this approach you avoid creating excess potential which means that the fifty percent probability that the forces will work against you is avoided. Secondly, when you are not obsessed with the idea of whether your feelings will be reciprocated, you are free of the dramatic and uncontrolled thoughts about unrequited love that pull you into corresponding life lines. Quite the opposite; if you simply love, without thought of possession, dependency is avoided and the parameters of the energy you radiate will correspond with those life lines where requited love exits. If you have already discovered requited love then you have no reason to be concerned with the issue of ownership and possession. Imagine how greatly your chances of being close to the one you love will increase for having given up the notion of possessing them. Besides, unconditional love is a very rare and attractive quality and so if you can embody it you will automatically draw people to you. Would you not be drawn towards a person who loved you simply for the sake of it without demanding anything in return?

The second extreme concerns the right to ownership, which is of course jealousy. In this case balanced forces have two potential means of action. If you are already in a relationship with the person you love then the first means of action is to bring you even closer together. Some people enjoy an element of jealousy in their relationship. The other option is for balanced forces to destroy whatever gave rise to the jealousy, i.e. the love itself. In this case, the stronger the jealousy the deeper the grave it digs for the love being shared in the relationship. The dynamics of love which becomes expressed as jealousy are just the same as the shift from simply savouring the aroma of the wild flowers to wanting to produce perfume.

All of the above relates as much to women as it does to men, but this is not the final word on the matter. We will return to this question later when we look at the other concepts that underpin Transurfing. Everything is so simple and yet at the same time so complex; complex because a person in love loses their ability to rationalise and so the recommendations above will probably fall to the wayside. I shall not however, upset myself with these things because I resist the need for the listener recognition.

Contempt and Vanity

Judging other people is a very powerful way of destroying balance, particularly when we have contempt for them. On an energetic level there are no good or bad people; there are simply those who observe the laws of nature and those who unsettle nature's 'status quo'. The latter always eventually succumb to the power of balanced forces which strive to restore balance.

Of course, situations often arise in which a person deserves to be judged; the question is whether you should be the one to judge them. This is no superficial question. If someone injures you personally then they have probably also destroyed the existing balance. In this case, your judgement is less likely to represent a source of unhealthy excess potential than it is a tool for balanced forces striving to restore balance. If you say what you think and take any necessary reasonable measures the disturber of the peace will get what they deserve. If, however, the person you judge has done nothing specifically to hurt you, then it is not for you to make accusations.

Look at it from a purely practical point of view, it would be pointless to feel hatred towards a wolf you saw tearing a sheep to pieces on television. It is our natural sense of justice that impels us to judge others but what originates as an innate feeling can quickly turn into habit with many over the years turning into professional prosecutors. Most of the time you cannot know what caused a person to act the way they did, and who knows, if you had been in their shoes, maybe you would have done something even worse.

This kind of judgement creates excess potential in your energy field, which is hardly surprising, because we tend to believe that to the same extent that the accused is bad–we are the epitome of goodness. If the accused has horns and hooves then you must be an angel, right? Nonetheless, because we have not actually grown a pair of wings yet, the forces that strive to restore balance are called into play. Their action will be different depending on the situation but the result is essentially the same: you get a slap. Depending on the force and form of the judgement, the slap may range from being hardly noticeable to so hard that you are swiped into one of the worst possible life lines you can imagine.

It is easy to imagine the different forms that judgement takes and the consequences of it however for clarity I will cite a few examples.

Whatever happens in life, never scorn anyone. It is the most dangerous form of judgement because you find yourself in the shoes of the person you scorned. For balanced forces this would be the most simple, direct means of restoring the harmony lost as a result of your bias and judgement. If you have contempt for beggars and tramps you too could one day lose all your money and your home as a way of restoring balance. If you have disdain for people with physical disabilities you could just as easily have an accident. If you turn your nose up at alcoholics and drug addicts you could end up in their shoes too. People are not born into these roles. The circumstances of life create the role. Why then should you be immune to such circumstances?

Never judge your work colleagues, whatever they do. At best you will find that at some point you will make the same mistake they did. At worst, a conflict could arise which ends with you losing your job even if you were not to blame.

If you judge a person for how they are dressed you could yourself end up one rung lower than them on the ladder of "good and bad" simply as a result of radiating negative thought energy.

There is nothing wrong with a person taking pride in their achievements or loving themselves. A general love for oneself is healthy and harms no-one. Balance is only destroyed if an overinflated sense of one's own worth is juxtaposed by a superior attitude to the weaknesses, shortcomings or humble achievements of others. Then healthy self-esteem becomes arrogance, pride and vanity. The action of balanced forces will again result in a slap on the cheek.

Contempt and vanity are the vices of man. Animals do not embody these characteristics in their behaviour. They are lead by the consistent purpose of fulfilling nature's will perfectly. Nature is more perfect than the human mind. The wolf like all predators feels no hate or contempt for its prey (try feeling hate or contempt towards a lamb chop). People, however, build their relationships with each other on masses of excess potential. The majesty of animals and plants lies in the fact that they are unaware of their greatness. Conscious awareness has given man many advantages, but it also brings with it the rubbish of feelings like guilt, inferiority, vanity and contempt.

Superiority and Inferiority

Feelings of superiority and inferiority are indicative of dependent relationships. When you compare your own qualities to those of others you inevitably create excess potential. On an energetic level it makes no difference whether you express your superiority publicly, or just secretly congratulate yourself on being better than others. Quite obviously, open expressions of superiority cause others to dislike you. People who make comparisons are often striving to artificially boost their own ego at the cost of others. This kind of behaviour always creates excess potential, even if it is just a shadow of the arrogance that is not expressed openly, and balanced forces will come in with a slap.

People compare themselves to the world around them as a means of establishing a sense of their own self worth. However, this type of self-assertion is as illusory as a fly trying to force its way through a pane of glass when the window next to it is wide open. When a person strives to prove their importance to the world, energy is wasted on supporting excess potential. Working on self-development, on the other hand, creates real virtues; no energy is wasted and no harmful excess potential created.

You might think that the amount of energy spent on making a comparison is minimal. In actual fact the energy involved is more than enough to support a relatively powerful charge of excess potential. What determines the charge is how you direct your energy. If your goal is to develop certain qualities in yourself then this intention will propel you forwards. If however, your goal is to demonstrate all your 'regalia' to the rest of the world, your wheels will spin helplessly as if caught in a deep rut, going nowhere but creating an irregularity in the energy field. The world will be 'stunned' by the shining regalia and balanced forces will take effect. The forces do not have a lot of choice. They can either freshen up the colours of the external world which has been paled by comparison, or reduce the shine of the misplaced star. The first option is of course far too labour intensive and so it only leaves the second. Balanced forces have numerous ways of doing things. They do not have to deprive the ambitious star of its regalia. They can simply send them an unpleasant situation to bring them down a peg or two.

We often perceive problems, obstacles and misfortune to be integral parts of the world we live in. No-one is at all surprised that difficulties, small and large, accompany them throughout their lives. We have all adopted the view that this is the way of the world. In actual fact, misfortune is an anomaly and not a normal phenomenon. Often it is not possible to find a logical explanation for why a problem occurred and why it happened to you in particular. The majority of unpleasant moments we experience are generated by the actions of balanced forces as part of their function in eliminating excess potential created either by you or those in your immediate environment. Most people are unaware of the fact that they have created excess potential and that balanced forces exist and so interpret the problems they face to be the manifestation of some unavoidable dark force.

You can eliminate the majority of the problems you usually face if you relieve yourself of the colossal effort of supporting excess potential. A huge amount of energy is wasted on excess potential that often produces a result which represents the complete opposite of your original intention. To free yourself from the action of balanced forces you have to stop buzzing like a fly against a pane of glass. Switch your intention from increasing your own sense of self-importance to developing the qualities you admire.

You also have to let go of any lurking idea that you are capable of controlling the external world. Irrespective of your place on the social ladder, if you believe you can manipulate the world around you things will definitely go wrong because attempts to change the world destroy the balance. Interference with the workings of the world has a negative affect on the interests of the majority. Transurfing enables you to choose your destiny without compromising anyone else's interests. This is ultimately much more effective than storming ahead and overcoming all the obstacles in your way. Your fate is truly in your hands but only in the sense that it has been given to you to choose it rather than change it. Many people have suffered failure because they have taken the idea of creating your own destiny literally. There is no place for battle in Transurfing, so you can lay down the weapons of war with relief.

Refusing to behave with superiority has nothing to do with self-deprecation. Belittling your own worth is just the other side of the coin. On an energetic level it is irrelevant which extreme of the complex you embody. The size of the potential created is in direct proportion to the extent with which a person's evaluation of the world differs from reality. When balanced forces encounter self-importance they knock it off its pedestal. In the case of an inferiority complex they force a person to raise their falsely reduced sense of worth. Balanced forces act directly and without concern for the subtleties of human relationships, and so often, once they start having an impact, a person begins to act less naturally, highlighting the aspects of themselves they would prefer to hide all the more.

For example, teenagers can be defiant as a way of compensating for their feelings of insecurity. Shy people can act in an overly overt fashion in order to hide their shyness. People with low self-esteem want to put their best side forward and so often behave in a manner which is affected and tense, etc. Whatever your psychological make-up, trying to battle against a complex can be more complicated and lead to more unpleasant consequences than the complex itself.

As you know, trying to hide a complex or battling against an inferiority complex is futile. The only way of mitigating its consequences is to eliminate the complex altogether which is no easy task. There is no point in repeatedly telling yourself that everything is wonderful because you cannot fool yourself. The slide technique can be helpful though and we will come to that later.

At this stage it is enough to establish the fact that a preoccupation with your own shortcomings in comparison to the qualities of others has the same effect as desiring to illustrate your comparative eminence. The result will be the opposite of what you originally intended. Do not think that others around you attribute to your shortcomings the same meaning that you do. Everyone is mostly concerned with themselves, and so you can freely relieve yourself of a huge burden. Excess potential will dissipate, balanced forces will cease from accentuating the situation and the freed energy can be used for self-development.

Rather than fighting your flaws or trying to hide them, they can be compensated for with other qualities. Charm can compensate for a lack of physical beauty. There are people who are relatively unattractive in their external appearance but who enthral others with their words. Self-confidence also compensates for physical flaws and many great historical figures were no picture to look at!

The inability to communicate freely can be compensated for by being a good listener: As the saying goes "They're all lying, but it doesn't matter because no-one is listening". Your eloquence may interest people but only to a lesser degree. *Everyone*, just like you, is focused on themselves and their problems and so a good listener who will let you pour your heart out to them is a real treasure. To those who are genuinely shy, take my advice; guard this quality like a precious jewel. Believe me, there is a hidden charm to shyness. When you let go of fighting your shyness it will stop coming across as clumsiness and you will notice how people begin to find you more attractive.

Here is another example of how one quality compensates for another. The conditioned need to "be cool" often causes people to imitate those individuals who have already achieved the status of being "cool". To mindlessly copy someone else's script creates nothing more than a parody. Everyone has their own script. All you need to do is choose your own credo and live by it. To imitate others in an attempt to gain the status of being "cool" is like using the method of the fly beating itself up against the window pane. For example, in a group of teenagers the leader will be the one who lives according to their own beliefs. The leader is therefore free not to take advice from others on how they should act. The leader does not need to imitate anyone; they simply have a worthy opinion of themselves. They know what they are doing; they do not need to suck up to anyone or prove anything to anybody. The leader is therefore free of excess potential and receives the deserved advantage. In any group the leader is always the person who lives according to their own beliefs. When a person has freed themselves from the burden of excess potential they have nothing to prove. They have an inner freedom, are self-sufficient and have more energy than those around them. These qualities give them the advantage of becoming leader.

Can you see where the open window is? Maybe you think that these types of dynamic do not concern you and that you don't suffer from issues like these. Do not deceive yourself. *Everyone* to some degree or another has a tendency to create excess potential in the energy fields around them but if you follow the principles of Transurfing, complexes of inferiority or superiority will simply vanish from your life.

Love to Have, Love to Hate

"I want, never gets!" There is truth in this childhood admonition although here I would rephrase it slightly to: "The stronger you want something the less likely you are to get it". When you want something so much that you are willing to place everything on the cards to get it, you create huge excess potential which destroys balance. Balanced forces can then throw you onto a life line where there is no trace of the object you desired.

On an energetic level, a person obsessed with desire is like a wild boar trying to catch a blue bird. The boar wants the bird badly, licking its lips, snorting loudly and rooting the ground in anticipation. Naturally, the bird flies away. If on the other hand the boar had simply wandered around somewhere nearby as if indifferent it would have had a good chance of grabbing the bird by the tail.

There are three types of desire. The first is when a strong desire transforms into the determined intention to have something and do whatever is required to get it. Then the desire is fulfilled. The potential created by the desire is dispersed because the energy behind it is fuelled into action. The second type of desire is inactive and tormenting and represents excess potential in its purest form. It lingers in the energy field. In a best case scenario, it wastes the energy of the suffering carrier, and in a worst case scenario attracts all kinds of unrelated problems.

The third kind of desire is the most insidious. This type of desire becomes dependent on the object of the desire. Attaching great significance to the desired object automatically creates a dependent relationship and strong excess potential, which in turn calls into effect equally powerful balanced forces. Usually, the person's thoughts run along the lines of: "If I achieve this, my situation will improve dramatically", "If I don't achieve this, my life will lose all meaning", "If I do this, I'll prove to myself and everybody else what I'm worth", "If I don't do this, I'm worth nothing", "If I got this, it would be great", "It will be terrible if I don't get this"; and so on. Once you become dependent on the object of your desire you are drawn into such a violent whirlpool that you will exhaust yourself in the struggle. Eventually, when you realise that your efforts have led to nothing you will let go of the desire. Balanced forces will have restored equilibrium remaining completely indifferent to your suffering and all because of a strong attachment to the fulfilment of a desire. This is what happens when a desire is placed on one dish of the scales and absolutely everything else is piled on the other.

Only the first type of desire can be fulfilled because desire is transformed into *pure intention* free of excess potential. It is a common view that there is no such thing as a free lunch and everything has to be paid for. In truth, we pay only for the excess potential we create. In the alternatives space everything is free. Since we are already using these terms, it could be said that absence of importance and dependent relationships are a kind of payment for the fulfilment of desire. The *energy of pure intention* is all that is required for you to transfer to a life line where the object of desire becomes a part of your reality. We will return later to the subject of intention. For now, we will simply note that pure intention is desire and action without the attribution of importance. For example, going to the shop to buy a newspaper is a pure intention because it is in no way inhibited.

The greater an event is valued the more likely it is to fall through in some way. If you attribute huge value to what you have, sooner or later balanced forces will take it from you. If what you want to receive is hugely important to you there is very little chance of you actually getting it unless you lower the stakes.

For example, you are mad about your new car. You blow the dust off it, cherish it, fear it may get scratched and generally worship it. The huge value you place on your car creates excess potential because in the reality of the information field its true meaning is close to nil. Balanced forces will soon find a clumsy driver to cripple your car or you may bump it somewhere by being overly cautious. All you have to do is level out your attitude towards it, treat it as the relatively ordinary object that it is and the chances of it being damaged will be sharply reduced. Treating your car as something ordinary does not mean carelessly. You can take perfectly good care of a car without idolizing it.

There is another aspect to the dynamics of strong desire. A lot of people believe that if you want something badly enough, you will get it. This would suggest that strength of desire can bring you onto a life line where your desire will be fulfilled but that is not the case. If your desire has become dependent, like a kind of psychosis, or you are hysterically driven to obtain something whatever the cost, then somewhere deep down inside you do not really believe that you can achieve it. This creates "strong interference" in the thought energy you are transmitting. If you do not truly have faith in something, you will try really hard to convince yourself that you can achieve what you want, thereby boosting the level of excess potential even more. With this kind of dynamic there is a risk that your "life-work" could actually take you all your life to achieve.

All you can do is reduce the significance your aim has for you personally and set about achieving what you desire in the same manner as you would if you were to go the shop to buy a newspaper.

The strong desire to avoid something is a logical continuation of being dissatisfied either with yourself or with something in your environment. The greater the negative attachment, the more powerful the excess potential will be. The more you want to avoid something the greater the probability that you will experience it because balanced forces have no attachment to the means of restoring balance. They simply have two alternatives which are either to draw you away from encountering the thing you want to avoid or to bring you into contact with it. It is better to consciously stop negating things in your environment so that you do not create excess potential in the first place. But this is not the only consequence of strong negative attachment. When you think about the thing you are negating you radiate energy at the frequency of a life line where that thing is present. You always get the things you love to hate.

In reality, this is what happens when you actively desire for something not to happen. Imagine a man attending a grand reception at an embassy. The atmosphere is formal, refined and sedate. Then the man starts waving his hands about uncontrollably, stamping his feet and screaming desperately how much he *would hate* to be forced to leave immediately. Naturally, the security guys would appear forthwith, grabbing the strange guest under the arms. The man whines and tries to resist but is nonetheless swiftly escorted out of the building. This is, of course, an exaggerated picture of reality, but on an energetic level the dynamic of negative attachment has the same level of force and intensity.

Let us take another example. In the middle of the night you are woken by your noisy neighbours. You really want to sleep because you have to go to work in the morning but it seems like your neighbour's party is just getting going. The more you want them to stop the more likely the party is to go on for some time. The angrier you get the noisier the party becomes and if you start to hate your neighbours with intensity you can guarantee that late night parties will become more frequent. To solve the problem you can apply the method of defeating or stopping the pendulum. You will stop the pendulum's sway if you choose to see the situation as a parody. You could also ignore the situation, refusing to show any sign of interest or emotion. Then the pendulum will be defeated and no excess potential is created. Take comfort in the awareness that you have freedom of choice and that you know how to use it. Soon the neighbours will settle down. This is how it works. Try it out for yourself.

Now you can think back and recognise what things in your life you have attributed excessive importance to and what problems you came up against as a result. If things are genuinely awful, let go of the idea of their importance totally; shake loose your dependency on the situation and start transmitting positive energy right away. The worse things are now, the better, as this will enable you to assess how the technique works if you feel that you have suffered great loss. Take heart! In this situation,

balanced forces are on your side because their task is to compensate bad with good. Things can no more be bad all the time than they can be good all the time. No-one can ride the wave of success all their lives. This is what it would look like on an energetic level if you were to re-attune your energy in this way. Imagine you were attacked, abused, beaten up and everything you had on you was taken, and then all of a sudden, you were shoved a bag which turned out to be full of money. The more you were wounded, the greater the amount of money in the bag there would be.

Guilt

Guilt is pure excess potential. In nature there are no notions of good and bad. For balanced forces both good and bad deeds are equivalent. The important thing in either case is to restore balance if excess potential arises. If you have behaved badly, became aware of it and then started to feel guilty (I should be punished) you will have created potential. If you have acted well, become aware of it and started feeling proud of yourself (I should be rewarded) then you will also have created potential. Balanced forces have no concept that some things should be rewarded and others punished. They simply eliminate inhomogeneity in the energy field.

The payment for feelings of guilt will always be punishment in one form or another. If you do not feel guilty then punishment might not be forthcoming. Unfortunately, feelings of pride that you experience when you have done something good will also lead to punishment rather than reward because the purpose of balanced forces is to eliminate the excess potential of pride, whereas a reward would only enhance it.

An induced feeling of guilt, i.e. guilt you feel when "proper" people are expecting you to feel guilty, creates excess potential squared. As well as your own conscience bothering you, you also have to bear the anger of the righteous as well. Finally, the greatest excess potential is generated by people who experience unwarranted feelings of guilt caused by an innate tendency to "always take the blame". In this case, there is absolutely no point in suffering pangs of conscience, because the reason for the guilt was made up in the first place. Having a guilt complex can ruin your life because you will be constantly subject to the impact of balanced forces appearing in order to eliminate the bias of guilt for imagined crimes.

There is a truth in the saying: "Impudence is second happiness". In general, people whose conscience does not bother them are not affected by balanced forces even if they have committed a wrong doing. It would be great if God automatically punished all villains and culprits. Justice would prevail and evil be overcome. Nonetheless, there is no 'justice' as such in nature and so, sad as it may be, the opposite happens; decent people who have an inherent feeling of guilt are the ones who constantly face misfortune, whereas the shameless and the cynical often go through life not only unpunished, but successful.

Feelings of guilt will always produce a script that includes punishment whether you are conscious of what is happening or not. Your subconscious follows the script and makes you pay. In a best case scenario you will get away with a few cuts or bruises, or some kind of problem will arise. In a worst case scenario, you could have an accident with serious repercussions. This is what the feeling of guilt does. It brings nothing useful or creative, only destruction. It is better to avoid doing anything that would later cause you to feel guilty than to torture yourself with a guilty conscience. Once you can say to yourself that you have not actually done anything wrong it is totally futile to continue torturing yourself with a guilt complex. The feelings you suffer will not benefit anyone, least of all you.

The Ten Commandments are not so much morals in the ethical sense as recommendations for how to maintain balance. It is we with our basic childlike outlook who have interpreted the Commandments as if they were our mother warning us not to be naughty, otherwise she will make us stand in the corner. On the contrary, nothing is said about punishing people who get up to a little mischief. People create their own problems by destroying the balance. The Commandments are simply a warning.

As we said earlier, guilt is like a thread that pendulums, and especially manipulators, can use to control you. Manipulators are people who act according to the construct of: "You have to do what I tell you to now because you are guilty" or "I am better than you because you are in the wrong". A manipulator tries to impose a feeling of guilt onto their "charges", to gain power over them, or for their own self-assertion. On the surface these people can seem very "proper." In their view, what is good and what is bad was established long ago. They always say the right thing and their actions are impeccably correct.

However, in fairness it should be said that not all people who are respectable and decent have a tendency to manipulate. The need to lecture and guide is a consequence of doubt and uncertainty that plagues a person's soul. They skilfully hide their inner struggle from themselves and those around them. Lacking the inner strength that truly decent people possess, the manipulator seeks self-assertion at the expense of others. The need to lecture and control stems from the desire to strengthen their own position, which they do by belittling their adopted ward. Thus, dependent relationships are created. It would be wonderful if balanced forces could make sure that manipulators got what they deserve. However, excess potential only arises where there is tension and a build-up of energy. In this case, there is no build up of excess potential because the ward gives their energy to the manipulator creating a flow. As a result, the manipulator stands uncorrected.

As soon as a person indicates that they are willing to absorb guilt, a manipulator will stick to that person like glue and feed on their energy. This dynamic can be avoided simply by refusing to take on feelings of guilt. You do not have to justify yourself to anyone and you do not owe anybody anything. If you are to blame for something then you can accept the punishment, as long as you do not get stuck in the position of the guilty party afterwards. You do not owe those close to you anything either; after all, you care about them because you love them not because you have been coerced into doing so. This is a completely different matter. If you have a tendency to justify yourself, start letting go of it; once manipulative individuals realize they no longer have a way of hooking into your energy they will leave you alone.

Guilt goes hand in hand with an inferiority complex. If you feel inferior in any way it is because you have compared yourself to others. It is as if you create trials where you play the role of judge over yourself. In reality, it only feels as if you are the judge. The true dynamic works out slightly differently. If you have a natural predisposition to take blame upon yourself irrespective of what the blame is about it follows that you can also be found guilty and punished. By comparing yourself with others you place them in a superior position of authority. In so doing you are enabling others to suppose that they are somehow better than you. The likelihood is that other people do not actually believe that they are better than you but if you have come to this conclusion yourself you end up playing the role of judge in their name. By assuming the role of the guilty party, willingly giving yourself to the court you are effectively inviting other people to judge you.

Appropriate action is to stand up from the accused bench and reclaim the right to be yourself. No-one will dare judge you if you do not consider yourself guilty. Only you can give others the privilege of being your judge. This might all seem like empty rhetoric because if someone has a real flaw we all know that there will always be someone willing to point it out. This only happens though, if they sense that you are predisposed to accepting the blame for your shortcomings. If you consider yourself guilty of being worse than others, even for a second, it will most certainly be used against you. The opposite is also true. If you are free of the feeling of guilt, it will never occur to anyone to assert themselves over you. Here, excess potential has a very subtle influence on the surrounding energetic environment. These ideas are difficult to accept and the technique cannot be proven in words. Do not just take my word for it, try it!

Power and courage also represent aspects of the guilt dynamic. People who have a tendency to feel guilty only subject their will to a person who is immune to the same tendency. If a person is in principle willing to admit guilt for anything at all, subconsciously, they are willing to endure punishment and subordinate themselves to others. If a person is not plagued by feelings of guilt but has a need to assert themselves then they can easily become a manipulator. I am not trying to say that the world is divided into manipulators and string puppets; I am just inviting you to observe a pattern. Rulers and leaders have a very poorly developed sense of guilt, or do not experience feelings of guilt at all. Feeling guilty is a foreign concept to cynics and other types who have no conscience. Their way of progressing in life is to wade through the slaughter and walk over other people. It is not surprising that it is often the unscrupulous that come to power. This does not mean that power of itself is bad or that any person in a position of power is bad. Who can say, perhaps your happiness also lies in becoming a pendulum's favourite. Every individual must decide for themselves how they wish to keep their conscience clear. No-one else has the right to tell you what to do; one thing is clear, indulging in feelings of guilt can only undermine your position.

Boldness indicates the absence of guilt. Fear lies in the subconscious and is evoked not only by the unknown but also by the dread of punishment. A person who is "guilty," theoretically agrees to bear punishment, and therefore experiences fear. Brave people are never tormented by pangs of conscience and they suffer not the slightest feeling of guilt. They have nothing to fear because their inner judge has declared that they are in the right. Quite the opposite position is true of the timid victim who is uncertain of whether they are behaving correctly or not. The victim fears being declared guilty, giving everyone the right to administer punishment. Even the faintest, most deeply hidden feeling of guilt can open the gates to punishment in the subconscious mind. A person, who feels guilty, theoretically agrees that robbers and bandits have the right to attack them as a form of punishment and so they are afraid.

People have learned that asking for forgiveness dissolves the excess potential of guilt and it really works. When a person carries feelings of guilt they hold on to negative energy which culminates as excess potential. In asking for forgiveness a person lets go of the energy allowing it to dissipate. Asking for forgiveness, admitting your mistakes, praying for forgiveness and confession are all ways of eliminating the excess potential of guilt. When a person allows themselves to be forgiven they can let go of the accusation they originally created and then feel better for it. The only thing to be careful of is indulging in remorse. If a person goes too far in their remorseful attitude they risk becoming dependent on manipulators who are just waiting for the next victim. When you ask for forgiveness, admit your mistake and release the potential. Manipulators will remind you of your mistake on more than one occasion trying to reawaken your feelings of guilt. Do not react to the provocation. Everyone has the right to ask for forgiveness once and once only.

Releasing feelings of guilt is the most effective way of surviving in an aggressive environment such as a prison, a gang, the army or street. It is with good reason that the unspoken rule: "Trust no one, fear nothing, and ask for nothing" exists in the criminal world. The rule warns against creating excess potential. Guilt lies at the core of all potential that will serve you ill in an aggressive environment. In a world based on the principle of survival of the fittest you can protect yourself by demonstrating your strength but this is sometimes too general an approach. It is much more effective to eliminate the idea of potential punishment from your subconscious. The following situation illustrates what I mean. In the former Soviet Union, political prisoners were intentionally jailed with common criminals as a way of breaking their spirit. What happened was that many political prisoners by virtue of their remarkable qualities not only avoided becoming victims of harassment and abuse; they became chosen authority figures among the harder criminals, demonstrating that personal independence and dignity are valued more highly than physical strength. Many people are strong physically, but strength of character is a rare trait. The key to personal dignity is the absence of guilt. True personal power rests on the ability to remain free of guilt and not on the ability to take someone by the throat.

The famous Russian writer, Anton Pavlovich Chekhov, once said: "Drop by drop I am squeezing the slave out of me." His phrase highlights his personal dedication to rid the conscience of any feeling of guilt. To get rid of something normally means to fight against it but in the context of Transurfing there is no need to battle or force yourself to do something. In Transurfing it is considered more preferable *to renounce i.e., to choose.* You do not have to squeeze the feeling of guilt out of yourself. It is enough to live by your own credo. *No one has the right to judge you and you have the right to be yourself.* If you allow yourself to be you, the need for self-justification will fall away and the fear of being punished will fade. Then, something truly remarkable will happen: no one will dare insult you.

Moreover, wherever you happen to be, in prison, in the army, in a gang, at work, on the street or in a bar, you will never again find yourself in a situation where somebody will threaten you with violence. Others may from time to time, be subject to violence in one form or another, but because you have renounced the feeling of guilt and driven it from your subconscious you will reside on life lines where scripts of punishment simply don't exist.

Money

It is almost impossible to avoid a dependent relationship on money because it is very hard to love money without wanting more of it. All one can do is attempt to limit the aspect of dependency to a minimum. Be happy if money has come to you but never kill yourself worrying about not having enough money, or spending it, otherwise you will have less and less of it. If a person does not earn much money they probably make the mistake of complaining that they never have enough because the parameters of this type of thought energy correspond to life lines in which there is no wealth.

It is particularly dangerous to give in to an anxiety that your income is gradually decreasing. Fear represents the most energetically intense emotion a human being can experience and so when a person fears losing money or not earning enough money they activate the most effective method there is for shifting to life lines where they really do have less and less money. Freeing oneself from the money trap is difficult but it can be done. First the cause of the excess potential has to be eliminated, which will either be strong dependency on money, or a very intense desire to have money.

Start by accepting and enjoying what you already have. Remember that things could always be worse. You do not have to stop wanting money entirely but you can relax about the fact that it is not rolling in with the force of a gushing river. Take the position of the gambler who could at any moment just as easily hit the jackpot as lose everything.

For pendulums, money is a universal means of rewarding their adherents. It is the activity of pendulums that has led to the widespread idolization of money. Money helps us to provide a good life for ourselves in the material world. Almost anything can be bought and sold. All pendulums use money as payment and there is a hidden danger in this. Having taken the falsely glittering bait it is easy to switch to a life line that lies far away from your true happiness.

In pursuing their own interests, pendulums have created the myth that in order to achieve your goals you have to have money. As a result, people replace their original goal with the artificial substitute of money. Money can be gained from different pendulums and so people shift their focus from the goal to money and come under the influence of a pendulum that is alien to them. People then lose a sense of what they really want from life and focus on the fruitless search for money.

This state of affairs is very profitable for the pendulum but not so profitable for the individual who becomes dependent and loses their way. No-one will ever make a lot of money working for a pendulum that functions outside of the context of their true purpose because they just end up serving someone else's objective. A lot of people live in exactly this position. This is how the myth arose that wealth is the privilege of the minority. In actual fact anyone can become rich if they serve their own goals.

Money is not the goal nor is it really even the means to reaching the goal. It is simply an accompanying attribute. The goal is what a person really wants in life such as to have their own house and grow roses; travel the world and visit faraway places; catch trout in Alaska; go skiing in the Alps; raise horses on their own farm; enjoy life on their own oceanic island; become a movie star or an artist.

It is true that certain goals can be achieved if you have a sack of money so this is what the majority of people do; they go after that sack. By focusing on the money they put the goal itself on the back burner. According to the principles of Transurfing, this is like trying to get onto a life line where a sack of money awaits but you find it almost impossible to get there because you are working for someone else's pendulum. In the end, the person loses out both on the money and their own goal because their thought energy is focused on a substitute for their true purpose.

We will return to this issue in the chapter "Goals and Doors". For now we can draw one general conclusion which is that if you have placed the likelihood of achieving your goal on the condition of getting rich first, drop the condition fast. Let us take an example. If your dream is to travel round the world then obviously this requires a lot of money. To fulfil you dream do not think about the money; keep your thoughts on the original goal. The money will come to you because it is an accompanying attribute to the goal. It is really very simple. It sounds unlikely I know but this is really how things work and soon you will realise that for yourself. In pursuing their own end, pendulums have turned everything upside down. It is not that the goal is achieved with the help of money but rather the money that follows on as you create the path to your goal.

Now you can see just what a powerful influence pendulums have and how many seeds have been sewn for myths and misunderstandings. Listening these lines you may object that it is obvious that first a person becomes a large industrialist or a banker or a film star and then they become a millionaire. It is true that those who become millionaires are those who think not of wealth but of following their own goal. The majority of people think and do the opposite. They either serve someone else's goal, replacing their own with an artificial substitute, or renounce their own dream entirely because the condition of having to be rich first seems unachievable.

In actual fact there are no limitations to wealth. You can desire anything you want. If it is truly yours to have you will receive it. If the goal has been imposed upon you by a pendulum you will not get anywhere. We will talk about goals in more detail later. I am rushing ahead a little but that is unavoidable because there is not anything else to be said about money. Money is nothing more than an accompanying attribute on the path to your goal. Do not worry about money and it will come to you of its own accord. The most important thing now is to reduce the importance of capital to a minimum so that you do not create excess potential. Think only of the thing you wish to achieve.

At the same time, you should be attentive to money and treat it carefully. If you see a small coin on the street and are too lazy to pick it up, it suggests that you do not respect money at all. The money pendulum will hardly be well disposed towards you if you treat its attributes carelessly.

Neither should you worry about spending money because this is a necessary part of fulfilling your mission. If you have made the decision to spend money on something have no regrets. When you try to save up a handsome sum and spend as little as possible you create strong excess potential because energy has been built up in one place. In this case it is highly likely that you could lose everything. Money should be spent wisely to keep a flow going as potential appears where there is no flow of energy. Wealthy people support charities with good reason as it reduces the excess potential of their accumulated wealth.

Perfection

Finally, we look at the most ambiguous and paradoxical way in which balance is compromised. Things that start small can turn out to have the severest of consequences. Usually, we are taught from childhood to do things carefully; to be thorough and always do our best. We are taught to be responsible and are instilled with a sense of what is right and what is wrong. Undoubtedly, this is how things should be; otherwise the next generation would turn into an entire army of slobs and slackers. The down side to this kind of upbringing is that in some of the pendulum's adherents the striving for perfection is so deeply instilled that it becomes part of their persona.

Some people become obsessed with perfection as a result of which their life becomes a constant battle. You can guess what they are battling with of course: balanced forces. The need to achieve perfection in everything creates complications on an energetic level because the assessments a perfectionist makes will inevitably be distorted.

There is nothing wrong with always trying to do your best, but if you attribute perfection too much importance, balanced forces will come in and ruin everything. In addition, a kind of vicious circle is created making the person even more immersed in their obsession. The person desires perfection but they get the opposite. Then they try desperately to right everything but that just makes things worse. In the end, striving for perfection becomes a habit, and can even develop into a mania. The idealist has a tendency not only to place high demands on themselves but to expect high standards of others too, which can poison the life of those they are close to. Their high expectations manifest as an intolerance towards other people's habits and tastes, which often causes small conflicts that easily escalate into bigger ones.

From the outside it is easy to see how ridiculous it is to seek perfection in everything at the same time as tyrannizing everyone else around you. The perfectionist, however, is deeply involved in their role and seduced by the thought that they are impeccable, infallible, in short, perfect. They think that because they strive to meet perfect standards they must be a model for those standards and yet they will not admit this to themselves because generally speaking most perfectionists are too clever not to realize that enjoying a sense of one's own supremacy does not quite fit with generally accepted notions of perfection. Nonetheless, in a person with these traits, the feeling of being right about everything is deeply rooted in the subconscious.

At this point the perfectionist risks succumbing to the temptation of placing themselves in the position of supreme judge over the rest of humanity and deciding how and what all other lost souls should be doing. Naturally, the perfectionist easily gives in to the temptation because they are motivated by the righteous desire to set everybody on the right path and they have no difficulty in justifying their behaviour because they know that they are always right.

From then onwards, having wrapped themselves in the mantle of "arbiter of fate" they assume the right to judge and condemn other people. In reality, of course, the trial does not go beyond everyday accusations and admonition. However, on an energetic level, powerful excess potential is created. The "judge" takes on the mission of deciding how the foolish ones should act and think, what they should value, what they should believe in and what they should strive for. If some feeble being should suddenly decide that they have a right to their own opinion they will be quickly put in their place. Anyone who dares show any resistance will be judged, sentenced and labelled, just to make it quite clear who is who.

Of course the listen is nothing like the picture of the idealist portrayed here. It is unlikely that a person who believed they were always right would be drawn to listen this book. The perfectionist who feels they know how others should run their lives is free of self-doubt. However, if you meet someone like the perfectionist portrayed here take a good look because here you have an extreme example of how crudely the laws of balance can be disregarded. We are all guests in this world. We have the freedom to choose our own path but no-one has the right to judge others, to sentence them or to label them (with the exception of criminal law).

What starts as an innocent striving for perfection ends in claims to the privileges of master. Accordingly, the resistance exerted by balanced forces which initially takes the form of minor problems increases in intensity. If the idealist is protected by a pendulum they will get away with their behaviour for a while but eventually the time will come when they will have to pay for their deeds. When a guest forgets that they are just a guest, and makes claims to the role of master they run the risk of being thrown out altogether.

Importance

Finally, we will look at the idea of importance as this is the most common cause of excess potential. Importance arises when something is attributed excess meaning. Importance represents excess potential in pure form. In the process of eliminating importance, balanced forces create problems for the person that created it.

Two forms of importance exist, *inner* and *outer*. Inner or personal importance represents an overestimation of your own virtues or shortcomings. The formula of inner importance goes along the lines of: “I am an important person” or “I do important work”. When the arrow of perceived personal importance goes right off the scale, balanced forces get involved and the “hot shot” gets a disappointing slap. They will discover that their work is either not needed at all, or that it is done badly. Puffing up your chest and sticking your nose in the air is only one side of the coin. The other side of the coin is excessive modesty and self-deprecation. The reader already knows what this leads to. The amount of excess potential is the same in both cases, the only difference being its positive or negative value.

Outer importance is created when a person attributes huge meaning to an object or event taking place in the external world. In this case the formula goes: “such and such means an awful lot to me” or “it is really important to me to do such and such”. Consequently, excess potential is created and things go wrong. Whereas the feeling of inner importance can be controlled it is much harder to do so with outer importance. Imagine that you have to walk along a plank lying on the ground. Nothing could be easier. Now imagine that you are forced to walk along the same plank which has been placed between the roofs of two high buildings. Walking the plank will have escalated in importance and there will be nothing you can do to persuade yourself otherwise. The only way of eliminating outer importance is to have a safety net. The form the safety net takes will be subjective and depend on each situation. The most important thing is not to place everything on one side of the scales. There has to be some kind of counterbalance, protection or alternative plan.

Essentially everything that can be said about importance has already been said above. There is nothing more to add. You may have made the connection already that in fact everything we have been talking about in this chapter is one variation or another on the theme of importance, inner and outer. All unbalanced feelings and reactions such as indignation, dissatisfaction, irritation, restlessness, anxiety, despondence, embarrassment, despair, fear, remorse, attachment, admiration, exaggerated affection, idealization, worship, delight, disappointment, pride, conceit, contempt, disgust, resentment etc, are all manifestations of importance in one form or another. Excess potential is only created when you attribute excess importance to an object or event that exists inside or outside of yourself.

Projected importance creates excess potential which calls forth the winds of balanced forces. These in turn lead to a mass of different problems and life becomes a battle for survival. Now you can judge for yourself how much inner and outer importance complicates your life.

But that is not all. Remember the *puppet strings*. Pendulums hook into your feelings and reactions: fear, anxiety, hatred, love, worship, call of duty, guilt etc. As you now know, all these states are as a consequence of projected importance. This is a description of what happens. Imagine an object is standing in front of you. On an energetic level the object is neutral: neither good nor bad. You approach the object, wrap it in *importance packaging*, step aside to look at it and gasp. Now you have created an attachment to the object you are willing to give the pendulum–your energy. Importance is like the carrot that makes a little donkey obediently plod along behind. A pendulum uses the same carrot to lock onto the frequency of your energy, drain it and then lead you wherever it wants you to go.

To return to a condition of harmony with the rest of the world and free yourself from the burden of the pendulum you have to be able to *diminish importance.* You have to be able to keep your inner Guardian from dozing off so that it can observe the level of importance you place upon yourself and the world around you. By reducing the level of importance you place on things you immediately re-establish a state of balance. The emptiness (absence of excess potential) gives pendulums nothing to hook onto and consequently, no means of establishing control over you. You may protest that I appear to be suggesting that we all numb ourselves into being lifeless statues. I am in no way urging anyone to reject all emotion or even reduce the intensity of the emotions they experience because, generally, it is futile to fight your emotions. Trying to keep yourself in check and struggling to stay calm on the outside, while everything is bubbling over on the inside just creates more and more excess potential. Emotions stem from attitudes, so rather than fighting your emotions it is more purposeful to change your *attitude.* Feelings and emotions are simply a consequence of your relationship or attitude to something and that attitude is caused by one thing – importance.

If for example, someone in my family has had a baby, a relative has passed away, or there is a wedding or other family gathering planned, these things are neither important to me nor am I indifferent to them. Do you see the difference? I do not make a problem out of the event or torture myself and those around me with my emotional response. So, what of compassion you may ask. I think I would be correct in saying that compassion and helping those who truly need it never did anyone any harm but it is still important even with compassion to observe how you attribute importance to it. I mentioned helping someone when they really need it but sometimes, people just want to suffer. They enjoy it, and evoking your compassion is just a way of indulging in self-validation at your expense. Or, for example, you see a cripple begging on the street and give them some money but the cripple smirks at you as you move on and it turns out that it is not a cripple at all but a professional beggar.

Importance does not exist in the animal and plant kingdoms like it does in human society, with the exception of pets that so closely identify themselves with humans and adopt aspects of human behaviour. Society affects pets as well it would seem. In the world of the wild behaviour is based on the fulfilment of purpose from the point of view of maintaining the laws of balance. Animal behaviour is purely guided by instinct. Importance is a solely human invention that is enjoyed by pendulums. Any extreme bias of assessment towards outer importance makes a person a fanatic, whilst any extreme bias of assessment towards inner importance makes a person a despot.

From the way I have portrayed reality you may be under the impression that one can hardly take a step without fearing the consequences. Fortunately, things are not that bad. Balanced forces will only noticeably affect your life if you are very strongly attached to your own ideas of how things should be; you are obsessive; or have just gone too far. The role of pendulums is also clear. We all come under their influence. The main thing is to be very aware of the mechanism for control; how they hook into you and how far you will let them go.

Reducing importance does not just significantly eliminate problems from your life. Once you have let go of inner and outer importance you obtain the treasure called *freedom of choice.* But, I hear you say, according to the primary principle of Transurfing we automatically have freedom of choice. This is true, we do have the freedom of choice, but often we do not know how to use it because balanced forces and pendulums get in the way. By projecting importance our entire lives are spent battling with the actions of balanced forces. There is simply not enough energy left over to make conscious choices or think about what we really want in life. Pendulums go out of their way to gain control and enforce their own ideas. What freedom can there be in this?

All the importance we attribute to things, be it inner or outer is simply a projection. No-one is of any true importance in this world and yet the riches of life are available to us. Children playing happily on the beach, splashing about and having fun in the waves do not think about whether they are good or bad, whether the water is good or bad or whether the other children are good or bad. Whilst the situation remains unchanged, they are simply happy and in harmony with nature. We all came into the world like that, as a child of nature. If a person maintains a state of harmony the best that life has to offer will be available to them but as soon as a person begins to project importance problems arise. People fail to see the causal link between their projections and the problems they experience and so they buy into the idea that the world is a truly hostile place, where it is really hard to get what you want.

In fact, *the only obstacle on the path to fulfilling your desires is the projection of artificial importance.* I may not have managed to convince you so far that this is the truth of things but I have not run out of arguments yet!

From Battle to Balance

You may wonder if there is a way of counteracting the action of balanced forces. In fact our day to day life is an ongoing battle with balanced forces. All the difficulties and problems we encounter are linked with the actions of balanced forces. Trying to resist balanced forces is futile as they will have their way no matter what. Any effort to avoid the consequences of their actions will only aggravate the situation. The only remedy for the impact of balanced forces is to reduce the excess potential of importance produced as a result of the underlying problem. The kind of situations life throws at us are so diverse it would be impossible to give a universal recipe to cover all of them. There are however, certain general recommendations that can be made to ease the way.

People spend a lot of time building walls based on a foundation of importance only to bang their heads against it or try crawling under it. Rather than trying to get over the obstacle would not it be better to remove bricks from the foundation so that it crumbled? People tend to have a very clear view of the obstacles in their way but a very dim view of the foundation the obstacles are constructed on. If you find yourself in a problematic situation try and determine where you might have placed too much intensity, gone too far, or become obsessive, consequently projecting excess importance. Determine the meaning something has for you and then let go of it. The wall will crumble, obstacles will disappear and problems will be resolved of their own accord. *Do not try to overcome obstacles; reduce their level of importance.*

Reducing importance does not mean fighting your feelings or trying to suppress them. Excessive emotions and worries are the direct consequence of projected importance. It is the cause that has to be dealt with, and the cause is your relationship to whatever the event or other object happens to be. I could advise you to take a philosophical stance in life as far as this is possible, although this approach has already been milked for all its worth. You have to make conscious the fact that projecting importance onto things will bring you nothing but trouble and with that understanding, intentionally reduce the importance you attribute to things.

Reducing outer importance has nothing to do with neglecting one's responsibilities or underestimating what is happening around you. On the contrary, neglect is the flip side of the coin where projected importance is concerned. There is a need to live simply, which includes maintaining a common sense attitude towards life. There is no place for carelessness or exaggeration. Rather than thinking so much about whether a person is good or bad, try to accept the limits of life.

Neither does reducing inner importance have anything in common with becoming resigned or putting yourself down. Indulgently repenting one's sins and mistakes in life is the same as showing off one's virtues and accomplishments. The only difference lies in the value sign each type of behaviour carries, be it positive or negative. Your remorse is only of any use to pendulums that want to establish control over you. Accept yourself the way you are. Allow yourself the luxury of being you. Neither exalt nor belittle your own virtues and flaws. Strive for a state of inner peace in which you understand that you are neither important nor totally insignificant.

If your situation very strongly depends on the outcome of a certain event try to find an alternative solution. In order to stay calm when walking along a plank you have to have a safety net. In each individual case, the safety net will be something different. Simply ask yourself what might serve as a safety net in a given situation and remember that it is useless battling against balanced forces. Neither should you try to suppress fear or excitement. You can only reduce the level of importance you have projected onto something and this can only be done if you have a safety net of some kind or a plan B. Never put all your eggs in one basket, no matter how safe the basket looks. The only thing that does not create excess potential is a sense of humour, the ability to laugh at yourself and others without causing offense. This alone is enough to stop you from becoming a kind of walking talking manikin. Humour deflates the intensity of importance.

When trying to solve a problem follow one golden rule: before you even start considering where the solution might lie, first reduce the level of importance you associate with the problem. That way balanced forces will not get in the way and the problem can be solved quickly and easily.

In order to reduce importance, first *remember* and be aware that the problem or situation has arisen as a consequence of projected excessive importance. Until you can explain to yourself that every single problem is created by excessive importance, you will continue to bury yourself in its intensity, as in a dream, remaining completely under the power of the pendulum. Stop, shake off the delusion and recall what projected importance leads to. Then intentionally change your attitude to the situation in question. It is not difficult to do. You already know that attributing excessive meaning to something will only get in the way. The main difficulty is to *remember* quickly enough that you are playing out projections of inner and outer importance. You need the help of your Guardian, your inner witness who constantly keeps track of all of your inner values.

A person's thoughts are gripped by the power of importance in the same way that muscles become tense. When something is bothering you the muscles in your back go into spasm. You do not notice the tension in these areas until you feel the pain it causes. If you had *remembered* in time and paid attention to your muscles you could have released the tension before it built up into spasm.

Try to catch yourself when you start attributing excess importance to some event you are preparing for. If the event is genuinely important to you, try not to blow it up out of all proportion. The best recipe for success is spontaneity, improvisation and a common sense attitude. Any preparation should be by way of creating a safety net, not by being intensely serious and over careful; this will only increase the level of importance you are attributing to the event. If you are worried about something and yet do nothing about it, this too magnifies the level of importance you give it. *The excessive potential of importance dissipates with action.* Do not think, act! If you cannot act then it is better not to think at all. Shift your attention to something else, and as far as possible, let go of the situation.

The highest level of efficiency in any action is achieved when a person manages to shift the focus of their attention from *self* and *the end goal*, to the *process* of performing the action. In this case the person is not "doing important work" nor is "the work itself important". Excess potential is eliminated and balanced forces will not interfere. The action is completed dispassionately but in no way carelessly or light-heartedly. You might be wondering why one should have to take the focus of attention off the end goal. After all, how can you do your work if you are not thinking about the end goal? Understanding of the meaning of this less obvious and curious fact will become clearer on reading the next few chapters of this book.

Why is it that sometimes you can get really anxious about a certain event? You think about it all the time imagining all kinds of things that could go wrong but in the end everything goes smoothly and so much better than expected? Other times the opposite happens. You are not particularly worried about a particular event which turns out to have completely unforeseen complications and unpleasant sides to it. In the first case, the personal assessment of the situation is off the charts negative whilst in the second case it is through the roof positive. What actually happens in the end is a result of the impact of balanced forces which have the function of balancing the excess potential created by the individual.

From this one might assume that a student, who intentionally pictures the worst possible scenarios immediately before an exam, is more likely to get a high grade. It does not work that way unfortunately because any intention that originates in the mind and not the soul lacks sincerity. You can try deceiving yourself but false sincerity has no energy behind it. Only an *intention that comes from the soul* has juice to it. This is why it does not work when you try to create a desired result simply via visualization, but this is a topic for later.

Never under any circumstances should you boast about what you have, even if you deserve those things and received them fairly, to say nothing of the things you have not yet achieved, because balanced forces will act against you.

Make yourself at home but do not forget that you are visiting. If you are in balance with surrounding pendulums, swaying with them in unison, your life will be pleasurable and flow with ease. When you are vibrating in resonant harmony with rest of the world it energizes you and you achieve your goals without any particular effort.

If you have driven yourself into a state where it is practically impossible to live in balance with the world around you (for example, your husband beats you), then you should think hard about how to take that crucial step to change your surroundings. If you feel that you have nowhere to go this is an idea that has been instilled in you by a pendulum that is trying to keep you under its control. There is always a way out, sometimes more than one. Remember that fly on the glass pane that did not spot the open window? Sudden movements that are badly thought out should be avoided. The best possible solution to any problem will come to you as soon as you reduce the level of importance you project onto it and free yourself from the influence of the destructive pendulum that prevents you from living in peace. You are already familiar with the two means of freeing yourself from a pendulum: defeat and stopping its sway.

With that thought I conclude this chapter on the complex and difficult theme of balance. Now that you understand how the mechanism of balanced forces works, you will easily be able to determine the reason for one failure or another. We conclude that it is essential to observe the principle of balance. It remains only to offer a word of caution against applying the principle too ardently, from becoming fixated with or fanatic about it, as this will only negate the very principle itself. If you try and explain to a centipede in minute detail how it should walk it will become so confused that it won't be able to move at all. All things in moderation. Allow yourself from time to time to disturb the balance at little. Nothing awful will happen as long as you do not force the arrow off the scales.

SUMMARY

Excess potential is only created when you attribute importance to your assessment.

Only the importance you personally attribute to something imbues your assessment with energy.

The force of the excess potential created, increases if your assessment represents a distortion of reality.

The impact of balanced forces is aimed at eliminating excess potential.

The action of balanced forces is often the opposite of the original intention that created the potential.

When renting yourself out, instruct your inner Guardian be help you remain impeccable.

Discontent and judgement will always turn balanced forces against you.

It is essential that habits of negative response be substituted with a transmission of positive energy.

Unconditional love is admiration without worship or the need to possess.

Setting conditions and making comparisons leads to dependent relationships.

Dependent relationships create excess potential.

Idealization and overestimation always end in disillusionment.

To experience reciprocal love you must let go of the right to possess.

You always have to pay for expressions of contempt and vanity.

Let go of the need to assert your superiority.

Striving to hide shortcomings creates the opposite effect.

Your positive qualities compensate for any inadequacies.

The greater the importance of your goal, the less likely you are to achieve it.

Desires are realized when they are free of excess potential created by projected importance and dependency.

Let go of feelings of guilt and the need to justify your actions.

To let go of guilt, it is enough to give yourself permission to be yourself.

No-one has the right to judge you. You have the right to be yourself.

Money comes of its own accord as an attribute on the path to your goal.

Greet money with love and attentiveness and part with it without regret.

Having let go of inner and outer importance you acquire freedom of choice.

The projection of importance is the only obstacle on the way to fulfilling your desires.

Do not try to overcome obstacles; reduce the amount of importance you project onto them.

Take care without worrying.

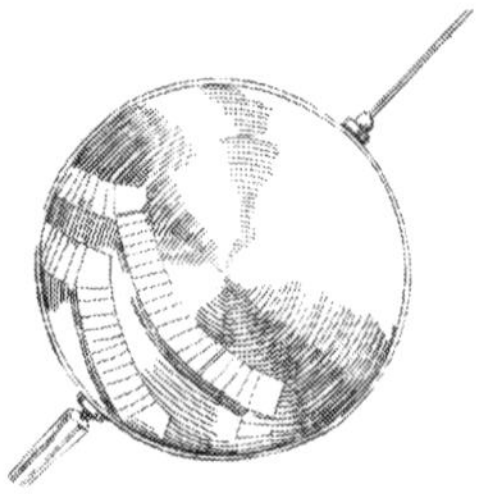

Chapter V. THE INDUCED TRANSITION

Do Not Absorb Negative Information

The Generation Shift

People have always hankered after "the good old days". With age life somehow seems to get worse. People turn to reminiscing about their youth and times when the colours were richer, first impressions more vivid, dreams attainable, music was better, the climate more favourable, people were more approachable, and meat was more tender, to say nothing of their health. Life was full of hope, pleasure and joy. Once a certain number of years have passed, people begin to sense that events do not make them as happy as they did before. Picnics, parties, concerts, films, celebrations, dates, warm sea water…from an objective point of view all these things are still pretty much the same quality as they were before. Parties are still fun, films are still interesting and sea water still feels warm. Nonetheless, life is not the same as it used to be. The colours have faded, our responses have dulled and enthusiasm has waned.

Why is it that everything is so much more wonderful when we are younger? Can it really be that our perception of things loses its sharpness as we grow older? We do not lose the ability to laugh, cry, perceive taste and colour, distinguish truth from deceit or differentiate between good and bad just because we are a little older. So, could the world gradually be going downhill? No, the world is not deteriorating. Things only seem to be getting worse to certain people. What actually happens is that a person shifts to a negative life line that runs in parallel with former life lines where everything is just as fine now as it was before the individual left them behind. By expressing dissatisfaction a person attunes themselves to life lines that draw them in and where things genuinely are 'worse' than before.

According to the principle of Transurfing, the alternatives space has everything for everybody. In one sector, the colours of life have become grey, while another life remains as bright and cheery as it always was. A person who emanates negative thought energy ends up drawn into a sector with a different type of scenery but the world remains the same for everyone else. This is true not only in extreme cases in which someone has become an invalid, lost their home, their loved ones or become an alcoholic and ruined their life. In most cases, during the course of their life a person regularly slides onto life lines where the colours of the scenery are duller than they were on the previous life line. When this happens a person begins to reminisce about how vivid and fresh everything was years ago.

When a child is born they accept the world the way it is. A child is unaware of the fact that life could change becoming better or worse. Young people have not yet been spoiled and so they are less picky. They are still busy with the task of discovering the world for themselves and enjoying life because they have more hope than cause for complaint. They think that life is pretty much ok and expect it to get even better. With time they experience misfortune and failure and begin to understand that not all dreams come true; that some people are better off and that they have to fight for their place in the sun. As time goes by, they can end up with more cause for complaint than hope. Discontentment and whining become a moving force that pushes a person onto unsuccessful life lines. Expressed in Transurfing terms, this type of person radiates negative energy, which transfers them onto life lines that correspond to the negative parameters of their own thought energy.

Life is less satisfactory the worse you think it to be. Children rarely contemplate whether their childhood is good or not. As children we take everything for granted. We have only just begun discovering the world and have not yet acquired the habit of criticism. The greatest insult we experience as children is not being bought a much wanted toy by a relative. It is only as we get a little older that we start to resent the world around us for fulfilling us less and less. The more we complain the worse things are as a result. Everyone who has survived their youth and reached a mature age will say that a lot of things were better when they were younger.

That is the paradox: you come up against circumstances that disappoint you and so you express your dissatisfaction which then aggravates the situation even more. Your discontent comes back to you like a triple force boomerang. Firstly, the excess potential created by your discontent turns balanced forces against you. Secondly, your discontent serves as a channel through which a pendulum being can draw on your energy. Thirdly, radiating negative energy, you shift onto life lines of a corresponding vibration.

The habit of reacting negatively is so deep-seated that human beings are beginning to lose their advantage over other creatures further down the food chain in their capacity for awareness. An oyster also reacts negatively to external irritants, but unlike the oyster, a human being is able to consciously and intentionally regulate their relationship with the external world. Nevertheless, most people do not use the benefit of awareness, instead responding aggressively to the slightest inconvenience. Aggression is mistakenly interpreted as strength but in fact a person who chooses to express themselves aggressively might as well, metaphorically speaking, be quivering helplessly in a pendulum's web.

You might think that life is not as good as it used to be but the younger generation happens to think that life is wonderful. Maybe they just do not know how great things were, when you were their age. Having said that, when you were young, the older generation complained about life too and reminisced about the good old days. This pattern cannot simply be explained by the tendency of the human psyche to erase all negative memories leaving just the positive ones. The criticism is aimed at the present moment which is supposedly worse than it used to be.

If you accept the fact that life is getting worse with every passing year then you would have to agree that the world should have simply fallen to pieces a long time ago. An uncountable number of generations have passed since the beginning of human history and each one believes that life's colours have faded. Many an old man will tell you with absolute certainty how much better Coca-Cola used to be. Coca-Cola was invented in 1886. Imagine how disgusting coke must be by now if it has been consistently worsening in quality since then! Or perhaps one's sense of taste weakens with age, although that is hardly the case. Anyway, the old man will probably tell you how everything else is of a poorer quality today too, be it furniture, clothes or any other item.

If the world were the same for everyone, after several dozen generations life would have become a nightmare for everybody. So how should we understand the paradoxical statement that the world is not the same for everyone? We all live in the same world comprised of the material realization of alternative life lines and yet every individual experiences a different possible alternative. On the surface of things there are obvious differences in people's fate. Some are rich, some are poor; some are successful and some are struggling; some are lucky and some unlucky. We all have our own personal reality within the common world we live in. It seems quite straightforward, just as there are rich and poor neighbourhoods in a single town.

The script, role and the scenery differ in different manifestations of reality. The difference in scenery is harder to track. One person looks at the world from the window of their luxurious car whilst another peeks at it from inside a rubbish container. One person enjoys the party whilst another is consumed in thought about their problems. One sees a group of happy youths, another at a gang of hooligans. They are all looking at the same things but the images they perceive differ as black and white film differs from colour. Every individual is attuned to their own sector in the alternatives space and so everyone lives in their own personal world. All these worlds exist in layers that exist one on top of the other forming what we understand to be the space we live in.

It might be difficult to imagine but no one layer can be separated from another. Every individual creates their own reality and that reality intersects and interacts with the rest of the world around us.

Imagine what the Earth was like before any single living creature existed. Winds blow, rains fall, volcanoes erupt and rivers flow. Then suddenly a person is born who begins to observe their environment. The energy of that person's thoughts stimulates the material manifestation of a certain sector of the alternatives space which represents their specific life in this specific world. That person's life represents a new layer in the world. Then another person is born who generates another layer. One person dies and a layer disappears, or perhaps is transformed depending on what happens beyond the threshold of death.

We are vaguely aware that other forms of life exist in parallel worlds of some kind. Let us suppose for a moment that there are no living creatures in these worlds whatsoever, at least not yet. What kind of energy would stimulate the material manifestation of space that contained no single living creature? We can only guess. Perhaps, once the last living creature dies, the world itself will disappear? Who can prove that the world exists if there is nobody in it? For if there are no people who would be around to say that the world (in our understanding) exists at all. There would be no world to speak of.

That is enough speculation for now. We do not want to get bogged down in abstract conjecture. Remember though, that Transurfing is just one of many models. All existing theories about the world and life in it are nothing but models. Remember also the notion of importance and try to avoid projecting any outer importance onto the Transurfing model of the universe; otherwise you could become an apologist for futile ideas and try proving to everyone the truth of your own subjective worldview. Truth is an abstract notion for we can only understand some of the world's forms and laws. Our goal here lies exclusively in attaining maximum practical benefit from our preferred model of the universe.

Now let us return to the topic of the generations. Throughout their lifetime a person re-attunes their energy from the vibration of one sector in the alternatives space to another, thereby transforming the layer of their personal world. The more a person readily expresses their discontent emanating large quantities of negative energy, the more strongly the tendency for the quality of their life to deteriorate is consolidated. A man could acquire great material wealth with age but not necessarily be any the happier for it. The colours of his scenery could just as well fade and life become less enjoyable. The older and the younger generation both drink the same Coca-Cola, swim in the same oceans, ski on the same mountain slopes and everything is pretty much the same as it was many years ago. However, the older man is convinced that in his day everything was better and the young person is convinced that things are better now and when the young person grows old the story will no doubt repeat itself.

There are deviations from this tendency, both for the better and for the worse. Sometimes a person only begins to develop a taste for life as they get older, and the opposite can happen; a successful young man can go downhill until he hits rock bottom. That said, in general, the generations agree that life gets worse as you get older. This is how the shift in generational layers takes place. The layer of the older generation shifts to a life line of poorer quality and the layer of the younger generation gradually follows on behind. The shift takes place gradually, each time starting from a point of optimism. This is precisely why the world as a whole never actually transforms into a living hell. Everyone has their own layer, which they choose themselves. By now you will have a clear picture of how the choice can be made to one's personal detriment.

In previous chapters we have already talked about how to avoid creating a living hell in your own life layer. You may also wonder whether it is possible for a person to retrieve an earlier section of their world, or return to a life line that was filled with colour and hope like it was in childhood. The Transurfing technique can help with this task but before we look at that it is first useful to understand how exactly a person can end up shifting from a life line full of success and hope to a life line where they would face the question: "So how exactly did your life end up like this?"

The Pendulum Vortex

The human psyche works in such a way that it reacts most strongly to negative irritants such as unwanted information, hostility, danger or any other form of negative energy. Of course, positive influences can also stir strong emotions but the intensity and force of emotions like fear and rage by far outweigh those of joy and happiness. The reason for this originates in ancient times when fear and rage were crucial to survival. What use is joy in a context like that? Joy is not as useful when it comes to defending yourself, avoiding danger and foraging for food. In addition, throughout the entire history of humanity life has been filled with burden and hardship that have brought more grief and fear than joy and happiness. This is generally speaking why man yields readily to thoughts of gloom and depression, while feelings of joy and happiness pass relatively quickly. Have you ever heard of a normal person suffering from too much joy? People who suffer from stress and depression however can be found in good number wherever you look.

Pendulums, in particular, the mass media, actively make use of these particular features of human perception. You rarely hear anything good in the news. Usually, in a news program you hear a negative fact followed up with news coverage. New details gradually emerge, and the details of the story are thoroughly savoured and dramatized.

Other negative news stories covering catastrophes, natural disasters, terrorist acts and armed conflicts are presented according to the same principle. Notice the pattern. Events develop in a spiral of intensity. First there is the catchy headline and then the story is unravelled exposing further details. The tension gradually peaks with emotions running equally high. Finally, the story comes to its conclusion and all of that emotional energy is released into space as a temporary calm descends upon the viewers. Endless TV series are based on the same pattern of build up and release like waves breaking on the shore. From an objective point of view, there is nothing special about these programmes. All the "drama" is literally created out of thin air. However, you only have to watch two or three episodes and you are hooked. Why is this, after all, nothing particularly interesting ever happens? You become hooked because the frequency of your thought energy is caught by the pendulum of the TV series, and your attention becomes fixed on that sector within the alternatives space.

This is the mechanism that winds the spiral mentioned above: At first a person is confronted with a fact which theoretically they may or may not find upsetting. Let us suppose that the fact is a fresh piece of news about a negative event that has taken place somewhere in another country. This represents the destructive pendulum's first prod. If a person is touched by the news story they respond to the stimulus by expressing their thoughts and feelings about it. If the news concerns them they will begin radiating energy at the same frequency as the pendulum's initial prod. Like thousands of others the person responds to the pendulum with interest thereby participating in the overall event. The vibration of the person's thought energy begins to resonate with the pendulum increasing the force of its energy. Meanwhile, the media continues its campaign. The person follows developments with interest making sure that the pendulum receives its nourishment. This is a typical example of how a pendulum entices adherents into its web so that it can continually suck energy from them. The person who becomes increasingly interested in the news piece absorbs some of its negative energy and whether they are aware of it or not they are now involved in a game, at least as an observer. At first glance, it does not look as if anything untoward has happened. Watching the news is a matter of course. So what if a person gives a bit of their energy to a destructive pendulum? It is not as if it will affect their health. When a person begins radiating energy at the frequency of a negative event, they shift onto a life line that is located closer to other life lines in which such events take place. They begin to play a part in the plot. They find themselves within the impact area of a spiral that rotates faster and faster, drawing them into a vortex, like water into the funnel of a whirlpool. The interaction between the individual and the pendulum becomes increasingly close, and the person accepts the event as an unavoidable part of their life. Their attention becomes selective and it will seem as if new facts about similar events in different countries are popping up everywhere. The person will discuss the news with their close friends and relatives who will no doubt respond with interest and compassion. The energy of the pendulum grows as a result and the individual is drawn ever closer, by the frequency of their thought energy to the life line of the original event except at this stage they are no longer an observer, but a direct participant.

The phenomenon of being drawn further towards the vortex can be described as an induced transition to a life line where the adherent becomes the victim of a destructive pendulum. The individual's response to the pendulum's initial prod and the mutual exchange of energy that follows induces a shift to a life line with a vibration very similar to that of the pendulum's sway. As a result, a negative event occurs in the layer of this person's life.

Disaster

Most people accept that theoretically they could end up being involved in a catastrophic event but not all actually allow the possibility into the layer of their personal world. There are people who do not watch TV serials, have no interest in the news, and are emotionally undisturbed by events taking place somewhere else in the world. They live in a different life layer to these events and are adherents of other pendulums. They remain undisturbed by the fact that somewhere in the world there has been a plane crash. They listen to the news indifferently whilst they eat their supper probably because they have enough to deal with in their own lives.

The type of person most likely to undergo an induced shift shows active interest in disasters that involve other people and take place in other areas. This kind of person is deeply disturbed by news of such events. Sometimes, when a person suffers few problems of their own there is a tendency to fill the empty space in their lives by giving their attention to events taking place in life layers other than their own. This type of person regularly reads the tabloids, watches TV series, or awaits news updates on tragic accidents and natural disasters. Tabloids and soap operas are the activities of small, harmless pendulums. Adherence to pendulums in this category does nothing more than make up for a deficit of information, emotion and experience in a person's own life. In contrast, displaying an active interest in catastrophes and natural disasters poses a real threat, for these are the manifestation of stronger, more aggressive pendulums.

The vibration of thought energy radiating from a person who gives their attention to tragic events is hooked in the same way as it is by a television series. Anyone who looks for negative information will always find an abundance of it. At first they play the innocent role of observer like a person watching a football match from the grandstand. The game gradually becomes more gripping and the observer becomes a fan. Then they walk onto the playing field and start to run about waiting for the ball. Gradually, unnoticeably, the fan becomes more involved in the game and in the end another player will pass them the ball. Metaphorically speaking, the original observer has become a player, a victim of disaster.

Could it really be otherwise? A person allows information related to disaster to become a part of their life. They unwittingly accept the fate of victim and eventually, materialize misfortune in an alternative life line. Of course, the person had no intention of becoming a victim but that is unfortunately of no consequence because once a person has agreed to join the role they will play is chosen by the pendulum. Whereas for many people personal involvement in a disaster would signify the result of a fatal train of events, for our victim, it would represent the logical end to a line of behaviour that increased the probability of their being in the wrong place at the wrong time.

If you ignore the prod of a destructive pendulum you will never end up involved in a catastrophic event or at least the probability of it happening will be close to zero. You may object that thousands of people have lost their lives in tragic accidents and natural disasters; surely not all these people were thinking about catastrophes simultaneously? The thing is that we do not live alone in the world. We are surrounded by other people who are actively working for destructive pendulums and radiating energy within the pendulum's spectrum. It is not possible to become totally and ideally isolated from these vibrational frequencies. The common field encompasses you, and without being consciously aware of it, you begin to radiate energy at the same frequencies as the surrounding field. The roots of this type of behaviour go back to very ancient times when the herd instinct helped to protect the group from danger. This is why the energy field of an induced shift grows, producing a snowball effect that pulls you in like water to the centre of a whirlpool.

The task is to stay as far away as possible from the pendulum's vortex. This means not absorbing negative information relating to catastrophic events and disasters; showing no interest; refraining from worry or discussion and generally, letting the information pass you by. Notice that we say 'let the information pass you by', rather than try to avoid it. As we know from previous chapters, trying to avoid a meeting with a pendulum is the same as seeking out a meeting with it. When you resist something, desire specifically to avoid something or express your enmity towards something you actively radiate energy at the frequency of the object you are trying to avoid. To 'let something pass you by' means not to absorb or react to negative information; simply ignore it and switch your attention to harmless television programs and books.

If you find it impossible to retain a positive outlook when confronted with negativity you can always turn to your Guardian Angel. For example, if you are afraid of flying, stay away from planes. If you are afraid it means that somewhere in the spectrum of your energy there is a frequency that resonates at the vibration of a life line in which a plane crash occurs. It does not mean that you will immediately transition to this life line, but nonetheless, the possibility exists. If you are the kind of person who does not think of the dangers of flying at all, then you have nothing to fear. On the other hand, if you experience unusually high levels of anxiety before boarding a plane it would be wise to skip the flight. If this is totally out of the question you would be wise to learn to listen to the rustle of the morning stars. What that is and how it can be heard, you have yet to discover.

War

Wars break out essentially for the same reason that fist fights do. One party expresses their opinion. The other party holds the opposite opinion and so the opinion expressed by the first is like the prod of a destructive pendulum. The second party takes offense at the prod and reacts with double the amplitude. The first shouts back even louder. Both parties become increasingly aggressive until things finally come to blows.

This metaphor illustrates the battle between two pendulums that knock against each other, causing each to swing higher and higher. Obviously the outbreak of war or build-up to a revolution involves all sorts of complex factors, but essentially the process is the same. The pendulum primes the people by telling them that they do not have a good life and the people are quick to agree. It is then explained that the reason they do not live well is because other people are preventing them doing so. This stirs resentment and the pendulum begins to swing. Then one side provokes the other evoking a storm of anger whereby the pendulum gathers force and the war or revolution can begin. Each swing of the pendulum generates a response, which strengthens the pendulum's sway still further. A snowball effect is initiated until a shift occurs to a life line with mounting tension.

The situation can only be changed at the outset before things escalate out of control, at the moment when the spiral begins to turn and the pendulum makes its first move. If the other party responds peacefully or simply walks away, the pendulum will be brought to rest or defeated. If however, the pendulum's prod is accepted, the participant's energy will correspond to the parameters of the life line on the next turn of the spiral. Unfortunately, there is no guarantee that an individual participant will not be pulled into the events of war or revolution even if they manage not to respond to the pendulum. If you get pulled into a powerful whirlpool, however hard you try, it is almost impossible to free yourself from the current that pulls towards the centre. If however, a participant refuses to play the pendulum's game they will at least have greater chances of surviving with minimal loss.

Here we should be clear about what it means not to tolerate war or revolution. You could hate war or be actively campaigning against it. It makes no difference to the pendulum which side of the fence you stand on. It will claim your energy in both cases. If energy is emanated at the frequency of war a shift will occur onto a corresponding life line. If you accept war and participate in it then you are effectively on the battle field. If you fight against war it will consume you anyway. Not to accept the pendulum's game means to ignore it. I realize that it is not always possible to ignore something like war but this is the danger of the induced shift. It is not worth taking the position of defender or opponent of war. There have always been neutral countries which have remained on the sideline and watched while entire nations destroyed each other. From the point of view of the pendulum trying to provoke a fight with its rivals, people who ardently protest against war at demonstrations are potentially just as committed and desirable adherents as the supporters of conflict. Active protest against war potentially provides the pendulum with just as much energy as the support of war, although naive adherents will be convinced of the opposite. The real way to prevent war is simply to support peaceful action and where possible expose a pendulum's true motives. Do you remember the metaphor of the hive of wild bees? The pendulum tells its adherents that the bees are dangerous and must be killed. But what is the pendulum's true motive. What does it really need? Honey perhaps...

Unemployment

As we have said, there are different ways of playing the game of a destructive pendulum, either by supporting it or negating it. The second option is probably the most perilous, since the desire to actively avoid a pendulum creates excess potential that can pull you into the vortex of an induced transition. Almost everyone nowadays experiences concern at some point or another about losing their job. An induced transition to finding yourself out on the street would be quite a crafty manoeuvre. Sometimes larger events start with something small and seemingly harmless; an initial feint signal. For example, you might hear that your company is not doing quite as well as it was before, or someone you know lost their job recently, or there are rumours at work that staff may have to be made redundant.

On a subconscious level, an otherwise unnoticeable red light comes on. Shortly afterwards, you pick up on another signal such as reports that inflation is sky high. This keeps you and those around you on their toes. People start talking about their concerns and the unemployment pendulum is provided with a source of energy. Then there is news about an impending drop in the stock market and the general tension increases. Concern quickly gives way to anxiety and then fear. By this time you are already generating energy to the vibration of a life line where you can see yourself without a job. If you are afraid that you will end up being one of the ones made redundant your fear is as perceptible to others as if you were wearing a placard saying, "I might be made redundant". If you think you can hide your fear you are mistaken. Body language and the slightest intonation in your voice say more than a thousand words. Once you lose confidence in yourself you become less efficient. Tasks that you found easy before seem more difficult. A certain tension seeps into your communication with colleagues who are in the same position. You take your anxiety home with you and instead of support you find your family begin to complain and criticize. Stress levels rise and you are no longer an efficient employee. At this stage you might as well be wearing a sign saying: "waiting to be sacked".

The fear of being sacked lies in a feeling of guilt which either smoulders away or burns brightly in your subconscious. They always fire the weakest employees first. If you allow yourself to consider that you might be weaker than your colleagues you effectively write you own name into the black list. Let go of guilt. Give yourself the luxury of being you. If that does not work start looking for another job because the excess potential of your emotional worries will be dissipated by taking action. Some people start looking for another job, as soon as they have taken on a new position, not because they intend to change jobs immediately, but because the idea of having a safety net makes them feel more confident. On the off chance that something unexpected does happen, they know they have an alternative avenue to follow. If you feel secure about the future, the action of balanced forces will not affect you.

Epidemic

You are probably thinking that an epidemic can have no relevance to life lines and that people get ill simply because they have become infected by some bacteria. This is correct, but only so far as a person allows themselves to become infected, and by this, I do not mean that they were not wearing a protective health mask.

That would not have saved them. I cannot prove my point with theoretical argument; just as I cannot prove anything I have said in this book, just as you would not walk around with a mask on during a flu epidemic, just to test whether the mask works or not. I am sharing what I know to be true. Whether it resonates with you or not only you can know.

So, let us unravel the stages of disease. The cause of an illness is your voluntary agreement to play the game called "Epidemic." It all begins with rumours that somewhere an epidemic, the flu for example, is going around. Everyone knows that the flu is transmitted through the respiratory system and so, you, like everyone else, totally accept the possibility that you could come down with something. You immediately run the 'being off sick' scenario through your mind. You imagine having a temperature, lying in bed coughing and sneezing. From this moment on you are playing the pendulum's game because your imagination is shaping your thought energy to the same frequency as the destructive pendulum.

Your subconscious starts searching for confirmation of the onset of an epidemic and your attention becomes selective. You seem suddenly to be surrounded by people sneezing. They were always there; it is just that you did not notice them before. From time to time, at work and at home, someone will raise the subject of the flu. Your suspicion that an epidemic is on its way is confirmed by more and more evidence. Even if you were not particularly looking for confirmation or the subject does not particularly worry you; somehow, confirmation is given of its own accord.

If, from the very beginning of the game, you have attuned yourself to the frequency of the destructive pendulum, your bond with it will become stronger, regardless of whether your participation is conscious. If you are not against the idea of getting sick or if you feel that you are for some reason bound to come down with something you become an active adherent. On the other hand, you decide that you cannot afford to be ill and keep telling yourself how totally healthy you are, but that does not work. Just thinking about the illness means that you are attuning your energy to its frequency. How exactly you think about it, positively or negatively is of no matter. Your efforts to convince yourself from the very beginning that you will not get ill enforce your acceptance of the likelihood that you will become ill, and because this is the case, no amount of self-indoctrination will keep you healthy.

Words spoken aloud are simply warm air and words spoken to oneself are nothing at all in comparison to the inaudible power of faith. Without faith you will not protect yourself from the flu even if you rush to get a flu vaccination. It makes no difference because whatever you do, you will be ill for as long as you need to be. The first symptoms provide you with a choice of whether you are going to come down with something serious or recover very quickly. You might make a weak attempt to resist but finally, you face the fact that you are going to be ill. With that the final adjustment is made to your energy vibration and you shift to a life line where illness is prevalent.

The induced shift actually starts from the very moment that you respond to the pendulum's prod. If you genuinely could not care about the epidemic you will not be affected. If you are on holiday, have not communicated very much with anyone, have not seen the news and know nothing about the epidemic, the pendulum will not affect you. It will simply disappear into thin air. Have you ever wondered why doctors are not infected by their patients? Many boldly work without wearing a mask. It is not because they have had the jabs. You cannot have a vaccine for everything. The thing is that doctors are also actively playing the game of the illness pendulum, but they are playing an entirely different role. By analogy, the next time you fly, notice the stewardesses on the plane. They whizz up and down the cabin like little angels insistently advising passengers to fasten their seat belts, and yet they are so mobile in the cabin one suspects that if anything happened they would simply hover in the air like hummingbirds.

"What about breast fed babies infected with AIDS?" the fastidious reader will ask. "Do they too radiate the energy of induced transition?" In response it should be said, that firstly, we are looking at the phenomenon of epidemic as a general tendency and secondly, I am not suggesting that the concept of infection is a delusion or that thought energy radiating at the frequency of illness is the sole cause of ill health. Transurfing is neither a dogma, nor does it claim to be the final authority on truth. No idea should be taken to be absolute truth. We can only take into account patterns and regularities. Truth is always "somewhere close by", but where exactly, nobody can say.

Panic

Panic generates the most intense and quickly induced transition. Panic very effectively highlights the distinctive features of an induced transition. Firstly, the spiral coils very strongly when a person panics because any signal of real danger always has a convincing sound to it. It is so easy then to be immediately drawn into the game of a destructive pendulum. The increase in the pendulum's sway also gathers speed very quickly for the same reason.

Secondly, when a person panics they almost completely lose their self-control, simultaneously becoming a sensitive receiver and active transmitter for the pendulum's sway. Finally, the pendulum itself can use panic as an ideal way of materializing itself in the crowd. Unfortunately, all these factors make it very difficult to defeat the pendulum or bring it to rest because in a moment of panic, considering how to overcome the problem of a pendulum is the last thing on your mind.

However, if you can somehow keep your head you may succeed in saving yourself and others. For example, when a ship is sinking a group of desperate passengers will clamber around a small number of lifeboats whilst other boats nearby remain empty. It only takes a second to look around and notice the empty crafts but this is the cunning quality of the induced shift that works like a whirlpool sucking in anything located at its periphery.

Poverty

From a logical point of view how does a simple man from the slums become rich, not including criminal means or beautiful stories about people becoming millionaires overnight? The rags to riches story is very difficult to explain using only common sense, so what, you may ask, is the use of logic? Transurfing does not entirely fit into the framework of common sense. On the other hand, it does enable you to achieve things that would otherwise appear impossible.

When your actions are based on logical deduction you get a corresponding result. If a person is born in poverty they will be accustomed to living in poor circumstances and their energy will be attuned to the frequency of their own misfortune. It is very difficult to shift to a life line of prosperity if you despise your own poverty, envy the wealthy, and constantly wish you were better off. Actually, I would say that with these three types of thought in mind it is totally impossible.

One of the first discoveries children make as they get older is the fact that just because you would hate for something to happen it does not mean you can avoid it happening. Sometimes, the soul simply cries out in despair: "But I don't want to! I hate it! Why does this always happen to me?" It is not only children who ask themselves this question in fits of anger, but adults too. It is difficult to accept the fact that even though you do not want something to happen there is nothing you can do about it and if you hate something, it will follow you around wherever you go. You can harbour a hatred for poverty, your work, your physical flaws, your neighbours, drunks, alcoholics, drug addicts, dogs, thieves, criminals, the impudent child, the government…the list goes on. The more you love to hate something, the more likely you are to have experience of it in your life. The reason for this is clear. When something gets to you, you think about it, which means that you radiate energy at the frequency of a life line where that thing exists in abundance. It does not matter which polarity you embody: "liking" or "not liking." The second is of greater benefit to the pendulum because emotions associated with 'not liking' are more powerful than emotions associated with 'liking'. The destructive pendulum sways even higher when you are suffering emotionally. Finally, when you actively hate something you create excess potential. Balanced forces are then directed against you, because it is easier for them to eliminate one opponent than to change a world that does not suit one individual. Who would have thought there could be so many harmful aspects to a negative attitude towards life!

In the case of the individual who is born in poverty but dreams of becoming rich, we know that desire itself is not enough to initiate change. Often people do their dreaming lounging about on the sofa having the occasional stretch and thinking how much they would like a bowl of strawberries but not knowing where to get them in the middle of winter.

If you are not prepared to take action to acquire what you want you will not get it. A poor person usually does not take action because of their own conviction that the fulfilment of their desire is not realistic. It is a vicious circle. Desire of itself has no power. Desire fails even to lift a finger. Intention i.e. the readiness to act is the force that lifts the finger. With intention a person could just as easily say: "You can't take this away from me! It's simple. I just want to be rich!"

Again, there is a huge chasm between "wanting" and "being ready to become". For example, a poor person tends to feel out of place in the company of the wealthy or an expensive shop, even if they are desperately trying to convince themselves and others that the opposite is true because in their heart they believe that they are not worthy of that environment. Wealth is not part of a poor person's comfort zone and not because it is uncomfortable to be wealthy, but because it is so unfamiliar. A new armchair is better but the old armchair is more comfortable.

A poor person only sees the external side of wealth: luxurious houses, expensive cars, ornaments, clubs, etc. If you placed a poor person in this type of environment, they would feel uncomfortable and if you were to give them a suitcase full of money, they would do all sorts of foolish things with it until they had spent it all. The frequency of energy a poor person transmits is sharply dissonant with that of a wealthy life. Until a person lets the attributes of wealth into their comfort zone and until they learn how it feels to be the owner of expensive things, they will remain poor, even if they find a buried treasure.

Another obstacle on the path to wealth is envy. To envy someone means to be annoyed by someone else's success. There is nothing constructive about envy at all. In fact, it has a very strong, destructive element. A person's psyche works in such a way, that if they envy something that another has they try to devalue it in every way possible. This is the logic of being "green with envy": "I envy what he has. I don't have it and probably never will have. He is no better than I am. That thing he has can't be that good then. Perhaps I don't need it after all."

The desire to posses something is transformed into a psychological defence which then develops into rejection. The aspect of rejection takes place on a subtle level because the subconscious mind takes everything literally. Your conscious mind only plays at devaluing the object of envy to comfort the person for not having it, but the subconscious mind takes it all seriously and bends over backwards to make sure that the person does not receive what has been so ardently devalued.

You can see what tenacious forces hold a person to their life line of poverty. Events can unfold even more dramatically when a person undergoes an induced transition from a life line of prosperity to a life line of destitution. It does sometimes happen that a successful person suddenly loses everything and ends up on the street. The most insidious thing about an induced transition to poverty is that the spiral begins to unwind slowly and then picks up speed until there is no stopping it.

The spiral starts with temporary financial difficulties. Anyone can experience temporary financial difficulties. They are an inevitable part of life, just like rain on the day you plan for a picnic.

As long as you do not get angry about it, depressed, excessively anxious or resentful, being deprived of a potential source of energy, the pendulum will come to rest. The induced shift only occurs if you somehow take a grip of the spiral's tail. The spiral can only start turning if you react to the destructive pendulum.

A person's initial response is often to be disappointed. This is quite a weak source of energy so if the emotional response stops here the pendulum will be stilled. Anger and resentment are stronger forms of emotional response which might lift the pendulum's spirits enough for it to convey the information that someone else is to blame for the person's financial difficulties. Their response to this second prod might be making negative comments taking action against those who are supposedly to blame. By this time the pendulum will be quite revived and begin the second turn of the spiral. At this stage the person may receive a reduced income payment, prices may rise, or some debt might suddenly be called in.

At this stage the person probably does not realize that a process has been set in motion. It could seem to be nothing more than the result of unfortunate circumstances, whereas in actual fact, it is the result of a directed process, which has been induced by responding emotionally to the pendulum's prod. The frequency of that person's energy will continue to change from a vibration characteristic of a prosperous life line to a vibration characteristic of a new life line in which they suffer deprivation and annoyance. As a result, they shift to life lines that correspond to a new set of financial circumstances.

The situation is compounded and bad news starts to come in from all sides. Prices rise and their company's performance level drops. They discuss the problem with close friends and relatives and the conversations are usually of a destructive nature full of complaint, resentment and aggression towards the guilty party. This can be particularly pronounced in companies where business is especially bad and the working day begins with the statement that "there's no money coming in", as solemnly as if it were a morning prayer.

At this stage the person is totally gripped by the spiral and their energy attuned to the frequency of the destructive pendulum. Seeing that things are consistently getting worse they become stressed and anxious. Despite its relatively insignificant magnitude the pendulum can easily assimilate the energy of anxiety and so it becomes all the more audacious. Because the adherent is so stressed they inevitably generate excess potential: discontent, aggression, depression, apathy, resentment and so on. As balanced forces connect with the pendulum the situation snowballs out of control. The fear they begin to experience drives them to distraction and things become frantic.

It is as if someone has taken them by the hands, spun them round and round, only to let go abruptly making them fly off to one side. The poor adherent falls to the ground where they lie in a state of shock. The finale is not a pretty picture although it all started with just a few financial difficulties. Of course, it is not money that the pendulum needs so much as the negative energy a person generates when they realize that their money is literally going down the drain. By the time the spiral has unwound itself the unfortunate individual has at best lost much of their wealth and at worst lost everything they had at which point they are no longer of any interest to the pendulum as there is nothing more that can be gained from them. The unfortunate adherent will either remain lying in shock on the unsuccessful life line, or try with difficulty to pick themselves up from the floor. Such an induced transition can happen to a private individual as easily as to a large group of people. In the latter case, as you can imagine, the spiral is like a massive whirlpool from which it is impossible to escape.

The only way to avoid an induced transition is to avoid gripping onto the tail of the spiral, thereby avoiding getting caught up in the pendulum's destructive game. It is not sufficient to know how the mechanism works. To remain free of the pendulum's power you must maintain a constant awareness of it. You must not allow your inner Guardian to doze off. Pull yourself up every time you realize that, out of habit, as if in a dream, you have accepted a pendulum's game, i.e. you have expressed discontentment, indignation, anxiety, or contributed to a destructive discussion and so on. Remember: everything that causes you to express a negative reaction is a provocative prod from a destructive pendulum. The same thing happens when you are dreaming; until you realize that what you are seeing is a dream, you are simply a pawn in someone else's game and there is nothing to stop you from being tormented by nightmares. As soon as you wake up, shake off the delusion and realize the nature of the game. You are in control. When you do this you will no longer be the victim of circumstances, while everyone around you continues to exist in a zombie-like state.

SUMMARY

Everyone creates the separate layer of their own world.

The world of humanity consists of individual layers, placed one on top of the other.

When a person emanates negative energy they compromise the quality of their own life layer.

Aggression is mistakenly taken to be a strength and dissatisfaction as a normal reaction.

Reacting to negative events induces a shift to negative life lines.

An induced transition is accompanied by a negative event in a personal life layer.

Do not allow negative information into your layer.

"Do not allow" does not mean strive to avoid, but rather, to intentionally ignore, to express no interest.

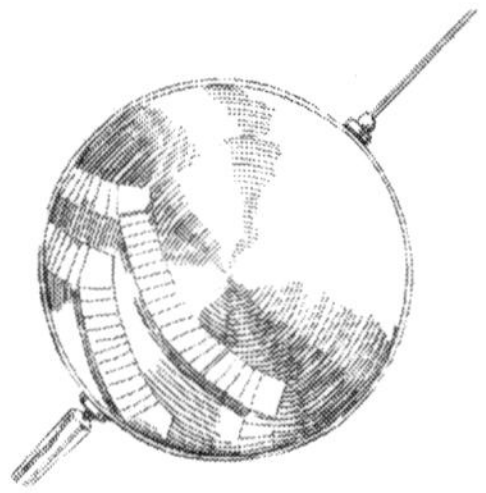

Chapter VI. THE ALTERNATIVES FLOW

When you go with the flow the world meets you halfway

The Information Field

The alternatives space is an information field or energy matrix, *a template for what things could be like*. When a sector of the matrix is lit up by an energy that has the same resonance, that part of the template is transformed into physical reality. The question is whether the information held in the matrix can be used whilst it exists in its intangible form.

You could say that we are using this information on an every day basis. The conscious mind might not be able to read the information held in the alternatives space but the subconscious mind can access it directly. This is where premonitions, intuition, prophecies, inventions and works of art originate.

The conscious mind sources information both by interpreting data from the external world and by receiving it from the subconscious via intuition. Put bluntly, the data recorded in the information field represents truth in its purest form. It represents objective information undistorted by interpretation. When truth passes through the filter of the mind it becomes an interpretation, i.e. knowledge. All living beings have their own way of interpreting the truth. A chicken for example sees and understands the world very differently to a human. Even different people will see and understand the same things in different ways. As a result, knowledge is a more or less distorted representation of the truth.

The data contained in the information field exists in the form of a complex energetic structure. The field is a record of everything that causes matter to move in accordance with the laws of nature. Initially, data from the information field is received by the subconscious, the soul, and then the conscious mind or reason, translates it into word and symbol. This is how any innovation is brought to life, be it a new genre of music, a work of art, or anything that a person could not have seen or understood directly. Intuitive knowledge and premonitions are received in the same way.

This explanation might be a little perturbing or hard to accept. Can it really be, you ask, that the mind is incapable of creating anything new independently and is actually drawing on data from an external source or information field? Perhaps it is too categorical to say that the mind can never create anything new. The mind can build a new object or solve a problem using knowledge of objects and logical constructions that it is already familiar with. In other words, the rational mind can build a new house but only from old bricks. It can construct something using ideas that have been made accessible to the conscious mind previously, but it cannot directly access information that is fundamentally new.

Scientific discoveries are not made as a result of logical reasoning, so much as from an 'aha moment' of insight when knowledge seems to come from nowhere. The same goes for genius inventions. Good music just comes to the musician. It is not created via the intelligent choice of notes. Works of art are created as a result of inspiration not professional and technical skill. A picture that from a technical point of view has been executed perfectly will not necessarily be proclaimed a work of art. The special quality that makes something a work of art lies beyond the realms of technical execution. Poetry that has the ability to touch your heart is not written by the process of choosing rhythms but comes from the depths of the poet's soul.

Creativity based on inspiration and insight is totally different to something produced by the rational mind. It is only later that a product of true creativity becomes an attribute of the mind. The mind may be capable of making a perfect copy of an old work of art but it is incapable of creating a new one. The mind analyzes data, received from the information field by the subconscious and endows it with symbolic form producing a painting, a melody, a poem, mathematical formula etc.

We do not yet know how the subconscious accesses the information field but we can witness the access. Clairvoyants for example are capable of perceiving events that have taken place in the past, have not yet taken place, or are happening somewhere beyond our field of vision. As we cannot yet explain the mechanism for such things we refer to them as paranormal phenomena. Not wishing to reveal their impotence the pendulums of fundamental science refuse to take such phenomena seriously. However, the fact that we cannot explain them does not stop them from being real or justify the tendency to dismiss them out of hand.

There are people who are capable of seeing events in the information field as clearly as if they were witnessing them in the material world. People like this are capable of attuning to manifest sectors in the alternatives space. A clairvoyant for example can attune to the sector of a missing person by looking at a photograph of that person or touching an item of their belongings. The police have even been known to make use of the services of clairvoyants in their investigations.

Not all clairvoyants can see perfectly and so mistakes are made. Mistakes can be made for two reasons. Firstly the clairvoyant may attune to a sector that has never been realised in the material plane and never will be. Confusion can also be caused by the fact that separate sectors differ in script and scenery to a lesser or greater degree depending on their relative distance from one another. This can effect how information is interpreted. For example, ancient prophesiers and prophets who observed unusual scenes from the future interpreted them according to the knowledge available to them at the time causing their predictions to be inaccurate.

Whether you believe in these things or not is a very personal thing. Remember, Transurfing is just a model that allows us to apply the laws of the universe to serve our own interests. It does not claim to provide a comprehensive description of the structure of the universe. Neither is Transurfing a monument in granite bearing the inscription: "Here lies the secret". Truth, as you know, is only ever somewhere close by. The idea that man is capable of synthesizing anything new using the rational mind alone is simply the product of a certain attitude. It is just that society has been relying on the model that generated that attitude for a long time now. It should be pointed out however, that the conventional worldview is as impossible to prove as the Transurfing model. Whether things actually happen according to one system or another does not concern us here too much. The fact remains, that information originating in the alternatives space is somehow available to us in the form of hunches, visions, insights and signs, and as far as we are able we must attempt to understanding its meaning.

Knowledge Out of Nowhere

Only a few very unique individuals are capable of reading data held in the information field. The majority of us receive reverberations of data in the form of momentary premonitions and vaguely perceived knowledge. People involved in the worlds of science and creativity often receive insights after many long days or years of contemplation. It can take such a long time to unveil something entirely new because thought energy, however deeply a person concentrates, can be more easily attuned to sectors of the alternatives space that have already been transformed into physical reality. Anything fundamentally new originates in sectors of the alternatives space that have not yet been transformed into physical reality. Unfortunately, we do not yet fully understand how to attune our thoughts to these sectors.

When the subconscious is somehow able to access information held in an unrealized sector of the field the conscious mind can be confused finding it vague and obscure. This is because the data has not before been interpreted using symbols that are familiar to the rational mind. If however, the brain manages to reach deeply into the essence of the information newly available, insight and clarity is achieved.

There is much that is unclear and contradictory about the mechanisms of the conscious and the subconscious mind. Rather than delve deeply into all these issues here, we will just look at a couple of themes related to how they function. Also, to avoid getting mixed up in semantics and terminology, for simplicity's sake we will define everything connected with the conscious mind as reason and with the subconscious as the heart or soul.

If the mind was capable of understanding everything the heart wished to share with it, humanity would have already gained full access to the information field. One can only imagine the heights human civilization would have reached as a result. The mind however, is not very good at listening to the heart and does not want to. Its attention is either taken up with things relating to the outside world or with its own inner bag of contemplation and anxiety. The mind is busy controlling its unceasing internal monologue and is by comparison highly inattentive to the feint signals of the heart. The mind authoritatively insists on doing things its own way. When reason "thinks", it draws on categories which it uses to mark the qualities of visible objects in materialized sectors of the information field. In other words, it thinks with the help of established *designations*: symbols, words, concepts, diagrams, rules etc. The mind unscrambles all the information it receives using appropriate designations.

Designations are attributed to everything that exists in the world around us. The sky is blue, water is wet, birds fly, tigers are dangerous, winter is cold etc. If the information received from a non-materialized sector has not yet been attributed rational designation the mind perceives it as unfathomable knowledge. If new designations can be introduced or if it can be explained within the context of conventional references then a discovery is made.

It is always extremely difficult to find designations for new knowledge. It is like when a person hears music for the first time, a type of information expressed in the form of sound. When a person hears the music their mind receives the information it carries. The mind knows it is hearing something but does not yet understand what it is hearing because it has nothing to make reference to. Understanding comes later, when the person has heard music many times and all the relevant designations and objects have been demonstrated: musicians, instruments, notes and songs. When music is heard for the first time it is perceived simultaneously as knowledge and a mystery.

Try explaining to a small child that "milk is white". Young children are only just learning to use abstract categories and so they ask a lot of questions. A child may know what milk is but not understand what white means and so the child asks: "What is white?" "White is a colour." "What is colour?" "It's a quality objects have." "What's quality? What's object?" And so it goes on! Rather than trying to explain it is easier to just show the child objects of different colours. Then the child's mind begins to recognise how to differentiate objects using the abstract notion of colour. This is how a child learns to define everything in the world around it and then think using these definitions. The heart, unlike the mind, does not use designations. How could the heart explain to a child that milk is white?

Ever since the mind began thinking in terms of abstract categories the connection between the heart and mind gradually atrophied. The heart does not work in terms of categories. It does not think or speak. It feels and knows. Because the heart is not able to express what it knows in words and symbols, the mind finds it difficult to understand. How then can the heart communicate with the mind if it has discovered something in the alternatives space that does not yet exist in the material world?

The mind is always busy with its own chatter. It has a logical explanation for everything and is constantly trying to control information. It picks up on vague signals from the heart which it is not always capable of defining with the help of categories. The vague feelings and knowledge signalled by the heart are drowned out by the vociferous thoughts of the mind. When control over the mind is released however, intuitive feelings and knowledge can break through to consciousness.

The signals of the heart are conveyed as an ambiguous premonition which we call the inner voice. In moments when the mind is distracted it allows you to experience the feelings and knowledge of the heart. This is the *rustle of the morning stars;* the voice without words; reflection without thought and sound without volume. When you hear this music you know that you have understood something but it still has an elusive quality. Do not think so much; feel and listen to your intuition. Everyone knows what intuition is. Everyone has sometime had the feeling that someone is about to arrive just before a visitor appears at the door; has had the feeling that something is going to happen and then it does; or has had the feeling that they *simply know something that requires no explanation.*

The mind is constantly generating thoughts and the voice of the heart is literally drowned out by the 'thought-churn' making it difficult to access intuitive knowledge. If you stop the train of thoughts and simply contemplate the emptiness, you will hear the rustle of the morning stars, the inner voice that has no words. The heart could provide answers to many of our questions if only we could hear its voice.

It is quite difficult to deliberately attune to unrealized sectors of the information field and to force your mind to listen to what the heart is trying to convey, so we will begin slowly. The heart has two quite clearly discernible states: comfort and discomfort. The mind has designations for these states: "I feel good" and "I do not feel good", "I feel confident" and "I am anxious", "I like it" and "I do not like it".

At every step we take in life we have to decide whether to do one thing or another. The thing we call life emerges when parts of the alternatives space are transformed into physical reality. Depending on our thoughts and actions one sector or another is realized on the material level. The heart has access to the information field and somehow the heart is given to see what lies ahead in as yet unrealized but impending sectors. When the soul has set its sights on a sector that has not yet been realized in the physical it knows what to expect and whether it will be a pleasant or unpleasant experience. The mind interprets these feelings as vague sensations of inner peace or the lack of it.

The soul often knows what lies ahead and tries patiently to communicate what it knows to the mind but the mind hardly hears the voice, or attributes very little meaning to the vague premonition. The mind is hooked by pendulums, preoccupied solving problems and convinced by the reasonableness of its actions. The mind makes resolute decisions guided by logical reasoning and common sense. As we know though, sensible reasoning is no guarantee of an ideal solution. Unlike the mind, the heart is rarely mistaken because it does not think. It feels and knows. How often do we hear people claim post factum: "I knew nothing good would come of it!"

The task is to learn to interpret what the heart is trying to communicate to the mind at the time a decision is being made. It is not difficult. All you have to do is instruct your inner Guardian to pay attention to your inner state before making a final decision. Your mind is usually trapped by pendulums or absorbed with the job of solving various problems. To hear the rustle of the morning stars it is enough to simply *remember* to note your inner condition. It sounds quite banal and commonplace but it works. The only problem is in *paying attention* to your feelings and sensations. People tend to be more inclined to trust arguments based on reason than their own feelings and so have forgotten how to pay attention to their own inner condition and the feeling of integrity that inner peace gives.

In the moment of considering a possible solution to a problem the mind is guided by sensible reasoning, not by feelings. In fact, in the moment of decision making the mind is unlikely to even notice that there are such things as feelings. If however, you have been able to *remember,* then take the next step and note what you are *feeling.* There might be something about a situation that puts you on your guard or worries you. There might be something you do not like about a situation. Once you have made a decision ask the mind to be quiet for a moment and ask yourself how you feel about it, good or bad. Then imagine having made a different decision and ask yourself the question again: "How does this make me feel, good or bad?"

If you cannot pick up on a clear feeling when you do this it suggests that your mind is still not very good at listening. Instruct your inner Guardian to alert you to your inner state more often. On the other hand, it may be that the question itself is ambiguous in which case it is better not to make a decision based on vague information. In this case you can rely on the judgement of your mind or simplify the question.

If you get a clear sense of "Yes, I feel good about this", or "No, I do not feel good about this", then you have clearly heard the rustle of the morning stars. Now you know the answer to your question. It does not mean that you will necessarily act according to the dictates of the heart for we are not always free to act as we would wish to, but at least you will know what to expect from a sector which has not yet been transformed into physical reality.

The Needy, the Indignant and the Fighter

In any situation a person can respond with two extremes of behaviour. One extreme is to be swept along by the current like a powerless paper boat and the other is to row stubbornly against the tide.

If a person is lazy, incapable of taking the initiative, has no goals and is happy to simply exist then they can be controlled by other forces. It is very easy for this kind of person to become a pendulum's puppet. People like this effectively decline from choosing their own fate or choose to believe that their fate is predestined or 'predoomed'. Through their choice they affirm the statement that there is no flying from fate; what will be, will be and they will be proved right because this life path also exists as a potential reality in the alternatives space. Having made this decision all a person can do is complain about their fate and, in their impotence, hope for the mercy of higher powers.

When a person gives up responsibility for their fate they take one of two paths in life. On one path they accept their circumstances and *beg* for handouts, cap in hand, appealing either to the pendulum or to some higher power. A pendulum will force the needy to work hard and the person will break their back earning a very humble living. They may naively call on higher powers for help but generally speaking higher powers have more important things to do. The needy abdicate responsibility for their own fate in the manner of "It's all in God's hands". Perhaps they believe that all you have to do is ask nicely, and as God is merciful, He will give you what you need. Imagine the prayer: "Mountains and valleys! Rivers and oceans! Oh, sky! Oh, earth! I bow before your power! My heart is filled with faith and reverence. I believe that you will help me buy my morning newspaper!" Perhaps this is too exaggerated an example, and yet why not, after all, it makes no difference surely to the higher powers whether you are asking for a newspaper or a palace, for they can do anything. If the needy for some reason ended up without a morning paper they would surely conclude that they just did not ask properly. So, carry on asking...

There is a Russian joke that goes: A man is lying on his sofa praying: "God!" he says, "Make me rich. I know you can. I totally believe in your greatness!" Annoyed, the Lord tells him: "Listen, mate, you could at least buy a lottery ticket!" It is a convenient position to abdicate all responsibility for your life at the same time as wallowing in your own self-importance, for it is self-important to imagine yourself so significant that God, in all his majesty and mercy, would see to your needs personally. God has already given man the ultimate gift: freedom of choice, and yet some people are too infantile to accept the gift preferring to remain constantly dissatisfied.

People will always find ways of justifying their actions claiming that their path is too densely strewn with obstacles and that for them, something always goes wrong. That something of course is balanced forces and pendulums that arise as a consequence of the excess potential generated by their self-importance. It is like in the children's game that goes: "Geese–geese!" – "Honk! Honk! Honk!"–"Are you hungry?" – "Yes, yes, yes!" – "Well, fly on home then!" – "We can't. We are afraid of the grey wolf that stands at the foot of the mountain!"

If a person does not fit the role of the needy they may choose the role of the indignant, expressing their dissatisfaction and demanding to be given what they are *supposedly due*. By being so very demanding the indignant person harms the potential shape of their destiny even more. Imagine a man who visits an art gallery but does not like the exhibition and so has a tantrum believing that he has the right to express his dissatisfaction. He stamps his feet making threats, breaking things and demanding that the organisers take the exhibition down. Naturally, the man would be punished for his actions which would make him even more resentful and all the more inclined to express his indignation. A person who believes that their own wants and needs should be a priority for others would never dream that they are merely a *guest* in this world.

From the point of view of Transurfing, both roles appear equally as absurd. Transurfing offers a different path: *if you want something, don't plead for it, don't demand it, just go ahead and get it.* There is nothing new in this position. It is the natural stance of a person who makes their own choices and believes that their destiny is in their own hands. However, people tend to take this too far in their struggle for a place in the sun. Taking a hard stand people declare war on pendulums, get drawn into competition and elbow their way forward. Their entire life becomes a continuous *struggle* for survival. This is their choice and the choice will be played out because it also exists as a possible reality in the alternatives space.

We already know that passive acceptance and overt dissatisfaction cause a person to become dependent on pendulums. Perhaps you recall the content of the chapter on importance and excess potential. The needy create excess potential via their feelings of guilt, voluntarily offering themselves into the hands of manipulators. The victim automatically assumes that they are condemned to have to ask for what they want and waits until someone decides to give it to them. The indignant person creates excess potential with their continuous expression of dissatisfaction and ruins their own life by endlessly invoking balanced forces.

Having chosen to battle, the fighter takes a more productive stance, but their life is hard and demands a huge amount of energy. No matter how hard a person tries to resist, if they take this position they will just get more and more entangled in the web. The fighter believes that they are battling for the sake of their own destiny, while in fact they are simply wasting huge amounts of personal energy. Sometimes a person wins but at what cost? Their example goes to convince everyone that the laurels of victory can only be hard won. With that the widespread belief that if you want to achieve something you have to slog away and fight for it is further consolidated.

Public opinion is mainly shaped by pendulums. The excess potential of self-importance serves as a feeding trough for pendulums and so beliefs based on some aspect of self-importance are widely supported. The belief that a personal goal is difficult to attain represents a projection of outer importance, whereas the belief that the goal can only be achieved by a personality with extraordinary qualities is a projection of inner importance. Either way the individual is fleeced. They may be allowed to reach the finish line which will no doubt make them very happy, but what the person will not realize is how much energy was wasted, not so much on reaching the goal, as on indulging the exactions of the pendulum.

Metaphorically speaking, it is like a person trying to make their way through a crowd of pleading beggars in order to reach their goal. The beggars bustle about, block the way, and grasp at the person's clothes and body. The person tries to justify themselves, apologises, gives the beggars money, pushes them aside and forces their way through the crowd. Finally, and not without great difficulty, the goal is reached. The energy that was spent on actually achieving the goal is comparatively small, enough *to place one foot in front of another*. The remaining portion of energy went on battling with the needy.

When a person learns to break the loop with the pendulum they will have their freedom. The scroungers will leave them in peace and focus on some other individual. To free yourself from the burden of pendulums you have to abandon inner and outer importance. If you manage to do this the obstacles you would have encountered on the way towards realizing your personal goals will simply fade away. Then you will be in a position *not to ask for what you want, not to demand it, and not to struggle for it, but simply to go ahead and get it.*

Now the question arises as to how the phrase "go ahead and get it" should be understood specifically and how to go about it. The rest of this book is devoted to answering this question, so soon you will have the answer. So far we have outlined general strategies for choosing one's personal destiny. None of the roles described above, the needy, the indignant or the fighter are for us. What role do you think Transurfing would ascribe to the master of their own fate in the game called life? That is the homework. The answer can be found in the next chapter.

Now we are going to look at different tactical ways of behaving in various situations.

Going With the Flow

The needy and the indignant go weakly with the flow of life while the fighter pushes against the flow. Of course, in life, no one person is a pure example of either role. We all adopt one or more of these roles to a greater or lesser extent as life changes and yet none of them are particularly effective. If it is not advisable to fight and going with the flow is too limp what other options are there?

Earlier we described how reason authoritatively asserts its will based on common sense. Some people rationalize in a very reasonable, intelligent manner and yet are totally incapable of solving their own problems. How useful can common sense be if the mind cannot use it to provide an ideal solution to a problem? The thing is that even though the mind is being rational it remains unaware of the fact that it is influenced by the thought patterns created by pendulums. Certainly, while a person is playing the role of the needy, the indignant or the fighter, there can be no question of freedom of movement. In reality, the fighter has no more freedom to assert their true will than the little paper boat.

Metaphorically speaking, this is how the fighter moves with the flow of life: pendulums provoke the fighter who then swims against the current, not understanding that it would be easier and more advantageous *to use* the flow. The fighter's mind is gripped by pendulums, but the fighter is resolutely set on battle and, by making resolute decisions, whips the water with all his might, in places where calm, smooth movements would have sufficed.

Now imagine a person who neither goes against the flow causing additional eddies in the water, nor lets the current carry them utterly, like a little paper boat. They would be intentionally moving in harmony with the flow noting the sand banks, obstacles and dangerous areas along the way, making smooth movements to keep to their chosen course. This is the person at the helm.

How useful is it to think of life in terms of flow and why is it so injurious to swim passively or try to resist the flow? The information that lies in the alternatives space is stationary, like a matrix. At the same time, the information structure is organized into chains of cause-and-effect which give birth to *the flow of alternatives*. This is what we mean when we talk about flow in the context of Transurfing.

The main reason to avoid actively resisting the flow is that in doing so you expend a huge amount of energy either in vain or to your own detriment. Neither can you rely entirely on the alternatives flow, for it could carry you into a calm lagoon as easily as to the edge of a waterfall. One should therefore, proceed with a sense of caution correcting one's movements with smooth actions. A person should also be aware of the general direction of the flow which is determined by their chosen goal and the means of achieving it. Once the general course has been determined one should rely on the flow as far as possible.

Everyone has a rough sense of the general flow of events in their life. Most people first study then get a job, have a family, work their way up the employment ladder, build a house, and so on. Many people make a lot of mistakes along the way, in retrospect wishing they had done things differently, but it is too late to change anything. What is done is done. The flow takes them in a direction far away from their goal and the rational mind is powerless to do anything about it. All they can do is regret, knowing that if only they had known where they would fall, they would have put something there to soften the landing.

Everyone wants to know what awaits them just around the corner. Not everyone is serious about turning to fortune-tellers and astrologers for advice, but many are interested in them, at least out of curiosity. The advantage of a listening is that an optimistic astrological forecast or prediction can light a spark of hope whereas an unpleasant prediction can be trivialised as meaningless and later forgotten. Despite the fact that astrological calculations and clairvoyance cannot guarantee one hundred percent accuracy the Transurfing model does not negate their value because prediction and sight are sourced in the alternatives space. In any case, if the accuracy rate was too low, no one would take these translunary predictions seriously. Astrology does not only exist because people are curious to take a peep into the future. The alternatives flow also allows us to take a glance at other sectors of the field that exist in physical reality.

How much one chooses to rely on forecasts and astrological predictions is also a very personal thing so we will respectfully place this subject to one side and consider what we can usefully conclude from the simple knowledge that the alternatives flow exists. The main questions that arise, are to what extent we can surrender ourselves to the flow, how to determine whether we are going in the right direction, and why we should surrender ourselves to it at all.

As we mentioned previously, the mind is constantly under pressure from projected levels of importance and so hindered from making truly efficient decisions. Inner and outer importance is, essentially, the main source of the problem causing balanced forces to manifest in the form of rapids and whirlpools along a person's path. If you reduce the intensity of projected importance, the flow will return to a calmer current. The question of whether one should surrender oneself to the flow is also important. Outer importance encourages the mind to look for complicated solutions to simple problems. Inner importance convinces the mind that its reasoning is sound and capable of making the only right decision.

If we reduce the intensity of projected importance the mind can breathe freely. Because it has been released from the influence of pendulums and the pressure of artificially created problems it can make more objective, appropriate decisions. The beauty of this lies in the fact that once the mind is free of the burden of importance it has no great need for a powerful intellect. Of course, to solve everyday problems you need logical thinking, knowledge and analytical skill, but this requires much less energy. The flow of alternatives is a luxurious gift which, paradoxically, the mind hardly ever uses.

The alternatives flow contains the solutions to all our problems. The majority of problems are in fact artificially created by the mind. Pendulums prod the anxious mind which sets about solving all sorts of problems just to try and keep the situation under control. Its wilful decisions are for the most part pointless like randomly slapping your hands on the surface of the water. The majority of problems, particularly minor problems, resolve themselves if the alternatives flow is allowed to take its course.

There is no essential need for a powerful intellect if the solution to a problem already exists in the alternatives space. The optimum solution will appear of its own accord as long as we do not go rooting around in the debris interfering with the alternatives flow. Optimality is a principle that is inherent in the structure of the information field. Chains of cause-and effect create separate *streams* in the flow of alternatives. These streams represent the best possible ways in which cause and effect can move. Everything exists in the alternatives space, but it is the optimal or most energy-efficient alternative that is more likely to be realized. Nature never wastes energy which is why people walk with their feet and not their ears. All processes strive to move along paths which are most energy efficient so the alternative streams are organized along the path of least resistance. This is where the optimal solution to any problem lies. The mind is constantly losing a sense of the flow because it is influenced by pendulums and acts in their interests. In other words, the mind gets caught up in a maze looking for complicated solutions to simple problems.

All these abstract notions may appear overly conjectural. However, you can try out some of the ideas in this book in practice and then decide whether you think the flow exists or not. The alternatives flow *is a truly sumptuous gift for the mind.* The keys to any problem are encoded within it. To access them you have to learn to move in the direction of least resistance. As a rule, people look for complicated solutions because they perceive the problem as an obstacle and as we know, obstacles can only be overcome by applying much effort. It helps to get into the habit of choosing the simplest possible solution to any given problem.

We all have to leam something new at some point, or think about how we can do familiar tasks in a more effective way. One approach to doing things in the most efficient manner is so simple it is hard to believe it actually works: *in accordance with the principle of harmonious movement everything should be done by the easiest and simplest means possible.*

The most optimal alternatives to any action are organised in streams which are like chains comprised of links which represent optimal cause and effect. Deciding to take the next step in a given action is like choosing the next link in the chain. It is a matter of deciding which link is a part of the stream. What normally happens though, is that a person makes a logical decision based on what they think would be most correct based on their day to day experience of life.

The mind makes wilful decisions believing that it is capable of calculating and explaining anything but this is not true. You can probably recall many occasions when you have suddenly seen how things could have been done differently and yet it was too late. It is not that the mind is scattered or lacking in sharpness so much as that the chain in the stream does not always correspond to logical construction.

However meticulous you are, you will rarely choose an optimal action relying solely on logic. Generally speaking, the mind is always under some kind of pressure, be it stress, anxiety, depression or heightened activity. In other words, the mind is constantly distracted by pendulums, which makes it a little bit pushy, or prepared to launch an attack on the outside world.

In order to choose the next chain in the stream all you have to do is free yourself from the puppet strings and have enough compliance to follow the flow. This means adopting a condition of balance and having enough mindfulness not to project inflated importance.

Once you feel that you are in a condition of balance and harmony with the world just follow the flow. You will notice a multitude of signs that will guide you. Let go of the situation. Be the objective observer rather than the participant. Perform your actions simply adopting neither the position of slave nor master. Instruct your inner Guardian to nudge you every time your mind tries to make a 'sensible' but nonetheless wilful decision. Detach yourself emotionally as if you were simply an administrator and observe your work from the outside. *Everything can be done a lot more simply than you think. Yield to the simplicity. It is the mind not the alternatives flow that carries you to the edge of the waterfall.*

Imagine that there is something you need to buy, but you do not know where to find a shop that sells it. You rely on your mind which suggests the most sensible and the most complicated way of finding the shop you need. You drive round half the town looking for the right shop, only to find one, right next door to your house. If you had attributed less importance to the search, the mind would not have been set on finding such a difficult solution.

Here is another example. You have a list of things to do and you are wondering which task to start with and which to put off until later. Do not think about it. If there is no particular need for the tasks to be done in a specific sequence, do the task that you feel most inclined to start with. Go with the flow; Separate your mind from the influence of the pendulums. It is about learning that smooth, light, simple movements are enough to navigate the water. You do not have to be an impotent paper boat or splash your hands wildly about in the water,

I will not go on with a long list of examples. If you spend even just one day truly going with the flow you will discover for yourself just how helpful and surprising living your life in this way can be. Every time you have to come up with a solution to a problem ask yourself which approach would be the easiest and go with that. Every time something or someone comes in to distract you, do not hurry to resist it or skirt around it. Try detaching yourself from the situation and then observing what happens next. Every time you face a new task, ask yourself: How can I do this as simply as possible? Then allow whatever it is to get done with as much ease as possible. Every time someone suggests something different or tries to prove their own point of view try not to jump in and argue back. Maybe the rational mind just cannot understand the advantage or see the alternative. Activate your inner Guardian. First observe and only then take action. Come down into the auditorium. Do not hurry to take control. Let the game develop as far as possible of its own accord under your supervision. There is no need to madly splash your hands about in the water. Try not to get in the way of the flow of life and you will feel much better for it.

Guiding Signs

How can we distinguish between an approaching sandbank or waterfall and a normal turn in current? There are always tangible signs that will help us navigate ourselves through life. Life is constantly sending us signs.

The most common, well-known sign is an omen. There are good and bad omens. Seeing a rainbow is a good omen. A black cat crossing the road is an omen of misfortune. Widely acknowledged omens are created as a result of multiple observations and comparisons. If the percentage of correctly predicted omens is high enough, a certain pattern is determined which then becomes public opinion, because people love to talk to one another about strange phenomena. However, omens do not always come true; far from it in fact.

In Russia, when you forget something and have to go back for it people worry because they say that returning to a place you have just left is a bad omen. Even if a person is not particularly superstitious the strong social stereotype throws a shadow across their subconscious. The person begins to fear that something unpleasant will happen and so decides that it is not worth returning to pick up the thing they left behind. Unfortunately, that does not help either, because an even flow has already been disturbed and the person is already slightly out of balance. The expectation of misfortune introduces change into the parameters of a person's thought energy and they shifts to a life line that corresponds in quality. Not surprisingly, they then end up experiencing whatever it was they feared. In effect, the person has allowed the possibility of the event to enter their personal script. This explains why an increasing percentage of omens are fulfilled.

As you can see, the omen of itself cannot serve as a law or pattern. Why is it that *everyone* considers a black cat in particular to be a bad omen? Or, put differently, how is it that a black cat can have any kind of influence on our lives? Of course it is not the cat that has the influence but a person's response to seeing a cat.

If you believe in omens they will play a role in shaping the events of your life. If you do not believe in omens, but still experience doubts when you realise you have seen one, the influence will be slight. If, however, you do not believe in omens at all and pay absolutely no attention to them, they will have no influence in your life whatsoever. The principle is very simple: *you experience what you allow into your personal life script.* A person who believes omens to be empty superstitions will experience no indication of their validity in the layer of their world. Omens may appear real in the layers of other people's worlds because those people look for confirmation of them, whereas the sceptic does not.

If omens have no direct influence on the events in our lives, then what do we mean when we talk about guiding signs? The black cat cannot have any direct influence over you but it can serve as a sign warning you of an event that will take place further down the line in the alternatives flow. It is amazing how many signs you can spot once you decide to be observant of what is happening around you. You can end up seeing them just about everywhere. So which signs should be considered guiding signs? The other issue is how signs should be interpreted but we will not go into that as it is too comprehensive and vague a topic. All you can reliably do is increase your inner Guardian's level of watchfulness and vigilance, notice the sign and take its presence into account.

Guiding signs are signs that indicate a possible turn in the alternatives flow. In other words, a guiding sign serves to herald an event that will substantially change the flow of everyday life. If you are expecting some sort of change in the current however small, a sign will appear to signal its onset. A characteristic sign may also appear if an unexpected turn is coming up in the near future.

When the alternatives flow makes a turn you shift onto a different life line. The life line will be more or less homogeneous, as far as quality of life is concerned. The stream in the alternatives flow can intersect many life lines that have different parameters. The changes may be relatively insignificant, but you will nonetheless experience the difference. The qualitative change is noticed either consciously or subconsciously with the knowing that something is not quite the same as it was a minute ago.

Guiding signs only appear when a shift to a different life line is initiated. If for example you pay no particular attention to a separate event such as a crow squawking, if it does not put you on your guard and you do not feel any qualitative difference in that moment it suggests that you are on the same life line as before. If, however, the phenomenon does attract your attention and you feel that there is something unusual or odd about it then it is probably a sign.

A sign differs from other everyday phenomena in that it signals the beginning of a shift to a life line that differs considerably from the current one. Often we find signs like this a little disturbing especially if they are spotted immediately after a shift to a different life line. This is because there is a qualitative difference in the current and former life line that we cannot rationally account for. Often it is hard to put your finger on what exactly has changed. You may just have the *feeling that something is not quite right.* When a shift has been made it is sensed intuitively and sometimes we even notice change in the type of signs we spot. It is as if out of the corner of our eye we see, or suspect that something new has appeared in the flow. So signs serve as indicators that a shift has occurred, or is in the process of occurring.

Some people are unaware of most of what is happening around them, and so are unlikely to notice even the most obvious signs. Generally speaking though, if we fail to notice anything unusual about an event that takes place on our current life line it is probably because it has the same quality as all the other phenomena we experience. The shift to a substantially different life line normally occurs gradually, passing through intermediate lines along the way. The signs on these lines can appear as warnings with different levels of severity. Sometimes a person ignores their first warning. The shift continues and then a second warning appears and then a third and if the person has still taken no heed of the danger an event finally occurs that is encoded in the final line of the shift.

Interpreting signs unambiguously is very difficult to do. Sometimes you cannot even be one hundred percent certain whether the phenomenon that attracted your attention is a sign or not. All you can do is take into account the fact that the world seems to be trying to communicate something to you. We are mostly interested in approaching sand banks and rapids so it would be nice to at least get a hint of what lies ahead. In most cases, you can explore the sign by phrasing a question in such a way that it will produce a yes or no answer. For example: "Will it work out or not? Will I get it done in time or not? "Will I be successful in doing something or not?" "Is it good or bad, dangerous or not", and so on. *The interpretation of a sign should be simplified enough to hint at a "positive" or "negative" type of answer.* There is no point in expecting a high level of precise detail.

The sign carries a *hint* of the quality of the forthcoming turn in the flow. If you associate the sign with an unpleasant sensetion or it fills you with misgiving, unpleasant surprise or anxiety it means that the sign signals a negative turn of events. If the sensation is ambiguous there is no point in trying to interpret the sign, as your evaluation of it will be too subjective to be reliable. A sign may bring a warning that you need to be more careful, change your behaviour in some way or stop doing something. For this reason it is important neither to negate a sign nor to let it worry you too much by attributing it too much significance.

Signs can take various forms but in each case the most useful thing to do is decide whether their meaning is positive or negative. For example, if you are in a hurry and an old lady with a stick blocks your way this could be interpreted as meaning that you will be delayed, that the bus that normally crawls along will for some reason fly past today; Perhaps you went too far in a situation and should be more careful, or maybe you are trying to do something that is not going very well and no matter what you do obstacles keep getting in the way bringing things to a grinding halt. Maybe you have chosen a dead-end road and should take a different route.

The main benefit of signs is that they have the capacity to wake you up in time making you see that you are acting in the interests of a destructive pendulum or to your own detriment. People often make fatal mistakes when they are under the zombifying anaesthesia of a pendulum, only later realizing that they were unaware of their actions and had forgotten to be vigilant. It can be useful to interpret even innocent signs as simple warnings. It is always wise to maintain a sense of caution and awareness with regard to what is happening around you as long as cautiousness does not deteriorate into anxiety and suspicion. You have to be able to take care without worrying. Be detached at the same time as impeccable in everything you do.

However strange it may seem, sometimes the clearest and most concise guiding signs are phrases, spoken spontaneously as if they were of no import. When someone is trying to force their opinion on you it is better to pay no attention, but a spontaneous phrase uttered as a casual recommendation or piece of advice might be worth taking seriously. Spontaneous phrases are spoken without the speaker planning what they are going to say beforehand. You can probably recall an occasion where you responded to a comment immediately, without thinking. It is as if the answer already exists somewhere deep in your consciousness and it just comes out, bypassing the analytical mind. The same thing happens when your mind is dozing or busy with something else and seemingly random phrases are uttered. When the mind is dozing the soul speaks and the soul, after all, has direct contact with the information field.

For example, someone just on the off chance says: "Don't forget your scarf. You'll catch cold". If you do not take their advice the likelihood is that you will regret it later. You might be absorbed in thoughts about some problem and someone makes a recommendation in passing that at the time does not seem very relevant. Listen to these words and phrases. Do not be too quick to discard them. You may be convinced you are right about something and then someone opens your eyes to see things differently without even intending to do so. Try not to be too stubborn to reconsider your point of view and ask yourself whether you were not in fact just randomly splashing your hands about in the water.

Feelings of inner discomfort are also a very clear sign, although as a rule, we do not pay these feelings due attention. If you have to make a decision, no one better than your own soul knows what that decision should be. It is often very difficult to understand what exactly the soul is trying to tell you but the principle is the same as with all other signs. You can quite unambiguously determine whether the decision is to the soul's liking or not. When you have to make a decision, stop and listen to the rustle of the morning stars. If in your mind you have already made the decision and remembered about the rustle too late, try to recall what type of feelings you were experiencing when you were making the decision. These feelings can be characterized either as "I feel good" about it or "I don't feel good" about it. If you made the decision reluctantly, and it left you feeling cold then this feeling would clearly fit into the "I don't feel good" category. If it is not too late to change your mind, do so.

Listening to your gut feeling, assessing how comfortable you feel is not difficult. What is difficult however, is remembering soon enough to listen to your heart, for the mind reasons with authority with no inclination of listening to anyone else. The loud drumming of common sense drowns out the whispering voice of the heart. The mind is always trying to substantiate and prove its position. Here you have a choice: "yes" or "no." The soul tries timidly to object: "no". The mind is aware of the soul saying "no," but pretends it does not hear, putting forward persuasive arguments based on "sound judgement" to support its own "yes". Having read these lines, store them away in a separate file in your memory and the next time you make a decision pull out the file. You will see that the process is just as I have described.

I would suggest keeping in mind this simple, reliable exercise as a way of recognising your inner "no": *if you have to convince yourself and talk yourself into saying "yes", then your soul is really saying "no." When your soul says "yes", you do not have to talk yourself round.* We will return to this later.

Pay attention to the signs the world is giving you without going over the top and looking for signs everywhere. It can get a little absurd if you say: "Look! The birds are flying high in the sky today. I wonder what that means" Maybe it just means that birds are not afraid of heights and so are able to fly at high altitudes. It is sufficient to be aware of what you notice and *keep in mind* that something you have seen might be a guiding sign. As soon as you forget to be vigilant pendulums will latch onto you and you could become the victim of circumstance.

It is also worth meticulously checking out desires and actions that could dramatically change the course of your destiny. If you get a negative gut feeling about something you are thinking of doing, if it is at all possible, do not do it because the negative feeling you are experiencing indicates that the original desire came from the mind, not the heart. Desires and actions that come from the mind are always imposed by pendulums. If you ignore a negative gut feeling in the majority of cases nothing awful will happen, but sometimes you may deeply regret doing so. Therefore, whenever possible, it is better *to forego* desires and actions that evoke feelings of guilt, doubt or apprehension. If you can get into the habit of doing this it will greatly simplify your life and free you from all sorts of problems.

There is just one 'but'. If a series of misplaced steps have got you all tied up in a knot it might not be enough simply to rethink certain desires and actions, because sometimes a person is called to do something which causes them "discomfort" like not telling the truth or going to work when you hate your job. However, once a knot has been untied and you are freed from a more complex situation you can confidently try out the principle of foregoing desires or actions that evoke a feeling of inner discomfort.

This is all that can be said about guiding signs within the context of the Transurfing model. Ultimately, only you can interpret the signs that are personal to you. There is no need to teach you how to interpret signs. You will instinctively understand their meaning if you are observant of yourself and the world around you. Be wary of attributing excess importance to signs that are not sufficiently clear or that would introduce negative interpretations into your personal life script. You will not get caught up on a sandbank or fly off down the rapids if you avoid creating excess potential. After all is said and done we can survive quite well without signs if we have to. It is not given to us to understand their meaning fully. The only sign particularly worth focusing on when you are making a decision is your gut feeling and intuition. It really is worth listening to the rustle of the morning stars.

Letting Go

The existence of streams in the alternatives flow can potentially free the mind of two overwhelming burdens: the need to solve problems rationally and the need to control. That is, if the mind will allow itself to be freed. The mind will require a more or less rational explanation to be comfortable enough to let go. As you may have noticed quite a lot of what is described in this book is irrational which is why, although it is not the purpose of Transurfing to offer a description of the structure of the universe, I try to validate the conclusions I have drawn that would otherwise be difficult for the mind to accept.

Providing an explanation the mind can accept is actually essential because the mind will not take anything on faith and it is extremely difficult to shake the monolith of common sense. The mind demands proof and circumstantiation which you can provide yourself if you try putting the principles of Transurfing into practice. I offer a couple of feasible explanations here to sooth the incredulous mind, for if I did not, the listener would be unlikely to try out the Transurfing principles or listen any further. And this is just the beginning. Many exciting revelations lie ahead.

The burdens of the mind are placed on us in childhood. As children we are constantly being reprimanded: "Think with your head!", "Do you realize what you are doing?", "Explain yourself!" "Do your homework. You won't get anywhere in life without a brain!", "Don't be so stupid. Will you ever learn?" Teachers and circumstances sculpt a soldier from our minds ready at any moment to produce an explanation, give an answer to a question, assess a situation, make a decision and control those around us. The mind is trained to act in a practical manner based on common sense.

I am not presumptuous enough to advocate getting rid of common sense altogether; quite the opposite. Common sense provides us with a minimal set of rules on how to behave in life in order to survive. The mistake of the mind is that it follows the behavioural code too literally. An obsession with common sense prevents the mind from opening up, looking around and noticing all the things that do not fit the rules.

There are many things in the world that are inconsistent with common sense. The rational mind is incapable of explaining all the phenomena we witness in the world. Neither is it very good at protecting a person from experiencing problems and disappointment. However, relying on the streams in the alternatives flow can compensate for the limitations of the mind. The justification for doing so is very simple; there is purposefulness to the streams in the alternatives flow and this is a quality the mind seeks. As we have said before, the streams take the route of least resistance. The mind strives to reason sensibly and logically relying on the principles of cause and effect but the imperfections of the mind prevent it from navigating correctly in the external world and finding the one prime solution to any given problem.

Nature is in essence perfect and so the streams of the alternatives flow have more purposefulness and logic than the wisest reasoning mind. However convinced the mind is that it reasons clearly, it will still be prone to making mistakes. The mind would make fewer mistakes if it did not try so hard to get involved and allowed problems to resolve themselves. When you *let go of the situation* and relax your controlling grip you allow the world around you more freedom and the flow can take its own course.

You already know that it is futile and even dangerous to try to pressure the world and yet when the mind loses a sense of harmonious flow it creates excess potential, which in turn creates obstacles. Transurfing demonstrates a different way of being. Firstly, if you reduce the importance you attribute to an obstacle it will fade of its own accord. Secondly, if the obstacle does not respond to your efforts to overcome it, move around it and guiding signs will appear to assist you.

The problem with the mind is that it tends to interpret any event that fails to fit its script as an obstacle. The mind likes to plan everything beforehand, make calculations and when something unexpected happens it fights against it trying to make it fit the script. Unfortunately, this only makes the situation worse. Obviously, the mind is not capable of planning events ideally. This is where more freedom should be given to the flow. The flow has no interest in ruining your life as such an action would lack purposefulness. Lives can however be ruined by ill-designed actions.

The mind would have it that purposefulness is what happens when everything is going according to the script and unwanted problems are what happens when something does not go along with the script. Problems have to be solved and so the mind sets about doing so with great gusto generating new problems and cluttering the path with endless obstacles.

Think about it, when are people happy, fulfilled and pleased with themselves, if not when everything is going according to plan. Self-importance prevents the mind from allowing any possibility of deviation from the original script which is automatically interpreted as a failure. The mind thinks: "But I planned it all and worked it all out beforehand. I know what is right for me and what is not. I'm rational". Life often delivers people gifts which they accept reluctantly because they were not planned. "I wanted a different toy!" Life rarely gives us the toys we planned on getting, and so we walk around dissatisfied and sad. Imagine how joyful life would be if the mind could forego some of its importance and accept the fact that deviations from the script also have their place.

We can all regulate how happy we are. Most people set their minimum happiness bar far too high and so do not consider themselves happy. I am not saying that you should always be satisfied with what you have in the spirit of the dubious slogan "if you want to be happy, just be happy". This is not what Transurfing is about. You can have the toy you want most but we will return to that later. For now we are concentrating on how to avoid disappointment and experience fewer problems.

It is the mind's unwillingness to accept deviations from its script that prevents it from making use of ready solutions present in the alternatives flow. The mind's compulsive desire to control everything turns life into an endless battle with the flow. If only the mind could allow the flow to go its own course rather than trying to force its will upon it. The mind's greatest error is that it *strives to control the flow itself rather than its own movement within the flow*. This is one of the main causes of the majority of problems and disappointments that people face.

The purposeful stream that takes the path of least resistance is incapable of generating problems and obstacles. These are created by the madness of the mind. Activate your inner witness and observe at least for one day how the mind tries to control the flow. Perhaps you are offered something but you refuse it. Maybe someone tries to tell you something but you fob them off. Somebody tells you their opinion and you argue. Someone does something their own way and you try to set them on the right path. You are offered a solution but you protest it will not work. You expect one thing but receive another and express your dissatisfaction. Someone bothers you and it makes you angry. Something contradicts your script and you go for the jugular to force the flow into the right channel. Maybe things are different for you, but there is undoubtedly a grain of truth in these words.

Now try releasing your grip and giving the flow more freedom. I am not suggesting that you must agree with everyone and accept anything that is happening but you could consider making a tactical adjustment: move the centre of gravity away from control towards observation. Do not be in a hurry to fob someone off, object, argue, prove yourself, get involved, manage or criticise. Give situations a chance to resolve themselves of their own accord without active involvement or resistance. If not dumbfounded, you will at least be surprised by the result, for something quite paradoxical will happen. *By being willing to release control you will acquire more control over a situation than you had before.* The objective observer always has the advantage over a direct participant. This is why I so often repeat the words: exercise detachment.

In retrospect you will see that the control you were exerting before was making you go against the flow; the suggestions other people were making did in fact make sense and it was not worth arguing about; your intervention was not actually necessary. What you thought were obstacles, were actually nothing of the kind. When you let go problems resolve themselves quite satisfactorily without your having to know how; the things that happen that do not fit with your plan turn out not to be so bad after all; chance phrases can actually have quite powerful meaning; your gut feeling and instincts are there to warn you; you do not waste the same amount of energy as you did before and find that you are quite happy. This is the sumptuous gift of flow I mentioned earlier.

Of course, in addition to all that has been said above we could not forget our old pendulum 'friends'. When people go with the flow it vexes the pendulums and so they try to provoke us at every step into beating our hands wildly on the water. Pendulums abhor streams in the flow for the simple reason that the stream moves in the direction of minimal energy expenditure. When a person goes with the flow of the stream they do not put energy into battling against the current, creating excess potential and fodder for the pendulums. The only form of control worth your attention is control over the intensity of projected inner and outer importance. Remember, that projected importance prevents the mind from letting go.

In many cases letting go of a situation is much more effective and productive than insisting on getting one's own way. Even from childhood our striving for self-assertion generates the habit of trying to proving ones personal significance. From this stems the harmful tendency to prove that one is right whatever the cost. This striving creates excess potential and a conflict of interests. People will go to great lengths to prove that they are right, even when the verdict either way will not directly affect their interests.

In some people the feeling of inner importance is so exaggerated, that they insist on their own way even in matters of very little relevance. Self-importance can develop into a mania that produces a compulsive need to control everything. "I'll prove I am right, whatever it takes." It is a grave habit that makes life much more complicated, especially for the one so intent on defending their truth.

As long as you do not risk seriously compromising your interests, let go of the situation and let others exercise their right to beat their hands on the water. If you practice letting go consciously the feeling of relief will be greater than when you succeed in proving your point. You will experience a sense of fulfilment knowing that you moved on. Instead of insisting on your own self-importance, you manage to act like a wise parent dealing with difficult children.

Here is another example. Excessive commitment to work is just as detrimental as neglecting one's responsibilities. Imagine that you have just taken on a new prestigious position that you have been dreaming of getting for a long while. You demand a lot of yourself because you want to prove your potential. There is nothing wrong with that in principle but if you throw yourself into the job too zealously you may find that you cannot take the pressure over time, particularly if the work tasks are very difficult. In any case, you will become less efficient and at worst you could earn yourself a nervous breakdown deciding wrongly that you are incapable of handling the position.

Another possible scenario is that you generate vigorous activity without observing the established order of things. You may see all sorts of things that could be improved on and initiate the necessary changes confident that you are behaving appropriately. However, if your innovations change the usual running of daily life for your colleagues no good will come of it. This is the kind of scenario in which using your initiative can become a punishable crime. You entered an environment with a slow, peaceful, even flow, and with your actions started wildly slapping the water with your hands, trying to swim faster.

Does this mean that you should keep your mouth closed and your head down? That would be a little extreme. The question should be approached with a sober mind. You should only consider getting annoyed and telling someone off if they are bothering you directly and then only if your criticism will change the situation for the better. Never criticize anything that happened in the past and cannot be changed. In everything else, go with the flow, not in a literal sense by agreeing with everything and everybody, but by moving the centre of gravity from control to observation. Observe more and do not be in a hurry to control things. There is no need to be concerned about getting the right balance. A healthy sense of moderation will come with practice.

SUMMARY

The mind interprets information using a set of established designations.

The heart does not think or speak. It feels and knows.

The mind is only capable of building a relatively new version of a house from old bricks.

Fundamentally new discoveries originate in unrealised sectors of the alternatives space.

The heart serves as a medium between new information and the mind.

The heart perceives unrealised information as knowledge beyond interpretation.

A discovery is made when the mind is able to interpret information accessed by the heart.

The mind is capable of perfectly assessing one's level of inner comfort.

Learn to pay attention to your inner state.

By foregoing the projection of importance you are free to choose your destiny.

Freedom of choice means being free not to ask, demand or fight for what you want but simply to go out and get it.

The information structure is organised in chains of cause and effect.

Chains of cause and effect generate the alternatives flow.

Paths of least resistance are organised into separate streams.

Streams in the alternatives flow contain the solutions to all our problems.

Inner and outer importance jolts the mind out of the optimal stream.

In the alternatives flow it is not the streams but your mind that brings you to the edge of the waterfall.

Everything works a lot more simply than you think. Yield to this simplicity.

What works is not the omen itself but your attitude to the omen.

Guiding signs indicate a possible bend in the flow of alternatives.

Life lines differ from each other in quality.

Signs put us on our guard because they appear during a shift to a different life line.

Signs are characterised by their tendency to evoke the feeling that something is not right.

Spontaneous phrases can be perceived as instructions.

The level of inner peace one feels represents a clear sign.

If you have to talk yourself into something it means that the heart is saying 'no'.

If it is possible to change a decision that causes you to feel uncomfortable in your gut, do so.

Soften your grip on things and allow unforeseen events into the script.

Projected importance hinders the mind from accepting a deviation from the script.

The mind strives to control the flow itself rather than its own manner of moving with the flow.

Shift the centre of gravity from control to observation.

Having let go of attachment to control you will find you have genuine control of a situation.

If you move harmoniously with the flow of alternatives the world will meet you half way.

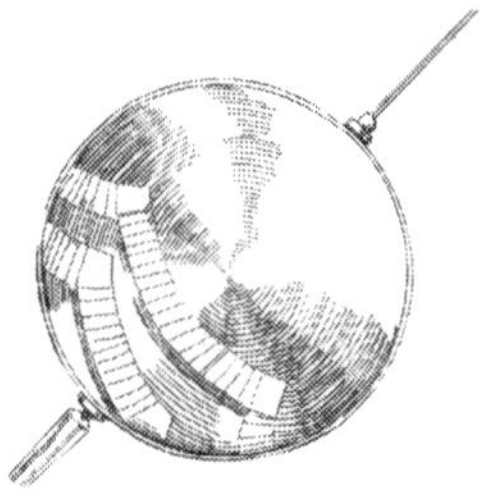

Chapter VII. INTENTION

Potential is only limited by intention

Lucid Dreaming

In this chapter we come closer to solving the Guardian's riddle about the fact that we are free to choose anything we want in life and how to go about it. One of the keys to the riddle lies in what we call dreaming. A person spends a third of their lifetime asleep. Unfortunately, scientific research can only offer us a limited understanding of the human sleep state and so what exactly happens to a person when they are asleep remains a mystery. Philosophical interpretations of dreams are no more enlightening, spanning from one extreme to another. Some say that dreams are an illusion whilst others claim that life itself is nothing more than a dream. Who should we believe? The Transurfing model of the universe supports neither position.

When adults remember their dreams they tell themselves that what they saw was not real. The mind is comforted by the interpretation that dreams are a product of the imagination, somehow generated in a state of rest. We know that children up to the age of four fail to distinguish between what they see in a dreaming and a waking state. They believe that the content of their dreams is happening in the same space as the rest of their life. When a child wakes terrified from a nightmare they are convinced that the monster is still somewhere in the bedroom and nothing their parents can say will comfort them. Gradually, the child's mind begins to accept the idea that dreams are not real.

We discussed previously how the mind quickly and willingly organises any new information that it receives according to abstract references and yet it takes a whole four years to convince the mind that dreams are not real. This must be the only thing that the mind cannot willingly accept. Most people have no memory of their life before the age of four and so as adults they cannot bear witness to the confusion the mind must have experienced upon wakening from a dream when it was still believed to be real.

Every night when the mind switches off it falls innocently into a kind of trap. It does not occur to us to take a critical view of events whilst we are asleep. Even on waking we are surprised by how real and very natural the virtual reality of our dreams appears. The mind is accustomed to finding a rational explanation for everything and so despite the fact that people see quite bizarre events in their dreams, for some reason, in the moment of dreaming the mind responds as if they were quite normal. Whenever we notice or experience something unusual the mind will instantly provide a rational explanation. And despite this we do not question the reality of what is happening in the world around us when we are in a conscious, waking state and the same is true of dreaming. Despite the mind's incessant need to control, the simple question "is this real?" slips through the prism of control and the mind falls into the dream trap.

Sometimes, if we are lucky, something quite miraculous happens and we wake up in a dream, suddenly aware that we are dreaming. Usually this happens when we dream about something extraordinary or have a nightmare. The rational mind is shocked into part waking and we understand what to do next in the dream. At this point the unconscious dream state shifts into *lucid dreaming*. In lucid dreaming a person can take part in their dream as if it were a virtual game, at the same time understanding that it is just a dream. If you have never experienced lucid dreaming or are reading about it here for the first time, you can be certain that it is not a product of our imagination. Numerous books have been published on the topic and there are many individuals who practice the technique consistently.

It is not difficult to try lucid dreaming because it can be brought on by the power of intention. To 'wake up' in a dream you have to train your mind to ask the question: "Is this real?" It is not that difficult to do if you are motivated. The process of training the mind is quite straightforward but it does require your focused attention. Over the course of a day you need to ask yourself whether what you are seeing is real at least ten times. Your inner Guardian will assist you. Instruct your inner Guardian to keep asking you whether you are asleep. It is important that you answer each time as conscientiously as possible so that the rational mind retains a critical attitude rather than it becoming a routine procedure. Shake yourself a little to increase your alertness, look around, assess the situation and ask yourself whether everything is as usual or whether something strange is happening. If you are persistent enough you will eventually 'wake up' in your dream.

You will probably find that it is quite difficult to remember to ask yourself this question even ten times a day and so you have to be really motivated if you want the technique to work. Depending on the strength of your intention you may begin to experience lucid dreaming within a few days or perhaps a few months.

It can be helpful to use a chiming clock. You can then program your inner Guardian to ask you whether you are asleep or not every time the clock chimes. The sound of the clock will be like a bridge to consciousness. When you are asleep and the clock chimes your inner Guardian will become more alert out of habit which should in turn waken your rational mind causing you to 'wake up' in the dream. You can use other bridges between waking and sleeping as long as you are using a sound that can be heard whilst you are asleep. Avoid linking your question to signals you cannot rely on such as the sound of an incoming telephone call. Unless you receive a call in the middle of the night you will not get the necessary trigger until you see a phone call in your dream.

As you can see, the basic principle is to develop the habit of regularly asking yourself whether what is happening is real. Try to answer the question with awareness rather than mechanically. It is important to train yourself to assess the situation critically and respond to the question conscientiously because for many dreamers the one thing that shifts them into lucid dreaming is recognising an anomaly, a contradiction or quirky element in their dream that normally, they would pay no attention to.

Why practice lucid dreaming? At the very least it is fun to consciously play with your dream like in a virtual game rather just have it 'happen'. No science fiction book or computer game can compare with lucid dreaming where you can do anything your imagination can conjure up.

When an unpleasant situation arises in a dream you can will it to change. For example, in a dream where someone is chasing you if you think that what is happening is real it will be very difficult to escape. If you are aware that you are dreaming, you will probably try to wake up from the dream which does not always work. However, once you are aware that it is just a dream you can act much more effectively by simply looking back at your pursuer and thinking: "Go away!" (Get lost! Disappear!). The pursuer will vanish immediately. You can even mentally lift them up and make them turn cartwheels in the air.

As long as two simple conditions are fulfilled the dreamer can control everything that happens in their dream. Firstly, they have to be aware that they are dreaming and secondly, there has to be the realisation that 'here' they can do anything. For example, if you are dreaming lucidly and want to fly nothing could be simpler. All it requires is your intention. An important distinction should be made between desire and intention. The desire alone to rise up into the air will lead to nothing, in dreaming as in waking. It is the same with raising your hand. You can say to yourself, that you want to raise your hand but you do not necessarily move it. Then you suddenly decide to act and you raise your hand, transforming desire into action by the power of intention. You do not think about how you are going to raise your hand, you just do it and it is the same with flying in a dream. You simply decide to rise up into the air and you can fly wherever you want to.

Returning to the example of the nightmare about being chased, the desire alone to be free of the pursuer is not enough. When fear takes hold, the rational mind loses the advantage at every turn of events. It is as if someone else decides the rules of the game. Even if you are aware that you are dreaming you will remain powerless to act until you decide to take control. Whilst you play the role of the passive victim the game will have control over you. It makes no difference that the game is a product of your own imagination. You are still effectively a slave to your imagination as you tremble in fear and run. In lucid dreaming you can choose the role you want to play. You can even stop and decide to swop roles with your pursuer, who will oblige you and turn on their heel. Imagine how comical that would be!

To *any* question that starts: "Is it possible to do such and such in a lucid dream?" the answer is yes. You can talk to people, the living and the deceased. You can do whatever you want with people and objects in your dream; fly around on other planets, solve problems, compose music, rehearse a scene, travel, etc. In comparison to what you can experience in a lucid dream, serious drugs are merely child's play and a lot more harmful. You can also bring information back from a dream. The only thing you cannot do is bring a material object back from a dream into physical reality. At least, I personally have never heard of this being done.

If you find that you do not remember your dreams note what direction you sleep in. It is considered best to sleep with your head to the north. Avoid sleeping with your head to the west as this can have a negative impact on your health. I cannot explain why exactly but it is connected with the impact of the Earth's magnetic fields on the body. Try sleeping with your head to the north and your dreams should become more vivid and diverse.

Do not worry if you have no desire to practice lucid dreaming or perhaps have tried to induce lucid dreams without success. Lucid dreaming does play a certain role in Transurfing but it is not essential to practicing the technique. In addition, lucid dreaming carries a subtle threat. You are probably wondering why I introduced the topic so positively if now I intend to caution you. Lucid dreaming is a secret door that opens into the unknown. It would be irresponsible of me not to mention the potential danger that lurks behind that door so I will explain this below.

The Dream Space

To solve the Guardian's riddle we have to be able to answer two questions: why is anything possible in lucid dreaming and why do dreams seem so real?

In lucid as in non-lucid dreams the pictures we see can be very vivid depicting the tiniest detail. Sometimes our dreams are sharper in form and richer in colour than everyday life. There is a hypothesis that the brain synthesizes certain pictures and during sleep perceives them in the same manner as it would in a waking state, similar to hypnosis. As yet, no-one has succeeded in proving this theory. The Transurfing model interprets the origin of the images we see in dreams slightly differently. Rather than independently creating these images *the subconscious directly connects to the alternatives space and the information it contains.*

If you look carefully at an object and then close your eyes and try to imagine it, you will not be able to 'see' it as clearly, even if you have excellent powers of visualization. The image your brain commits to memory is like a low resolution photograph. Even if the brain stores the photograph as a group of neurons in a certain condition no quantity of neurons would be enough to reproduce all the photographs of all our memories.

If our memories and dreams are a product of the information recorded by neurons, imagine how many of these cells would have to be contained in our heads. In the Transurfing model neurons are not defined as information carriers like memory bites in a computer. *The brain does not store information itself. It stores the address to where the information is located in the alternatives space.*

The brain is capable of retaining a certain volume of data. However, despite the fact that the brain represents a perfect biological system it is not capable of holding everything that we are willing to commit to memory. Neither can the brain synthesize the perfect virtual reality that we see in our dreams. It is difficult even in a waking state to close your eyes and mentally imagine pictures as naturally as one would see them in a dream and so it is pointless to indulge in flimsy arguments that claim that the mind suddenly acquires the ability to perceive imagined images perfectly as soon as it switches off in the sleep state.

As we said earlier the mind is not capable of creating anything fundamentally new. It can only build a new version of a house from old bricks. The rational mind only contains primitive information about the building bricks and how to put them together. We store more detailed information on paper or other forms of memory. All other information is channelled to the mind via the heart from the alternatives space.

In the Transurfing model the brain represents a comparatively primitive system whose function can be replicated by technology. Scientists have tried to replicate the functioning of the brain and yet attempts to create artificial intelligence have not yet been successful. The mind may be capable of understanding itself to some degree, but it is still incapable of understanding the nature of the heart. The secret of the intellect in any living being lies in the harmonious connection between heart and mind. So far, efforts in the sphere of cybernetics have been limited to modelling thought processes familiar to the mind. Maybe one day someone will design a machine capable of retrieving information from the alternatives space as the heart does.

Somehow the mind is capable of remembering the address of relevant sectors in the alternatives space. If it needs to remember something the mind turns to the heart which attunes to the corresponding sector in the information field. Perhaps the heart is not very good at attuning to sectors in the field; perhaps the mind is not very efficient when it comes to retrieving addresses in the information field; or maybe the mind and heart are just not very good at collaborating. Whatever the explanation, human memory is far from perfect.

The heart is capable of randomly attuning to sectors of the alternatives space that have not been transformed into physical reality. These are the pictures we see in our dreams and this is why the dream space appears so real. *Dreams are not illusions in the usual sense of the word. They are not simply imagined. The mind genuinely sees them.*

We know that people see pictures in their dreams that do not seem to be of this world. For example, one might see an architectural construction in minute detail that in principle could not exist anywhere on the planet. If a dream is simply the brain's memory of reality, where then are images sourced that we could never have observed with the waking eye?

As we have said previously, sectors of the alternatives space contain various versions of scripts and scenery. The scenery includes our surroundings as well as living beings. If you remember seeing someone you know in a dream, someone close to you or an acquaintance, you may have noted that they looked slightly different to how they are in waking. They may have a different hairstyle, unusual clothes, display different personality traits or behave in an uncharacteristic manner. In a dream you can recognize your friends, at the same time noticing something strange about them. This is a manifestation of the diversity of the alternatives space. In waking we observe the alternative of possible realities that has been realized in the physical domain. In dreams we are able to see things that have not been realized in the physical.

If you are ever lucky enough to see your reflection in a mirror when dreaming what you see may shock or scare you. The face you see reflected will not be the same as the face you are used to seeing when you look in the mirror. You will immediately sense that something has changed. This is because in dreams a person's appearance corresponds to the sector of the dream space that is being accessed. Depending on the difference between the virtual sector in the dream and current reality your appearance may differ to a greater or lesser extent.

The surroundings you see in a dream may also change depending on how far the virtual sector is from the sector that is manifest as your current reality. You might see your home town in a dream but it will appear slightly different. The same streets and houses will have a strange look to them and you will be confused as if you were seeing an apparition. If the energy body travels far from its current sector you may end up in a completely unfamiliar environment seeing places and people that live their own virtual life but do not exist on the material plane. Whatever role you play in that setting everything that happens there is happening on a non-physical level. Your role is also virtual, but not quite an illusion.

An alternative to your personality may or may not be present in that sector. If it is, you might be able to meet your energy double, although personally, I have not yet come to a conclusion concerning whether this can be done. It is more likely, that the soul simply appears in a role written into that sector's script. Perhaps this is why when people look in a mirror in a dream they see someone else's reflection.

Another interesting point about the dream state is that we see movement and take part in a virtual game despite the fact that information in the alternatives space is stationary, like a film roll stored on a shelf. All events are stored in the information field simultaneously. All that ever has been and all that will ever be already exists in the field. Why is it then, that when the soul flies in the alternatives space it sees life in motion and not in the form of still images? Maybe our powers of perception are such that we can only perceive information from the field in the form of a moving film roll. Or perhaps it is a quality of the space that it can only show itself to us in the form of moving alternatives. If the soul can fly around different sectors in the alternatives space it means that the soul observes movement, and if this is so, what time period is the soul accessing in the dream state, the past, the future, or the present?

Everything about the dream space generates more questions than answers. One thing however is certain. Dreams are not an illusion. It might seem weird to say that every night we move into the alternatives space and live a virtual life there. The alternatives space may not have a tangible, physical foundation, but it is real nonetheless.

What can be said about interpreting the meaning of dreams? The answer to this question may surprise you. You probably think that in the light of the above dreams would have every right to be messengers of future events. However, in the context of Transurfing dreams are not interpreted as signs unlike those described in the previous chapter.

Dreams demonstrate what *could have happened* in the past or what *could happen* in the future. We already know what actually happened in the past and the future in the alternatives space is too diverse to guarantee that what we see in our dreams is an image of the sector that is about to become realised in the physical. Adjacent sectors contain very similar scripts and scenery and so if the sector occurring in a dream lies close to the dreamer's current life line, it may well contain information relevant to impending events in that person's life. However, you can never be sure that the sector you see in a dream does in fact run close to your current life line.

The heart is capable of sensing approaching events and gut feeling is the most reliable sign a person can work with. In waking, the heart signals how comfortable it feels in response to what is happening both on the current life line and in relation to an imminent change in the flow. Other signs also relate to sectors currently *manifest on the material level* and those sectors immediately adjacent to them. In dreams, however, only God can know which sector the soul is exploring. No-one can totally rely on the information perceived in dreams precisely because the soul can fly into any sector at all within the alternatives space.

Another interesting question about dreams is the choice of script. Who chooses the script for the events we witness if they are not simply a product of our own imagination? A script is an essential part of every sector in the alternatives space. How events develop when the mind is sleeping so deeply that we do not remember our dreams nobody can say. In everyday life events are controlled by a person's mind and behaviour, but in our dreams the mind plays the role of passive observer taking things for granted.

Events are staged according to the script belonging to a given sector. As soon as the soul enters that sector events develop in accordance with the same expectations, anxieties and opinions that are a part of that person in waking. In dreams personal expectations and anxieties are realized instantly. For example, if a being comes onto the stage that the dreamer is afraid of a threat script will materialize instantly. You only have to have the slightest whiff of the thought that you might be in danger of being pursued and a monster will appear to start chasing you.

The soul *chooses a script that corresponds to the dreamer's thoughts and expectations* and moves through the alternatives space as their thoughts change. The film roll is turned by the driving force of the dreamer's thoughts and expectations. If you could completely stop your mind from functioning the film would freeze instantly. Thoughts however, do not stop; they continually chatter away in the mind.

Events in dreams do not necessarily conform to our usual perception of things because the mind's control is weakened. Things can appear all topsy-turvy; inconceivable visions can appear in which the laws of physics are defied. Incredible things can happen in lucid dreaming too because the rational mind, understanding that it is just a fantasy, will accept all sorts of strange things.

Now you can see why anything can happen in a dream. *Dreaming is the soul's travel through the alternatives space, where all types of script exist.* In lucid dreaming it is not so much that the script changes of its own accord, so much as it is *selected* via intention. As soon as the intention emerges in your thoughts to swop roles with your pursuer the soul re-attunes itself to a sector with the opposite script. This is the mechanism for lucid dreaming: *intention selects the script.*

If the mind realizes that it can control the script it forms a desire, for example, the desire to fly. This thought flashes through consciousness and is transformed by the soul into an intention. Intention is the force that carries the dreamer into the sector with a corresponding script.

Because the soul's travel through the alternatives space is unburdened by the density of matter our dreams are very fluid and the chosen script is realized instantly. In principle, the same thing happens in physical reality, the only difference being the speed at which the script is played out. In waking life events develop according to the same laws that govern dreams but not at such lightening speed because the material transformation of an alternative into physical reality involves inert matter. In this context the claim that our life is no more than a dream is unfounded and yet in other contexts the statement is not totally devoid of meaning. I have already described how thoughts are reproduced in the form of external, physical action, and are gradually transformed into the events of physical reality. You always create the object of your mind's most dominating thoughts.

Thought is energy vibrating at the frequency of a particular life line. In physical reality the shift to the life line that corresponds to the vibration of your thought energy is delayed by various physical factors. In comparison to a sector that exists purely as information, a sector realized on the material level has a heavy glutinous quality, like resin is dense in comparison to water. This quality hinders the material transformation of a potential reality. In dreams inert matter poses no obstacle and so the process of shifting between sectors occurs instantly.

Now you can see why I brought up the theme of dreams. In order to create the destiny you desire it is important to be clear about how thought carries us from one sector to another and why not all our desires find expression on the material level. You do not have to practice lucid dreaming in order to attain your purpose though. Our goal is simply to learn the knack of choosing the script we want in waking. *It is much more important to learn to 'wake up' in real life than in a virtual one* not least because, as we mentioned before, the activities of lucid dreaming involve an element of risk.

Anyone who practices lucid dreaming would probably assure you that lucid dreaming it is not dangerous at all, but perhaps these people fail to realize that they are walking a knife edge. No-one can guarantee that you will return from a lucid dream. There is no danger of this whilst your soul is flying in unrealized sectors of the field, but what do you think happens if the soul accidentally ends up in a realized sector of the alternatives space? There is a hypothesis that a person can end up physically manifesting in that sector. I know the listener is unlikely to be easily frightened by wild conjecture, but as you can see, the supposition does point to a certain risk, and what if it were true?

It is a well known fact that there were sorcerers of old who had perfected the art of dreaming and could intentionally pass over into other worlds forever. Their physical bodies literally disappeared from their own world. These sorcerers were either very reckless, or knew exactly what they were doing. Today, tens of thousands of people go missing every year without trace. Some people believe that some of these people are abducted by aliens. I cannot corroborate this theory, but I do wonder whether some of these missing people are lost in dreaming and do not return from a sector of physical reality that they have visited in their dream. The soul does not necessarily have to be dreaming lucidly to fly into a physically manifest sector of the field.

In this context, lucid dreaming can be risky because the mind, having had a taste of unlimited freedom, is tempted to throw caution to the wind and fly off into unknown corners of the field not knowing whether the soul will be able to return. If the physical body fails to return from a foreign sector of the field to the place that person usually inhabits they are simply said to have died in their sleep. It is not my intention to scare the listener but it is worth remembering that dreaming is not an illusion and in lucid dreaming it can be tempting to go a little wild knowing that you can do whatever you want without being punished or hurting anyone.

The dreamer may simply enjoy flying into other worlds to explore. There is no reason why not whilst the soul is visiting sectors of the field that only exists within the information field. The only danger is if the soul wanders into a sector of the field that is manifest as physical reality. It may take the mind a little while to realize that virtual reality has become physical reality. It would be foolish to comfort yourself with the thought that our visible world is the only world that exists in the universe. The alternatives space is boundless and without doubt contains many manifest sectors inhabited by all sorts of living beings.

You could just as easily wander into a world that fits your picture of paradise as you could into a world that fits your vision of hell with no idea of where that world is located in relation to your own. It could be a million light years from Earth, or it could be right here in your coffee cup. It could be very far away or close by but in another dimension. As we said in the first chapter, eternity appears to cover an infinite distance only if you are looking directly down at it. That said, whether the parallel world is near or far from home is irrelevant. It is very easy to lose your way but much more difficult to find your way home again, however little or far you have actually wandered from your home sector.

We will not go into the theme of travel via astral projection here. Astral projection is something very different to lucid dreaming although it is also not without its risks. Most importantly, it bears no relation to Transurfing. The connection between dreaming and Transurfing is fairly minor as our task is not to escape from harsh reality by residing in the parallel worlds of dreams, but to make reality itself more comfortable.

There is no need to be particularly afraid of dreaming but it should be taken seriously. *If you get a negative feeling in your gut when you read about lucid dreaming it indicates that this is not an activity you should become involved in.* Your gut feeling will tell you whether something is risky for you personally or not. The heart is better than the mind at sensing impending danger and so dreaming without the active intrusion of the rational mind is far safer.

However, if you are quite decided that lucid dreaming is for you, be cautious. Do not go sticking your head in the lion's mouth and be careful to retain maximum levels of awareness. In dreaming as in waking, make yourself at home but do not forget you are a guest.

The Magical Power of Intention

We have explained that our thoughts and desires direct how we move through the alternatives space and that when we are asleep this movement is free of the burden of inert matter inherent in material realization. The slightest hint of a thought is enough to instantly carry the dreamer into a corresponding sector of the field. In sectors manifest in the physical everything happens more slowly due to the heavy density of matter. The principle however, is the same: our thoughts have a direct impact on the course of events in our life.

"Is that a fact?" The listener may ask, not without a touch of irony, as yet untouched by the miracles of the strange Transurfing model. "And there was I thinking that it was action and not thought that determined the course of my life. How lucky I am to have been informed that it does not matter what I do as long as I think the right things".

In actual fact, there is no contradiction here and it is not really about what a person first thinks and then does. As a rule people pay more attention to the consequences of their actions than their thoughts because they are more clearly evident. This is connected with the impact of balanced forces. We have already described examples of events in which balanced forces engender a result that is the direct opposite of one's original striving. You want one thing but you experience the opposite. The more excess potential you channel into a situation, the more reality will take on a different shape to your original desire. Unable to find a rational explanation for how strangely the world behaves, people imagine that they must either have slipped up somewhere, or that it is just very difficult to get what you really want in life.

It might seem that there is a contradiction in the Transurfing model. On the one hand it states that our thoughts program the energy that passes through us and this carries us onto the life lines that match those them, or, as you now know, thoughts transfer us into sectors of the alternatives space that have a corresponding script and scenery. This is indeed what happens when we are dreaming. On the other hand, it seems as if our thoughts do not really have much weight at all in the physical reality of our day to day life because we cannot achieve the things we desire with our thinking alone. No amount of thinking will initiate a shift to another life line, even accounting for the density matter, whilst you sit on the sofa doing nothing. "Exactly!" I hear the pragmatic listener cry... "You have to act! It has nothing to do with thought and transition." In principle the listener would be right, but only in principle.

There only appears to be a contradiction in how we have presented the role of thought. We are gradually working towards a more comprehensive explanation of why attempts at visualization rarely achieve the desired result. As you know, the most obvious reason for this lies in the excess potential which we create when we are intensely attached to the fulfilment of our desires.

The second reason why visualization does not necessarily work has to do with the inert quality of material realization. Sometimes people fail to reach their goals simply because they are not persistent enough and so the goal does not have time to materialize before the person loses their passion and gives it up as a 'lost cause'. You may even recall situations from your own life where the thing you wanted came much later than you expected, once you had given up hope and forgotten about your original 'order'.

Another widespread mistake is the expectation that everything about the goal can be achieved instantly. Also, if you set several goals at the same time that are not connected your thought energy will be spread too thin and dissipate into emptiness. The alternatives flow will not allow you to swim in different directions at the same time. Attuning to a targeted sector is most effective when focused on one specific goal. We will return to this idea in the next chapter.

In dreaming, none of the inauspicious factors described above apply. In dreams the excess potential of projected importance is much less burdensome, the quality of density plays no part and the mind rests from the daily struggle to achieve its goals. That said, even in dreaming not all our desires are fulfilled. Those who practice lucid dreaming will know that not every whim will carry the dreamer to the matching sector. So what is the problem?

The answer is as simple as it is fundamental. There is no problem, and it has nothing to do with a person's thoughts. The secret is that *realization is brought about not by desire but by one's attitude to that which is desired.* It is not a person's thoughts about the object of their desire that is significant but something else difficult to describe in words. There is a certain force that has the last word and yet it lingers in the wings whilst the thinking game takes centre stage. You will of course have guessed that this force is *intention.* The rational mind has not yet found a comprehensive definition for intention among the shelves of its chosen designations. Here we will roughly define intention as *resoluteness in the decision to have and act.*

Now you can see that thoughts of themselves really do not mean anything in the process of attuning to a specific sector in the alternatives space. Thoughts are just foam on the crest of the wave of intention. *It is not desire that is fulfilled so much as intention.*

Here is another metaphor to describe the idea of wanting. You want to raise your hand. The desire is registered in your thoughts at which point you become aware of the desire. But it is not the desire that actually makes you raise your hand. Desire of itself does not have the power to generate action. The hand only lifts when your thoughts about the desire have been fully processed leaving only the decision to act. Neither is it decisiveness that raises your hand. You may have made a firm decision to raise your hand but not do so. So, what in the end makes you lift your hand? What can we call this thing that lies beyond decisiveness? The rational mind is powerless to provide a clear and comprehensive explanation of what intention actually is. Our definition of intention as resoluteness in the decision to have and to act only demonstrates the prelude to the force that creates action. All we can do is state the fact that the hand is lifted not by desire and not by decisiveness but by intention. The thing designated as 'resoluteness' is introduced to cause your muscles to finally contract.

It really is very difficult to explain what intention represents. We do not even question how we move our arms and legs. We forgot that there was a time when we did not know how to walk or what to do when we first sat on a bicycle without stabilisers. Even when we learn to ride a bike we cannot explain how exactly we did it. Intention is a very subtle thing. It is difficult to acquire and easily lost. For example, someone who is paralysed totally loses the power of intention. The desire to move the legs exists but the ability to enact the desire is lost. There are known incidents where people who were paralyzed have been able to walk again thanks to hypnosis or a miraculous healing which returns the power of intention.

Desire of itself leads to nothing. On the contrary, the more intensely you desire something the more active the backlash of balanced forces. Desire focuses on the goal whereas intention focuses on the *process of achieving* the goal. Desire is realized via the creation of excess potential in relation to the goal. Intention is realized via action. Intention does not intellectualize about whether the goal is achievable or not. Once the decision is made all you have to do is act. If in a dream when you want to fly you start analyzing whether it is possible or not, nothing will happen. If you want to fly you just have to intend yourself up into the air. *In dreams the choice of any script is brought about not by desire as such, but by the firm expectation of having the object of your desire. You do not analyze; you do not desire; you simply have and act.*

We have talked about the futility of wanting something already, but what about asking for something to be given to you? There is not much that can be said about asking for things. There is no point in asking the Angels, God or higher powers for the things you want. The laws of the universe are absolutely dispassionate, completely indifferent to your complaints, pain and lament. Gratitude however is another matter because gratitude is by nature similar to unconditional love. When a person experiences feelings of sincere gratitude they *radiate* creative energy. The excess potential created by a request, on the contrary, *delays* action leading to a concentration of energy. Complaints, requests and demands are the invention of pendulums aimed at harvesting energy. Thoughts expressed in the words 'give' and 'want' automatically create excess potential. When you speak these words it suggests that you do not have something you want and are trying to attract it with the power of your thoughts.

There really is no point in trying to solicit something from higher powers or any other power. It is the same as walking into a shop and asking the owner to give you some of what they sell for free. You can request things of people within certain limits if they are well disposed towards you but everything else in this world is built on objective law and not the desire to have someone help you.

Imagine how absurd it would be if the Earth asked the Sun for permission to shift into a different orbit. It is equally as absurd to ask for something of anything other than another human being. *The only thing that does make sense is your intention to choose.* When you choose you really are creating your own destiny. If the parameters of the energy you radiate match your choice and no laws are being contradicted then you will receive what you choose. *Choice is about the decision to have and to take action, not about request.*

Intention does not create excess potential because the energy inherent in the desire's potential is dissipated through action. *Intention unites desire and action.* Intention in action discharges the excess potential created by the desire quite naturally, without invoking the medium of balanced forces. If you need to solve a problem, act. Contemplating the complexity of the problem simply creates excess potential and feeds the pendulum your energy. When you take action you realize the energy behind intention. "The hands do what the eyes fear to pursue", as they say. When you set about realizing an intention, trust the alternatives flow and the problem will resolve of its own accord.

Waiting, worrying, doubt and desire only drain your energy. Intention in action not only dissipates the energy behind excess potential, it uploads that energy to the person's energy field. You can see how true this is when you are studying. Swotting and cramming requires a lot of energy for a relatively minor result. In contrast, rather than leaving you feeling exhausted, learning via action, physical work or applied problem-solving is inspiring and fulfilling.

Intention is the driving force that transforms sectors of the alternatives space into physical reality. The question is why our fears are also realized. Surely our fears cannot be categorized as intention? In real life, just as in dreams, we are constantly chased by alternatives with a script to match our fears, anxieties, aversions and hates. Why should these scripts be transformed into physical reality if we neither desire them, nor intend to have them? And yet we do experience the things we love to hate. It would appear that the nature of our desires, whether it is something we love or something we love to hate, is ultimately irrelevant. Why? The mystery is unveiled by an even more enigmatic and powerful force we refer to as *outer intention.*

Outer Intention

Intention is a combination of desire and action. The intention to do something by your own efforts is obviously a personal *inner intention.* It is much more difficult to extend the action of intention to the external world. We refer to this kind of intention as *outer intention.* Outer intention has the potential to rule the world, or rather, to choose the model of behaviour the external world lives by, as well as determine the script and scenery.

The concept of outer intention is critical to the alternatives model. Today, all manipulations of time, space and matter that cannot be explained logically tend to be described as magic or paranormal phenomena. These things are the work of outer intention which works to *choose life lines in the alternatives space.*

Inner intention could never transform an apple tree into an avenue of pear trees. Outer intention does not transform anything either but it is capable of choosing an avenue of pear trees instead of an apple tree in the alternatives space and executing the shift to the relevant sector, as a result of which, the apple tree is substituted with a pear. Nothing happens to the apple tree. There is simply a substitution: material realization shifts in the alternatives space from one life line to another. No power on earth is actually capable of magically transforming one object into another. Inner intention may try but its capacities are sorely limited.

You cannot move a pencil that is lying on a table with the power of thought but if you hold the firm intention to imagine that the pencil has moved you may be successful. Let us say that you were able to move the pencil (some people with extra-sensory abilities are capable of doing this). What I am about to tell you may seem strange but physically, the pencil will not actually have gone anywhere. At the same time, you are not simply fantasizing that the pencil has moved. In the first instance the pencil is subjected to thought energy which is clearly too weak to shift a material object. In the second case, you slip across life lines in which the pencil has a different location. Can you see the difference?

The pencil is lying on the table. With the power of your intention you imagine that it is beginning to move. Your attention scans sectors in the alternatives space where the pencil is placed in all sorts of other positions. If the thought energy you radiate at this stage is powerful enough, the pencil will materialize at different points in the space of physical reality. It is the separate pencil 'layer' that moves whilst the remaining layers, including the layer of the observer, remain unmoved. *It is not the object itself that moves, but its point of realization in the alternatives space.*

It is hardly surprising that most people cannot get the pencil to move. In the majority of people capabilities such as these are weakly developed, not because they have a weak energy field but because it is so difficult to evoke pure outer intention if you struggle to believe that such things are possible at all. People who have the ability of telekinesis do not move objects. Rather they have a unique capacity for the power of intention that enables them to shift the location of a point of material realization in the alternatives space.

Everything connected with outer intention is generally considered mysticism, magic or at best inexplicable phenomena, proof of which is successfully stored away on distant, dusty shelves. The predominant worldview totally negates these things and so anything irrational evokes a strange fear. People who witness UFOs also experience high levels of fear and consternation. UFOs are so far from our day to day reality that we do not want to believe they exist. When they display the stunning audacity of being real they evoke a weird kind of horror.

Outer intention is a case of "if the mountain won't come to Mohammed, then Mohammed must go to the mountain." Did you think it was just a saying? Outer intention does not have to be all about paranormal phenomena. In day to day life we constantly come up against the results of outer intention. Outer intention is the force or mechanism that causes our misgivings and worst expectations can to be realized in the physical. Because the dynamics of outer intention function independently of our will, we do not necessarily realize what is happening. It is much harder to work with the force of outer intention than it is to work with personal inner intention.

Imagine that you landed on an island where you had to face a tribe of savages. Your life would depend on what you did next. One possible outcome is that you would become the victim, apologising for your presence, making gifts, justifying yourself and trying to ingratiate yourself with the natives. In this case, you would be likely to get eaten. The second possible outcome is that you would become the conqueror, showing signs of aggression, launching an attack and trying to assert your control over the tribe. You would either be victorious or lose your life. The third alternative is that you would present yourself as master and leader. If you were to reach out your hand like the powers that be you would be obeyed. When you have no doubt in your own might, your thought energy is attuned to life lines where you are king and everyone else assumes that this is how things should be.

The first two types of behaviour demonstrate inner intention, whereas the third type demonstrates how outer intention works. Outer intention simply chooses a certain alternative.

The fly that beats itself against a window pane right next to an open window acts on the basis of inner intention. What do you think outer intention would look like in the case of the fly? You would think the answer would be for the fly to discover the open window and escape but it is not. If the fly were just to take a step backwards and look around it would see the pane of glass and spot the open window. In the case of the fly it is just a matter of having a slightly wider perspective on reality. Outer intention literally opens the window for the fly.

Inner intention aims to impact the outside world of your current life line. Everything that is possible within the confines of a *materialized sector* can be described by the laws of the natural sciences and fits nicely with the limits of a material worldview. Outer intention by contrast chooses a life line on which your desire can be realized.

The analogy of the fly in relation to intention is probably quite clear by now. Insisting on flying through a closed window is an expression of inner intention, whereas shifting to a life line where the window is opened is an expression of outer intention. You can make a superhuman effort to move the pencil with your thoughts or, working with outer intention simply scan the alternatives space for the pencil where it is placed differently.

Let us imagine that it is Christmas Eve and you are certain you will not be able to find a parking spot just outside the supermarket. The voice of inner intention would say there could not possibly be a free parking space because the whole world is out shopping. Outer intention allows for the possibility that one space might become free just as you arriving at the supermarket. It is not so much that in the case of working with outer intention you solidly believe in the possibility. It is more that you simply claim the possibility of what you deem necessary, dispassionately and unconditionally.

Outer intention is born of improvisation, like insight. You cannot prepare for outer intention. All magic rituals are aimed at evoking the power of outer intention but ritual is just the preparation for magic, a theatrical prelude. Imagine that you fell from a cliff in a dream. You would have to evoke the intention to float in the air. You would not have time to prepare yourself or speak an incantation. All you could do is take it into your head to fly and you would do so. Spells and magical attributes can help to awaken the power inherent in each and every individual but they cannot directly apply it.

Unfortunately, in contemporary man the ability to direct the power of outer intention has all but atrophied. People have even contrived to erase the ability from memory although ancient legends vaguely hint at it. Today it is pointless trying to prove that the Egyptian pyramids and similar constructions were built with the power of outer intention. Any hypothesis explaining the principle of their construction will be considered, just not this one. The ancients who built the pyramids would no doubt be quite amused to learn that their descendants considered the ancestors a more primitive civilization and were bending over backwards trying to guess the secret of their construction within the limited context of inner intention.

Time has not totally deprived us of working with outer intention; the ability is just blocked. Everything that can come to be called magic is nothing more than an attempt to work with outer intention. For centuries the alchemists sought in vain for the philosopher's stone that would turn any base metal into gold. There are many complicated and misguided books dedicated to the topic of alchemy. Legend has it that the secret of the philosopher's stone fits into just a few lines inscribed on an emerald tablet, the so-called Smaragdine Table. If the secret is so succinct why are there so many books on the subject? No doubt, because of the desire to understand the meaning of those few lines…

You will have heard of the Holy Grail that has been so ardently sought including by representatives of the Third Reich. There are many legends about ritual objects that supposedly endow their owner with unlimited power and strength. Such legends are of course naïve misconceptions. Fetishes, incantations and other magical attributes have no power at all. Belief in the magical power of ritual attributes can to some extent help the subconscious to waken from the daydream and stimulate the weakly developed capacity for outer intention. However, the power is not in the objects themselves but in outer intention and the individuals who use the objects.

Ancient civilizations so perfected the skill of working with outer intention that they no longer required the prop of magic ritual. Naturally, their power in this regard created intense excess potential which is why civilizations like Atlantis which had conquered the secrets of outer potential were destroyed by balanced forces. Shards of secret knowledge have been passed on to us in the form of magical practice with the aim of restoring what was lost. In general however, these are frail and superficial attempts often undermined by false understanding and confusion with inner intention. The essence of the power of outer intention as such has remained a mystery.

The priority placed on the development of inner intention and the loss of knowledge concerning outer intention is the work of pendulums which feed on the energy of inner intention. A person can only truly develop the ability to work with outer intention once they are as free as they can be from the manipulation of pendulums. You could say that the pendulums have so far managed to keep the upper hand in the battle with man.

We have established that the nature of thought energy aimed at achieving set goals manifests in three different forms: desire, inner and outer intention. *Desire is the concentration of attention on the goal itself.* As you can see, desire has no power. You can think about your desire to reach a goal for as long as you like but there will be no change. *Inner intention is the concentration of attention on the process of moving towards the goal.* This can work but demands a lot of effort. *Outer intention is the concentration of attention on how the goal is realized of its own accord.* Outer intention simply *allows* the goal to realize itself. Outer intention presupposes the firm belief that the alternative of the goal's realization already exists and only remains to be chosen. *Inner intention achieves the goal, outer intention chooses it.*

Inner intention can be characterised by the thought pattern: "I insist that....", whilst outer intention follows a totally different principle: "Circumstances are such that....", or "It turns out that...". The difference between these two thought patterns is huge. In the first case you actively exert pressure on the world making it obey your wish. In the second case you take the position of an outside observer where everything happens according to your will but without the slightest coercion. It is the difference between changing and choosing. You fly in your dream because of the thought pattern: "Oh! I'm flying", not "I insist on being able to fly".

Inner intention strives directly towards the *goal.* Outer intention is focused on the *process of its independent realization.* Outer intention does not hurry to achieve the goal as it is already a done deal. The fact that the goal will indeed be achieved is neither doubted nor discussed. Outer intention is unremitting, cool-headed, detached and moves the goal indomitably towards its realization. The following bilateral comparisons can help discern where inner intention and outer intention come into play: you try to get something from life – life freely gives you what you want; fight for your place in the sun – the world offers you its embrace; bang on a locked door – the door opens wide before you; try passing through a wall – the wall moves aside for you; you try and generate certain events in your life – the events come of their own accord. Using inner intention a person tries to reposition their own fact of material realization relative to the alternatives space, whereas outer intention shifts the alternatives space so that your material realization is where it needs to be. Can you see the difference? The end is the same in both cases, but it is achieved by very different means.

If the second part of the comparisons listed above describes your actions then you have understood the principle of outer intention. When you battle for something it is like you are trying to push your realization into the alternatives space, whereas when you choose something the space comes to you. Of course, the alternatives space does not totally independently reposition itself in relation to where you are within it. You have to take certain actions first which lie beyond the widely accepted perception of things. Throughout this book I will provide examples of the difference in approach between inner and outer intention. Outer intention is the cornerstone of Transurfing. It is the key to the Guardian's riddle about why there is no need for us to fight with the world and why we can simply choose the things we want.

Nothing is beyond the capacity of outer intention. You can fly in waking or walk on water if you have the outer intention of a Christ and it would not represent a contradiction of the laws of physics for the laws of physics work in just one sector of material realization. Outer intention is manifest in the movement of realization through different sectors of the alternatives space. It is impossible for a person to fly within the limits of a sector that is manifest in physical reality because you would have to resist the gravitational pull of the Earth. Trying to do so would be an example of inner intention demanding a massive input of energy in order to overcome the force of gravity. Free flight in dreaming as in waking is not really movement through space in physical reality. It is a shift in the relative position of your realization point. In other words, the body consequently materializes in new points of the physical space.

You could also put it this way: *it is not that you fly through space but that space moves relative to you in accordance with the choice of your outer intention.* This probably does not sound quite right. Nonetheless, we will not go any deeper into the theory of relativity here. We can only guess how it really happens.

In order to fly you have to have absolute faith in the idea that it is possible to do so. Why did Jesus so matter-of-factly say: "According to your faith, be it unto you"? Perhaps because nothing can be received or completed without intention and there is no intention without faith. We would not be able to take a single step unless we believed it was possible to do so. However, you will never be able to convince the rational mind that it is possible to fly in waking as it is in dreaming, at least in a normal state of consciousness. There are yogis in India who can leave the ground during meditation. (These are the only reliable cases of levitation that I have come across personally). Their intention may only be sufficient to attune to the movement of alternatives in which the body floats in mid air. Taking into account the incredible capacities of yogis in comparison to ordinary people you can imagine just how difficult it must be to overlay one's personal will on the power of outer intention.S

The dozing mind can accept the possibility of flight during sleep but in conscious waking, however hard you might try to convince yourself otherwise, human flight will always seem impossible. For the mind to accept something there has to be faith as well as knowledge. Faith presupposes the possibility of doubt for where there is belief there is also room for doubt. Knowledge eradicates doubt. You have no doubt that when you throw an apple it will fall to the ground. You do not have to believe in this, you just know it to be true. Pure outer intention is free of doubt and consequently, of belief also. Whereas in the sleep state a mere hint of outer intention is enough for flight to occur, in the world of inert material realization the intention has to be absolutely pure. There is no need to be overly concerned with acquiring a knack for creating pure intention. To realize your personal goals run-of-the-mill intention will do! It just takes some time for material realization to build up momentum.

It is interesting to consider outer intention in the context of hypnosis. It is difficult to say whether hypnosis is a result of inner or outer intention. Thought energy alone is clearly insufficient to enable personal will or inner intention to move physical objects, even very light ones. Thought energy is sufficient however, for one person to send a suggestion to the unconscious mind of another. Some people seem to have a marked ability to radiate and direct powerful waves of energy. If that energy is programmed with specific thoughts the person the energy is aimed at comes under the effect of hypnotic suggestion. I hope you do not think that the effect of hypnosis is occasioned simply by magnetic gaze or mesmeric passes. The impact of the hypnotist's energy does not rely on visual or voice contact. However, as far as I am aware, hypnosis works mainly at close distances suggesting that the impact results from a transmission of thought energy directed by inner intention. In cases where hypnosis works across greater distances, outer intention undoubtedly plays an important role, unless some other technique is being used.

To experience the power of outer intention you have to escape Procrustes' bed of everyday thinking and feeling. The rational mind usually exists within the narrow confines of the predominant worldview. It can be very difficult to move beyond the limits of the conventional mind set because outer intention is essential to make the leap and the rational mind will not easily yield its position. It is a vicious circle because you have to apply outer intention in order to experience it. Not an easy task.

I am afraid I will have to disappoint the listener as I am not aware of any exercises that specifically develop a feeling for outer intention. The aim of such an exercise if it existed would probably be something strange like "to intend to have intention". The only way of understanding the nature of outer intention more deeply is to practice lucid dreaming. In place of some targeted exercise however, I would recommend simply practising conscious living in the sphere of physical reality; not so much training outer intention as living it. The reality of the waking state differs from dreaming only in the inert quality of material realization in the alternatives space. In all other ways they are the same.

You may wonder what we have to work with if we are not able to direct the power of outer intention. Of course, you are highly unlikely to move slabs of stone weighing several tonnes, but the density of the material world can be overcome by time. Conventional methods of achieving goals are based on activating the power of inner intention. The essence of the Transurfing method in contrast is based on leaving inner intention alone and applying the principle of outer intention.

Inner intention transforms into outer intention when the conscious mind meets and merges with the subconscious. The boundary between the conscious and the subconscious mind is so elusive that it is almost impossible to draw a clear line marking exactly where inner intention ends and outer intention begins. It is like the feeling of free fall or the feeling you have when you first manage to keep your balance riding a bicycle. The closest feeling to the point of merging between the conscious and the subconscious is when you deliberately raise your body into the air in a dream and find that you can fly.

The conscious mind merges in total harmony with the subconscious in a very narrow segment. It is easy to deliberately move your finger, a little harder to move your toes and even harder to wiggle your ears, to say nothing of manipulating your inner organs. By comparison, the muscle of outer intention is even less developed. Hence, to join the conscious and the subconscious mind in the intention to leave the ground and fly is considered practically impossible.

Levitation is the highest embodiment of outer intention but we will set ourselves more grounded goals than meditating several feet off the ground. The power of outer intention is so great that even its tiniest part is enough to achieve formidable results. In everyday life outer intention works independently from our personal will and can even be detrimental such as when it manifests in the form of our worst expectations. We have already discussed situations in which a person experiences the things they love to hate. On the one hand you are followed by the things you fear, hate or wish to free of because your thought energy focused on the unwanted event carries you into a sector where it exists. On the other hand, it was never your intention to experience these things, so how does intention function in this instance?

Inner intention is focused on avoiding the things you see as negative, that are oppressive, cause you anxiety or evoke resentment.

There are some things we just want to avoid with all our heart, things that cut us to the quick, that evoke fear and aversion. The rational mind is fearful and the soul too is anxious. The rational mind experiences enmity and the heart feels the same. The mind experiences hate and the heart all the more so. The heart and the mind are in complete agreement. It is in these moments of union between the conscious and the subconscious that outer intention is activated. The only problem is that it is not directed in accordance with your personal will. It is probably not quite accurate to speak here of outer intention being directed. Whereas inner intention has the focus of staving off the negative, outer intention would be more accurately described as *giving the green light for the realization of whatever the soul and mind agree on*. What they agree on of course, is their assessment of a given event. Whether it is a desired event or not is irrelevant. It is as if outer intention, on seeing that the mind and the heart are united, automatically chooses the matching sector in the alternatives space.

The heart and the mind most often agree over the things they would rather avoid in life and so the cases where a person's worst expectations are realized provide the most indicative illustration of how outer intention works. As we have said before, people usually have an excellent idea of the things they do not wish to experience and only have a vague sense of what they desire with a passion. To subject outer intention to your will you have to wipe all negative thought from your mind and establish harmony between the heart and mind in your positive striving. You already understand what a harmful effect a negative attitude can have on your life. When you express resentment and dissatisfaction you become subject to the impact of balanced forces. Then you become dependent on destructive pendulums and your thought energy becomes focused on negative sectors of the alternatives space. Attracted by the negativity outer intention transforms the sector into the physical reality of life.

This is why outer intention can work independently from your will. It is difficult to harness the power of outer intention but there are ways of making it work for you. This is our next task. We have already established that to avoid experiencing the undesired results of outer intention it is essential not to create the potential of projected importance and to refuse to have anything to do with negativity. Now we need to grapple with the task of how to make outer intention serve the goals you set for yourself. It may not be quite as simple as rubbing Aladdin's lamp but methods to activate the mechanism of outer intention do exist.

Much of what has been described above may be a little obscure. It is a theme that is hard to understand because outer intention defies literal description. The picture will become clearer however. I have no desire to surround these ideas in a fog of mystery, just to intrigue you, as adepts of certain schools and spiritual groups have a tendency to do. Everything you need to know about outer intention is contained in this book and all the skills you need to have to work with it can be acquired from personal experience if you put the principles of the Transurfing method into practice. No special classes or seminars are required, neither is there anything mystical or mysterious about the Transurfing technique.

"Secret knowledge" is often clouded by metaphor and allusion but a person who thinks clearly also tends to express their ideas clearly. If a guru claims to carry "secret knowledge" so precious that it can only be whispered into the ear of a disciple, the rest of the time being alluded to only allegorically or with profound rhetoric, they probably have not fully penetrated the essence of this knowledge either.

It is not our goal to acquire the power of absolute intention capable of lifting the body into the air. If we knew how to levitate there would be nothing left to say. The alternatives space exists and the freedom of choice exists. You choose which possible pathway in the alternatives space manifests as your physical reality. The task we have set ourselves is to learn how to achieve goals given the capabilities and resources we already have at our disposal. Even though these may have their limitations Transurfing represents knowledge that can awaken a power we rarely make use of. Transurfing does not require you to exhaust yourself with meditations, various practices, lucid dreaming and other mystical activities that are enough to make the head spin. I understand that the Transurfing model seems unlikely to work but all you have to do is reconsider your established views of the world and you will be able to achieve things you previously thought were beyond you. Likely as not you will soon become convinced that you really can make the power of outer intention work in your favour.

The Game Script

Dreams are very malleable and so they serve as an excellent model by which to demonstrate how outer intention works. So, we will return now to the theme of dreams. As we said, in essence dreaming is very similar to real life. Everything that happens in a dream is a result of a game played according to a script chosen by the soul. When the rational mind sleeps we dream but we do not remember our dreams. The soul travels uninhibitedly through the alternatives space. Where exactly the soul is gallivanting whilst the mind sleeps, no-one can say. All our conscious memories are controlled by the mind. Dreams that we remember occur when the mind is just dozing. The mind's control is weaker during this stage of sleep being reduced to the role of passive observer. The mind is not imagining things when we dream; it simply perceives what the soul witnesses in sectors of the alternatives space that have not been transformed into physical reality. In non-lucid dreaming the mind does not weigh on the soul with its need to control. It is like a cinema-goer watching a film. On some level though the mind does experience what it sees and the sensations evoked are communicated to the heart which immediately attunes itself to a matching sector. The script therefore, changes as it goes along, the scenery and characters likewise adjusting to the changing script. The imagination plays a part in dreaming only to the extent that it generates ideas.

In a dream, when you have the passing thought that a person may act aggressively towards you the thought is instantly materialised and someone appears on the scene to threaten you. As soon as the weather vane of your opinion turns in a different direction foe is immediately transformed into friend. It is a bit like a kitten playing in front of a mirror whose mood smoothly shifts from friendly to aggressive as it jumps about. The kitten sees a figure in front of it and wonders what to expect from it. At first its attitude is neutral and curious. Then the kitten lifts a paw and the assessment instantly shifts towards possible danger. The kitten puts its hackles up, makes an attack and then dodges to protect itself. The kitten jumps backwards, sees its comic image in the mirror and its mood changes to one more playful. Then the ritual is repeated as the kitten dynamically corrects the script either attacking its reflection or substituting aggression with playfulness.

A person corrects the script in non-lucid dreaming in exactly the same way. The kitten is not aware that it is looking at its own reflection just as a person is not aware that they are dreaming. Did you know that when a person looks in the mirror the facial expression they see is not the facial expression they usually have. A person's expression changes the moment they look in the mirror, too quickly for them to notice. This is because of habits and desires we have since childhood to look a certain way. As soon as you say to a child: "Look in the mirror. See how awful you look when you cry!", their face will change. Adults also have certain expectations when they look at their reflection. They say to themselves: "I like myself" or "How do I look", or "I look terrible", etc. The facial expression is immediately corrected depending on the thought.

The mirror is an example of how we dynamically correct our own script, only the mirror is an example of how inner intention functions, whereas the dream is an example of outer intention. In waking a person sees their reflection in the mirror and immediately inner intention changes the expression on their face according to their expectations. *A dream is like a play, and the script that will direct the role of the outside world is chosen by the dreamer's out-*

er intention in accordance with their experience and expectations but irrespective of whether they will experience pain.

Participants in a dream behave exactly as the dreamer expects them to. The original idea is nothing more than the initial impetus; the rest is orchestrated by outer intention. The dreamer's own behaviour in a dream is determined by inner intention, whereas everything else is subject to the dreamer's outer intention, whether they like it or not. As we have already said, inner intention tries to *impact* the world directly, whereas outer intention allows the external world to *become realised* in accordance with intention.

In dreams events can only unfold according to a script you can tolerate. Nothing could happen in a dream that the dreamer could not conceive of. This partly explains the low level of critique the mind applies to the events that take place in dreams. Even total absurdities are taken for granted because the dreamer writes and produces their own dream script. It is not that the absurd is considered the norm so much that the subconscious does not rule out the possibility of the absurd, for in a dream the rational mind dozes whilst the subconscious can easily anticipate all sorts of unlikely events.

Over the course of a lifetime a person's brain deals with a huge mass of information from external sources as well as from the world of its own fantasies. Some of that information is filtered out by the rational mind as unreal and is scrapped. The information does not actually go anywhere. It may be locked in a closet but the subconscious still has access to it. When sleep approaches the soul tiptoes into the closet and unbeknown to the rational mind experiments with all sorts of outlandish scripts. Moreover, in non-lucid dreaming the soul is free to choose which sectors of the alternatives space it wishes to visit. The majority of these sectors are never realised because their events are irrational which means they require large inputs of energy to create. Only God can know how exactly the soul chooses its dreams.

However wildly the soul chooses its dreams the rational mind witnesses them and corrects the script according to its experience and expectations. As we have already established it is a person's worst fears and all that they strive to avoid that is most quickly realized. In this case outer intention functions with no regard for personal will and often to their detriment.

In physical reality a person is also very likely to end up experiencing the things they fear. The mind is capable of making inner intention work through willpower but outer intention functions irrespective of the will of the rational mind. It does not follow orders and manifests freely when there is agreement between the heart and mind. In dreaming the rational mind has no direct control and does not even realize that outer intention is working. To some degree dreams continue after the dreamer has woken up and so at this point the mind can have more say in what happens.

In a dream the dreamer can be completely absorbed in the most ridiculous, meaningless games, unaware of their absurdity. The same can be true in real life. When a group of people involved in a very narrow specialized activity, be it professional, religious or special interest groups, they often come up with their own understanding of things, vocabulary and actions that to anyone outside the group would appear unnatural and even silly.

The mind's uncritical attitude to waking reality is what allows phenomena such as hypnotism and entrancement to work. Gypsy hypnosis, for example, is based on three "yes's"'. A person answers yes to three separate questions which makes them feel that everything is going as it should. The person consequently becomes less vigilant and, in a sense, dozes off, their critical abilities being reduced to a minimum. People in this state are almost literally daydreaming automatically going about their daily affairs. This is particularly the case with individuals who have a strict daily regime.

When you talk to someone it is like you are in a deep sleep. Fully engaged in the game you naturally understand what is happening but your active participation makes you incapable of behaving or evaluating the situation objectively as an outside observer would. Any football fan who understands the game criticizes the players for their mistakes. What would happen though if that fan were to be brought onto the field to play? Would they do any better as a participant? Everyone acts unconsciously to a certain extent. When a person is lieing their eyes tend to shift to the right. They make involuntary movements with their hands totally immersed in the game.

The state of hypnotic suggestion is an extreme case of daydreaming but everyone is to some extent asleep in their day to day physical reality. In this moment, as you listen, you can shake yourself and say that you are aware of what you are doing and what is happening. Later, however, a person, event or problem will distract you and you will again get drawn into the game and doze off. You will remain sleeping all the while that you are on the stage and conscientiously playing your role. You will wake up when you come down into the auditorium and rouse your inner Guardian. Once in the auditorium you will continue to play your role, speak the necessary words, carry out the necessary actions following the established rules, only now you will play your role consciously, in a more detached manner assessing what is happening around you with a sober mind.

In non-lucid dreaming, the dream just 'happens'. Outer intention acts independently of your will and there is nothing you can do about it. In lucid dreaming a person steps down into the auditorium and consciously directs the script. It is not that outer intention deliberately aligns itself with a person's will, it just ceases to contradict it. In this case the mind gives the heart more freedom and in exchange receives its sanction. The unity of heart and mind in turn activates outer intention. In the forthcoming chapters we will describe how to work with outer intention on the path towards one's goal.

The level of conscious awareness is higher in waking than it is in dreaming and this is sufficient to direct inner intention. Outer intention requires an even higher level of conscious awareness. In lucid dreaming, as in waking reality in order *to work with outer intention you have to wake up*.

The Game According to Your Rules

What can you do if you are attacked in a dream? There are four types of inner intention: flight, fight, awakening and realization. Opposition and retreat, in response to being attacked in a dream, are primitive forms of response generated by inner intention. If you are attacked in a dream and you fight back events will unfold in much the same way as they would in waking reality, i.e. in accordance with the standard model of behaviour. Your conscious mind already has a script for how the fight should end. If you are accustomed to losing, you will lose the fight and vice versa. Your dream will shift around the alternatives space in accordance with your script.

In a dream you tend to behave in the same way as you are used to behaving in waking reality, but because in a dream anything is possible, working with outer intention can be very effective. With the power of outer intention you can quietly turn to your opponent and imagine them retreating before finally turning into a frog. It is not that you yearn or strive for your opponent to turn into a frog for this would be to actively will a change on the outside world using the power of inner intention. When you work with outer intention you simply imagine that your opponent is turning into a frog. In other words, you accept that their turning into a frog is a potential reality. *Outer intention only imagines an event to be true and accepts the possibility of a different script.* If the mind can fully accept the idea that there can be an alternative to the usual development of events, the heart will not object. Union between the heart and mind activates outer intention which transforms the chosen script into physical reality.

As you can see, *outer intention arises not as a result of will but as a consequence of harmony between the heart and mind.* Outer intention acts independently of personal will and so inner intention (personal will) should only be directed towards achieving a harmonious connection between heart and mind. To successfully set outer intention you have to first *acknowledge* that the script can be controlled. *Awareness* is also essential if you want outer intention to work in your favour.

Whilst the dreamer is not lucid the dream cannot be controlled; it just 'happens'. In dreaming and in waking the majority of human actions are carried out relatively unconsciously. When a person's relationship to their surroundings is unconscious they experience a situation as something determined and conditioned by external factors which they have neither the strength nor the capacity to influence. If a person believes this to be true, other people and the vagaries of fate will have a greater impact on their life. In this sense, reality also just 'happens', the rules of the game being set not by the individual but by the outside world.

To gain control both in dreaming and in real life it is essential to switch from the role of immersed participant to the role of witness. You continue to take part and play your role in the game but your inner Guardian is always vigilant. It is as if you detach yourself, enough to be playing the part of an actor at the same time as observing your role and the theatricals of others from the auditorium. The Guardian is always switched on in the background. It does not get involved; it just follows carefully and soberly assessing all that it observes.

In non-lucid dreaming it is as if the observer has switched off leaving the actor alone to get involved. In this state the individual becomes totally absorbed in their role unable to see the situation from the outside. To avoid getting completely absorbed in a role the intensity of inner importance and the projection of outer importance must be kept to a minimum and the Guardian must be always ready. Even without taking outer intention into account, a person's ability to control a situation is directly proportionate to their level of conscious awareness. In dreaming the level of awareness is minor and so the dream 'happens'. If however, a person is aware that they are dreaming the situation is under control and they can do whatever they wish.

Susceptibility to the influence of other people and destructive pendulums is in inverse proportionality to a person's level of conscious awareness. In sleep many people behave like zombies. If they are being chased in a nightmare they run away unable to do anything else about it. The script belongs to the individual but it has been given over to a different producer for staging. The individual is prisoner of their own conditioned perceptions of how an event may develop. Despite the fact that the perceptions originate with the individual they dictate their own will reducing their owner to the position of victim.

Remember what happens when you become totally immersed in a problem. Imagine, for example, that you are approached by a colleague who announces that some job has to be done. If doing the job is a problem your first response would probably be concern, perhaps a feeling of dejection. You would then run various scenarios around in your mind for events might develop: "That's not going to be an easy task. How will I do it? I so do not want to! My life is so difficult and stressful but if I do not do it such and such will happen, etc." At this stage you have joined in the game, becoming susceptible to outside influence; in other words you have dozed off. You can now be taken by the hand and lead like an obedient child into a room where difficult, exacting work awaits you, ending up on a life line where this is exactly what happens.

This is what happens if you allow the pendulum to hypnotise you and make its own game your problem. By turning the problematic script round in your conscious mind you reach a point where the heart and mind are in agreement over their concern, at which point outer intention immediately shifts you onto a problematic life line. This can happen quite easily as feelings such as fear, despair, dissatisfaction and worry can take hold of a person quite quickly. The underlying cause is of course, importance, both inner and outer. You can be pulled into the game or lulled into a slumber whenever you assess the game to be important either of itself or for you personally.

Now imagine a different version of events. A person comes up to you with a problem. In this moment you shake yourself and tell yourself that you are not sleeping and can decide whether the first prod of the pendulum will become a problem for you or not. This is the first condition to establishing control over the situation. The second condition is to take it into your head to defeat the pendulum. Even before you learn the nature of the problem, program yourself to perceive whatever it is as a mere trifle. The most important thing is not to allow yourself to be lead by the hand. Do not take any assertive steps, refuse to get involved, prevaricate or become irritated. Simply listen to what the person wants from you. Externally it is best to nod your head, make the right noises and internally remain the witness, not the participant. This is the role of the observer who takes part, like a trainer who sometimes plays as well.

To be detached in this case does not mean to be distracted or lacking in concentration. Quite the opposite; control over a situation presupposes attentiveness and total clarity of mind. To stand back from something means to be aware of the fact that you make up the rules of the game deciding whether the play will turn either into a tragedy or a comic sketch or light vaudeville. It depends on what you want which is probably for everything to be resolved quickly and easily. If you fear that there will always be complex problems just around the corner to be wrestled with for ages, do not worry. There is always a simply solution to any complex problem. The simple solution lies on the 'vaudeville' life line. *To shift to this life line all that is required is the intention to imagine to yourself that it is so.*

Once you start practicing this technique you will be pleasantly surprised. The outcome may be most improbable. At the very least the problem will be solved easily, or it may disappear or given to someone else to resolve. There simply are no complex problems on the 'vaudeville' life line. You do not have total power over outer intention but you can act in such a way that firstly, it does not act against you and secondly, that you get the opportunity to help it work in your interests. Circumstances may unfold in various ways and not necessarily in your favour but by taking this position you significantly increase your chances of coming up roses. Do not forget to trust the alternatives flow as well. If the level of unity between heart and mind in the vaudeville attitude to the problem is sufficiently high you will receive mind boggling results that you could only have dreamed of.

You are no longer a puppet on a string. I should warn you though to be careful of the temptation of considering yourself the puppeteer. You understand that this would disturb the balance and you would instantly receive a slap at the first sign of any conceit, feeling of superiority, contempt or (heaven forbid) disdain towards others. No individual can ever have complete control over all that happens in life even in dreaming. Remember, *you only have the right to choose, not to change.* Make yourself at home but do not forget you are a guest. It is also important to remember that when you detach yourself from a situation it is essential to act with complete integrity. *A 'vaudeville' attitude to a problem does not suggest being slack or nonchalant but it does mean being capable of soberly assessing the importance of things.*

It would be a mistake to interpret conscious awareness as the striving to establish control over the surrounding world. The rational mind is accustomed to insisting on its own view of things, trying to alter the course of events, and fighting against the current. Sometimes, when a person steps off the stage into the auditorium they are seduced by the desire to change the script by force, imposing their will on the remaining actors. This type of behaviour has nothing in common with Transurfing because it depends exclusively on personal will (inner intention) to push against the current. You have to remind yourself again and again of the need to go with the flow. *Conscious awareness lies in observation, not in the ability to control.* Control should only be directed towards imagining an auspicious script, allowing it into your life and embracing it with all your heart, instead of floundering about in negativity. *It is not about forcing your own script on the world so much as considering it possible, allowing an alternative to be realized and allowing yourself to receive it. You will only succeed in ceasing to do battle with the world and allowing yourself to choose if the heart and mind are one.*

In the previous chapter we looked at different models of behaviour and the roles of the beggar, the indignant and the fighter, neither of which fit the context of the Transurfing model. So what role could be worthy of the one who is master of their own fate in this game called Life? By now you have probably guessed that in the Transurfing model it is considered to be *the Guardian*. The more conscious awareness you have in waking, the more effectively you will be able to take charge of your own destiny.

The role of the Guardian is much more engaging than the role of the administrator. Captains, managers and other leaders tend to take a more proactive position in life than simple administrators and not only because they have greater responsibilities. Senior management personnel are more likely to adopt the role of guardian because their position requires them to be 'more awake' in comparison to other workers, who are able to remain asleep fulfilling their responsibilities simply because they have to. As soon as you embrace the position of Guardian you will feel a burst of energy and increased levels of vitality because now, rather than dejectedly carrying out actions that are the will of another, you are creating your own destiny. *Taking responsibility for your own fate is not a burden, but an act of freedom.*

Man differs from animals not so much in level of intellect as in level of awareness. Animals embody a sleepier state. Their behaviour is mainly determined by stereotypical scripts, instilled in them by nature, and which manifest in the form of instinct and reflexes. Animal behaviour is like that of an actor in a play with a fixed script. In this sense, human beings are 'more awake'. Man is by nature more inclined to self awareness and understanding of their place in the world. At the same time, the general level of human awareness is still very limited with most people too completely immersed in the script to have the necessary detachment for awareness.

The secret of so-called clever people lies in their awareness. Awareness gives clarity of mind. Some people are able to think and express their thoughts clearly whilst others are muddled. The relative sharpness or dullness of one's mind depends more on awareness than it does on intellect. Choosing simplicity of mind can also be means of protection from unwanted information: "I don't want to know. Leave me alone!", in contrast to an astute mind that embodies openness, curiosity and the desire to receive and process information in the spirit of: "I want to know everything!" Obtuseness is sometimes a result of retardation and both these traits can be developed in childhood, for example, when a child is forced to learn or psychologically manipulated.

The more we daydream in everyday life, the more mistakes we make. The fly that beats itself against the window pane is also deeply asleep. When you are totally immersed in the script you are not able to take a wider, more objective view of reality. Obsession with the game narrows perception and puts up a barrier. People are surprised when they realize they have made a mistake because they were too immersed in something to see more clearly, and ask themselves: "Where was I looking?" as if they had been seduced by some apparition. Even on April Fool's Day when people know they may have tricks played on them, they still fall into the trap. What is this if not a daydream?

Lack of awareness is the result of not wanting to look reality in the eye. The ostrich hides its head in the sand to escape the threat of reality. When people have their head in the sand it reflects the desire to insulate themselves from the outside world in the sense of: "I cannot see anything, I can't hear anything, I don't want anything. Leave me alone!" It is not possible in life to totally pull your head under the blanket and sleep and so people try to dull their powers of perception. Unfortunately this compromises their awareness. For example, a mild, harmless person may try to hide from the imminent threat of aggression but they will not be able to dodge the blow because their awareness is blocked by fear. Their reactions are dulled as if their eyes were covered in a film. Rage also dims understanding. When a person is immersed in the game they are incapable of seeing or hearing anything else around them, hence the phrase 'blind rage'.

Fear and anger are extreme examples of the absence of awareness. Pendulums will also try to gently dull your vigilance with a zombifying effect, playing on the fact that most people spend the majority of their time in a semi-aware state, only experiencing acute awareness and clarity of perception when the right circumstances give them an adrenalin rush. This is why it is so difficult to do something as seemingly simple as wake up in a dream and say: "Hey! You! Stop messing me about. It is just a dream and what's more, it's my dream, so I say what goes, not you."

Intuitive knowledge can be drawn from the subconscious by the power of awareness. Intuitive knowledge can be more easily perceived if you can catch yourself thinking: "Why do I suddenly want to do this?" The soul's reply will be soft and barely audible. The rational mind however will shout: "Shut up. I know very well what I want and what I should be doing!" You have to develop the habit of constantly listening for the rustle of the morning stars to hear the music of intuition. In a semi-conscious state it is almost impossible to remember quickly enough to note what your inner voice is trying to say. Even if early in the morning you set yourself the strict task of listening to the voice of your soul you will not remember to do so at the appropriate moment if you sink into the daydream.

So, harmony between heart and mind generates outer intention, and mindfulness enables you to have it work in your favour. Unity of heart and mind is so easily achieved in dreams for the simple reason that in dreams, the heart is free of the authoritative control of the mind. In lucid dreaming there is still an element of control but it is limited to adjusting the script. In dreams the mind will accept all manner of miraculous event. In 'The Tinderbox' a fairytale by Hans Christian Anderson, there is a scene in which the princess, convinced that she is dreaming, agrees to walk on the roof with the soldier. In dreams the rational mind will accept anything, but in waking reality it fitfully grabs hold of its familiar worldview.

It is not easy to achieve a state of harmony between heart and mind once you step beyond the realms of common sense. Common sense is like a lifetime cell, from which is difficult to escape. A person may be interested in mystical teachings, have their head in the clouds and believe in the impossible but there will always be place for doubt. The mind will go along with things but at the end of the day, it knows that apples really fall to the ground. This is why it is so difficult to completely align outer intention with your own will. Nonetheless, personal experience will show that mindfulness greatly increases your chances.

Maximum awareness can be achieved as long as the inner Guardian is constantly present in your consciousness. The Guardian objectively evaluates what is happening and assesses in whose interests the game is being played. It makes sure that you will not get drawn into the game like a puppet. You have to remember to ask yourself every minute of the day: "Are you asleep or not?" so that it becomes an attitude. You can also practice lucid dreaming if you are unafraid to do so but the dream will come to an end and everyday reality will return. Surely it makes more sense to focus on developing conscious awareness and mindfulness in your everyday life. As you can now see, this alternative gives you the chance to furnish your life layer according to your own taste. It is your choice.

The Purification of Intention

Outer intention is a huge, unfathomable force. At the same time you can see how fluid and subtle it is. It is control and at the same time, the renunciation of control. It is the decision to have at the same time as the abandonment of the need to achieve. It is something unfamiliar to the mind. We are used to securing what we desire by setting an inner intention. We are used to thinking that if we have the right direct impact on the world it will respond immediately. The idea of inner intention is clear and straight forward. Even so, things do not always come that easily. You still have to make an effort, insist on your goals, struggle for what you want and fight your way forward. The method of Transurfing suggests that if you let go of launching an advance the world will offer its embrace. Obviously, such an unconventional approach is bound to leave the rational mind confused.

How can you achieve a state of balance in which you combine the decision to have with the abandonment of direct action? The answer is obvious. You have to maintain balanced intention, which means to want without desiring, to take care without worrying, to strive without being distracted and to act without demanding. Balance is destroyed by the excess potential of projected importance. As you already know, the more important the goal the harder it becomes to reach.

The saying "if you really want something you will eventually get it" will have quite the opposite effect if the wanting is intensely driven and frantic attempts are made to acquire the object of your desire. Frantic actions are taken only when a person does not really believe that their wish will come true. Compare these two positions. This is the first: "I really want to achieve what I desire. For me personally it is a matter of life and death. Whatever happens I have to have it. I will do everything I possibly can to make sure I get it." This is the second: "I have decided that I will get what I desire. I want it. What's the problem? It will be mine, full-stop." It is clear which position will be successful.

Desire also differs from intention in that it includes the possibility of nonfulfillment. If something we desire is difficult to obtain it makes us want it even more. Desire always creates excess potential. Desire is potential by definition. Desire is when somewhere, something is absent but thought energy is aimed at attracting that something to make is present. *Intention neither believes nor desires; it simply does.*

Pure intention never creates excess potential. Pure intention assumes that everything is already in the bag. You simply decide that it will be so. It is like an almost accomplished fact. It is the calm realization that something will come into being. For example, I intend to go to the newsagents and buy a paper. There is no desire in this. Desire was present up until the moment I decided to buy a paper. The chances of nonfulfillment are extremely low and if I fail it is not the end of the world. In this case intention is free of desire and, consequently, of excess potential too.

The thought energy of desire is focused on the goal. The energy of intention is focused on the process of its being achieved. When a person wants something they create perturbance in the energetic picture of the immediate environment which bring about the impact of balanced forces. When a person simply walks to the newsagents to get a paper no heterogeneity in the energy field is created.

Within the context of a life line this is what desire looks like: I want it but am afraid I cannot actually have it and so I think of failure (because it is important to me!) and radiate energy at the vibrational frequency of a failure ridden life line. Here outer intention has the opposite effect: I know that I will have what I claim. It is already decided and so I radiate energy at the frequency of a life line where I have what I want.

So, achieving the goal is inhibited by two types of excess potential: desire and belief, or rather, the passionate desire whatever the cost to achieve the goal and the battle with one's doubts concerning the possibility of achieving it. The more strongly the goal is desired, the weightier one's doubts over a successful outcome become. Doubt in turn makes the thing we desire appear more valuable. We have already established that desire, rather than helping, just makes things harder. The secret to fulfilling one's desires lies in the understanding that *desire must be replaced by intention, total resoluteness in the decision to have and act.*

The importance one attaches to the goal makes one determined to follow through, continuing to impact the outside world with the strength of one's inner intention. When the mind sets an intention it launches headlong into battle. It is the feeling of importance that creates the mental habit of trying to put pressure on the outside world. You will not get a single step closer to working with outer intention unless you reduce the level of importance and emotional intensity you associate with your goals. Outer intention is totally different to inner intention in that it has no striving to impact the outside world.

You will never learn to work with outer intention by setting an inner intention to do so, however strong it is. The force is referred to as outer intention precisely because it lies outside of yourself. So just what exactly is outer intention? I confess I have no idea and I am not afraid to say so. It is extremely difficult to talk about intention within the limited context of reference familiar to the rational mind, and yet we can bear witness to certain aspects of it. For example, outer intention emerges in moments when there is harmonious connection between the heart and mind. As soon as this condition is fulfilled a kind of resonance is created between thought energy and the outer power of intention that picks us up and carries us into the corresponding sector of the alternatives space.

Outer intention is the force that makes Transurfing possible, i.e. switching life lines, or in other words, moving the point of material realization through sectors of the alternatives space. To ask why this force exists and wherefrom it originates would be as futile as asking why God exists or wondering whether there is a connection between God and outer intention. No-one can know these things. The main thing is that this force exists and all that remains is to take joy in the fact of using it, just as we take joy in the sunshine.

Outer intention makes it possible to shift the point of material realization from one sector to another in the alternatives space. It is the same principle as the force of gravity that indicates the possibility of falling from the roof of a building. Nothing happens whilst you are standing on the roof but as soon as you take a step off the edge and give yourself up to gravity, it will grab hold of you and throw you to the ground.

To give yourself up to outer intention you have to achieve unity of heart and mind. This can only be done if the intensity of importance is absent. Importance gives rise to doubt which stands as an obstacle on the path to unity. When there is doubt the rational mind desires something and the heart resists or the heart strives towards something but the mind suppresses the urge. Importance beats the mind against a window pane whilst the heart sees the open window. The heart asks for what it truly wants but importance has the mind trapped in a web of common sense which says no. Finally, unity may be reached but usually the agreement is over the non-acceptance of something, as a result of which, outer intention goes out of its way to fob you off with something you do not need or want. Lack of harmony between the motives of the heart and mind is conditioned by the fact that the mind is under the power of preconceptions and false ideas referred to here as pendulums, and as we know, pendulums pull us by the strings of projected importance.

This leads us on to the second condition to using outer intention: *reducing the intensity of importance and abandoning attachment to achieving one's goal*. It sounds paradoxical of course that in order to achieve your goal you have to abandon the desire to achieve it. We understand all aspects of how inner intention works because we are so used to functioning exclusively within these narrow confines. We have defined intention as resoluteness in the decision to have and act. The difference between inner and outer intention lies in the first and second parts of the definition. *If inner intention is the decision to act, outer intention is closer to the decision to have.* In the first case you decide to fall, so you run until you drop. In the second case you want to be on the ground so you let go of control and give yourself up to the force of gravity.

The thought pattern described below will help you to cleanse your intention of desire: to start with you consider the goal you want to achieve. As soon as doubts enter your head you know you have desire. If you start worrying about whether you have the necessary qualities and skills to achieve the goal it means you have desire. Even if you believe that you can and will achieve your goal, desire can still be present. You have to want and act without fuelling the emotion of desire. The intention to lift your hand up and scratch the back of you head is an example of intention free of excess potential. There should be the pure intention to act, not the desire to act. This requires reducing the levels of inner and outer importance you associate with the goal. There is a very simply way of reducing importance which is to *come to terms with the possibility of defeat* at the very beginning. Unless you accept the possibility of defeat you will not eliminate desire.

Make sure that in the process of purifying intention of desire that you do not lose a grip on the intention itself. Set the intention to achieve your goal and start by accepting the possibility that you may fail. Run the scenario of defeat round in your mind a few times and consider what you would do if that happened; what might serve as a plan B or safety net. Invite the realization into your mind, that not achieving the goal would not be the end of the world.

Imagining the scenario of defeat should be a one-time event. There is no point in constantly returning to the scene of failure in your mind. The exercise is only intended to free you from the need of achieving the goal exactly as you had imagined. You cannot know how the goal with will achieved, but we will return to this point later. Once you have consciously accepted the possibility of failure do not think about failure or success, just move in the direction of your goal and set off just as you would if you were going to the newsagents to buy a paper. Success will be in the bag, and if for some reason it is not, then there is no cause for sorrow or regret. If you do not succeed the first time, you will succeed the next as long as you do not tear yourself apart over the initial failure.

Finally, letting go into outer intention does not necessarily mean completely rejecting your personal intentions, sitting at home with your arms folded waiting for harmony between heart and mind to magically appear. No-one is stopping you from achieving your goals in the usual way. Eliminating desire and importance has the same beneficial effect when applied to inner intention. It is just that now, the powerful force of outer intention can also work in your favour helping you achieve things you previously thought impossible.

SUMMARY

In conscious dreaming the mind controls the game script.

Dreaming is the virtual journey of the soul through the alternatives space.

Dreams should not be interpreted as signs.

The soul will not necessarily return if it flies into a realized sector of the alternatives space.

It is not desire that is realized but intention, i.e. the resoluteness to have and to act.

Desire is the concentration of attention on the goal.

Inner intention is the concentration of attention on the process of moving in the direction of the goal.

Outer intention is the concentration of attention on how the goal realizes itself.

The goal is achieved by inner intention and by outer intention simply chosen.

Inner intention strives to impact the outside world directly.

Outer intention gives the green light for the autonomous realization of the goal.

The laws of natural science only work in one given sector of the alternatives space.

Outer intention works by moving through different sectors of the space.

Outer intention is the unity of heart and mind.

Imagination takes part in dreaming only to the extent that generates the initial idea.

The heart and mind are united in negative expectation, which is why they are easily realized.

In reality a dream continues in waking to some degree or another.

If you want to exercise control over outer intention you have to wake up.

Whilst you live without conscious awareness, reality cannot be controlled, it just 'happens'.

Any game must be played with an element of detachment like a participating observer.

Awareness is achieved by being detached from the game.

Detachment presupposes vigilance and complete mental clarity.

Conscious awareness is not so much about control as observation.

Control should be exercised only to the extent that it allows desired scripts into your life.

In order to choose the necessary script you have to imagine that it will be exactly as you desire it.

Inner intention is resoluteness in the decision to act.

Outer intention is resoluteness in the decision to have.

Outer intention is the power that makes Transurfing possible.

In order to reduce the importance associated with the goal the possibility of failure must be accepted at the outset.

Once you have accepted the possibility of failure, do not think, just move in the direction of your goal.

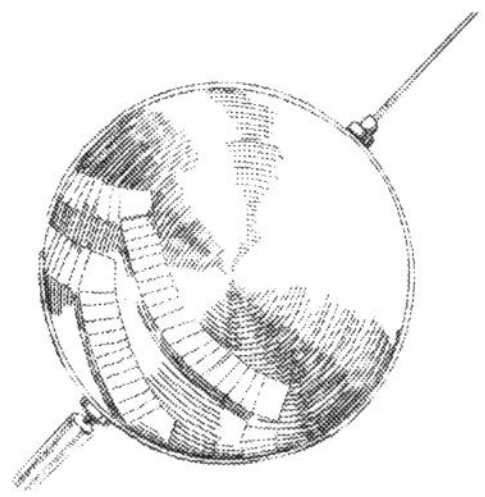

Chapter VIII. SLIDES

You Deserve the Best

Illusion

Transurfing suggests that we should be careful when tempted to interpret illusion as pure fantasy of the mind. Dreams, hallucinations, psychotic reality perception and even reality itself are all generally referred to as illusion. With the exception of psychosis, the perception of a different reality is more than just a fantasy of the mind. Dreams and hallucinations are experienced as a result of the soul's journeying through the alternatives space. Illusory perceptions of reality are often experienced when we glimpse other sectors of the information field that have not yet been streamed into the pathways of material reality; and finally, reality itself is no illusion. Anyone bold enough to claim that all they perceive is nothing more than an illusion, has too high an opinion of themselves.

For some reason, man has assumed that he must be capable of understanding and providing a rational explanation for all natural phenomena, when in fact, we are only capable of understanding some of the laws of the universe and some of life's many manifestations; for not all natural phenomena are subject to rational explanation. On the one hand, declaring that some of the things we witness are illusions is an acknowledgement of our failure to provide a logical explanation for everything, and yet on the other hand, the capacity of the intellect is overestimated in the claim that the illusion is generated by the brain or imagined by the mind.

When people are under the powerful influence of drugs or alcohol they lose control of their awareness as we do in dreaming. When this happens, the subconscious mind becomes attuned to unrealized areas of the alternatives space. Perception roams the virtual sector while the body remains in the physical sector i.e. the material world. We may walk along familiar streets and buildings, but see things in a distorted light. People and places will look strangely different because the scenery has changed, becoming half dream and half reality.

Similarly, psychotic patients may perceive an unrealized sector of the field whilst their body is present in a realized sector. In this case, the individual's perception is attuned to a sector in the alternatives space where not only the scenery is different but the scripts and roles have also changed. People with mental health issues are not necessarily ill in the normal sense of the word. It is assumed that a patient simply imagines themselves in the role of a Napoleon or other odious personality, but they may in fact be experiencing an alternative reality. The alternatives space contains infinite possible realities; the individual simply chooses the alternative they feel most drawn to. When the conflict between heart and mind reaches its peak and the tortured soul can no longer bear the harshness of physical reality, personal perception usually ends up in a virtual sector of the information field, leaving the body to continue living out its existence in the material sector.

A psychiatrist once shared the story of a female patient who suffered a pathological desire to have the ideal husband and children. Expressed using the terms of Transurfing, the importance the poor woman had attributed to having the ideal family was right off the scale. In the end, she married a man who brutally abused her and was herself unable to conceive a child. Real life became unbearable and the woman ended up in a psychiatric unit having lost all awareness of the materialized sector of the alternatives space. Her body remained in the material world but her awareness had attuned to a virtual sector of the alternatives space in which she was idyllically happy playing the role of wife to an English lord and mother to her perfect children. The woman's perception was totally focused on a virtual sector of the field and yet to all intent and purpose she appeared to be living in the same material world as everyone else.

Why is it that virtual sectors of the field that are the focus of the mentally ill are not transformed into physical reality? Doctors try to help psychiatric patients with contemporary medicine but many patients are actually happier living in an illusory world which they find a great deal more pleasurable than the physical reality they previously had to endure. What these people are experiencing is not really an illusion as such, but an unrealized alternative of reality which exists in the information field just as fully as the sector that exists as a physical manifestation. As we have already said, an alternative reality is transformed into physical reality when thought energy is programmed in a state of complete harmony between the heart and mind. Obviously, it is not possible for a psychiatric patient to embody this kind of connection. Perhaps the distortion between the material and virtual sectors is too great and so it would require too much energy to realize the virtual sector in the material plane. A contemporary Napoleon for example, would be an extraordinary occurrence, and an alternative reality that lies far beyond the potential limits of the alternatives flow. There may also be other reasons that we are currently unaware of.

As well as perceiving alternative realities, we are also capable of experiencing a false, distorted perception of our physical reality. A person's manner of perception greatly depends on the information they have absorbed in childhood. In a well known experiment, two kittens were kept in different environments; one kitten was kept in an environment that contained no vertical objects and the other in an environment that contained no horizontal objects.

After some time, the kittens were both brought into an ordinary room. The first kitten was constantly bumping into chair legs because in its perception vertical lines simply did not exist and the second kitten, who could not comprehend the phenomenon of horizontal lines, constantly slipped down the stairs.

Of course the mind is capable of great imagination and fantasy but only within the relatively narrow limits of its accumulated experience. The mind can only construct a new model of a house from the bricks of a previous design. So where is the line between imagination and actual perception of another reality? It is a fine line that has no concrete boundaries, and yet this of no great relevance to the purpose of this book. What is important, however, is how our internal beliefs affect our perception of reality and how this reflects on a person's life. Next we will explore what lies at the root of a distorted perception of reality and how strongly this distortion can influence the shape of one's physical reality.

Distorting Reality

No individual is capable of a totally objective perception of the world around them. It is like inserting a slide into a video projector. Uniform light passes through the film and is transformed into an image that becomes visible on the screen. Metaphorically speaking, the light represents the world around us; the slide represents our worldview, i.e. the model of our understanding of the world; and the image on the screen is our perception of things.

How individuals perceive themselves and their environment is always relative to the truth. It is our personal *slides* that introduce the element of distortion. For example, when a person is obsessively concerned with some symptom or personal shortcoming they tend to experience a feeling of inferiority and low self-esteem. They also tend to assume that their weaknesses matter to other people as much as they do to themselves. So when they are communicating with others they insert an inferiority complex slide into their projector which makes them see things in a distorted light.

You might for example be worried about how you are dressed. It might even seem to you that other people are looking at you with disdain or sneering at you. However, the people around you will not be thinking anything of the sort. The negative thoughts are all in your own head in the form of a slide which distorts your picture of reality. As a rule, most people are ninety percent preoccupied with thoughts of their own person. Even if you are sitting through a job interview you can be certain that the interviewer is thinking more about how well they are playing their own role than they are about the suitability of the interviewee.

Slides distort your perception of what other people think about you. *A slide is a distorted picture of reality.* A slide is something you carry around in your brain that others do not have in theirs. For example, you might consider your looks to be insufficiently attractive. If the thought does not particularly bother you then no distortion is created. Things are what they are. The issue is not so much what you think of your personal appearance, so much as the wider influence the corresponding slide can have on your life. If you are worried about your appearance you will create a slide in your head that reads: "I am not beautiful (handsome)" and you will look at the external world through the slide as through a filter. The corresponding image is a slide because it exists solely in your own thoughts.

Only potential partners, a very small percentage of the people you come into contact with, actually evaluate i.e. attribute importance to your external appearance. No-one else particularly notices what you look like. If you do not believe me, ask the severest arbitrator you know, yourself, how much the outward appearance of people you meet matters to you if they are not part of your immediate circle as a potential partner or competitor. It probably does not even occur to you to question whether you find these people attractive or not. Other people think the same way (or do not think at all) with regard to yourself. Even if you think you are ugly you can be certain that the same principle applies. Ugliness makes an impression only in the first moment of meeting but after that, ceases to attract attention, like any other part of the scenery.

So, let us suppose that you have inserted a slide into the metal projector relating to your seemingly unattractive appearance. You will perceive other people's behaviour, be it a look, facial expression or other aspect of body language through the perspective of the slide. What will you see as a result? You will see a sneer in a welcoming smile and hear mockery in the sound of happy laughter. You will be convinced that quiet whispering is other people gossiping about you. A random glance is interpreted as an askance look. All someone has to do is wince from indigestion and you think: Lord! What must they be thinking of me! Finally, any compliment makes you feel patronised. Yet, people will be thinking nothing of the sort. It will all be in your head, fashioned by a slide of your own making.

Your behaviour is also affected by your thoughts which can make you genuinely unattractive. You may start making awkward gestures with your hands not knowing where to put them. Your face will become distorted by tension and all intelligent thought will disappear as the inferiority complex claims the seat of domination in your mind. As a result, the slide in your imagination is played out in the material dimension.

The action of slides is two-fold. Firstly, their bias skews the perception of your true place in the world and how others relate to you. Secondly, they distort your perception of the external world. In addition, people have a tendency to perceive the self-deprecating qualities of their own slides in the people around them. For example, when a person dislikes certain innate qualities in their own character they try to hide them so that they will not have to look at that part of themselves and yet it is impossible to conceal an unsightly slide. It sits in the person's head doing its own thing. If you buy into the basic illusion that others think and act just as you do, you will tend to perceive in others the qualities you dislike in yourself, i.e. hang your *projections* on others.

A projection is when a person's dissatisfaction with self that has been forced into the subconscious pours out onto others. No-one wants to criticise themselves for their own unacceptable attributes and so they tend to ascribe them to other people instead. People are often quick to criticize others for the very things they dislike in themselves. You have probably done the same thing yourself without being aware you were doing it. Of course, this does not necessarily mean that whenever a person blames someone for something negative they necessarily embody the same quality themselves, but this is often the case. Observe yourself. The position of the inner Guardian in role plays will enable you to quickly tell whether someone is trying to hang a projection on you. If someone is unfairly accusing you of something or accusing you of being something that you are not, ask yourself whether that person embodies the same trait themselves. It is probable that they do because if you are genuinely not guilty of what you are being accused of, the accuser probably has a slide in their own head that is projecting its image onto you.

What serves as the foundation for the slide? What film roll does it belong to? The answer is importance. We keep coming back to importance! You worry about your outward appearance because it is *important* to you. The slide lives in your head alone, given that your appearance does not matter to anyone else for any particular reason. Ugliness or physical deformity is just part of the scenery to everyone else because to them it is of no personal significance. Other people note the appearance as unusual but nothing more. It is the biased slide of importance that claims an unusual appearance to be ugly.

Henri De Toulouse-Lautrec, the famous French painter, broke both his legs in childhood and was physically handicapped for his entire life. Whilst growing up, Lautrec suffered depression caused by the realization of his own ugliness. As the years passed his physical deformity became all the more evident causing him to suffer even more deeply. There came a point at which his distress reached its peak and Lautrec was forced to accept the inevitable. He finally overcame the limitations of his deformity and threw himself into life. As soon as he let go of the importance of his condition the slide ceased to exist and good fortune came his way. Aside from realizing his talent as a painter, he was also extremely popular with the ladies. Lautrec was one of the founders of the famous Moulin Rouge cabaret in Paris. He was loved by many women, and not only for his paintings.

Slides are created when you attribute too much meaning to other people's opinions of you. If it matters to you what other people think of you and yet you do not know what their opinions are exactly, a slide will take firm root in your mind. The slide is a product of the imagination and so it can be called an illusion and yet it is an illusion that can deeply affect a person's life. Slides are one example of how outer intention can act to your detriment irrespective of your personal will.

As a rule, a negative slide is generated by unity between the heart and mind. As you may remember, outer intention works flawlessly under these conditions. It catches the owner of the negative slide and carries them to a sector where the content of the slide is expressed to its full extent. The transition does not take place straight away. It is a gradual and consistent process which lasts for as long as the slide remains in the person's mind. The light strokes a person sketches onto their negative slide when they first get a whiff of importance become sharper and eventually end up 'larger than life'. If a person hates being plump they will continue to put on weight and if a birthmark bothers them it will continue to get bigger. If a person considers themselves basically inadequate they will quickly receive confirmation that this is the case. The more a person worries about being unattractive the greater the problem will become, just as a person tortured by feelings of guilt will find punishment to be forthcoming and plentiful.

The behavioural pattern will continue until such time as the person stops ascribing the slide such great importance or switches to creating a positive slide. As soon as importance disappears the negative slide loses its foundation, crumbles and ceases to function.

All you have to do is insert a positive, coloured slide and you will see that it works just as flawlessly as a negative one. Focus on the most positive sides of your personality and people will perceive you in that light. This is the other positive aspect of slides which can and should be exploited.

Positive slides

When you concentrate your attention on the unwanted parts of yourself that you would rather conceal or be rid of altogether you create a negative slide. The task in this case is to switch your attention to the qualities you do like about yourself and other attributes you would like to acquire. As we have shown previously, it is not possible to totally disguise your imperfections but if you want to you can easily emphasize and develop your strengths and virtues.

First of all, you should take stock and look at your negative slides. Ask yourself what it is you do not like about yourself, what you would rather hide or be rid of. Slides are created subconsciously but now you can wake up and consciously look your slides in the eye. In a conscious state of awareness negative you can easily determine what your negative slides are. The mind needs to be cleared of negative slides like we clear our space of unnecessary junk, but it is much harder to clear the mind of slides than it is to locate them. Clearing a negative slide is not like shaving off a beard. So how can you root out your negative slides? If you battle with a negative slide it will assert itself even more forcibly. You have to deprive slides of their essential foundation; namely your attention and the significance you attribute them. You have to switch your attention from negative to positive. Dismiss with a wave of the hand anything that has been getting you down and give up the internal battle. Turn your attention away from your shortcomings and towards your virtues and any other positive qualities you would like to acquire.

Is it *important* to you to disguise your shortcomings? If so, this is the basis of a negative slide. Is it *important* to you to make a good impression? If so, this is the foundation of a positive slide. Nothing changes except the focus of your attention and the importance you ascribe to things.

Draw yourself as you would wish to see yourself. You do not have to worry about the danger of indulging in self-deception because you are playing this game consciously. Battling with your failings on the other hand thinking you can hide them or dismantle them by setting personal intentions is self-deception. Create a slide where you see yourself shining in all your glory. Love the you that you see in the slide; Work on the image embellishing it with detail.

The slide does not have to depict a static image. It can be a representation of how gracefully and confidently you move; how elegantly you dress; your aristocratic manners, shining wit and charm, how quickly other people warm to you or what brilliant problem-solving skills you have. Feed the slide into your mind and 'forward'! Just like a negative slide, a positive slide will directly effect your actions and overall behaviour. You will unwittingly, unconsciously, begin to adjust to the slide. The main task though, is for outer intention to fulfil the picture in the slide.

You have to recreate the picture in your thoughts until the slide dissolves. What I mean by this is that with time the slide will become an integrated part of your personality, at which point, it will cease to exist. Once you achieve your desire, the slide will cease to be significant. Importance will disappear and the slide will melt away, but not without first fulfilling its mission. When this happens, the heart will be in harmony with the mind. The slide's mission cannot fail to be fulfilled because you desire it with both your heart and your mind. When the mind tries to transform a slide into reality by itself, your heart knows that it is just playing a game of masks. On the other hand, if you systematically and consecutively consolidate the slide's image in your thoughts the heart will get used to it and agree to integrate the slide into its essence. Remember, that outer intention will not realize the slide immediately. It requires time and the effect is gradual.

As you can see, it really is not that difficult to achieve the desired result. It is all about the will to have. The pictures you draw on your slides can be connected to any qualities you think you are lacking. However, it is important to be aware of how realistic it is to manifest your slide in physical reality. It is better to start with steps that are realistically achievable than to start by drawing a picture of your absolute ideal. With time you can progress to closer versions of it.

One thing you must avoid doing is creating an image that is a copy of someone else you believe already has the qualities you wish to embody! Your slide must be truly yours and not a copy of someone else's. We will return to this idea in more detail in the next chapter. For now it is enough to say that any quality you admire will have an aspect to it that you can apply in the initial stages. Bravery can be represented by resoluteness, beauty by charm, strength by dexterity, the ability to talk by the ability to listen, intellectuality by awareness and physical perfection by confidence. By setting realistically achievable goals you give outer intention the opportunity to fulfil your minimum order more quickly which means it can then set about realizing more complex tasks.

Positive slides will take effect more rapidly and effectively if you interact with people you have not met before, as they will have no previous conception of you. This could be at an interview, a competition, a party or some other event. Feed the necessary slide boldly and fearlessly into your mind. Remember the picture on the slide and hold it constantly in your awareness. Indulge yourself and disregard any doubt or wavering that might pop up such as: "What if it does not work?" Avoid the trap of thinking you have something to lose; let go of your doubts and anxieties. If your will to have is strong enough you will achieve your maximum potential and sometimes even, incredible success.

Positive slides can be created not only in connection with your personality but also in relation to the outside world. This type of slide lets the positive in but blocks the negative out. If you remember, in the chapter "The Wave of Fortune" we discussed the *transmission* of positive energy. In any scenario it is most advantageous to be open to all that is good and to ignore anything bad. At an exhibition, you stop to look at the exhibits you find attractive and walk indifferently past the others. The outside world differs from an exhibition in that *if you do not pass negativity by indifferently, it will start following you around.* By the same token, if you accept it joyfully the positive will never leave you.

It might seem that positive slides are like rose-tinted glasses. Contrary to the established view of things, rose-tinted glasses are the invention of pessimists, not optimists. Pessimists are pragmatically fearful of seeing everything in a rosy light and hence instructively warn optimists against doing so. This pragmatism is nothing more than a negative slide. The pessimist cannot allow themselves the luxury of having and so they receive accordingly.

There is no need to worry that the positive slide will skew your perception. In the majority of cases the element of inner control will make sure that any distortion is relatively minor. The distortion brought about by a positive slide will be beneficial, as long as you do not go to the extremes of imagining yourself to be a Napoleon. Everything should be approached in good measure, not forgetting the dangers of excess potential. In contrast, the distortion created by a negative slide can do immeasurable harm, but the fact of the distortion is not the primary issue. The main feature of a slide lies in that fact that outer intention will slowly transform it into physical reality.

Widening Your Comfort Zone

Are you filled with the ambitious desire to become a star or a millionaire? If so, can you give yourself permission to become one? Most people believe that fame, money and power are the privilege of the chosen few, but if this is the case, who chooses the chosen ones? Primarily, they chose themselves, and only later, is the choice confirmed by others. If you dream of something but cannot allow yourself to have the dream, it just will not happen.

A homeless person may stand in the street gazing through a window at a Christmas table, but can they allow themselves to sit at the table and eat? Of course, if invited, they would accept. It takes decisiveness to walk into a house and sit at the table, i.e. inner intention, but as the homeless person is well aware, who would extend such an invitation to them? The Christmas table exists in the layer of someone else's world. Is the homeless person ready to have this table in their own home, in the layer of their own life? They know that they do not have the house or the money, or the means to earn it. Outer intention will not give the homeless person anything because at the level of pure common sense they are not actually ready to *have.*

Suppose you want to get rich. Would you be ready to accept this gift of fate? Of course, if someone were giving away a spare million we would all find it in ourselves to accept the gift without any problem. Wealth will not ruin your life as some films with a moral try to teach us. But this is not my point. Are you ready to take the million? You are probably thinking that I mean that the million must be earned and won but this is not what I mean either. Are you ready to simply choose and *allow yourself to have?*

You have to come to terms with the idea that you will achieve your goal. If you want to be wealthy but are afraid of walking into expensive shops you will not achieve your goal. If you experience discomfort when visiting an expensive shop it means you are not ready to give yourself permission to own expensive things. The shops assistants in such places can tell immediately who they are dealing with: a potential buyer or a window shopper with an empty wallet. A buyer acts as if they are in control, and holds themselves in a calm, confident and dignified manner aware of their right to look around and choose. The curious window shopper, who is hungry with desire but poor, behaves like an unwanted guest. They have a tense, stiff, slightly inhibited manner; they sense the evaluating looks of the shop assistants and all but apologise for daring to appear in such a prestigious place. The merely curious visitor simultaneously creates a whole range of importance potential: desire, envy, feelings of inferiority, irritation and dissatisfaction because, not only is the shopper not ready to allow themselves to have all this material wealth and luxury, they *do not even consider themselves worthy of it;* for the mind harps on: "None of this is for us. We are poor. We need something a little more modest", and the heart takes what the mind tells it literally.

Give yourself permission to be worthy of the luxury. You genuinely deserve the best. Destructive pendulums only instil the idea that you must "cut your coat according to your cloth" because it is to their advantage to keep you under control. Walk boldly into expensive shops and look at their wares with the manner of an owner and not a servant to a wealthy house. Using self-suggestion to persuade yourself that you can afford to buy expensive things is of course futile. So how can you find a way of believing and giving yourself permission to have?

To begin with, let us distinguish between the realms of inner and outer intention with the phrase "be willing to give yourself permission". People who are used to thinking and acting within the limits of inner intention tend to be quite categorical: "I cannot afford this, full stop. What else is there to say?" Well, it is true that there is not any point in trying to persuade yourself that you can afford something expensive when all you can feel in your pocket is an empty wallet. Here though, we are talking about something else. Inner intention entails the decision to act, i.e. to find the money. However, because the money is not there to find the mind announces a pragmatic verdict. You really will not achieve anything at all if you act solely within the realms of inner intention. Outer intention will not hand the goods to you on a plate like manna from heaven either; for how can something come to you, if even you will not give yourself permission to have it? Outer intention requires the will to have, in other words, considering yourself worthy and knowing that it all comes down to your personal choice. With outer intention it is not so much a matter of believing as knowing.

In your heart you always doubt that a dream can really come true and so *just being willing to take the necessary action is not enough.* If you do not actually believe that your dream can come true you will not feel worthy of it either, or you will doubt that the goal is realistic. People who become celebrities and millionaires are no different to the rest of us in their abilities but they do distinguish themselves in being able to give themselves permission to have the things they want. *It is essential to give yourself permis-*

sion to have. The feeling is similar to riding a bicycle without stabilizers for the first time when suddenly all doubt, hesitation and verbiage disappears leaving nothing but the wordless clarity of knowing. *The feeling of clarity without words, knowledge without faith, confidence without hesitation comes from the unity that exists between heart and mind.* When you experience this state, you sense your own oneness with the silent force that rules the Universe. This force catches you and carries you into a sector where the subject of agreement between heart and mind can be manifest.

Everyone is free to choose whatever they desire but far from everyone believes in this overriding principle of indulgence and leniency. No matter what I say, you may not yet fully believe in freedom of choice. Because the majority of people still live under the power of pendulums life tends to give examples of the opposite. Even if you have freed yourself from the clutches of pendulums, freedom of choice may still lie beyond the limits of your comfort zone. It seems too unreal, too implausible, to have freedom of choice in a world of pendulums. In your heart you probably do not believe that achieving a remote goal is down to personal choice. However, *positive slides can help include the implausible into your comfort zone.* When the idea that any dream is achievable no longer makes you uneasy, doubt will melt away and faith will be transformed into knowledge. The heart will come into harmony with the mind and the will to have appears.

It is futile to try and convince the heart of anything. The heart does not reason, it just knows. The heart can be taught however, and it is capable of embracing a new comfort zone. This requires a slide. With the help of slides unity between heart and mind can gradually be achieved. The fortress is taken by lengthy siege. Create the dream slide in your mind and hold it in your awareness constantly. Return to the picture you have created again and again and refine the details constantly adding new elements to it.

Do not look at the slide from the standpoint of the objective observer; delve into it, live it, at least virtually. Pinch yourself every time you find yourself picturing the slide like an image from a film on a flat screen, as this is not very effective. You have to mentally play out the scenes experiencing yourself as a direct participant rather than a cinemagoer. Whatever you are doing conjure up the slide in your mind's eye as often as you can. You can think about other things but the picture should always be there in the background. Seeing the slide has to become a habit. *A slide will only bring results if it is reproduced systematically over a period of time.*

Express an active interest in anything that relates to the object of your dream. *Absorb all the necessary information allowing it to penetrate the layer of your world.* It helps to play your slide out in real life, at least formally. For example, in those expensive shops you can practise how you would like to choose. Do not think about the money and do not look at the price tags because money is not the goal so much as what you can buy with it. It is enough simply to be around expensive items, to feel the taste of them, to spend time choosing calmly looking around and evaluating the items on display. Allow all these things into your personal space. Look at the items as if you were planning to purchase them soon and not as if they represented an unattainable luxury. Pretend you own the goods already. Let the shop assistants think you are a potential buyer. Play at being a buyer who is discerning in their tastes, (being careful not to be superior). By letting these things into the layer of your world you will gradually attune to a life line in which they can be yours.

There is no need to be concerned with how the things you want will become yours. If you are resolute in your desire to have, outer intention will, without your knowing how, find a way you would never have suspected. When this happens, do not be surprised; do not try to convince yourself that it is a coincidence or show of mysticism. I do not remember now who exactly said: "Coincidence is a pseudonym for God, when he does not want to leave his signature".

Whenever you feel the slightest sense of awe for the world of your dream, drive the feeling out of your mind. Outer and inner importance are obstacles on the path to unity of heart and mind. This is your world and there is nothing in it that is unavailable to you. The world of your dream should be joyful and at the same time commonplace. When something is yours it seems unremarkable and has an everyday quality to it, so in order to attune yourself to a life line that corresponds to your dream you have to feel as if you already had it. You are consciously playing a game not just kidding yourself.

There is no better example of the will to have than the new Russian billionaires who are now more numerous in Russia than in the developed countries of the west. During perestroika at the end of the nineteen eighties, certain lightweight politicians decided that a socialist economy could immediately be transformed into a market economy if everything were to be privatised. Those who understood the significance of the moment and happened to be right next to the feed box got rich straight away without any particular effort or man-power. Everything that had belonged to the state during the socialist epoch such as oil, gas, gold and diamonds etc, as well as various natural, industrial and intellectual resources instantly became the property of a small handful of oligarchs. What had been common property now belonged to a small handful, who had never studied business management unlike the real, billionaires who had to actually earn their millions. All those who found themselves close to the feed box had to do was put their hand out, shout: "Mine!" and then seal it with a legal document.

On what basis did property that was previously common come to be owned by this elite group of individuals? This period in Russia's history is of course unique, but there were many other talented people around at the time, who ended up with nothing; so why these few? The individuals who finally reaped the resources, were the ones who gave themselves the permission to have. The newfound wealthy few suffered no feelings of guilt, qualms of conscience, doubt or sense of inferiority. They did not consider themselves in any way undeserving and it never occurred to them to feel guilty for shopping in expensive boutiques. They had the will to have and so dispassionate outer intention gave them what they wanted; and yet you would find this approach implausible!

Visualising the Goal

The Transurfing methods proposed for reaching personal goals lie beyond the realms of common sense and conventional worldview. Of all known unconventional methods, visualising one's goals has most in common with the methods of Transurfing. Visualisation involves using the imagination to create a mental picture of a goal in as much detail as possible and carrying the picture in your mind.

The conventional worldview would say that visualisation is a waste of time. It is true that distance is covered by the one who walks the road and not by the one who sits around lost in daydreams. However, imagining a mental picture of the goal has the same deciding weight as the actual process of achieving it for reasons you are already aware of. The one who simply walks the road will achieve average results and live the same life as everyone else making their own fine contribution to the majesty of common sense. In contrast, the pilgrim who has the methods of Transurfing at their disposal is capable of achieving the kind of results that common sense can only attempt to explain grasping at the notions of 'luck', 'coincidence', and fate's 'chosen few'.

From the point of view of common sense, Transurfing seems to turn everything on its head. The same of course can be said of common sense from the point of view of Transurfing. If you do not want to live like everyone else; if you do not want to be content with mediocre achievements; if you strive to experience life to the maximum then you are a *Pilgrim.* In Transurfing the Pilgrim is not lady fortune's chosen one. On the contrary, lady fortune is the Pilgrim's choice. You can achieve anything you want if you succeed in toppling the monolith of common sense. This does not mean floating in the clouds; quite the opposite, it means coming back to earth and grounding because the majority of what we call common sense is nothing of the kind. You will have seen the truth of this several times already and many more unusual ideas await you yet.

We still need to answer the question of why visualisation does not always bring about the desired result. Even dedicated followers of alternative psychology and all things esoteric cannot totally depend on visualisation for success. Various visualisation techniques exist, ranging from quite simple to more complex versions and they all work to varying degrees of success. Sometimes they work and sometimes they do not. Like me you may find this level of reliability unsatisfactory and so I would like to reassure you from the outset that the technique used in Transurfing is slightly different. As long as it is practiced according to the rules Transurfing offers a no-fail visualisation technique.

There are three common types of visualisation technique. The first type is the dream. From a practical point of view this is the weakest and most unreliable form of visualisation. There is no harm in dreaming but in terms of transformation it is fairly useless. *Dreams do not come true!* As a rule, those who love to fantasize are not actually expecting their dream to be realized. They might think they do but deep down they either do not believe it is really possible or they lack the intent to have and act. Dreamers look at their dreams in the same way as they gaze at the distant stars. When you hint to them of castles in the sky they close up like an oyster clamps its shells shut: "Leave my dream alone!" When you define the goal of the dreamer with more precision you find that it is in fact just the process of dreaming and nothing more.

The second type of visualisation is the film. I do not mean the kind of film one watches at the cinema but the kind of film people watch in their mind in relation to their desires. This is different to simply dreaming because the process is initiated consciously. There is the intent to have and to act and one action undertaken includes visualising the realization of your desire as if you were watching a film. For example, you want to have your own house and so you imagine the house of your dreams in all sorts of different ways and in all its detail, i.e. according to all the rules of visualisation. In your mind you will probably have a very clear picture of what the house looks like and will hold the image in your mind's eye every day.

If you fulfil this task perfectly you would expect the desire to materialize but, guess what, you will see much the same or exactly the same house that you imagined but it will not actually belong to you. It will be a house that belongs to someone else because you get what you order. If you work conscientiously on visualising your perfect house but do not explain to the 'waiter' that the house belongs to you, the 'waiter' will simply carry out your order perfectly. You can end up being so busy with the quality of the visualisation process, like they teach in the books on the subject, that you forget about the most important thing: who owns the house. This is the key mistake most people make when they practice this type of visualisation. The film remains a film they will never participate in. *They end up staring at it like a beggar stares into a shop window!*

In the third type of visualisation the person plays a role in the film rather than simply observing it. This type of visualisation is much more effective. By playing an active role in the visualised material you set the parameters of your thought energy to the corresponding life line. For example, if your goal is to have a new home there is no point in looking at it in your thoughts as you would at a painting. Create a kind of virtual waking dream. Enter the house, walk through the rooms touching things as you go; sink into an armchair across from the fireplace and feel the cosy warmth and smell of smoke; put a couple of logs on the fire; go into the kitchen, take a look in the fridge to see what you can find. Go to sleep in a comfortable bed. Do you feel relaxed? Sit at the table with your family. Have a house warming party. Move the furniture around. Touch the grass in the garden noticing how green and soft it is. Plant some flowers. What are your favourite? Pick an apple from the tree and eat it. Make yourself at home because it is your home. Do not look at it with the eyes of a suffering dreamer, with awe as if it were something unavailable or some distant prospect. The house is already yours; act as if it were real.

As you know, the visualisation described above represents a slide. This kind of slide will widen your comfort zone and with time is sure to be materialized although when exactly no-one can say. You may have to wait a long time. It all depends on how you work with the slide. If all you do is play with it for a while and then forget about it you will not have much to hope for; there really are no miracles.

It is important to remember the following points when working with a slide. Firstly, if you lose passion for your goal it will dissipate and if you have to force yourself to work with a goal you will soon become fed up with it. If this is the case you should ask yourself whether you really need the slide or not. Secondly, it is worth remembering that outer intention does not manifest slides straight away. It gradually brings you closer to the targeted life lines. It requires patience and perseverance.

Perseverance is essential only in the initial stages. Once visualising the slide becomes a habit you will not have to force yourself to remember to do the exercise. Finally, if the goal itself is not your personal goal but a goal mixed up with pendulums you will not be able to generate the necessary state of unity between heart and mind required to achieve it. We will talk more about this in the forthcoming chapters. If you strive towards your goal with all your heart, then visualisation of the slide will definitely bring results. When you acquire the genuine will to have, outer intention will find a way of realizing your goal.

If you think the slide represents the entire method of visualisation in Transurfing you are mistaken. Even a slide of the highest quality can take a long time to materialize, particularly if the goal lies in a fairly remote sector of the alternatives space in relation to your current life line. The process of reaching the goal however, can be quickened with the help of the Transurfing visualisation technique. Soon you will learn what this is.

Visualising the Process

Let us practice this task a little and imagine that your main goal is to get rich. In an attempt to reach this goal you practice visualising a suitcase stuffed full of notes. You do the exercise according to all the rules of the third visualisation type over a relatively long period of time. What will the result be from this practice and when will it show itself?

The answer is that there will never be any result. You can practice this exercise every day for the rest of your life and at best you will see suitcases crammed full of money a little more often, most probably in films. Your chances of finding the treasure or winning the lottery are very slim and who wants to rely on chance?

You will wonder why this is, after all, in your thoughts you constantly open the case, take out the money, rearrange the notes, stroke them and all but eat them! If the third type of visualisation is more than just a film what is the problem? And what about that all-powerful outer intention?

From the point of view of Transurfing there are two mistakes that undermine the example of visualisation shown above. The first is that your true goal is not really a suitcase filled with money. Money is an attribute, not a means and certainly not a goal. We will talk more about personal goals later. For now we will push ahead. The second mistake is that *concentrating attention on the end goal will not move you towards that goal unless you are already just one step away from achieving it.* Of course, your comfort zone will be widened and outer intention will gradually take effect *but you are not helping it.* You have to at least put one foot in front of the other. And yet, the fact that you have to act as well as visualise is not the point here as we are still discussing the practice of visualisation.

Until now experience has told you that if you want to achieve something you have to focus all your thoughts and efforts on your goal. Now you have to forget this idea. As I promised in the beginning, Transurfing undoubtedly works but you have to let go of commonly held ideas and embrace new ones that may seem a little incredible from a more conventional standpoint.

We will explain how visualisation in Transurfing is fundamentally different to other visualisation techniques. As you know, desire is the concentration of attention on a goal. Intention is the concentration of attention on movement towards the goal. The driving force behind any action is intention and not desire. Hence what moves you towards the goal is to *visualise the process of moving towards the goal* rather than to contemplate the goal itself. Intention becoming realized is a process, not a fixation on one single frame, although of course, that does not mean that the goal cannot be part of the mental picture. The mental picture of the goal should serve as the background to the central focus which is the process.

Visualisation of the process differs from visualisation of the goal in the same way that intention differs from desire. Desire is ineffective. We return once again to the example of lifting your arm. Imagine that you want to raise your arm. First think about the fact that you want to raise your arm and the result of that desire, i.e. the arm in a raised position. Now lift up your arm. At the first stage desire is strong but nothing happens. There is simply a statement of the fact of the desire and a mental picture of the goal – the raised arm. At the second stage intention is in action and continues to take effect for the whole time the arm remains in a raised position. During this process the goal is understood to be the final image towards which one strives but attention must be concentrated specifically on the process of achieving the goal. Finally, to desire something, to imagine oneself at the desired destination is sufficient in the early stages but to progress any further you have to move and carry out a concrete process.

These comments might seem trivial but look at the conclusion they prompt us to make: *visualisation of your goals is the work of desire which will not bring you a single step closer to your goal.* Your visualisation will effectively be a dummy run.

In Transurfing the visualisation practice involves *imagining a mental picture of the process of moving towards your goal* based on the principle that the goal must be reached sooner or later because the power of intention is working. Movement towards the goal does not take place in waking as quickly as it does in dreams but there is tangible movement nonetheless. If you study the chapter "Forward to the Past" you will even *learn to see movement along life lines.*

Whatever you are doing, if it involves a lengthy process, visualising the process will help. This type of visualisation method is particularly helpful in creative work where the end goal may not yet have acquired distinct contours. What should be understood by visualisation of the process in this context? You might be working on a piece of artwork and have an idea of the general qualities you wish the piece to convey but not yet know how exactly it will turn out. When you take a break from your work, imagine that the piece you are creating is constantly improving. Today you complete certain details; tomorrow you plan to add a few new touches. Imagine to yourself that your creation is becoming all the more transformed. You give it ever new qualities and it becomes a work of art in front of your very eyes. You are content; engrossed in the creative process watching your baby grow with you. You will automatically know what to visualise in any situation. The secret is to go beyond contemplating the nature of your piece to imagining the very process of its birth, development and perfection. There is no point in assuming that in your mental picture the creation or artistic piece will paint, sculpt or construct itself. You are the one creating it and the piece will reach its perfection in your hands. *An artist creates and admires their work simultaneously.*

A perfect example of this is how a mother cares for her child when it is growing up. A mother feeds her child, puts it to bed and imagines her tiny tot continuing to grow with each passing day. She takes care of her child at the same time as constantly confirming her admiration of its beauty. The mother plays with her child, constantly giving it instruction. She contemplates her child's intellectual development anticipating the onset of schooling. As you can see, in relation to her child, the mother is not focusing on an end result so much as simultaneously creating and visualising an ongoing process. The mother does not simply observe her child's growth. She takes part in it, all the time imagining the child's development and the kind of person they will become.

If what you are creating is a computer program, every day when you finish work imagine that the program is gradually becoming more effective and easier to use and how the next day you will impress everyone with new enhancements.

If on the other hand you are working on a business project, imagine that innovative ideas suddenly occur to you and that every day you introduce unique proposals. Observe the growth of your project and give yourself permission to feel assured that it is being transformed into an example of best professional standards.

If you are working with your body nourish it, as a mother does her child. Imagine that your body is gradually acquiring perfect form. Look after it, train it and then imagine that you are building more muscle making your body look more toned.

Whatever the focus, visualise the process. Visualise the means by which your project will reach completion. *Contemplating the end result will expand the limits of your comfort zone and so in this sense it has its value, but visualising the process of moving towards your goal will significantly quicken the work of outer intention.*

Do not worry if you do not yet know how your goal can be realized. Continue to visualise your slide calmly and systematically. Once the goal fits easily within the limits of your comfort zone outer intention will present you with a means. There is no need to rush about stressing over how to find a way of achieving your goal. Do away with importance and trust the alternatives flow. Watch the slide; live it and you will automatically take the right type of action.

The method does not stop at visualising the process either. The material realisation of the alternatives space is inert, like resin, which is why, unless you have a messiah's mastery of outer intention, the transition has to occur gradually. Gradually not only means continually but also progressively. Herein lies the secret of another aspect of visualisation in Transurfing.

Transfer Chains

If the realization of your personal goal lies in life lines which are quite distant from your current coordinates it is practically impossible to attune your energy to these life lines directly. For example, if you are intending to sit an exam but have absolutely no knowledge of the relevant subject matter you cannot attune your energy to a life line in which you pass the exam with flying colours. If you know nothing about the relevant subject you will not be able to visualise your answer to a single question.

The path that leads from your current position to your future goal may be quite long, although not necessarily in a temporal sense. It is not only your position that must change, but also your way of thinking, your manner and perhaps even your character. You cannot attune the parameters of your energy to any level of precision without actually walking the path.

If you try to visualise the process of moving towards a very distant goal you may be tempted to jump ahead and rush events which is ineffective and leads to frustration and annoyance which in turn will set balanced forces against you.

You can play a slide with a mental picture of the distant future in your mind as often as you like; it will not do any harm, *but visualising the process of moving along a part of the path that you would not naturally be treading for a while yet could end up getting you lost.* Imagine that you have to head down a winding river. If you had the option would not you walk along the river bank instead pulling the boat behind you and making a short cut of the winding river bends?

If the goal needs to be reached progressively you will have to work through all the different stages towards it, whether you want to or not. For example, you cannot become a professional in any given field in one fell swoop. You have to first finish your studies, then find work, polish your professional skills etc. This consecutive path towards a goal in the alternatives space is called a *transfer chain.* Every link in the chain represents a separate stage. Because the individual stages are linked together in a chain it is impossible to move onto any given stage without having completed the one immediately before it. For example, you cannot study for a master's before finishing your first university degree.

Each link in a transfer chain is made up of interconnected and relatively homogeneous sectors of the alternatives space. The path to the goal is made up of transfer chains and the alternatives flow. The alternatives space is inherently an ordered structure which means that if you try to create a path to your goals in an unordered fashion you will never reach them. You already know that in order to avoid disrupting the balance and losing a sense of the alternatives flow you have to be careful not to create excess potential; do not slap your hands on the surface of the water; and do not fight against the current. That just leaves one more rule, which is to practice visualising the process of moving towards your goal at your current stage only. You can picture the end result as often as you like in the form of a slide but the process should only be imagined within the context of your current link in the transfer chain. There is no need to hurry. Everything happens at the right time.

Now we can give a final definition of *visualisation in the Transurfing method* as *mentally picturing the realization process of your current link in the transfer chain.* Mentally picturing an image helps to direct thought in the necessary direction. If thoughts are just given a little push they will continue of their own momentum both in a script as in dreaming. The goal is achieved by living out the link's realization process in both thought and action.

As you can see, the approach is actually quite straight forward. It is not difficult to determine the separate links in your personal transfer chain. What if the sequence of movements towards the goal is not known to you yet, or you have no idea by what means or paths your goal might be achieved? Do not worry. We will repeat the steps you can take below.

If you do not know yet how your goal might be realized do not worry; just continue visualising your slide calmly and systematically. Once the limits of your comfort zone have been widened enough to embrace the goal, outer intention will offer up a suitable means to achieve it. There is no need to stress over finding the right way of achieving your goal. The slide itself will nudge you to take the necessary actions automatically, even subconsciously. Eliminate importance, remain calm, and trust the alternatives flow.

Here I would like to add a few more words about signs. If you interpret a sign which you believe might point towards the possibility of achieving your goal you should be aware that signs only relate to your current link in the transfer chain and only have a very tenuous connection to the final goal. In other words, indicators only relate to the particular road you are walking at the current time. You can interpret signs that relate to anything about the current link in the transfer chain. However, if several chains separate your current life line from your target line the signs you perceive will not serve as indicators for the goal itself. This does not mean that signs symbolic of a distant goal do not exist; it just means that you will not be able to interpret them sufficiently reliably from your current position. In Transurfing, with the exception of a negative response from the inner voice, sign interpretation is considered to be the least reliable technique one can use, so it is not recommended that you attribute them a great deal of meaning.

It remains only to clarify the place the third type of visualisation has in Transurfing and whether it is worth practicing goal-based visualisation techniques. The answer is unequivocal. It is essential to practice goal-based visualisation in any form that is convenient. The goal should be held in the mind in the form of a slide which helps widen the limits of the comfort zone and attune the frequency of your thought energy to the target lifeline. This is the sole function of third type visualisation. In contrast, the physical shift to a target life line is accomplished by the workhorse of Transurfing, i.e. visualisation of the process of moving towards the goal. By visualising the process you unite your personal, inner intention with outer intention.

SUMMARY

Illusions are not the result of fantasy but the perception of a different reality.

People present in the material world are capable of perceiving other realities.

Inner convictions can distort a person's objective perception of the world.

A slide is something you carry around in your own mind that others are not.

Slides distort the perception of true reality.

People have a tendency to hang their projections on others around them.

Importance lies at the foundation of all slides.

As soon as importance disappears the slide ceases to exist.

Outer intention gradually but consistently realizes the content of the slide.

Stop battling with yourself and switch your attention from the negative to the positive.

Create a positive slide that is pleasing both to your heart and mind.

Look at your slide more often each time embellishing it with more detail.

Never portray an image in your slide that is copied from another person.

You will never receive anything that does not trigger your will to have .

Allow yourself the luxury of deserving the absolute best.

The will to have is the immutable knowledge that you deserve what you want and that it is your choice.

Positive slides help you to push open the limits of your comfort zone to include things that previously seemed implausible.

Do not treat the slide as if it were just a picture; live it, at least in the virtual world.

Allow in any information relating to the world of your dream.

It is not contemplation of the result but visualisation of the process that moves you towards your goal.

Rather than contemplating the result imagine the process of birth and growth.

In Transurfing, visualisation is understood to be the act of focusing on a mental image of the realization process of a current link in the transfer chain.

If it is not clear to you how to achieve your goal, focus on visualising the slide instead.

The slide will take you in the necessary direction.

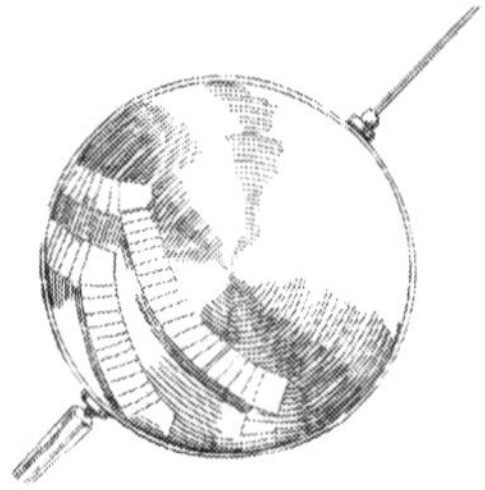

Chapter IX. THE HEART AND MIND

The soul comes into the world reaching out trustingly with a child's arms.

The Wind of Intention

Everyone is born an individual, unique creature that later develops a personality. Thoughts, knowledge, convictions, habits, even character, gradually build up like layers of plaque. These parts of the self obviously do not come out of nowhere and yet what is there of us originally? Could we all really have begun as a completely clean sheet? Just try for a moment being a completely clean sheet. Close your eyes and stop the mental chatter. If you contemplate the blackness you will manage not to think for a short period of time. For a moment your mind will be completely empty and yet you do not stop being yourself in this moment. The activity of the mind is temporarily halted but a sense of the integrity of the self remains.

How do you explain that you are in fact you? An awareness of personal identity usually comes from one's position in society. Yet imagine for a moment that the social environment has disappeared and that you are just hanging in the empty space of the Cosmos.

There is no Earth, no sun, no past and no future; just black emptiness. Everything else has disappeared. All that remains is you. So what of your former personality? All knowledge and thoughts, manners, habits, desires, fears, character and pursuits were dependent on your previous environment. What would remain of the self?

It is difficult to discuss this question within the framework of reason and yet a discussion on the eternal theme of the existence of the soul goes beyond the scope and purpose of this book. It would also take up a lot of time and lead to nothing. Neither is the issue of the existence of the human soul of particular importance to the aims of Transurfing. It may suit you to believe in the soul, or as you might prefer to call it–the subconscious. You may or may not agree with the concept of the eternal nature of the soul but it is inarguable that the human psyche consists of the conscious and the unconscious.

We previously agreed that all conscious experience would be referred to as the mind and all unconscious experience as related to the heart or soul. For the sake of simplicity and practical purposes we need only to draw a rough distinction between the heart and the mind by suggesting that feelings relate to the former and thoughts to the latter. States of elation, openness and inspiration as well as oppression and depression depend on the inner feelings of the heart.

The mind is entirely in the power of pendulums which impose limiting perceptions and beliefs. The extent of human freedom is narrowed to what pendulums will permit. This may explain why people tend to identify their position in the world mistakenly as servant or master. From the point of view of Transurfing neither of these positions is correct; for man is nothing more than a drop that flies in from the ocean for a brief moment.

Sea spray that forms when an ocean wave crashes serves as a good illustration of birth and death. A drop of spray that has become separated from the waves cannot experience oneness with the ocean or receive energy from it. The individual drop of spray thinks that it exists separately and has nothing in common with the ocean until such time as it falls back into the waters and its awareness of oneness is restored. At this point the drop merges with the ocean into a single whole, for in essence they are made up of the same element–water.

An individual particle of water can take various forms. It can be a drop, a snowflake, an icicle, or a cloud of steam. The form differs but the essence is the same. The particle does not remember that it is the same as the ocean. It believes that it exists in the form of a drop, a snowflake or a cloud of steam and that the ocean is made up of waves, foam, spray, icebergs, currents and calm. It is very difficult for the particle to see the common essence inherent in all these external manifestations of water. Despite being familiar the essential communality remains elusive.

Biblical texts on the subject reveal the truth coloured by the distortion of the mind. The statement that God created man in his image and likeness is true, only this truth is normally distorted. God can take any form but His essence does not lie in the fact that he has a head, two hands and two feet. If you compare God with the ocean and the individual with the drop both have the same essence, which is water.

According to the testimony of people who have had near-death experiences when death is close by the soul experiences an inexplicable serenity and bliss that comes from a feeling of oneness with the Cosmos. In a sense, the drop has returned to the ocean and rediscovered the awareness of its true essence knowing that it consists of the same substance as the ocean. In that moment the entire energy of the ocean passes through the drop.

Throughout the history of human civilization man has always sought a feeling of connectedness with universe. In pursuit of spiritual perfection all religious schools have ultimately striven for the same goal of reaching enlightenment, of experiencing a sense of oneness with the world, of dissolving into the ocean of energy losing awareness of the self as a separate essence.

An enlightened master has all the energy of the Universe at their disposal. They see no fundamental difference between themselves and infinity. Their thought energy enters into resonance with the energy of the ocean. Then the *intention of the enlightened becomes identical to outer intention,* the powerful and unfathomable force that rules the world.

When a kite is the right shape it will climb up through the airstreams. In the same way, the wind of outer intention lifts a person up and carries them through the field to a sector that corresponds to the quality of their thought energy. In order to travel purposefully through the space you have to be able to feel the wind of outer intention as clearly as you feel currents of air or water.

Until a person becomes conscious of their essence and the nature of their oneness with the ocean, the workings of outer intention will be beyond their grasp. We are not going to set ourselves the task of reaching enlightenment for this would be too hard a task, and in any case, it is not essential to the realization of your personal goals. You do not have to hide away in Tibet and meditate. Transurfing provides a loophole which allows you to compel outer intention to your personal will, to a small degree perhaps, but nonetheless, enough for you to fulfil your desires.

The principle of the loophole is relatively simple. The mind has will but is not capable of ruling outer intention. The heart on the other hand can experience oneness with outer intention but has no will, flying through the alternatives space like an uncontrolled kite. *Achieving unity between heart and mind is enough to bring outer intention under the sway of your will.*

Creating a harmonious connection between heart and mind is a difficult but nonetheless realistically achievable task. As we saw earlier, the effect of outer intention is quite tangible when it comes to working against the will of the conscious mind and materialising our worst expectations. What we need to do now is to understand how our best expectations can also be realized. In the chapter on 'Intention' we defined the key conditions for mastering outer intention: *awareness, reducing importance, and letting go of the goal.* Soon you will discover new secrets of Transurfing which will open more doors onto the mysterious world of outer intention.

The Heart's Sail

People generally tend to interpret themselves and other physical phenomena in the world as essentially material objects. Yet all material objects have one informational and energetic essence in common which defies conventional perception. It is this essence that directs the behaviour of material realization in the alternatives space. The language of abstract symbols we are used to referring to is only sufficient to describe the outer manifestations of this informational and energetic essence. The original essence itself cannot be unambiguously described using the language of the mind, hence the magnitude of philosophical and religious movements that have attempted to do so.

Human perception is like this because we have been taught since early childhood to concentrate our attention on separate elements. "Look at Lyalya! These are your hands and these are your feet. And this is your porridge! Look at the bird!" Our perception continues to be shaped and conditioned throughout our entire life and so the mind constantly channels data according to an established template of how the world is described.

For example, if someone has never seen another person's energy field, the mind will be reluctant for the eyes to perceive it because it is not consistent with the established template. In childhood, no-one ever drew our attention to auras and so they were excluded from the template we use to describe the world. Now we understand theoretically that the aura exists but our ability to perceive it visually is poorly developed.

The mechanism of perception still remains a puzzle. Our current understanding is such that only certain elements of it can be discussed with any clarity. Ants for example, have never seen the stars. They have never seen the sun, mountains, or even the forest. Their vision is designed so that from birth they only focus on objects that lie in close proximity. An ant's perception of the world differs radically from our own.

When we ask: "what does the world really look like?" we are attempting to pose an objective question in the hope of receiving an objective answer; but the question is not really objective. *The world looks just as we see it,* because the notion 'looks like' is also an element of the template that colours our perception. In the template of a blind mole for example, the notion 'looks like' simply does not exist. The world demonstrates itself to us in accordance with our template of perception and at the same time, the world does not actually 'look like' anything. There is no point in claiming that the world looks as it always has done, or looks like an accumulation of illuminated energy or anything else. There is only any point to speaking of the individual manifestations of reality that we are capable of perceiving.

Consciousness is a product of human society and emerges from the concepts and definitions that surround us. Whereas the soul (subconscious) is part of man from birth, consciousness is acquired as the surrounding world becomes defined by ideas and definitions in terms of human language. The world does not only exist because people have described it using their own concepts. In this sense the human soul will always be illiterate for it does not understand the human language of words. The heart is only capable of understanding the things we call feelings. First a thought emerges and only afterwards is it formulated in words. You do not have to have words to think. Thoughts are primary, not words, and thoughts are the language the subconscious can understand. There is no point in trying to communicate with the subconscious in the *language of the intellect.*

The existing set of concepts society uses is far from sufficient to express the entirety of human experience. As you can see, I was not able to fully describe the nature of outer intention. Fortunately, humanity has preserved one means of universal expression through art. We do not need words in order to understand works of art. Everyone can understand the *language of the heart.* This is the language of things created with love and passion. When a person walks towards their innermost dream through the right door, i.e. does the thing that suits their soul best, they become capable of creating a masterpiece. This is how art is born.

You can graduate from a conservatory and compose colourless music that no-one remembers and you can paint empty paintings that are technically immaculate but no-one would proclaim them a master piece. Yet, if you can say of a created work that 'it has something' then it can at least be considered a work of art. What specifically that something is, the critics will explain, but one thing is certain, that something can be understood by all without words.

The Mona Lisa's smile speaks in a language everyone can understand. There are no words. Words fall short of expressing the things we understand instinctively. What exactly is being comprehended is not important as everyone has their own unique way of divining and feeling. You could of course explain that the Mona Lisa's smile is mysterious or that it has an elusive quality etc, but words are still powerless to explain that special something that makes the painting nothing less than a master piece.

It is not just the elusive quality of the Mona Lisa smile that evokes such avid interest. Have you ever noticed that the Mona Lisa's smile is similar to the Buddha's smile? People say that the Buddha achieved enlightenment during his own lifetime. In other words, people say that the Buddha, like the droplet of water, experienced a sense of oneness with the entire ocean. In all the pictures of the Buddha his smile is totally dispassionate and at the same time it expresses serenity and bliss. It is a smile that can be characterised as an expression of the 'contemplation of eternity'. When you see the Buddha's smile for the first time it evokes a strange mixture of bewilderment and curiosity because it reminds you of a drop of something distant and forgotten – the feeling of oneness with the ocean.

Any reminder of this distant oneness touches a chord in the heart. When human language emerged the language of the soul gradually began to atrophy. People focused too exclusively on the language of the mind and so with time it began to take primary position in our experience. Even the story that explains how this occurred is told in the context of an intellectual concept. A distortion of the process is described in the legend of the Tower of Babel in accordance with which the gods became angry with man for failing to construct a building that reached the height of the heavens and so they confounded the languages of man so that the people would no longer be able to understand one another.

In essence the majority of myths and legends express a truth which has been interpreted via mental constructs. Perhaps the high tower serves as a metaphor for the power the people received when they learned to express their will consciously in the language of the mind. As we have said already, *the heart can feel the wind of outer intention but it is not capable of putting up a sail to harness the wind's force. The will of the mind however, can put up a sail. Will is an attribute of conscious awareness.*

The subconscious flight of the heart on the winds of outer intention is spontaneous and uncontrolled whereas conscious awareness allows personal will to be expressed deliberately. Initially, before the languages of the heart and mind became so divorced from one another, harmonious connection between heart and mind was easily achieved. Later, the mind focused so intently on constructing a worldview based on its own references that its knowledge of outer intention was left far behind.

Due to colossal intellectual effort the mind has achieved outstanding success in the technotronic world of material realisation but has lost connection with everything that is in any way related to the unrealised alternatives space. It is because the mind has radically distanced itself from an understanding of outer intention that so many ideas within the Transurfing model seem implausible. The mind can retrieve the knowledge that has been lost but de"in or to do so there must be a connection between heart and mind.

The difficulty is that the heart, unlike the mind does not think; it knows. While the mind considers the information it receives passing it through the analytical filter of the template worldview, the heart receives knowledge from the information field directly, without subjecting it to analysis, and communicates with outer intention in the same manner. In order to make this communication more focused there has to be agreement between the will of the mind and the strivings of the heart. Union between heart and mind is essential. If you can achieve this connection your heart's sail will fill up with the wind of outer intention and carry you directly to your goal.

The Wizard Within

Your heart already has everything you need to know to realize your desires. Do you remember the story about the Wizard of Oz? The clever Tin Man dreams of having a brain, the kind Scarecrow longs for a heart, the brave lion strives to acquire courage and the girl Ellie wants to go home. All the characters already have the things they desire but if Great and powerfull Oz the Wizard tells them so it will sound too implausible to be true and so he creates a magic ritual instead.

In reality, all that was needed was for the Tin Man, Scarecrow and Lion to give themselves permission to have the qualities they so desired because they already existed in their soul. For the girl Dorothy the task was a little more complicated. She had to express total will in the will to have in order to return home. The magic ritual helped her to strengthen her faith and then the wind of intention carried her home.

As we have already said, not everything that is connected with outer intention fits into the framework of the concepts of the mind. The mind is responsible for this scenario. Pendulums also assisted in the process because freedom and individual control over outer intention would have severely undermined the pendulum's interests.

The pendulum monsters only benefit from people who do not stand out in any way and are content to work for them as a cog in a wheel. The realization of individual potential is a pernicious threat to the pendulum because an individual who is free works for their own development and prosperity. Hence from childhood we are instilled with conditioned standards and rules which conveniently mould us into obedient adherents.

On the one hand there is a positive need to teach the individual certain rules that will help them to get along in life, as the people who break these rules become losers or outcasts. On the other hand, social conditioning strongly suppresses a person's unique individuality and so people generally cannot say what they really want and have no idea of their true capabilities.

If you want to suppress a person's ability to master outer intention, it is enough to break the heart's connection with the mind. Throughout the history of humanity, huge efforts have been made to divorce the heart from the mind. The mind has worked constantly to perfect its language of symbols at the same time becoming ever less practiced in the language of the heart. Pendulums of religion like pendulums of science have pulled the mind in different directions as far as possible from the true nature of the heart and finally, the development of industrial and information technologies witnessed over recent centuries has dissolved the connection altogether.

The influence of pendulums is particularly great at the present time because everyone is now reading books, listening to the radio, watching television and accessing information via the internet. Humanity has absorbed a huge volume of knowledge and equally as much delusion which holds just as steadfastly in the psyche. The separation of heart and mind is humanity's greatest loss. The idea that real success, be it in business, science, art, sport or any other sphere can only be achieved by a few individuals is widely accepted as the normal state of affairs. Nobody seems to question it or consider it abnormal.

There is no point in you and I trying to 'save humanity'. I simply wish to suggest that you, dear Pilgrim, ask yourself the following question: "Why him (her) and not me? What do I have to do to become one of these chosen few?" I am no Great and powerfull the Wizard, and so cannot create magic rituals for you; I will simply answer the question directly. *You already have everything you need. All you have to do is use it. You are capable of anything, it is just that no-one has told this yet.*

You are capable of creating incredible works of art, making unique discoveries, achieving phenomenal results in sport, business and any other profession. All you have to do is turn to your heart, for the heart has access to all knowledge, as well as the previous achievements of all humanity. You just have not asked your heart yet. All great geniuses of art, science, and business have only succeeded in creating masterpieces because they turned to their hearts. *What makes your heart any worse than theirs? Nothing!*

All masterpieces speak to us in the language of the heart. Whatever you do your work will only create an impression if it comes from the heart. The mind can build a new house using bricks from a previous model but no-one will be astounded by the new design. The mind can make a perfect copy but only the heart is capable of an original.

All you have to do is accept the axiom that the heart has everything it needs and then give yourself the joy of making the most of it. It is incredibly simple and at the same time totally incomprehensible and still, you can allow yourself the luxury of having. The will to have depends on you alone. You can do anything.

The listener may doubt what I claim to be true and yet we rarely experience doubt when we are persuaded that we lack the necessary calibre, ability, and quality, or that we are not as worthy or as talented as others. We easily believe the statements that erect high walls on the path to our goals. So do yourself (not me!) a favour and embrace the knowing that you are worthy and do deserve the absolute best and are capable of achieving whatever you desire with all your heart.

The fact that everyone is worthy of the best and capable of anything is meticulously hidden from us. We are told we are naïve to believe we have unlimited capabilities; but the opposite is true. Wake up and shake off the delusion. You can dictate the rules of the game if you consciously exercise your rights.

No-one can forbid you from trying but the conventional worldview and pendulums will try to convince you in every way possible that your goal is unattainable. There will be all kinds of reasonable arguments put forward to prove that your capabilities are limited. Ignore these arguments and shield yourself with the 'unreasonable and frivolous' conviction that *together your heart and mind are capable of anything.* After all, you have nothing to lose; for what have you really achieved living within the framework of those other very reasonable arguments?

You only have one life. Is it not time to shake up the pile of commonly held beliefs? What if they turn out to be false and you would never have known? Do it now, otherwise, you will not have time to find out whether they are true or not. Life will pass you by; all the possibilities will have been exhausted and the gifts of this miraculous life given to others, and perhaps indeed they will only be given to a few, but nonetheless, they will not come to you.

Only you can decide whether you want to fully exercise your rights or not. If you can allow yourself to have something you will achieve it. Begin by believing in the unlimited possibilities of the heart and then turning your mind round to face it. False beliefs make this more difficult to do but the Transurfing model helps to deconstruct many erroneous ideas.

One of these beliefs stands as follows: "it is hardest of all to overcome the self" or "it is hardest of all to battle with the self" or the predatory Russian saying: "You have to be able to stamp on the throat of your own song", i.e. sacrifice your own desires and act in the interests of others. This is one of humanity's greatest delusions. How can one possibly battle with the amazingly beautiful creature that lives within you, and what would be the point? Negativity does not live within; it lies on the surface like a layer of dust on the surface of a painting. If you wipe the dust away a pure heart is revealed underneath.

The creature that hides behind many different masks and costumes is imbued with truly wonderful qualities. *The task is to allow yourself to be you.* Surely the masks you wear are not capable of achieving success, abundance and happiness? It is futile to try and change yourself, because all you do is create another mask. If you remove the masks destructive pendulums force us to wear, you will reveal the treasure that is hidden in your heart. You really do deserve the best because you really are an, amazing, unique, special being. Just allow yourself to be so.

If you admire the geniuses of the art world, science or cinema, know that you too can join their ranks. The reason the work of a genius appeals to you so much is because these creative works are born of the heart. What you choose to create will please others just the same, as long as it originates from the uniqueness of your soul. Everything that is ordinary and mediocre is created by the mind. There is nothing unsurpassable about the mind or its creations. You carry a real treasure within you; for *the heart is unique.* Only the heart can produce an ingenious creation. Make sure the mind allows it to do so.

The Mirage

All their lives people are forced to believe that success, wealth and fame only befall the chosen few. At university, in tournaments, competitions and similar events people are constantly made to understand that they are far from perfect and that other people are better and more deserving than they are. The ones who achieve success, wealth and fame in abundance are the ones who *do not buy into the deception.* It is that simple. It might be difficult to believe that everyone deserves these things and is capable of achieving them, but you can begin to believe it if this is your *intention.*

Many people dream of becoming a star and achieving huge success and the general standards for success are actively and widely promoted. The pendulums love to demonstrate the achievements of their favourites to the silent majority. They introduce their favourites as an example of the success we should all strive for if we want to reap the full range of benefits life has to offer. A star has everything the life can give swimming in the rays of wealth and fame. Who would not want to be rich and famous? Even if you do not particularly want to be a huge success and are not the type that hankers after material luxury you probably would not turn down the chance of material wellbeing and fulfilment from personal achievement.

Stars are born independently, but they are lit up by pendulums. By this I mean that star worship is intentionally set up and flourishes thanks to pendulums. In films, on stage, in stadiums and on TV we are constantly being shown the society's best representatives – the chosen ones. The way the fans greet the stars with such ravish admiration is always emphasized, and we cannot but see how incredible they are, and how phenomenal their achievements. The same immutable fact is always being instilled: everyone loves the stars and we must strive to be like them.

What aim are the pendulums pursuing by putting their favourites on pedestals? Could it be that they are concerned for the personal achievements and wellbeing of their adherents? Indeed not. Pendulums demonstrate the achievements of their favourites so that the majority of adherents are stimulated to serve them even more conscientiously; for how does your average Joe Bloggs become a star if not by hard work? Stars are the best of the best. Anyone can become a star but they have to work really hard. The stars are a good example; do what they do and you will be successful. The stars also have unique abilities and qualities that the ordinary person does not have, which is all the more reason for them to labour intensely if they want to be a success.

These are the slogans the pendulums use. They do not deny the fact that anyone can be successful but they do carefully hide the fact that everyone without exception has unique qualities and abilities. It would mean certain death for pendulums if every individual were to discover their own remarkable abilities. If the adherents were to become free, escaping the control exerted over them, the pendulum would simply disintegrate. The pendulum is most comfortable when its adherents are thinking and acting in the same way. As you may remember from the second chapter the pendulum's very origin and survival depends on the uniformity of its adherents' thinking. The star's colourful individuality is supposedly an exception, and serves to prove the rule by the very fact of being an exception. The rule is: "Do what I do!"

This is why many young people fall into the pendulum's trap striving to be like their idols, copying them and hanging up posters of them on their bedroom walls. The mind blindly follows the pendulum. Thoughtless reason tells the heart that she is less than perfect, as if by saying: "Even with my superb abilities success is beyond me, so you have no chance! These people, now that's a different story. Look at them! We need to learn from them. Sit there quietly in your imperfection whilst I try as hard as I can to be become their copy."

The younger generation emulate their idols as if trying to *catch hold of a mirage*. The desire to emulate the success of others is the work of inner intention, like the fly beating itself against the window pane. They are effectively attuning to a foreign sector of the field in which they would be nothing more than a parody. The mind can create various versions of a copy but they will never astound anyone. A person becomes a star because of their willingness to be different and their own unique individuality. The soul of every living being is inimitable in its own way. A unique soul has its own sector in the alternatives space where its exceptional qualities can be manifest in all their magnificence.

Every soul has its own individual 'star' sector in the information field. It is clear that there may be an infinite number of star sectors but for the purposes of the explanation we will conditionally assume that the individual soul has one unique sector of the field in the form of an individual goal or path. Distracted by the lure of the pendulum the mind will senselessly stagnate in some-one else's star sector trying to copy their qualities or repeat the script of their success. Copying someone else's script always creates a parody. The heart's potential can never be fully realized in a sector that does not belong to it. So how do you find your true sector? There is no need for the mind to worry about this because when left unhindered *the heart will find the path of self-expression*. The mind's task is to forget about other peoples' experience, to acknowledge the heart's extraordinary nature and to allow it to find its own path.

Teenagers are particularly susceptible to the influence of pendulums because they are still new to the world and do not yet know what to do or how to behave. It is easier, more reliable and safer to mix in with the crowd, living life in the same way as everyone else rather than to stand out for any particular reason. The crowd instinct provides a feeling of security but fundamentally severs the buds from the stem of individuality. You will have noticed how the majority of young people dress in the same style, use the same vocabulary ('Ace', 'wicked', 'cool'), and behave quite consistently with each other. Despite their superficial gloss of independence and autonomy they submissively follow the pendulum's rule to: "do as I do!" They believe they embody the modernism of the contemporary generation but who among them would actually risk *creating* and valorising the new?

Among the teenage population it is always the few that have given themselves permission to reveal the hidden qualities of the soul that become the leaders and the mavericks. It is these few, who develop their own individuality, that later become the trend-setters, the ones to set the tone, to create new movements and chase new opportunities and prospects. They do not copy other people or religiously obey the rules. They allow themselves to realize the distinctive qualities of their own soul. *Pendulums will not ordinarily put up with any expression of individuality but in the case of the upcoming star they are left with no choice but to accept them as a favourite.* Then the next round of favourites is put on a pedestal and spotlighted as new models for the adherent masses to worship.

There is nothing wrong with a young boy wanting to be strong like his hero or a girl wanting to be beautiful like her heroine, but they should not only copy them or, for example, set themselves the task of building the same muscles, acquiring the same way of moving, talking, singing or playing as someone else. The reason we like these people is because they have realized their own unique qualities right within their own sector of the alternatives space.

Of course, there should be some kind of initial role model that can serve as an example like a demonstration copy, but not as a yardstick or template to be emulated. Your yardstick is your soul. Simply allow it to explore all its qualities within your current sector. It is better to put a photograph of yourself up on the wall and admire that than someone else's image. Loving yourself is extremely beneficial and constructive. Loving yourself leads to self-approval and is only punishable by balanced forces if accompanied by disregard for others.

You really are a unique individual and in this sense no-one can compete with you. Just give yourself permission to be yourself. There can be no competitors to your personal uniqueness. Remember that you have a right to your own individuality and you will have a huge advantage over those who try to copy the experience of others. You will not get anywhere by striving to become like a him or a her; become yourself. Allow yourself this luxury. Whilst you wear the mask of an existing star at most you will be a copy and at worst a parody. Stars do not become stars by copying other people.

When you give up on futile attempts to be like someone else, everything will work out. Likewise, when you cease futile attempts to repeat other peoples' scripts everything will work out. When you acknowledge the brilliance of your own individuality other people will have no option but to agree with you. Allow yourself to be presumptuous enough to have.

All great actors play themselves. This might seem strange because the roles they play differ, but personality, character and charm give an actor away immediately. The hardest role to play is the one where you play yourself and allow yourself to remove the mask and be yourself. It is much easier to play someone else because putting on a mask is comparatively easy, and the actor will have the professional skills to pull the role off. It is infinitely more difficult to remove the mask but if you can take off the mask what ensues is not role play but what they call 'life on the stage'.

It only seems difficult but in fact deciding to have is quite straight forward. All it requires is for you to shake off the stereotypes imposed by pendulums and once and for all claim belief in the infinite possibilities of your own soul. There is nothing pendulums can do to stop you if you reject the experience of others and give yourself permission to be a star. All they can do is imbue you with oppressive thoughts like: "a star has to be beautiful and I am not beautiful. A star has to be able to sing well, act and dance but I cannot. A star has to have talent which I do not have. I have not got what it takes. I am better of watching how other people do it".

Do take a good look at the stars of the pop, science, sporting and business worlds etc. Many, if not all, fail to meet the perfect standards and expectations of what a star should look like. Every celebrity has their own bundle of flaws that could potentially eclipse their positive traits. For example, one star has a long nose but people still think she is beautiful. Another star cannot sing but people are mad about her songs. Another has no acting ability and all the directors have sent her packing but she still climbed to the ranks of the celebrities. Another is short and fat and you can only guess why the women love him so much. Another is a right nobody. Just what do people see in him? You look at another and he turns out to be really nondescript. You ask yourself: Could he really be famous?

Individuality does not fit with the rule "do as I do", but you will agree that individuality is an essential prerequisite for the birth of a star. So, a bright personality breaks the rule and the pendulums have to acknowledge them as an exception, whilst the other stereotypes remain in force. All stars are exceptions. You too will become an exception from the conventional stereotypes.

You can sing with a well-trained voice and languish in obscurity or sing terribly but in your own curious manner and everyone will love it. You may boast brilliant intellectual abilities and never achieve anything whilst the pathetic C pupil who is constantly harping on about his mad ideas in the end makes a brilliant discovery. You may have outstanding physical qualities but never become a sport's star whereas the one who dares to break the conventional stereotype leads the game on the field in an unexpected way and ends up the golden player. I will not continue the list of contradicted stereotypes. You understand the principle. *Do not be afraid of breaking the pendulums' stereotypes and find the boldness to direct you mind's attention towards your own unique and inimitable soul.*

Watch out that you do not get caught up on another pendulum hook by being provoked into chasing after someone else's goal. This will only lead to disappointment. What good is another person's goal? Listen to your heart and not your mind. Your heart knows best of all where you can shine like a star.

There is a law in the world of pendulums which has it that only the occasional few may become a favourite and everyone else must fulfil the function of ordinary adherents and observe the rules of the system. Transurfing cannot get rid of this law but it can help you personally to break away from it. Then if you make the most of the unique qualities of your soul the pendulums will be obliged to include you among their favourites.

Guardian Angels

Many people believe that they have a Guardian Angel who helps them. If you believe in your personal Guardian Angel that is wonderful because it means that it exists. When you think about you Guardian Angel, turn to it with confidence and are grateful and you can be sure that these thoughts make your Angel real. There is nothing that cannot exist in the alternatives space. You may even believe that thoughts can create an independent informational energetic being if it pleases you to do so. The more sincerely you love your Angel and express your gratitude for any small thing it helps you with, the stronger the little Angel will become and the more it will support you. Ultimately, it does not really matter whether the Angel exists independently or whether it is created by your thoughts.

There is nothing wrong with not believing in Guardian Angels. If do not feel the need for a Guardian Angel you obviously feel comfortable and good about your life which is great. In the end, you get what you believe in, although if I was you, I would believe in my Guardian Angel. What if Guardian Angels do exist irrespective of whether you believe in them or not? What if they love us, look after us as best they can but we have forgotten them and turned away from them? The Angel might need your love and be weakened by your lack of attention. It might be drained of energy and unable to assist its ward whilst you give your energy away left and right to destructive pendulums. Pendulums may also assist you but only if it serves their interests. The wellbeing of a specific individual is of no consequence to pendulums at all, whereas your Guardian Angel takes care of you alone.

Imagine your angel in any form: a cherub with wings, a fluffy cloud, a bird; whatever. It really does not mater how you see your angel for, of itself it does not actually *'look like' anything.* It only takes a specific form within your imagination so imagine your angel in the way that you find most comfortable. You can even identify it with your soul if you want to. People with extrasensory abilities can communicate with their Angel. Do not worry if you are not one of these people. Your angel will find a way of setting you on the right path. *It is important not to take offense at your angel, or even worse, get angry with it.* Your angel knows what to protect you from and where to send you because in comparison to your angel you are like a blind kitten. It is not for you to reproach your angel. You have no idea of the misfortunes your angel might be bending over backwards to protect you from.

There is a parable about a man who meets with God in heaven. God is showing the man his entire life's path and the man can see from the footprints that God had been walking beside him his entire life. Then the man noticed that in the bleakest periods of his life there was only one set of footprints on the ground. The man turned to God reproachfully: "Why God did you leave me at the times that were hardest to endure?", to which God replied: "You are mistaken. Those are not your footprints but mine. In those most challenging moments I carried you in my arms".

You cannot overestimate the role of a Gurdian Angel. Just the knowledge that there is another being, who looks after and protects you as far as they are able helps to balance your confidence levels. Confidence which generates inner calm can play a huge role in a person's life. If you feel lonely you can share your loneliness with your Angel. Angels have yet another wonderful quality that you can benefit from: *your angel is not affected by the influence of balanced forces.*

If you are pleased with your success, give yourself a slap on the back and be proud of yourself. This is a good thing. It is better to praise yourself too much than to be reproachful or self-critical. The only negative thing about being very pleased with yourself, is that it can create excess potential, perhaps just a little but enough and so balanced forces can end up spoiling your soul's celebration. You praise yourself and as a result you error or experience some unpleasantness. So does this mean that one should fear even a secret enjoyment of one's personal achievements?

There is one way of taking joy and pride in one's triumphs without creating excess potential which is to *share your glee and satisfaction with your Guardian Angel.* Your angel took care of you and helped you get there and so it deserves your praise and gratitude. When you are relishing in the delight of a positive result and feel satisfied with yourself remember your Angel and delight in these moments together. Talk to your Angel; be unsparing in your praise and thanks. It is in fact better to praise your Angel than to praise yourself. Have sincerity; give away the gift of your right to reward wholeheartedly. You have nothing to lose because you have already received what is yours leaving you free to thank and congratulate your Angel.

Consider your success to be your Angel's merit. What will happen if you do? The excess potential of your pride will be dissipated and at the same time, you can give yourself the space to celebrate in your heart without caution. *Feel the joy but give the pride away to your Angel;* for obviously, no one can take your achievement from you.

It is better to give the reward and thanks to your Angel than create the excess potential associated with pride, or express your gratitude to a pendulum that has bestowed a little joy upon you. *Your Angel needs your energy but it will not ask you for it.* If you think you have received help from a pendulum there is no harm in thanking the pendulum too but be aware that the pendulum will always automatically receive a portion of your energy because with a pendulum there is no such thing as a free lunch, ever. Whatever you do, do not neglect your Angel. *Remind your Angel constantly that you love it and are grateful to it.* It will become stronger as a result and reward you handsomely.

A Soul Box

Your soul came into the world wide eyed, full of hope and trust but the pendulums promptly picked it up and assured it that no one had been waiting to meet it, no-one was particularly pleased to see it and that it will be expected to do hard, dirty work just to earn a small crust of bread. Of course, not everyone is born into poverty but the wealthy have their problems too, just of a different kind. In the world of pendulums the wealthy suffer no less than the poor.

Your soul did not come into the material world to suffer. It just benefits the pendulums when the battle for a place in the sun becomes the norm. As you already know, in accordance with the laws of informational and energetic matter a pendulum emerges from the shared thoughts and actions of a group of individuals and later carries on to exist independently of the group. Via the process of informational energetic exchange the pendulum compels adherents to its will and forces them to think and act in its own interests. Pendulums harvest human energy when emotions such as dissatisfaction, irritation, frustration, anger, worry and fear are expressed and when people are taken in battles between other pendulums.

We are accustomed to living in a world of pendulums where oppression, feud, competition, war and many other examples of rivalry are considered par for the course. It does not occur to us that this might not be normal and that things could easily be different. Look at the world from the point of view of the pendulum model. If you remember all the many different manifestations of a pendulum's insatiable thirst for energy, imagine what the world might be like if they did not exist. If these types of informational energetic exchange were not taking place there would be no structures that absorb the energy of others by drumming up rivalry. It is difficult to imagine, but in a world such as this there would be much happiness and very little suffering. We could live in a world where there are enough natural resources and opportunities for everyone.

The idea has been instilled in us that the battle for survival and natural selection is an essential process that facilitates the evolution of life. It is true that these processes do support the development of the world, albeit of an aggressive kind. However, natural selection is not an essential condition for the growth of life. Life could equally as well develop in accordance with other more humane laws.

In the world of pendulums natural selection occurs according to a negative script by which *the one who suffers loses their life.* Selection relies on the methods of oppression and destruction. Have you ever wondered whether there could be a different, more positive script in which *the one who feels well survives*? These two scripts differ only in as much as negativity differs from positivity. One could argue that both scripts have a place in the context of natural selection but negativity is still the predominant factor. The weakest one dies. Whatever the case may be, the system that pendulums have established in the human world is far harsher than any system supported by nature.

The battle for survival as it occurs in nature does not exhibit the same hardened and aggressive features that it does in the human world. The pendulums people have created are considerably more powerful and hostile than any of nature's pendulums. Just because in nature someone is always getting eaten does not mean there is a constant war going on. The lion feeds on the cow just as the cow eats the grass. Importance is a trait unique to human beings. Because plants and animals have zero understanding of importance the law of balance is maintained. It is only because man observes natural phenomena from the human belfry of importance that the normal coexistence of living organisms is perceived to be a fierce struggle.

Even animal kingdom rivalry over territory and mate is purely nominal in comparison to the constant warring of man. Animals very rarely inflict physical injury on each other unless they are hunting for prey. In the majority of cases any conflict is decided in the best interests of the one that barks loudest and pulls the most intimidating grin and if blood should be drawn it is most likely because paws cannot avoid being heavy. Emotions such as anger and hatred are not characteristic of animals. Neither do they show signs of courage or cowardliness. It all comes down to survival instinct. Daring wolves and timid rabbits only exist in our imagination.

We cannot change the world. We have to accept that how the world is does not depend on us. Myriad limitations and conditioning literally stuff the soul into a box. The mind captured by convention becomes the soul's jailer prohibiting it from realizing its potential. The individual is simply forced to behave in the way the pendulum world demands: to express dissatisfaction, to get irritated, to fear, to compete and to fight. *Human thinking and behaviour is determined by reliance on the pendulum world.* As you have already understood from previous chapters, this type of conditioning drains a person's energy, sets balanced forces against them and distracts them from their true path sending them out in search of false objectives. To top it all, outer intention manages to realize our worst expectations. Most people would be happy to free themselves of conditioning and dependency, they just do not know how to.

Now you know that the pendulums' power relies on their adherents' importance and lack of awareness. *People are not usually aware that they are reacting to provocation.* They give in to worry, fear and frustration automatically expressing dissatisfaction and anger out of habit. They easily succumb to gloom and will exert maximum effort when met with obstacles. People live as if in a dream, complying with the script enforced by pendulums. They are oblivious to the fact that they can take control of the script believing that very little depends on their own actions. Importance sucks people into the pendulums' game and lack of awareness deprives them of their final chance to shape the script. *The game is played by the pendulums' rules.*

As you can see, sometimes I repeat the same point several times. This is because, although the insights set forth in this book might seem obvious, the conventional pendulum-constructed worldview is so deeply rooted in the human psyche that they can be difficult to feel and comprehend in their full depth and entirety. You can however break out of the box of conditioning if you follow the principles of Transurfing. The power of the pendulums is great but as long as you abandon importance their power is insufficient to prevent you from consciously exercising your right to choose and to write the scripts in your life.

It is in the pendulum's interests to keep people under control so that they can pursue their own goals. To the pendulums the individual is just an instrument, a means to an end, a puppet. Your soul came into this world as to a celebration, so go ahead and give yourself permission to have this experience. Only you can decide whether you want to spend your entire life working for the good of someone else's pendulum or living for your own enjoyment. If you chose to live life as a celebration, it is essential that you free yourself from the pendulums that bind and seek out your own goal and your own doorway.

Your mind has to understand that you do not owe destructive pendulums anything and are not obligated to do their bidding. Establish union between the heart and the mind and you will have anything you could wish for, literally and figuratively. All you have to do is free yourself from pendulums and soften the discord that exists between your heart and mind. Allow yourself the luxury of deserving the best.

If someone tries to persuade you that you must work for the good of someone or something else do not believe them. If someone tries to prove to you that everything in life comes through hard work alone, do not believe them. If someone is imposing a harsh battle on you to secure your place in the sun, do not believe them. If they try to tell you what your place is, do not believe them. If someone tries to draw you into a religious sect or community because you can make 'an essential contribution to the common goal', do not believe them. If they tell you that you have to live your entire life in poverty because that is how you were born, do not believe them. If they tell you that you have limited options, do not believe them.

You will soon see that pendulums will not leave you alone that easily. As soon as shoots of your will to have begin to show themselves pendulums will create a situation designed to force you to accept that your options are limited. The moment you feel strong enough to choose and determine the script yourself, pendulums will upset your plans. As soon as you begin to feel calm and confident they will get their claws into you. *Do not respond to provocation and do not let them shake you off balance. Keep the importance you attribute to things to a minimal level and be conscious of your actions. Keeping importance at zero is what the situation calls for, not massive effort and tenacity.*

In this game the only limitation on your options is your personal intention and the only limitation that can be placed on the pendulum's options are your zero importance level and conscious awareness. Remember: if I am empty there is nothing for the pendulum to hook into; if I am aware of the meaning of the game pendulums will not be able to enforce their scripts on me. If they still manage to disappoint you, upset you, or throw you off balance take a good look at where you have attributed inflated importance.

Change your relationship to whatever threw you off balance in the first place. Try to be consciously aware of the fact that *it is the pendulum and not you that is desperate for importance.* The box that inhibits your soul is made from the importance you attribute to things. Do not attribute excessive importance to *anything.* You must simply *take what is yours, calmly and without insistence.* If it does not work, do not make that important either. The pendulums are just waiting for your spirits to fall. If something distresses you, make it seem less important. Be aware that it is just a game; and precisely that, a game and not a fight; for in essence the pendulums are like clay goons.

The game is harsh and relies on human weakness. The moment you give any slack to importance you lose. If you keep importance at zero the pendulums fall through your emptiness and the clay golem disintegrates. You will source strength in the awareness that you understand the rules of the game. As soon as you notice that a pendulum is trying to hook into you and knock you off balance have a chuckle to yourself and adamantly reduce the level of importance. Gradually, this will become a habit and when it does you will feel your strength and understand that you can determine the script yourself. By winning the pendulum game you beget *freedom of choice*.

Fraile

Until now we have been talking about how sectors of the alternatives space have specific characteristics or parameters. For the sake of simplicity we agreed to consider these characteristics frequencies. If when there is unity between heart and mind, the frequency of your thought energy corresponds to the frequency of a sector in the alternatives space, the power of outer intention will facilitate your transition to that same sector. In other words, the scripts and scenery of the sector in question will become materialized in the layer of your physical world.

The soul also has a unique range of parameters which in the context of Transurfing is referred to as *fraile*. Again, for the sake of the simplicity of the model we will consider the soul's fraile its characteristic frequency. Everyone's fraile is unique like the structure of a snow flake; no two are the same. The fraile *characterizes the unique and incomparable essence of a person's soul.*

We can only guess at the form fraile takes because it manifests implicitly, hidden under the *masks of the intellect* which every individual wears. For this reason there would not be much point in going into this notion more deeply here. It is beyond doubt however, that every individual has a unique soul essence. You can describe the character, habits, manner and appearance of a person you know and yet there will be something else beyond these characteristics, an integral image of that person that you understand without words. It is this individual essence that requires no explanation that we call fraile.

You may have come across people who emanate an elusive and indefinable charm. Surprisingly, they may be relatively unattractive in their outward appearance and yet as soon as they begin to speak you immediately forget their physical shortcomings and are entirely spellbound. When asked wherein lies that person's charm, you can only mutter: 'there is something about them', finding no other explanation. Such people are extremely rare. If there are none in your circle of acquaintances look for them among the stars of show business. The hallmark of these personalities is the exceptional beauty and charm which seems to radiate from the depths of their soul. You will immediately recognise that their beauty is different to a doll-like beauty, for doll-like beauty is purely external and corresponds to conventional, established standards.

From the point of view of fraile, the secret of this type of charming beauty lies not in the fact that a person has a beautiful heart or other special spiritual quality. You will come to accept (or not, as you wish) another paradox of the Transurfing view: *beauty lies not in the heart or soul but rather in the harmonious connection between heart and mind.*

No-one who has not yet learned to love themselves, who is self-critical, begrudges their work, lives in mental turmoil or at odds with their own soul can ever radiate the beauty of charm. Conflict between the heart and the mind is reflected in a person's outward appearance and their character. If a person is happy and has learned to love themselves, if they enjoy life and do what they want to do, then they will exude a certain inner light which indicates that *the mind is attuned to the soul's fraile.*

Unity between heart and mind equates thought energy with the nature of outer intention. Self-fulfilment, and a balanced relationship between heart and mind generate something very similar. Inner peace ignites an inner light that reminds the heart of its true nature, which is why the beauty of harmony is interpreted as charm or spiritual beauty. This kind of beauty sometimes evokes hidden envy and people ask: "How come you look so radiant?"

The heart is not at peace when the mind is suffocating it in a case but when it is caressing the heart like a rose in an orangery, admiring and caring for it, allowing every petal to open freely. This is that rare thing we call happiness.

Fraile can manifest in the form of a hobby or other pursuit, and anything that is done with love and enthusiasm. Often the strings of the fraile rest silent for a long time. Sometimes a sign of some kind will cause a string to sound. It could be an unexpected, passing comment that for some reason strikes a cord in your soul or something you see that has a special magnetism that immediately draws you to it and you begin to sense a vaguely perceptible urging over and over. This is the outer intention of the soul working. But since it is a vague yearning outer intention works without a specific aim. It is important to listen to the dictates of your heart so that the mind can pick up on them. Then you can catch hold of outer intention and quickly achieve your desire.

What prevents the mind from entering into a relationship with the heart? Once again, importance is the problem along with our old friends, the pendulums that install false aims and values. As we said earlier, it is pendulums that set the standards of our notions of beauty, success and abundance and inner and outer importance that motivate the individual to compare themselves with these standards. Naturally, the mind finds a bundle of shortcomings and starts to hate itself and consequently the heart too. It tries on all sorts of masks trying to make the fraile fit the standards, but as a rule nothing good comes of it. As a result, the rift that exists between heart and mind widens. How then can there be any question of inner peace! The mind waters its rose with reproach and dissatisfaction and the rose becomes ever more feeble.

The mind will search for treasure anywhere except in its own heart. Pendulums tout loudly and seductively while the heart tries quietly and delicately to make its abilities and inclinations known.

The mind does not listen to the heart and tries to change fraile. Naturally nothing good comes of this either. As a result, the heart and mind converge in their decision to negate these imaginary imperfections. Outer intention immediately transfers the individual to a lifeline where hostility intensifies because the imperfections have literally materialized.

The mind assumes that if it wears a correcting mask it will be able to meet the established standards. As you know, this is fruitless like chasing after a mirage. Rather then making the most of fraile's precious uniqueness, people beat against the window pane chasing after the success of another. And yet the star's success is born from having attuned the mind to fraile. The one hunting the mirage achieves nothing and is deeply dissatisfied with self. *No-one can ever reach a life line where they accept themselves and feel fulfilled by expressing fundamental dissatisfaction with the self.* The parameters of their energy field will simply correspond to life lines where they have even more reason to feel unfulfilled.

This is the game that pendulums inflict upon us. It appears senseless but from the pendulums' standpoint the game has a very definite meaning; dissatisfaction and lack of fulfilment are their favourite dishes.

How can you attune the mind to the heart's fraile? The only way is to convince the mind that above all the heart is worthy of love. You have to first love yourself and only then pay attention to the virtues of others. Love for the self should not be confused with self-satisfaction, vanity or complacency. Complacent self-satisfaction comes from considering oneself superior to others and creates dangerous excess potential. To love yourself means to understand your own uniqueness and accept yourself the way you are warts and all. The love you have for yourself must be unconditional otherwise it will turn into excess potential. Surely you are worthy of your own love; for you are the only one there is of you.

If a person has gone too far in the battle with their fraile it will be difficult for them to just up and love themselves. "How can I love myself if I do not even like myself?" This is pure excess potential born of increased inner and outer importance. Outer importance lies in the fact that I take someone else's standards to be the immutable truth. Perhaps I am valuing the virtues of others too highly? Internal importance lies in the fact that I force myself to follow other people's standards. Who said that I am any less than they are? I am just me. Could my self-esteem be too low?

To learn to love yourself, shake outer importance off its pedestal and give up worshipping other peoples' standards. Who is stopping you from creating your own standards? Let others chase after your standards. Release inner importance and let yourself go. You are not obliged to follow or live up to other peoples' standards. You have to remain aware of the fact that the pendulums need importance, not you. When you love your heart with all your mind outer intention will carry you to a life line where you will be totally accepting of yourself. If you like yourself, no matter what, you will succeed in deceiving outer intention and reveal qualities you never suspected having. When your thought energy radiates at the frequency of self acceptance and self-fulfilment outer intention will pick you up and carry you onto life lines where you really do have something to be proud of.

One of the commandments says: "Love your neighbour as yourself". For some reason everyone seems to focus on the necessity to love your neighbour but the commandment presupposes that one already has love for the self. Leave the game enforced by the pendulums and begin to love yourself starting today. Buy yourself a favourite treat and have a personal party. Give yourself some tender loving care. Some may maliciously continue: "indulge in all your weaknesses and bad habits..." but this is the demagoguery of pendulums and I see no reason why I should debate with them. You already know what it means to love the self. Weaknesses and bad habits are only induced by pendulums.

There is no need to set out in search of the Holy Grail somewhere in the depths of the jungle. *The Holy Grail is within you. It is the fraile of your soul.*

Unity of Heart and Mind

The heart comes into the world trustingly reaching out with a child's arms. Then it discovers that pendulums have conquered the world and transformed it into a jungle. Pendulums immediately try and convince the heart that no-one was expecting it and that in this world everyone has to fight for a place under the sun and pay tribute to the pendulums. The naïve, direct heart must be put in its place straight away. The heart is told that no-one is interested in her desires, that there is more suffering than happiness in the world, that holidays are only held on prearranged dates and that it will have to work extremely hard just to earn a crust of bread. That is it. The heart is crestfallen. The eyes well up with tears of despair or the heart is increasingly indignant. That's not right, it's not fair! The hackles are up and it looks as if the only choice is to plod dejectedly along a path enforced by pendulums or scratch away desperately in an attempt to pursue one's own goals.

The pendulums take hold of the mind on all levels: mental, emotional and energetic. The conventional worldview and human behavioural responses are also shaped by pendulums. People think and act in a way that is advantageous to them. The heart like the mind also ends up in the conditioning box. There is an element of conditioning in literally everything. People have to come to terms with the limitations placed on them and play their role in the game that has been forced upon them. In conditions such as these the heart gradually retreats to the back burner whilst the mind takes the reins into its own hands.

The mind counsels the heart as if it were a small, unreasonable child: "I know better than you what needs to be done. Your foolish babble makes no sense." In the majority of people the heart shrinks into a frightened, powerless creature that is left in the corner mournfully observing all the frantic mind gets up to. Sometimes moments of union between the heart and mind occur. In these moments the heart sings and the mind rubs its hands in satisfaction, but such moments are rare. More often than not agreement between the heart and mind arises in moments of negation, fear and hatred.

The heart is given no voice in issues of choice. The mind treats the heart as if it were a child asking for a toy in a shop. The mind usually answers in the standard fashion that sounds: "We cannot afford it", and with that the dream is instantly nipped in the bud.

Look at what happens. The child needs the toy now. If you genuinely cannot afford to buy the child the toy there is nothing wrong with refusing the child their desire, but the heart is willing to wait! And yet the mind places a crucifix on the entire situation with the conviction of an idiot: "We do not have enough money". It turns out that the dream is fundamentally unattainable in principle.

The mind has a logic imposed by pendulums who gain from keeping adherents on a leash denying them even of the freedom to choose their own dream. The heart has no logic and understands everything literally. The mind insists that there is not enough money and yet the heart is not asking for money. It is asking for a toy! Arguing that there is no money the mind places a taboo on the toy (it is unrealistic, elusive), and the heart has nothing else except to close up inside and not mention the toy again. And the dream's funeral is over.

The mind cannot see how to realize the dream and so will not let it into the layer of its physical life, for in life everything should be logical and clear. The mind should have agreed to having the toy and then outer intention would have taken care of how to find the money for it. However, the worldview constructed by pendulums does not allow for such miracles. That adherents should have freedom of choice just does not fit with the pendulums interests.

People erroneously accept the rational worldview as an immutable law. This law however, is a 'sham' and can easily be 'deconstructed'. Sometimes in life little, inexplicable 'miracles' happen, so why not allow one of these miracles into your own life? All you have to do is allow yourself to have what the heart desires. If you brush away the web of prejudice and limitation the pendulums weave around us and genuinely believe that you deserve your dream and allow yourself to have what you desire, it will come to you. *Allowing yourself to have is the most important condition for wishes to come true.*

The mind has other responses for the heart in the toy shop as well that sound: "Do not be silly. I know what you need better than you do. We are simple people. It is not possible. Not everyone can have these things. You do not have the right qualities or abilities. You can hardly compare yourself with him/her! Just live like everyone else does", etc, etc. If it were not for the impact of pendulums as a mitigating factor, one would accuse the mind of extreme stupidity. One can only listening these lines it will wake up from its tenacious illusion and comprehend the absurdity of its 'reasonable arguments'.

Without the heart the mind is not capable of very much at all and yet together, the heart and mind are capable of almost anything because their merging generates the magical power of outer intention. The mind governs internal intention and the heart governs outer intention. Without help the heart is not able to direct outer intention in a goal-orientated manner and yet when the heart and mind merge outer intention becomes controllable and can be used in pursuit of specific goals.

Everything that you think is unattainable is indeed impossible to achieve via internal intention which is governed by the mind. No-one is arguing against that. Whatever goal you set yourself I agree that it would probably be hard to achieve within the limits of a rational worldview. And yet why should you have to walk away from your dreams simply because some puffed up authority claimed the right to determine what is real and what is not. Why should not you claim your right to a personal miracle?

The secret of happiness is just as straightforward as the secret of unhappiness. In both cases it comes down to unity or disunity between the heart and mind. The older a person gets the greater the discord becomes. The mind succumbs to the influence of pendulums making the heart unhappy. In childhood the heart still hopes that someone will give it the toy it wants to badly, but with time, hope fades. The mind finds more and more confirmation that the dream is difficult to achieve and puts off realizing it until later. Usually, the putting off till later lasts for a life time. Life comes to an end and the dream is stored away in a dusty box.

In order to achieve unity between heart and mind first of all one has to determine what exactly there should be agreement on, i.e. identify ones goals. Despite seeming obvious, this question is not as trivial as it might first appear. As a rule, people know exactly what they do not want but find it difficult to express their true desires. This can be explained by the fact that pendulums strive to subdue people enough to impose their own false goals upon them. There can be no question of unity of heart and mind if the mind is chasing after a seductive mirage and the heart longs for something else entirely.

On top of that people are so intensely busy and concerned with carrying out various types of work for pendulums that they have no time to simply sit quietly and consider their true desires. You have to deliberately set aside time and remember what your heart longed for in childhood. What did you like, what did you want, what really attracted you and what dreams did you have to give up on over time? Ask yourself: does the goal from that distant past still attract you? Think about what you really want. Could it be a false goal? Do you really desire it with all your heart or do you just *want to desire it?*

When you think about your goal you must reduce inner and outer importance. If outer importance is heightened the goal will appear seductively prestigious and unattainable. Are you sure you have not been caught on a pendulum's hook? If internal importance is heightened you will think the goal is beyond your capabilities. In this case you will again be attracted to the goal because it appears unattainable. Do you really need it?

When considering your goal, do not think about whether it is prestigious. Shake the goal from the pedestal of unattainability. This will reduce outer importance. *Likewise, when you are thinking about your goal do not think about how to achieve it.* This will reduce internal importance. *Only think about how comfortable you feel.* Imagine how you would feel if you had already reached your goal. Do you genuinely feel good about it, or is it like a heavy weight in your heart? Doubting whether your desired goal is realistic or not does not mean that it is not needed. The important thing is that your heart sings when you think about your innermost goal. However attractive something might appear to you, if it evokes a heavy feeling in your heart the goal could be false. We will look at all these questions in more detail in the next chapter.

If you have no specific goal and do not desire anything in particular you either have a weak life force or your mind has finally driven your heart into its box. In the first case, you could increase your vitality by looking after your health better. It might be that you do not truly know what good health is. When a person is in good health life is pleasurable and they want to experience everything all at once. The heart is incapable of not wanting anything because for the heart this life is a unique opportunity.

In the second case you only have one option which is to love yourself. Might you have gone a little overboard looking after everyone else? Put yourself first. You cannot do anyone any good if your own heart has been pushed onto the back burner. You can waste your entire life sacrificing yourself to serve others, even if it is for the sake of those closest to you, to say nothing of pendulums. We are not given this life to serve others. We are given this life to realize our own individual potential. Shutting away your heart in a box creates powerful excess potential in the shape of a hidden lack of inner fulfilment which will spill out in all kinds of trials and tribulations for yourself and those close to you. You will think you are doing good deeds whereas in fact, from a wider perspective, all those good deeds are to the greater detriment.

Look after yourself tenderly, attentively and enthusiastically. Then your soul will be warmed through and spread its wings.

Do not believe anyone who tells you that you have to *change yourself* in order to be successful. No doubt you have heard such things said. This is the pendulums' favourite recipe. Apparently if something is not working you have to work on yourself. What do the pendulums mean when they say that you should change? They mean, turn away from yourself, face the pendulums and follow the rule "do as I do" in order to fulfil their demands and act in their interests. In order to change yourself you have to struggle to overcome yourself. What question can there be of unity of heart and mind if you cannot accept or love yourself and are in conflict with your inner self? The soul will not accept false aims; it has its own inclinations and needs. When you work towards false goals you either end up achieving nothing or, when you arrive at your destination, you finally understand that it was not where you wanted to be after all.

Transurfing has no relationship to pendulums and so recommends a completely different path; do not change yourself – accept yourself. Turn away from the husks the pendulums impose and lure the mind's attention towards your heart. *Listen to the dictates of the heart consciously reducing importance as you go; allow yourself to have, and you will receive anything your heart desires.*

To bring your heart and mind to unity you have to pay attention more often to your level of inner peace. You feel comfortable, calm and at peace when nothing is worrying you or getting you down. Inner tension signals the opposite: you feel uneasy, oppressed, afraid; you feel down or something is weighing on you. If these are the feelings that arise and you know what is causing them then the tension begins in the mind. As a rule the mind knows what is frightening, worrying or oppressing it and so you can rely on the mind to find a solution.

The heart's tension is a little more complicated because the discomfort is manifest furtively as a vague presentiment. The mind will insist that everything is fine, that everything is going as it should and there is no need for concern. And yet despite all these reasonable arguments you know that something is getting you down. This is the rustle of the morning stars. It is not difficult to hear the voice of the heart. The task lies simply in *paying more attention to it.* The mind with its logical reasoning sounds too loudly for the individual to attach any meaning to a vague and elusive presentiment. Absorbed in its own logical analysis and prognosis of events the mind simply is not in the mood to listen to the feelings of the heart.

There is no other way of learning how to listen to the rustle of the morning stars than to develop the habit of paying attention to your level of inner peace. Every time you have to make a decision, first listen to the voice of reason and then the feelings of the heart. As soon as the mind has made a decision, the heart will react to it either positively or negatively. In the case of the latter you will experience a vague feeling of inner tension.

If you forget to pay attention to your level of inner peace until it is too late try and remember in retrospect which feelings the decision evoked. You will have experienced a fleeting feeling precisely at the moment the decision was made. In this moment the mind was so involved in analyzing the situation that it was too busy to take note of any whispering from the heart. Now try and remember what this first fleeting feeling felt like. If it was an oppressive feeling on the background of the mind's optimistic reasoning this is the heart's way of saying 'no'.

To what extent can you trust the presentiments of the heart? If you think you have experienced a premonition of a particular event that is going to happen it is not advisable to place too much trust in these feelings. There is no guarantee that the mind will correctly interpret the information the heart is providing. *Only a feeling of inner tension in response to a decision made by the mind can serve as a reliable guideline.*

A feeling of inner peace however, is not necessarily a guarantee that the heart is saying 'yes'. It might be that the heart simply has no particular response to your decision. Yet when the heart says 'no', you will feel it distinctly. As you know from the material in previous chapters, the soul is capable of seeing sectors in the alternatives space that will be transformed into physical reality as a result of an intellectual decision being put in action. When the heart sees the result it will express its response to it as positive or negative. You will know from your own experience, that when the heart says 'no', it is always right.

You now have the reliable criteria of inner tension as a way of determining the truth when you have to make a decision. If the heart says 'no' and the mind says 'yes' boldly refuse, if at all possible. The heart is not capable of desiring anything bad. If, however, the mind still insists that 'we have to', act as best you can in the circumstances. Sometimes in life we do have to accept the inevitable. In any case, the criteria of inner tension will help bring clarity and certainty to situations where the scales fluctuate.

Once you have achieved unity of heart and mind on the issue of your chosen goals the next step is to *attain unity in the decision to have and to act*. Internal intention of the mind has to merge with outer intention of the heart. If you act within the framework of internal intention at the same time as directing outer intention in the necessary direction, you can consider that the goal is in the bag. If you are uncertain of the internal intention because you cannot see clearly how to achieve the goal, work on the decision to have. Outer intention is much stronger than internal intention and will find a way.

You have to achieve the same unity of heart and mind over the decision to have that is present when you experience powerful emotions. The heart and mind are usually united in strong feelings such as adoration, hostility, fear and our worst expectations. We love, hate and fear with all our heart. When the heart and mind are united, a passionate feeling is born. As the famous Russian writer Nikolai Chernyshevskiy said: "The one who does not know how to hate will never learn to love."

If the goal is chosen correctly the heart and mind will both be satisfied. The feeling of pleasure that arises can only be marred by thoughts of how inaccessible the goal seems, or if the goal is beyond the person's individual comfort zone. Slides can help correct the situation if the mind doubts the potential reality of the goal and the heart feels bashful in the 'director's chair'. You already know how slides work. By widening the limits of your comfort zone you will achieve the passionate joy of unity in which the heart sings and the mind rubs its hands in glee.

I repeat: *when considering your goal, don't think about how prestigious it is or how achievable it is, or how exactly you might achieve it; the only thing you should pay any attention to is how comfortable it makes you feel.* Does thinking about it make you feel good or bad? This is the only thing that matters; otherwise you may end up confusing feelings of inhibition with feelings of inner tension. When faced with a challenging or unfamiliar situation it is natural to experience some reluctance, inhibition or shyness. You may wonder: "Can all this really be for me?", whereas gut feelings and inner *tension are associated with dejection, chore, oppressive responsibility, despondency, apprehension and painful anxiety.* If creating slides does not ease feelings of inhibition then what you are experiencing is clearly a negative gut feeling of inner tension. In this case you should be totally honest with yourself and decide whether the goal really is that essential after all.

Sound Bite Slides

Human perception can be divided into three main types: auditory, visual and kinetic. Some people can better operate with visual images, others are more sensitive to sensation and the third group is particularly receptive to sound. Until now we have talked about creating slides with a preference for visual and sensory objects.

Some spiritual development practices use positive affirmation which involves a person repeating their goal as a positive statement many times over in their mind, for example, "I have perfect health, a powerful energy field and inner peace. I am calm and confident". Multiple repetitions of phrases like this spoken aloud or silently are most suited to people with auditory perception. However, there is no such thing as an absolute type so anyone can use the positive affirmation technique successfully.

Affirmations work in the same way as slides but when you use a positive affirmation, you have to take into account the difference between the language of the heart and the language of the mind. Firstly, the heart does not understand words and so mindless repetition will have no effect on it. The heart only understands feeling and thought which go beyond words. Words can be used to simulate thoughts and feelings to a certain degree but they are not as efficient because speech is a secondary medium. It is more effective to feel something once than to repeat it a thousand times in words. *Strive to experience the feeling and repeat the affirmation simultaneously.*

Secondly, *each affirmation should have a narrow focus.* There is no point in grouping several goals together in the same affirmation. For example, the affirmation cited above would seem to have great content because it includes everything you might need in life, but you will not be able to evoke the whole set of associated sensations when you are repeating the affirmation.

Thirdly, *avoid humdrum monotony and uniformity.* Every new series of repetitions should be accompanied by fresh elements of feeling and experience. For example, if you consistently repeat to yourself: "I am calm and confident" these words will very soon lose their meaning. Desire has to be nurtured and persuaded. Intention on the other hand acts instantly with confidence appearing in the moment of your intention to be confident. Therefore, if you want to be confident be confident with intent.

Finally, *there is no point in creating an affirmation that fights against an effect*, without first eliminating the cause. For example, there is no point in repeating: "I have nothing to fear and nothing to be worried about" if the cause for concern is still present in your life. Moreover, the affirmation should be designed to have a positive note. Instead of endlessly repeating what you would like to avoid, program yourself to the result you wish to achieve. For example, the negative affirmation: "I am not afraid or concerned" would be more effectively replaced with a positive affirmation such as: "Everything is working out well for me". Be specific about what would have to be going well for you to have no cause for concern as a result.

Note also that you should say "everything is working out fine" and not "everything will work out fine". If you write the affirmation using the future tense, the future will never become the present being simply transformed into an oasis somewhere just ahead of you. You have to set the parameters of your energy *as if you already have the thing you are ordering.*

Neither is there any point in ordering inner peace. Inner peace results from a harmonious connection between heart and mind on a specific issue. Harmony cannot be achieved as a general principle, by abstract autosuggestion. The heart can however, be taught and soothed with the help of a slide.

Affirmations work most effectively when you are in a *zero emotion state* i.e. when there is no excess potential. The subconscious cannot be persuaded, instructed or ordered to do anything. As soon as you switch on any emotion you destroy the balance. If you try to beat a thought into your brain, your heart will simply stick its fingers in its ears and ignore you. An affirmation is most effective when it is repeated dispassionately in a relaxed state. Then perhaps, your mind will get through to your subconscious. If the mind has to desperately try and convince the heart of something it means that the mind does not really believe it either and no amount of repetition will dispel its doubts.

Nothing can be achieved by the mind pressuring the heart. Neither can you generate will to have with intent when you are riding an emotional high. The things that belong to you seem mundane and you take them for granted. You handle things that are yours calmly without insistence, in the same manner that you take letters out of your post box. If you mistake assertiveness for will and the intent to have you will end up spinning circles on the spot and taking a pendulum by the hand. Before you have time to blink the pendulum will let go of your hand and send you sliding headlong into the pit of your former indecision. When your *will to have with intent* is free of your *desire to have* the pendulum will have nothing to hook into.

As you can see, an affirmation represents a kind of *sound slide.* You can use affirmations and film slides and of course, they are additionally effective when integrated into the same practice. Here is an example of an integrated slide. It contains a picture of your new home. You are sitting beside an open fire, in a creaking rocking chair with the logs in the fire happily spitting and crackling away. It is so nice to sit and watch the fire! You can hear the sound of the rain outside where a cold wind blows but you are warm and cosy beside the fire. You have your favourite treat on a small table beside you and there is an interesting film on television. You see, hear and sense the whole scene and say to yourself: "I feel comfortable". You are not simply watching the slide; you are living it.

A Window onto the Alternatives Space

People always have controlled and uncontrolled thoughts running through their mind. Some people refer to this as the inner dialogue but in essence it is not a dialogue but a *monologue* because the mind really has no-one else to chat to aside from itself. The heart is not capable of thinking and talking; it only feels and knows. The inner dialogue is loud in comparison to the silent sensations of the heart and so intuition manifests itself very rarely and is barely noticeable. Some people believe that if you can quiet the inner monologue, the mind will give you access to intuitive information. This is true, but it is not possible to switch the monologue off totally when you are in a conscious state. Imagine that you have concentrated on being still and have managed to relax the flow of thoughts and words. You may have no apparent thoughts, experiencing the emptiness within, but this does not mean that the monologue has been silenced. The mind is not asleep; quite the opposite in fact. It is very alert because its task has changed. It must not think or chatter. It is as if the mind is saying: "Ok. I'll be quiet. We'll see how you get along without me." That the monologue appears to have been silenced is an illusion. The inner monologue can only be truly quieted when the mind relinquishes its control or at least relaxes its vigilance. When the monologue only appears to have been stopped the mind is still on the look-out and you could say drowns out the feelings of the heart even more with its very deafening 'silence'.

When the mind really surrenders its control your perception falls through into the alternatives space. The inner monologue is only truly muted when you are sleeping or experiencing deep meditation. This only has any practical benefit if a person practices lucid dreaming or deep meditation in which a state of consciousness is maintained.

Lucid dreaming can be used as an experimental way of training the skill of outer intention, but what about in waking? Can you silence your inner dialogue when you are in a conscious state? Fortunately, there is a loophole. In moments when the mind gives some slack on its control a narrow window spontaneously opens and through it the intuitive feelings of the heart erupt into consciousness.

Intuition is felt as a vague presage, also called the inner voice. In moments when the mind is distracted it is easy to intuit the feelings and knowledge of the heart, to hear the rustle of the morning stars, the voice without words, meditation without thought, and sound without volume. In these moments you begin to get a sense of something but it still has an elusive quality to it. Do not think; feel intuitively. Everyone has experienced the thing we call intuition at some time or another in their life. For example, you get the feeling that someone is about to arrive; you sense that something is about to happen; you have an unconscious urge to do something or you realize that there is something *you just know*.

In the game of thinking the referee is the mind's analytical apparatus. The mind quickly sorts any data it receives onto shelves reserved for different signs to make everything logical and rational. Silencing the inner monologue is like confiscating the referee's whistle and making him sit out the game on the reserve's bench. The mind continues to observe but is incapable of controlling the game.

The mind occasionally takes short breaks from juggling data as if for a brief moment sitting down on the bench for a rest. During these breaks the window opens to intuitive information. In these moments you fall asleep. This may be news to you, but this really is how it all works. Everyone falls asleep during the day several times it is just that they are not aware of doing it because the window is open for a very brief instant.

The dozing mind wakes up and continues with its monologue. Sometimes an impression of what was glimpsed through the window reaches the conscious mind in the form of intuitive information, but more often than not, the mind pays no attention to these brief visions because it is so engrossed in its own thoughts.

In sleep the soul can travel anywhere and flies about purposelessly but when the window opens during waking the heart specifically sees the sector of the alternatives space that backgrounds the mind's current thoughts.

The soul's gaze is directed towards the corresponding sector of the alternatives space, where it sees knowledge related to the mind's current thought content. As soon as the window opens, this knowledge breaks through to consciousness. If on waking the mind pays attention to the impressions of the soul, i.e. remembers the short burst that took place during sleep it will receive what is called intuitive knowledge, information that comes as if from nowhere, as if 'pulled out of a hat'.

An intuitive revelation is sometimes claimed to be a spontaneous flash of mental insight, or a solution that suddenly falls into the mind as if 'out of a hat', as well as a solution the mind comes to of its own accord. So where exactly does this knowledge out of nowhere come from? In the conventional worldview people usually close their eyes to this strange type of occurrence and make allowances for it accepting it as a quirky feature of the mind.

Based on the Transurfing model we can see that inspiration works quite differently to the explanations people usually come up with. The mind finds a solution to a problem via logical inference. Revelation i.e. the missing link that cannot be obtained from the existing chain of logic comes from the alternatives space through medium of the heart.

The subtle feelings of the heart are manifest as anxiety and depression or excitement and high emotion. All these feelings can be covered by one term – vexation. It is as if the heart is striving to communicate something to the mind but cannot quite explain what it wants to say. Lingering anxiety, guilt, the burden of responsibility and depression can become transformed into physical reality in the shape of our worst expectations. In all these feelings there is unity of heart and mind. Our worst expectations become a reality due to outer intention.

We know that misfortune never comes alone. With these energy parameters we shift onto the worst life lines where misfortune has no chance of getting lonely. Sometimes an induced shift shoves us into a run of bad luck that takes us a long time to free ourselves from. You will notice that when you experience this state of lingering anxiety your worst expectations are immediately realized. Outer intention moves you onto unsuccessful life lines where the situation escalates before your very eyes.

The heart actually helps to materialize the misfortune it has foreseen because it is united with the mind over its worst expectations. You can turn outer intention to your advantage by establishing unity of heart and mind on the question of your best expectation.

Transurfing recommends abandoning importance and negativity and consciously directing your thought energy towards the achievement of your goal. As you are already aware, the conscious use of slides can help attune your thought energy and the same technique can be applied when the window opens as long as you can catch the moment.

Intuitive knowledge and premonitions come to us spontaneously. When this happens the mind uses the heart's capacity for premonition in standby mode. It simply receives information from the sector the soul has randomly wandered into. So, our task is to learn *to generate intuitive premonitions intentionally* in order to set the heart's sail in the right direction.

How is this done? Rather than simply being intuition the premonition must be intentionally induced. You have to seize the moment when the mind is distracted and quickly place a slide in the window. The image must contain the feelings you experience from living inside the slide. When you place a slide in the open window information is deliberately dispatched into the target sector of the alternatives space as opposed to being received randomly from the heart. If you manage to insert the slide in the open window your mind will have touched on outer intention.

You might think that you can create the same effect by running a slide lying in bed before you fall asleep. You would think that the slide would gradually slip into a dream and the heart and mind would be united; yet as strange as it may seem, this approach does not work. I will explain why in the next section. Before I do though, see if you can answer the question: *why is there no point in trying to run a slide in your sleep?*

The Frame

A transitional zone exists between the moment in which we have an intuitive premonition of an event and the actual event as it is shaped by outer intention. In other words, when you intuitively sense that a certain event is going to happen, your thoughts brush across it without thinking. Then, ordinarily, the event is later materialized, particularly if the mind agrees with the heart's premonition. It makes you wonder whether you simply had a premonition that the event was going to happen, or whether your subconscious thoughts actually induced the event working in a similar way to outer intention.

There is no unequivocal answer as to which serves as the original cause. Both explanations have their place. In dreams everything is much clearer. You barely have to think or rather sense that an event will develop in a particular way and the scenario is realized instantly. During sleep outer intention works flawlessly. So where does that leave us?

It leaves us with just that. We see the realization of a foreseen scenario in a dream but *dreaming has no impact on material reality*. Virtual reality remains just that – virtual, so why does not outer intention materialize a virtual sector as a result of our dreaming?

You might think that is it because of the inert quality of material realization. Dreaming in comparison to physical reality is as a paper boat to a large frigate. The paper boat flies off at the slightest whiff of outer intention, whereas only a large sail and extended period of time will shift a heavy frigate along.

Yet inertness is not the reason why outer intention does not transform virtual sectors into physical reality as a result of our dreams. You can run your slide as much as you like, even in lucid dreaming, but it will not bring you a single step closer to your goal. The thing is, that in dreaming outer intention only has one function, which is to carry the soul from one virtual sector to another. This is how it works in dreaming: the mind sets the rudder of the heart's sail in line with its expectations, outer intention instantly shifts the paper boat to the corresponding sector, and with that it is done; the mission of outer intention is complete.

In physical reality the work of outer intention can never be completed with one small puff. The wind of intention blows but the frigate is unmoved. If there is unity of heart and mind the sail will adopt the necessary position. The size of the sail depends on the power of unity that exists. The wind cannot instantly shift the frigate to the necessary sector. The qualities of a person's thought energy may already correspond to the target sector but material realization lags behind in the previous sector. In order for the target sector to be realized, the wind of intention has to work for much longer.

The outer intention that works in dreaming has no chance of shifting a frigate for the simple reason that the frigate's sail has been taken down leaving just the small rudder of a paper boat to do its work. *The wind of intention can propel the paper boat of dreaming but its capacity for material realization is powerless to work on a frigate.*

This is why running a slide in your sleep will not help the process of material realization. The heart's sail is sufficient to power flight around virtual space but is totally different to the kind of movement that occurs in material realization. In lucid dreaming the slide's only function is to widen your comfort zone, and this is enough. If you practice lucid dreaming the slide can be an excellent way of widening the limits of your comfort zone in your sleep.

In waking both your conscious and subconscious mind are firmly anchored in the material world. The mind keeps the heart clearly focused on the sector of material realization. As we showed earlier, the mind is constantly correcting its perception to fit in with the established template. By running the slide in waking you attune your thought energy to an unrealized sector of the information field. Depending on the strength of connection between heart and mind the sail fills up with the wind of outer intention and the frigate begins to move slowly but surely towards the target sector. Outer intention will continue to do its work until such time as material realisation reaches its destination.

Can you see the difference? In dreaming the work of outer intention culminates quickly whereas in waking it continues over time. In dreaming, the parameters of thought energy and the targeted sector correspond instantly and with that the job is done; whereas in waking the process is slow and gradual. *When you run the slide in waking, the frigate's sail of material realization is set and outer intention works on moving the powerful frigate rather than the little boat of the dreaming realm.*

You must not be put off by my bold use of such simple metaphors to describe these complex processes. They help to convey the essence of things more clearly and in any case, there are no other analogies in the mind's list of symbols that would be more apt.

When the mind has momentarily switched off and the window opens onto the alternatives space the focus of one's perception remains within the *context* of the current sector that has been realized materially. Unlike in ordinary dreaming, through the window the frigate's sail is still up. If in this instant you place a slide through the window, a gust of the wind of intention will propel material realisation a considerable distance. The window is so effective because in this moment the connection between heart and mind is at its strongest. The dozing mind relaxes its control and allows something unreal into its perception template just as it does in dreaming. As a result, the sail takes on significant proportions and outer intention acts with greater force.

This technique is more complex than the others we have introduced, but that is not to stop you from giving it a go. Start by paying consistent attention to your intuition and observing the self. Then you will realize that during the course of the day the window opens quite often. From time to time the mind gets tired of control and chatter and loses its concentration for a few moments. This is the time to deliberately insert the feelings associated with the event you want to induce. It has to be the feelings specifically, rather than an expression of those feelings in words.

Imagine how you would feel if the imagined event had already been streamed into physical reality. Run the slide over in your mind picturing the fulfilment of the goal and then take one integral exposure or *frame* from it. For example, you sign a contract and feel contented, or you pass an exam and the teacher shakes your hand, or you win the race you push your chest through the tape at the finish line. This exposure is the formula you need to insert into the open window. You can give the frame a one word title such as: "Victory!", "Yes!", "I did it!" or anything else you prefer. The title just serves as a reference point for the frame.

It is difficult to catch the moment when the window opens because your mind is involved, even though it is dozing, which means that as you set about inserting the frame the mind will wake up and the window will be instantly slammed shut. With time you will get the knack for it. The important thing is to be patient and keep your intention strong. First your mind has to develop a frame for the feeling associated with the material realization of your goal event. The mind should actively participate in the development of the slide. Then, without yet trying to catch the open window, turn the slide over in your mind to get a clear sense of the final feeling associated with the event. Create a hook for this integral feeling. Then you will be ready to deftly insert the frame the moment the window opens.

Ideally, the dozing mind becomes aware of its sleeping condition and immediately throws the frame through the window before it has time to come to fully. This is how outer intention works when the mind has silenced its inner monologue.

Repeated attempts, even if they are at first unsuccessful, gradually become habit making it easier for your mind to instinctively throw the frame through the window. The point of having the frame is that the mind can activate it rapidly and automatically before fully waking up.

If you find the frame technique very difficult to work with, do not worry. Leave it for the time being. The frame technique is described here more for the sake of information than anything else. If it does not work for you straight away maybe the technique is not for you. Focus on the standard slides and practice the visualisation process instead.

In any case, it is very useful to acquire the habit of being attentive to the window. If you can learn to catch the open window moment you will begin to have intuitive insights more often.

SUMMARY

The mind has will but is incapable of feeling outer intention.

The heart can feel outer intention but is not capable of will.

When heart and mind are united they harness the will of outer intention.

Your heart is just as good as the heart of others. You deserve the absolute best.

You have everything you need. All you have to do is use it.

Stars are born independently but pendulums light them up.

Pendulums hide the fact that every individual has unique abilities.

The rule 'Do as I do", creates the pendulums' widely accepted stereotypes.

Every soul has its own individual 'star' sector.

If the mind allows it to, the heart will find its sector.

Allow yourself the boldness to sneeze at stereotypes.

Allow yourself the boldness to believe in the unlimited capabilities of your soul.

Allow yourself the boldness to exercise the right to your own amazing individuality.

Keep the joy and give the pride to your Angel.

Human thought and behaviour is conditioned by dependency on pendulums.

Keep importance to a minimum and act with conscious awareness.

Do not attribute anything excessively meaning.

You do not need importance; pendulums do.

It is not effort and steadfastness but conscious intention that keeps importance at zero.

Fraile characterises the individual essence of the human soul.

In chasing after other peoples' standards the mind becomes all the more divorced from the heart.

You will acquire many hidden virtues by attuning your mind to the soul's Fraile.

In a state of unity the heart sings and the mind rubs its hands in satisfaction.

Focusing on the means the mind places a fatal cross on the elusive goal.

Allowing yourself to have is the most important condition to fulfilling your desires.

Despite all its attractiveness, if something weighs on you the goal may be false.

Never believe anyone who expects you to change yourself.

Inner discomfort manifests as heavy anxiety, a feeling of being burdened and oppression.

A feeling of inner comfort does not signal an unequivocal 'yes'.

A feeling of inner discomfort signals an unequivocal 'no'.

When considering your goal, do not think about how prestigious or realistic it is; do not think about the means to achieving it.

Give your attention to how comfortable thinking about it makes you feel.

Any affirmation should be accompanied by corresponding feelings.

Every affirmation should be positive and have a narrow focus.

Focus the affirmation on the cause, not the effect.

Formulate the affirmation in the present tense.

When the will to have is free of the desire to have the pendulum has nothing to hook into.

You calmly take what is yours without insistence, just like you take the post from your letter box.

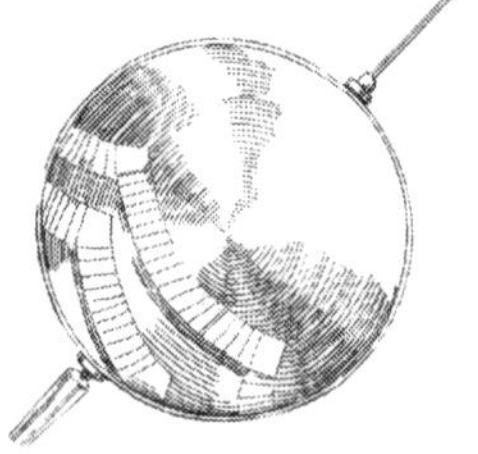

Chapter X. GOALS AND DOORS

By breaking through stereotypes,
You open doors.

How to Choose Your Own Things

In this chapter we will talk about how to discern the true strivings of the soul from the false goals pendulums are everywhere trying to impose upon us. The problem is that a false goal, however attractive it may seem, ultimately will not bring you anything but disappointment. When you chase after a false goal you either achieve nothing, your efforts simply providing feed for pendulums, or you achieve the goal but discover it was not really what you wanted after all. Is it really worth missing the unique opportunity of this life spending valuable time correcting your mistakes? Despite the fact that a lifespan seems a long time it passes quickly and unnoticeably and so it is essential that you learn to find the things that bring you personal happiness.

I do not want to start this chapter with theory as the listener is no doubt tired of complex theoretical explanations. I have tried as much as possible to keep the expression of ideas from being too heavy but fear I may not have always succeeded in doing so. This is perhaps unavoidable, as the questions we have touched on are a little offbeat and the conclusions drawn no less unusual. Your mind would never have taken the ideas of Transurfing seriously if I had not given at least some kind of theoretical basis for them. However, the worst is behind us and I will begin this chapter with questions of a more practical nature.

The clearest and simplest mark of your ability to determine your own goals is evident in the way you choose your clothes. Searching for new clothes can also be a good exercise in helping you to choose your own goals effectively. If you think back, there have probably been occasions when you have purchased something you thought was suitable, only later to discover that you do not like it any more, it no longer suits you, or it has some kind of defect. There may also have been occasions when you saw something you liked and bought it straight away without hesitation and are happy with it still. The difference between these items is that in the second scenario they are meant for you and in the first scenario they are meant for someone else.

The first type that attracted you is meant for someone else. It may be something you saw on a manikin or something a friend was wearing. Just because something looks good on someone else does not mean it will necessarily look good on you. It may have nothing to do with a shortcoming in your figure or other virtues. It is terrible being a manikin that everything looks great on. It is individuality successfully emphasized that makes an impression, not a copy of the widely accepted notion of beauty.

I know I am not the first person to have said this, but nonetheless, people spend a lot of time out shopping not knowing what to buy. Knowledge of style, a feeling for fashion and even good taste does not help. Even if you have bought something having searched for it for a long time you may still not be totally satisfied with your purchase. If you always want to be able to always to find exactly the thing you are looking for you have to learn to distinguish between things that are yours and things that are meant for someone else. So, how is this done? You will not believe how simple it is!

Firstly, never torture yourself with the problem of choosing because this destroys the balance. The more stressed you become over it, the worse the result. There is no point spending a long time looking at things analyzing their strong points and weaknesses. The mind should not be involved in the choice because in this case the mind is not you; it is the build up of plaque from pendulums. Just walk around the shops and observe, as if you were at an exhibition. Do not think.

First, make sure you have a general picture of what you would like to buy. There is no need to focus on the details necessarily. It is enough to describe the type of item you want. For example, if you need a coat set yourself the goal of choosing a coat without insisting any other superfluous conditions. Let your heart choose because the heart is much closer to knowing who you really are. Your heart will not miss the tiniest detail and will point to the right item at the right time. You will know immediately when you have found the right thing lying among numerous other items because you will see it and feel instantly drawn to it.

I emphasize once again that you should not analyze why you are attracted to any particular item. You just like it and that is all. You can say about it: "This is exactly what I was looking for" and then you should buy it without any further thought.

Even if you have been looking for something for a long time without finding it, have no doubt that exactly the right item for you is lying in a shop somewhere. If you do not find it in the third place you look, you will find it in the tenth. It is waiting there for you patiently and so you should show some patience too. Do not rush about stressing yourself with doubts or getting cross with yourself. Just so that you can be completely confident I will tell you a little secret about the difference between your things and the things meant for others. It is as simple as it is reliable.

As I have already said, there is no point in weighing up the strengths and weaknesses of the things you are choosing. There comes a moment when you have to say "yes" or "no" to the shop assistant. In this moment you are sleeping soundly even if it does not seem that way to you. If the shop assistant or your friend makes a comment about the things you are choosing between the sleep will be particularly deep.

When you are busy making a decision only your mind is working. It is analyzing the fors and the against and building a conceptual justification that is both sound and rational at the same time as listening to the opinion of someone else present. The mind is so immersed in the process that it pays no attention at all to feelings of the heart. In this sense the mind is deeply asleep; and so be it.

Do not disturb the mind until it has made a final decision. Wait for the decision and immediately afterwards stop listening to anyone else, *wake up and tune into the feelings you experienced at the moment you made the decision.* How comfortable you felt in this moment will reveal your heart's attitude to the mind's decision.

As you know inner peace does not signify an unequivocal answer. The heart cannot always know what it wants and is also capable of being indecisive. If you love something the moment you set eyes on it and you feel delighted straight away then the soul is saying "yes". Then the mind switches on and begins to analyze and justify its decision. If at the end of the analysis the mind also says "yes" it means the thing is yours. If however, you decide to buy something not because you fell in love with it at first sight but because it is practical then you should pay particular attention to the slightest hint of inner tension. *The soul always knows exactly what it does not want.*

If you find yourself hesitating, or something about the item is inconvenient or causes you slight concern, if you feel that a slight shadow of doubt or heaviness has been cast you can be sure that the item is meant for someone else. The mind will try to persuade you otherwise and eloquently list the items positive points. If you catch yourself *persuading* or trying to convince yourself that something is right for you because of the style or size you should immediately put the thing to one side without an ounce of regret because it is not yours.

An unequivocal criterion for personal choice can be expressed in one simple phrase: *if you have to persuade yourself to have something, it is not yours*. Remember, *if a thing is meant for you, you will not have to convince yourself of anything.*

Finally, is it worth listening to other peoples' opinions when you are choosing something? I do not think so. No-one but you can choose the things that are yours. If you like a thing so much you just have to have it, you can be absolutely sure that other people will be very impressed when they see it on you.

As far as pricing goes all I can say is that your things do not necessarily have to be found in expensive shops. However, if it really comes to it Transurfing can eliminate the problem of money from your life. If you define the goal that is meant for you and strive towards it, rather than striving for money the resources will come to you of their own accord, in great abundance.

The next step is to abandon the desire to achieve your goal. You are calmly aware that your thing is waiting for you somewhere and you know exactly how to distinguish it from things that are meant for another. This assures that importance is kept at a minimum level. Immediately after having made your decision you wake up and allow in the awareness of what the decision felt like. This means that you are acting consciously and determining the game script. Having made a final decision you rely on how comfortable it makes you feel inwardly. You will not be mistaken because fortunately there is reliable support available in this shaky world – unity of heart and mind. Finally, you will make the task much easier if you forget about strict planning. Rather than tying yourself to circumstances or stubbornly insisting on your own ways of doing things trust the alternatives flow. Life can be an easy holiday if you allow it to be. Take what is meant for you calmly and without insistence.

As you can see the process of choosing things encompasses all the main principles of Transurfing. You wander around the shops as if you were at an exhibition. You simply observe without necessarily setting yourself the concrete task of buying something.

Now you have a simple but powerful tool at your disposal. Now you can go shopping with ease and even if you do not buy anything this time you will know that you have protected yourself from the things that are meant for others. You will be calm and confident in yourself because you know that the thing you need is somewhere waiting for you and you are sure to find it. The main thing is to remember that before you finally answer "yes" or "no", you have to wake up and listen consciously to your feelings.

This technique will not work if you are choosing clothes for someone else, for a child perhaps. At least it will not work with the same level of accuracy. Your soul cannot choose something meant for another so you have to rely on being guided by practical concerns. At the same time, you can give the child the chance to choose for itself. Unlike adults, children are very good at finding the things that are theirs.

Of course, this technique does not only apply to clothes but to any other case where you have to choose something for yourself. I would very much like to hope that the book you are listening is 'yours'.

How to Become a Trendsetter

Do you ever want to become a trendsetter? Previously, you had to watch how others dressed and try to keep up with the fashion, but did you ever ask yourself who created fashion? Fashions already exist before they reach the salons of the leading couturiers. New trends are created by people who are relatively free from pendulums. They are ruled by their own independent judgements and preferences. They dress by listening to their heart and hit the mark. Then their idea is noticed, picked up on by others and begins to spread spontaneously. This is how they begin to dictate fashion.

If you blindly follow the latest fashions you can totally cripple your outward appearance. If you observe other people you will notice that certain individuals dress extremely elegantly but not in the latest fashions. You can see immediately that these individuals have a certain edge and it would not occur to anyone to accuse them of being unfashionable. Quite the opposite in fact; everywhere you see people dressed strictly to fashion but you cannot help feeling sorry for them because it just does not suit them. They are imitators blindly travelling the road of inner intention towards another's goal buying into a fashion created by pendulums. Rather than understanding their own preferences and what really suits them they follow the pendulum's rule: "do as I do". A French saying comes to mind that goes: "Do not be afraid of looking unfashionable; be afraid of looking silly".

Style is just the outer , superficial side of fashion. The essence of fashion is conveyed when a person finds clothes that fit the style context and compliment their individuality. You have to be sure of what you really want; to look fashionable or to look elegant, because these are not the same thing. What do you think is better? You can dress in some weird retro style way off the spirit of the era, but if the style is yours everyone will be green with envy!

You have probably already realised that following the fashion is nothing other than participation in the pendulum fashion game. The fads of fashion come as quickly as they go. They are one of the most perennial pendulums. There is nothing wrong with succumbing to its influence. The important thing is to be aware you are doing it and gain the benefit of the fashion for yourself rather than simply paying tribute to it.

You can create your own fashion pendulum. It is very simple to do. You just have to turn away from the pendulums and towards yourself. Set yourself the goal of looking elegant and interesting. You do not have to make anything too specific. Just walk around the shops and look at what is on display using the method described above. Forget about the current fashion. Pay attention only to what you are feeling when you look at things. Turn off the analysis apparatus; stop thinking, comparing and expostulating. The moment you catch yourself trying to reason and speculate, stop the process immediately because it is futile. Instead, listen to the rustle of the morning stars.

You might not be very successful at it when you first start so it is better not to set a time limit on things. Let go off the desire to achieve your goal. If it does not work, well, you have not lost anything. Take off the pressure of having to achieve your goal. Reduce importance and relax control. Just window shop; try things on out of curiosity. Trust the alternatives flow.

It can be useful to run the slide of your goal in your mind whilst you are shopping. The slide must include the quality of how you feel when you attract a lot of attention because you are looking so elegant, interesting and different rather than being a detailed picture of what exactly you look like when that is happening.

Give up on the desire to find something artsy and extraordinary. The extraordinaire does not necessarily guarantee success. Believe me you will stumble upon all sorts of unexpected discoveries. After a while you are sure to discover unusual and original ways of putting things together. As soon as the heart and mind are united you will experience an incomparable feeling; a combination of surprise and delight. You will recognise it straight away and rather than saying to yourself: “That is what I was looking for” you will want to cry out something more like: “No way! That’s amazing.” That is how it works. Your potential is only limited by your own intention.

The secret to success lies in freeing yourself from pendulums and going your own way. So what do pendulums do when they see a new star rising on the horizon? As you know from previous chapters, they light it up. They have no other option than to make you a star, i.e. their favourite. Because pendulums need to be in control of everything they will even help you. If you are lucky, you will become the favourite of your own pendulum creation.

All that has just been said relates to more than clothes of course. You can apply the same principles to everything you do. It is such a luxurious privilege to be yourself! It is the one privilege everyone can afford but only a few muster up the courage to enjoy. The only reason for this is that people are dependent on pendulums who need obedient puppets not free-minded individuals. You just have to understand the principle, free yourself from their needless influence and be yourself.

In other words, the mind has to include one simple truth into its list of references: *everyone owns a precious treasure – the uniqueness of their soul.* Every individual carries the key to success in their pocket and yet leaves off using it. Have your mind take the heart by the hand, take it to the shops and let it choose its own toy.

Unity of heart and mind is such a rarity that you can literally sell at a huge profit. All great achievements of art and culture are an expression of this unity. Stars become stars only because people are interested in what is missing from their own lives – unity of heart and mind.

Other People's Goals

Until now we have looked at the outside world as an alternatives space with sectors linked together in life lines. If the parameters of a person's thought energy correspond to the energy of a given sector that sector is then transformed into physical reality through the process of material realization. On an energetic level the individual also represents a unique essence imbued with its own inimitable spectrum of emission. There is a life line in the alternatives space that matches every individual's fraile perfectly.

When a person lives out this life line they encounter minimal obstacles and circumstances always work in their favour. The soul's fraile successfully fits into its own true life line and easily reaches its goal in the same way that your own key easily turns in the lock and opens the door. We do not necessarily need to know why and how this happens. What is significant is the fact that each individual has their own path. When a person walks towards the right goal along the path meant for them everything turns out favourably.

When the opposite happens and a person turns off the path they were travelling they meet with all kind of adversity and life becomes a continual battle for survival. This is a tragedy for the soul. You get upset if the weather is foul at the weekend so just imagine how the soul feels when it sees the unique chance given to it in this lifetime being wasted.

The soul can see how the mind, infatuated with pendulums, ruins its life, but it is powerless to change things. When the soul comes into this world it does not know exactly what to do, what it wants and what to strive for. If the soul does not know exactly, it can at least guess, but the mind will not listen. Then the pendulums put the mind into circulation imposing on it their own goals and game rules. They force people to choose goals that are not their own and to crowd around other people's doorways. The soul's feeble attempts to influence the mind come to nothing, so powerful is the pendulum's influence.

For many of us the idea that success only comes from gruelling hard work is instilled in us from childhood. Equally engrained is the idea that you have to stubbornly strive towards your goal overcoming all obstacles along the way if you want to succeed. One of our greatest delusions is that we have to fight for happiness, be stubborn, persevering, overcoming countless obstacles, and basically, fighting for a place in the sun. This is a particularly misleading and undermining formula.

Let us look more closely at how this received idea was formed. Normally a person turns off their path when they succumb to the influence of a pendulum. Naturally, numerous obstacles start piling up in front of them. If a person wants to be happy they have to overcome the obstacles, do not they? Can you guess where the delusion is? Perhaps the delusion lies in the fact that the person effectively begins working towards someone else's goal passing through someone else's door. But no, this is not it. Again the answer is surprising, like everything else in this book.

The fundamental misconception lies in the erroneous conviction that if a person overcomes the obstacles in front of them, happiness will be waiting for them on the other side. This is the illusion. There is no happiness on the other side! However hard a person tries they will always find themselves chasing after the setting sun. *No happiness awaits a person in the near or the distant future when they are living a life line that is not their true path.*

Many people just feel depleted when not without great difficulty, they finally reach their goal. What happened to happiness? Well, it was never there in the first place. It was just a *mirage* of illusory happiness created by pendulums to make people give up their energy. I say again: *happiness is not out there, somewhere just ahead of you. It is either in your current life line right here right now or it is not there at all.*

What does happiness look like in the Transurfing model? Maybe it is something you achieve when you have attained your true goal? You guessed wrong again. *Happiness is what you experience on the journey towards your own goal on the path through your own door.* When a person is on a life line meant for them and following their own true path, they experience happiness in the present moment even if attainment of the actual goal still lies ahead. Life becomes transformed into an ongoing celebration. When the goal is achieved they will be doubly happy but in the meantime the process of striving makes every day a holiday. *Movement towards someone else's goal always places happiness in an illusory future. Achieving a goal that is not truly yours will bring disappointment and depletion but never happiness.*

Your goal is the thing that makes you feel deeply fulfilled. It is not something that fulfils you temporarily. It is the thing that gives you *a sense of the real joy of life.* Your personal door represents your journeying along the path towards your goal experienced with passion and inspiration. It is not necessarily that everything comes easily but when you are using your own door *you do not feel depleted. On the contrary, you feel energized.*

When you work towards your own goal through your own door obstacles are easily overcome and work does not feel like a burden. If you are making maximum effort to achieve your goal, but left feeling uninspired and fatigued either the goal is not meant for you, or you are banging on the wrong door. These are the features of goals that are not your own:

A foreign goal always feels like an obligation. It is punishing and forced. If you feel that your goal represents an enforced obligation in the slightest way you should dump it boldly. If the goal is yours you should not have to persuade yourself to work on it because you will be enjoying it so much. When you work towards a foreign goal there will always be numerous obstacles to overcome along the way and it will always be a struggle. The pendulum requires everyone to work like a cog in the greater machine and so when you are working for a foreign goal, you will continue working even though it is a slog, because you have been programmed to believe that everything will come to you eventually if you can just work hard enough. If you are strong and cool you will master yourself, clear everything from your path, survive hell and high water, and finally win your place in the sun. If you are weak – shut up and know your place.

A foreign goal is presented as being fashionable and prestigious. Pendulums need to lure you away from your perfect life line and so they do their best to offer a really delicious looking carrot to trigger the adherent's mind into rushing headlong after it. Pendulums cannot always force you to follow the rule "do as I do". You have to want to observe the rule and so myths are created that tell the story of the star's successful career. The pendulums demonstrate the pattern of their success and leave you with a choice of either repeating someone else's experience or ending up with nothing, for how could you possibly know how to achieve success? The pendulums clearly know exactly what a person must do to become successful and the results are there to prove it. As we have already demonstrated, stars achieve success precisely because they do not follow the rule "do as I do". They go their own way. *Only your soul can know the algorithm of your own individual success.*

A foreign goal attracts you by nature of seeming unachievable. The human psyche is such that we are attracted by everything kept under lock and key. It is human nature to long to possess things that are unavailable. This feature of the human psyche originates in childhood when we have many desires but very little is accessible to us. When a child is refused a toy it will often play up until it gets it and yet when it finally receives the toy it so longed for it suddenly loses all interest. Adults have their own toys and get themselves just as wound up over then as children do. For example, a grown up child with a terrible voice and no ear for music thinks they love to sing. In reality the little 'nightingale' just does not want to accept the fact that singing is not for them. "Everyone else can sing. Why should they be any better than me?" So, when considering your goals drop the importance of the goal and ask yourself: Do I really want this with all my heart and soul or do I just enjoy wanting it? *If achieving the goal would mean that you could prove something either to yourself or to others then the goal is also misguided.* Your goal does not hang around your neck like a lead weight. It gives you genuine pleasure.

A foreign goal is imposed by others. No-one but you can define your goal. You can calmly hear out the teachings of 'those who know better' on how you should *act* but afterwards you must draw your own conclusions and act as you see fit. No-one should presume to teach you what you should be *striving* towards and such a rude intrusion into your soul should be quickly nipped in the bud. Your heart has enough to put up with listening to the foolish ideas of the mind. No-one can point to your goal; the only exception perhaps being via the casual passing phrase. As you remember, phrases mentioned in passing can serve as signs. When a passing phrase is a sign you will sense it instantly. An unintentional phrase can unexpectedly ignite a flame in your soul. If the phrase touches on your goal the heart will become enlivened prompting you to the awareness that this is 'what you need'. It has to be an incidental remark or recommendation spoken with no agenda and absolutely no intention of setting you on the right path.

A foreign goal always serves to better someone else's wellbeing. If a goal does nothing to improve the quality of your life then it certainly is not meant for you. True goals always work for you, for your wellbeing and success. You are the only person that has need of your individual goal. If a goal serves *directly* to fulfil other people's needs and improve other people's prosperity then it is a foreign goal. Pendulums will use any pretext and any means to try and force you to serve others. Words like "must", "obligated" and "have to" usually have the necessary effect on people with a heightened sense of guilt. People like this often find solace in absolving their imaginary sins. For others the slogan "your help is needed" is more effective and it works. As you now understand these methods rely on outer and internal importance. You have to remember that first and foremost you live for yourself. You do not owe anyone anything and you are not beholden to anyone. You cannot make other people happy but you can easily injure others with your own unhappiness.

A foreign goal evokes inner tension. Foreign goals are usually very attractive. The mind will paint a lavish picture of the goal's virtues in all its various hues. But despite its lure if something about the goal does not sit right with you then you have to be honest with yourself. Obviously, the mind will not want to listen because it is sure that everything is fine. So where does the shadow of apprehension come from? This is a good time to repeat an important rule from the previous chapter. *When considering your goal do not think about how prestigious or seemingly unattainable it is, or the means to achieve it. Focus your attention on inviting your inner voice to speak. How comfortable does thinking about the goal make you feel inwardly?* Imagine that you have already achieved your goal and all this is behind you. Does it make you feel good or not? If the pleasurable feeling is mixed with anxiety, or the heavy feeling of burden, this is inner tension. Is it really worth committing to someone else's goal? Your own goal will be even more attractive and will give you even more pleasure without having to put up with inner tension. All you have to do is turn away from pendulums and discover your true goal.

If you are unfulfilled by your current position in life or have been plagued by a wave of misfortune it means that at some point you have come under the influence of a destructive pendulum and passed through a foreign door towards a foreign goal. Foreign goals demand a lot of energy and hard work. Your own goals on the other hand seem to achieve themselves and everything goes like clockwork. Foreign goals and doors are always fraught with suffering and yet when you find your own goals and doors, all your problems will disappear.

You might ask: "How can I discover what I really want if I do not already know what that is?" I would answer this with another question: have you ever once seriously thought about it? However strange it might seem the majority of people are so preoccupied with the affairs of pendulums, spending all their time running round in circles like the proverbial hamster in the spinning wheel, that they just do not find the down time for their own soul. People think about what they really want in life in random moments when they are under pressure, rushing from one place to another, fleetingly catching ideas in snatches. Determining what your true goal is does not have to involve any deep navel-gazing. It is enough to take a time alone to relax and finally, listen to the rustle of the morning stars.

What if you find there is nothing you really want? If you look inside yourself and have no sense of an innermost desire this suggests that your life force is depleted. Depression and apathy is a clear sign that your current energy levels are only sufficient to support your basic existence. In this case you should focus on increasing your energy reserves. It is not possible for your heart to have no desires but you do have to have the strength to hear it.

Breaking Through Stereotypes

Despite the fact that we have said a lot about pendulums already I would like to introduce some new examples of how they can knock you off track. Ask yourself whether a pendulum is imposing a foreign goal on you under the guise of some noble pretext. For example, an appeal is being made to "kind souls" to help protect defenceless animals, injured soldiers, starving children or other vulnerable groups. Or perhaps someone somewhere is fighting for their freedom and they need your courageous heart. The kind soul flies off there and then to wherever it is needed.

In reality it is not the 'kind heart' that responds but the 'kind mind' and it is not so much kind as *soulless*. The mind forgets about the soul and drops everything to run to the aid of others. It is like leaving your own children in trouble to save someone else's child. The 'kind mind' stuffs the heart back into its box to be left in peace with its 'reasonable' thoughts. Spiritual emptiness grows and the mind needs something to fill it with.

Pendulums are quick to offer all kinds of compensation. They will demonstrate a wide range of ways that you can contribute your energy to the benefit of others. And yet could not be that spiritual emptiness is what prompts people to respond to the call of others so enthusiastically? The kind-heartedness and charitable feeling associated with the positive stereotype is really the effect of spiritual emptiness. Caring for others is the mind's way of compensating for spiritual emptiness leaving the heart's needs unfulfilled. It is in the pendulums' interests to pass up caring for others as compassionate altruism.

As you can see, pendulums are very sophisticated when it comes to creating convincing stereotypes but it is nothing more than a beautiful demagoguery. What about your own soul? Surely your mind will not abandon it to save another? This is why I so strongly recommend that you turn your back on pendulums and let the heart out of the box. When you learn to love yourself you will find your goal. Once you are securely on the path to your true goal you will commit many good deeds and be better able to help those who are poor and unfortunate along the way because you will be attracting greater resources and opportunities into your life.

Until your own goal is clearly defined you should be extremely cautious in responding to appeals for help. Internal and outer importance should be kept to a minimum.

Pendulums particularly need more energy during their battles. When two pendulums are about to start a fight, one will announce itself the earnest liberator and accuse the other of being a dictator and potentially dangerous aggressor. What the righteous pendulum really wants is to swallow its competitor and take over its oil or other resources but this is kept under wraps whilst an extensive propaganda campaign is developed in defence of justice and freedom.

The person who becomes inspired with importance and takes the pendulum's bait says to themselves: "I will free the oppressed people; I will show that dictator and aggressor!" At the same time the other pendulum prepares its own camp of adherents. The pendulum-dictator claims that it is the goodie and that the pendulum claiming to be the liberator is in fact the true aggressor. Another person filled equally as inflated with importance boils with indignation: "How can they have declared war without consulting me?" "I'll take to the streets in protest!" They may even rush into the war and give up their life for someone else's freedom.

As you can see, the adherents in both camps are drawn into the pendulums' battle. Internal and outer importance is revved up on a background of spiritual emptiness. Rather than filling the emptiness the problem is further exacerbated; for what do the adherents who have been pulled into the battle receive? The supporters of war tell themselves that they have been tricked; the war turned out not to be necessary after all and brought misery to all its participants. The supporters of peace also take a slap. The defenceless nation attacked by the pendulum-aggressor hastily disowns its conquered ruler and overthrows the embassy of the protector-country of peace, steals its humanitarian aid and starts to lick the aggressor's boots.

The lofty ideals the adherents fight for are like soap bubbles. The surface of the bubble is covered with a rainbow-coloured film of pumped up importance but they are empty inside. Do the souls of the adherents really need all this fuss?

There is a very simple way of telling whether the goal you have set yourself serves you or others. *If the idea of needing to take care of others originates somewhere outside yourself, whatever the source, it represents a foreign goal.* If the impulse to take care of others comes from deep within your heart, then the goal may be yours. For example, "I love spending time with my pets. It is not a chore at all" or: "I love the kids (grandchildren) and I enjoy looking after them, watching them grow up, having fun with them." When the kids grow up of course, you will have to find a new goal.

No-one else can identify your goal for you. There is only one way of finding your innermost goal which is to reduce importance, turn your back on pendulums and appeal to your heart; to love yourself first and foremost and to take care of yourself. This is the only way of finding the path to your own goal.

The mind's mistake is that it tries from the very outset to evaluate how realistically achievable the goal is and calculate in advance all the ways and means to achieve it. Everything has to be logical and reasoned. If there is doubt as to whether the goal is realistically achievable then the mind either drops the goal in principle or stores it away in a distant drawer. With this attitude you will never attune your thought energy to your target life line. *By thinking about the means to achieve a goal you attune your thought energy to a life line of bad luck* because it involves the mind running through all the potential scenarios of defeat. No goal is ever reached by the obvious means and it will not by a miracle either. Any challenging task is rarely fulfilled within the context of the conventional worldview, which is not surprising because the frequency of a person's thought energy when they are in doubt differs so intently from the frequency of the target line.

Miracles only happen when you break the conventional stereotype by thinking about the goal rather than the means to achieve it. Then, what previously seemed so unrealistic will suddenly present itself in a different light. As if quite randomly, a totally realistic path will open up in front of you. According to the conventional worldview this would be called a miraculous coincidence. All the mind can do is shrug, for "who would have thought it!"

From the point of view of Transurfing, there is no miracle here. You have simply attuned to the frequency of the target line, decided to have with intent, and outer intention has carried you to a life line where new opportunities appear and new doors open which you would never have suspected existed when your vision was limited to the previous life line.

We have become so accustomed to stereotypes that we consider them representative of the valuable experience accumulated by humanity over the years. In reality, the pendulums generate stereotypes and people are obliged to conform to them. All society is based on pendulums that develop independently according to their own laws as informational energetic beings and then subjugate adherents to their will. Their influence on man is so great that the mind is literally becoming clouded losing its capacity for independent, conscious thought.

Take for example the terrible crimes of the German Nazis during the years of the Second World War. Could it be that the fascists were just particularly cruel people with pathological sadistic tendencies? No, the majority were normal people like you and I. They too had families; loved their close ones and took care of them. After the war, they returned to living a peaceful life like all other normal, good-natured burghers.

Why is it that respectable, family men are transformed into beasts when they enter a war? It is because their mind succumbs to the power of a pendulum. Adherents drawn into the battles of pendulums literally know not what they do. This is particularly evident in the cruel, senseless acts sometimes committed by teenagers. A young and shaky psyche is particularly vulnerable and susceptible to influence. If you took any of these teenagers individually would you really say that they were cruel? Indeed not, and their parents would swear to it. And yet when they come under the influence of a pendulum, for example, becoming part of a crowd they cease to be consciously aware of what they are really doing. The mind of a member of a crowd is literally sleeping because it has been caught in the pendulum's trap. You might remember how the induced shift works.

All the evil, cruelty and violence in the world, originates not in the darker side of human nature but in the greedy nature of the pendulum. The human heart knows no evil. All evil is concentrated in the mind like a plaque that builds up from the destructive influence of pendulums.

Pendulums provoke people to use violence not only against others but against themselves. What do you think of the brave slogan: "No risk, no champagne", "Nothing ventured, nothing gained"? Its content is provocative, a challenge to put your wellbeing or your life on the line in the name of someone else's idea. Of course, if the idea is your own and the risk is justified then maybe it is worth it, but there is nothing more foolish than taking reckless action that may threaten your health or even your life.

Pendulums provoke people into taking risks because the fear, tension and excitement the risk-taker experiences are the pendulum's favourite energy dishes. Using the stereotype of false courage or the help of another adherent the pendulum tries to hook its prey: "Stick to your guns! Show them what you're worth! Do you want people to think you are a coward?" The person filled with internal importance rushes to prove the opposite to themselves and to everyone else! Firmly in the trap of a misguided stereotype it does not occur to them that they do not have anything to prove and can disdain the opinion of their manipulators.

A person suffering from a feeling of inferiority is easily led by the nose. Rather than a display of courage, taking undue risks is usually an attempt to conceal one's false complexes. The mind irresponsibly throws the life of the heart around in order to accommodate dubious stereotypes. The poor little heart rolls into a ball and observes the frantic mind's actions in horror, powerless to do anything about it. The way the mind behaves towards the heart is at best like a chronic loser venting their inadequacy on their loved ones and at worst like a mad animal that slaughters its defenceless offspring.

May your mind awake from its heavy apparition to see that it has a wonderful priceless treasure in the heart. By uniting the heart and mind you acquire true freedom and strength. Do not be afraid to break through stereotypes created by pendulums; if you do, you will discover the true nature of many things in the world. *Breaking through stereotypes you open locked doors.*

Your Goals

I suspect that you already have an innermost goal and at least a rough idea of how to achieve it. It does not really matter though if you cannot yet see how to make your dream a reality. If you have the will a way will present itself. The important thing is to define your innermost desire and acquire the will to have and act with intent. Intention transforms desire into a concrete goal. Without intention a desire can never be fulfilled. First of all however, you have to be distinctly aware of what you want in life. Obscure wording such as "I want to be rich and happy" will not work.

Imagine that you are strolling around town without any particular purpose. You are simply wandering wherever your nose takes you. Where you will end up no-one can say, but if you have somewhere specific in mind, you will eventually end up there, even if you do not know the way. It is the same in life: if you have no goal, you are a paper boat in a raging river. If you have set a goal and are striving towards it, you might achieve it, or you might not…

The only one hundred percent guarantee of reaching a goal is if it really is your own innermost goal and you head towards it through your door. No-one and nothing can stop you then because the heart's fraile key fits the lock to your path perfectly. No-one can take anything from you that is truly yours so there will be no problem in achieving your goal. The only issue is how to find your real goal and your real door.

Firstly, your goal cannot be determined by a temporary need. Your goal should be the answer to the question: *what do you want most out of life? What will make your life happy and joyful*? This is all that matters. You can consider anything else to be pendulum husks.

Settle on one main goal. *Achieve that goal and the fulfilment of all your others desires will follow on behind.* If nothing specific comes to mind, you start by defining a general type of general goal such as comfort and wellbeing in life. Ask yourself what comfort and wellbeing mean to you personally. The need for a house, a car, beautiful clothes and other attributes can be replaced with the single goal to have a high-paying job, but as you know this would not be a goal so much as a door, and a fairly vague one at that.

A high-paying job can be replaced by a more specific expression of the goal: to become an excellent or even unique specialist in your field. *What is your heart drawn to?* The question is whether this job alone will bring complete meaning to your life. If it can then you are lucky because your goal matches your door. You may be drawn towards a certain field of science, culture or art and whilst doing the thing you love, make a brilliant discovery or create a masterpiece. On a life line such as this happiness is to be found right here, right now, not somewhere just around the corner. All the attributes of a comfortable life that other people obtain with great effort will come to you seemingly automatically; for you are following your own path.

Even if you love what you do, if your work does not *solely* represent the one thing that brings you joy and will fill your life with things that make you feel good, it means your work is a door but not strictly speaking a goal. Do not forget that your goal should make your life feel like one continuous holiday with all its accompanying attributes. Do not think about the door i.e. the means to achieve your goal at this stage. The important thing is to define the goal and then with time the door will find itself.

Ask yourself the following question: *what does your heart long for? What would make your life feel like a continual holiday?* Put all thoughts aside that focus on the prestige associated with the goal or how difficult it may be to achieve. You should not be inhibited by any sense of limitation. If you do not believe that anything is possible for you at least pretend you believe it and then you will be free to make a real choice. Do not be shy. Go for it and order whatever you want.

If you want to have a boat, what about your own yacht? If you want to have a flat, what about your own mansion? If you want to be head of your department, what about being president of the corporation? If you want to work hard and earn a lot of money, what about not working at all and living a happy life? If you want to purchase a piece of land that is not too expensive and build your own house, what about having your own island in the Mediterranean?

The list of 'what abouts' goes on forever. You cannot begin to imagine how modest your requests are in comparison to what you could have if you went your own path, through your own door.

Do not make a wish with your mind. No time spent trying to clarify what your heart really wants is wasted. The expression that something is "after your own heart' speaks for itself. It expresses your relationship to something, not your opinion. An opinion is the result of the mind's intellectual activity. Your relationship to something comes from deep within your heart, and only this can serve to discern between your personal and foreign goals. When you are defining your goal ask yourself: "How comfortable do I feel in the bubble of the goal now that I have achieved it?

Once you have made a wish, in order to check whether it is truly meant for you ask yourself two more questions. Firstly: "Do I really need it?" and secondly: "But seriously now, do I really need it?" Try and measure all aspects of a foreign goal up against this wish.

Do you really want this thing with all your heart or do you just *want to desire it?* Are you trying to prove something to yourself or others? Do you really want it? Might it be a tribute to fashion or prestige? An invalid might think that they want to ice skate with all their heart whereas really the goal comes not from the heart but from the pain caused by their handicap. A goal will lure you by being unattainable. If the goal is difficult to achieve try letting go of it and observing how you feel afterwards. If you feel relieved in any way it means that it was a foreign goal. If, however, you feel indignant or find yourself wanting to protest it means that the goal may well be yours.

The only reliable criteria you can use when choosing your goal is inner tension, *the heart's negative reaction to a decision that has already been made by the mind.* You can only use this test of how comfortable you feel about something after the mind has made a decision about its goal. Imagine that you have already achieved you goal and all this is behind you. As soon as you can feel it yon must stop discussing the goal and listen to the promptings of the heart. Is your immediate reaction negative or positive? If the feeling of pleasure is mixed with fear, a heavy sense of burden, a sense of urgency or obligation then the heart is clearly saying "no". The mind might not suspect the troubles the goal hides under its beautiful packaging, but the heart can sense it.

The feeling of inner tension can be elusive and vague. Try not to confuse inner inhibition with discomfort. As we mentioned in the previous chapter, it is natural to feel some inhibition or a kind of shyness when we experience an unfamiliar situation: "Can this really all be for me?" *Inner tension is an onerous feeling of oppression or strain that appears quietly amid the optimistic reasoning of the mind.* Inner inhibition can be overcome with the help of slides but inner tension – never. The worst mistake would be to consider yourself unworthy as a result of the tension. Absolute rubbish! This is a primitive label pendulums have forced you to wear. You deserve the absolute best. At the very least, do not be in a hurry to make a final decision. Try testing your goal against the slide technique. If after some time the onerous feeling has not passed it means that you are dealing with inner tension.

If you experience inner tension because of some aspect connected with the goal itself this means that it is a foreign goal. If you experience inner tension from the awareness that the goal is difficult to achieve this means that it lies beyond the limits of your current comfort zone or that you have chosen a foreign door. *Do not think about the means of achieving your goal until you have firmly decided on what the goal should be.* If you cannot see yourself clearly in your imagined role it might be that you are not ready for it yet. The limits of your personal comfort zone can be widened with the help of slides and there is no need to worry about doors. All that is required of you is the will to have and then sooner or later outer intention will lead you to the right door.

Do not be tempted to make money your goal as if all your problems would disappear if only you had more money because after all, you know what to spend it on. Remember the suitcase full of notes in the chapter on slides. There we said that money of itself cannot serve as a goal and can only serve as an accompanying attribute to another goal. You may readily agree, but the statement is less trivial than it appears. We are so accustomed to money that we can translate almost anything into a monetary equivalent. Money is an abstract category designed to help the mind, but in no way intended for the heart. The heart has no idea what to do with money because it is not capable of abstract thinking. The thing is that your end goal has to be comprehensible to the heart. The heart has to know what you want to buy with the amount you have requested, be it a house, casino or private island etc. It's not a matter of the means, but the heart must like it.

All the time that your inner accountant is calculating the means to the end you will not be able to determine your goal or attune your energy to your target life line. Activate your inner Guardian and give yourself a nudge every time you catch your mind trying to evade the question: "What do I want in life?" The stereotype of the unattainable goal is the most deeply ingrained and so you will need to be patient. The mind will be trying to find the answer to different question: "But how do I achieve it? Here your heart needs to tell the mind to "be quiet. That's not your problem. We are choosing a toy!"

It is important to strive for freedom from destructive pendulums but this does not mean that you have to isolate yourself entirely. All society is constructed on pendulums and so you are left with no choice other than to seek out your own pendulum or disappear to the Himalayas. It is easy for hermits to "converse with Eternity" when they are living in distant solitude but as soon as they return to the aggressive environment where pendulums function they instantly lose their inner balance and meditative detachment.

Your goal will also belong to a pendulum but that will not be a threat as long as the goal truly represents your innermost desire. Find your goal and the pendulum will be obliged to make you its favourite. You can even create a new pendulum. The important thing is to practice your right to freedom of choice and not allow pendulums to establish control over you.

You cannot determine your goal through analysis and reasoning because analysis is the activity of the mind. Only your heart can identify a true goal and the heart is not capable of thinking. It can only see and feel.

It is not the task of the mind to do the searching in your process of choosing a goal. The mind will search in its usual way, by method of analysis and the construction of logical connection based on common stereotypes and clichés. If a person's true path in life could be determined in this way everyone would be happy without exception.

It is the task of the mind to process all external information, at the same time as paying particular attention to the inner voice. The mind has only to establish the precept that it is looking for what will make life feel like a holiday, then allow in external information and observe the inner feelings of the heart within the context of that precept.

Active searching for your path will lead to nothing. Do not worry about it; wait and observe. If the instruction for the search has been given, the right information will present itself. A moment will come when you will receive certain information that inspires your interest. At this point simply pay attention to your inner voice. Do not let the mind get involved.

You can quicken the coming of the necessary information by extending your circle of interests. Visit places you have never been to before: the museum, an excursion, the cinema, trekking, a different part of town, a bookshop, wherever. There is no need to actively search for information; simply widen the diapason of external information you receive and observe.

Do not set any particular timescale. Do not pressure yourself with temporal limitations or turn the search into a chore. Simply hold the following statement in mind: *I am looking for the thing that will make my life feel like a holiday.*

Be more attentive to your inner feelings than you have been before. Have the statement working constantly in the background of your mind. Pass any information that comes to you through the questioning filter: how do I feel about this, do I like it or not?

Sooner or later you will come across a sign or some information that makes something inside reverberate: "Oh! I like it!" Think the information through from all angles remaining carefully attentive to the small voice inside.

So finally, you will have succeeded in resisting the temptation of obsessing about the means and can concentrate on defining your goal. When your desire to have with intent and act in the name of achieving your goal your world layer will undergo an amazing transformation and when it does, this is what will happen…

Your chest will breathe freely having freed yourself from the burden of false goals. You will no longer feel that you have to force yourself to do things your heart does not feel drawn towards. You will give yourself permission to be happy right here, right now having abandoned the struggle for an illusory happiness that only exists in the future. The mind will let the heart out of its box and discover the wonderful feeling of lightness and freedom that comes with the onset of spring after a long hibernation instead of trying desperately to fill the spiritual emptiness with cheap pendulum surrogates. The onerous feelings of depression and strain will be gone. It is much more pleasurable, is it not, to head towards your own goal knowing that it comes from within you than to search in vain for your goal in the outside world. Your mind will have rid itself of useless junk and things that belong to others. It will abandon the futile search for the means and simply launch the necessary task into the layer of your world. The heart will choose its own toy and jump up and down clapping its hands in delight. You will have broken through the conditioned stereotype giving yourself permission to have, despite the seeming unattainability of the goal. As a result, doors will fly open before you that previously had been closed. The mind will at last have accepted the idea that the goal can be realistically achieved. Life will be transformed into an ongoing holiday. The heart will skip joyfully after the mind. The heart and mind will walk hand in hand together along the smooth, cheery road to the kind of happiness that exists right here, right now.

Your Doors

If on the path towards your goal you find yourself constantly with obstacles it suggests that either you have chosen a foreign goal or that you have set off through a foreign door. The only thing in life that is genuinely important is the process of defining your own goal and finding your own door. You can spend your entire life working and yet achieving nothing because it is not the right goal for you. Nothing is more disappointing than finally coming to the realisation that your efforts were all in vain and life has not worked out the way you dreamed it would.

Pendulums have taught people to do what is essential and moreover, to accept without question, that this is the way things are meant to be. The stereotype of *forced necessity* has been taken to the absurd. One would think that life is a term of sentence or compulsory labour that must be served. People are so used to demands being made of them that the heart's true inclinations are pushed to the farthest corner of their consciousness and made to wait for better times. Then life comes to its end without better times ever having presented themselves.

The erroneous stereotype depicts happiness as something that looms in the near future and which must be achieved, earned and hard won in order for it to be become part of the present. People often abandon the thing they love doing for financial reasons. They divide their activities into leisure and paid work. Aside from setting false goals, enforced necessity is just another method used by pendulums to draw the individual away from their true path.

In reality, you can even make a hobby profitable if the hobby fits your goal. If you are forced to abandon the thing you love doing most because it does not provide you with an income you should look at whether the activity is related to your heart's innermost desire or not. Would doing the activity you love make your life feel like a continual holiday? If the activity is not related to your innermost goal it is difficult to say whether it will provide you with an income or not. However, if you are certain that the activity you love doing is strongly connected to your personal goal you can expect it to bring all the attributes of a comfortable lifestyle. When your goal coincides with the door you no longer have to worry about material prosperity. If a person desires material wellbeing it will come into their life automatically.

However, the rigid stereotype of enforced necessity deprives people of the opportunity to throw themselves completely into the things they love doing that fits with their innermost goals. There are numerous examples to illustrate how this happens such as the eccentric, who has to go to work like everyone else, and in his spare time creates and invents things. It never occurs to the eccentric that his creations could be sold to fetch a good price. He lives poorly with total conviction that a mere crust of bread has to be hard-earned, and that his passion for invention is just 'for pleasure'. Do you see what is happening? People spend the majority of their lifetime sweating on behalf of the 'boss man' because this apparently is essential for their survival while the soul receives crumbs of time left over after the main job is done. Who are these people living for; the boss man?

If your door fits your goal you will become rich doing the hobby you love most. In the process of achieving the goal all your other desires will be fulfilled and what is more, *the results will far exceed your expectations*. Have no doubt that everything in this world that comes from the heart is extremely expensive. Products of the mind on the contrary are less highly valued. As you know, a genuine masterpiece is born of union between the heart and mind. You will create masterpieces on the path to your goal as long as you do not allow pendulums to lead you astray. It is very simple. All you have to do is calmly follow your path without succumbing to their wily tricks and sooner or later you will achieve huge success.

If the door does not coincide with your goal things can get a little more complicated. However, think very carefully before drawing this conclusion. Your goal should not have to complicate your life. Quite the opposite in fact, defining your goal will simplify your life significantly and free you of a mountain of problems. Do not be in a hurry to choose a door. When you find the will to have, a door will present itself. If you cannot see clearly where your door lies, work with slides and widen the limits of your comfort zone. Reduce the importance and abandon your attachment to achieving the goal. As soon as you give yourself permission to have, outer intention will offer you an appropriate alternative.

The right door is the path that will lead you to your goal. Once you have defined your goal you can ask yourself the following question: How might this goal be achieved? Sooner or later, outer intention will present you with various opportunities. Your task lies in deciding which among them specifically represents the right door for you. Consider all the possible options. Every option should be tested against the inner voice. Here you can be guided by the same principles for choosing your goal.

Let us suppose that your goal presumes you to be a very wealthy individual. You will have to decide by what means you are going to become wealthy; for money is attracted not to the individual as such, but to what the individual represents, a star of show-business, a large industrialist, a financial expert, a leading specialist or perhaps an heir. So, who do you want to be? You have to find your own true path to wealth; the thing that calls to your heart and what calls to the heart must be asked of the soul, not the mind. The mind is a product of the social environment and society hangs on pendulums. Society says: "become a celebrity, a politician, rich; it's prestigious." However, a pendulum can never determine your niche in life because it has absolutely no interest in your personal happiness.

Your mind and acquaintances will advise you to look for a highly-paid job, as a lawyer for example. They will tell you that "once you become a qualified lawyer, you will be earning big bucks." Of course, everyone wants to earn a lot of money but this might not be the door that is meant for you and if you walk through it you will end up feeling out of place. If the goal has been chosen wisely the door will open up opportunities such that you never dreamed of. Let us suppose that your requests include a house, a car and a good salary. When you walk through the right door, meant for you alone you will receive so much that your original requests will appear ridiculous, but you must not error in your choice of door.

Do not hurry and never regret the time it takes you to make your choice. You will waste a lot more time and effort if you rush in and make a choice you later regret. *Choosing your goal and door can take months.* During this time you will have to observe a kind of "fast of impeccability" as strictly as possible following the main principles of Transurfing with which you are now familiar.

Primarily this is conscious awareness. You have to be aware of the motives for your subsequent actions. Do you behave with awareness and understanding of the rules of the game or are you limply obeying a pendulum.

Keep an eye on levels of internal and outer importance. Think about your goal and door as if you had already acquired them. There is no such thing as prestige, unattainability or necessity. Be rid of all importance. There is nothing unusual in what you have.

Come to terms at the onset with the idea of possible failure. If things work out well then great, but if things do not work out it obviously was not right for you and there will be nothing to mourn. Allow yourself to make mistakes. Allocate a place in your life for defeat where you can keep an eye on it. From the text that follows you will also learn that a disappointing failure need not necessarily mark defeat so much as a landmark on the path to your goal.

Find a safety-net and a substitute for the door. Do not leave your previous door straight away or burn all your bridges in one go. Proceed cautiously. Do not put all your eggs in one basket. Give yourself alternative paths.

Continue to picture the slide of your goal. This will enable you to widen the limits of your comfort zone and attune to the frequency of your target line. Outer intention will present you with the information you need.

To guard against missing any information outer intention is sending your way, *conjure up a slide in your mind depicting the search for your personal goal and door.* Filter any information you receive from the outside world through this slide. Assess whether the information is relevant to you or not. At the same time, listen to the rustle of the morning stars and not your mind. *Do not track your thoughts in this process; track whether the information inspires you or weighs heavily in your heart.* Take note of the heart's response to any information you perceive. There will be a moment when the heart will zing and exclaim: "That is exactly what I was looking for!"

And again, do not be in a hurry to rush ahead. Expand your comfort zone and attune your thoughts to your target line until such time as the goal and door have been expressed in a clear concept. You have to come to the distinct conclusion: "Yes, this is what I want; this will transform my life into one ongoing holiday." Your heart will sing and your mind will rub its hands together in satisfaction.

If the heart is singing but the mind is still in doubt work again on expanding your comfort zone. This will enable you to break through the delusion that will hold you back that the goal is not realistically achievable. Do you know why the door seems impregnable? It is because it is padlocked with the false stereotype of unattainability that sits in your mind. When you break through the stereotype the door will open.

I am not calling you to believe me, or yourself or anyone else for that matter. You will never succeed in forcing the mind to believe anything. The mind only accepts facts on an unconditional basis, nothing else. In order for the door to become real you have to transition to your target life line and only your target slide can help you achieve that shift. At the beginning of your line the goal lies ahead of you in the future but the mind will be able to see a clear path to it. *It is futile to try and convince yourself that some-*

thing is achievable, or to fight to overcome a stereotype. This is not what breaking through the stereotype is about. *The stereotype will crumble automatically when outer intention shows you the new opportunities that await you on your target line.* This is why I draw your attention to the fact of not trying to persuade yourself of anything and not battling with the stereotype. All you have to do is *systematically run the target slide in your mind.* Far from being a meaningless, speculative exercise picturing your target slide represents a concrete step towards your goal.

Do not forget, that material realization is inert and so outer intention cannot carry out your order instantly. You will need to be patient. If you run out of patience then you obviously have a passionate desire to achieve your goal as quickly as possible. If this is the case, go back to the beginning and reduce the level of importance. If you desire something, it suggests that you doubt whether the goal is realistically achievable, so work on expanding the limits of your comfort zone once again until you can see real prospects unfolding.

Pendulums may disguise your true door with the mask of insignificance and low value. *Everything you are capable of doing easily, comfortably and willingly has meaning and value.* You do not have a single meaningless virtue. Any characteristic folly that appears to have no meaning within the context of rigid stereotypes can be the key to the right door. Try holding your characteristic 'foolishness' and 'silliness' up against serious doors.

For example, if you have a reputation for being a clown perhaps you could become a great comedian. If everyone says that you are no use and you spend all your time dressing up and titivating your appearance maybe your door leads to the profession of top model, make-up artist or designer. If you are irritated by bad adverts and love to shout about how the advertising should have been presented totally differently it is not because you are in a bad mood, it is an expression of a hidden desire to demonstrate your abilities in that area. I have listed specific examples but generally speaking personal qualities that are usually considered 'useless' can be expressed in unexpected ways. You will discover this for yourself if you turn away from pendulums to face your heart. Think about it. If you really do display some kind of 'silly' behaviour willingly and with ease there will be a purpose to it.

Everything said above relates to the process of choosing the right door. If you are already on the path to your chosen goal there is a way of determining whether you have chosen the right door or not. It is not the right door if you get tired on the path to your goal, becoming drained. If however, *when you are busy doing something that brings you closer to your goal you are filled with inspiration you can boldly claim that this is the door meant for you.*

There is another way of testing whether a door is yours or not. A foreign door might pretend to be yours, opening up before you, but at a critical moment it will slam shut in your face. Everything may go quite well initially as you pass through a foreign door but eventually, when you find yourself right at the cutting edge of things, failure will befall you. When this happens you will know that you passed through a foreign door. That they deliberately open *public doors* to lure in new adherents illustrates just how insidious pendulums are.

As a rule, private individual doors do not have a crowd of people hustling around the entrance. Even if you meet people who say they would like to pass through your door they will step aside instantly clearing the way for you to walk through unhindered. Public doors are open to all and sundry but only a few will walk through them. Remember how the pendulums create myths surrounding the star's successful career in an attempt to force everyone to observe the "do as I do" rule. People are entranced by the mirage and cram together around the same entrance whilst the true doorway for them stands just next to it entirely empty.

Even a door meant for you personally will close if you crudely contradict the law of balance by giving it too much importance or putting all your eggs in one basket. Yet if you reduce importance the door will reopen. We will return to this idea at the end of the chapter.

Intention

I believe that if you have taken the time to choose the goal and door for you it shows that you have intention. *Intention is what transforms a desire into a goal.* Without intention, desires are never realized and dreams do not come true. A goal is different to a dream in the same way that intention is different to desire. When you have intent your dream becomes a specific goal. Empty dreams and castles in the air will not change anything in life. Only intention i.e. the will to have and act can change your life.

Let us suppose that you have managed to define your goal and are full of the will essential to achieving it. You are burning with impatience to get going. This is the moment to release the grip. Reduce the importance surrounding your goal and abandon any attachment to reaching it, so that all that is left is intent. All that remains, then, is to act within the context of purified intention i.e. to do everything that is expected of you, *without desiring or pushing for the end result.*

The only thing that can spoil your progress along the path to your goal is taking on the burden of excessive responsibility, making excessive effort, extreme diligence or coercion. In the context of the conventional worldview this may sound strange and unfamiliar. However, I hope that by now, you at least will not find the idea absurd or hair-brained. Now we are going to turn everything on its head.

When you are moving towards your goal through the right door there is no need to apply excessive effort. Nor should you have to force yourself to do anything. If you find the opposite is true you have either chosen the wrong goal or the wrong door. The mind is accustomed to struggle and having to overcome obstacles and yet the mind creates all these problems itself by attributing excessive meaning and fighting against the alternatives flow. Your ideal life line will contain minimal obstacles as long as you do not lean too hard on importance.

Go after your goal in the same way that you go to get the post from the letter-box. What will remain of intention if you purify it of importance and desire? All that will remain is the will to have and the need to place one foot in front of the other. Stop imagining the post to be a problem and simply put one foot in front of the other in the direction of the letter box. Do not think about the problem; act, create momentum, irrespective of how things might turn out, and then the problem will be resolved in the process.

Inner intention of the mind will urge you to slap your hands about in the water: "I insist that such and such happen...." Outer intention functions entirely differently to internal intention: "It turns out that such and such has happened..." *All the time that you are insisting on something, pressuring for something to happen, you are preventing outer intention from realizing your goal in harmony with the alternatives flow;* for how can the mind know exactly how the goal should be realized?

Moving towards a true goal through the door that is meant for you is like passing along a well-trodden road. No-one and nothing can stop you as long as importance is kept at a minimal level and you refrain from fighting against the alternatives flow. Because you are walking your true path you have nothing to worry about, even if difficulties temporarily arise. Give yourself permission to enjoy life and accept everything that comes to you as a gift. As soon as you feel a cloud forming over your holiday, try to discern *where you have increased importance*. What is it that is preying on your mind? There is a ready answer to this question: you are forcing yourself to do something; you are overly impatient to achieve your goal; or you are attributing something excessive importance. Relax your grip.

Oppressive thoughts and feelings can arise as a result of a narrow comfort zone. For example, if as a result of achieving your goal you plan to receive a large sum of money, a whole range of anxious thoughts may instantly pop up. Where should you keep it? How should you invest it? What if I lose it? How should I spend it most wisely? What if they take it back? With this state of mind you are not ready to have the money. When the realization of the dream is fraught with these kinds of issues, inner inhibitions will inevitably arise and with it the subconscious striving to free yourself of the cause. In this case outer intention will work against you.

The will to have must be constantly maintained although it is not essential to be picturing the target slide in your mind all the time. It is a pleasant thing to think about the goal you desire and so you do not have to use persuasion and coercion. You can try and convince yourself of something until the cows come home but you will never be successful. Unlike auto-suggestion, with intention the decision has been made and the decision is final. Nothing is open to discussion. The goal will be reached. That is self-evident. *Any doubts will fall away of their own accord as you continue widening the limits of your comfort zone.*

I wish to warn you against making a major mistake. There is one more false stereotype to be aware of. This stereotype encourages you to think positively and only examine successful potential outcomes. However strange it sounds, this is indeed a false stereotype and there are so many! Do you think you could manage to limit your thinking exclusively to successful outcomes? Hardly. If you strive to exclude negative potential outcomes from your script it will not work because it is almost impossible to convince the mind that everything could go so smoothly. The mind is perfectly capable of acting the part, pretending that it believes the scenario you are presenting, but deep in your heart you will still have doubts because the mind is doubting. The heart will unquestionably come across the negative alternative which the mind has chucked in the closet.

You do not need to include any scenarios in your target slide that depict you in the act of achieving your goal. The target slide must simply depict a final picture of what life looks like to you once the goal has already been achieved as if you already have it. All that is required is that you take pleasure in watching the slide and that you put one foot in front of the other with the help of purified inner intention. Visualisation of the process involves working on the scenery but in a completely different way. You convince the mind *not that everything will go smoothly but that everything is already going smoothly.* Visualisation of the current link in the transfer chain should keep pace with what you are doing now and what you will be doing just one step ahead of that. In convincing yourself that everything will come to favourable fruition you continue to hold the deadly grip of control. Relax the grip. Do not think about problems that have not happened yet; just go calmly with the alternatives flow.

Realisation

I walked on the wet pavement…

It had rained in the morning and so the worms had crawled out of the lawns onto the pavement in search of the meaning of life and new horizons. The fate of the worms concluded differently. The lucky ones managed to crawl to the neighbouring flowerbed lain with deep black soil. Some were pecked at by the birds. Others were squashed by the soles of monsters walking along the pavement. Then the sun came out and warmed and dried the moisture. The sun's rays reached one worm who had crawled to the middle of the path. By the time it realised its mistake it was too late. It would not have the strength to crawl to safety. A slow and painful death would hover above it until the worm dried out completely. Suddenly, some mysterious power lifted it up and threw it onto the wet ground. From the point of view of the worm what happened was theoretically impossible and it had no way of understanding let alone explaining what had saved its life; whereas from my point of view nothing supernatural had taken place at all. I was simply sorry for the little worm and so picked it up and threw it onto the flowerbed. Evidently, the lonely Pilgrim had chosen his goal and door very well.

If your goal seems unattainable the entire holiday will be spoiled by doubt and depressing thoughts of possible failure. How do you ultimately believe in the impossible in order for it to become possible? Well, you cannot. That is impossible! What a stupid question. You just cannot! So I return once again to what I have said above. *There is no way of successfully persuading, convincing or forcing yourself to believe something.* Put these meaningless cares to one side and get back to doing something more beneficial i.e. the process of putting one foot in front of the other in the direction of your goal.

Do not worry if the goal seems unattainable. It might be difficult for you to imagine how your goal could be at all possible to achieve but really, it is a useless concern. All you have to do is make your order properly and leave the rest to the waiter. Many people who have achieved phenomenal success all say that in hindsight they would never have believed that they were capable of achieving such amazing results.

When the heart wants to strive towards the goal and the mind is worried about the means, mutual understanding between them is blocked. The heart has no concept of the notions of a means. In dreaming the heart is used to getting anything it desires because any striving is instantly brought about by dream intention. Where the soul flies off to whilst the mind is in deep sleep no-one knows. We only remember the dreams we have in a lighter sleep state when the mind is dozing. Unfortunately though, our dreams cannot serve as a criterion for the desires of the heart, because as soon as we wake from a deep sleep the mind resets the heart's sail in accordance with its own expectations and experiences.

We are unable to remember the soul's past lives for the same reason; if of course they actually happened. Unlike the heart, the mind comes into this world as a clean sheet of paper. There are many accounts of how the human mind has had access to information from past lives under the right circumstances. However, past lives are a separate issue and go beyond the scope of this book.

The mind has to consider the means because it is used to acting within the limits of inner intention. Within these limits, there will undoubtedly be potential scenarios with an unfavourable ending and so in this case outer intention not only will not help you, it will act to your detriment. This is why I so insistently recommend that you stop thinking about possible scenarios of how events might develop. On the path to your goal, the will to have must prevail. This is what you should focus on above all else, and the remaining aspect of intention, i.e. the will to act, must be purified to the maximum from the undesirable elements of desire and importance.

The will to place one foot in front of the other represents the inscrutable intent to do the minimum of what is required of you. To act dispassionately does not mean to act indecisively or sluggishly. I am sure you know what I am trying to say. Excessive will is also a consequence of importance. Your actions will be effectively to the degree that you manage to purify inner intention from desire and importance.

You should think through scenarios of actually achieving the goal in general terms only, enough to determine the main stages of the path i.e. the links in the transfer chain. Once this is done it is important to let go of thinking about the general scenario altogether. At this stage, only the target slide should occupy your thoughts. The target slide should only include the final picture of your life once the goal has been achieved without any additional scripts. Turn this slide over in your mind continuously; live inside it. Your comfort zone will begin to expand and the parameters of your thought energy will become attuned to the target life line.

Eradicate any desire or importance from your attitude to it all. If you are trying to make a huge effort to achieve the goal as soon as possible, or you doubt your abilities or fear difficulties it means your importance level is embellished. Give yourself permission not to be perfect and to make mistakes. If you do not allow yourself to make mistakes you cannot expect others to be lenient towards you either. If you fear that the goal is unachievable it means you have strong desire. But how can one not have desire? Accept the possibility of defeat in advance and consider emergency exits and back-up plans. Have them prepared. Unless you take this step you will not be able to free yourself of desire.

Most importantly, whatever happens, *never put all your eggs in one basket*. For example, never ditch everything and throw yourself into an infatuation. What if you suddenly discover that you have made a mistake and taken a foreign goal and door to be your own? Then, having placed all your bets on one card you destroy the balance. There must always be some kind of counterbalance, fallback option or retreat because when you have these your heart is calmed and balanced forces will leave you be. For example, do not leave your previous job until you are guaranteed of finding a new one. Do not slam doors behind you or burn bridges; be careful and prudent. Even if you are absolutely certain that the goal and the door are your own, it is still better not to make any sudden movements that could, in the case of misfortune, leave you without a crust of bread and a roof over your head. No-one is immune to misfortune.

In any case, you are now armed with the powerful Transurfing technique and so you should have less cause for fear and anxiety. Now you at least understand the rules of the game, which is something in itself. People normally participate in the games of the pendulum world without knowing the rules and so lose straight away. The methods you have become acquainted with here will give you a huge advantage, but that is not all. In the remaining chapters you have yet to learn about Transurfing's 'heavy artillery'.

If you do not get in outer intention's way with intense actions motivated by heightened importance it will most certainly deliver you to your goal. Go with the alternatives flow; do not try to fight against it. The mind's habit of controlling everything may cause you to go against the tide but you will agree that it is better to trust the flow; for no-one is given the gift of anticipating every move ahead of time. If you practice visualising your target slide outer intention will guide you and because outer intention works beyond the limits of familiar scenarios and stereotypes it will introduce unexpected changes.

The mind will perceive these changes as unfavourable and respond by slapping its hands in the water spoiling everything. To avoid this happening allow the dynamic of change to take place organically. Let go your grip of control on the situation. If something does not turn out as you expected do not hurry to correct the situation; instead, try and see the unexpected event in a positive light that shines in your favour. At first it may not be obvious but in the majority of cases you can begin to see the truly positive nature of the event. People upset themselves unnecessarily; for in reality, things really are not too bad at all.

I am not suggesting that you should blindly believe the saying: "All's for the best in the best of all possible worlds". There are two seeds of truth in this saying, one is obvious and one is more obscure. The obvious part relates to standard stereotypes and presupposes that things are not that bad *overall*. Indeed, the alternatives flow always takes the path of least energy expenditure. Problems always involve huge expenditure of energy and what is more, are generated when a person fights against the current. People only interpret changes in the direction of the current as a problem because it does not fit with their plan.

The hidden grain of truth in the saying has much greater weight. The point is that if you can take it into your head to perceive the seemingly unfavourable change in the scenario as a positive thing playing for your hand, this is exactly how things will be. This statement might seem harmless as well as doubtful. Nonetheless, here there lurks a great force, which we will talk about more in the next chapter.

When you are going with the alternatives flow you can accelerate your speed by using a "paddle". The paddle is the visualisation of links in the transfer chain. Unlike the slide, this type of visualisation includes a script of how you move towards the goal. But as you know, visualisation of the current link does not include the entire script, just a fragment of it that relates to the present time. You place one foot in front of the other, guided by your current intention. Whilst you are taking one step you simultaneously set the intention to take the next.

Remember how a mother watches over her child as it grows. In every moment, the mother is visualising the current link in the transfer chain. In her mind the chain consists of several tiny links. She delights from the fact that today her child stood up unaided and imagines that the child may take its first step the next day. A mother does not imagine her child growing up into an adult overnight. She takes joy from the present; she caresses the moment of now, in the firm knowledge that tomorrow, new achievements will be made.

Visualisation of the current stage in the process of achieving your goal should be practiced according to this same principle. *Today is better then yesterday and tomorrow will be better than today.* There is no point in trying to anticipate every coming turn in the alternatives flow. It is better to take pleasure in the present moment and simply dispassionately and impeccably place one foot in front of the other. Imagine that you wanted to go for a swim in a pool but in order to do so you have to first run one hundred meters and jump into the water. Now imagine that you "dive" to the ground straight away, sweeping your arms before you have reached the water. Absurd?

When visualising the current link in the chain a statement is made about the successful status of the course of events at the present time: Everything is going well. This provides the foundation for the next rung of the ladder: tomorrow will be even better. You mentally intend to step onto the next rung higher than the previous one. When this happens a feedback circuit is created. As a result, the stages of moving towards your goal are imagined as climbing up a ladder. Coming success is mentally imagined not as a cloud hanging in the air but as a ladder on which every rung supports the one above it. Your level of success has a rising tendency, like climbing a ladder. Every day brings with it a particle of your coming success. *Do not worry about the future; live the present.*

On the path to your goal pendulums will find all sorts of ways of knocking you off course. Take any setbacks as par for the course. Nothing ever goes entirely smooth. When you upset yourself over a setback the rung you are currently standing on breaks and you end up sliding back down the ladder. This makes you cross and sets off the inner critic because things have stopped going according to the mind's plan. When this happens you are caught on the pendulum's hook. You will never cross onto a life line filled with happiness and good fortune whilst you are dissatisfied with yourself; for when well-being and good fortune shine upon you, are you not pleased with yourself? How can you get onto these lines if the parameters of your thought energy are attuned to self-criticism?

Do not forget, that the mind only perceives an unforeseen change in the alternatives flow as a failure because it is not written into the mind's script. Why not accept the change and see the setback as a success? Try playing the flowing game: *greet every setback with joyful surprise rather than annoyance;* for apparent setbacks are the work of outer intention that moves us towards our goal in ways unforeseen to us. How can the mind possibly know exactly which path leads towards the goal? The mind thinks the goal is difficult to attain precisely because it does not see the single path among the well-beaten tracks that leads to your goal. Naturally, you will not achieve anything unless you give in to the alternatives flow and allow outer intention to nudge you onto the right path.

Do not watch how other people walk their path to success or try to keep up with them. Do not give in to the herd instinct. You have your own calling. The majority take the roads well-trodden but true success is achieved by the few who refuse to follow the rule "do as I do" and independently tread their own path.

That brings me to a final word of warning. If you associate your dream with the idea of helping those close to you everything could go very wrong. For example, you may think along the lines of: when I realize my dream I will be able to help my loved ones. The heart is selfish by nature and as things stand it receives just a modicum of what it desires in life, so one can hardly imagine it possible for the heart to think of anyone else's happiness besides its own. The heart does not really care about other people, no matter how near and dear they are. It thinks only of its own wellbeing. Its life in this world is a remarkable and unique opportunity. Contrary to popular belief, all gestures of altruism originate in the mind, not the heart. The heart will do anything possible to achieve its innermost goal, but if the goal serves someone else instead it will lose all interest and leave the mind free to exhaust itself battling to find the solution to its one task.

In the well known fairytale of Pinocchio the wooden boy sets himself the task of getting rich in order to help his father. He reasons that if he plants golden coins in the field of Miracles a golden tree will grow and then he will be able to buy Papa Carlo a theatre. Naturally, he does not achieve his goal and it causes the small boy all sorts of troubles.

Pinocchio makes two major mistakes when he sets his goal. His first mistake is that the goal does not serve himself but someone else. Pinocchio's heart dreams of something for itself whilst his mind envisages Papa Carlo's future wellbeing. Altruism is a wonderful quality to have but if you choose to devote yourself to serving others you will never find your own happiness. To perceive your personal fulfilment in service to something or someone else, in helping the weak and defenceless, or in giving yourself fully to someone else's vision or idea is nothing more than an illusion and self-deception. In the illusion the mind has been seriously gripped by a pendulum and sees its happiness exclusively in service to it. However hard the mind tries to convince itself that it has found happiness in service to other people or to some lofty idea, this person's heart will be miserable and forced back into its box with no strength to even verbalise its rights to personal happiness. The conviction that another person's idea is one's own or that another person's happiness represents one's own fulfilment is a misconception held by people who have been unable to find their own goal, or perhaps have not even tried.

Pinocchio's second mistake is that he sees money as a means to an end. As you will remember, money can serve neither as a means nor a goal. Money is simply an accompanying attribute along the way to your goal. There is no point in sharpening your focus on money. Quite the opposite; as a rule, chewing over money thoughts only creates harmful, excess potential. If the set goal is truly yours money will come to you of its own accord and you will not need to worry about it at all. The tale of Pinocchio is the perfect illustration of this.

The fairytale confirms the idea that if you find your own happiness first you can make other people happy as a result because when you achieve your goal, money and wellbeing come to you. Then obviously you have ample opportunity to help the ones you love because you will have greater resources at your fingertips.

For now, whilst you are only on the path to your goal you should put your own happiness first. Then you will avoid frightening your heart away from the goal. On the path to your goal allow your heart to think only of itself. Once you have achieved your goal you can afford your altruistic mind as much freedom as it desires in looking after your loved ones, nature, homeless animals, starving children and whoever else you feel drawn to help.

Inspiration

Once on the path to your goal through the right door you will be racing the crest of the wave of good fortune. You will radiate harmonious energy because of the feeling of ease that has entered your heart. We have already talked about transmission in the chapter on the wave of fortune and how to drum up and maintain an emotional high. It can be quite difficult to maintain this feeling consistently but once you are experiencing the joy and peace that comes from unity of heart and mind, the quality of energy radiating from you will adjust itself. Everything will start to pick up. Various problems will find a way of disappearing and inspiration will visit you often provided you do not try to evoke the feeling intentionally.

Inspiration is a wonderful thing but for some reason it has become cloaked in an aura of mystery and inscrutability. It is assumed that inspiration is extremely difficult to find and that it appears spontaneously and always unexpectedly like a muse that pops in for a bit without prior warning. Then the muse flies away just as suddenly as she appeared without returning for long periods of time. The suffering one agonizingly awaits his lady's next visit but nothing he can do brings her to him and the solution eludes him.

In reality, everything is a lot simpler. *Inspiration comes from union between heart and mind in the absence of importance.* The first part of the definition will be clear to you. Inspiration is the state of elation which makes the creative process easy, simple and most importantly, brilliant. It is quite clear that this can only happen when there is union between heart and mind. You are never truly inspired when you are working on something you do not feel passionate about.

When you are focused on working towards the realisation of your goal you will definitely achieve unity of heart and mind and this will serve as the essential condition for inspiration. However, this unity alone is not enough. Why is it that inspiration suddenly appears and then disappears somewhere? Perhaps it leaves when we are fatigued. And yet, in an inspired state you can usually work for many hours before being overcome with tiredness.

The second part of the definition of inspiration gives us to understand where inspiration comes from and where it disappears to. You can probably already guess what this is about. The thing is, inspiration does not appear from anywhere. It is simply freed up when the importance potential drops. Wherein lies importance? Firstly, in the passionate desire to achieve your goal and secondly, in the insistent striving to find a source of inspiration.

As I have said many times before, desire will not help you achieve your goals. Painful hankering after a goal whips up a whirlwind of balanced forces instead of the wind of outer intention which quickly scares all your kind fairies and muses away. The desire to invoke inspiration has the same effect. Any preparation and subsequent expectation of inspiration creates the excess potential of importance.

You may carefully arrange your work area in minute detail, tidy up, put everything in its proper place, be well rested, prepared and in general have created all the necessary conditions for a meeting with your muse. In your intense preparation you will have materialised the potential of importance causing the wind of balanced forces to start howling alarmingly outside your window. Then you set the table, light the candles and sit in expectation of a visit from the temperamental lady but she still does not appear. And you can be sure she will not appear because inactive waiting is like desire squared. Outside the window such a hurricane of balanced forces is raging that no winged lady would dream of flying up to your house.

If you show signs of impatience bordering on despair, the raging wind will smash the windows making chaos of the energy in your house. The commotion will build like a wall standing between your heart and mind and it will take some time to re-establish the connection that existed previously. Can you see how charged preparation, anticipation and desire really are?

Likewise, inspiration will not come to you until you release the stranglehold of anticipation. *Inspiration does not arrive; it is freed up in the moment that the potential of importance leaves* and the other way around; inspiration is clamped the moment the impatient mind drives the heart back into its box to wait. In the end, the mind's nasty habit of subjugating everything to its control ruins the whole party.

Nonetheless, despite inspiration's apparent insubordinate and unpredictable nature the mind has an excellent way of bringing inspiration under its control. It is just that the element of control has to be used totally differently to how the mind is used to exercising control. Usually the mind beats against the window pane with its inner intention whilst next to it another window is open. Now the mind must do the exact opposite.

Firstly, *abandon the desire to achieve the goal* for if the goal is truly yours you will not succeed in getting rid of it for long anyway. Sooner or later, the goal will be fulfilled. The will to have and the complete absence of insistence and determination on your part play the key role. Take what is yours calmly and without pressurising the situation just as you would take the post from your letterbox. All inner intention should do is place one foot in front of the other on the way to the letterbox.

Secondly, *forget about specially preparing for the "mystery"*. Any preparation for inspiration to come to you, in whatever form, creates excess potential because all the time that you are busy getting ready for it you are signalling that you wish to attract something you do not currently have. The more carefully you carry out the preparatory ritual, the worse the outcome will be. If you think back, you can probably recall situations when you conscientiously prepared for an action, event or meeting but things did not work out, the meeting did not happen and the plan fell apart. If balanced forces are capable of disturbing the interaction between material objects, they can blow away a barely discernible whiff of inspiration as lightly as a feather.

Thirdly, *abandon the habit of waiting for inspiration.* Is it not right that inspiration comes when you least expect it? So, why wait for it and negate the condition required for it to appear?

So, let us suppose that you have observed these three conditions. All that is left of your personal, inner intention is the will to put one foot in front of the other i.e. to take action. Just start, and what is more, start without waiting to feel inspired first and in the process of doing, inspiration will come to you. *Inspiration is freed up in act of working.* You cannot disperse the potential of desire and anticipation fully until you begin, irrespective of whether the initial results are good or not. As you know intention in action disperses excess potential.

So this is the scene you end up with. You set the table for yourself, light the candles for yourself, make yourself comfortable and begin drinking tea for your own pleasure without waiting for anyone else to arrive. You can be certain that the whimsical muse will be affected by your display of indifference wondering how you could have forgotten about her. She will appear and instantly fall in beside you. That is the secret.

Reviving the Goal

What should you do if you have set about achieving someone else's goal but do not want to abandon it? Can a foreign goal be achieved? Indeed it can. Armed with the Transurfing method you will have a huge advantage in comparison to those who do not know the rules of the game in the pendulum world. However, achieving a foreign goal requires considerably more effort and you should be aware of this fact. On the path to achieving a foreign goal you should allow yourself to be guided by the same principles described for following your own goal. The only difference being that all these principles have to be followed with the utmost impeccability. That is all that remains to be said on the subject of achieving a foreign goal.

If you have chosen to work towards a foreign goal and feel that you would like my advice on whether you should abandon the goal or not you have not fully grasped the principles of the Transurfing method. This book only gives a map of the general area and discloses the rules of the game. You have to make the decisions yourself. Transurfing cannot help you if you are not ready to take full responsibility for your own destiny. These methods will only work if you take the helm of intention into your own hands. You now know how to handle the helm but it is for you to decide in which direction you wish to travel. Only pendulums can provide ready solutions but *relying on other people's decisions you place your destiny in their hands.*

If it is too late to abandon a foreign goal you can achieve it quite easily by freeing yourself of desire and the excess potential of importance. There may be many obstacles on the path to a foreign goal but the majority are born of the mind itself when it fights against the alternatives flow and pumps up importance. *Detach yourself.* Act in a manner that is both emotionally detached at the same consciously aware. Do not battle with problems and obstacles. Reduce importance and they will withdraw.

Suppose that you are moving towards your goal but have met with formidable obstacles along the way. What causes them? Now you can pinpoint the reason more easily. Analyse the situation to discover where you have overindulged the level of importance. Examine what you have attributed excessive meaning to and where you have tried to fight against the alternatives flow. Reduce importance, detach yourself from the situation, trust the alternatives flow and things will improve.

The goal may remain equally elusive if you are setting off towards it through a foreign door. Perhaps it would be worth looking around and choosing a different door. However, before you boldly swop doors, be sure to reduce importance first and see what effect that has. *Even your own door can slam shut if you have somewhere attributed significantly embellished importance.* For example, if you place all your eggs in one basket the goal will have too great a value. The door will reopen if you reduce importance and give yourself the protection of having an alternative route.

As a rule, foreign doors that once stood wide open will at some stage in the game slam shut quite unexpectedly. There is such a rational explanation for this that the mind will take its hat off and shrug its shoulders in bewilderment: "Who would have thought it?" What happens is the opposite to what happens when the mind puzzles too deeply over the means to achieve the goal to see a realistic strategy i.e. the right door. The thing is that if the goal is genuinely yours and you are ready to give yourself permission to have, your true door will open just as suddenly as a foreign door closes. If you give yourself permission to have even foreign doors will open before you.

Just as you may have more than one goal, you have more than one door. In fact, you may have several. Hence it is *never too late to look for a new goal even if several previous goals have become objectively impossible to attain.* There is no reason why you should not go after a foreign goal through a foreign door searching for your own goal along the way. There is no need necessarily to abandon something that has already been started. The shift to your target life line can be orchestrated quite smoothly. You can be working towards a foreign goal and holding a mental picture of your own goal slide in your mind at the same time. Then, outer intention will with time open unseen doors that will allow you to painlessly change your activities.

It is unlikely that anyone can free themselves totally from the influence of pendulums that strive to impose foreign doors. It is likely that you previously burst through the wrong doors. Even now that you have more knowledge you are not immune to error. Everyone makes mistakes. The important thing is not to fall into despair or criticise yourself too harshly. You will eventually find your own door. A person who never made a mistake never tried anything new. You are surrounded by people who live like robots, who do not set themselves goals and do not read books like this one. These people want more but they do not have the intent to act. The advantage people like this have, is that they do not make mistakes. You on the other hand will undoubtedly make mistakes; all you have to do is use them. *True success grows from the ruins of past failures.*

You will inevitably encounter difficulties when you knock at foreign doors. From the outside it will be obvious to everyone that you are having to overcome obstacles and are battling with various problems but that is just the superficial view of things. No-one including you will see that deep down your heart is strongly opposed to having to walk through a foreign door.

The mind oppresses the heart with its forceful will insisting that they fight to the end, but even in people who are very strong-willed there is a limit to how long the heart can take being oppressed and things end in crisis. The annoying thing is that the crisis can take the form of committing an unforgiveable faux pas. When a person is in a state like this they easily make very basic mistakes. It can happen to anyone including "the powers that be".

On the path that leads through a foreign door you can expect there to be moments of crisis and you can expect to make mistakes, but try to avoid making blunders. *Rent yourself out–proceed with impeccability.* The paradox is that a major mistake tends to be forgiven more easily than a minor oversight. Do not expect any sympathy, even from those closest to you. If your loved ones are the slightest bit dependent on you either materially or socially, the worse it will be, for you will have failed their expectations.

Accusers and manipulators do not set themselves high goals, which is why they do not make mistakes. Do not give them reason to accuse you of an unforgiveable, if relatively minor offence. *Be impeccable in the small things* then any crisis you have on the path through a foreign door will be less traumatic.

It is also advisable to be cautious of the advice given by loved ones who definitely "want the absolute best for you". (It can be awful to watch compassionate parents predetermining their child's goal in life from very early on.) If you are decidedly going your own way in life and suffer some kind of defeat you can expect no mercy. They will cry: "We told you so, but you never listen to us!" At this moment your position will be very weak, upset by the misfortune you have had to endure and the manipulators around you will exploit your weakness trying to get their claws into you. It is more convenient for them that way because they get to assert themselves while you are on hand, resigned and submissive.

Anyone who finds themselves in a quandary will always attract advisors and manipulators pursuing the same goal: to put you in your place, to seize the opportunity of manipulating you or of going up in their own estimation by coming all the old solider over the newfound foul-up! Their words, clothed in the packaging of "sincere participation" can be translated as follows: "Whatever did you think you getting yourself into? Did you think you were better than us? Sit here and keep your head down. Live like we do. We know more about life than you do". In a moment of weakness doubts will sneak in: "Maybe they are right, I do not know what I am doing?"

You inevitably ask yourself whether it is worth listening to the advisors and manipulators. How might they be right? Only in the fact that you have made a mistake. Anyone who ever tries to achieve something will have times when they make mistakes, even if they are guided by the advice of those who supposedly know better. Only you can find your goal. *No-one else can do this for you.* Even those who genuinely wish you well cannot look right into your soul for even you hear the whisperings of your heart as the rustle of the morning stars i.e. barely audibly. *Do not give in to the influence of other people. Believe in yourself. In the search for your goal do not listen to anyone and follow your heart.* As far as choosing your innermost goal in life is concerned you have to be persistent and adamant in relation to pendulums and extremely attentive to your own heart.

As you can see, the only excuse in the process of choosing your destiny is the fact that not all goals and doors in the alternatives space are truly meant for you. This does not mean however, that you cannot choose them. Nothing prohibits you from making such a choice but you can expect to encounter problems as a result. Do you really need that? When you choose foreign goals and doors you are taking the path of greatest resistance. The whole beauty of the freedom of choice lies in the fact that personal goals and doors appear to the individual to be so much better than any other. But in order to indulge in freedom of choice you have to free yourself from the influence of pendulums that impose foreign goals and doors.

SUMMARY

A foreign goal is always punishing, coerced and feels like an obligation.

A foreign goal appears in the guise of fashion and prestige.

A foreign goal attracts you with its apparent unattainability.

A foreign goal forces you to prove something to yourself and others.

A foreign goal is imposed upon you by others.

A foreign goal serves to improve someone else's material wellbeing.

A foreign goal makes you feel uneasy.

In the process of achieving the goal you will fulfil all other desires along the way.

What is your heart drawn to? What would make your life joyful and happy?

Do not think about the means until you have clearly determined your goal.

Having made the decision, be aware of how your inner voice responds.

Slides can eliminate inner inhibitions but never inner discomfort.

The heart always knows exactly what it does not want.

It is not the mind's task to do the searching when you are looking for your goal.

It is the mind's task to absorb information from the outside world at the same time as paying particular attention to the still, inner voice within.

Your door is the path that will lead you to your goal.

If you cannot see the path, picture the mental image of your target slide.

Outer intention will open your door for you to your target life line.

If you experience a feeling of inspiration on the path to your goal you know that you have chosen the door meant specifically for you.

Everything you do willingly and easily has meaning and value.

Do not include any scripts in the target slide. You already have what you want.

Do not put your goal and door in one basket. Find a potential substitute.

Do not slam any doors or burn any bridges.

Do not allow yourself to be influenced by others. Trust yourself.

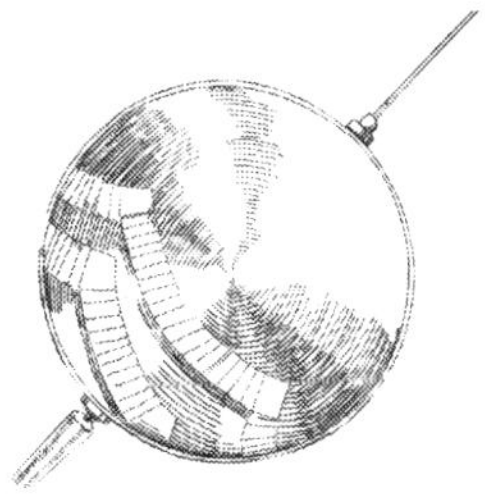

Chapter XI. ENERGY

You do not have to fight for your health
or store up energy.
Simply let it in.

Energy levels

To practice Transurfing effectively you have to be in a good state of health and have a relatively powerful energy field. You may think that your health is quite good as it is but not really know what true health feels like. If you struggle to get out of bed in the morning and do not want to go to work or university; if you feel sluggish after lunch and find yourself nodding off, and in the evening wish for nothing better then to plonk yourself down in front of the television, you cannot say that you are in good health. If this describes your lifestyle, your energy levels are clearly only sufficient to support a measured existence.

You will already have additional energy by reclaiming the vitality that was previously being spent on the burden of excess potentials and pendulums. However, you can never have too much energy and so later in this chapter I am going to introduce a number of recommendations for ways to increase your energy levels even further.

What we understand here by 'energy levels' is the ability to absorb and use energy. There are basically two forms of energy in the human body: *physiological energy and free energy.* Physiological energy is attained via the digestive system. Free energy is the energy of the Cosmos that passes through the human body. Together both make up our energy body. Human energy is spent on fulfilling various biological functions but it also radiates out from the body into the space around us.

There is an infinite supply of Cosmic energy in the world, but as humans we only absorb a tiny fraction of it. It passes through the body in two directions. The first current passes in an *upward direction* and runs one inch in front of the spine in men and two inches in front of the spine in women. The second current of energy passes in a *downward* direction and runs very close to the spine. The amount of free energy a person has depends on the width of their central meridians. The wider the meridians, the greater a person's energy levels will be.

The meridian system was discovered long ago. We are not going to delve too deeply into a detailed description of the structure of the human energy body here. If you are interested in this topic there is plenty of relevant literature available. The circulation of energy round the human body is a relatively complex process but that should not overly concern you. For our purposes it is enough to concentrate on these two central meridians.

A disruption in the normal flow of energy caused because somewhere 'blocks' and 'holes' have appeared, can manifest in the form of physical illness. The opposite is also true. An inner organ that is affected by an illness can also distort the overall picture of the energy body. It is difficult to draw a clear distinction between cases where physiological symptoms such as toxicity in the body have caused problems in the energy flow and where disturbances in the energy flow have resulted in a physiological disorder. Acupuncture and acupressure and many others methods besides can help restore the normal circulation of energy in the body curing illnesses caused by poor energy flow. However, these methods can only guarantee a short-term effect. In order to maintain a good state of health one has to take care of the physical and the subtle bodies.

Human energy levels are closely linked with the condition of the body's muscles. Muscle tension hinders the normal flow of invisible currents which disturbs the transmission of energy throughout the energy field. A person who feels tense can enter a relaxed group of people and change the general mood in the group without uttering a word: the tension just seems to hang in the air. The other people in the group absorb the negative energy without necessarily being aware of it. Tension creates inhomogeneity in the general field calling up balanced forces as a result. Equilibrium can be re-established either by bringing the group energy to a common denominator or by quashing the energy potential of the opposite sign. For example, the group may tease the overly inhibited individual who has recently joined them, to get them to relax.

Mood and vitality are directly linked to energy levels. Depression, stress, ennui, tiredness and apathy all indicate a lack of sufficient energy in the body. Physiological energy alone is not enough to support high levels of vitality. A person can be feeling physically tired but comfortable and cheerful at the same time. Likewise, a person who is well fed and rested can feel down and listless.

Free energy plays the most important role in assuring a person has a proactive approach to life. When a person has no desire to do anything at all they clearly lack free energy. A person may be able to force themselves to carry out routine functions on a background deficit of free energy but they will find it difficult to be creative or physically active. Intention is the driver for any proactive behaviour and yet when a person has no free energy they can have no intention.

Physiological energy is spent in the physical execution of our actions. Here we will focus primarily on the first type of energy that goes into creating intention. This is in effect the energy of intention and it is thanks to this energy that we experience the motivation to have and act.

Stress and relaxation

When a person is depressed or tense their central meridians become blocked. The meridians narrow and the circulation of free energy either slows down or stops altogether. In this state intention loses its energy supply. When intention is blocked a person usually becomes incapable of dealing with stressful situations effectively. Stress can also have the opposite effect on the meridians making them suddenly dilate. When this happens a person is capable of doing incredible things that ordinarily they would never be capable of doing. There are known examples of this although they are rare. In the majority of cases a person's abilities and resources are severely reduced when the body experiences high levels of stress.

Every day people come up against numerous stressful situations of varying intensity from fairly minor incidences that are usually quickly forgotten to extremely stressful situations which can knock them off kilter for quite some time. The body's natural response to stress is to tense one or another muscle group. This tensing has become such a deeply engrained habit that we do not really notice it. For example, whilst you read these lines you are tensing individual facial muscles but as soon as you pay attention to them they relax. After a few minutes you will forget about your face and it will freeze once again into a mask that reflects your emotional condition.

There is an erroneous but widely held belief that stress can be relieved through relaxation. By trying to relax you are in effect railing against the symptom without eliminating the cause. Physical tension is caused by psychological tension. States of oppression, anxiety, irritation and fear cause spasmodic muscle tension. Naturally, conscious relaxation of the muscles will give some temporary relief but unless the mental tension is dealt with the body will reassume its previous condition. *To eliminate mental tension it is essential and sufficient for importance to be reduced.* The reason you are tense in the first place is because of the excess meaning you attribute to whatever is bringing you down.

Stress is a consequence of importance. Stress can be instantaneously relieved by reducing importance. It is futile and harmful to create ongoing importance. You will never succeed in changing a situation for the better and acting effectively if you are carrying the heavy load of importance. When you are severely stressed it is enough to wake up, open your eyes and become conscious of the fact that a pendulum has hooked into your importance. It is easy enough to see what the importance relates to in each specific instance. Remind yourself: by reducing importance you free yourself of the pendulum and can act effectively. You have to be aware of the fact that attributing something inflated meaning will *always* work against you.

To change any difficult situation it is enough to remember about importance and consciously reduce any excessive meaning you have connected with it. The only challenge is *to remember* in time. When you are stressed your awareness is sleeping and so you will forget that something called Transurfing ever existed. *To eliminate stress from your life you have to wake up and reduce importance.*

If you have made a habit of paying attention to your inner voice, it will not be at all difficult to remember about importance at the necessary moment. Every time you experience a feeling of unease ask yourself why. Where has meaning been inflated? However 'important' the specific circumstances are to you consciously let go of your attachment to their importance. Only after the purification of intention can you act effectively.

To become immune to stress you have to replace the old habit of stressing out over any small thing with the new habit of maintaining a relaxed state. Being in a relaxed state does not mean being listless or apathetic. It is a state of harmonious interaction with the outside world: *balance*. Balance presupposes the absence of internal and outer importance: I am neither good nor bad and the world is neither bad nor good; I am not pathetic and insignificant and the world is not pathetic and insignificant either.

The absence of importance or at least a low level of importance is the main condition essential to becoming relaxed. There is no point in trying to relax when importance is inflated. For example, you can hardly expect to be able to stay superbly relaxed when you are standing at the edge of a high rooftop and have a fear of heights. *If reducing importance is not an option, you can at least avoid wasting energy on trying to relax.* This only increases your energy expenditure because as well as trying to control a critical situation, you are also holding back on what you feel which is totally futile. Instead *let go and worry to your heart's content!*

For the practice of Transurfing you have to be able to swiftly induce a relaxed state in any circumstances. This does not require any verbal self-suggestion because the muscles are governed by intention and not words. The majority of the body's muscles can be relaxed consciously simply by being aware of them. It can be enough to simply scan your body with your inner eye to release any contraction. We do not usually focus our attention on our muscles until we experience physical discomfort and so there will also be certain muscle groups that have forgotten how to obey intention. This is connected with the modern day, sedentary lifestyle that most people lead. For example, it is difficult to control the back muscles consciously and so with age people tend to develop back pain. However banal it may sound, it is absolutely essential to regularly stretch and exercise the back.

The whole procedure of inducing a relaxed state consists in the following. Without hurrying quickly scan your body with your inner eye and release any contraction. Focus your attention on the entire surface of your body in one go. Imagine that your skin is a membrane that suddenly and rapidly warms through from the inside out. Focus your attention on the surface of your body. Imagine this stage in any way you like: your skin is warming up, covered in a tingling sensation or electrical discharge. The important thing is to feel your skin. Now imagine that energy is sparkling all over the surface of your body like iridescence on a soap bubble. In this moment you are a part of the Universe and are in perfect balance with it. There is no need to try and simulate any special sensation. Everyone experiences these things differently. There is no need to try at all in fact. Do the exercise as if in passing but decisively nonetheless. The integral feeling you experience when you feel the entire surface of your body overflowing with energy is equivalent to a state of relaxation, balance and oneness with the world. After you have practiced the exercise a few times you will begin to achieve this state instantly and soon, inducing a relaxed state will be as easy as folding your arms.

Energy vampires

We are all swimming in an ocean of energy. But accessing this energy is not that simple because it is not differentially distributed in relation to man. To consciously access this energy a person has to intentionally widen their meridians and consciously draw the flow into the body. You drink water consciously and intentionally but are unable to draw in energy with the same clarity of sensation. People are in principle capable of intentionally "recharging" from the Cosmos but this ability remains limited to its embryonic stage.

It is much easier to absorb someone else's energy that has already been assimilated by the human body than to draw energy from the Cosmos. So-called energy vampires exploit this fact. The human form of energy is easy to assimilate because it has a specific frequency. To take someone else's energy it is enough to tune into their frequency in the same way that an oscillation circuit radio does not pick up all radio waves, but picks up on those for which it is configured. Vampires feed on energy that has already been assimilated by other people and to do this they attune themselves to the frequency of the energy their victim is emanating.

A vampire subconsciously finds various ways of attuning to the frequency of their victim's energy. An energy vampire may sidle up to you with innocent questions, stare you in the eyes, try to touch you, hold your hand or pester you with intrusive conversation. The energy vampire knows how to adapt and respond to character and temperament looking for a way of stealing into the victim's soul to get to their fraile. This is the behaviour of the "stealthy" vampire.

As a rule the energy vampire is a good psychologist, communicative but not charming, as well as tenaciously intrusive. Usually this comes across straight away although being aware that their behaviour is irritating the energy vampire will try very hard to present themselves in a different light.

Another type of vampire is the manipulator. As you know the manipulator plays on feelings of guilt. The manipulator vampire unconsciously seeks out people who are inclined to give themselves up to another's judgement or request advice when they are in a quandary. Anyone with the slightest guilt complex is likewise subconsciously searching for the one who will accuse and then immediately pardon them. Support and advice is sought by those who doubt their own convictions and are willing to give themselves up to another's judgement. So, the vampire and the donor find each other and fulfil each other's needs. The manipulator easily attunes to the frequency of its victim. The technique here is very simple: the manipulator has only to touch the surface of the problem that is worrying their victim and they will open up immediately making their energy freely available.

The third type of vampire, the "provocateur" is more coarse and aggressive. Without really thinking about it, this type makes a direct assault on the aura trying to throw its victim off balance. You already know very well how provocateurs behave. They will use all means available to them from implicit bullying to overt aggression. Their priority is to make the donor lose it, so that rudeness, irritation, resentment, fear and hostility gush from them. It does not really matter what the emotion is specifically…anything will do.

People become energy vampires unconsciously and their need to suck other people's energy is equally as unconscious. Throughout their life they notice that certain situations give them a lift, and sense of fulfilment, and they are compelled to recreate the experience. After a 'session' the vampire's donor usually feels very drained, so if after talking to someone you feel exposed, vulnerable, weak or shaky you can assume that your energy has been 'sucked'.

That said, it is pendulums that take the lion's share of free human energy. We have described how they do this already. Pendulums take energy through the importance meridian. Unlike the vampire that may pose a threat for a short period of time, pendulums can suck energy constantly the whole time a person is transmitting energy at the pendulum's frequency.

When something is worrying you or bringing you down your energy levels are weakened and other people and animals can intuit this on an energetic level. When your awareness and self-confidence are at a low point of all the other people walking along the street the dog will choose to bark furiously at you and the gypsy will choose you to pester and pressure into giving her your money. An energy vampire can take a good dosage of energy from you when your defences are low and you can easily find yourself drawn into a tricky situation.

There is no need to start looking out for potential energy vampires in everyone you meet. By being obsessively cautious you create access to your biofield. Strengthening your energy body, keeping an eye on your importance levels and developing conscious awareness will help protect you from negative influence.

A developed awareness will help you to remain conscious in the moment that someone tries to pull you into a game or a trap. Maintaining a low importance level makes it much harder for someone to attune to your frequency. You should also remain very aware of any feelings of guilt that might plague you. Whilst I am empty there is nothing for anyone to hook into. Most manipulator vampires will leave you alone if they have made one or two unsuccessful attempts to hook into you to no avail, and a strong auric field will provide you with reliable protection from any unwanted interference.

The Protective Shield

The human body is surrounded by an invisible energy field called an aura. The average person is not aware of feeling their aura but they can imagine it. To sense your aura feel the surface of your whole body like you do when you slide into a hot bath. Notice that I did not say: 'try to feel the surface of your body'. Just do it. When you dive straight in and do not assume that you must first try to do something before it will work, you will find that you can do it first time around and do not have to practice. Energy moves in a slow wave from the centre of your body and then spills over onto the surface forming a ball. Imagine being surrounded by the ball of your energy body. It does not matter that you cannot physically touch it. With your imagination alone you have taken the first step towards managing your energy body and with time you will begin to get a physical sense of it.

People who have psychic abilities can see auras as well as any defects in the aura. In fact, everyone is born with extrasensory perception abilities but they do not use them and so the talent lies dormant. Latent abilities can be awakened instantly or over a lengthy period of time by practising exercises. It is all a matter of the power of your intention. Of course, it is not easy to acquire the full power of intention, but for our purposes it is enough to have sufficient power of intention to keep your energy levels healthy. A weak aura will always leave you open to the possibility of assault upon your energy field.

You can develop and maintain healthy energy levels by regularly performing the following exercise. It is very simple and does not take up much time. First stand in a comfortable, relaxed position. Breathe in and imagine a flow of energy coming out of the ground, entering the perinea region and moving up the spine (roughly at the distance indicated above) exiting the head and extending upwards into the sky. Now breathe out and imagine that a flow of energy is descending from the sky. The flow of energy enters the head, moves along the spine and passes out and down into the ground. You do not necessarily have to have a sense of the physical flow of the energy. It is enough just to imagine it. With time your sensitivity will develop and you will learn to feel the energy moving.

Next imagine both currents moving towards each other simultaneously without crossing, each in its own meridian. At first practice on the in-breath and out-breath but after a while, try to let go of tying the flows of energy to the rhythm of your breathing. You can quicken the flow imbuing it with power using the strength of your imagination (intention). Now imagine that the ascending flow exits the body and pours downwards over the head in a fountain shape. Similarly, the descending flow exits the body and passes in the opposite direction directly under the feet. You now have two fountains, one above you and one below you. Mentally unite the spray of both fountains so that you are enveloped inside a sphere of energy. Then draw your attention to the surface of your body. Feel the surface of your skin and extend this same feeling out into the sphere like a balloon that gets bigger when you blow into it. When you mentally inflate the surface of your skin the sphere created by the meeting fountains of energy becomes firmly established. You should remain relaxed throughout the exercise and avoid creating tension by trying too hard to feel the energy physically.

Do not worry initially about not being able to get a physical sense of the central meridians. You are so used to them that you have stopped feeling them, just as you no longer feel any other healthy inner organ. From time to time practice regularly concentrating your attention on your energy currents and you will soon come to sense them physically, perhaps not with the same immediacy as touch, but tangibly nonetheless.

This is energy training. By joining the currents into a sphere you create a protective shield around your body. By extending the surface energy of the body into the sphere you strengthen the shield until it acquires a stable condition. This exercise is invaluable. Firstly, the shield protects your energy from being undermined. Secondly, by training your energy levels you cleanse the subtle meridians. The blocks that prevent the flow of energy dissipate, and the holes in the aura that cause energy to be lost close up. This is a gradual process. Nothing is going to happen just like that. On the other hand, you will save yourself from constantly having to seek the assistance of psychics and reflexologists being able to restore the healthy circulation of your energy independently.

You should be aware that of itself your energy body will not protect you from vampires and pendulums because the freeloaders pump energy by adjusting their settings to your frequency. When a pendulum tries to hook into its prey the victim's state of balance is undermined. In this moment, you have to wake up and reduce importance if you are to defeat the pendulum. Then the muscles will relax, your energy levels will be restored to a state of balance and the pendulum will fall through into emptiness. If you are not swaying the swaying pendulum cannot take your energy. Conscious awareness is essential if you are to develop control in moments when you involuntarily lose your inner balance.

Increasing Your Energy Levels

Increasing your energy levels does not involve accumulating large reserves of energy. This might sound a little strange because we are so used to popular phrases such as: "I do not have enough energy" or "I am full of energy". Only physiological energy can be stored. All you have to do is eat good food and get enough rest and the energy is stored as calories. However, the human body has no way of storing free energy which it takes from the Cosmos. If a person's meridians are wide enough they will run free energy but if they are narrow, the flow of energy will be impaired. So, high energy levels first and foremost depend on the width of the meridians.

Free energy is permanently present in a limitless quantity at every point of the field. You can literally take as much as you can carry. You have to learn to draw in free energy and experience yourself as part of the universe, and rather than doing it once you should work to establish a continuous feeling of oneness with the world around you on an energetic level.

People think that if they build up huge energy reserves they will become strong and successful. They try and accumulate energy as a way of preparing to impact the outside world with inner intention. As you already know, the attempt to alter or conquer the world by force is a difficult, fruitless, ineffective task that requires a huge expenditure of energy. Anyone who relies solely on inner intention in their interaction with the world thinks too highly of themselves, for in reality, we are all just a single drop in a massive ocean.

Outer intention does not try to change the world or fight it. Outer intention simply chooses what it needs from life. In the "alternatives space shop" outer intention does not need to haggle for goods or wrangle them out of the shop assistant. You do not have to build up energy to work with outer intention because it is superabundant and all-present. We are practically swimming in it. To focus on deliberately accumulating energy is like swimming in a lake and filling your cheeks to keep some water in reserve just in case the lake water runs out. *Do not try to accumulate energy; just allow it to pass freely through you in the form of two counter directional currents.* It can be helpful to imagine these two currents joining in counter directional fountains, but that is all you need to do.

Do not strive to become a bundle of energy; rather, imagine yourself to be a drop in the ocean. Allow your consciousness to feel that it is an integral part of the Universe, in oneness with it and then its entire energy will be at your disposal. Rather than accumulating energy in your body, merge with the energy of the universe. Expand your sphere of energy and dissolve it into the space around retaining the awareness that in form you are a separate particle. Then, by just touching on outer intention with your little finger you will achieve in a short period of time things that would never have been possible to achieve with the power of inner intention. I am talking of course about achieving your personal goals, not the intention to rearrange someone's face; for one's immediate needs can only really be met by the power of inner intention.

A person should have plenty of free energy if their meridians are not restricted. The meridians suffer two major limitations: the body getting clogged up, and continual stress. Energy cannot flow freely if the body is toxic and stress causes the meridians to narrow even further. When the meridians are compromised short bursts of energy are usually followed by long periods of recovery. This makes it difficult for a person to live a full active life, instead of just eking out a measured existence.

As a person gets older they stop developing; life takes on a slower rhythm. Work with the meridians all but comes to a halt and the meridians gradually atrophy. The meridians are worked at times when life requires you to power intention to its highest level of intensity. We stimulate intention and consequently our meridians when we work towards vital goals, but as soon as the main peaks have been taken, the bar of intention is gradually lowered. The time comes when all you want to do in the evenings (and perhaps during the day too) is to sink into an armchair in front of the television. The meridians narrow, the energy of intention fades and life becomes a burden not a joy.

Fortunately, this can all be easily put to rights in a way that does not involve forcing your intention to conquer new peaks. *Meridians can be developed by doing energy exercises.* The positive effect will be compounded the more that you tune in to the feeling of your central energy currents and subtle body. This condition has a number of advantages. It helps induce a feeling of balance and harmony with the world; it increases your sensitivity to changes in the environment and enables you to easily go with the flow; it plugs you into the information field, an unlimited source of creativity; it gives you access to the energy of the cosmos; you radiate harmonious energy, which creates an oasis of prosperity and success around you. Most importantly, it keeps you functioning at the meeting point between heart and mind, bringing you closer to outer intention. Your ability to direct outer intention develops which means that your desires are met more quickly and more easily.

You can begin the process of change by turning on the energy fountains from time to time during the day and trying to strengthen them by picturing them in your mind, without trying too hard. If during the exercise your head begins to feel heavy it means the ascending flow is stronger than the descending current. Focus your attention on the descending current and strengthen it slightly. The energy currents have to be balanced so that they meet half way up the body. From this point in the body mentally picture the currents radiating throughout the energy sphere and your sense of the subtle body should become clearer. You should experience an integral feeling of the ascending and descending currents together with a sense of your entire energy body.

If you concentrate your attention on the descending current your energy centre will shift downwards and vice versa; if you concentrate on the ascending current your energy will accumulate in the upper part of the body. Aside from this, your physical centre of gravity will shift in accordance with your energy centre. You can use this quality to your advantage in sport. If you require good stability in the legs such as in skiing you can strengthen the descending current, whereas if you need to jump high you can work on strengthening the ascending current. Martial arts masters have a good understanding of the quality of energy currents in the body. There are other types of energy masters who can stay so firmly fixed to a certain spot when they are concentrating on the descending current that it is impossible to move them. And likewise, there are energy masters who can concentrate on the ascending current and jump to unimaginable heights.

You can practice paying attention to the central meridians when doing any kind of physical exercise. Just do not try too hard. Being overly diligent never pays off. From time to time turn your inner sight to the area just in front of the spine. Imagine the ascending current rising and the descending current moving downwards. If you regularly practice running your central meridians you will gradually develop the skill of feeling them. It might seem as if some movements are totally at odds with how you are visualising your energy. Be patient. With time you will learn to easily correlate any movement with a sense of your energy flow.

Concentrating your attention on the central meridians during weight training can significantly increase your energy levels. During the exertion stage of a lift focus your attention on the muscles. Then when you make the opposite movement and the muscles relax shift your attention to the central meridians. The moment of relaxing the muscles should be held for one or two seconds to give sufficient time to feel the movement of energy.

Take pulling on the bar as an example. At the start of the lift the breath is held, then the lift is completed and followed by an out-breath. Attention is focused on the exertion. Then on the return there is an in-breath, the muscles relax and attention shifts to the central meridians. During the return imagine your energy moving simultaneously in both directions. You should fully extend the arms and hang with arms relaxed for one to two seconds. At this point you should clearly sense the flow of energy as if it had been suddenly freed and was gradually beginning to move. Do not try to quicken the flow of energy when the muscles are relaxed. Let go and allow the currents to pass freely.

In contrast, the central meridians can be pushed with force when doing press ups. Once you have positioned your hands on the floor with your elbows bent, on the out-breath mentally picture pushing the energy hard. Do the in-breath and out-breath in any order you feel comfortable with to avoid creating unnecessary tension but as in the majority of strength-building exercises the breath is held or the out-breath is made at the exertion stage and an in-breath at the relaxed stage.

You stimulate the strengthening of the meridians just by giving them your attention. Alternate contraction and relaxation will stimulate them still further if you direct your attention properly. At the stage of contraction the meridians stop and tighten like springs. During relaxation the springs straighten and the power of the energy flow increases. After contraction accumulated, compressed energy is released and literally forces its way through the central meridians.

Increasing your energy levels not only gives you more vitality, it increases your power of influence. The quality of your energy becomes richer which can be very useful when you need to influence or persuade someone of something. Techniques exist that enable a person to exert dominant energetic influence over others. However, these techniques contradict the principle of Transurfing which asserts that we have the right to choose but not the right to change things. The world does not need to be pressured or fought and taking this approach is a highly ineffective way of achieving your goals. As you know, the world usually responds to being pressured by pressuring in return.

The higher your energy levels the better people will treat you because subconsciously they will sense your energy and even to some extent benefit from it. However, the majority of people do not feed on personal energy deliberately like pendulums do. It is as if they are simply swimming in your energy because your 'fountains' are abundantly overflowing.

People inevitably become well-disposed towards you because you are providing them with a source of excess energy. People are so used to giving their energy away to pendulums that they are always delighted to be on the receiving end. So-called magnetic or charismatic personalities are one such source. It is hardly surprising that people like this are said to have an inexplicable charm or magnetism. What would you find more attractive, a pool of stagnating water or a pure spring? There is no need to worry that other people are using your energy. The small quantity of excess energy you give away to others will only work in your favour.

When you are waiting for a very important meeting, abandon importance and activate your central meridians until they are flowing in fountains. When your energy is running well, you do not need half as many clever words and convincing arguments. Simply turn on the fountains.

By drawing free energy towards you and letting it pass through your energy body you make the same energy available to others. They will be able to feel it on a subconscious level and without being aware of the reason they will feel well-disposed towards you. The secret of your charm will be a mystery to them.

The Energy of Intention

As we said at the beginning, energy enters the human body in the form of central currents of energy flow which are programmed by a person's thoughts and on exiting the body adopt the same parameters as that person's thoughts. The programmed energy builds up in the corresponding sector of the alternatives space which causes that reality alternative to be realized materially. The programming is appropriate only if the heart and mind are one, otherwise the thought energy is like radio frequency interference.

You can fulfil basic actions in the material world with the power of inner intention but the material realisation of a potential reality in the alternatives space can only be powered by outer intention, generated when the heart and mind are united in their aspirations. *The power of outer intention is proportional to your energy levels.* Outer intention is total commitment combined with high energetic potential.

Energy levels can be increased by training the central meridians and cleansing the body. Transurfing also recommends another excellent technique to widen the channels – *visualising the process.*

You need to have some initial intention to increase the energy of intention. The technique involves the following affirmation: my channels are widening and my intention energy is increasing. During the energy exercise visualise the affirmation as a process. As you know, the essence of the visualisation technique lies in the statement that: today is better than yesterday and tomorrow will be better than today. Switch on your energy fountains and repeat the affirmation in your mind that your intention energy is increasing with every passing day. This way, intention will support itself and your energy levels will increasingly rise.

Do not forget, that the intention to improve your biofield must be purified of importance and desire potentials. Diligence and gusto in the attempt to enhance the energy flow will cause the reverse and create a block. *Intention relies on focus, not gusto.* It is only by focusing on the process that you achieve the desired result. Performing the exercises with maximum effort is a waste of time and energy if the mind is busy dreaming of something else whilst you are doing them. Loosen the grip of diligence and focus on action.

The Step of Intention

Imagine an average newborn brought into a society where people age very slowly and live to the age of around three hundred years old. How long do you think the child will live for? What I am trying to say is that from birth people are taught the standard script that health deteriorates with age, the body withers and in the end, we all die which can undoubtedly be explained by standard physiological causes.

However, if you look at the ageing process from the point of view of Transurfing it is really just another induced transition. You could even say that ageing is the lengthiest induced transition we experience occurring slowly but very surely. The ageing script is so familiar and obvious that it would never occur to anyone to doubt it. All attempts to change the script have been reduced to the discovery of all sorts of elixirs. Even the achievements of contemporary pharmacology and genetics fail to deliver tangible results.

One can only conclude that the physiological factor comprises just one portion of the ageing process. Exactly what portion the induced transition accounts for is impossible to say, but that does not really matter. The important thing is to be conscious of the fact that the transition exists.

From early childhood we are convinced that the ageing process is inevitable. Over the course of a person's life they receive endless confirmation of the ageing process from their own personal experience and the experience of others. At every birthday celebration theatrical demonstrations of good wishes are made calling for good health and longevity but everyone knows that these good wishes mean nothing and have absolutely no impact on the script. On the contrary, translated into the language of fact what these well meaning words are really saying is that your health is far from what it used to be and the years are passing. These are the slight oscillations or flirtations of a destructive pendulum.

Sooner or later you will begin to feel that ten years or so ago you had so much more strength and energy. You will want to share these thoughts with someone else. That someone will instantly appear to enthusiastically develop the topic of conversation. The theme of illness is no less popular in polite small talk now than the weather. By participating in such conversations you radiate energy at the same frequency as the destructive pendulum, i.e. you agree to play the game.

The pendulum may send you a prod in the form of exhaustion or malaise. Your condition will worry you deeply and you think to yourself: "I must be unwell". This is your response to the pendulum's sway. Having received a bout of energy the pendulum prods you again, making it hurt even more. You go to the doctor who confirms your illness and the process continues to unfold. The pendulum receives energy and sways even harder. By the time the crisis hits, the pendulum will already have taken everything it can take leaving you alone to begin your recovery, if of course the induced transition has not thrown its 'victim' onto an invalid life line.

Does this mean that you should not go to the doctor or take any medicine and should refuse all help in coping with your illness? No. To refuse a possible cure for an illness that has reached a developed stage is irresponsible and reckless and certainly no way to leave the game. The issue is how to avoid being drawn into the game in the first place.

You may comment to a colleague: "I have not seen you for a while. Why were not you at work?", to which your colleague will undoubtedly answer: "I was ill". Note that they do not say they were *healing,* they say they were *ill.* To the question "What is wrong?" the answer will be: "I am ill". Of course, it would sound unnatural to answer these questions with: "I was (am) healing". People are so used to playing the Illness game that cure is seen as an attribute or side effect of the game but not a goal in its own right.

The pendulum's game begins with you willingly accepting the symptoms of the illness, in other words, gripping the end of the spiral of an induced transition. The pendulum's first push can be defeated if you do not take the symptoms seriously, quietly turn away and there and then and forget about them. If that does not work you can still the pendulum's sway by taking basic preventive measures. If you do get sick, play the Treatment game, not the Illness game.

To play the Illness game means to suffer passively, to take part in conversations about various maladies, to whinge, complain and capriciously demand care and sympathy from those around you; to consider your malaise an indispensable attribute; to flaunt your ill-health like a child that must be constantly fussed over; and to eagerly seek out information connected with various ailments.

To play the healing game means to take active interest in possible cures, to make efforts to live a healthy lifestyle, to treat your illness with humour and to focus your attention on improving how you feel, striving towards health and communicating with like-minded individuals.

You can see that these are two totally different games. In the illness game you participate in the role of passive victim radiating energy at the frequency of the destructive pendulum. The vortex of the induced transition drags you ever closer towards its centre. In the healing game you participate as a proactive creator and master of your own life, ruling your own destiny and thereby shifting onto healthy life lines.

If you are already trying to play the Healing game ask yourself whether you are playing it sufficiently sincerely. The problem is that it is so easy to kid yourself. You might know in your mind that you should be leading a healthy lifestyle, giving up bad habits, getting more physical exercise and eating good foods etc., but in reality, old habits die hard. You try to follow the rules of a healthy lifestyle because you know it will be good for you, but in the end, laziness gets in the way and you just cannot be bothered.

That is not a clean game. That is the "I am ill and they will make me better" game. On an energetic level this game is no different from the Illness game because you are playing at healing from a position of duress rather than personal conviction. When the intention is neither clean nor sincere the results will be the same.

Attempts made by representatives of the fairer sex to lose weight are a perfect illustration of a tainted game. They torture themselves with diets forcing themselves to do the unwanted to get rid of the weight ("I am ill, but they will heal me"). They abhor their weight and figure which as you know, is the perfect requirement to radiate energy at the frequency of lines where their weight and figure will be exactly the way they currently feel about them. Women do not actually like their diets. They would much rather have the food they usually eat. If this is the game you are playing, abandon self-coercion. At best it will bring temporary, minor results. Self-coercion frightens the subconscious which makes it resist. In the end, the subconscious will have its own way, so you can expect to ditch the diet and gain even more weight than before.

The only conclusion worth drawing is that if you want to be healthy and beautiful you have to change your lifestyle. This means giving up old habits and acquiring new ones, not from necessity but from a place of conviction. You must have strong motivation and intention and your intention must be pure. You cannot hope to radiate energy at the frequency of healthy life lines or to transition to these life lines if you do the same as you have always done. It is not as difficult as it might seem to make a change in lifestyle. Changing old habits is a matter of intention and time, and not much time at that. The choice is yours.

Illness Pendulums

Everyone has been ill as some point in their life. Being ill usually brings a mass of problems and anxieties with it making one prone to negative thoughts and emotions. This energy then emanates through your personal space providing fertile soil for the development of pendulum related illnesses that absorb negative energy so efficiently.

Pendulums generated by illness are among the most powerful of all pendulums. They are primarily the diseases and epidemics themselves as well as the various pendulums of the medical world that stand in opposition to them. You can imagine what influential structures these encompass: whole clinics, sanatoriums, research agencies, factories, pharmacies, educational institutions...

The medical pendulums declare their goal to be the battle against disease. In practice, this battle generates a massive spectrum of negative phenomena characteristic of destructive pendulums, because their main idea is still to hold onto existing adherents and attract new ones.

For example, classical medicine is hostile to all traditional healing methods (i.e. any method not belonging to it). Any criticism of outdated or mistaken ideas originating from adherents of alternative healing methods is automatically proclaimed unscientific. Any new age healing method will be met with extreme cynicism. In turn, adherents of alternative medicine have nothing against throwing the odd stone into the garden of the orthodox should it come to that.

No-one gripped by the leverage of an illness or medicine pendulum can reclaim the feeling of their youth, or the time in their life when health related issues were the last thing on their mind. If your health is not causing you any problems you just do not give it any thought and consequently, your energy lacks the kind of frequency characteristic of illness pendulums.

To one degree or another everyone becomes gradually more susceptible to pendulums with age. Once you begin radiating energy at the frequency of the pendulum you lose energy and create dependency which facilitates your transition to life lines saturated with illness. To reclaim your former state of health all ties with pendulums must be cut. To cut the ties you have to block any information generated by illness pendulums and refuse to participate in their games, i.e. applying the approach of defeating the pendulum. If you are seriously ill you should play the Healing game and care for your whole body, i.e. applying the approach of stilling the pendulum's sway.

Every day, drug companies show advertisements featuring happy people depending on a certain medicine for their health and because they have their health they are highly successful in all areas of their life. It is a tempting carrot and works every time because, as we have already discussed, the majority of people live their lives in a semi-conscious state. Your brain is programmed to: "go to the chemist, take the medicine and receive your reward: complete order in all your affairs". But that is the least of it. There is another deeper, more insidious program that is subtly planted into the advertising.

Think about it: The people shown in the adverts are generally normal, attractive and thoroughly successful individuals. (Are they really any better than you?) All these individuals have some kind of health problem but quickly recover thanks to the medicine they are taking. (And you are the same!) It is drummed into our conscious and subconscious minds that we are all either predisposed to illness, are already sick or will soon come down with something and most people accept these game conditions. This is the true face as opposed to the declared face of the destructive pendulum. Its true task is not to cure the individual but to claim them as an adherent, to successfully convey the idea that they are ill and therefore, must take their medicine.

Another curious method used to attract adherents is a poor weather forecast. The core of the forecast is made up of information on magnetic storms, fluctuations in atmospheric pressure and other adverse factors. (Note that these phenomena occur to one degree or another practically on a daily basis.) A prognosis is then formed on the basis of these data detailing which health issues will be most affected by the weather conditions and who can expect to particularly suffer that day or the next. At first it is amusing to hear the pendulum almost chocking its way through the list of illnesses and inevitable consequences for those who suffer from them. Then it seems freakishly disturbing as it dawns on you what terribly destructive thought patterns are being programmed into the minds of conscious and less conscious individuals who are already unwell. When you hear such a negative prognosis you might think that it would be better not to go out of the house at all and that you might as well get ready to climb into your own grave. It is natural that adverse factors will have some effect on our health but why create the expectation from the very outset? Many people, particularly the elderly listen to the pendulum's effusions and program themselves beforehand for ailments and aggravations as if they had been sentenced to suffering. The weather forecast and its prognosis for ill health is a perfect illustration of the pendulums' brazen and cynical desire to subjugate people to its will.

The most classical topic is the conversations we have with friends and relatives about our health. As a rule the conversation does not focus on the theme of strengthening one's health. It centres around the theme of illness and medication. One gleefully describes how they suffer from various ailments and the other readily grunts in response that this is what happens when you get a bit long in the tooth. People who participate in this kind of conversation actively radiate energy at the frequency of illness pendulums and their energy is just as infectious as pathogenic microbes. Avoid this kind of company otherwise the frequencies of illness will unexpectedly creep up on you.

It is easy to spot an illness pendulum. *It lures you with information about various diseases and their treatments*. If you decide to ignore the information and let it pass by you without taking it so seriously the pendulum will be discouraged and leave you alone. This is its defeat. If you respond to the information with healthy laughter and take a couple of digs at it the pendulum will bolt in terror in the opposite direction. This is the stilling of the pendulum's sway.

By parting with illness pendulums you become completely free, but the freedom does not last for long. It is human nature to want to become the adherent of one pendulum or another and so sooner or later you will again risk falling under the influence of their illnesses. To protect yourself you have to shift out of the state of limbo that can set in once you have sided with recovery pendulums that govern everything related to strengthening the body and spirit. Become an adherent of a healthy lifestyle and you will see how joyful and exciting it is compared with the dull, burdensome battle with disease.

Obviously if a person consistently takes good care of themselves they will radiate energy at the frequency of healthy life lines and be far too busy to have anything to do with illness. You can see that there are two completely contrasting life styles: one based on healing illness and the other on looking after your health. Clearly, in relation to ill-health the first relates to inner intention and the second to outer intention. Which lifestyle you will live is entirely your choice.

SUMMARY

Physiological energy is spent on the execution of physical action.

Intention depends on free energy.

Free energy passes through the body in two opposing currents.

The energy of intention is blocked when you are stressed.

To get rid of stress, wake up and drop importance.

If reducing importance is not possible there is no point in wasting energy trying to relax.

You can strengthen your protective shield by performing energy exercises.

Do not try and accumulate energy just let it freely pass through you.

High energy levels depend on wide central meridians.

Performing energy exercises is an effective way of strengthening the meridians.

Cleansing the body will significantly widen the meridians.

Inner intention is focused on being ill and getting better.

Outer intention is focused on leading a healthy lifestyle.

Never accept the game of destructive illness pendulums.

During the exercises pay attention to the central meridians.

Intention lies in focused concentration not gusto and diligence.

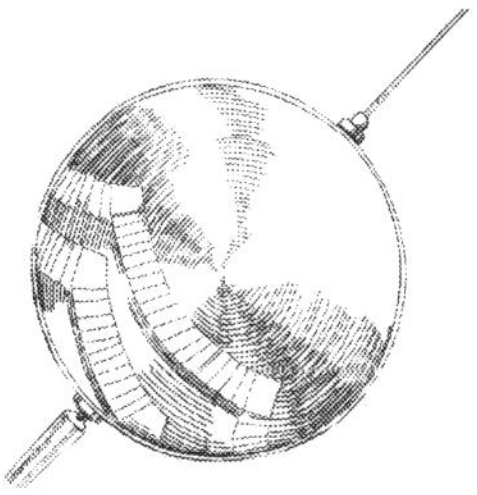

Chapter XII. FRAILING

Abandon the intention of receiving; replace it with the intention of giving, and you will receive the very thing you gave up.

Intention in Relationships

We tend to measure our success in life on the one hand by the level of our achievements and on the other, by the volume of problems we have amassed. Transurfing helps us not to fight problems and rather than how to solve them, how to avoid coming up against them in the first place. In the context of Transurfing, our goals are also achieved in an uncommon way with the help of outer intention. One way or another, all our problems and achievements are born of our relationships with other people, personal and professional.

The question is: can outer intention be applied to relationships? The trouble is that outer intention is elusive, difficult to control or subject to personal will. However, there are techniques you can use to activate its function implicitly. With a certain approach, outer intention can be set in motion so that it works independently, irrespective of your will, but nonetheless, in your favour.

Instead of working with personal inner intention you can learn to work with the inner intention that motivates others. If you let go of your own inner intention, outer intention will activate the workings of inner intention in others. Outer intention can give you what you want in life with the simple wave of a hand because it does not want anything for itself, and it does not particularly have to do anything. It simply allows inner intention which is attuned to the frequencies of the external world to work unhindered. *Use other people's inner intention to achieve your goals.*

Despite how selfish this last phrase may sound, it does not actually mean that you are using or abusing other people. It is more a matter of not getting in the way of letting them do what they really want to do. At the end of the day, all problems arise due to a conflict of interests surrounding inner intention. Motivated by personal interest one person tries to get something from another, who has different plans and is intent on having things their own way. How can different interests be balanced and the needs of both fulfilled? It is a difficult task is it not? And yet, it is not really; it comes down to finding the common ground in each other's inner intentions.

A sense of self worth lies at the core of inner intention. In the world of pendulums the only things that truly motivate a person, at the same time as limiting their freedom, are inner and outer intention. Our sense of self-worth is linked with inner importance. As informational energy entities, pendulums are created by groups of people and later continue to exist independently, finally subjecting people to their own laws. The pendulums use importance to establish their control. This is why for the majority of people, enhancing their sense of self-worth is a key determinant in the formation of their intentions. Other determinants relate to fraile, and the needs of the heart but to a much lesser extent. As a rule, fraile accounts for a very minor portion of our motivations and is poorly developed, muffled by the constant need to maintain one's self-esteem in a world based on pendulums.

To activate the power of outer intention in human relationships you have to first break down one more false belief. You may often hear what would appear to be very appropriate advice: "if trying to change others does not work, start by changing yourself." This saying immediately evokes a feeling of inner discomfort and protest: so I am imperfect and need to change, but I so do not want to!" And quite right that you do not want to! *Do not try to change others, but do not try to change yourself either.* Whatever you do to try and change yourself or others will be the ineffective and harmful work of inner intention. Problems can be better solved using a different approach. *Allow others to realise their inner intention.* The act of allowing will stir outer intention which will cause your inner intention to be realised seemingly of its own accord.

Imagine a woman who is itching to get married but for reasons she cannot understand her husband is resisting and fobbing her off with excuses. Working with inner intention the woman focuses all her thoughts on trying to persuade her partner to get married. Pressuring him will not resolve the situation and she will end up creating excess potential with her powerful desire and the importance she attributes to getting married. As a result, balanced forces will no doubt steal her loved one away. So what was the problem? Maybe her partner was not committed to the relationship or was no longer in love with her? Of course not. The woman transformed their love relationship into a dependent relationship making marriage the deal-breaker: "If you loved me you would agree to marry me".

For outer intention to work the woman would have to let go of her attachment to persuade her partner to marry her and ask herself: what does a man look for in a marriage? The answer is not difficult to find. He undoubtedly wants to know that his needs will be met and that he will feel loved, valued, respected and admired etc. If the woman were to direct her energy towards helping him meet these needs she would not only meet her own goal but would succeed in having her own similar needs met. What if you feel the man in question does not deserve your love and respect? Well, why be with someone in the first place if you feel that way about them? Everyone is free to choose.

As you can see, *there is no need to change yourself.* The thing is that the open window is in a different place than where we usually look for it. As a rule people are so consumed with what they want to get from others that they do not bother to find out what those other people want. By shifting your attention to the desires and motivations of others you will easily find your own needs met. All it takes is for you to ask yourself *what the focus is of your partner's inner intention.* This is effectively like flying backwards from the pane of glass and finally spotting the open window. Next, all that remains is to *refocus your inner intention on realising your partner's inner intention.* By doing this you transform your personal inner intention into outer intention.

Very often inner intention is aimed at attracting attention and presenting oneself in the best possible light or you may be worried about something that is not going very well. Imagine that you are going to a party. You may imagine that all the other people invited will have their eyes on you and be aware of where you are all the time; for they have gathered with the sole purpose of discussing what you are wearing, how you move and what you talk about. If you were to hear someone in the group laughing you would assume they were laughing at you and you would catch so many disparaging looks! I sympathise!

You have of course twigged, that the situation should be interpreted in the opposite way. Everyone else at the party is primarily concerned with themselves and what other people think about them. How they treat other people is the last thing on their mind. So, you can relax, take it easy and feel free. Do not try to act with a lack of pretension or affectation; just gift yourself the quality of naturalness and ease.

Remember, that setting yourself the *goal of acting in an unaffected manner* does not work. Of course, you might get somewhere with the help of slides but that takes time and the party is today. You can only achieve a state of being unaffected if you eliminate importance. However, reducing importance is not always easy. You will not be able to totally abandon the desire to present yourself in the best possible light just like that in an instant.

The solution is simple. When someone is talking to you what they need most is for you to give them your attention and show an interest in them as a person. You can be quite certain that people are exclusively interested in themselves, *so be interested in them too.* Shift your attention from yourself to others. Activate your Guardian and *stop playing the game of enhancing your own self-worth. Play the game of increasing the significance of others.* Show an interest in other people, listen to what they have to say and observe. You do not need to curry their favour, just go with the flow. As soon as you shift your attention from self to others the excess potential of your own importance will fade automatically. Then you will succeed in behaving naturally.

You attract attention to yourself, by showing interest in others. Do not talk to people about what you are interested in, talk to them about what they are interested in, including themselves. Then your inner intention will be transformed into outer intention. Other people will immediately become interested in making your acquaintance. They will have nowhere to retreat from the power of your outer intention, which is always completely subtle in its workings. It is useless trying to get people interested in your own being. This desire is a reflection of inner intention. Showing interest in others is a reflection of outer intention. By abandoning inner intention and switching your attention to other people, you effortlessly achieve the result you wanted initially; only outer intention has done it for you.

You may wonder how you can attract attention to yourself by showing interest in others thinking: "OK, so I show some curiosity. Will this really make me seem a more interesting person?" The thing is, that even if you were a thousand times more attractive than you are now, other people would still be primarily interested in themselves, and only interested in others as an afterthought. All the time that you are trying to attract attention you are thinking solely of yourself. *When you show interest in another person, you fulfil their inner intention.* Where does their feeling of fulfilment come from if not from you, and having realised that, who else would that person then be interested in if not you?

People are interested in other people when they are well-known personalities, like the stars of show business and the cinema. But this is a different kind of interest. Unless you are a film star, people look at you as a potential partner for business, friendship or love. Fanatics are extreme in their fascination with the stars, swooning over them, gobbling up every tiny detail of their lives, but it would never enter their mind to consider the celebrity as a potential partner in a personal relationship. *In everyday communication it does not matter how interesting you are. What matters is how well the other person thinks you would suit them in a relationship* and this is what they are evaluating whilst communicating with you.

When a person is with you they are generally thinking of their own interests and consciously and unconsciously evaluating how well you would fit a relationship script in which they feel personally fulfilled. A person feels fulfilled when their sense of self-worth is confirmed: they feel liked, interesting, respected, as worthy as anyone else and valued.

Now consider what the result would be of imposing yourself on someone in one case and showing interest in someone in another. Naturally, you will fit all their criteria if you fulfil their need for confirmation of their own self-worth. If you are good for a person's self-esteem they will be lenient to any evident failings you may have and forgive your weaknesses; you may be concerned with your shortcomings, trying to cover them up and put your best qualities forward, but this is the last thing on the other person's mind. I repeat, your positive qualities and failings are not your partner's prime concern. *The sense of self-worth they experience when talking to you however, is their utmost priority.*

You might be 'gorgeous' in all respects but that will not help you in the search for a friend or partner. On the contrary, many stars suffer from loneliness. Your superb qualities may even set limitations on your search for a partner. People can see your full 'gorgeousness' but *first and foremost they are evaluating to what extent they will feel significant standing next to your perfection.* If you shine before them in all your glory they will probably decide that their personality can only fade in the glaring light. Wave your hand at all your fabulous qualities and give your full attention to the person facing you. Make them feel that when they stand next to you they will know their true worth, and you will steal their heart.

When you are talking to someone and displaying an interest in them do it with sincerity. Do not let them feel that you are trying to win their favour by manipulating them with a learned psychological technique, or that you have a hidden agenda. If you care enough to want a certain person to be well-disposed towards you, then at the very least, they deserve your sincerity.

People who present themselves as an interesting conversationalist try to show themselves in the best possible light by proving how clever they are, and dropping names to show how much they have seen and experienced in life. This way of acting is inner intention directed, and this is how the majority of people behave when they want to appear interesting to others. Take a step back from the uniformity and take a different stance. Set yourself the task of *giving your partner the opportunity to appear interesting* rather than trying to be an entertaining conversant. Adjust to their frequency and listen attentively, asking questions and showing interest in your partner's chosen topic of conversation and their life. You will find that you can support a conversation in this way for up to several hours with your partner doing most of the talking. Towards the end of your conversation they will be *absolutely convinced* that they have met a very interesting confidante and a wonderful person all round.

Outer intention works by allowing the inner intention of others to be fulfilled. You sacrifice putting your own personality in the spot light to allow the personality of another to shine; a*nd as a result you receive the very thing you sacrificed.* The person in question will be won over instantly and become an avid fan because you have allowed them to fulfil their inner intention; something they would never experience in the company of a celebrity.

What can you do if you wish to gain the attention of a person who does not currently wish to enter into dialogue with you such as the person you would like to accept your business proposal who is not remotely interested. In a situation such as this there is all the more reason to believe that you will only gain their interest by putting yourself and your proposal to one side and giving them your full attention. Take a genuine interest in everything that person is involved in, and take time to talk to them. Only then will they show any interest in your problem.

You may ask why you should have to listen to others, take an interest in their life, give them your attention, and love and respect, when they are completely self-centered and cannot even be bothered to talk to you. Ok, well, why should they take an interest, admire, love and respect you? Everything you imagine to be true about yourself, how wonderful you are and oh how wonderful in comparison to them, is just a fantasy of inner intention clothed in the excess potential of dependent and importance relationships. Your inner intention is to be worthy but *you will only become genuinely significant in the eyes of others if you abandon your inner intention and allow the inner intention of others to be fulfilled instead.* Your advantage lies in the fact that you are outer intention directed whereas others are the inner intention directed. Make the most of your advantage.

Generally speaking, when you want something from someone you should bear one universal principle in mind: let go of the inner intention to *receive* and substitute it with the intention to give. It is very easy to do.

If you want someone to respect and acknowledge you, do not wait for their respect. Treat them with respect on your part. Make them feel that in your eyes they are important. If what you need is compassion and gratitude, do not expect others to give these things to you. Participate in other people's problems and look after them with sincerity. If you want to be thought attractive it will not happen just on account of a pair of beautiful eyes. Show someone else that you find them attractive by definition. If you need help and support be the one to help someone else. That way you increase your worth and will not be the one left owing. Finally, if you want to find mutual love abandon possessiveness and dependent relationships. You will find love if you can be the one just doing the loving without expecting anything in return. This kind of love is very rare and no-one can resist it. In all these cases *you will inevitably receive the very thing you let go off.*

There is one more question: how can you make someone do what you need them to do. You can force a person to do something with inner intention if you are in the necessary position of power. You can also persuade a person that it is essential that they do something. However, outer intention offers the most effective method: arrange things in such a way that the person wants to help you. Arrange things so that it corresponds to their goals and aspirations. *Ask yourself how you can connect what you want with another person's needs.*

Start by defining the other person's needs, what they strive for, what they lack, be it money power, the respect of others, a sense of fulfilment from work well done, care for their children, prestige, a leading role in their team, social recognition, etc. All these things are variations on the theme of self-worth.

Everyone feels bad about themselves when they feel they are of little significance to the world. When a person does not feel needed or worth anything they naturally try and increase their sense of self-worth. When a person achieves a result they feel more confident and ready to set new tasks as the bar of their self-worth is raised. There is nothing wrong with this. No-one should be judged for their desire to feel more worthy. Everyone is trying to increase their sense of self-worth, they just go about it in different ways. On the contrary, it is much worse when a person stops developing and does not want anything at all although this happens very rarely. Usually, people are in some way dissatisfied with their current position in life and so strive for something however modest.

So, work out how the task that is important to you might improve that person's sense of self-worth. Then, *present the task to them in the context of how it would increase their stature.* Allow a person to feel more valued and they will experience greater faith in themselves. When they do, be generously appreciative of them.

If you let yourself be guided by this principle you will easily prompt other people to act in their interest. Directed by inner intention you may try and force or cajole someone into doing something. Directed by outer intention you simply express the desire for everything to work out in your favour. To fulfil outer intention you have to arrange things in such a way that people act in your interests whilst thinking about their own concerns and doing what is important to them. All you have to do is wake up, drag yourself away from your own interests and think about the needs of others.

For example, if you are involved in retail you will be thinking about how you can *sell* your products to potential customers. The buyer however, will not be thinking about how to please you and neither do they wish to be sold to. They want *to buy*. Can you see the difference? The buyer is more likely to be thinking: "I wish everyone would stop trying to flog things to me and just let me choose what I want to buy."

Do not think about how to sell your products. Think about what the buyer might want to purchase. The desire to sell is a reflection of inner intention. Outer intention takes a totally different approach which is *to find out what the buyer wants*. You do not necessarily have to know what product the buyer wants exactly. If they suffer from rheumatism and you take a genuine interest in them by recommending a doctor or form of treatment, the buyer will make their purchase from you. This is an over-simplified example of course but the principle is infallible.

Every time you need something from someone or need to have them do something, let go of inner intention. Ask yourself what the other person's inner intention might be. Act in a way that assists that person in fulfilling inner intention. Once you are already helping someone else to fulfil their inner intention consider casually what you need from that person. Whilst you are busy realising the other person's intention, make your request in passing. You might find that you do not even have to hint at your own need and everything unfolds of its own accord. This is the magical power of outer intention.

An even more effective way of influencing other people is to try and induce their inner intention. When you break it down step by step, the method is quite simple. Enhancing one's sense of self-worth almost always serves as the motivation for another intention. Everyone is trying to emphasize and increase their sense of self-worth to one degree or another and by one means of another. If you need something from someone all you have to do is think of how doing what you require of them would increase their sense of self-worth. This is what they call issuing a challenge.

You can issue a challenge to a group as well as an individual in the form of: "So, who among you is the best?" If you are playing on feelings of professional honour then the challenge may sound: "Let's not lose face!" You can also appeal to inner importance: "Let's show them what we are made of!" *If a person accepts the challenge in the context of their self-worth they will carry out your will as if it were their own* and you will have their commitment precisely because you have abandoned your own inner intention and paid attention to that of another. *Work with other peoples' inner intention, not your own.*

The Flow of Relationships

Most people or companies produce some kind of product for consumption. So, how do you motivate consumers to want to buy your product? If you think they will choose yours simply because it is such a fantastic product you are sadly mistaken. A typical mistake people make when they are directed by inner intention is to assume the standpoint that: "People are bound to buy our product because ours is a masterpiece".

This position is flawed on three accounts. Firstly, the phrase "ours is a masterpiece" is strongly directed by inner importance. You assume your creation is perfect, which means that it is important to you, and if this is the case, you will not be able to evaluate it objectively because you are not sufficiently indifferent. Secondly, inner intention is aimed at *selling,* but people will not want to buy because, in their eyes, your creation is not a masterpiece at all, and someone else's intention *to sell* is of no interest to them whatsoever. Finally, the greatest mistake of this approach directed by inner intention is that it centres around the product, rather than the customers' needs. The narrow focus of inner intention creates the perfect product that no-one needs and it happens all the time.

The position of outer intention lies in determining what people want, what they are missing, what they need, what motivates them and what their interests are. Outer intention follows the alternatives flow. All the time that you are busy creating a "masterpiece" taken from the glass ceiling of your own mind, you are going against the flow. The mind is always prone to idealise its own abilities and it becomes so totally and utterly absorbed in the creative process that it fails to notice what is happening outside of that. The mind strives to subordinate everything to its control. However consumer demand is a difficult thing to control because it goes with the flow and always follows its own course. It takes huge resources to influence the flow of demand and even then, it does not always work.

The mind cannot predict market trends but fortunately, it does not have to. All you need to do is stay abreast of the flow and note any minor changes in its course. There is no need to invent the object of demand. Almost all inventions that are ahead of their time do not end up being implemented and neither do they pay off. This does not mean that innovation has no place. The point here is that *if you are counting on earning an income from a personal masterpiece that is ahead of its time you are likely to lose the bet.* Of course, if your discovery is totally brilliant it might claim a winner-takes-all market but this does not happen all the time.

Only ventures that aim to fulfil their customers' current demands can be guaranteed of success. Now we can return to the question of how to make people *want* to buy your product. The answer is: *you cannot.* Trying to make someone want to buy something is, if not impossible, then extremely difficult. *Acting from inner intention you inevitably try to push or impose your product.*

Going with the flow, outer intention works towards tracking what the customers want and where their needs have already been satisfied. Changes in demand are shaped by the alternatives flow. The alternatives flow contains all the answers and is the only thing that can guarantee success.

It is no coincidence that fundamental discoveries and inventions are sometimes made by different people practically simultaneously. This is an example of the phenomenon of material realisation and how it moves through the alternatives space. Everything that must come into being has its time. Only very recently, have many inventions accredited to Leonardo da Vinci been implemented in physical form.

This would all seem quite obvious. However, the mind is liable to forget as it endeavours to break away from the stream and take control of the current. We have already talked about how *the alternatives flow is a sumptuous gift for the mind.* Remember this and make the most of the good fortune. If you do, many an obstacle will pass you by untouched.

Many problems in relationships occur as a result of the mind battling against the alternatives flow. *Criticism is one aspect of the battle* and is the direct fruit of inner intention. Encouragement and trust in a person's positive qualities is more concordant with outer intention. Criticising people is the same as fighting against the outside world. It will not bring any dividends unless you consider the need to vent your bile and provoke your enemy a dividend. In contrast, encouragement is a true driver in human relationships. We blame and criticise others when we are trying to influence them with inner intention. Yet, when you emphasise a person's positive qualities, no matter what, you lose nothing and allow the situation to develop to your benefit.

Never blame anyone. Many people reproach themselves and carry a sense of guilt around with them, but nobody likes to be reproached by others. People can be extremely condemning in relationship to themselves, even to the point of sadomasochism, and yet they will take any accusation made by another very badly indeed.

People will always take offense at criticism, irrespective of whether they are in the wrong, or whether the accusation is fair or not, so where does criticism get you? You might get to vent your bile but at the same time you create excess potential and end up being the one to suffer. You will never persuade someone that they are in the wrong. They may listen to your accusations but are unlikely to fully acknowledge being in the wrong, even if they agree with you superficially. You may be successful in asserting yourself at someone else's expense or at establishing your power over them, but not without adopting the role of manipulator.

If this is not your goal, abandon criticism and blame. When you are disapproving of others and find them at fault you are in effect slapping your hands about on the water trying to swim against the current. When you resign yourself to other people's shortcomings and concentrate on their strengths you go with the flow which is immensely beneficial.

Unless it is dozing your Guardian will always find an explanation for the behaviour of the person you wished to judge. As the inner witness your Guardian will stop you from leaping headfirst into the game and starting a dispute or quarrel. Stand back and observe the game, as a spectator. Remember that criticism only causes harm, and go with the flow.

Blame and criticism can never lead to anything positive because they catch a person off balance, and knock them off the course they were following. Everyone is guided by their own motives and aspirations and is in a flow that is carrying them in the direction of a specific goal. When you encourage a person, no matter what, you urge them in a favourable direction without making them lose the flow or undermining their inner most hopes. When you encourage someone nobody's rights are impinged upon and nobody's pride is knocked. Your interests become one and their desires run parallel to your own.

How do you feel when you are criticised? You probably either refuse to take the criticism on board or try to convince yourself that the criticism is well-founded. In neither case do you actually accept the criticism outright unless of course you have developed your own personal guilt complex in the meantime. Criticism can spur you on or make you behave 'as you should'. However, only the mind can be coerced. It is impossible to force the hand of the heart. The heart will always either do what it wants to do or hinder the mind from doing what it thinks it should do. Criticism makes the heart an enemy of the mind – encouragement makes it an ally.

Encouragement is a creative force; criticism a destructive force. The successful applicants for business management positions are not the managers who focus on criticising poor quality work which any idiot can do, but individuals capable of creating an atmosphere of enthusiasm in which people are motivated to work efficiently. People feel driven to work hard in contributing to a common goal when they feel their individual worth is being valued.

Arguing to the end to prove your point is a sure way of making enemies. We have already discussed how senseless and harmful it is to try and prove you are right at any cost in the chapter "The Alternatives Flow". If the argument is critical and your interests in no way allow you to step down, then go ahead and argue. In all other cases, leave the job of exercising the right to slap your hands around in the water to others.

Winning a debate will never pay dividends. Your enemy however may well benefit from your efforts. No-one will never thank you for pointing out that they have been talking rubbish with absolute confidence and if they do it is only because they have a tendency for self-flagellation and a heightened sense of guilt. Yet, what good is winning one over on a person like that? If it is not going to compromise your interests in any way, allow others to freely state what they feel they cannot agree with. You on the other hand will avoid creating excess potential and battling against the current.

People who argue are usually oblivious to anything else but the game. They are in such a deep sleep that they cannot be awakened. *To protect yourself from being drawn into the game you have to wake up and switch on your inner Guardian.* If several people are taking part in a debate come down into the auditorium and watch the performance from there. There is a huge advantage in playing the role of the judicious spectator. Whilst everyone else is trying to fulfil their inner intention insisting on their personal opinion you have flown backwards from the window pane and are taking a good look around. You will see a solution that would not have occurred to any of the disputants. Do not try and force it upon them though. All you can do is make a suggestion; leave the horn locking to the others.

If you win the argument, you can consider yourself defeated. Even if your opponents have formally acknowledged that you are right you can be sure that in their minds they will have found numerous informal arguments in their own favour. Whatever the case, the one who loses the argument takes a knock to their self-esteem and who delivered the blow? The one who succeeded in proving their own point of view.

You would not want to punch another person in the face, after all; s*o why would you possibly want to deliver the same blow to their feeling of self-worth?* People often offend each other in this way and the insult always has a hidden quality to it because the hurt is taken silently. People do not like to demonstrate their need to assert their self-worth openly. We are all supposed to have a sense of worth automatically, so no-one wants to reveal that they have to fight for theirs, despite the fact that we are all looking for confirmation at every step we take.

Just because a person keeps quiet when their self-esteem has taken a knock does not mean that they were not hurt or had simply accepted the knock. The hurt will continue to live in them, not in their conscious mind but in their subconscious. When you win an argument you feel confident that you have risen in standing. However, you have only won by compromising the integrity of your opponent. We all know that the hidden hurt will end in tears eventually. Moreover, the defeated opponent will never acknowledge your newly acclaimed worth.

There is one sure way to set a person against you which is to let them know how much better you are then they. "Do not make idols for yourselves and do not create enemies" is the most important slogan you could have for creating relationships that go with the flow. *Avoid injuring other peoples' sense of self-esteem like the plague.* Make it a kind of taboo. In so doing, you will save yourself from endless problems and niggling unpleasantries you will never know the reason for because of the hidden nature of the blow to self-worth.

What the person arguing with you is really trying to do is protect their own sense of worth in one way or another so meet them half-way. Agree with what they are trying to say. By agreeing you will have given the person what they wanted enabling you to calmly express your own point of view without having to insist or prove anything. When you take this approach you not only go with the flow; you implement outer intention. The results will be beyond compare and far superior to anything you could have achieved via sophisticated intellectual contrivances.

It is essential that the tone of the conversation be set to one of agreement from the very beginning. If the first thing a person utters in response to your opening phrase is "No", you can consider that trying to convince them of anything is totally out of the question. The person you are talking to has taken a different turning and there is no chance of them now going with the flow together with their conversation partner. It is important to start a conversation in such a way that the first word a person says is "yes". Never begin a conversation with a sensitive issue. It does not matter what topic of conversation you choose to start with, as long as your conversant agrees with you. Later, you can smoothly navigate the conversation towards more contentious issues. There will now be a much greater chance of achieving the outcome you desire because by inertia both are moving in the same direction and going with the flow. The thought energy of the conversants will avoid being brought into dissonance.

If somewhere you have slipped up and are expecting to be blamed fairly, try not to get all prepared to defend yourself. *Come forward in admitting your mistake.* Then, the person who had intended to vent the wrath of justice upon you is likely to take a more generous and gracious stance. In this instance the saying 'attack is the greatest form of defence' does not apply. You have effectively agreed in advance with your opponent's line of argument giving their intention the green light. Your anticipatory submissiveness realises their inner intention to put you in your place at the same time as increasing their own magnitude. Because you have taken the step voluntarily without being forced into it your self-esteem will not suffer in the slightest. You end up killing two birds with one stone: you increase the standing of your opponent for which they will be grateful, and you keep your own integrity.

By defending yourself and trying to justify your mistakes you end up rowing against the tide and giving your energy over to pendulums. Whatever the circumstances, the desire to justify yourself comes from heightened inner importance. Lay down this crippling burden, gift yourself the right to make mistakes and allow yourself to make them. *Do not justify your mistakes, acknowledge them* and you will immediately feel relieved.

In the chapter "The Alternatives Flow" I mentioned that irritating comments other people sometimes make can actually be very helpful. Other people's suggestions that you may at first have been inclined to take coldly can in the end turn out to have more sense than you initially thought. The comments and suggestions of others only hurt if we have somewhere heightened inner importance. Drop importance and stop fighting the current. Accept that the other person was right or at the very least, try to bear it in mind.

Tell the person that they were right about what they said and you will see the result. You are not obliged to say anything, but do it anyway. You have nothing to lose. Everyone makes mistakes, fools and thinkers alike, but unlike fools people with brains can acknowledge their mistakes. By admitting aloud, that the person was indeed right you win their good grace.

People live in an aggressive world of pendulums where at any moment they may be forced to stand their ground and protect themselves. Suddenly you are offering to do that for them. In this moment the problem of having to defend their position to you is pre-empted. They immediately feel a sense of relief and are grateful for the assistance afforded during battle. You are no longer a potential opponent but an ally. All this information passes through your partner's subconscious in a matter of seconds. People think in exactly the same way in lucid dreaming. If however you practice mindfulness you will find it easy and even fun to adopt the role of *witnessing others peoples' right-mindedness*.

When someone turns out to be right, other people usually keep quiet whereas you openly express your opinion that the person was right. For that person the moment will have huge significance and they will feel indebted or at the very least grateful to you, although for the most part the realisation will be subconscious.

Imagine what a jungle we live in. People have to be constantly on the look out, ready to spot potential opponents even in relationships that, on the surface of things, look relatively friendly. Everyone puts themselves first and is ever ready to defend themselves. This is no over-exaggeration. It just seems that way because we have long become used to the current state of affairs.

Given the nature of the environment we live in, you can become a real treasure for those who are already tired of the battle. Can you just imagine how many allies you could find?! All it takes is to ditch importance and not hold back in acknowledging other people when you know that they are proven right. Your advantage is that you act with conscious awareness whereas other people are asleep and will therefore never thank you in return. If they could wake up and express their opinion or attitudes mindfully you would hear them say something along the lines of: "Yes, this person is far from stupid. They are nice. I would like to get to know them better. What a sweetie."

No-one will say these words aloud and they may not even say them to themselves but this is what their subconscious feeling would sound like if it could be expressed. Imagine the gold that lies at your feet. People are usually so anxious and burdened with importance that they wander around failing to notice the nuggets lying right under their noses. You have a huge advantage: mindfulness, the absence of importance as well as the willingness to give others your attention. Make the most of your advantage and you will see gold where others can only see stones.

Attuning to Fraile

When people communicate with each other they tend to make adjustments and allowances to take account of the character, temperament, intellectual level, manners etc of the person they are talking to. If two people cannot adjust to each other's differences they will not achieve a level of mutual understanding and any communication between them will be no more than empty words and hot air. You cannot achieve mutual understanding without attuning to the frequency of your partner.

The term "attuning to the frequency of your partner" is of course purely customary. You know by now that I am using an over-simplified model for the sake of convenience. It does not matter too much exactly how the attunement takes place on the physical level. The essential idea is that every individual is bestowed with a unique range of personality characteristics which we refer to in Transurfing as fraile.

When you manage to establish a close connection with another person you are actually frailing, i.e. attuning to that person's special characteristics. How successfully you are able to communicate with another person is directly dependant on how well you have been able to grasp the essence of your partner's fraile. Frailing is not as difficult as it might sound. Giving your full attention is the most important aspect to successfully attuning to another's fraile. Without the power of attention there can be no question of even beginning to attune to each other's frequencies. On the one hand, this is an obvious thing to say; and yet as a rule, people forget it and in conversation with another concentrate solely on their own thoughts.

A successful businessman once said: "Everyone wants to offer me something, but no-one ever asks me what I need". People who want something from another are usually concerned with their own problems and wondering how they can solve them with the help of other people. This is pure inner intention. Accordingly, if you think about what other people want you activate the functioning of outer intention.

How can you connect what you want with the needs of another? First of all you have to consciously focus your attention on their interests. *Shift your inner sight from yourself to your conversation partner.* A person will only be interested in delivering a counter question in the context of their own problems and aspirations. Your thoughts are currently focused on what you want but this is of absolutely no interest to anyone else. Is it really of any significance to you what others want? They feel exactly the same way about their own concerns. They do not really care about anyone else's needs. So, *the only way of finding a common language and understanding your partner's wavelength is to lead the conversation within the context of the other person's interests.* You are sure to have mulled your own problems over for more than long enough. Now switch your attention to your partner's concerns. Set your partner's intention at the foundation of your communication and only build your own concerns on top.

For example, you might want to take a holiday in August. It is essential that you take a break. You are thinking of your interests. What does your boss think about you taking leave? He is thinking about your work and not even remotely interested in your need for a holiday. There are two ways around this. The first is to go up to your boss and start groaning about your problems and needs. The second is to explain that your workload is expected to increase in September and so you would like to take a break in August to be back at work and working efficiently by September. Which approach do you think would be most effective? Your boss might suggest that you wait and take a break in October, but likely as not he will agree with you because he hears a suggestion expressed at his own frequency. You attune yourself to the frequency of another person's thought energy when you talk to them in the language of their own interests.

When the rider and the donkey are both lost in their own thoughts the donkey will not do what the rider tells it to stubbornly refusing to go in the right direction. The donkey is thinking about carrots and so if you show the donkey a carrot it will go wherever you want it to. You are in effect inserting your own intention into the context of the donkey's intention. How does fulfilling someone else's desire benefit the donkey? Ask yourself this question every time you need someone to do something for you. If you can find an answer to the question they will do what you need them to do.

Listening attentively to what a person is trying to tell you is essential to attuning to their frequency unless of course your intent is to dominate the conversation with your own themes of interest and opinions. In large groups everyone talks at the same time, but it does not really matter because no-one is listening anyway. Of course, some people will pretend to be listening but ninety percent of their attention is aligned with their own thoughts. You do not have to shine with wit and erudition to stand out as an interesting conversationalist. It is enough just to listen to your conversation partner.

If a person is indifferent to you but for some reason you need to stimulate their interest or participation *talk about what interests them.* Just for a while forget about what interests you personally because that radiates at a completely different frequency. Adjust to the frequency of your conversation partner. Put yourself in their shoes and you will begin to understand what motivates them, and the reasons for their actions and attitudes. When you attune to your partner's frequency you can smoothly move on to the issue that interests you.

A person's name is the simplest key to their frequency. You cannot get away from the fact that since birth a person has been appealed to by name. Use their name in the course of the conversation more often and it will have an effect. Calling someone by their name is like a password indicating that you come as a friend with good intentions and acknowledge that person's worth.

Everyone to some extent or another maintains a protective field around them that jealously guards their self-worth. You will not be able to attune to your partner's frequency if they are surrounded by a protective wall of formality or distrust. Sometimes the obstacle can be overcome with the help of a certain disarming directness. If you show that you are not trying to hold up a field of protection around your self-worth and have no intention of pouncing, the other person will be encouraged to let down their screen of protection. The most effective way of dissolving a barrier of separation is to *demonstrate your genuine liking for that person.*

Why do we love our pets so much? It is because they always show us how genuinely pleased they are to see us. They wag their tails, purr, jump up at us, squeal and show their delight in any number of ways. There are other less communicative beings such as aquarium fish but these creatures do not inspire love. They are like plants or a part of the furniture. It is as if the creatures we love are saying to us: "I do not need anything from you. I am just so pleased to see you!" This is one of the main reasons people adore their pets.

In dealing with people, if you want to inspire a sense of fellow-feeling *in someone, show them how happy you are to see them.* You do not have to go as far as expressing canine delight but you can smile and greet them enthusiastically, call them by their name and listen attentively. If you behave with the warmth of an aquarium fish you can expect the relationship to develop accordingly.

The way it works is very simple. On a subconscious level your partner will think: "I have met a person who is happy to see me. I must mean something in this world. This person confirms it. What a pleasant, attractive person!" People ask: "How are you?" out of habit expecting the standard response.

Attention and participation in any dialogue must be genuine. *There is nothing more off-putting and sterile than a dialogue raised to the order of etiquette.* People pull on a smile as if it were just another accessory. It might as well be a tie than a smile. Any answer that deviates from the norm is considered an anomaly. Nobody cares about other peoples' problems really, so what is the point in asking?

You can be in resonance with someone you are communicating with by radiating energy at their characteristic frequency. Everyone has their own resonant frequency, their own "forte"; the thing they are particularly passionate about, interested in or proud of. A person's forte is like a musical string that sounds at their resonant frequency. If you can determine a person's true passion, discuss it with them; give them the chance to express themselves. This is the most effective way of establishing a connection with someone. If you can catch the thread of their 'forte' wooing them will be easy.

You can easily win a person's favour by asking for their help with some difficulty or asking them to do you a small favour. When you ask your partner for a favour you abandon your own importance and increase theirs. Your partner will feel more significant if you convey that you need their help and give them an opportunity to express themselves, emphasizing their significance.

If the person can provide you with the service you requested they will feel needed when they are with you and you will no doubt win their favour. The feeling of personal self-worth means a great deal to people. Anyone you manage to inspire this feeling in will remember your generosity to the end of their days. No doubt you are still grateful to people who have valued your strengths in the past.

You might think that I exaggerate the significance of self-worth and it is true, if you look at people from the point of view of frailing, it can seem like everyone considers themselves king. Nonetheless, self-worth plays an essential role in shaping human behaviour and motivation. What do you think causes a person to feel the most hurt? Perhaps when they feel ignored, insulted, are beaten or maimed? No, a person is wounded most deeply when they are *degraded.*

Aside from life itself, people cherish nothing more dearly than their sense of self-worth. The most powerful hunger, aside from feeling physical hungry, is being hungry for power. This naturally represents the extreme and final stage of the battle for self-worth. Not many people get to this stage and yet when there is nothing more a person could wish for in a material sense they are left with the battle for power. Nothing excites people more than power so you can imagine the role the feeling of self-worth plays in people's actions and motivations.

Criticism in any form knocks a person's self-worth. Criticism is a kind of anti-frailing. *Never tell anyone to their face that they are wrong.* Even if you are confident that you are in the right it is much more beneficial to retain a position of neutrality. That way you will avoid undermining the other person's sense of self-worth and protect yourself from the action of balanced forces.

Another way that we hurt each other is by touching on our negative slides. The slide hangs on the film of importance and so when you knock the slide you touch on an open wound. The negative slide is a picture of what the person does not like about themselves. As you know, people with negative slides try to hide their unwanted qualities and project them onto others. Try making a counter accusation, i.e. handing the projection back to its owner, and you will be surprised by the turbulent reaction it evokes. Nothing will persuade that person to admit that you are right and they are more likely to become your worst enemy. It is better to leave other people's negative slides alone, to say nothing of trying to explain to them that it is all a negative slide in their head.

Being in love is of course the most perfect way of attuning to another's fraile. It is difficult if not impossible to explain how and why love happens and so much has been written on this theme already. Mutual love demands that we let go of the right to possess and simply give our love unconditionally. As long as it is not turned into a dependent relationship love can be preserved once it has already flowered, but there is nothing you can do to make yourself fall in love. That is all I can say on the subject of love.

So here I have roughly described the principles of frailing. The way I have described relationships as those directed by intention and those that go with the flow is purely relative. Relationships that go with the flow can be examined from the position of intention and vice versa. In the end it is all down to frailing. You attune to your partner's frequency; you both turn in the same way; you act in that person's interests moving in the same direction and as a result, you achieve something you could never have achieved via the standard methods of inner intention.

Energy in Relationships

In the chapter "pendulums" I talked about the benefit of visualisation. Just to remind you, the essence of visualisation is the following: Let us suppose that someone is causing you a problem, annoying you or even attacking you. Or perhaps the situation is the opposite and you need something from someone. If this is the case, you need to roughly determine what is driving that person; what is eating at them and what they are lacking: health, confidence, inner calm? Everyone has something that eats away at them, even if it is something relatively small and niggling, especially if that person is causing you problems or it may be you causing them a problem! Now imagine a situation in which that person receives exactly what they need.

For example, imagine that person doing what they love most, the thing that gives them a feeling of pleasure, fulfilment and peace. There is no need to think too hard about the details of the favourable scenario. Just visualise the first picture that comes to mind. They might be sitting at home by the fire with a glass of beer, swimming happily in the sea, wandering through a valley of wild flowers, riding a bicycle or jumping for joy. If you manage to "please" this person with the picture in your mind they will become well-disposed towards you seemingly for no reason, and will do what you ask of them, or ease the problematic situation.

What is really happening here? It is pretty much the same as watching a good film and by that I mean a film that conveys a sense of the joy of life. You watch a film like that and you begin to feel good, and your heart is filled with a light festive feeling. The film creates a celebration for the soul both on an intellectual and an emotional level. Beneficial visualisation also creates this feeling on an energetic level. If you have been able to successfully attune to a person's fraile and guess what their needs are, they will feel as if a comforting wave has suddenly come over them.

The difference between the feeling of celebration on an intellectual and an energetic level is this: when a person receives the energy delicacy of your visualisation they experience a comforting feeling without being aware of its source. That does not actually matter. The important thing is that the person will now feel comfortable when they are with you and you will have won their good-will. It is important to remember that a beneficial visualisation like this should be carried out with sincerity by uniting the heart and mind. If you genuinely wish the other person well, the effect can be quite substantial.

As you know, it is the abundance of free energy that makes a person charming, magnetic, powerful and charismatic. People mostly pick up on the energy of a powerful personality subconsciously. Depending on whether the person's energy is softer or harsher they will come across as more or less charming or powerful. In any case, *the force of a person's energy is proportional to the volume of free energy they run and the strength of their connection between their heart and mind.* The excess of free energy overflows in a fountain and is felt by others. Free energy is programmed by thought. The closer the strivings of the heart and mind the purer the programming will be. It is no coincidence that strong personalities come across as having strong integrity and wholeness.

As I have already said, charm is in fact mutual love between the heart and mind. When the heart is let out of its box it makes a person more attractive and magnetic. Their attractiveness lies not so much in their personal power as in the connection between their heart and mind. This is what people are lacking and so they feel drawn to such people as moths are drawn to the light. On an energetic level charm represents the energy a person radiates when they have union of heart and mind. If the force of their energy fountains is great enough they will literally shine with inimitable charm.

People with heaps of charm live in a condition of harmony between the heart and mind, that is, in accordance with their own credo. People like this are happy; they enjoy life and bathe in their own love without the slightest whiff of narcissism. Other people can sense their constant feeling of celebration.

Such people are few and far between but you could be one of them. You just have to turn to face your heart, love yourself and set out on the path to your innermost goal. Not only will your personal qualities change but your body will become more attractive, your face softer and your smile enchanting. When you are firmly on your target life line your external appearance, i.e. part of the scenery of that sector, will correspond to the characteristics of the energy you radiate when you see your own perfection. This is not as unlikely as it might seem. If you do not believe me, just look through some photographs of yourself that were taken when you were going through a dark period in your life.

By training your meridians and increasing your energy levels you will develop the unusual ability to influence people and inspire their good will towards you. To become the life and soul of the party all you have to do is abandon importance and turn on your energy fountains. A person with an abundance of free energy always evokes the interest and good will of others. This is particularly evident when free energy is attuned to the thought energy of those present.

You might find yourself having a discussion with a group of colleagues or friends. The frequency of the thought energy of those present will be attuned roughly to the same theme as if they were all swaying in unison. Turn on your fountains and let them flood your group. Feel your energy field and sense it expanding to encompass everyone taking part in the discussion. Then your comments will have greater weight and the other people present will feel the power of your thoughts.

When talking to a person one to one you can mentally launch a beneficial visualisation for them. If your energy fountains are working at the same time you will create a most favourable impression. This technique will grant you a huge advantage in situations that require your personal charm or strength making you successful in negotiations, exams, job interviews and personal relationships.

A favourable visualisation is an effective and tolerant means of attuning to the frequency of the person you are conversing with. Energy vampires attune to fraile by pulling on painful strings or invading your soul space. Unlike energy vampires you are not 'pawing' at the other person's fraile or draining their energy. They will appreciate it and be grateful to you.

Pardon

If you know you have shortcomings that could hinder you from achieving your goal or think that you lack the necessary knowledge and skills accept it. Accept yourself just the way you are. *Allow yourself the luxury of having shortcomings and lacking the necessary qualities*. This will help and give you a sense of relief and inner calm. If you try to hide the fact that you lack the necessary qualities and conceal your shortcomings they will undoubtedly show themselves at a critical moment.

Lack of self-acceptance will always manifest in the form of obstacles. We create the obstacles in our lives ourselves: firstly, feeling guilty or inadequate creates excess potential and balanced forces then exacerbate the situation; secondly, outer intention inevitably realises your fears. Anything you try to block out will become part of the script. For example, someone will always ask you the one question you fear to answer or request that you demonstrate the one thing you do not know how to do. But worst of all, you will be overcome with tension or freeze up at the critical moment.

Where does your free energy go? Your free energy is spent on supporting the excess potential of importance, on battling with balanced forces and managing situations that are fast threatening to roll out of control. The more importance you attribute to your shortcomings the more insistent the resistance of balanced forces will be. The tighter your grip of control, the stronger the pressure exerted by the alternatives flow, because it has no intention of stopping. Eventually, the energy of intention is exhausted. What would you expect to be capable of in this condition?

Imagine if you had to carry a piglet around with you wherever you went. The piglet would be squealing, trying to wriggle free and you would constantly be trying to keep it tucked tightly under your arm and somehow quieten it down. Then you would finally let the piglet go and immediately feel free and light with relief. The energy you had been spending holding on to the squeaker would now be entirely at your disposal to channel into other things.

The piglet comparison is not as obtuse as it might seem. It is unlikely that you will be able to hide your shortcomings and so it is better to concentrate on your strengths. You will see for yourself how much freer and at ease you feel if you let go and accept your shortcomings before an event where you have to be at your best. It may be an interview, an exam, a performance, a contest, or even a romantic date. Take off your cloak of inner importance. Give yourself pardon (in the sense of absolution) for your shortcomings and you will feel as if a huge weight has been lifted from your shoulders as the excess potential disappears and the energy of intention is released.

The battle with your own shortcomings is the work of inner intention. It is the work of the fly beating itself against the window pane. In contrast, eliminating excess potential and freeing up energy gives you a huge advantage.

There is a grain of truth in the saying: "What the eye fears, the hands do". What is better, to be tortured by doubt, to wallow in your hang ups, to lick your lips in desire and fitfully conceal your weaknesses or to simply shake off the baggage and calmly fulfil the work of purified intention? If you cannot drop importance, you must at least let go of the grip of control and shift from worrying to taking action. Just begin the process of doing, in whatever way you can. It does not matter whether your actions are effective initially or not. Allow yourself to act badly. The potential of importance will be dissipated in the course of action; the energy of intention will be released and everything will work out fine.

Job Hunting

To conclude this chapter I would like to demonstrate how the principles of Transurfing, including frailing, work in practice in a situation that is relevant to everyone. You have probably read various sources giving instruction on how to write your resume and how to behave in a job interview. You may gain new and useful insights from the material I am going to share with you below.

First you have to decide which job is right for you. In making your decision you can rely totally on the method of choosing goals and doors so there is no need for me to repeat the details of those steps here. You must just keep in mind that you genuinely do have the right to choose and that your potential is only limited by your intention and the level of importance you attribute to it. In the process of coming to a decision about the kind of job that would most suit you, do not think about prestige, the means to achieving it or your shortcomings. Focus on whether the job is really for you or not.

You may have doubts about whether there will be a vacancy for you at the position of your choice. If this is the case, you should be aware that pendulums will create the necessary conditions for anxiety, disappointment and even despair. You must remain aware of this and constantly affirm that *you have the right to choose and that if you make an order, sooner or later it will be delivered.*

In dreaming, your intention works instantly, but material realisation is inert like tar and so it takes time, patience and indomitable conviction that you have the right to choose. In a restaurant with poor service you may have to wait a long time for the waiter but you are certain that your order will appear eventually. In this instance I recommend using the following slide: *You make your own choice deciding on the kind of job you want, but how you will find it is nothing to do with you.* Anything is possible in the alternatives space although pendulums will do their best to convince you otherwise. All you have to do is choose and hold the firm intention to receive your order.

Of course, if your financial situation does not allow you to wait you will have to resign yourself to taking whatever is currently available. That should be obvious. However, once you have work that provides at least a minimum wage you can make your order for the best and calmly await its arrival. If you enjoy your work but feel a little tense or inhibited carry a slide in your mind picturing how well you do your work and the feelings of pleasure and self-fulfilment you get from it. *If the feeling of tension does not dissipate over time it is a case of inner discomfort.* In this case it would be worth looking for something else instead.

Once you have decided upon the job you would like to have, you can begin running the slide in your mind picturing that *your goal has already been achieved.* At the same time it is essential that you do your part and do not sit around with your arms folded. Before you set about writing your resume and preparing for interviews focus your intention in the right direction.

It would be a mistake to make *being offered the job* the focus of your goal. The goal should sit in your thoughts as a slide featuring *you, already having been offered the job with the application process behind you.* By wondering whether you will be chosen or not you inevitably create scenarios of defeat. *Remember the transfer chains.* The first link is writing your cv. This is where you must focus inner intention.

When you are writing your resume, stipulate all your skills but *only indicate one position, the one you are currently applying for.* There is a good reason for this. Firstly, displaying the willingness to do this, that or the other, will not evoke confidence in your potential employer who will assume that you are desperate enough to accept any position as long as they take you on somewhere. Secondly, by setting yourself several goals all at the same time you spread yourself too thin and intention is transformed from a firm central core to a formless amoeba. Thirdly, when you take on too much at once you concentrate excess potentials around you and as a result, end up with nothing. You have the right to choose but on each occasion choose just one quality. When you are choosing a toy you do not demand that it combine all the qualities of a doll, a gun and board game all at the same time!

Decide who you really want to be and what position would suit you best. There is no need to be shy or hold back; for you are choosing this position for yourself. Remember, you do not have to fight for your place in the sun. You have the right to choose. Indicate the specialisation you have chosen and do not worry about the fact that jobs of that kind might be scarce. *If you can allow yourself to have you will get exactly what you want.* How it happens should not concern you. Give this task to outer intention.

When you are writing your resume *inner intention will be intent on showing what a brilliant specialist you are but outer intention focuses on what the employer is looking for.* Do you see the difference? Of course, everyone needs brilliant specialists but if you are new to job hunting you might be completely bewildered to find that the employer has favoured another brilliant specialist with more modest strengths.

Your competitor will beat you to the post because their characteristics are a better match for the employer's perception of the position. You may protest that you are a match too and a perfect one at that! But that is the problem; 'a perfect one at that' creates a situation in which 'perfect' is the enemy of the good. The employer is completely focused on the inner intention to select a specialist in accordance with the characteristics he considers necessary. He is beating against the window pane failing to notice the wide open window that you represent.

The mind is not capable of predicting demand. It will do what it can to present you as the 'masterpiece' it perceives you to be. Yet the market dictates totally different criteria. Naturally you should show yourself in the best possible light, without over exaggerating, but in the process of writing focus all your thoughts and motives on the problems faced by the employer. Ask yourself *what he wants from you and what he needs.* Put yourself in the employer's shoes.

You can take the easy approach and simply read through the vacancies that match your specialisation and make a note of all the responsibilities and qualities required of the candidates. You will see that many things are repeated. From the general mass of information select everything that relates to you. Then adjust and adapt to the responsibilities and qualities required and you will be left with a picture of what the employer wishes to see in your resume. You can literally copy into your resume everything the employer expects from the successful applicant. When you are looking for ways to embellish your resume make sure that you *express yourself using the employer's language rather than conjuring up your own eloquent phrases.*

Imagine that rather than being a job applicant you are actually the employer compiling a template of the ideal resume of your future employee. Then your resume will meet the employer's criteria rather than your own. To do this successfully, you need to look through an abundance of vacancies and put yourself in the shoes of those who posted them. You should indicate all your skills beyond those required. However, make sure that you *especially highlight and emphasise the requirements indicated.* Your resume should sound a chord with the employer's conditions.

Before you upload your resume to the Internet for example, *put yourself in your employer's position and do a search for the resume of specialists in your field.* It will give you a huge advantage and you will discover all sorts of useful details. The majority of applicants directed solely by inner intention go directly to the search vacancies section and upload their resume straightaway. Try first doing a search for the resumes of specialists in your desired position. Imagine that you are the one choosing the best candidate. Then you will become aware of all the strengths and weaknesses of your competitors and will understand what the employer feels when he reads the same resumes. Then you will understand what you might need to change in your own.

Once you have compiled your resume send it off to various companies but be careful not to bang on the door too fervently. Allow the door to open to you. You need to recommend yourself without pressurising. *Let them choose you.* For example, publish your resume in various media forms. Do not pressure the world with your desires and aspirations. *Shift the centre of gravity from searching for work to announcing your presence in the work market. As far as possible allow the work to find you.* Never send your resume to the same address twice. Have respect for yourself and know your worth. If you are an exclusive specialist send your resume to recruiting agencies and calmly await the catch.

Do not expect an immediate response. You may have to wait for a long time for your order to be processed. It all depends on the purification of the intention. If your desire is burning like a bright flame balanced forces will interfere in all kinds of ways. Often an order is fulfilled just as all hope has been lost. *The greater your indifference to your order the sooner it will be completed.* The absence of desire grants a freedom that allows you to concentrate on the intention to act rather than on worrying about the possibility of failing.

Eventually you will be invited to an interview. At this point you must be extremely careful of your intention. The narrow-mindedness of inner intention will prompt thoughts such as how working for that particular company would benefit you. *Inner intention will concentrate your thoughts on what you can bring to the company.* This is the moment to clear the target slide from your mind, forget about yourself and focus totally on the needs of the employer. *You should now be solely interested in the employer's inner intention.*

Learn as much as you can about the company beforehand from their promotional material. *Identify what the company prides itself in and how they choose to differentiate themselves from their competitors.* Make sure you have a clear picture of these things in your mind and be sure to bring them up during the interview. Every company, just like every pendulum, has its own resonant frequency which is characterised by a number of qualities. Get a sense of the spirit of the company. Are their corporate ethics regulated or unregulated? Is the preferred form of in house communication official or informal? What is more greatly valued in the employees' relationship to their work, enthusiasm and initiative or discipline and a can-do attitude? Do they favour team work or individual creativity, etc? All these factors place certain restrictions on the company's employees and determine the behavioural style that makes them a part of the group. *If you manage to get a clear sense of the spirit of the company even at interview stage you will be considered 'their type of person'.*

Before the interview give yourself pardon for your shortcomings and weaknesses. If you know that you have shortcomings that could weaken your chances of achieving your goal or think that you lack certain knowledge and skills *accept it.* Accept yourself the way you are. Accept everything you would rather conceal and walk calmly into the interview. There is no such thing as the ideal candidate just as there is no such thing as the ideal employer, so you can boldly abandon internal and outer importance. You do not have to justify your actions to yourself or anyone else. Of course this does not mean that you should not work on your shortcomings but during the interview it is essential that you give yourself permission not to be perfect.

Everyone knows that it does not help to feel nervous during your interview. People try and control their anxiety with the power of inner intention but however insistently you try to convince yourself that you are calm, and however much you try not to get anxious it will not work. You cannot do anything about your nerves unless you eliminate the cause. Battling with inner panic can make you freeze and then you will behave like the mummy of an Egyptian pharaoh. *The only effective way of reducing stress when you are in the hot-seat is to accept the possibility of failure beforehand.*

The desire to be chosen creates excess potential. The more meaning you attribute to a successful outcome and the more important the job is to you the fewer your chances become. *It is essential that you purify your intention of desire.* You are going to the interview *not to be offered the job but simply to get through the interview;* not to pass the interview but literally, to get through it. *Do not strive for your goal, concentrate on the process.* Enjoy the interview process like any other event in life. Nobody is going to eat you and you have nothing to lose. This is the time to relax and take pleasure in the proceedings. *Set your mind on this thought; for the interview is a wonderful opportunity to show yourself in the best possible light.* Grant yourself the rewarding experience. Cast away any thoughts of messing things up. You have already accepted the possibility of defeat so you really do have nothing to lose.

At interview all the applicant's thoughts are usually focused on showing themselves in the best possible light. This is inner intention. In what light exactly can you show yourself to be best? *Outer intention is focused on expressing a genuine interest in the issues of the employer.* Only in the light of the employers concerns can you be the best.

Your task lies in answering questions in such a way that you return to the context of the employer's concerns. The skill lies in doing this at the same time as *giving precise answers without talking profusely or deviating from the subject.* It always irritates an employer when an applicant gives vague answers to a question and indulges in lengthy explanations. That said, as soon as the opportunity arises try to touch on issues related to what the company-employer does, what it takes pride in and what problems it may be facing. You should develop the conversation within this context. *Your strengths should be conveyed in the light of the company's problems.* Talk to the employer about these problems and how your professional qualities are relevant to their solution. This is outer intention. *If you have been able to lead the conversation in the direction of the employer's concerns you can be confident that the game is being played according to your script.*

Finally, if you were not the successful applicant the job obviously was not meant for you. You never know what problems you may have escaped so luckily. Be calm–wait for the job that is meant for you and you will be the successful applicant. If you have been accepted to a position that is meant for another you can expect to come into problems. So, carry on searching for the job that is yours. How to go about this you already know. The issue of work should not be grounds for the slightest wave of inner discomfort. This is the time to go to work as if to a celebration.

SUMMARY

Use other people's inner intention to achieve your own goals.

The feeling of self-worth lies at core of inner intention.

Do not try and change others; do not try and change yourself either.

To act more naturally switch your attention from self to others.

Play the game of increasing other people's sense of self-worth.

If you want to attract attention, show an interest in those around you.

In conversation people are not inclined to evaluate how interesting you are; they are evaluating how well you might suit the role of realising their self-worth.

Express your interest in others with sincerity.

Outer intention helps you to realise the inner intention of others.

Let go of the intention to get and replace it with the intention to give.

As a result, you will get the very thing you gave up.

Argument and criticism are the mind's battle with the alternatives flow.

Avoid any action that injures another's self-esteem.

At the beginning of any conversation, take a turn with your partner so that you are moving in the same flow direction together.

Do not justify your mistakes – consciously admit them.

Adopt the role of defending other people when they are right.

A display of genuine liking for someone brings down their protective barrier.

Asking a small favour of someone is the best way of befriending them.

Healthy visualisation creates a condition of comfort on an energetic level.

An individual's personal power and influence is proportional to their free energy.

Charm is the result of mutual love between heart and mind.

Allow yourself the luxury of having shortcomings and lacking strengths.

The excess potential of inner importance is dissipated through action.

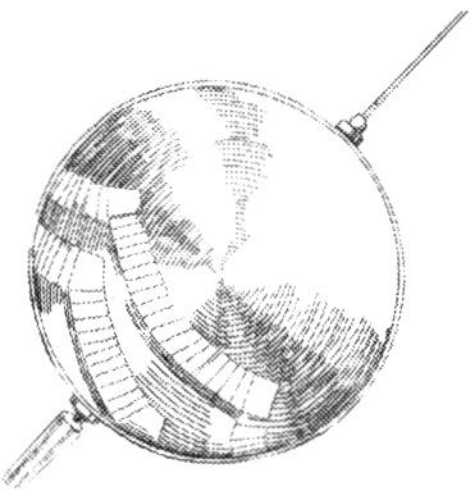

Chapter XIII. COORDINATION

I do not want or hope – I intend.

The Insecurity Labyrinth

No-one and no thing can prevent you from reaching your goal once you have taken the path through the right door except yourself. In other words, only lack of faith and lack of confidence can hinder your progress. Lack of self-belief and lack of confidence are basically one and the same thing. Both undermine the effectiveness of inner intention and make outer intention practically impossible.

Nothing you do when you are lacking in confidence will be done well. The more stressed you are about the need to do something well the worse the result will be. Lack of self-belief, together with the tendency to exaggerate the complexity of challenges, leads to a state of extreme tension or feeling of being totally overwhelmed. The extreme feeling of being overwhelmed is caused by the initial tension squeezing in on itself. The outer importance you associate with your goal makes the desire to reach it excruciating or wearying, whereas inner importance makes you doubt your own ability. Together this all leads to feelings of insecurity.

Insecurity tightens the grip of inner intention as hard as it can in its efforts to achieve the goal. Even without taking the impact of balanced forces into consideration, the effect of this intense grip is always the direct opposite of the original intention. The effort required to maintain several excess potentials at once takes up all your personal energy. You can see how many potentials are involved: inner and outer importance, frustration and the effort required to keep yourself in check and the situation under control. There just is not enough free energy to go round. It is no wonder people end up feeling inhibited and tense which makes them clumsy and awkward and in turn causes them to tighten the grip of control even further.

This is why people end up feeling overwhelmed, unable to move or utter anything intelligible. When a person is in this state it might appear as if their intention is being held in a vice but actually, once things get to this stage intention is absent altogether. All the energy that would fuel intention has gone on maintaining excess potentials. Insecurity in the form of anxiety and panic is pure feed for pendulums. Panic generates prognoses that start: "But what if…?" When a person is feeling insecure the prognosis is usually pessimistic in nature. In this case energy is channelled into running negative scenarios around in your mind and worrying about them. This also uses up the energy of intention. The fact that the energy is being used up is not as bad as what the energy is being used for. Stress, panic and fear are all powerful generators for our worst expectations, which, as you know, do come true.

Guilt feelings are another rich source of insecurity that blossom into a bouquet of inadequacy inferiority, lameness and worthlessness. What question can there be of any self-confidence with that array of feeling? Guilt and everything connected with it causes the meridians to narrow. At the same time the energy of intention is only sufficient to motivate actions that are feeble, indecisive and mediocre. If you have a propensity to indulge in feelings of guilt there will always be manipulators around you, like moths around a light bulb. Sensing your weakness they assert themselves at your expense happily devouring your unprotected energy. They play constantly on your feeling of guilt while you endlessly explain and justify your behaviour deepening your insecurity even further.

Insecurity creates a vicious circle. The stronger the importance and desire, the deeper the insecurity. The tighter the grip of control over yourself personally and the situation the more intense your tension. The more you feel panic and anxiety the more likely they are to become justified. Guilt eventually turns life into the wretched existence of the loser.

In an attempt to find a way out of the labyrinth people desperately try and acquire confidence. One way in which they do this is to launch an outright attack on the world. In a pre-emptive manoeuvre they attempt to demonstrate their strength and hide their lack of confidence. People try and erect a wall of confidence by impacting the world with their head-on vigourous decisiveness. This kind of approach takes a lot of energy but the wall of confidence will keep on crumbling. The energy behind forceful impact is spent on creating excess potentials and resisting the alternatives flow. In any case the approach inevitably leads to failure and the battle to construct a wall of confidence starts all over again.

Another way of trying to acquire confidence is not to bother building a foundation for confidence but simply to put everything at stake. This kind of self-confidence is the same sheepish manner turned inside out. It is a way of creating the impression of something that is not really there. If confidence is not based on anything is generates excess potential, but excess potential is not the only problem. You usually end up injuring someone else's interests when you act in a cock-sure or over-confident manner. A man standing in the middle of a desert shouting: "The world is my oyster" can shout all they like. As long as he is not bothering anyone else, balanced forces will leave him alone. However, when unfounded self-assuredness begins to compare itself with the abilities of others dependent relationships are created. Confidence that is based on comparing oneself with others is pure excess potential, especially if one's confidence is based on a scornful or contemptuous attitude to other people. False confidence will sooner or later be punished with a clip round the ear, or, if you will excuse the expression, a kick up the back-side.

There is also a kind of ecstatic confidence that a shy person feels when they suddenly experience a whiff of self-confidence. This is also a false kind of confidence because it is based on a temporary emotional high that quickly passes.

So, how can you acquire true self-confidence? Fighting feelings of insecurity is futile and neither can insecurity be hidden behind a screen of false courage. You cannot hide the insecurity anyway and the energy spent on trying to create it will turn against you. Trying to force confidence is also pointless. Any efforts made to artificially instigate courage and determination when they are not already present will also be wasted. Force yourself to keep it together when you are actually falling apart is totally impossible. As we said above, the energy of intention cannot be grasped or clenched; it just ends up being spent on maintaining the grip of control, leaving nothing behind to motivate action.

It is ridiculous to try and develop confidence in any way at all. You might think that confidence grows by taking decisive action but in reality when a person stops fighting and starts taking action the energy of intention releases its grip and switches from excess potentials to the implementation of action. In the end "the hands do what the eyes fear" and everything turns out well. *Confidence is not developed through action – it is the energy of intention released.* You cannot develop confidence. Confidence is like energy – it is either present or not present.

Confidence like self-belief cannot be acquired by the means of auto-suggestion. You can repeat affirmations on how self-confident you are until you are blue in the face but it will remain a naïve and fruitless exercise. It is no different to fighting the symptoms of an illness without curing the cause. Whatever you try and do with your insecurity it is not going anywhere. Wherever you look for confidence you will not find it. Neither will you be able to maintain the corresponding thought transmission necessary to be on a constant wave of confidence. You might say to yourself in the morning: "That's it. I am confident. Nothing can shake my self-confidence. I am solid as a rock". Try it and you will see what happens afterwards. For a while you really will feel more confident which will make you feel extremely happy and even more confident. But very soon a pendulum will arrange some nasty provocation and you will not even notice how you come crashing down from the wave of confidence. Once again you will be irritated and depressed, a problem will come out of nowhere, something will get you down and you will have reason to fear and hate the world as before. You thought you glimpsed a light at the end of the tunnel but you came to a dead end instead.

So how can you free yourself from the intricate labyrinth? You cannot actually because there is no exit. *The secret to the labyrinth is that its walls will crumble when you give up looking for the exit and abandon importance.* The reasons for insecurity can be separated into two groups. The first group consists of internal causes such as obsessive concern with one's personal qualities. This gives rise to feelings like dissatisfaction with self on account of one's shortcomings and lack of certain strengths, feelings of inferiority in comparison to others, bashfulness, fear of failure, looking stupid, etc. The second group consists of external factors linked with unrealistic overestimation of external factors. As a result unfounded fears arise in relation to the gap between one's meagre inner qualities and the high demands of the external world, feeling very small in a big city, and finally, fear of reality.

The paradox lies in the fact that *to acquire self-confidence you have to let go of wanting to acquire it.* The labyrinth's walls are made out of importance. You are walking round the labyrinth trying to get rid of your insecurity and acquire self-confidence. Confidence is a wild goose chase, another pendulum invention, a deceptive mirage, a trap for importance. Confidence is a pendulum game in which they always win. Where there is belief there is always room for doubt. Likewise, where there is confidence, there is always room for hesitation and indecisiveness. Confidence is a kind of belief in success. A negative adjustment can be made to any scenario and one small adjustment is more than enough to bring down the walls of confidence.

The notion of confidence is constructed on excess potentials and dependent relationships. Any variation on the theme of confidence takes roughly the following format: "I am determined. I am resolute and unshakeable. I am better than everyone else. Nothing can stop me. I overcome all obstacles. I am stronger and braver than the rest" and it goes on in the same vein.

Confidence is nothing more than temporary excess potential. Whatever packaging you wrap it up in it remains nothing more than excess potential. Even self-control is nothing more than a temporary concentration of tension; for confidence is just the opposite value of insecurity. Both potentials demand an output of energy and the first will be inevitably destroyed by balanced forces. Therefore, the pursuit of confidence is as fruitless as chasing after an illusory happiness that hovers somewhere in the future.

And so, we have just successfully broken through another false belief but how are we to manage without confidence? Transurfing offers an alternative – *coordination.* What coordination represents you will find out very shortly in the next section.

Coordinating Importance

Why do we need confidence? To boldly and determinedly conquer our place in the sun. Pendulums have imposed one sacrosanct postulate which sounds: there is no such thing as a free lunch; if you want to achieve something you have to fight for it, insist, demand, outstrip your rivals and elbow your way forwards, but in order to act boldly and decisively you have to have confidence.

As you know, the path of battle and rivalry is not the only way. If you reject the pendulum's scenario you can calmly take what is yours without having to put pressure on, without having to fight but simply by finding the will to have. Freedom of choice represents a pernicious threat to pendulums. If everyone were to claim what was rightfully theirs without fighting for it, without spending energy creating obstacles and then overcoming them the pendulums would be left with nothing. Despite the fact that it is extremely difficult to imagine the world without pendulums the false stereotypes and beliefs they create are not as hard and fast as the laws of motion for example. Awareness and intention enable you to ignore the pendulum's game and claim what is yours without having to fight for it. *When there is freedom without struggle there is no need for confidence.*

Confidence has only one origin–importance. Confidence represents the same potential as insecurity. It is just the opposite polarity of the same quality and both polarities are rooted in *dependency on external factors and circumstances.* The following metaphor describes the nature of this dependency. The pendulum leads a person along a path like a puppet on a string. The person does not believe that they can choose their own path or even walk independently. If the strings are kept even the person walks with confidence like a child holding onto its mother's hand but as soon as the strings relax and give some slack or start to jerk about the person feels insecure and tries to tighten the strings.

It is not that the pendulum is holding onto the person tightly, it is that the person will not let go of the strings of importance. *They are afraid to let go because they are under the power of dependency which creates the illusion of support and confidence.* In the end, the child will let go of its mother's hand and walk on its own and the mother will encourage the child to do so. Pendulums, on the other hand, will try to convince the person that they will not be able to choose their own path by themselves or walk without the support of the strings. If the person were to shake off the delusion and let go of the strings of importance they would find that they were able to walk freely wherever they wished and simply *choose* their goal without having to fight for it.

Once a person has their freedom they no longer need confidence and the illusion of support that it creates. All they really need is coordination to stop them from falling. Of course they have become used to the stability and support they received when they were under the pendulum's power and holding on to the strings of importance. However, when they were giving their energy away to the pendulums they would constantly disturb the balance and end up dangling helplessly at the end of their pseudo safety ropes. If a person could let go of the strings, all they would have to do to maintain their balance would be to avoid creating importance and excess potential.

Confidence as a support would no longer be necessary, because where there is no importance, there is nothing to guard or conquer. There is nothing to fear or be anxious about. As long as I do not attribute excessive meaning to anything, the layer of my world will not be distorted by excess potentials. Instead I abandon the struggle and go with the flow. I am empty and so there is nothing that can be hooked into although this does not mean that I am hanging suspended in a vacuum. Finally, if I want it, the freedom of choice is mine. There is no need to struggle anymore. I just calmly walk my path and take what is mine. Unlike shaky confidence this is a new state of conscious, composed coordination.

Where does the feeling of peace come from? The feeling of inner calm comes from not creating inner importance and so having nothing to prove. When you carry the belief that you are an important person the desire arises to prove it to others and excess potential is created. Then, balanced forces will do all they can to demystify the myth of your importance, repeatedly creating conditions designed to test your confidence to the limit.

The slightest pang of inferiority prompts a person into struggling to raise and assert their sense of worth. Let go of the need to prove anything to yourself or others and just accept whatever you needed to prove as a fundamental truth. You can spend your whole life battling to prove your worth and yet the moment you let go of the battle you acquire it.

A feeling of insecurity is intrinsically the same as low self-esteem, so how can you improve your self-esteem? You probably think that I am now going to try and make you believe that you are much better than you give yourself credit for. This is what many psychologists do without a second thought. It is true, that the opinion others have of us is directly proportional to our own opinion of ourselves as long as it does not border on arrogance. The moment you acknowledge your true value, free of any self-deception, others will agree with you. The only problem is that it is not that easy to convince yourself of your own true worth. Try it. If you suffer from low self-esteem you will not succeed in persuading yourself of the opposite. However much you try and convince yourself of your own true worth you will never quite be able to believe that you are special. Thoughts will creep in along the lines of: "So where are they then, these special qualities of mine? I can see the shortcomings. They are obvious".

So I am not going to urge you to believe in your special qualities and raise your self-esteem because I know that it would either make you smug and over-confident or shove you deeper into despair. My advice would be to *abandon the struggle for worth* altogether. Do not try to believe or convince yourself of your own value. Simply let go of the battle and observe what happens: the people around you will start treating you with more respect as if they valued you more highly. As soon as you appreciate the fact of their attitude the need to convince yourself or try to believe in something will fall away and you will simply *know*.

It is a paradox but it works every time. The battle for self-worth drains your free energy and channels it into the battle with the alternatives flow and the creation of excess potentials that drums up the winds of balanced forces. Together all these circumstances create a tangled ball of problems fraught with all sorts of negative consequences. You cannot untangle the ball. Just abandon the struggle for self-worth and you will be surprised and delighted with the result. Your sense of self-worth will grow before your very eyes and your self-esteem will be enhanced, and in turn, the people around you will affirm your new sense of self.

It is as pointless to try and deny or stamp out feelings of guilt as it is to artificially raise your self-esteem. If you have a disposition to feel guilt you will never be able to stifle or banish the feelings of guilt you experience. So what can you do? The same thing as with low self-esteem: *stop justifying yourself to others.* Only ever justify yourself when it is absolutely necessary to explain your actions. Remember, no-one has the right to judge you, whatever you have done, as long as you have not harmed anyone else. Do not take the blame publicly and do not justify your actions. Let the manipulators fall through the emptiness. Resisting the temptation to slam the door behind you, silently leave the court room where people gather to profit from the guilt feelings of others. Give them nothing. If you have quite a deep guilt complex then initially it will not hurt to put the lid on your conscience for a while. *Do not invite others to judge your self-worth.* Only by taking this attitude and not by means of inner battle will you rid your conscience of feelings of guilt. You will see how guilt just disappears into thin air.

Having abandoned the battle for self-worth and given up justifying yourself you will have settled the score with a significant portion of inner importance as feelings of guilt and low self-worth are the predominant manifestations of inner importance. All other types of excess potential are derivative of these two. You will no longer feel the need for protection as there is no longer anything to protect. Neither will you need to pounce on others to pre-empt their attack. There is a saying that goes: "Do not frighten anyone, and you will have nothing to fear".

By the same token, if you reduce the importance of external factors they will cease to reign over you with their pre-eminence. The two most oppressive kinds of outer importance are fear of the unknown and feeling overwhelmed by challenges. Both generate the dismal potential of panic and stress. Everyone is always concerned about something. People who are insecure prefer to bow under the weight of their problems somehow dragging their burden along with them. Strong personalities strive to overcome their difficulties with force and decisiveness. They take the fortress by storm penetrating its walls with the excess potential of overt confidence.

Insecurity like confidence requires energy. In the case of insecurity the energy mainly goes into panic and anxiety and in the case of confidence the energy goes into overcoming obstacles. These are fairly elaborate methods of interacting with the outside world. In reality, everything is much simpler than it seems. *As soon as you consciously reduce outer importance and abandon fighting against the alternatives flow, the obstacles you perceive will be cleared from your path.* Do you really think you would need confidence? No, all you need now is good coordination to move with the flow and consciously control, not the script, but your importance levels. Energy that was previously channelled into maintaining all sorts of excess potential now goes on supporting the balance and just slightly helping the flow along with the oar of purified intention.

Of course, you cannot ever totally stop attributing meaning to things in life, how ever hard you might try, so do not fight to negate importance; just release the grip and transform the energy of anxiety into the energy of action. *Begin the process of doing in any way you can, without insistence or pressure.* The energy of excess potential will disperse through action releasing the energy of intention and with that, complex problems will be transformed into minor ones.

As far as fear of the unknown is concerned neither blind faith, nor auto-suggestion, nor false confidence will help you deal with it effectively. You may remember that I advised not thinking about the means to achieving your goal. You will never force yourself to believe in the possibility of a distant goal or total one hundred percent success, so abandon futile attempts to do so, as your faith will come to nothing and temporary bursts of confidence quickly fade.

You do not need confidence or faith. You need *coordination.* Coordination means: *taking pleasure in thinking about the goal as if it had already been reached; letting go of the grip of control over the script and going with the alternatives flow, helping it along with the oar of pure intention.* This is totally different to blind faith in success. Where there is faith, particularly blind faith, there is always room for doubt. It is the forced potential of importance that blinds. *When you go with the flow in conscious awareness everything falls into place without excessive effort.*

When you act in accordance with coordination, what you previously wanted to believe in but could not because it frightened you with the unknown will soon appear from around a bend in the current. Doubts disappear when the mind is confronted with fact. Then faith is transformed into knowledge and fear of the unknown becomes satisfaction at the feeling of your own strength. The most important thing is to reduce importance and let go of controlling the script. It is also important to remember that you decide the level of complexity a challenge represents and that adjustments to the script will play in your favour if you let them.

Finally, absolute coordination is achieved as a result of harmony between heart and mind. If on a conscious level you are certain of what you want but a worm of doubt or glimpse of depression sits in your subconscious, coordination remains an elusive quality. Harmony of heart and mind is achieved by *listening to the whisperings of the heart and living true to your own credo.* A lot has already been said about how and why to listen to the voice of the heart. All I will add here is that living according to your own credo means loving yourself, accepting yourself the way you are, not suffering from pangs of conscience or guilt and firmly acting according to the dictates of the heart and mind.

Efforts to live true to your personal credo fall apart when self-esteem suffers and conflict arises between the heart and mind. It is as you know a wonderful thing to be able to live according to your true values and beliefs. It is even more wonderful to know that you do not have to create your credo, change it or battle with it, although many people do, chipping away at their own credo as if it were literally a statue in marble. Titivating your credo will not bring you anything but fruitless soul searching, spiritual torment and self-doubt. Your personal credo cannot be shaped or drummed up as a result of struggle or other wilful effort. You already have a credo, it is just that, like the heart it gets sealed up in the box of importance. As soon as you let go of inner and outer importance you will immediately sense that your credo has been freed. When importance is at zero, you have nothing to protect or conquer. You simply live in accordance with it and calmly take what is yours.

By abandoning the battle for self-worth, not inviting others to judge your worth and reducing outer importance you finally acquire what is normally considered to be true confidence. This type of confidence is not the frail confidence built on excess potential but a calm inner strength-coordination.

True, calm coordination does not relate to anything external and so it requires neither confirmation nor proof. No doubt you have seen characters in films whose confidence is beyond question. True, calm self-confidence can only come from inner self-sufficiency and the integrity of wholeness. You do not compare yourself to anyone; you are simply in a state of total balance. This kind of balance is achieved when there is unity of heart and mind; when there is no feeling of guilt, dependency, superiority, obligation, fear or stress; in other words, when you do not disturb the balance inside yourself or in the world around you. *Live in harmony with the outside world, yourself and your credo.* This is the ideal we should strive towards in order to have complete confidence, that is, coordination. Achieved by any other means confidence can only be artificial.

Coordination grants you freedom from pendulums allowing you to move independently in whatever direction you wish to claim whatever you desire. If at the present time you have to fulfil tiresome obligations, detach yourself and imagine that you are being filmed for a movie. Hang on, for you will have to play your role to the end, at least until the end of the current series until you walk through the right door. Practice visualising your target slide without thinking about the means and wait for outer intention to open the door to you.

The Battle with the Clay Golem

At last I am free of the unnecessary burden of excess potential. Inner and outer importance no longer exist. I have no need to assert my superiority or hide my inferiority. I fear neither the past nor the future. I have nothing to protect and nothing to conquer. I am finally free of the influence of pendulums and can take care of myself. If only this were true…

Pendulums have great power, and part of the reason for their power is that people do not suspect they exist. It would not be right to talk about pendulums as if they were a secret group of aliens hatching a plot against the human race because pendulums are an integral part of our world. They have a genuine impact on people exerting their control via informational energy. Their influence takes effect on three levels: mental, emotional and energetic. Pendulums pump free energy from people via the strings of importance. It has always been this way, except that recently, the purely informational impact has been greatly accelerated.

Human civilization has evolved over many thousands of years but it is only over the last decade that the picture has radically changed due to developments in the field of information technology. The volume of accumulated data stored on all kinds of servers is growing exponentially. The threat lies not so much in the volume of data being stored but the methods and means of its distribution. We are ensnared in a web of telecommunications that become more dangerous with every passing day. We do not sense the danger however, because the growth of the information industry takes place under the jovial anaesthesia of new forms of entertainment and convenient tools that are fun to use.

It is quite evident that the pendulums's goal is not to entertain its adherents but to subject them to its power. The expansion and intricate elaboration of the information network has enabled the pendulum to attract a phenomenal number of adherents simultaneously. The greater the percentage of the population that watches the same program the more energy the pendulum can harvest. The stronger the pendulum becomes, the greater its influence and the more easily adherents are persuaded to follow the rule "Do as I do".

The pendulum's rule works well and succeeds in drawing people away from their innermost goals. The process is now approaching its final stage in which man is ultimately deprived of the freedom of choice. One day, people will find themselves in a situation in which thy represent nothing more than an element of a monstrous, informational energy *matrix*. The individual will be shut in a box of conditioning and transformed into a detail of the greater machine. The matrix grid will determine how each element should function and what they should wish for. As you know, science fiction has a tendency to become reality in its time.

This process is already taking place steadily and unnoticeably. There is nothing that can be done about it. Subordination does not necessarily have to be brought about by force. *It is sufficient to shape the individual's worldview in such a way that they have no notion of their freedom.* This is what is happening now. It is relatively difficult to preserve a sense of freedom under these conditions and so we will take a closer look at specific aspects of pendulum protection methods.

As you know, importance is the only thing a pendulum can use to hook into. A pendulum can even hook into your attributing great importance to keeping importance at zero. Everything that has been said in relation to pendulums is quite serious but here lies the paradox: if you now declare war on pendulums in earnest you will be destined to fail. *The most important principle in the battle with the pendulum is to refuse to fight them.*

You have to understand that this is not a fight with a tangible object but a battle with a clay golem, a game and so it is up to you what kind of fight you want it to be. If you perceive the process as a fight you will lose whatever happens because you cannot beat a pendulum in battle. If you challenge the golem even along the lines of: "Now I know it is just a clay golem, I will show it!", you can consider yourself defeated. If you perceive it as a game you will at worst lose the round, but not the fight.

The pendulum is just a golem whilst you are conscious of the essence of the game and refuse to observe its rules. Pendulums will lie in wait for their victim every time they feel confident. Be prepared for the fact that they will try to throw you off balance in any way they can. This is the nature of the game. You take the bait, lose your sense of balance, get very upset and feed you energy to the pendulum.

You start off clam, happy and balanced but it does not last long before the pendulum provokes you. You get involved in a dodgy situation or receive bad news. In accordance with the script you should get stressed, become afraid, despair, feel dejected, and express your irritation or dissatisfaction. All you have to do when this happens is wake up and remember what the game is and then instantly reduce importance. If you do this with conscious awareness the pendulum will fall through into emptiness.

You can break the game rules as long as you are not day dreaming. In non-lucid dreaming the dreamer is always a victim of circumstance. The dream just happens and you cannot do anything about it. In waking life people have long been accustomed to reacting just as automatically to any negative influence, and I do not have to explain what follows. However, you are not an oyster and are more than capable of responding in an *inadequate manner*. If you deliberately act strangely the pendulums plans will be ruined. You just have to *come to your senses* in time and break the rules of the game.

You will see for yourself just how pleasant it is when you realise that you are aware the pendulum is desperately trying to provoke you and you do not take the bait. The pleasant feeling does not only come from being proud of yourself for being strong, there is another reason too. When you give your energy to a pendulum you become weaker, but when a pendulum tries to provoke you and you resist *you become the receiver of the energy the pendulum channelled into the provocation,* making you stronger. This additional strength is experienced as a pleasant feeling. Now you can imagine how great the pendulum feels when it feeds on your energy. Do not give the pendulum the opportunity. It will pursue you time and again, but do not weaken. Let it spend its energy on you.

During the game where you are breaking the rules do not be tempted to get angry or frustrated with the game. All the time that you are playing with conscious awareness, you are having fun, fighting a golem with sugar sabres and it will not be able to touch you. If you break the rules and manage to retain a condition of inner balance the golem will shatter into pieces. However, as soon as you begin to lose your temper the pendulum's sugar sabre will be transformed into a dangerous blade. Then the game could turn into a battle and end in an induced transition.

Do not fight your reaction to being provoked. Look at it from a different perspective. The emotions you experience are the effect, the cause of which is your relationship to what is happening. You have to consciously change your response to the negative factor. It is not difficult to display an inadequate attitude because you are aware that it is just a game. Let the jester jump. It is as if you are fighting an invisible opponent in a room of mirrors. It seems as if the pendulum is right next to you but in reality what you are seeing is not the pendulum or even the pendulum's reflection. The reflection in the mirror is your importance. All the time that something has exaggeratedly important meaning you have an opponent that constantly looms at you in the mirrors. Whilst importance is kept at zero there is nothing to fear, nothing to protect and no-one to attack. Then the mirrors of importance will splinter into tiny pieces and you will see that the golem has crumbled.

You do not need toughness in the battle with the pendulum. Emptiness is considerably more effective. The expressions "impenetrable, nerves of steel, iron will, steadfast, endurance and self-control" among others imply protection, tension, and readiness to fight back. Maintaining this type of protective field requires a huge amount of energy. As you know, all this energy is feed for the pendulum. Yet if I am empty I have no need to maintain the protective field. Energy is not wasted and the golem falls into the emptiness and crumbles. All you have to do is consistently remind yourself of the rules of the game and be conscious to keep importance at zero.

The need to keep importance at zero should not escalate into a permanent state of readiness for defence combat. You should not attach excessive meaning to the game itself. Relax and allow yourself to lose from time to time. There is no need to strive for victory at all cost. Whilst you maintain your grip of control the pendulum can twist you about. It will drag you about like a dog grips onto a stick it does not want to let go of. If the game is not any fun, display the maximum level of indifference possible by losing and not caring at all.

If the pendulum wins a round, do not be stubborn; accept that you lost that game. There is nothing wrong with losing your inner balance and getting upset. Do not give yourself a hard time over it; the next game will be yours. *And do not promise yourself that this time will be the last, or set an ultimatum or trap to fall into.* You think you are setting an ultimatum for yourself but actually, you are setting it for the pendulum which is exactly what it is waiting for. Ultimatums are nothing but a powerful wall of protection. By putting up a protective wall you turn the game into a battle in which you will inevitably suffer defeat.

Be prepared for pendulums to provoke you gently and softly. Many people look for a prop in cigarettes, alcohol and drugs when they are flagging under the weight of their problems. The next time you give up a harmful habit and tell yourself: "That is it. This is the last one" this is not you talking. A pendulum can so capture your thought wave that it can literally impose thoughts on you. Every time you swear to yourself "just one last time and then that is it", wake up and shake off the delusion. This is the pendulum speaking. Being consciously aware of this fact will help you to indifferently 'split' with the bad habit; not decisively but indifferently.

There is nothing that pendulums will not do to attract adherents. They have completely whittled away everything sacred, from ethical principles to religion. The world is a manifestation of the One Spirit, an affirmation of multiplicity in oneness. The divine essence penetrates all living and non-living beings. God lives in each and every one of us. We touched on this previously when we compared the human soul to a drop in the ocean. As soon as God informed human beings of his existence via his manifestation on Earth the pendulums instantly took religion under their control. You can see this for yourself if you look at the original Ten Commandments.

The First Commandment despite its various interpretations is in essence the following: "Thou shall have no other gods before me". This statement demands that man believe in the existence of the one God who rules over all creation but people broke the commandment straight away and created numerous other religions, i.e. pendulums. Rather, they allowed themselves to become subordinated to the pendulums of religion. The pendulums of religion hide behind the name of the Lord. Spiritual ministers genuinely try to preach the word and work of the Lord but being adherents themselves, they are held under the power of pendulums and so very little actually depends on their actions. Can religious war and conflict really please God?

The Second Commandment: "Thou shalt not make unto thee any graven image, or any likeness of any thing that is in heaven above, or that is in the earth beneath, or that is in the water under the earth. Thou shalt not bow down thyself to them, nor serve them". This also refers to pendulums. The pendulum subjects adherents to its will and forces them to act in its interests, whatever the circumstances, and no matter what the good intentions are that conceal its true purpose.

All the Commandments can basically be reduced to two. In the words of Jesus responding to the question: "Teacher, which is the greatest commandment in the law?", Jesus said "You shall love the Lord your God with all your heart and with all your soul and with all your mind." This is the first and greatest commandment; the second is similar to the first: "You shall love your neighbour as yourself". "The whole of the law and the prophets depends upon these two commandments". Love God in yourself and others without worshipping pendulums. This is all that the Commandments urge you to do.

The negative impact of the mass media on the human psyche requires the individual to be very *consciously aware.* Do not let negative information affect you. Everywhere you look someone is trying to seduce you, capture your attention, or force something on you. Any group of people has its pendulum. When adherents carry out the pendulum's will they are often unaware of its true goals so you should always ask yourself the question: Who needs this and why? Do I need it? At the same time, actively search for any information that relates to your goal. "Yes, yes" your mind impatiently replies, "I know all that already". And what of it, that your mind already knows? Despite all that the mind already knows it still carelessly nods off every time the pendulum starts a game. Do not let the pendulum come and lead you away by the hand.

Generally speaking, your task comes down to consciously breaking the rules. This can be done in two ways. Either drop importance and scupper the pendulum in the emptiness of your indifference, or still its sway by reacting in an inadequate manner. If you struggle with reducing importance you can always stick with the second method. Any inadequate reaction to provocation is a gross violation of the rules of the game.

Ending the Battle

The freedom of choice lies in one incredibly simple fact. *There is no need to fight to achieve your goal. All you need is the will to have.* As soon as you allow yourself to have you can begin the process of calmly placing one foot in front of the other in the direction of your goal. Pendulums will impose a different scenario *forcing* you to fight for your goal, declaring war on the world and yourself. Pendulums recommend starting with yourself. They make you believe that you are not perfect and so will not achieve your goal until you change. Once you have changed, then you must join the battle for a place in the sun. There is only one motivation behind this scenario which is to drain the victim's energy. By battling with yourself you give your energy to the pendulum and you do just the same when you join the battle against the outside world.

The word battle in this context presupposes constant tension, struggle and discipline. You have to be ever ready for battle, as warriors are who vaguely understand that somewhere in the world there is *freedom*. The mistake of the warrior is that they think they have to *fight for* their freedom. They spend their lives at war always putting off their main fight until later. Warriors do not believe that you can just walk up and take your freedom. They tell themselves and others that it is an extremely challenging task requiring years of hard work and sweat.

The Transurfing Pilgrim does not get involved in the fight for freedom because they know that freedom is already theirs. No-one can *force you* to fight and yet if you are filled with inner and outer importance you really do not have any other choice. The closest thing to battle in Transurfing is the intention to act impeccably but rather then requiring tactical efficiency and discipline it requires conscious awareness.

If you find it difficult to just claim and allow yourself the idea of having you may put it off to return to later. But for how long? The yarn of postponement can go on all your life. Putting it off until the next time makes life in the present moment a mere dress rehearsal for some better future. People are always unsatisfied by the present moment and console themselves with the hope that things will soon improve. With this attitude the better future will *never* come. It will *always* hover just in front of you for you to chase after, and it will be just the same as trying to catch up with the setting sun.

The idea that you still have plenty of time is an illusion. You can spend your entire life in expectation of a better future. There is the saying; "There is nothing more permanent than the temporary". In reality there is no time to wait. Do not wait for the future but insert it into the current moment. Allow yourself to have, here and now. That does not mean that your goal will be realized instantly. *We are talking about will, i.e. the intention to have in contradistinction to the ongoing battle with the self.* The will to have is infinitely more powerful than the will to act.

If you have spent your whole life taking part in the battle for a place in the sun, how far has it got you? Did you have to drag yourself to your boring job or to college as if to forced labour whilst someone else was relaxing at a ski resort or warming themselves in the sunshine by the ocean? Perhaps they won their battle and are now able to enjoy life?

The majority of people who participate in the battle would not be able to afford to go to a ski resort even if they saved up for it their whole life and if you can afford to give yourself a few days pleasure once a year then that is always an achievement. But what often happens is you arrive and the weather is bad or the ski lift is broken or you have to deal with other problems you could not have foreseen. Even if everything goes well, the thought will still be in your mind that you should be economical and you will remember how hard you worked to earn the money to pay for these few days of holiday which is so quickly coming to an end. You will have had a nice time in principle but then you will have to return to the grey days of working life and slave away again.

You won the battle and earned a holiday and yet from time to time a dark shadow creeps into your thoughts. You are convinced that you have to work long and hard to earn just a short time of pleasure. You are not ready to totally *give yourself permission to have*.

Those who give themselves permission to have do not take part in the battle. They are too busy. For example, a lucky couple were taking a break at a ski resort in Switzerland last week. They had a ball. All balls eventually come to an end but in different ways for different people. Now the couple is arguing about where to go next. He wants to go to the Australian Alps but she would rather go to the French Alps. The whole scene may remind you of some superficial soap opera, but for the couple it is more than a serious matter. The difference in perception is caused by different *levels of willingness to have*. You will trudge away for another year until you have a holiday whereas the couple expect to have their next holiday in a week's time.

The rational mind may be upset protesting: "But how can that be, after all, they were born with their millions whereas I have to earn my money! Where would I get the money?" How many times have we already said, that you do not have to think about the money. *When you end the battle and give yourself permission to have outer intention will find away of giving you what you need.* I cannot prove this to you right here and now but you can test the principle for yourself and do not try it, just do it and not tomorrow but today. Allow yourself to have from this moment onwards, unconditionally and unreservedly and not occasionally but all the time. If you do not expect instant results and continue to allow yourself to have one fine day something will happen that others will want to call a miracle. Those who are born with millions are already imbued with the will to have. They do not even have to think about it whereas you will have to work with slides. The mind will worry about how realistic the goal is and the means to achieve it, but this is the path of battle that leads nowhere. If you take this path you will never earn enough money. *Earn the will to have, not the money.*

If you concentrate on the goal as if you had already achieved it your doors will open and the means will take care of themselves. The freedom of it all is enough to make your head spin. You may choose not to accept this freedom. It is your choice. Nothing would be easier than to say that this is all rubbish and continue toiling away the rest of your life. Everyone makes their choice and receives what they are willing to have. *Your choice is immutable law and with it you shape your own reality.*

Choice in the alternatives space takes place roughly in the following way: people wander into a supermarket where they are asked: "What would you like?" One customer replies: I would like to become a star in show business. The shop assistant replies: "No Problem. Here is a great version, especially for you. World fame, wealth, shine! Will you take it?" Surprised the customer says: "Well, how can I put this…It is not that easy. Only a handful ever really make it, and the chosen few have unique talents whereas I am just your average Jo blogs." The shop assistant shrugs their shoulders: "What has talent got to do with it. Here's your item. Take it!" The customer then says: "It is really hard to get into show business. It is a bit of a jungle, a world full of sharks.." The shop assistant comes back with: "Ok, so here's a massive shark to help you make it. Take it, you will not regret it." The customer replies: "The stars of show business have such luxurious homes, fancy cars, top society...could all that really be mine. I can hardly believe it", at which point the shop assistant says: "Oh well, it is a shame of course. I do not think we can help you", and puts the item back on the shelf.

In the same way a person might cautiously ask another: "Do you know how to fly on a commercial airliner?" "Of course", the other replies, "I simply sit in the seat, fasten my seat-belt and the aeroplane lifts up into the air." As soon as you allow for the idea that achieving the goal is simply a matter of choice you will begin to feel just how absurd the customer's concerns are in the alternatives space shop. It is just a matter of being willing to have. That is all.

You might fall into the trap of battling with yourself for the will to have. *Whatever you do, do not force yourself to allow yourself to have.* Do not force yourself to picture the target slide. You should not need to push yourself. Do not pressure yourself or tense up over it for that again makes it a battle. *Simply take pleasure in having exciting thoughts.* Abandon importance and end the battle. Nothing is achieved by battling. The reason you continue battling is because everything around you has been elevated in importance. You cannot allow yourself to have at the same time as fighting ardently for your place in the sun.

You may be resolute and full of confidence that you will have what is yours and are enthusiastically convincing yourself that it is all down to your personal choice. Yet to act forcefully entails creating excess potential. *What is required is more like a carefree, light-hearted resolve.*

Relax, let go your grip of control and just be aware of the fact that you are taking what is yours. You do not need to drum up momentum and enthusiasm to go to buy a paper. If they do not have the paper you want you just walk to other newsagents. Release your deadly grip.

By *trying* to release your grip it becomes even tighter. Any kind of diligence or effort only aggravates excess potential. Importance is the underlying cause of effort and compulsive grip. You cannot relax the grip if you are battling with it. Abandon importance and the grip will relax of its own accord.

Reducing importance shifts the arrow that indicates the direction of intention from the inner intention zone to the outer intention zone. Any pressure that is applied is the result of importance. When you try to put pressure on a situation your actions are directed by inner intention. Will power is essential in overcoming obstacles but as we now know, obstacles are born of importance. Obstacles disintegrate the moment you reduce importance and will power is no longer required. When importance disappears the need to *push* for your goals transforms into the will to have and then outer intention sets in.

You do not have to win the right to choose. You already have it. If you feel filled with decisiveness *to win* your right to choose, prepare to be disappointed. If you are filled with decisiveness and vigour you again hold the deadly grip. Balanced forces will quickly cool your smouldering coals. And pendulums, having sensed your importance will immediately try to provoke you. You will see for yourself that this is how it works.

Do not let unsuccessful attempts to acquire dispassionate will worry or upset you. People are very used to channelling their energy not so much towards their goals as towards the feed for pendulums. Eventually, you will learn to differentiate between decisiveness and will. The will to have is the dispassionate, unemotional intention to take what is unquestionably yours. Does not it sound weird to say: "I am absolutely full of decisiveness to get the post from the letter-box"? You must exercise your right to choose just as calmly and uninsistently as you would retrieve your post from the letter box.

In life people are always having to take tests, exams, take part in contests, and all sorts of personal assessments but the will to have depends only on yourself. You are your own examiner. Any mark you give yourself is usually a reflection either of the belief that you are incapable and unworthy, or that the goal is unrealistic. People do this automatically, out of habit. All you have to do is allow yourself to have whatever else is happening. It is unfamiliar of course, but why not dare to try it and allow yourself to have. Newton's and anyone else's apples may fall to the ground but let yours fall to the sky. You might desperately wish to acquire the will to have but nonetheless, abandon desire. Enough of desiring; you are going to get what you need anyway. Just think about taking what already belongs to you. Take it calmly without demanding or insisting with the thought of: If I want it, what is the problem? I will have it"

Release

The will to have is created by the free energy of intention. Two things get in the way of allowing yourself to have. The first is conflict between the heart and mind. The second is the excess potential of inner and outer importance, which use up free energy. One would be mistaken to think that the will to have is equal to banal thinking that sounds "I want and I will". In reality, such thoughts must be filled with the energy of intention otherwise they will just be the mumbling of the mind and nothing more. Thoughts must flow from the unity of heart and mind. Otherwise, the programming of the energy of intention will not be pure. *If a large portion of free energy is consumed by excess potential intention will have no power to it.*

The difficulties we experience in acquiring will are similar to the reservations a person feels when they sit at the handlebars of bicycle without stabilizers for the very first time. The person knows that it is possible in principle but they also know that they will not manage it on their first attempt. They doubt their abilities and yet are filled with the desire to learn. The person tries to control the learning process but does not understand what to do. Three types of excess potential are immediately created – doubt, desire and control and all three drain the energy of intention.

The mind tries to keep balance this way and that but the bicycle keeps falling over because there is not enough unity of heart and mind or free energy. Then there comes a point at which the mind gives some slack on control and the unity of heart and mind appears that is so essential to maintaining balance. As a result, you can suddenly do it although the mind has no idea how. But that is the whole point! The mind always thinks about the means and how one should act. It takes control and tries various options. The heart in contrast does not think. It is simply *unreservedly willing to have*. The mind is also willing to have but only on the condition that things are clear and rational. The conflict between heart and mind arises because the mind doubts the goal can be realistically achieved. *As soon as the grip of control weakens the limiting conditions of the mind fall away to reveal unity between heart and mind.*

The mind is surprised by the fact that its control is not necessary and that everything works of its own accord. However, this fact is enough for the mind to accept, even if it does not totally understand what happened. The rider can balance and so the mind accepts it. The mind gives up enforcing its control because it is now convinced that it is not necessary. After a little practice, the other excess potentials disappear as well and the energy of intention is released at which point riding the bicycle goes from being a challenge to a pleasure.

In order to acquire the will to have you have to achieve unity of heart and mind and release the energy of intention. Unity of heart and mind is achieved when you are on the path to your goal through the right door. It remains only to determine your innermost aspirations and set out on the path. By laying down the useless burden of inner and outer intention you release the energy of intention, the moving force for transition in the alternatives space. When you are dragging inner and outer importance around with you, you waste ninety nine percent of your energy on supporting excess potential. How can you source free energy if it is all tied up in potential?

In order to drop importance you need to take action consciously. You need to be aware of what you are attributing excess meaning to and the consequences of doing so. Unfortunately, our attempts to consciously abandon importance on an intellectual level are not always successful. The answer then is to *take action* because the power behind excess potential dissipates in the process of doing. *The action you take can be turning the target slide round in your mind; visualising the process and calmly placing one foot in front of the other in the direction of your goal.*

How not to be afraid? – Get a safety net. The hardest excess potential to overcome is fear. You cannot force yourself to be unafraid. If something that has excessively important meaning in your life is threatened, something that you cannot let go of, such as your life, career or home, the only way to stop fuelling the potential is to find cover, a plan B or alternative route.

How not to worry or get anxious? – Act. The potential of anxiety and panic is dispersed through action. Idle worrying will continue to plague you until you take proactive action. The type of activity you turn to does not necessarily have to be related to the cause of your stress. As long as you do something your anxiety will be reduced.

How not to desire? – Accept the possibility of defeat and act. It is just as difficult to eradicate the potential of desire as the potential of fear *because letting go totally of your desire to reach your goals is almost impossible.* However, if you accept the possibility of defeat beforehand and find alternatives roues the potential of desire will at least become more balanced. Desire can always be transformed into action. Desire is what comes before intention. When desire is translated into the determination to act the energy channelled into the potential disperses. The energy of desire then goes towards shaping your intention.

How not to wait? – Act. The potential of waiting is dispersed through action by definition. Dissolve desire and expectation in action.

How to let go of self-worth? If you have understood this book thus far, this question ought to sound a little out of keeping with what has been said before. Of course, Transurfing encourages you to *stand up and accept your worth as an axiom rather than resigning yourself to feelings of personal worthlessness.* The difficulty with this is that the mind only senses its worth when other people treat you accordingly. Taking this into consideration, the secret to increasing your standing is as simple as it is effectual. *All it requires is for you to abandon the tendency to take action aimed at increasing your sense of self-worth.*

Examine your behaviour. How do you respond when you feel the need to protect your sense of self-worth? Whatever your knee-jerk reaction is, be it demanding attention and respect, feeling you have to prove that you are right, taking offense, being defensive and justifying your actions, getting drawn into conflict, acting superior and arrogant, insisting on being the leader, belittling someone else and pointing out their shortcomings or showing off your strengths; whatever it is, other people will subconsciously pick up on it.

If you do not automatically rush to protect your sense of self-esteem it suggests that you have a healthy sense of your own worth. People will start to treat you differently. When the mind sees that it is being treated with more respect it starts to acknowledge its own worth. *When you start to realise your own value other people around you will see it too, without exception.* By letting go you receive the very thing you gave up.

How to not get irritated so easily? Play the pendulum's game and break the rules. This is the only way to ditch the habit of reacting negatively to unpleasant information. You already know how this is done; you just have to *remember* quickly enough, that it is just a game, and then humorously break the rules by reacting inadequately. When you hear a piece of good news rather than reacting limply, respond happily with overt enthusiasm so that you radiate energy at the vibration of the wave of good fortune. Pendulums will cause you problems to make you lose your sense of inner balance and generate negative energy. By reacting in an inadequate manner you disturb the pendulum's rhythm leaving it with nothing. Have a go at playing the game in this way. It is quite entertaining.

How to get over feeling guilty? Stop trying to justify yourself. As I have already said, only you keep yourself in the courtroom to be judged. You are the one playing all the roles of prosecutor, lawyer and defendant and the manipulators exploit that. Leave the courthouse. No-one can detain you. Those who gather to listen will sit there for a while and then go their own way once they realise there is no defendant. With time your case will be closed. This is the only way you can get rid of your guilty feelings.

How to deal with resentment and indignation? You will not experience these feelings of anger if you rid yourself of guilt and acknowledge your worth. *End the battle and go with the flow.* You might sometimes find that you are quietly going with the flow when someone grabs hold of you and starts to pull you against the current. What should you do?

People who have a skill are generally capable of finding solutions to their problems, and then there are other people who only know how to find problems. They seek out problems and then triumphantly present them as if they were some huge achievement. They seem to genuinely believe that others are obliged to offer a solution in response. If you start trying to find the solution for them you will soon be surrounded by an entire crowd of idle rags. Some will criticise, and the others will find new problems, give advice, or take charge and make demands. However hard you try to go with the flow there will be others to make it more difficult. Naturally, this evokes resentment and indignation.

What should you do if you are not able to deal with the resentment and indignation you feel? Simply allow yourself not to be able to deal with it. Giving excessive meaning to the need to keep importance to a minimum will only make things worse. And who do you work for? For some 'boss man'? If you do, you will inevitably regularly experience feelings of resentment and indignation. Move on to the path that leads towards your goal and then with time when you do work, you will work only for yourself. Until that day comes allow yourself occasionally to blow up and create excess potential. *Do not pressure yourself to win all the time.*

Instead of fighting with the different kinds of excess potential you create, *you should act with purified intention and intention is purified in the process of doing, through movement.* As you can see, achieving the will to have takes more than just speculative exercises. It requires concrete action. *Begin placing one foot in front of the other in the direction of your goal in whatever way you can.* Your actions will become more effective in the process of doing.

The will to have has three stages. The first stage is inhibition caused by an unfamiliar situation: "Surely this cannot all be for me?" When you run the target slide in your mind you will not quite be able to take in the fact that it might all be possible. The second stage is delight, a feeling close to weightlessness. There will come a point when you accept the goal into your comfort zone and feel the sense of restriction fall away. The realisation that the goal is actually quite realistic evokes a feeling of elation. The feeling of weightlessness is also quite real being caused by the release of the energy of intention from excess potential. This is what you will feel.

With time the will to have shifts into its third stage of ordinariness. Because you are constantly turning the target slide around in your mind you think yourself into its content and gradually, everything in the slide starts to become ordinary. The slide is based on the film roll of importance. All the time that you desire, doubt and puzzle over the means, the will to have is standing on a shaky foundation. As soon as importance dissolves the will to have gains power. At the same time, it is important not to let go of the will to act, i.e. the intention to place one foot in front of the other in the direction of your goal. If you have moved through all three stages of the will to have you are undoubtedly on the right road.

And finally, how not to give way under the weight of your problems? There is always something that will get us down to one degree or another. It is extremely difficult to just up and let go of all importance but there is one very interesting and powerful method in Transurfing that can help – *coordinating intention.*

Coordinating Intention

People normally feel that they are subject to circumstances, powerless to change the way things are. Sometimes they are lucky and fly on the wave of fortune for a short time. Sometimes it even looks as if success is just within reach. All you have to do is act decisively and put up a good fight and yet despite all your efforts defeat follows victory.

It is as if people are walking along a road lined with high hills and deep pits. The ones who are confident and determined turn off the even road and for some reason start scrambling up the hillsides towards seductively shining prizes left there by the pendulums. Sometimes, a person makes an incredible effort and manages to take the prize but more often than not, the attempt is unsuccessful. Having found themselves at the top of the hill, the person is then pulled off their feet by the wind of balanced forces and sent tumbling head over heels to the bottom of the hill once again feeling powerless to change anything.

Then there are the negativists who believe that they are totally powerless to change anything and therefore prefer to wallow feebly in the holes of their worst expectations. Naturally, their worst expectations are instantly realised. The negativists do not only suffer from their own impotence. In their infantilism they also hand over their destiny to others in the manner of 'God's will be done'. They do not move with the alternatives flow, neither do they go against it, they simply wallow in their own discontent poisoning the atmosphere around them. The only thing they do well is realise their worst expectations and they get a kick out of the fact that they are at least right about something. They have perfected the art of confirming their own negative attitude.

People like this take a kind of sadomasochistic pleasure from negativity. They can make a mountain out of the tiniest molehill. Their motto is: "Life is loathsome and gets worse with every passing day" and having made this choice they find confirmation of it in everything. They are such natural sufferers that they are constantly being blamed and punished; such is the bitter lot of the martyr. They are literally swimming in a sea of negativity. Why? Because negativity is the only thing they have that the world can agree with them on and meet them half way. They find strength in the assurance that their worst expectations will be confirmed.

Sometimes a negativist will accidentally find themselves on a wave of fortune. For a while they might actually feel happy and content but it does not last long because they cannot resist looking about intently for the spell of bad luck they are so comfortable with. And why not, after all, anything good comes to an end and good luck, well, it just is not normal. It is not natural! The negativist sets out to catch hold of a tail of bad luck so that they can return to their familiar ditch where everything is terrible but predictable. They search for something to which they can attach their discontent, listening to the disasters in the news, complaining, blaming and generally making demands. If making demands does not work, they crawl into the role of victim who everyone must calm and sooth.

It is extremely difficult to wean a negativist off the habit of finding comfort in self-torture. It is an extreme case. The tragedy is that the negativity does not only poison one life; by negatively transforming the layer of their own world the negativist drags those they are closest to, whose layers intersect, into their own pitiful hell. The paradox lies in the fact that although the negativist seems impotent in reality they have a power that they exploit to its full force. The negativist's power lies in the firm conviction that life is terrible and gets worse with every passing day. The firm conviction is nothing other than the will to have which is why the negativist's choices are successfully transformed into physical reality. The negativist makes the choice and the world meets them half way.

In reality, we are not impotent and we do have the power to make change in our lives. The fact that the negativist's worst expectations are realised proves that *everyone is capable of influencing the course of events*, capable of determining the script, not only in dreaming but in waking also. Perhaps it is just a matter of substituting the negative attitude with a positive one: "Life is wonderful and gets better with every passing day". And yet, if you adopt this motto you embark on a journey across the clouds. If you doubt for one moment or look down out of fear, you will instantly come to a halt and fall downwards from a great height.

A negative outlook persists so firmly because from birth a person is sued to thinking that the world is out to get them. A huge wave of aggression sweeps over little people soon after they are born. There they were lying in the womb all cosy, warm and peaceful when suddenly the poor child is roughly squeezed out of their comfortable home hearing the mother's screams and possibly aware of the fact that they are the cause of her suffering. With this the foundation for a guilt complex is laid. Light glare in the child's face making it crinkle up its face to protect its eyes. Moist warmth is replaced with harsh, dry cold. The child just wants to crawl up into a ball and hide from the horror of what is happening but with that they cut the umbilical chord crudely severing the only connection with the source of life. The child is already experiencing a fatal shock. It is suffocating and does not know yet that it must breathe. It then suffers the trauma of being slapped on the back. It then cuts into the lungs with the sharpness of a razor. It is painful to breathe but the child has no other choice. The conditions are harsh: either fight for your life or die. The innocent, pure mind is forced to take in its first lesson: the battle for survival is an integral part of life. The child is afraid and in pain and to top it all is then taken away from its mother and shut up in a sterile box. Exhausted the child attempts to hide from life in the safety of its dreams.

Such is our first encounter with the outside world, filled with fear, loneliness, hopelessness, resentment, anger and total impotence. These are the initial lessons that are harshly and indelibly printed marked on the clean sheet of the mind. The inroad so essential to pendulums has been successfully made. It is no coincidence that these shocking methods of child birth are to this day widespread and considered civilised practice. Rarely does it occur to anyone that a birth of this nature is a terrible shock for the child that leaves a deep wound in the subconscious for life. No creature in the animal kingdom experiences anything even remotely similar at birth. Only in occasional and very expensive clinics can one be assured of a more 'personable' birth.

The first harsh lessons of the world of pendulums are well assimilated and consolidated even further over the course of one's life. There comes a time when the child lets go of its mother's hand and runs out with joyous, innocent courage to meet life. But the world of pendulums shows the child that life is not that safe after all. Suddenly, bang, the child falls over. The mother is worried that her child may have been hit by a car. I am saying this simply to convey how very deeply the *predisposition to negativity* is rooted in our consciousness while the good intentions of positivism often end up carrying you up into the clouds building castles in the air or drumming up all your strength to take by storm the fortresses on the ground.

So, what do you have to do to make sure that you maintain coordination and walk upon even ground without plunging into holes in the ground or clambering over obstacles? Reduce importance and go with the flow? Exactly. It is not easy, however, because it is not possible to free yourself from importance completely and the anxious mind that day dreams and wants to control everything prevents you from going with the flow.

Nonetheless, there is a solution, simple and yet ingenious. You can make use of the mind's inclination to control everything and offer it a new game. The idea of the game is, every time something bad happens, the mind has to wake up, consciously evaluate the level of importance being attributed and then change its relationship to the problem. Your mind is sure to like it. We have already looked at the principles of the game. They are the same as the humorous battle with the golem; but that is not all. Here we come to the main principle of coordination. If you allow yourself to be guided by this principle you will achieve the same level of success in realising the positive as negativists do in realising their worst expectations. It goes like this: *If you choose to perceive seemingly negative changes in the script as positive, that is what their outcome will be.*

If not absurd it still sounds a little unconvincing, does it not? What could possibly be positive about an obvious setback and what good is there to be found in misfortune? And yet however strange it might sound, the principle works every time. Once again, I assure you, that I am not asking you to believe in the principle I describe. Simply experiment with it. Try it out in practice. There is also a logical explanation for the mind.

As you know, the world is constructed on the principle of dualism. Everything has an opposite manifestation: light and dark, black and white, positive and negative, full and empty, etc. When you walk across a log and fall to one side, you automatically lift your arm on the opposite side of your body to compensate for the movement. Likewise, every event on a life line has two branches of potential realisation: one favourable and one unfavourable. Every time you come up against one event or another you make a choice about what your relationship to that event will be. If you choose to perceive the event as something positive you position yourself on a favourable branch of the life line. A predisposition for negativity however, causes a person to express their discontent and choose an unfavourable branch on the life line.

From first thing in the morning people get irritated by the slightest little thing and then the next thing until their whole day has turned into a constant trail of trouble. Obviously, even with the small things, as soon as you lose your inner balance, the negative scenario evolves into a drama. As soon as the one thing brings you down the next thing follows. This is why we say, that 'things always happen in threes'. *The trail of trouble does not follow on from the initial irritation so much as from your attitude towards it.* How the pattern is formed depends on the choice you make when you are standing at the fork in the road. It might only be a minor irritation that has shaken you out of sorts but irrespective of the magnitude of the irritation, you are already radiating energy at the frequency of the unfavourable branch in your life line. Moreover, a negative attitude creates tension potential which drains your intention energy. Your actions become ineffective and you stumble upon the next bigger irritation. You can imagine where you will end up in life if you keep following the map of negative branches. Essentially this is what facilitates the generation shift.

Now imagine a different scenario. Something happens that irritates you. Take a moment before rushing in with a negative attitude and responding in the primitive manner of the oyster. Say to yourself: "Stop! It is just a game with a golem. Ok, golem, let's play!" Whatever is happening, stay positive and pretend that you are pleased. There is a reason why we have the phrases "a blessing in disguise" and "every cloud has a silver lining".

Try to look for the positive in any difficult or annoying situation. Be glad, even if you fail to find anything positive to hang on to. *Adopt the foolish habit of rejoicing in setbacks.* It is much more fun than getting irritated and whining at every little inconvenience. You will see that in the majority of cases your inconvenience will act in your favour. And even if that is not the case you can be certain that your positive attitude has shielded you from other misfortune and carried you onto a favourable branch in your life line.

As a rule, annoyances are a deviation from the norm. They are only displeasing to you because they represent a strong deviation from balance and require additional energy use. You are the one providing the source of energy when you create the obstacles and then you spend even more energy in overcoming them. By contrast, good fortune and feeling happy is the norm. We are usually only discontent when we come up against a deviation in the script. Whenever the mind spots a deviation from a script it has accepted, it automatically perceives the change in a negative light and expresses the corresponding attitude towards it. The mind then strives to bring the situation back under control in its understanding.

So, now explain the rules of the game to your mind. Tell your mind that it will still be in control but that the function of control now consists in perceiving all events as positive. Switch on your Guardian at the very beginning of the performance, at the beginning of the day. Normally you have a rough idea of how the events of the day should unfold. In the moment that you see the scenario changing you must *accept the change and agree to them.* You only perceive an event to be negative because it does not fit into your scenario. Pretend that the event is just what was needed.

This way you get a sliding and dynamic element of *control over changes to the scenario*. Do not rush to express your dissatisfaction or try to fight the situation just because ongoing changes are being introduced to the script. *By giving up your control over the scenario, you have it returned to you only this time control is aimed at going with the alternatives flow rather than fighting against it.*

The secret to coordination lies in letting go your grip of control at the same time as taking the situation into your own hands. When the mind keeps things under its tight grip of control the situation cannot develop in harmony with the alternatives flow. However, when you accept changes to the script as par for the course, you let go of imposing your own sense of control. When you let go of the need to control you actually become able to keep your own attitude and consequently the situation itself under control.

At the end of the day, everyone wants to avoid problems and have everything turn out well in their life. If you begin practising the principle of coordination this is exactly what will happen. The coordination principle is even more effective than trying to influence events with the power of outer intention. The mind is incapable of anticipating perfectly every move that is to come; as we have already said you are not alone in the world. The layer of your own world intersects with endless layers of other people's worlds who are constantly adding their own thing to the picture. And yet the mind does not have to work out in advance what moves lie ahead. All is has to do is to run your target slide and follow the principle of coordination. Then outer intention will successfully bring you to your goal.

Coordination develops with practice. It is not enough to understand the coordination principle on an intellectual level only. You have to be constantly developing and perfecting the ability. Your Guardian must be working constantly too. You must not be oblivious to the moment that you are being drawn into a negative game.

Coordination is the most effective means of moving through the alternatives space. You perceive every event as positive and so always move onto a favourable branch of your life line and more frequently encounter the wave of fortune. You must be careful not to end up with your head in the clouds. You are not meant to be floating in the air but rather taking conscious, intentional action that enables you to *balance as you ride the wave of fortune.* This is the essence of Transurfing.

Apples Fall to the Sky

As it is written in the Holy Scripture: "According to your faith be it unto you". There is so much truth in this line. You only ever receive as much as you are willing to receive. Whatever this is, outer intention will fulfil your orders impeccably. You have what you have because it corresponds to the template of your worldview and vision of your place in the world. Now that you are acquainted with all the main principles of Transurfing you can manage your fate according to your own *free will.* Your fate will be shaped to reflect your personal choices and beliefs.

You know how to choose. That just leaves the question of how to believe in it all. As I have said before, you cannot convince the mind of anything until it is confronted with fact. The mind however, is capable of pretending. It is also capable of blind, fanatic belief, but usually a false belief based on intense excess potential created when inflated meaning is attributed to conviction. When the mind is absorbed with false belief it becomes so deafened by its own fanaticism that it is incapable of seeing or hearing anything else. When the mind climbs into the box where it has stuffed the heart, belief is blind.

The sail of false belief will never fill with the wind of outer intention. False belief is a trap that the pendulum sets in the labyrinth of insecurity. When you buy into a false belief you might think that you have escaped the labyrinth but this is an illusion. Deep down inside you will be plagued with doubt, but you will not acknowledge them because you have put up a protective wall of faith that blocks them out.

How can false belief be distinguished from true belief? True belief is more than belief; it is knowledge. *A belief is false if you have to persuade or convince yourself of it, no matter what approach you take, enthusiasm or duresse.* Knowledge is shaped by facts, not conviction. When the mind is faced with a fact it simply knows, whereas false belief is maintained by the mind's control. The mind makes absolutely certain that no trace of doubt can slip into its illusory room inside the labyrinth. When the mind *wants to hope* it refuses to listen.

When you try and convince yourself, or try to believe in something, you run the risk of adopting false beliefs. And yet, when you begin to listen to the rustle of the morning stars the illusions are revealed. Relax the mind's control and shift your attention towards being more attentive to the slightest signs of inner discomfort. If you reveal a pang of discomfort step back from trying to convince yourself of the idea you want to adopt. *When you achieve a state of unity of heart and mind you will not have to convince yourself of anything.*

Neither is there any point in trying to talk yourself round with positive affirmations. Any doubts you feel will not disappear by repeating to yourself: "I will have my way!" On the contrary, this just creates fertile ground for the doubts to grow stronger. The heart will not be persuaded, however hard you try because the heart does not understand logic or the language of the mind. Nor does it communicate in half tones. If you ask the heart: "Will I reach my goal?", it will answer either "yes" or "no" but never "maybe" or "probably". If the heart feels the slightest shadow of a doubt the answer will also be "no".

When the heart has doubts there is absolutely nothing you can say to persuade it otherwise. So what should you do? The answer lies in the statement above: the heart does not work with half tones. Doubt is what you experience when you believe in something to a certain extent, but not totally. The heart turns "not exactly" into "absolutely not". It neither believes nor doubts; it simply *knows* what will happen and whether the answer is "yes" or "no".

You have to take the radical step of removing the word 'believe' from your worldview template and replacing it with 'know'. If the mind knows that such and such a thing is going to happen the heart will agree without question. Do you believe that you are holding this book? No, because belief does not come into it. You just know that you are holding it. Where there is belief there is always room for doubt.

Now that you have removed the notion of belief from your mind, allow yourself *to have the knowing* that your desire will be fulfilled; for the law has it that: the goal will be reached if there is will to have and if there is the will to act by moving through the right door. It is your choice. You are in charge. If the decision is truly yours any thoughts along the lines of: "what if it does not happen", will become irrelevant.

Any event can develop in one of two ways: it will either work out or it will not. It is pointless trying to convince yourself that something will work out but when you have the knowing of the heart you can determine the outcome. Knowledge is the foundation on which confidence is built.

There is just one small step to go, which is how to acquire the *knowing*. To properly acquire knowing you have to get used to it and accept it. With time people get used to all sorts of incredible things: telephones, televisions and aeroplanes...have we not seen many examples of things that were thought 'absolutely incredible'. Apply the slide technique. Harbour knowledge in your mind and look after it until outer intention makes it fact. Remember, the task is not to convince yourself but to remind yourself of the knowledge that you will achieve your goal.

Whenever you think about your goal you will catch your self being involuntarily drawn back into doubt and thoughts about how the goal might be achieved will inevitably creep back in. Doubts will naturally creep up on you but you have to fish them out of your mind and put them in their proper place straight away with thoughts that sound: "I know success depends on my choice and I have made my choice so why hesitate?" If you do this the doubts will gradually fade. Where there is knowledge without belief, doubt cannot exist. There is no need to set about eliminating them or battle against their presence for this is a guarantee of defeat. You can however, console yourself with the knowledge that doubts do not necessarily guarantee failure, although the road might just get a little bit bumpy at times.

I want to emphasize that the most important thing is to remember that you alone decide whether you will achieve your goal or not. Remind yourself of this fact every time the doubts set in. I also draw your attention once again to the habit of forgetting and living a semiconscious existence. New knowledge is easily forgotten and old habits run deep. Never forget that you are in charge of your own fate.

I do not imagine that Jesus was particularly astounded when he walked on water. It must have been as natural for him as walking on the ground is for us. Other people would also be able to walk on water if they could be rid of the doubt, anxiety and emotion connected with doing so. Sounds improbable? Yet the entire history of humanity is a continual chain of the surprising and incredible. For example, it was once said that "iron ships will never float on water, let alone fly". And yet as soon as people saw that they could cross the water in iron ships and fly through the sky in heavy aeroplanes they ceased to contemplate the lack of probability that these things were possible.

Dragging doubts around with you is a sure way of reducing your chances of success. There are two life lines in the alternatives space: on one the goal is achieved and on the other you meet with failure. When you wallow in doubt you radiate energy at the frequency of the line of failure and then you can hardly hope for success. If encountered, failure will be caused by circumstances that have appeared as a direct result of your own thoughts.

The question needs to be put differently: "Will it happen or not?" should be replaced by "What do I choose, success or failure?" It can be difficult to get used to posing the question in this manner. Your entire life you have been convinced that apples fall to the ground and could hardly fall to the sky. However, if you can regularly catch yourself in the moment that you succumb to doubt, and remind yourself that success is just a question of choice, you will soon get used to it. Imagine to yourself that as of today, apples have started falling to the sky. It feels quite strange initially but then you get used to the idea and accept it. What can you say? That is just what apples do. Is anyone surprised when balloons fly off and upwards into the sky?

Now wake up and look at what I have just tried to convince you of with conscious awareness. Did you get the feeling that I might have been leading you into a labyrinth in search of belief? If you 'believed' me you fell into the trap. Do not be offended dear listener. I only wanted to demonstrate how easily the mind falls to wandering about in the pointless labyrinth of belief. Our stroll began with the words: "You have to take the pivotal step..." Then we tried to substitute belief with knowledge that has not been obtained yet. However, that does not change the essence of the nature of faith. Pendulums do exactly the same thing when they are trying to win your faith and trust.

Do not worry; Transurfing is not a trap for the mind and everything I have shared in this book is more than a product of speculative exercise. Even our little stroll ceases to be a trap if you think about it from the point of view of *hoping to obtain freedom* rather than calling you to believe. Only pendulums have a need of other people's faith. In the context of Transurfing, winning people over so that they hold a certain belief has no purpose whatsoever.

My goal is not to convince you. My goal is *to break through the stereotypes and false thought patterns of the conventional worldview in order to assist you in breaking out of the box of conditioning and waking up into the dream of waking*. When you wake up you realise that you can direct your own dream and without having to rely on belief. Take action and you will see what happens as a result. Do not believe; verify and prove and when you see that Transurfing really works you will then simply *know*.

You have probably heard it said that you can achieve anything if you have unshakeable faith in your own strength and victory. It is easy to say: "According to your faith be it unto you", but you cannot help wondering where this faith and strength of conviction is to be found, and how doubts can be eradicated. In reality you cannot avoid doubt and it is futile to try and acquire faith. If a shadow of doubt has crept into your heart no act of persuasion will ever drive it out. You can only deceive the mind. The mind will pretend that it has forgotten all about its previous doubts, but they will continue to live in the heart as before.

Abandon fruitless attempts to acquire absolute faith. There is another more realistic way of dealing with doubt. *Do not think about the means; run the target slide in your mind and place one foot in front of the other in the direction of your goal.* This exercise is not just another form of abstract dreaming. It consists of real work on attuning the energy you transmit. After all, your worst expectations are realised, are they not? So make it a concrete task to *consciously and deliberately re-attune your energy towards realising your best expectations.*

If you have a goal but doubt whether things will work out for you or not, your doubts will hinder your progress. You will not be able to discard them totally, but neither it is necessary to do so. The mind looks for faith to help it confirm that the goal is realistic. Nonetheless, do not think about the means. Brush faith aside. *Live out the slide that pictures your life as it would be were the goal already achieved.* By practicing this exercise you work on the quality of your energy without fuelling it with conviction. Take pleasure in the task, then outer intention will do its work and apples will fall to the sky.

When the mind is faced with fact, apples fall to the sky; the mind relinquishes its control and allows the fact to come to life. It does not matter whether the situation's development can be clearly seen or not. What matters is that the goal appear realistic to the mind. We live in a world where people do ride bicycles. If we were born into a world where everyone could fly, we would learn to fly too.

I have already explained, that when a person attunes the energy they radiate to their target life line they activate the workings of outer intention. You turn the target slide around in your mind and practice visualising the process. Whilst you are busy with these exercises the wind of outer intention slowly and surely pushes the frigate of the material realisation of your world through the alternatives space. Opportunities begin to arise in ways you would never have suspected. Moreover, outer intention begins to direct your actions in a way that brings you closer to your goal.

Note, that *sometimes it might seem as if circumstances are unfolding in a bizarre way.* And yet how could you know *which road specifically* leads to your goal. Would you expect to teach a top chef how to prepare a dish in their own restaurant? Always remember that the mind is incapable of anticipating all the moves that lie ahead and so cannot possibly know how to realise the goal. After all, it could not be achieved by ordinary means could it? And there we go again trying to crawl into Procrustes' bed of stereotypes and false patterns of thinking! Leave the matter of the means and ways to outer intention. Trust the alternatives flow. You will act in a way that brings you to your goal irrespective of your own will.

This is how outer intention works. If right now you are walking to a job you hate through the mud and rain but with a sense of the celebration of life in your heart all the difficulties you were experiencing will soon disappear. Quite simply, the quality of your energy will no longer correspond to the frequency of the scene.

I am not trying to convince you with these words for there is no way out of the labyrinth of faith. I am just trying to inspire *hope.* There has to be hope that the walls of the labyrinth will crumble when outer intention demonstrates to you that apples fall to the sky. It is impossible to practice Transurfing without this hope and you would not have started if you did not have hope. When there is hope the mind feels firm ground beneath its feet and the heart becomes vibrant.

When people encounter misfortune and disappointment or come up against a difficult problem they give their energy away to pendulums and feel anxious, exhausted and depressed as a result. People tend to get all psyched up and ready to battle with the situation or they give up entirely. Neither position is very positive, and both lead to stress and depression. There is no calm in these states. The inner core of confidence is undermined and people turn to cigarettes, alcohol, and drugs etc as a way out only to find themselves in bondage to new pendulums.

You can always find strength inside yourself if you wake up and become conscious of how the situation was created in the first place. The problem was created by pendulums and there is nothing wrong with this. The danger lies not in the problem itself but in your relationship to it. If you accept the importance of the problem you are giving your energy to the pendulum. It is important to be conscious of the fact that in any difficult situation the pendulum requires you either to tense up and fight or to lose heart and succumb to despair. You must not do either and yet what can you do when there is no support and the inner strength of confidence has been lost? Support is found in the awareness that you know that the pendulum is trying to subject you to its will and feed on your energy.

You might wonder how such simple knowledge can help, embolden and give heart but it can. Hope is also a kind of knowledge, that not all is lost and that there is a solution. Understanding how a problematic situation works has the same weight as hope; for it puts you above being the puppet and the little paper boat. You now understand what is really happening and you can consciously smile to yourself and say: "No, pendulum, you will not get your hands on my energy. I know what you are after and how you are trying to get your claws into me. It will not work. You will not get me to buy into the importance of the problem. I have the right to choose and I choose to be free of you".

Everyone makes their mistakes in life which they later have cause to regret. You might think that you are too far now from your original goal to make it real but nothing is ever lost. Transurfing can help to get things back on track. Even if your previous goal is objectively speaking closed to you now, you can also find a new goal. Everyone has more than one goal and so at any age there is the chance to set a new goal and the chance must be taken.

The mistakes of the past serve as your capital. If you take this position you will achieve shining success. Everyone who has achieved success has passed through a whole forest of setbacks and failures. There is a grain of truth in the saying that 'one man caned is worth two that were not' and 'failure breeds success'. All prominent figures at the height of success have had to go through many difficulties in life. It is just that this side of their life is not particularly advertised. So, if you have made a big mistake and met with failure, be glad, for you are on the sure path to success. If you beat yourself up, whine and complain about life, failure will repeat itself again and again. All the life experience that you consider worthless will undoubtedly benefit you in your target life line.

Apathy dissipates when fresh hope emerges. Both animals and human beings who walk the desert to the point of exhaustion forget their weariness when they spot the oasis on the horizon. Picture the fly that beats itself against the window pane next to the open window. Its entire life the fly has had it pummelled into its head that when you see a goal you should fly directly towards it. And yet the fly sees its goal and beats against the window pain in vain. It is the same with people when they fail to understand how to achieve their goal, deprived of choice and forced to accept the little they have. Now that you know that the open window exists, and it is just close by, even if you cannot see it yet, you will have *hope* and where there is hope, the energy of intention is released.

We need hope to begin taking action. Begin taking action and you will see that apples fall to the sky. When hope has done its work, you will become conscious of the freedom of choice. Then you will say to yourself: *I do not want and I do not hope. I intend.*

SUMMARY

Self-confidence is the same as a sheepish manner turned inside out.

When you abandon importance the walls of the labyrinth of insecurity crumble.

Where there is freedom without struggle confidence is no longer necessary.

When I have no importance, I have nothing to defend and nothing to conquer.

Do not fight your response to provocation; change your relationship to it.

Be indifferent to losing and avoid setting yourself ultimatums.

Treat all information with conscious awareness.

You have freedom of choice. All you need is the will to have.

Earn the will to have, not money.

Concentrate on the goal as if you had already achieved it.

The fact of personal choice is an immutable law. You shape your own reality.

How not to be afraid? — Find a safety net, plan B or alternative route.

How not to worry or get anxious? – Act.

How not to desire? — Accept the possibility of defeat and act.

How not to wait in expectation? — Act.

How to increase your worth? — End the battle for self-worth.

How not to get irritated? — Play with the pendulum and break its game rules.

How to be rid of feelings of guilt? — Stop justifying yourself.

How to deal with resentment? — End the battle and go with the flow.

If you cannot deal with your resentment, allow yourself not to be able to deal with it.

Life lines fork into positive and negative branches.

You make your choice by expressing your relationship to the event that stands at the fork in the line.

You step onto the positive branch of a life line when you intend to perceive apparent negative changes to the script as positive.

Adopt the foolish habit of taking joy in setbacks.

Switch control from battling against the alternative flow to going with it.

Do not think about the means of achieving your goal; turn the target slide in your mind and place one foot in front of the other in the direction of your goal. Live your slide where the goal has already been achieved.

Then outer intention will have its way and apples will fall to the sky.

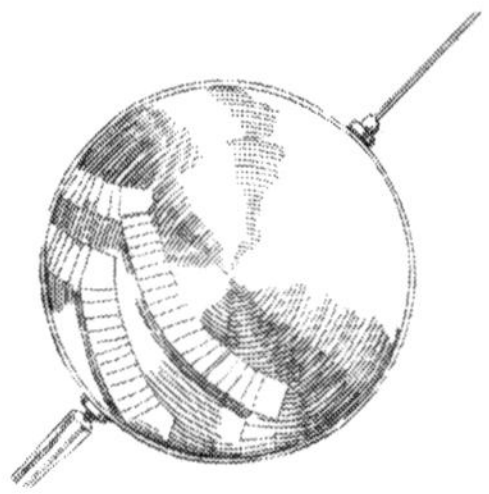

Chapter XIV. FORWARD TO THE PAST

The Past Lies Just Ahead.

Transaction

Sometimes we hear a random song that suddenly reminds us of times in our life when we were happy or we will catch the fleeting edge of a feeling we had when we were full of hope and life felt, if not like a holiday, then at least like the preparation for one. In these moments we feel a wave of nostalgia for what has been lost. It is sad to know that these moments were somewhere in the past and we can never return to them. Are these moments really lost forever?

In the foreword I promised to reveal the meaning of the words "forward to the past" towards the end of the book. Now the time has come to fulfil this promise. Transurfing has already presented you with more than a few remarkable insights. You are probably intrigued as to what I will share with you this time. All tricks of time travel are distinctly limited to the realm of science fiction. Despite the fact that theoretically physics does not exclude the possibility of time travel its physical application is still shrouded in doubt.

Moving through time does indeed seem unrealistic, and yet it all depends on your perspective. It is like the model of the two dimensional beings on a flat surface, who cannot see where the third dimension could be. From the point of view of fourth dimensional space, our three dimensional space also looks like a flat surface. The rational mind would say: "All these theoretical models are just abstractions, but I know what I see."

There is much in Transurfing that seems incredible, and yet I do not call you to believe the principle of Transurfing, I urge you to test them out. Of course, this will require your intention, some effort and patience because the results will not be immediately obvious. In the majority of cases, outer intention works slowly and barely noticeably. It might be difficult for you to believe that this mysterious, invisible force exists that acts in a way unseen by the eye, particularly if you are still just reading about it and have not yet tried to apply the principles of Transurfing in practice.

The moment has now come for you to see your movement through the alternatives space with your own eyes. You will see that you are capable of moving through time, both forwards and backwards. It will not be like the time travel they depict in science fiction movies for we are only concerned with the shape of reality. This time you will not have to wait for the results of outer intention. You will see the results straight away with your own eyes. It is no trick; neither does it involve experiments with moving into the astral plane or the dream space. For a few moments you will really feel movement in time and space. In practice the process comes down to a simple, single action – *transaction*, which consists of three elements.

To carry out the first element you must remember your central meridians. If you have already been doing the energy exercises you should be familiar with the feel of the meridians. You start by running scanning your body relaxing any tension in the muscles. Then picture your energy moving in the rising and descending currents along your spine.

A useful method to activate your energy fountains quickly is to imagine that two arrows run horizontally from the centre of your body extending in opposite directions. One points forward and the other backwards. The arrows extend twenty to thirty centimetres or more from the body. Now picture both arrows turning at the same time, the front arrow turns upwards and the arrow at the back turns downwards until they are in a vertical position to the spine. You will immediately feel a boost in the flow of energy.

You can practice this exercise either standing still or when you are walking. It is as if you are turning a *key* that switches on the central energy currents. There is no need to turn the arrows into fountains or to bring them together into a sphere. The important thing is to imagine being permeated by the flow of energy. It does not matter if you cannot actually feel the energy moving through you. A real sense of this will come with practice. Do this exercise when you are going somewhere, or simply out on a walk. It will give you a feeling of lightness and relaxation. *Turning the key is the first element of transaction.*

You can apply this exercise at any time that you need to quickly enter a more relaxed state. Try turning the key many times during the day, particularly when something is troubling you. You will notice straight away how the key releases tension. We are constantly carrying problems around with us, some small some large and the weight of our problems is automatically reflected in our muscles. When you are walking along and catch yourself thinking about something unpleasant, troublesome or worrying *remember* the key and turn it. You will feel a wave of relief as your muscles relax.

It is good to get into the habit of turning the key as many times as possible during the course of your day, then you will always have a way of releasing and cleansing the energy of intention from the excess potential that brings you down. Consider the exercise the *key to the conditioning box* that oppressive circumstances like to lock you up in. It will not free you of importance but it will considerably ease the process of release on an energetic and a physical level.

The second element of transaction is to visualise the target slide. Once you have turned the key, picture your target slide. Do not forget to imagine yourself inside the slide rather than watching it like a scene in a film. See yourself in a situation where the goal has already been achieved. To connect yourself with the slide imagine what you would be feeling if you were living it in reality. Touch the scene with you hands, imagine the sounds, smells or any other sensations that easily come to you. Turn the slide in your thoughts for a minute or more. The transaction process is most effective if you practice it when you are relaxed and walking in a familiar place. You can look to the side but in order to focus more clearly on the slide it is better to lightly hold your gaze somewhere on the ground just in front of you.

Once you can more or less clearly see yourself in the slide *gaze ahead of you with a look of conscious awareness.* Do not think or analyze anything; just take in with clear sight whatever you see ahead of you and further into the distance. *Clear sight is the third and final element of transaction.*

For a few seconds there will appear to be a change in nuances of the scenery. When you look at a familiar view with clear sight you will notice that although the picture is basically the same, there is something new about it as if some new yet barely perceptible hue had been added. It will be as if you had seen it before somewhere, not the specific details of the scene but a certain feeling, mood or after-taste – *a hue.*

You might for example look at a house that you have seen many times before but on this occasion notice its colour or lighting and understand that somewhere in different circumstances you have experienced something similar. In some cases you might have a distinct feeling that you know the scene from something that has happened in the past. You will no doubt have already come across the bizarre effect of when a *feeling from the past suddenly streams into your conscious memory.* It is not a memory of the past so much as a feeling from the past, a déjà-vue.

We experience the déjà-vue effect quite often it is just that we do not always notice it because we accept situations at face value, in other words, we are sleeping through a daydream. Transaction on the other hand enables you to notice how the world is changing before your very eyes. You may experience a vague sense of something familiar or the opposite, sense the appearance of a new, unfamiliar hue.

So, what is really happening in these moments? The material realisation of the layer of your world is moving in the alternatives space. Essentially, *what you are seeing is a change in the shades of the scenery in the stage set.*

As you know different sectors in the alternative space have different scripts and scenery. Depending on their relative distance from one another the differences between the sectors may be more or less pronounced. As a rule, the movement of material realisation takes place evenly and for this reason barely noticeably. You will not perceive the movement just as we do not perceive the movement of the minute hand on small clocks. Dramatic changes in shade are only felt when there is a sharper shift from one life line to another. This is also when you begin to see signs that clearly draw your attention.

During the transaction process visualising the slide strengthens the force of the wind of intention. In these moments the quality of your thought energy significantly differs from the frequencies of your current life line. The turning of the key strengthens the energy that programs your thoughts and as a result the movement of material realisation through the sectors accelerates. Clear sight attunes you to waking up and capturing the moment of change. Clear sight enables you to perceive the changing shades in the scenery for the short moments that the gust of wind lasts.

The transaction exercise should be performed dispassionately in the same manner that you would clean your teeth or brush your hair. You might not get it straight away, like riding a bicycle. We cannot ignore the fact that during the process of transaction you touch on outer intention, that elusive power that cannot be controlled.

I advise that you do not get too hung up about it if the transaction exercise does not work straight away. It will work. Make your attempts spontaneous. Do not try too hard. Do not strain to achieve the desired effect or place too much importance on the technique itself. You might happen upon a completely different technique that works for you. Do what feels right and comfortable and practice lightly at odd moments during the day. *The less important you make the transaction exercise the better the results will be.* As long as you do not take it too seriously or try too hard it should come easily.

You might think that if you repeat the transaction often the process of moving towards your goal will be rapidly accelerated. And you would be right. The problem is that you cannot always consistently perform the transaction exercise impeccably, i.e. dispassionately because the old habit of desire spoils things. If you set to burdening yourself with the transaction exercise you will be expressing the powerful excess potential of the desire to get a result as quickly as possible. Potential will also be created if you become absorbed with the necessity to act and put pressure on yourself to do the transaction. Necessity is also an excess potential which is why I always urge you to simply enjoy the process of visualising your target slide rather than making demands of yourself.

The potentials of desire and necessity drain the energy of intention to such an extent that there can be no gust of wind and without the wind of intention the transaction will not work. The desire to see results is particularly great in the initial stages and so I would recommend keeping a look out for desire. As soon as you catch yourself desiring to see a result, take a break and begin again later. Likewise, if you find yourself tensing up because you are trying really hard to fulfil the transaction perfectly, leave it and try again later.

Only practice the transaction exercise from time to time out of curiosity and with the aim of enjoying it. Do not take the transaction exercise too seriously. Its only purpose is to enable you to see the movement of the force of material realisation in the alternatives space. Of all the Transurfing exercises most attention should be given to running the target slide and visualising the current link in the transfer chain stream into realised pathways of reality. Outer intention works whether you see it or not. It is just that now you have a kind of porthole into the alternatives space and the opportunity to observe your movement there. It is quite impressive. You will not be disappointed.

Shades in the Scenery

Now we shall take a more detailed look at what you are really seeing as a result of transaction. It all sounds so unlikely that doubts will naturally arise. Might it be the effect of some kind of illusion created by the workings of human perception? Where is the guarantee that what you are seeing is the change in shades of scenery as you shift from one sector to another?

As I have already said, and as you know yourself, in dreams we see the external appearance of people differently from normal. When you see your reflection in a mirror the face you see is yours and at the same time someone else's. Familiar scenes take on a totally different look. You recognise the streets and the houses but they look different. The real world also changes with time. Trees grow, houses are painted different colours and all these changes are natural. At the same time, the movement of material realisation through the alternatives space does not follow a single straight line. So how can you distinguish the scenery of one line from that of another?

You could say that this would be impossible if it was not for the old invention of photography. Look through an old photo album. If you look at the background view captured in the photographs you will not be able to distinguish difference in the shades of the scenery in different life lines because the appearance of a physical location changes anyway due to natural causes. There is a more reliable method of distinguishing between life lines. Compare the faces of the people in the photographs taken at different times. You would expect the faces to change in a linear fashion as a reflection of the ageing process. And yet what you are seeing is something else.

A person's appearance significantly differs in different photographs and yet the change is not purely linear. Even if you discard the effect of different hairstyles and compare photographs of the same person from the middle of their life when the face has not greatly matured or aged you can see tangible differences. You are looking at the same face but it is somehow *different* and it is nothing to do with getting older, changing one's hair or even expressing different emotions. The face seems to have taken on a different countenance having acquired a different quality. This is the difference in the shades of the scenery. You already know that people change you just might not have paid particular attention to *characteristic differences in shade*. Leaf through old photo albums and you will be surprised.

In some people the difference can be so pronounced that when you meet them several years later you do not even recognise them. If you compare photographs of yourself taken at qualitatively different periods of your life, you will notice significant differences in shade. You will begin to get a picture of what your realisation looks like in qualitatively different sectors of the alternatives space.

Surely the photographs in the album must also take on different shades whilst you are moving through sectors of the alternatives space? Indeed they do, but it is almost impossible to catch changing shades and nuances in basic objects. If you practice transaction focusing your clear sight on a bed or cupboard you will not notice any change. This is why I recommend practicing the transaction exercise outside where changes can be perceived, rather than in a very simple environment.

A life line is a chain of sectors that are relatively uniform in quality. The sceneries of a single life line are also relatively uniform. When the layer of your world shifts to another life line, there is a change in scenery. Depending on the extent and quality of the difference between the lines changes in the scenery will manifest either as nuances and shades or significant transformation. In any case you will observe a qualitative change in shade.

So where is the time travel I mentioned in all of this? When we move along life lines in an organic manner we swim synchronously with time, as with the current of a river. Material realisation proceeds through the alternatives space like a roll of film in a projector and it is this movement that we perceive as time. In order to move relative to time you would have to move forwards or backwards, against the flow at a faster speed than the flow itself. It would be as if a picture in the film had suddenly started moving along the film roll. In this sense, time travel is genuinely impossible.

In other words, you cannot move forward or backwards in time within the same life line. This would be a contradiction of the laws of cause and effect. However, theoretically it is possible to move through time between different life lines. Transurfing does not claim to have the answer to how this can be done. Besides, we are looking at time travel here from a slightly different angle. Why is it that a feeling of the past sometimes bleeds through during transaction? The following gives a rough explanation of this phenomenon.

From early childhood the heart intuitively moves towards its goals through the necessary doors. In childhood we are still on life lines that would lead us to our goals. Maybe you had a childhood dream. Or maybe you were not aware of what you really wanted but your heart will have known nonetheless. And yet in life we are more influenced by destructive pendulums than we are by the dictates of the heart to say nothing of the long line of negative branches which everyone passes through due to a tendency for negativism. All this taken into account you gradually shifted further and further away from those initial lines that lead to your goal.

By performing transaction you are being shifted in the opposite direction and arrive at a life line where you have been previously, only now your position in time has changed. That section of the former life line that you may have travelled along is now in the past but you have returned to the line itself. Every line has its specific inherent features, taste and tones. It is these shades that you experience in the moment of clear sight towards the end of the transaction. Do not be confused by other differences such as the way a house looks in the morning and how it looks in the evening. The contrasts between different life lines are something quite different. You will know what I mean by this when you have experienced that feeling.

This is the return to the past we are talking about, by going forward to previous life lines. It might not be quite as exotic as what you were expecting but it is real. Imagine what a huge detour you have made by straying from the path and wandering around the forest for so long. However, now is not the time for regret. Now is the time to delight in the fact that you once again are gradually returning to your own path; for the majority of people never return.

You may not necessarily experience the shades of a line you have been on before if the path to your goal lies via new lines you have not previously travelled through. In this case, a return to former life lines happens rarely or not at all. Life lines in the alternatives space are deeply intertwined and indeed there is no need for us to know how exactly Transurfing works. At times you may think that you recognise the shades of the scenery and at other times everything will appear new. It may occur to you as you observe a familiar view that there is something new to the scene, particularly a tone or shade. I would like to emphasise that these new details are not the kind of change that you could perceive without doing the transaction exercise; they are new, subtle tones, styles, moods, meanings, themes or fleeting feelings.

You will understand exactly what I mean when you try it. You can do it. The only thing is to avoid trying too hard. The mind can spoil everything with its addiction to control. If you catch yourself straining to perceive the shades it is better to pause and come back to the exercise later once the desire to get an immediate result has faded. Remember the rules of the transaction exercise. It will not work if you are in any way tense. Believe me when I say that you will experience the result easily and naturally if you just "lift your little finger of outer intention". The opposite is also true. Your efforts will be transformed into the futile straining of inner intention if you try to force a result.

If no change in shades is noticed during the transaction exercise it means that the quality of the current line already meets the necessary quality of the visualisation. This indicates that you are transmitting the energy of the current life line and that your goal lies ahead on this same line. Whatever the case, if you do the transaction exercise, from time to time you will notice a transformation reflected in the shades of the scenery.

Shades are not only perceived in familiar views and landscapes. Even when your clear sight rests on a scene you are seeing for the first time, you may experience a fleeting sense of something long-forgotten or a sense of something fresh and new. There is a difference between the feeling of experiencing something new and observing something that is unfamiliar to you. When you look at an unfamiliar view you simply state as fact that you are seeing the place for the first time; you do not notice anything peculiar about it. During transaction you will have the distinct feeling that something new has appeared in the scene that was not there a few seconds ago. You will definitely feel it.

When you do perceive the shades you will amazed at how real they are. Admit it, reading this book you probably are not fully convinced by the reality of the alternatives space and life lines. When you do see what I am talking about with your own eyes, do not be afraid. It is no mysticism and neither is it purely a result of the nature of human perception as you might think. Soon you will discover other signs indicative of the shift to new life lines that cannot be explained solely by the nature of perception. You might begin to feel, that the way other people treat you has changed for the better without any evident reason or that certain day to day problems have disappeared. Generally you will notice that certain attributes of everyday life have changed although you cannot see any particular reason why this should be so. For example, a clock that stopped working many years ago has unexpectedly started working again.

Under normal circumstances, clocks stop working due to a natural clogging up of their moving parts. If you clean them they will work fine. However, very often clocks, household appliances and electrical equipment will suddenly stop working for no apparent reason, or break down when their owners lose a state of balance due to stress or conflict. The breakdown of equipment is not caused by excess potential for this energy is too minor by comparison and is not directed differentially such that it could cause any kind of mechanical change.

The energy connected with negative experiences induces a shift to a life line where balance is disturbed, life has lost its peaceful flow and where there are deviations from the norm. Nothing appears to have changed and yet something is not right, something seems unsettled and awry. It is as if the scenery of the stage set is the same but the lighting is different, the transparent air has become clouded with a pall of dust, or the water is muddied. These slight changes are capable of affecting sensitive household appliances and other complex technology for which a pall of dust is a tangible phenomena.

There is a certain type of person whose life always seems to be falling apart. People like this are always off balance due to being too absent-minded, excitable, tense or worried. Sensitive appliances that find themselves on the muddy life lines of these poor individuals fail. So, if your clock has suddenly started working again it suggests that you have managed to shift to purer life lines. Do not be overly concerned if you cannot get your clock to work at all. It might just need to be repaired.

Now you know that as well as travelling through the alternatives space you are also in a sense travelling through time. You cannot return the past but it is possible to retrieve that free feeling of the new, hope, and happiness that was lost as a result of moving down a chain of negative branches. Earlier on in the book we talked about why the feeling of freshness in life fades with time. Moving towards your goal is like returning to the past when ice-cream was delicious, hope was bright and life was still joyful and promising. Do not despair – the past lies just ahead!

Gliding

Finally we have arrived at the moment when I can reveal the answer to the Guardian's Riddle. The statement that everyone has the absolute freedom to choose their own destiny is only a riddle until you clearly understand the origins of bondage. Based on all that has been said so far in this book, I can now share the answer with you.

Freedom is yours when you end the battle. As you can see, the answer is short and simple like the alchemist's secret on the Emerald Tablet. If I had told you the answer to the riddle at the very beginning of the book, you would not have understood all its implications, would you? Our dependence lies in taking part in the battle imposed upon us. Once you wake up from the day-dream, once you stop being hard on yourself and end the battle with yourself and the world, nothing can hold you down. The battle will continue but without your participation and you will be free to go wherever you wish and choose anything you desire. *The world is a mirror that reflects your relationship to it. When you are discontent with the world, it turns away from you. When you fight the world it fights you back. When you end the battle the world meets you halfway.*

From birth the pendulums show you your place in life. They install a template of the worldview you must accept, explain the rules of the game, assign you a role and with that, you are locked up in a box of conditioning. At the same time, the pendulums falsely declare you independent. Their declaration states that you can choose. You are hung on puppet strings and allowed to go 'free', to desire whatever you want and to achieve it in any way you see fit. You begin to pull at the strings working towards your goals but are unsuccessful. Then you are made to understand that if you want to win your place in the sun you will have to fight even harder, both with yourself and with the world. This is the pendulum's rule: "Fight and do as I do".

The only freedom you exercise is the right to take part in the battle for this too is a choice and you always get what you choose; that is an immutable law. A person can never beat a pendulum in battle. They may perhaps receive a prize but even this is achieved by a mere handful of individuals. The pendulum's objective is to conceal your true freedom. No-one can force you to take part in the battle but they can *instil* the belief in our minds that no other choice exists. In a sense they are right: *there can be no other choice until you stop clinging to the strings of importance.*

To gain your real freedom you must abandon importance – do not attribute excess meaning to anything either inside yourself or outside in the world. In the majority of cases it is enough to wake up and consciously change your relationship. We are all dreaming, mechanically playing out our roles. The depth of our dream is likewise proportional to the meaning we attribute to the attributes of the game which makes us prisoners of our own attachment to importance.

Is not trying to change your relationship to something just another part of the same battle? No. You battle with yourself when you try to control your *emotions.* Now that you know the nature of the pendulum's game you can consciously change your *relationship* to it without being hard on yourself. In this way you make a choice for freedom from the battle. Now you can decide the rules of the game yourself. Your game with the pendulum revolves around breaking the pendulum's game rules. Then the battle is transformed into a ridiculous fight with a golem. It is as if you realize that it is all a daydream. By distancing yourself from the stage and watching from the auditorium, you suddenly understand that it is entirely up to you to decide whether you want to continue participating in the battle or simply take what is yours.

Of course, you will not be able to tear off the strings of importance straight away. You cannot just decide to be rid of all your excess values and complexes just like that. Neither should you set about being rid of them, for that just sets up another battle. The strings of importance will drop off by themselves when you stop battling. Any importance that can be consciously dropped should be. Anything that cannot be consciously dropped can be transformed through action. Turn your target slide round in your mind, visualise the process and calmly place one foot in front of the other in the direction of your goal. This is your proactive step. Rejecting the game also counts as action. Give yourself and the rest of the world the opportunity to be as they are. There is no need to change yourself or fight with life. As soon as you turn your back on the battle, your freedom will become more tangible with every passing day.

It is not possible to be rid of the burden of the problems that you have accumulated over the course of your life in one foul swoop. However, by observing the principle of coordination you will make your way out of the mesh of wind-fallen trees onto a clear, even road. There is no guarantee that everything will go smoothly at the outset. You can expect to be provoked by pendulums, obstacles and disappointment. The main thing is not to lose heart or sink into despair. Everything will work out with time, for now you have a powerful technique at your fingertips for managing your own destiny.

If you have felt enlightened by the insight that you can control the events of your life, if you have sufficient confidence and the necessary enthusiasm, you can also expect to come up against unpleasant surprises. You are likely to get a slap from one force or another, depending on the intensity of your confidence and emotional high as balanced forces will respond to your excess potential. Do not succumb to the temptation of imagining yourself to be the puppeteer or director-producer of the play called "My Life".

Of course, you are a director, but solely in relation to your own fate. You are not the only one acting in the play called "My Life" and so the slightest expression of arrogance and self-importance will create excess potential. You might think that you do not have a high opinion of yourself at all, but no-one is perfect. You have received the key to an extremely powerful force and so the slightest deviation from integrity and impeccability will have tangible consequences.

Ideally, the awareness that every individual is the master of their own fate should be quite obvious. Imagine that you were given a document that certified your right to purchase a newspaper at any stall across the city. The document would hardly fill you with excitement because you have this right anyway, irrespective of any document. Would you get upset if you could not buy a paper at one particular newsstand? No, you would simply go to the next or forget about buying a paper after all. Your attitude towards your new ability to control the events of your life should be no different to your attitude towards buying a newspaper.

There is one more thing I must warn you about. Transurfing is not designed with the intention of causing any other person harm. It is possible to use Transurfing to direct hostile intent towards a person or group of people that you wish to take vengeance on, but doing so would entail serious consequences. I really do not recommend that you practice black magic. Even if it seems to you that retribution is entirely justified, do not get involved. If you have not been able to resist sending negativity towards your enemy you can expect to receive an initial warning. You will see a sign. If then you do not stop, you will be punished. Never forget that we are all guests in this world. The conditions of freedom are that we get to choose but we do not have the right to change anything or anyone.

As you know, many ancient civilisations perished leaving nothing but shards of physical construction such as the Egyptian pyramids and the muffled echoes of some secret, mystical knowledge. Those people who mastered the power of outer intention became too powerful and were not only punished but totally destroyed by balanced forces. There have been many civilisations like Atlantis and every time the people mastered the power of outer intention they forgot that they were just guests in this world. And you know what happens to guests that push the limits – they get kicked out.

You should also be particularly wary of boasting to your friends and family. If you make claims aloud that you will get what is rightfully yours, your chances of success will decrease significantly. It is one of those cases where confidence must grow into inner confidence. When you know in yourself that you will achieve your goal you do not disturb the balance. When you carry this knowledge inside it becomes a thing of itself. However, if you declare to others that you will acquire something you do not yet have you create excess potential. Then balanced forces become involved aimed at eliminating the excess potential. One should conclude therefore, that it is better to act with some humility and keep silent. Naturally, once you have achieved your goal you can kick up your heels but without foolish extremes or euphoria, otherwise balanced forces will confiscate your newfound toy.

Transform your joy into the intention of celebration. Use your right to choose and allow yourself the luxury of perceiving the life you are currently disenchanted with as a celebration. This will give you a real rather than an illusory cause for celebration; for then you have the hope of acquiring freedom. You will experience a quiet delight knowing that you are moving towards your goal and this will keep the feeling of celebration close. Even balanced forces will not be able to darken your quite delight. *In accordance with the principle of coordination, if you perceive life as a celebration whatever is happening, it will become one.*

Now there is no need to continue battling. You will get what is yours in the end. By turning your back on the battle you tear off the strings and acquire your true freedom, without losing the prop they gave. The new prop is the alternatives flow. Remember that your choice will be fulfilled. Attune your thoughts to your target line and then the flow will be directed towards your goal. There is no force capable of preventing you on the path towards your goal if you go with the flow, stay balanced and observe the principle of coordination. You are no longer a small paper boat on the wave of circumstance and no puppet in the hands of pendulums. You have a sail, unity of heart and mind. You have a helm, your choice. You glide through the alternatives space on the wind of outer intention.

SUMMARY

Turning the key releases tension and frees the energy of intention.

Transaction: turning the key, visualisation and clear focused sight.

Transaction enables you to see the changing shades in the scenery.

Do not give the transaction technique excess meaning.

Carry out transactions in a relaxed manner.

Do not push yourself to do the transaction exercise too often.

The target slide and visualisation process are quite sufficient.

The only purpose of transaction is to enable you to perceive movement through the alternatives space.

Moving towards your goal refreshes the layer of your world.

The world is a mirror that reflects your relationship to it.

You win your freedom by ending the battle.

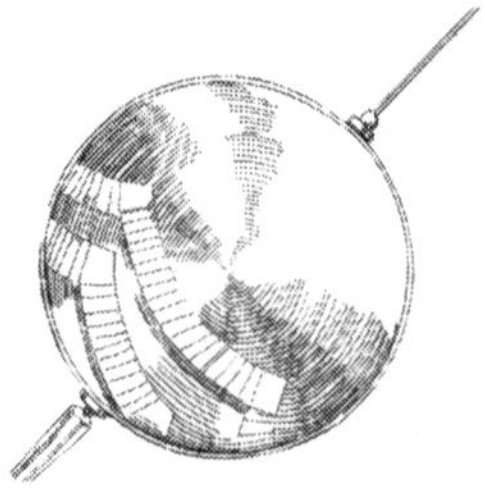

Chapter XV. LETTERS FROM THE PAST

"But you yourself must not distinguish your victory from your defeat"
B. Pasternak

A Run of Bad Luck

"I have some questions I have not been able to find the answers to. According to your theory, if I look for the good in everything I should end up riding a wave of positive events. I tried that but it did not work for me, and it was not just the once, otherwise I would not have noticed it.

I will give you an example. About six months ago I had a great job that suited me perfectly and made me happy. I lived for my work. I had good friends, a partner, a home and my parents lived close by. I was genuinely happy, and what is more, I knew I was happy. I even envied myself a little I was so happy. Life was chilled and everything made sense, but I knew it could not last forever. Then I had to leave and now I have no home, very few friends and a job that does not match my qualifications or personal plans...

Here is another example. I was about to graduate from university. For the two years prior to graduation I spent a lot of time at the faculty building close relationships with the lecturers and other students. During the final term I even had a physical sense of what a wonderful, unrepeatable period in my life this was and so I tried to commit every day to memory. Then I had an offer to stay and work at the institute. I was beside myself with joy! But then there were cut backs in university staff and I was not offered a position after all and spent six months unemployed just sitting around at home. These were truly dark days.

In other words, there have been many times in my life when I have been truly happy and thanked God for it only for it all to be ruined by a run of bad luck. In my case, the law you talk about did not work and I got drawn onto a negative wave of events. And when I was really low and started to whine and complain about things it is as if I was given a clue or some kind of help, although according to your theory this should have swept me way off course...

These are the kinds of contradictions I have been experiencing. I would be grateful if you could help me understand them better".

There are no contradictions in your case. On the contrary, everything is working out just as it should and although it may not be clear to you why it suddenly rains after the sun has shone, you express the reason for this wonderfully clearly in your letter.

The reason has always been and will always be the same: *the world is a mirror of your relationship to it.* The difference between the former and the latter only lies in the fact that a mirror reflects change instantly whereas the world's response may take a few days or even several months.

Look at what you have written: "Life was chilled and everything made sense *but I knew it could not last forever. ... During the final term I even had a physical sense of what a wonderful, unrepeatable period in my life this was."*

Where in your opinion is the contradiction? In your relationship to these periods in your life you chose the program and the world fulfilled it impeccably. The world always manifests your personal choice perfectly. This in fact is all it ever does.

You express your complaint about the mirror in the following way: "*...there have been many times in my life when I have been* *truly happy and thanked God for it only to then have a run of bad luck!"* So, what caused the run of bad luck?

If I tell you where a run of bad luck comes from you will not believe me. Even if your letter had not contained the key phrases I have quoted it would not be difficult to name the reason for the phases of bad luck you describe. There is nothing unique about what you write, for we always make the same mistake.

The thing is, that the run of bad luck that followed the run of good luck, was not a run of bad luck at all. You just decided to paint it in dark colours. Nothing bad can follow from something good. In reality, after *something good, something better always follows* but you did not see it this way. You could not accept the changes that were underway and so put your negative relationship to the world out there. The world gave you a mirror reflection of it and transformed your choice into physical reality.

Such is the nature of the human mind that it stubbornly insists on its own script. Anything that does not fit the script is considered a failure. And vice versa, only things that the mind has already imagined are accepted as a sign of success. The mind is quite obstinate in this regard and this quality originates in an inflated sense of self-importance and established social stereotypes.

How can your mind know what is really good for it and what is not? Can it possibly foresee how things will turn out? Great success never knocks on the door beforehand; it always literally drops out of the sky. Have you never wondered why this is? It is because in this instance the mind is distracted and has not been able to hinder success from being realised.

Only in the moment when the mind releases its deadly grip of control over the script can success break through the solid line of defence. If success could be planned there would be no need for us to have all these conversations in the first place. Plan and get what you planned for? Only very rarely.

The mind is not capable of designing an algorithm of success. Sometimes listeners ask me how they should act in one specific situation or another. How could I possibly know how they should act? Never believe anyone who claims to know the recipe for success in any given situation. *No-one is given to know these things.*

So, where does the answer lie? The answer lies in the world that is your mirror! Transurfing offers the most amazing discovery. All you have to do is make a choice and then get out of the way of its material realisation.

The paradox is that we do not have to know precisely how to find success and in fact it is actually better that we do not know. Did you really think that Transurfing would give you yet another recipe for success? It is beyond the calibre of the mind to make up such a recipe. The whole beauty of it all is that *the recipe writes itself!*

The mind's task is to avoid hindering the alternatives flow, the natural course of events, with its tendency for control. *The alternatives flow always runs in the direction of your choice.* This is why, once you have made a choice you can boldly depend on the coordination of intention principle: *my intention is being realised; everything is working towards its realisation and everything is unfolding as it should.*

Let us return to the run of bad luck. Every time you encountered a run of bad luck you missed an opportunity of some kind; the chance to make the run of good luck even luckier. The mind could not accept the nature of forthcoming events or interpreted them as negative, as a result of which, the negativity became manifest in all its glory.

Do not be upset at the thought of opportunities lost. If you define your goal and hold fast to the principle of coordination, a wonderful discovery will await you. You will see that all the mistakes you made previously served towards this goal. You would never have achieved it if you had not encountered the previous setbacks. On the other hand, if you had not made those mistakes you would still have reached your goal it is just that it would have taken a different shape. You do not have to limit yourself to the potential of one goal only. There are infinite goals at your disposal. This is how mysterious, magnificent and generous the world really is.

So, do not despair: if you move towards your innermost goal the past will lie before you. Perhaps until now you have allowed yourself to be distracted by other people's goals?

The Game of Partners

"You said that seemingly incompatible individuals marry as if to punish one another. When I read this I thought it described my situation perfectly. Could you give me any practical advice as to how to find a way out of the situation, what to do and think.

I have tried many times to improve my relationship. Sometimes things get better but the effect is always temporary, and then I understand that my wife and I are just fundamentally incompatible and I should try to build a relationship with a different woman. I have chosen to get a divorce. I really want to end the relationship but there is shared property involved and so circumstances prevent me from carrying out my plans quickly and smoothly with minimum losses.

Sometimes when I get angry and feel prepared to end it all there and then, whatever the circumstances and consequences the relationship seems to improve for no apparent reason, but soon after, it all kicks off again. What can I do from the point of view of Transurfing to change the situation?"

It is true that the majority of divorces come about for the relatively trivial reason that the partners involved refuse to accept each other as they are. You might be thinking that this explanation is wrong and that I will show you why but you would be mistaken.

It is not a matter of who is right and who is wrong. *Awareness, or rather the lack of it*, is the one banal yet key cause of conflicts that seems to arise over the trivial things in life.

Annoyance reflects a lack of awareness. In non-lucid dreaming the dream just happens to the dreamer; they are not aware that what they are seeing is just a dream because they are so totally absorbed in the game. In the same way, people who are living asleep in the waking world react negatively like an oyster reacts to any external irritant. Everyone understands theoretically that each individual has a right to their own weird personality traits and eccentricities and that they are not obliged to change if they are a little different to us. Yet most people are only aware of this when they are asked about it directly. In all other cases, the annoyance factor is triggered unconsciously.

The type of person who is asleep in the waking world cannot allow themselves or others to be themselves. They create dependent relationships which generate polarisation and evoke the wind of balanced forces which brings people with diametrically opposed personality traits together in order to cancel out the dissimilarity between them.

In addition to everything else, sensing a polarity of qualities, pendulums induce actions that cause even more annoyance. You may have noticed that sometimes your partner seems to do things deliberately to annoy you. Be aware that in the majority of cases they are not conscious of what they are doing. Their actions are influenced by a pendulum that wants to annoy you even more so that it can then feed on the energy of your irritation.

You illustrate how polarisation works in your letter when you write: "*Sometimes when I get angry and feel prepared to end it all there and then, whatever the circumstances and consequences, the relationship seems to improve for no apparent reason.*"

When you agree, "whatever the circumstances" you let go your grip as if saying: "Let it burn!" In this moment, the effect of polarisation is weakened; the wind of balanced forces quietens and the pendulum leaves you alone. As a result, the relationship temporarily improves.

It would be more accurate to say that people who are similar in character are more incompatible than people who are very different. Translated into the language of fact, when people say "we are not compatible" or "our personalities clash" what they really mean is "we could not accept each other the way we are".

In reality, people with opposite characters can and should be able to live happily together in harmony. There is a reason why balanced forces bring opposites together thereby supporting the status quo. You may know, as I do, of couples who have split up many times during the course of a long-term relationship, each time believing the split was serious, packing suitcases, smashing plates, burning family photographs, tearing up certificates of marriage and carrying out other equally as inflammatory rituals. Each act of drama is likewise accompanied by terrible oaths that this time it is for real and there is no going back. Yet the storm subsides and both warriors calm down and go back to living together again.

All these conflicts armed with rolling pins and plates could be avoided if those involved could step down from the stage into the auditorium and observe the act, i.e. their life together from a different perspective. It is essential that at least one of the partners do this.

Why is a life shared by two people like a play? Because each takes on a role: I will be this person and I will do such and such, and such and such that you do irritates me. People become immersed in the play and behave without conscious awareness as if they were sleeping in the waking world. Life 'happens' to them and so they are incapable of influencing the script however hard they try, and try they do.

Remember how when you were little you used to play at being grown-ups? Unlike adults, children are aware of the fact that it is all just 'for fun'. Children always remember that this is a game and so they act consciously like a theatre-goer who simultaneously acts in the play. Children are capable of changing the script in their game because they know that it is not real. Likewise, in lucid dreaming the dreamer is capable of controlling the events that are taking place because they are aware that it is a dream.

When people grow up they lose the ability to play indifferently and become mentally immersed in their games as in a deep sleep losing conscious awareness of what is happening as a result. Because people are asleep in waking they turn into weak-willed puppets, obedient to the pendulums and life begins to just happen to them in the nature of a dream.

Try to live your life together as children. Adopt the roles you have attributed each other and play at them indifferently, 'just for fun'. For example, as soon as your partner begins to do something you do not like and you find yourself getting irritated as before, play your role in picturesque or grotesque manner, with humour. As a result the dynamics of the conflict caused by dreaming unconsciously when you are awake will become crystal clear. Then you will begin to realise just how many arguments are pulled out of thin air like in the soap-operas. When you become aware of this moment you will at last be able to accept yourself and others just the way they are.

Charity

"For the past two years I have been totally immersed in trading currency (FOREX) but have not been able to get to a point where I could trade stably and profitably. For two years now I have suffered constant losses. Maybe my colleague is right who writes that the market is the invention of the devil "Give what is Caesar's to Caesar and what is God's to God". They say that when you play on the market you trade in your own soul, and unfortunately it is true. That is how it is. The only way out for me now is to donate everything to the church, but this will not resolve the karmic consequences...

And what about the multivariance of fate? Why should not one provide for one's life by trading in the currency market? Are the stories of the millionaires all just a myth? Should I eliminate the very idea of getting rich from my mind and replace it with the idea of helping others? I am no theorist and neither am I just dabbling in ideas. Everything I write I have experienced personally and not once but hundreds of times. What do you think I should go for?"

You are asking *me* what *you* should choose. Can I or anyone else really show you your true path? Only your soul can know what you should choose. All I can do is evaluate your mistakes, and even that is a subjective opinion.

You write: "The only way out for me now is to donate everything to the church". Naturally, I realise that you do not really believe that this is the only solution available to you. Yet, why would you consider making donations a solution at all? It is not the adherents of God, but the adherents of pendulums that have instilled the idea that you 'save your soul' or are absolved of certain karmic issues by giving your money away to the church. Any true servant of God will tell you, that absolution or pardon can never be bought for any amount of money.

Let us call a spade a spade: the religion pendulum is not the same as God. The church is required by the pendulum, not the Almighty. God does not need your donations. If you see making a donation as a solution to your problem it means that you are trying to make a deal with Him.

Charity can eliminate the excess potential of accrued sums of money if you have a surplus of stagnant resources. However, given that you are involved in trading currency you probably are not suffering from financial stagnation.

Charity is a good deed in the true sense only if it is sincere. For example, a wealthy individual financially supports an orphanage but never visits. This is not a good deed but a deal. The support is indifferently directed and simply serves a nice idea framed with the pious phrase: "I help children!"

The motivation however, is not sincere. The sponsor does not have a passion to communicate with the children they are helping and so does not have any love for these children. *They have regard for themselves as someone helping children.* Can it really be bad that a person helps without love and sincerity or not? It is not necessarily bad. It is fine, but there should be any reason to hope that the act will somehow 'count'.

Such a sponsor may increase their rating in public opinion but in terms of compensation, the soul will get diddly quat. It is better to love yourself sincerely than to love others insincerely. I would even go so far as to say, that it is absolutely essential to love oneself.

You wrote: *"Should I eliminate the very idea of getting rich from my mind and replace it with the idea of helping others?"* Do not burden yourself with the idea of having to help others if you do not genuinely feel motivated to do so. On the contrary, work on accumulating *your own* wealth. This you will do sincerely and there is absolutely nothing to be ashamed of in doing so. Pay no attention to the cries of pendulum supporters who try to force their "spiritual" values upon you. Remember, that a truly spiritual person *will never try and force anything upon you.*

The highest spiritual value you can have is your own soul. Turn away from pendulums and turn to face your soul. Think of yourself, for example, creating your own well-being. That said the approach to creating your own wealth needs to be different to the one you are currently taking. The soul does not want money. It wants the things that money can buy. Do you really know what you want? Perhaps not. Ask yourself what you really want in life. *What would turn your life into one continuous celebration?* Define the goal.

Your mind takes the direct approach: money will buy almost anything, consequently, it makes sense, to go straight for the money. The problem is that the soul is direct in its own manner and does not share the minds desire for cash. The soul has no understanding of what money is, basically because, put simply, it does not know how to 'think' in abstract terms, so the soul will never become the mind's ally when it comes to accruing money. The mind is powerless without the soul just as the soul is powerless without the mind.

So what should you do? *Define your goal and take steps towards it without considering the how to achieve the goal.* The means will appear – that is the whole trick. In other words, if the soul and the mind move towards the goal together, arm in arm, doors will open before you that previously appeared impregnably locked.

Could the currency market be your true door? I am not the one to judge. Yet you write: "…I have not been able to get to a point where I could trade stably and profitably. For two years now I have suffered constant losses." You can draw your own conclusions. Those who become millionaires work towards their innermost goals, not for the sake of money.

When a person moves towards their innermost goal via the right door for them the soul sings and the mind rubs its hands in glee. Does working the currency exchange bring joy to your heart? Does this vocation satisfy your mind? Only you can know the answer to these questions.

Esoteric Knowledge

"I have read a lot of literature of this kind and the interesting thing is that in principle the authors are all saying the same thing with some differences.

I for example get confused from all the available material as to what is right and what is not. Almost everyone says that it is not worth letting all the information you perceive into your heart. But what should people who are sensitive do and for example people who give alms daily? For if we stop perceiving or understanding the grief of others the world will become a callous and evil place.

In the future I want to be a journalist and already work for one publication. I mainly write newspaper stories based on the problems faced by women. You cannot write productively unless you are prepared to let their cares touch you. What should journalists do who come up against information of all kinds on a daily basis? Surely it does not mean that my entire life I will have to push pendulums or suffer myself? Perhaps I am just not getting it?

Sometimes I even wonder whether all these ideas, including Transurfing, are not just different versions of a utopia, because if you think about it, Transurfing is also a pendulum that you have created which you keep swaying with the thoughts of others. Why not simplify the laws and principles you describe?

Transurfing has not simply been 'made up' and so its laws cannot be remade. It would be impossible to 'make up' anything of this kind. Neither is it possible to learn this kind of thing from someone else. Esoteric knowledge can neither be made up nor learned. It simply resides in a commonly accessible place which I happen to call the alternatives space. Someone else might call it something else, but that does not change its essence.

In your letter you mention that you get confused about certain issues. How do you make sense of the myriad different teachings which, as you put it, although being different pretty much say the same thing? You will not believe how simple it is.

Once you have read a sea of literature on psychology and the esoteric you reach a certain point where you can stop and forget everything other people have written in books. Once you have established a basic foundation of knowledge in any given area you can source further relevant information directly from the alternatives space.

It requires boldness to rely on yourself rather than continuing to search for the answers in books. Whilst your mind is attentively focused on the words of the wise people in this world you will find confusion and be confined to the position of the eternal student. Change direction. Turn the focus of your mind to your soul and there you will find the answers to all your questions.

Do you know what differentiates those who make discoveries, create masterpieces of culture and art and write books from others who are surprised by the discovery, delighted by the masterpiece and who listen the books? How is the creator different to the critic or the teacher different to the student?

The former have the boldness to tear their mind away from the creations of others and give their attention to their soul. It is not that the critics and students have no talent. It is just that they direct the power of intention differently, towards valuing what belongs to others and learning from them.

You might think that I enjoy appealing to your emotions in a kind of empty demagoguery or chewing over common truths. When I tell you to turn the attention of your mind to your soul it probably sounds a bit vague and reeks of the kind of spirituality that is indulgently sweet.

However, the things I am talking about are quite real. It would not be quite accurate to say that your soul already knows it all. It is not that your soul already knows, it is more that unlike the mind, it has access to an information field that contains data relating to the past and the future and likewise that contains all masterpieces and discoveries.

The mind perceives the feelings of the soul as intuitive knowledge and inspiration and then interprets them in the form of commonly held ideas and classifications.

The mind can never invent anything totally new. The mind is only capable of building a new house from old blocks. Everything that is totally new is created from the unity of heart and mind. There are simple, concrete steps that can be taken to achieve this unity.

Accept as fact that all knowledge is accessible to you. Look to yourself for the answers. Walk your own path. Exercise your right to individuality. Use your access to knowledge.

Knowledge will become accessible to you as soon as you manage to change the focus of the power of your intention from others to self. You must just tell yourself that you are a unique individual and know everything. Ask yourself a question and wait for the answer. The answer will come to you, perhaps instantly, perhaps a few days later or perhaps even months later, depending on the complexity of the question, but the answer will definitely come!

Everyone's connection between heart and mind is different but whatever form the connection takes, the most important thing is to be mindful of the heart, so that the power of intention is with the heart. *The whole secret lies in the fact that it does not occur to many people to do this, but those who do begin to make discoveries and create masterpieces.*

The only thing that obscures unity of heart and mind is inner and outer importance. Importance locks the creative essence up in a box of established stereotypes. This is what you write about your listeners' problems: *"It is impossible to work productively without letting their cares touch you".*

It is a phrase stamped with correctness do you not think? It just begs to be followed with something like: "how can you help them, unless you let their problems touch you?" This sounds very correct but underneath it is a false stereotype created by pendulums.

You help solve other people's problems not because you let them touch you but in spite of the fact that you are touched. Moreover, when you become mentally immersed in other peoples' problems you become incapable of solving them objectively.

People experience problems in the first place because they are totally immersed in their own enactment. Life 'happens' to them and they, like in non-lucid dreaming are subject to the power of circumstances. As soon as they come down into the auditorium and observe the theatrical from a different perspective they will see many things more clearly.

Whilst your mind is immersed in the problems of others you are in the same position as they are. In order to understand and solve someone else's problem you have to act dispassionately.

This does not mean heartlessly or indifferently but with detachment. This is the difference between the absence of importance and the absence of compassion.

You can only find solutions to problems, both your own and others' if you adopt the role of the participating spectator. All the time that you are 'living' your problems or the problems of others you remain powerless. Many Listeners struggle to discern the difference between detachment and heartlessness. *The absence of importance is a matter of detachment not indifference.* Play your role 'just for fun' as children do. Then you will be the puppeteer and master of the situation but whilst your mind is immersed in the enactment you are the puppet on the string.

It really is not worth identifying emotionally with everything you encounter. When it comes to it, things are not as important as they at first seem. You should help those who need your help but the help should be given with detachment, without distressing yourself or sympathising on a deep emotional level as this only causes more harm. In addition, help should only be given when it is asked for.

In response to your question: "...what should sensitive people do, people who give alms daily for example? There is a very straightforward answer, but one you may not be expecting: abandon guilt.

Anyone who regularly gives alms feels a sense of duty and duty comes from feelings of guilt. There is a difference between *compassion* for the needy and feeling *a duty* to help them. Duty is not a reflection of compassion so much as a manifestation of importance.

If you suddenly feel overcome with a wave of sympathy for a particular poor old woman then this is compassion. If on the other hand you are incapable of walking past any beggar without feeling tortured by your conscience this is not compassion but a sense of duty. So, what should you do?

Acknowledge your freedom. You do not owe anyone anything. Claim your right to knowledge. You are equally as capable of creating and providing answers. Yet if you are not free of importance you will be tortured by feelings of doubt. If you are free of importance then you are right and when you are free you can allow yourself to sympathise and empathise.

How to Win Back the One You Love

"I beg you to tell me how to win back the man I love."

If the man you love left of his own choosing then it is highly unlikely that you can win him back. At least you will not be able to return him to your life with the efforts of inner intention, that is, by taking any actions directly aimed at 'getting him back'. This would include any attempt to directly influence the person in question. Even if you were to have some success, the person would not be the same.

Only outer intention will win him back. With inner intention you try to influence the world directly in pursuit of your goals. Outer intention works in such a way that the world itself meets you half way. I can briefly explain how outer intention works.

In relationships partners are guided by inner intention, i.e. they want to receive something from the other and if they do not get it they break off the relationship.

Everyone has their own way of finding fulfilment in their relationships. They may need love, sex, respect, acknowledgement, approval of certain personal qualities, closeness, mutual understanding, escape from loneliness, fun etc. Might there be one common element that unites these different needs? This common element has always existed and it remains the protection and confirmation of individual self-worth. Whatever guiding principles inform a person's actions all personal motives are linked with the feeling of self-worth. It is human nature.

Inner intention in human relationships is always aimed at protecting and confirming one's self-worth in one form or another. This is what the inner intention of your loved one is aimed at – on finding a partner that will fulfil their sense of self-worth.

So what is your inner intention aimed at? Returning your loved one and in doing so, firstly restoring your own sense of self-worth and secondly, renewing a relationship which gave you a sense of fulfilment.

Now ask yourself whether you can fulfil your partner's need if you allow yourself to be guided by inner intention alone.

If you wish to win your partner back you will have to give him the focus of his inner intention. Do not judge him for wanting to find confirmation of his worth in you, for you also wish to receive something from him.

You may recall that the first principle of Frailing sounds: *abandon the intention to receive, replace it with the intention of giving and you will receive the very thing you gave up.*

Abandon inner intention, whatever it is aimed at. Define the focus of your partner's inner intention. Turn your aspirations towards fulfilling your partner's intention. As soon as your actions are redirected towards fulfilling your partner's needs your own inner intention will be transformed into outer intention.

You will find that by adopting this approach you not only make your partner happy, but you receive from your partner everything you desired *and more*. If you can abandon the intention of receiving and replace it with the intention of giving you will instantly receive the thing you let go of.

This principle works so effectively that it makes you feel as if some magic power were at play. This is real magic. No spells or love potions are required.

Despite all we have said it is as difficult to return something that has been lost as it is to step twice into the same river. It is better to try and adhere to the principles of Frailing before the relationship starts to suffer.

In any case, before you take any kind of action if I were in your shoes I would think very carefully about whether you really want to win this man back or whether what you really have is a burning desire to restore your lost (dumped by him) self-esteem.

It is very painful to feel rejected or neglected, I know. But even if I knew all the details and circumstances of your relationship I would still be incapable of advising anything more specific. All I can do is give you the tool. How you choose to use it only you can decide.

Do not forget that the layer of your world is your mirror. If you prefer to suffer this is what will happen. If you apply the principle of coordinating intention and evaluate the current circumstances as exclusively positive, this is also how things will be.

You think that everything has gone wrong, but has it occurred to you that the aplit with your loved one might be saving you from as yet unseen problems? Tell yourself that everything is unfolding as it should for it is up to you whether you choose to delight or to suffer. If I was you I would take heart, jump for joy and clap my hands in delight. Let the mirror give you pleasure.

"I have the same problem. The woman I love is leaving me – my wife (we were going out for three years and have been married for four).

The main reason for the separation is my own financial insecurity. In many ways I am too soft, timid and overly cautious. My wife thinks that with my knowledge and experience I should create my own business because it is difficult when you have a gentle nature as I do to climb to the top of the career ladder. And building a career is not really the thing for a creative type.

In some ways I agree with my wife. I tend to be too thorough always looking for additional information or ways of gaining more experience. Over the course of my career I have not worked at any one position for longer than two years (which has given me varied experience and knowledge in business). One of the strong points of my personality is that I am very receptive. This is also a disadvantage as it is a personality trait that makes it harder for me to build a career.

My wife wants stability, reliability and children. These are my personal motivations too but I do not see them developing in the context of a career, so much as on the principle of designing a profitable system (business model). This requires knowledge and experience which have always been among my highest priorities.

Three months ago my wife and I finally divorced and now my wife is renting a separate flat which her salary enables her to do. She is searching for herself but our relationship is becoming colder and she does not seem to want to see me. How can I win her back?"

I cannot give you a specific recipe to solve your problems. I offer specific solutions only in cases where the situation is crystal clear. And yet even then my opinion is purely subjective and so fallible. If I do not know the answer to a problem I ask my intuition. If my intuition does not help I recommend applying one of the principles of Transurfing because I know that this will not do any harm.

In this case, my intuition coincides with the principle according to which you must totally listen to the voice of your heart. Others would say that success lies in a good career, stability and a high-paying salary, but these things have no relation to our goals. Surely one cannot call one's true path in life climbing up the career ladder?

Careers, stability, high-paying salaries really are not goals in themselves. They are the accompanying attributes of goals. Your true goal is the thing that will turn your life into a celebration. You will never achieve anything by substituting a goal for an accompanying attribute. Attributes come of their own accord as a result of achieving the goal. For example, you receive all the benefits of life as a result of becoming a leading specialist in your field.

It makes sense to strive for your goal and not for the benefits it will bring. It seems obvious. It is something anyone can understand but the paradox is that this notion rises up in a small flash in people's awareness and is thereby eclipsed in the sticky gloss of attributes.

People strive after attributes like moths to a light-bulb except that it does not get them anywhere. How can you achieve success if you work towards the goal's attributes rather than the goal itself. This is where the myth comes from that great abundance is the pleasure of a chose few.

Public opinion imposes its stereotypes but the image of the stereotype is solely taken from the visible end results whereas success comes in the process of moving towards the goal. The end results are always visible, whereas the process that tells the story of how the goal was achieved remains concealed in the shadows. As a result the stereotype is created: go after a career and good money, in other words "make straight for the light-bulb!"

All people see is the gloss of stars already risen. There are few who turn their attention to the path that brought the star to the peaks of their success. All stars pass through a thick forest of setbacks and failure. Success only smiles on those who are convinced they walk their true path. Move towards your goal with indomitable spirit and remember: whatever happens, the alternatives flow unfolds in the direction it should. No-one can know when or how the goal will be achieved.

If you walk in the footsteps of stereotypes you are certain to be successful but the level of your success will be mediocre and require immense effort. To achieve huge success you must define your goal and move towards it *unfalteringly* irrespective of what anyone else might try and tell you. There is no harm in taking other people's advice into account but ultimately decision must be made with the heart. Only then will you stop beating your wings up against the light bulb like a moth in the dark.

The appropriate decision is always born from unity of heart and mind. A categorically inappropriate decision is a decision that is based on a feeling of inner discomfort. If a decision causes you the slightest feeling of unease in your gut similar to feelings of obligation your heart is saying "no". If on the other hand the decision you have made does not cause you any inner discomfort the heart is saying "yes" or "I do not know". In this case your mind makes the final choice. If the decision is right for you *the heart will sing and the mind will rub its hands in glee.*

On the other hand, if you cannot define your goal do not torment yourself with trying. It is not like you cannot live without a goal. Why not just live without striving towards something, if that is what you want. If this is the case then there is only one piece of advice I can give which is *to move* with the flow, and not just be carried along by the flow. In other words, you need to observe the principle of coordination and then life will take a calm, comfortable course. Your goal will no doubt reveal itself when you cease fitful attempts to find it.

As far as your question goes concerning how to win back your wife I am afraid there is nothing I can advise you. The key phrase: "*She is searching for herself but our relationship is becoming colder and she does not seem to want to see me*" it is clear that the problem is not financial stability and the lack of it. If she does not love you it is impossible to win her back.

Intention

"My question is this: can the laws of Transurfing be extended to other people? For example, in the case that a mother wants to heal her children (mine suffer from mental illness) or has (I have) the intention for Russia to become a wealthy country and for its people to be happy".

Intention is capable of anything. The issue is one of force. If you have intention with the force of a Jesus Christ then of course you can heal but the power of intention is not the power of desire. If you want something very strongly then you are unlikely to get it. Neither is it a case of faith, because where there is faith there is always room for doubt.

Intention is the dispassionate, unconditional resolve to see your will manifest in reality and the calm knowledge that this will be the case. Intention is pure when it is free of desire, fear, doubt and other importance potentials. The intention to get your mail from the post box is, for example, a pure intention.

If your willingness to heal your children is equally as pure then you will heal them but do not fall into the trap of thinking that the result will be achieved by making effort. No matter how much effort they put into it, a person who is paralyzed will never get up and move. On the other hand, they will easily reclaim their mobility if they can by chance 'remember' how they used to move.

No-one can teach the power of intention, not I, nor anyone else but Transurfing does offer methods that cause intention to work irrespective of your will. I am talking about outer intention.

In this case, if the treatment does not help you must stop trying to heal your children. What is a psychological disturbance? It is when the soul is attuned to an area of the alternatives space that has not been streamed into physical reality. Most healthy people are attuned to our physical world whereas, the mentally ill are not sick as such, they simply 'soar' in an area of the field which from our point of view seems abnormal because it has not been transformed into physical reality.

Accept your children as they are. They are not sick they are just different to other people. It is great when a person is not the same as every one else. This is what should be normal. What is not normal is the current situation in which everyone thinks and acts in the same way.

You will not achieve anything by trying to make your children normal. As I have already said, the power of intention cannot be forced. By trying, making effort and getting frustrated you simply create excess potential which in turn only aggravates the situation.

If however, you are able to accept your children the way they are and acknowledge their sanity the power of intention will come indirectly and the power of your inner intention will be transformed into outer intention.

Give your children your attention, love and as far as it is possible their freedom. Release your children from the necessity of being 'normal' and yourself from the need to make them 'normal'. Then perhaps not straight away but over the course of time, you will begin to see results.

You must also decide for yourself whether to take my advice or not. Obviously, my advice is not that of a specialist psychiatrist. Do I even have the right to give such advice at all?

You're heart will provide you with the answers to any question that relates to you personally. Trust the voice of your heart above other people's opinions including my own.

The only advantage I have is that I have no emotional attachment to your children. In this sense I have no excess potential in relationship to them and so my intention to answer your question is pure.

What I do not understand however, is why you are care so much about the fate of Russia if your own children are ill. Is this not a little too large scale for a personal concern? I am no fan of ideas aimed at making everyone happy.

Each individual can only create the layer of their world and so no one individual could possibly bestow happiness upon all of Russia. This could only be achieved if everyone were to work at it together. But people who are united by a common idea end up creating a pendulum which sooner or later engenders the destructive activities of leading adherents away from their true path and unleashing wars upon its competitors.

You know as well as I do what comes of ideas to make everyone happy. Any idea of this kind, even spiritual ones based on love for God generates a pendulum. Entire nations have been wiped out in the name of God and happiness on Earth.

No pendulum is capable of making everyone happy and any attempt to do so will cause much suffering and woe. Happiness is not a common thing that can be shared. Happiness is a very individual notion. When a nation takes action to build a happy society for all, it can only lead to the kind of shambles that according to Bulgakov reigns "not in the closet, but in the mind".

Pendulums benefit from passing off a caring for others as great heartedness and have a sophisticated knack of creating extremely convincing stereotypes. However, this is just a beautiful demagoguery. All people will be happy only when each individual sets out towards their innermost Goal through their own Door. In this sense Transurfing is a kind of pendulum for individualists but it is the only true path to a genuine rather than ephemeral happiness.

It is essential that you turn away from pendulums, let your soul out of the box of stereotypes and work on your own happiness. On the path towards your goal you will have the opportunity to do plenty of truly good deeds and of course, you will be able to help the poor and the needy because you will have greater resources.

> *"You say that when a person rides the wave of success they are happy and fortunate in all respects and that the main thing is not to give in to the influence of destructive pendulums. What about the fact that life is not perfect and it is rarely the case that one person is lucky in everything? Either you have growth and success at work and in your career or you are lucky in that everything is cosy and calm and loving at home. Most people want everything to be wonderful in both."*

You are the one who says that no man is lucky in everything. That is your personal choice. If this is what *you* think, this will be true for you. The world always manifests the choice *you* make for *yourself*. You write: "*Most people want everything to be wonderful in both.*" Here the world also manifests your choice. It impeccably reflects the fact that you *want* everything to be wonderful but nothing more than that. You want it do you not, so what you will receive is exactly that, *your wanting self.*

When you stop simply *wanting* and *intend to have* then you will receive. Take note of the Transurfing motto: *"I do not want or hope, I intend".*

Importance Potential

"Tell me how to overcome fear, anxiety and panic. How do you avoid getting brought down by these emotions on a practical level? When someone close to me leaves like my daughter or son for example, the fear comes over me in a wave and consumes me: Did they land ok, why do not they ring to say they have arrived?"

The issue you have touched upon here is interesting but quite complex. There is no universal recipe for fear. If you found a simple and effective way of dissolving fear that did not involved having to change your conscious awareness it would be one of the greatest discoveries of all time.

In the terminology of Transurfing fear is an excess energy potential that emerges when excessive meaning is attributed to the object of one's fear. Excess potential disrupts the balance in the field consequently giving rise to forces that eliminate the imbalance.

Suppose you found yourself having to walk along the edge of a cliff and were terrified of falling over the edge. By what means could balanced forces eliminate the excess potential? The least energy-consuming method would be to throw you into the abyss and be done with it. Nature always takes the path of least resistance.

However, since this alternative is not to your liking you overcome the resistance of balanced forces, that is, you control yourself. It turns out that in order to balance the fear potential you have to make even more effort. As a result your energy expenditure is twofold, spent on the potential itself and on retaining it. Hardly any free energy remains leaving one in a kind of stupor.

If the fear potential has enough force it will not be possible to keep it under control and then balanced forces will do with you what they will. In other words, a feeling of panic arises and you are carried away by forces aimed at extinguishing the potential, that is, towards your death. If you could manage to consciously reduce the level of importance surrounding the situation, fear would disappear. The problem is that in a situation of this kind it is impossible to consciously reduce importance. So, the only effective approach you can use is to have some kind of safety net or alternative route set up. Whatever form this takes it will be unique to each situation.

If you have no safety net all you can do is avoid struggling to control the anxiety. Trying to talk yourself out of being afraid is futile. Self-deception will not help. Any form of inner battle with fear only drains your energy and exacerbates the problem of excess potential. If it is not possible not to feel fear, then feel the fear. Act as best you can in the circumstances but do not fight the fear itself.

For example, if you are nervous before making a presentation, go for it. Be nervous naturally and with pleasure. Give yourself completely to this wonderful feeling. Allow yourself to lose your mind in the way that it pleases you most to do so. As soon as you allow yourself this freedom all the anxiety will magically dissipate eventually vanishing into thin air. This happens because a significant part of your energy was otherwise spent fighting the anxiety.

Anxiety and worry are less powerful manifestations of fear. Importance here is generated by anticipation of the unknown. In this case it is possible to reduce the bar of importance. If something is worrying you tell yourself that it is self-defeating to worry about it for as a rule, our suspicions and worst expectations become reality.

One way to eliminate anxiety is through action, whatever the kind. The potential created by anxiety and worry is dissipated in action. Idle worry will hang in the air around you until you take action. The form of action you take may not even necessarily have any connection to the object of your anxiety. It is enough to busy yourself with something and you will see straight away that the intensity of your anxiety has subsided.

The coordination of intention principle (everything is unfolding as it should) can serve as a useful reference point for lowering the bar of importance. Allow yourself not to know how events should develop. Let go the grip of control over the situation and give the situation the opportunity to successfully resolve itself successfully.

Circumstances will begin to unfold in a positive way if you consciously go with the flow rather than beating your hands on the water. You can rest assured that the coordination of intention principle works. The world has no intention of causing anyone difficulties and not because forces exist which take care of you specifically, but because it involves expending less energy.

Nature does not waste energy and it is not profitable for nature to spend energy on you. The difficulties we experience are always related to an excessive expenditure of energy. By contrast, prosperity is the norm and demands minimum expenditure of energy. The mind has no understanding of the path of least resistance and battles with the alternatives flow thereby bringing obstacles and problems upon itself. Where else could they come from? No-one has yet eradicated the law of the conservation of energy.

The coordination principle should not be taken literally or categorically. You cannot walk right into the thick of things and at the same time assure yourself that everything is unfolding as it should. But generally speaking you can rely on this principle.

> *"My problem is this: I have set myself very high goals but I am constantly surrounded by pendulums that get in the way of achieving them. I cannot talk about my goals or discuss my interests with anyone else and even my relatives tell me I will not make it. When I observe other people they all pretty much look the same to me. Please give me some advice."*

Of course pendulums get in your way. They get in everyone's way. The way of keeping their counter impact to a minimum is to keep the bar of importance to a minimum, i.e. do not attribute anything excessive meaning. This might seem an unusual recommendation but the majority of problems are due to high inner and outer importance.

"Very high goals" are not difficult to achieve per se. It is the accepted stereotypes and the mind's false thought patterns that make them difficult to achieve. The coordination of intention principle can help you in breaking these stereotypes and thought patterns.

You can achieve any goal if it is truly yours. If the goal has been set by someone else you can expect to experience a feeling of inner discomfort when you run the mental image of the goal as it would look had it already been achieved.

As far as the choice of your goal and how to achieve it is concerned, here you can take into account what other people say to you, but their words should be given no more meaning than that. You should take instruction from the dictates of the heart and not the advice of others, particularly relatives who "only wish the best for you".

That said, I cannot detect the precise nature of the problem from your letter. The phrase: "When I observe other people they all pretty much look the same to me" is particularly vague.

> *"Let me explain: no-one understands me, including my friends and parents. They do not understand my desires and try to pressure me into doing what they want. They do not understand how any one could think the way I do. I am the kind of person who likes strict discipline. I plan my day, I am proactive, persistent and persevering in relation to my goals; I am eager to acquire new knowledge etc. My parents tell me to forget about all of that, find a job and have a problem free life which I consider to be very modest goals. The position of my friends is, I feel, even worse. All they think about is how to skip the next class. They insult the teachers and discuss topics of conversation which I find totally uninteresting. They also make it impossible for me to concentrate on the lesson. To top it all, my parents are constantly arguing."*

Now the picture is a little clearer. You may not like my response but it is mine to make a suggestion and yours to decide whether it is relevant or not. I do not force my views on anyone but you asked me and therefore I will reply.

The solution to your problem is to play the fool. I mean it quite literally. Do not think that I am humouring you. Choose the image of the fool very carefully, one that allows you to display all your positive qualities: scrupulousness, being organised and focused. Ideally the thing you choose to be the fool should be an inanimate object so that you do not cause any discomfort. Consider carefully the object you will choose. I would suggest for example using a teddy bear.

Once you have found the appropriate dummy make a neat plan of where, when and how you will fool the fool around. It would be best to come up with a set of instructions detailing its actions, something like: "To fool around with the said fool rotate it around a longitudinal axis. The fool should be placed on an even surface in a position that will not prevent it from being rotated. The rotating of the fool is accomplished by the application of consecutive effort by means of the hands of the one fooling the fool around" and so on and so forth.

The instructions and plan should be scrupulously put together with great attention to detail including safety measures. Take the task seriously and you will end up with quite an impressive project. I recommend that you format the project in a professional manner and present it in a business folder.

Once this stage of the project is complete you can set about its implementation. Prepare thoroughly and carry out all the necessary actions conscientiously in strict accordance with the instructions. Your facial expression should be intelligent and focused. If you find yourself bursting into fits of laughter take a break, laugh as much as necessary to get it all out, then when you are calm you can continue.

You think I mock you? The thing is that the root of your problem lies in the heightened potential of inner importance. You write: "…. *I am the kind of person who likes strict discipline, to plan my day, to be proactive, persistent and persevering in my goals…but I am constantly surrounded by pendulums that get in my way".*

You demand too much of yourself (and possibly of others too). I do not know but I suspect that you have placed upon yourself the role of a "serious and responsible person with an important task". If this is the case you will always find others fussing around you who display the opposite qualities. For example, you will be irritated by those who are irresponsible, disorganised, undisciplined and trouble-making. Basically, all kinds of birdbrains intent on messing up your careful planning.

Why is life like this? Because your excess potential of inner importance creates an instance of powerful polarisation. People with the opposite traits will be attracted to you like iron chips to a magnet. This is how balanced forces work in their aim to eliminate potential. The world you experience is your mirror. But if you create the excess potential of inner or outer importance the mirror curves and the distortion of reality manifests in the fact of being surrounded by pendulums that get in your way.

Put more precisely, the people that get in your way are not pendulums so much as their puppets. Pendulums sense the energy of your potential and make other people behave in such a way that will get to you. As a result you get irritated and the harlequin jumps even higher. The pendulum makes it swing and receives the energy of your irritation.

As soon as you reduce the potential of importance the picture of the outside world will gradually be transformed. You will be surrounded by the same people but they will behave very differently towards you. As soon as polarisation disappears the mirror is smoothed out and reality returns to normal.

So what causes the polarisation, surely not your positive qualities? Indeed not. You obviously have very positive qualities which will undoubtedly serve you well in life. Polarisation appears as a result of dependent relationships.

Your positive qualities only create change in the external energy picture when you start comparing yourself to others. For example, you think: I am disciplined and they are slobs; they are unfocused and I am goal-oriented. Making these kinds of contrasts is what attracts polarisation.

By carrying out this ritual you will nullify your inner importance. You might think that the ritual is not for you. In that case it would be better if you simply resisted the temptation of comparing yourself to others around you. *Be yourself and allow others to do the same. Let go your grip.* As soon as you do this, polarisation will disappear and the rest of the world will inexplicably look different and it will stop getting in your way. Then you will understand what "Transurfing Reality" is.

> *"You advised one serious reader to 'play the fool'. What about those who are too busy 'fooling around'? How can they be made to do something more serious with their lives?"*

No-one wants to do anything serious, not because they are serious as such, but because the things we consider serious are not the things that are meant for us. Laziness is a condition of the soul. It is quite natural for the soul not to want to busy itself with other people's affairs. Perhaps the soul did not come into this world to slave away for a pendulum but to warm itself in the sunshine by the ocean, go skiing in the Alps or travelling or any other of life's many pleasures.

"Right, so who is going to actually do some work around here?" asks the angry pendulum, to which one may reply with the words of a humorous student song: "Leave the job to the shaggy bear, who has nothing to do but roam the forest and roar there". Quite right too, for feelings of duty and obligation are the inventions of pendulums.

In reality, our world is so rich and generous that it has enough wealth to go round as long as each individual moves towards their own goal through their own door. It is unlikely that this will ever happen but that is not to stop a given individual transforming the layer of their world into a very cosy little corner.

You have to find your true goal and door. When you are moving towards your own goal you do not have to persuade or force yourself to act. The soul will skip towards its goal through its own door. To others your door might seem a burdensome task but to you it will be a pleasure.

All the time that you are moving towards someone else's goal through someone else's door you are working for a pendulum. When you are on this path the soul will always say "I do not want to" and the mind will keep insisting that you "must". This is a path to nowhere whatever reasonable arguments and beautiful scenery it is dressed in. There is only one solution – define your own goal and strive towards it.

In the meantime the remedy for forced obligation can be play. Remember how in childhood you played grown-ups at the shop or at the hospital. Imagine now that what you are doing is playing, not labouring.

You only suffer from forced obligation if your mind becomes immersed in the game. Adopt the role of the acting member of the audience, the participating spectator. Act in a detached manner. Do not give yourself entirely to the work you are forced to do. Make as if it were a game. *Rent yourself out.*

Reality Inversion

Reality moves its frames indomitably along the film roll of time. Holidays come and go. It is just a shame that they end so quickly. Hemmingway was right when he said that life is a moveable feast that stays with you, although rarely does anyone manage to live that way. The moveable feast is unexpectedly lost somewhere along the way after which all life's colours fade. Emptiness and oppressive melancholy fill the space in the soul sometimes for obvious reasons and sometimes not.

The worst part is that the world sinks into darkness swiftly and willingly whereas enlightenment emerges slowly with much anticipation. The tendency of man for negativity has its murky way and an oppressed state results in which heart and mind agree how bad life is.

When this happens outer intention steadily shifts reality into the darker areas of the alternatives space. The mirror responds quickly without hesitation or delay whereas enlightenment is then slow to appear because when a person feels depressed their attitude paints the layer of their world in ever darker shades. Sometimes everything seems so dreadful that you do not have the energy to recall Transurfing or anything else. How are you supposed to break the vicious circle and straighten reality out? Generally speaking it is pretty difficult to do and yet, there is a radical method that can be applied called *reality inversion.*

A long time ago, and still, quite recently, just twenty years ago when we were physics students we studied at a positively awful faculty where the teachers embodied the brutality of cavemen. The first year started with seventy five students but no more than twenty-five made it to the finish line. In an environment like this the working law was: *if you want to make it out alive, learn to laugh.*

We made up a game which I forgot about afterwards and only later came more fully to understand: the game was played according to all the rules of Transurfing. The essence of the game lay in turning your relationship to a situation on its head, that is, to initiate a kind of inversion. When things are bad the pendulum rules make you suffer, worry, crumble under the weight of your problems and generally lose it or go on a complete bender. Our game rules dictated that you had to do the opposite. How well we managed it you can judge for yourself.

"I was delightfully disappointed!" "Luckily, something terribly unfortunate has happened!"

"Something irreparable happened and my affairs instantly took off!"

"A fine gentleman in a car has just been so charming as to drench me in mud!"

"All my attempts were in vain which secured my success!"

"She does not love me! No, that would be too good to be true. She is faking it beautifully!"

"He dumped me and I laughed like a Budenny horse!"

And so on in the same vein of artful wit. The only thing that got in the way was the hysterical laughter that followed all our attempts to transform misfortune. You are not allowed to laugh out loud in the middle of a lecture and so suppressed laughter turned into rumbling, snorting, chuckling and gurgling and various other sounds characteristic of ungulates and amphibians. During break times the energy that accumulated poured out into roars of laughter quite Castaneda-like in style.

It is clear what was happening from the point of view of Transurfing. Firstly, any associated importance is reduced and consequently excess potential also. Secondly, the parameters of the thought energy of delight, even if it was silly, were far from corresponding to sorry life lines and so a more positive shift occurred at once. The mirror responds quickly and so the heart and mind sigh with relief and as a result reality is evened out.

Once we were preparing for an exam on the theory of probability. The teacher was a fearsome man putting it mildly. It was a sinister night in the student rooms in the shadow of the exam next day. My friend and I were racking our brains as to how we could even out the situation.

"Who knows what probability is and how to calculate it?"

"It is a mystery shrouded in darkness."

"They are like old hags sitting there cramming."

"That is not for us. Are we real men or what?"

"Half-baked bastards." One of the 'hags' overhearing our conversation stuck their head round the door: " Shut up low-life, we are Gentleman!" "Assholes."

"Young scientists!"

"Morons."

Eventually someone came up with the idea of playing cards all night at which point I said: "No guys, that is over the top. I am going to bed". But the 'gentlemen' dressed up in proper suits and ties and with cheap cigars in their mouths and bottles of some suspicious looking liquid on the table they sat down to play.

When I woke in the morning I found them sitting at the table still.

"You idiots" I said, "you are all going to fail!"

They stood up, shook themselves a little and set off for the slaughter.

As a result of their prank they did not do well at all. They all got a 'C'. Not me though. No. I got an 'F'. That was a true success! How they envied me! They all came up to me afterwards with a searching look and asked me earnestly how I did it.

I held my head up proudly.

"You see. I told you so. I hope you understand gentlemen where you can stuff your sorry 'C's."

That same day we celebrated my victory and it was great fun. The next day I had to re-sit the exam and got an 'A'. I am not making it up. Believe me, if you do the inversion well, you will not be kept waiting for the result.

If your mood is so low that you just cannot bear to bring yourself to do an inversion then you have to make your mood even worse taking it to the extreme, the grotesque, the absurd. If you increase the level of contrast in a slide to the maximum there comes a point when it changes into a negative. That is pretty much what we were doing.

One girl was feeling depressed. To make the situation worse she dressed up in black so everyone would know she was in mourning. Her friends came up to her expressing their condolences and enquiring about how exactly she intended to commit suicide and when she was planning to do so. Eventually the group surrounded her and started wholeheartedly singing a depressing, sorrowful song with wailing and wringing of hands worthy of savages–the whole shebang. Gradually, the primitive song became a prolonged cry and wolfish howl and when they could hold it in no longer everyone including the lady in black broke out into uncontrolled laughter.

Of course, it is easy if you have a fun group of friends but if you do not have then you must manage alone. How you do it, is a personal thing. Joking aside it really does work to take your condition to the absurd. Substances that bring about a change in consciousness should be avoided however as the results of taking something can be even worse.

Personally, I am no fan of using the contrast method in solitude, so I do not so much recommend it as offer the option up for information's sake. A low depressed state indicates that the energy levels of intention are extremely low. It is better to try and keep your energy levels at a healthier level in the first place and avoid depression that way.

As you can see, reality inversion is similar to the principle of coordination of intention. The only difference is that inversion is a more radical approach based on humour.

SUMMARY

If you do not control reality, reality will control you.

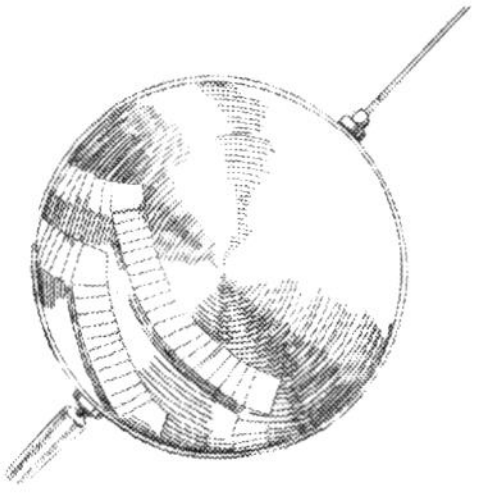

Chapter XVI. DANCES WITH SHADOWS

My world and I are going for a walk.

The Origin of Intention

A characteristic feature of the relationship people have with the outside world is that anything new is eventually treated as something mundane. Like clouds in the sky, reality constantly changes in appearance, but the rate of change is too slow for us to perceive. The movement of material realisation through the alternatives space is like the movement involved in cloud formation. We can only perceive it when it is captured on film and the footage is sped up.

Even the freshness of change that brightens life in short bursts dulls just as quickly. The unusual becomes the ordinary and the delight of the feast dissolves into the everyday routine. Life becomes boring…

Just as a rhetorical question I would like to ask: What is boredom? It is difficult to give a comprehensive and intelligible definition of boredom. It would be easier to describe how to fight boredom. In an attempt to survive the monotony of everyday life the heart and mind make up all kinds of toys and games to help us experience something new and unusual. A toy is a good remedy for boredom and a game is an even better one.

Besides skating, games like hide-and-seek, catch etc are great fun and extremely popular. As a person gets older they think up more sophisticated means of amusing themselves from sports contests to virtual reality. Many professions are in essence nothing other than a game.

Why do I say many? Try and name a profession that could not be perceived as a game. Whatever a person does, in reality they are just playing. In their superiority grown-ups call what children do a game but adults are also playing. It is just that they self-importantly refer to their 'play' as work.

Both take a very responsible attitude towards their activities. Ask a child what they are doing and they will answer you with great seriousness, even earnestness: "I am playing!" Try distracting an adult from their work and they will respond with indignation; "I am doing something important".

So the game is a serious matter. What does a child do when they are not occupied with a game? As a rule they just muck about. So what about the grown-ups? They slob out; that is just what the adults call it. But doing nothing soon becomes boring and then you want to play a new game.

So why do we need games if only to relieve the boredom of life? Let us put the question differently: what causes boredom? Insufficient stimulus perhaps?

This question is not as trivial as it might seem. The basis of our passion for games and play is as ancient as the world we live in. What is the fundamental need of living beings? Survival and the instinct for self-preservation? This is the accepted stereotype, although it is not the correct answer. Could it be the desire to reproduce? Again this is not the right answer. So, what is it then?

The primary need is to be able to independently manage our own lives. This is the fundamental principle underlying the behaviour of all living beings. Everything else, including survival and reproductive instincts are a consequence of this main principle. In other words, *the goal and purpose of all living beings is to control their reality.*

However, it is impossible to control reality if the outside world exists independently of you and behaves in a totally uncontrollable or even hostile manner. There will always be others who want to steal your food, drive you out of a cosy corner or even devour you as their next meal. It is hard and even scary when you are not choosing how to live your life and you feel that life is just happening to you instead and there is nothing you can do about it. This gives rise to the insistent and sometimes unconscious desire to control the world around you.

This conclusion will come as a surprise to many: "It has always been obvious that the survival instinct was primary and now you are telling us that is it in fact just a consequence of something more fundamental?"

It only seems strange at first. When you think about it, whatever activity a living creature is engaged in (including survival and reproduction) everything comes down to the attempt to *bring the reality of the world under control.* This is the key motive and primary origin of all intention underlying the activities of living beings.

Inactivity is the absence of control. Consequently, *boredom as such does not exist. What exists is a consistent and insatiable thirst to control one's reality;* to somehow subject it to your own will. In this sense, a game is a way of modelling controllable reality.

Some kinds of birds for example love to play with pine cones. The pine cone is a particle of an independent, uncontrollable reality. As soon as the bird makes the pine cone a piece of its game that particle and to some degree reality itself becomes controllable.

Skating or sliding is also a kind of control. Reality carries me but in the way I want it to. To some extent any other type of game follows the same rule: "Be what I want you to be". The game script is more or less predetermined which makes the situation fairly predictable. There are, of course, other games in which is it more difficult to lead but all games can basically be reduced to one and the same thing: to control what is happening with your will.

To the observer any kind of visible spectacle represents a game which models the control of reality. Music, books, films and shows are all swings for the heart and mind. The exhausting stream of tense thoughts ceases and is transformed into a flight on the wings of an elegant melody or captivating story. Whatever might happen to the main characters in a film what we are watching is a tamed, trained version of reality and so the observer can relax and enjoy the show.

Games in which we play with reality never cease even when we are sleeping. The heart and mind take pleasure in the world of dreaming where reality is subtly shaped to the light puff of intention.

Finally, games of the imagination are another acceptable method of shaping reality. A person will even make up a reality that does not exist yet just to play at being in control. Science-fiction is unusual. It remains unusual for as long as it is unreal and far removed from our lives. Reality is commonplace because of its proximity and yet it retains a quality of being inaccessible because it is hard to influence.

Generally speaking none of these games are made up in the effort against boredom. Everyday reality is not boring; it is mundane because it is uncontrollable. It is difficult to make everyday reality conform to the rule: "be as I want you to be". Hence as human beings we strive to hide from the nature of reality in a game where everything is simple and predictable.

Nonetheless, there is nowhere to hide from the inevitability of reality. The life of any individual is conditioned by their circumstances and position in society. Mostly, reality develops irrespective of personal will. To every "I want" there seems to be a "you cannot". To every "give me" you will hear "you are not getting it". So what is to be done given these conditions?

As a rule people are fairly unambiguous in their behaviour. In trying to get what they want they try to influence their environment in a linear, direct way according to the principle of "give it to me". Direct influence based on immediate contact is one form of control. But it is not the only form and is by far the most effective.

We will go about things in a different way. We will hide our hands behind our back and make the world meet our desires halfway. Everything that comes next will relate to how we can do this. Transurfing is a technique for controlling reality without direct impact, only not for fun as in a game, but for real.

The Law of Bad Luck

In order to learn how to control reality you must at the very least understand how reality is created. Every individual is the direct creator of the layer of their own world but the majority of people do not understand how this process works.

People try to make everything "the way I want it to be" and they apply this straightforward principle to the outside world. "I will go in the direction I turn", "It will cave in where I press it". But for some reason the world does not want to obey, and when you turn one way, you find yourself going in the opposite direction.

It makes you wonder. If reality behaves so strangely perhaps our attempts to shape it require a different approach? Maybe reality does not work according to the laws we thought. But people do not want to stop and look around and ask themselves these questions. Instead they stubbornly insist on having things their own way.

As a result of this stubborn kind of 'creativity' the person's individual layer is created in which nothing is "the way I want it to be". Reality seems strange, capricious and hard-line.

Sometimes you get the feeling that the world is doing it on purpose, to spite you. It is as if problems and unwanted events are drawn to you by some inexplicable force. Our fears are realised and our worst expectations justified. We are relentlessly pursued by the things we are adverse to and wish to avoid. So why is this?

In the beginner's Transurfing course we already talked about why you often "get what you do not want", particularly if the aversion is intense. When you hate or fear something with all your heart *outer intention* will deliver it to you in abundance.

Thought energy that is born from *unity of heart and mind* embodies potential in reality. In other words, the *sector of the alternatives space* that corresponds to the qualities of your thought energy will be streamed into physical reality if the feelings of the heart are one with the thoughts of the mind.

However, this is not the only reason that our worst expectations are realised. Life should be free of problems. That is the norm. If you do not disturb the balance and go with the alternatives flow everything should unfold very smoothly. Nature does not like wasting energy and has no intention of spending it on plotting against us.

Unwanted circumstances and events occur as a result of the distortion that *excess potential* creates in the surrounding energy field, while *dependent relationships* exacerbate the situation even further.

Excess potential appears when excessive meaning is attributed to a particular quality. Dependent relationships are created when people begin to compare and contrast themselves with others and place conditions upon a relationship such as "if you are going to be like that, then I am going to be like this".

The *excess potential* that is created when a distorted evaluation is made will have no grievous effect whilst it stands relative only to itself. However, as soon as an inflated evaluation of a given object is placed in comparative relationship with another, polarisation occurs which generates the winds of balanced forces.

Balanced forces strive to eliminate the polarisation that has occurred and for the most part their action is aimed against the individual who created the polarisation in the first place.

The following are examples of non-relative potentials: I love you; I love myself; I hate you; I do not like myself: I am a good person; you are a bad person. These evaluations are self-contained because they are not based on comparison or contradistinction.

The following however, are examples of potentials based on dependent relationships: I love you on the condition that you love me; I love myself because I am greater than the rest of you; you are a bad person because I am a better person than you are; I am a good person because you are a bad person; I do not like myself because I am less attractive than others; I am repulsed by you because you are not the same as me.

There is a huge difference between the first and second group of evaluations. Evaluations based on the principle of comparison generate polarisation. Balanced forces eliminate the heterogeneity by bringing the opposite values together just as the opposite poles of two magnets are drawn towards each other.

This is why problems, as if deliberately, push their way so importunately into our lives For example, married couples are often made up of two personalities that seem totally incompatible as if they were a punishment the other must bear. In various types of groups there will only be at least one person who will make your life difficult. Murphy's or as we call it, Sod's law is of the same nature. And putting up with nasty neighbours seems to be an essential condition of any form of close habitation.

The example of nuisance neighbours is a perfect illustration of the polarisation effect. This issue, despite its seemingly mundane nature, is directly related to the field of metaphysics. The problem is that some people prevent others from getting on with their lives. But why? Because wherever you are there will always be 'bad' old women and old men who will not leave other 'good' people in peace?

So should we conclude, that people really can be discriminated into two groups? And yet if you were to carry out a survey asking people which group they thought they belonged to only a small handful would acknowledge themselves as belonging to the 'bad' group. On the whole, your neighbours are just like you.

The tendency to discriminate is created by the wind of balanced forced that blows in the direction of your aversion. The direction the wind takes is determined by that same old principle–'sod's law: *you will experience anything you do not like.*

Some may protest; "It has nothing to do with balances forces. Some people just have no conscience. There is no point in philosophising about it". I will prove to you now that there is more to these situations than convoluted speculation.

Let us suppose that your neighbours are annoying you. Do you annoy them too? Probably not but why? "Because they are this and they are that, bad basically, and we are like we are", you will say. And yet there are no good and bad people. Any judgement is relative because it is generated by comparison and contradistinction.

So why is it then, that you do not annoy your neighbours? My answer may surprise you: *The reason you do not annoy your neighbours is because they could not care less about you.* "Exactly", you will say, "because they are bad people and have no shame."

With this attitude to your neighbours you switch on polarisation, like an electromagnet which will draw to you ever more problems related to your neighbours. To them it will all be water off a duck's back because you are of no interest to them whatsoever. It does not occur to them to look at you and make comparative discriminations, i.e. enter into a dependent relationship with you. It is in this sense that they could not care less about you. *They do not attach any importance to you or allow you to enter the layer of their world* and as a result they have no suffering they connect with you.

Your neighbours experience no polarisation in relationship to you whilst they are busy with their own lives and pay you no attention. And yet if they were to attach importance to your neighbourly existence begin comparing themselves to you it would be instantly apparent that you are not like they are. If this were to trouble them or touch a raw nerve in any way then you would undoubtedly start annoying them and you would cease to be a good neighbour and be transformed into a bad neighbour.

The situation will develop even more unexpectedly. You will begin to create the kind of problems for your neighbours that you would never have dreamed could possibly trouble anyone. *You will begin to annoy your neighbours without being aware that you are doing so,* just as they now have no awareness of the fact that they are annoying you.

When sharing a house for example noise pollution is problem number one. The more you do dislike the noise, the more intensely it will pursue you despite the fact that peace and quiet is the ideal condition for cohabiting not only for you but for your neighbours also. Less energy is expended that way. Any disturbance of the peace and quiet is always an anomaly, and does not arise without a reason. So where does the energy originate?

The noise your neighbours or flatmates make throws you off balance and you begin to quietly (or not so quietly) hate them for it. Your irritation serves as the source of the energy in the situation. A dependent relationship is created which in turn generates polarisation. Intense and aggressive feelings like "I hate these noisy neighbours" create a powerful magnet that draws ever new forms of irritating provocation towards you.

New neighbours will move in next door who have a tendency for a noisy lifestyle and your old neighbours or flatmates will buy new sound equipment as if deliberately to taunt you.

You should also be aware that your neighbours' neighbours also contribute to the situation and if the common feeling in response to the noisy neighbours coincides the effect will be magnified.

Of course, having nice neighbours depends on more than noise levels. It all depends on what kind of things you feel an aversion to. They might overwhelm you with their rubbish, suffocate you with unpleasant smells, cover the walls in the entrance hall with graffiti etc. An aversion to neighbours as a species may attract even more tangible consequences, such as a flood or even a fire.

In any other situation this kind of law of bad luck works in the same way. An object or characteristic that is attributed particular meaning attracts objects with the opposite qualities.

Meaning as we know is intensified via comparison and contradistinction. Where there is one magnetic pole the other will not be far away. Polarisation creates a magnet for problems and attracts everything that you feel an aversion to. Everything you find irritating will follow you. Everything that is highly undesirable happens. There is no mysticism in this. It is quite natural.

Polarisation distorts the lay of the energy field and gives rise to whirlwinds of balanced forces as a result of which the reflection of reality is warped like a reflection given by a curved mirror. Few people understand that any deformity represents a consequence of balance being disturbed and so they try to battle with the outside world rather than trying to eliminate the polarisation effect.

All you have to do is follow the main rule of Transurfing: *be yourself and let others be themselves.* You have to *loosen your grip* and give the world free reign.

The more you insist on your own desires and rights the more powerfully the magnet attracts the opposite. Figuratively speaking it is as if you have grabbed the world by the throat and it is resisting, fighting to get free.

It is futile to try and pressure a situation or insist on something. That just makes things worse. Instead, *consciously change your relationship to the situation in accordance with the Transurfing rule.*

For example, try at least for a while to forget about your neighbours, stop judging them and pretend they simply do not exist. Say to yourself: "to hell with them!" Rid the layer of your world of neighbours.

As soon as you are able to pull off the suction pad of your relationship, your neighbours' polarisation will disappear and they will gradually cease to bother you. And if you manage to completely break the dependent relationship you might make room for something incomprehensible to happen; your toxic neighbours may just end up becoming your best friends!

Everything Happens to Spite You

Is it strange, do not you think, that Sod's law should exist at all? Why should the world be so cruel? Or perhaps it is not, and Sod's law is just speculation and prejudice? And yet there is no getting away from it, Sod's law as a tendency definitely exists. Fortunately, the Transurfing model not only reveals the reason for this, it can also explain how to avoid getting caught out by this frustrating phenomenon.

The Transurfing rule works without fail freeing anyone who follows it from all sorts of problems they otherwise would have been unable to explain. All you have to do is let go the grip of control;

stop "grabbing the world by the throat", and life will instantly become welcoming and pliable.

If you do not 'let go' you will end up walking around like a magnet drawing the opposite to you. And it does not just stop at Sod's Law. The collision that occurs when opposites meet causes things to escalate even further.

The well-known law of the unity and conflict of opposites, the essence of which is apparent in its name, has become accepted text-book knowledge. The Volga River empties into the Caspian Sea and the Mississippi into the Gulf of Mexico. But it is not quite as simple as that. Let us start by asking ourselves why this law exists at all.

We have already explained why the unity of opposites is omnipresent: balanced forces bring opposites into contact with one another to restore the state of balance. This does not explain however, why opposing forces should be in a constant state of conflict.

You would think the opposite would be true: two opposites collide, neutralise each other and calm down. But no, the opposite forces will continue to anger each other to the point where they end up 'fighting'. If you do not pull them apart, they will go on scrapping forever.

You do not have to look too far afield to find examples. You will agree that the world gets on your nerves from time to time. Of course, it gets on everyone's nerves in different ways and to different degrees but the essence remains the same: *when something does manage to throw you off balance it always seems to happen as if to spite you.*

This is what happens. When you are worried or anxious about something your nerves are strained even if just a little. Then, as if in consequence, a jester appears and starts jumping and leaping about enough to play on your nerves even more. It starts to irritate you and then the jester jumps even faster.

There are many things that play on our nerves making us increasingly irritated. When you are in a hurry and afraid of being late the jester claps his hands in glee and shouts "Ok, let's go!"

From this moment onwards everything seems to work against you. People block your way or ceremoniously parade themselves making it impossible for you to pass. You need to go through a certain door but in front of you there is a whole queue of the laziest people in the world who can barely place one foot in front of the other. It is the same with the traffic. It is as if all the other drivers have secretly conspired against you.

Of course, some things can be put down to perception: when you are in a hurry it appears as if the rest of the world is going really slowly. But there are other more obvious signs. The lift or your car breaks down, the bus is late of there is a massive traffic jam. These things reek of a more ill-intentioned objectivity.

I could give other examples. When you are stressed and anxious other people around you do the very thing that irritates you and they do it right at the moment when you want to be left alone.

The children start going wild even though they had been behaving themselves previously. Someone sitting next to you will start slurping and swallowing loudly. All kinds of people will get under your feet and pester you with their problems. Everywhere things will get in the way. If you are desperate to see someone you will end up waiting for them for ages, and if you do not want to see anyone, someone will definitely turn up uninvited, and so on and so forth.

External pressures mount all the more intensely in direct proportion to your irritation. The more tense you are the more actively other people will annoy you. The interesting thing is that people are not deliberately trying to annoy you. It would not occur to them that their behaviour might be annoying someone.

There are many grey areas in the psychology of the subconscious. However strange it may seem people are mostly driven by subconscious motives. But even more peculiar is that *the driving force that creates these subconscious motives originates external to the human psyche.*

Despite being invisible this force consists of real informational energetic entities born of the thought energy of living beings –

pendulums. A lot has been said about pendulums in the first part of the Transurfing series. Pendulums are always present where there is potential for conflicting energies.

It would be a mistake to think that these entities are capable of conspiring or of making conscious intention a physical reality. Like leeches, pendulums sense polarisation as an irregularity in the energy field and try to feed on it. There is nothing particularly wrong with that.

The nightmare is that pendulums not only gulp down conflict energy they somehow make people behave in such a way that they give out even more of this type of energy.

They will do anything to make sure the energy keeps abundantly flowing. Pendulums pull people with invisible strings and people comply like puppets. It is not clear exactly how pendulums manage to influence people's motivations but they are very good at it.

Clear conscious awareness is off limits to pendulums but they get along very well without it as the subconscious is enough to satisfy their needs. Most people are asleep in waking to one degree or another. There are many things we do automatically, when we are relaxed without being soberly aware: "In this moment I am awake and am clearly aware of what I am doing, why and wherefore I am doing it".

A person's level of awareness is particularly low when they are at home or in a crowd. In the conditions of one's home there is a minimal requirement for heightened self-control and so people are relaxed to the point that their awareness is low to the point of dozing off. In a situation outside of the home setting but nonetheless with a close circle of friends are conscious awareness is more alert and concerned with self-control. In larger groups a person's actions once again are quite spontaneous and at the same time in strong correlation with the overall impulses of the crowd.

To clearly demonstrate how the pendulum works we will take the simple example of a pedestrian who you follow on the street and then overtake. As soon as you take a step to the left preparing to over take the person in front of you they take a spontaneous step in the same direction blocking your way. So you try and overtake them to the right but they inadvertently move in the same direction again.

What makes the pedestrian change direction? They cannot see you because you are behind them and why should they be at all concerned by the fact that you wish to walk past them? Perhaps the pedestrian somehow senses something approaching their back and instinctively does not want to let their 'competitor' pass in front of them? This supposition ends itself as an explanation and yet this is not the reason. In nature competitiveness is always expressed in situations where the two opposing parties stand facing one another. It is the pendulum that makes the pedestrian shift to the side.

People walk without thinking about how to place their feet so that they follow a perfectly straight line. In this sense we are asleep and so from time to time the line created by our footsteps spontaneously deviates to the left or the right. The motivation, that is, the choice of direction lies in the subconscious, which in the given moment is not controllable and so is potentially accessible to pendulums.

Then you turn up and attempt to overtake the person in front of you. Essentially, the situation is a conflict, albeit a minor one. With the objective of drawing on the conflict energy the pendulum forces the pedestrian to take a small step to the side to block your way and fuel the situation with intensity.

Having said that, the pendulum does not act deliberately as such because it is incapable of conscious intention. Balanced forces are equally as subconscious in their actions. I should emphasise that here we are talking about certain processes the mechanism for which is not entirely clear, but certainly not the premeditated behaviour of conscious beings. We are simply noting individual laws and phenomena connected with the nature of the world of informational energy.

There is no point in discussing the specific kind of pendulum that comes into play in this situation, how it appears, how it manages to have this kind of effect and what exactly is happening on an energetic level as we can never give a comprehensive answer to these questions. We can however draw the following significant conclusion: when balanced forces bring opposites into collision *pendulums will do everything possible to inflame the energy of the emerging conflict.* This is the *law of the pendulum.*

All pendulum battles, be they domestic arguments or armed conflicts, take place in accordance with this law. In case of resistance events will always develop towards an escalation of the conflict irrespective of any temporary or decorative reconciliations.

When the law of the pendulum is at work the rational mind has no power. This is why the actions of individuals as well as governments seem to make no sense at all. *In conflict situations the individual's motives are under the power of the pendulum.*

This is also why we sometimes look back on our actions as if they were a dream wondering how we could have been devoid of common sense and reason and what could have made us behave so strangely. The reason is of course that a person acts without awareness. Consequently, when one's consciousness is no longer subject to external influence events are perceived from a clearer perspective.

People who are in close relationships argue and separate becoming convinced that their personalities are incompatible and yet there must have been moments of happiness when everything was going wonderfully. But then one partner changes as if out of the blue and starts behaving coldly or with hostility. They are suddenly nothing like the person they were just a short time ago. No doubt this type of situation is familiar to you.

In reality is has nothing to do with the fact that one partner or the other has changed. One person behaves in a manner that is totally unacceptable to the other because they are pushed into it by a pendulum.

Pendulums control the subconscious motives of people who oppose one another and the control is aimed at increasing the energy of conflict. People fail to realise that they are being pushed into a confrontation and are capable of acting illogically and inappropriately.

This effect is particularly noticeable in crimes of inexplicable cruelty. It is only afterwards when the criminal is in the dock that they recall their actions in bewilderment: "I do not know what came over me." They are not lying. This is exactly what happens. The criminal is totally shocked and recalls their crime as if it were a terrible dream.

The dream is particularly heavy if a person's attention has been caught in the pendulum's noose. In certain communities such as for example the army, a gang or sect an environment is created with its specific stereotypes of behaviour and patterns of thinking. This numbs the mind and the subconscious becomes totally open to the zombifying effect of pendulums. Then things happen that to the objective bystander seem totally incomprehensible.

Why do people kill others just like them with such ferocity simply because they worship a different god? What harm were they doing? People suffer in these wars and dozens, hundreds, thousands, millions even lose their lives. Whatever happened to the survival instinct? One could just about understand the violent battle for wealth or territory but how are we supposed to understand the battle for a belief?

Peace is an idea that everyone believes in but there is no end to war. The notion of one God is obvious, and likewise kindness, justice and equality. The list goes on. We all understand these things and yet common sense does not work and evil prevails. So, where does evil come from?

Pendulums are a universal source of evil. You only have to observe for a short while for it to become quite obvious: whatever the circumstances in any confrontation events always move in the direction of the increasing energy of conflict. If the fight dies down then the reprieve is short-lived and bound to flare up again with renewed fury.

Of course there are many different types of pendulums but all are destructive albeit to varying degrees. Many are relatively harmless. The Transurfing pendulum for example is necessary so that as many people as possible start to think about what is really happening.

It is not about freeing oneself from pendulums altogether for this is pretty impossible. The important thing is not to be a puppet on a string, to act with conscious awareness and to use these structures in your own interests. So how can you free yourself from their negative influence?

Wake up and be aware of how pendulums are trying to manipulate you. Understanding what is happening is half the battle. The power of the pendulums' influence is inversely proportionate to awareness. They only have power over you whilst your consciousness is asleep in waking life.

Above all, do not get involved in the pendulums' destructive battles unless is it necessary to you personally. When you find yourself in crowd leave the stage and stand in the auditorium, look around and wake up. Ask yourself: "Why am I here? What am I doing here? Am I aware of what is happening?

Waking up from sleeping in waking life must be articulated very precisely as above: *"In this moment I am awake and I am perfectly aware of what I am doing and why I am doing it specifically in this way."* If you have this kind of awareness then all will be well. If you do not then even in the smallest, most insignificant conflict situation you are still a puppet.

This is hardest to do when something is annoying you. Usually the jester will continue with its jumping all the time that your nerves are on edge. Normally, this means that the pendulum has caught you in its noose. You can free yourself from the pendulum by falling into indifference but this is not easy to do.

For example, your neighbours' are getting to you playing music you really hate. In this case your task is to disentangle yourself from the pendulum in whatever way possible but bear in mind that it is almost impossible not to react. *Suppressing your emotions is useless.* Instead, direct your attention to something else.

Try listening to your own music, but do not turn the volume up too loud, just enough to fade out your neighbours' music. Find other ways of distracting yourself. If you can find something else to occupy your thoughts, your neighbours will gradually quieten down.

The same thing applies in other cases. If the 'jester is jumping' it means that your attention has been caught in the pendulum's noose and you have been enticed into the pendulum's game, the objective of which is to increase the energy of conflict. *To free yourself from the pendulum's noose you must refocus your attention on something else.*

In general, things are not too bad. Things will not happen 'to spite you' if your consciousness is awake. You may of course be thinking that the above is some kind of weird nonsense. It can be hard to get your head round the idea that certain entities can control us. Whether you accept this knowledge or not is a matter of personal choice. Do not take it on faith either. Observe and then draw your own conclusions.

The Pendulum Rule

In the world today at every turn we are forced to encounter direct or indirect material related to sexual relationships. In the Transurfing model this theme, just like many others, is approached from an unusual angle. Sex, or rather our *relationship* to sex, plays a hugely significant role in our personal lives whether we want to acknowledge it or not. It does not matter whether a person has an active sex life. From time to time everyone has flashes of thought that express their *relationship* to sex.

There can be no neutral attitude to sex. Human nature will always reveal itself eventually. Some people's relationship to sex is expressed in annoyance, ridicule and rejection. In others it is transformed into *intention.* If the intention is left unrealised or is realised unsuccessfully all sorts of complexes or, as expressed in Transurfing terms, *negative slides* emerge in the human psyche.

It is fair to say that to some extent the issues of sex concern if not everybody then the vast majority of people. And many people have hang-ups when it comes to sexual relationships. Pendulums play a significant role here too because they will try their hardest to convince you that you are less than perfect and have certain problems. You are not alone in this belief. You would not imagine how many other people think the same about themselves.

You are deeply mistaken if you think that you have difficulties in your sex life whilst everyone else's is fantastic. This is an illusion artificially created by pendulums with the help of the media. You may have noticed that wherever the theme of sex comes up we are shown people who are totally ok.

If you were to take a stadium full of people and then remove everyone who 'had a problem' there would be no more people left standing than the fingers on your hands. Imagine standing in the middle of a huge stadium that has suddenly emptied and you are looking about you in search of the remaining 'normal' few. This would be more realistically reflective of the actual proportions.

Even if your friends, who brag about their conquests, are not exaggerating, you can be sure that they too have their issues which they carefully hide, not only from others but from themselves.

We are not going to indulge in Freudian references here as Freud could hardly have imagined the scale of 'sexomania' that has developed today, but it is worth asking yourself why such a simple function, perfected by nature should cause so many problems.

The answer to this question is to be found in a quite unexpected area which is to some extent linked with the flash-mob phenomenon. If you do not know exactly what this is let me explain.

Imagine a busy street or town square on a Sunday. Everything is the same as normal and then suddenly several dozen people get out umbrellas and act as if it was raining. The 'ordinary' passerby stand with their jaws dropping whilst the 'rain people' have a blast.

This type of trick is very easy to organise. A group of people that are not necessarily already acquainted agree over the internet that at a pre-arranged time in a specified place there will be a signal to carry out some kind of silly activity.

What is actually happening during the event? As you know, when a group of people starts thinking in the same way a pendulum is created. The flash-mob thinks: "Look at us with our umbrellas!" The other passersby stand with their mouths open, and bewildered ask: "whatever are they up to?" The uniform thought energy of the group creates a resonant energy which is swallowed by the pendulum.

The flash-pendulum is the shortest lived of all the pendulums. It flares up and then burns out without causing anyone any harm. This harmless example illustrates how longer lasting and more destructive pendulums are created and how they work.

What makes people emit energy in a specific direction? It requires a code of behaviour and agreed type of thinking. There must be a set *rule*. Naturally the rules are made by people, not by the pendulum. Pendulums emerge spontaneously, generated by the rule that has been created and are not capable of manifesting conscious intention. The *pendulum rule* is the worst and most harmful thing humanity has ever created and it sounds: *"Do as I do!"*

Any codes of behaviour or thinking come down to following the pendulum rule. If you spend a little time observing life you will see examples of this rule time and time again. Of course, it does not always cause harm. For example, a wave made by fans at a stadium creates a flash-pendulum which feeds from the resonant energy but no-one is any the worse for it.

In a concert hall the pendulum will be enthusiastically consuming the energy of the audience. There is no harm in this either. However, watch how performers sometimes behave on stage when they use the pendulum rule to stir up the audience: "Higher, raise your arms! All together now!" The audience obediently starts clapping and the energy created, which would be tiny if it were emanated by just one individual, develops into a resonance creating an invisible monster that hangs above the stage.

If the pendulum did not swallow the energy the artist would literally fly up into the air. As it is, the artist just gets a few crumbs that are left after the pendulum has devoured the rest. Whilst the audience follows the rule: "Do as I do!" the monster lives.

Ok, so what? Nothing bad has happened after all. Flash-mobs are harmless, this is true. But what does this all have to do with sex? You will never guess.

We started by talking about sex and then moved on to flash mobs. So, what do they have in common? You probably think that it is something to do with energy and in fact whilst two people are having sex a flash pendulum emerges that swallows the resonance energy. People in ancient times suspected or knew that a certain entity hangs above 'the act'.

In various cultures this essence or entity, which is referred to in the Transurfing model as a flash-pendulum, is usually attributed an emotionally laden symbol such as "the amusement of Satan". And some followers of occult practice believe that during the sexual act energy is radiated that attracts various representatives of the subtle planes that settle in and have their devilish orgy.

Whatever people tell you, there is no need to be concerned because a flash-pendulum cannot harm you. It simply feeds on energy that you are spending anyway. But that is not the point I am trying to make. The main thing that unites sex in its modern day form is the pendulum rule: "Do as I do!"

With the development of digital media the pendulum rule has achieved total domination. At every step the human psyche is constantly being subjected to invisible but highly efficient conditioning stereotypes of behaviour and thinking. I am cautious to use the word "zombify" here but essentially, this is where it is all going.

The modern information and entertainment industry is based on one simple principle: watch how other people become successful and follow them; let them be your example. What the industry is trying to demonstrate is the *benchmark of success*. You know this perfectly well already but you may not have stopped to consider the magnitude of the propaganda's influence which is sometimes obvious but more often that not is subtle and gradual.

In particular, this is the case with everything relating to intimacy. In this context the stereotypes of *what it should be like* are very deeply rooted. Printed materials and videos on the theme demonstrate relationships which we are supposed to believe meet the necessary standards.

I do not want to create the impression that I am talking about some kind of plot or intentional propaganda. No-one actually sets themselves the goal of instilling certain patterns or moulds. It happens automatically. The problem is that people always have room for doubt in their thoughts: "am I doing the right thing?" There is always the need to compare for success is relative. Hence when a person witnesses someone else's success they naturally tend to perceive it as a benchmark in their own life.

Intimate relationships and sex in particular normally have their place in a tight, closed circle and consequently the need for confirmation that "we are ok" increases. If a person does not currently have a partner or if they have never had a partner they start frantically searching for an example of how things should be. Of course, the media fulfils this need offering all its audience a huge choice of models.

This is how common stereotypes of how to do *it* and what your image should be etc emerge. For example, he is tough and "macho" and she is sultry and "sexy". You are supposed to observe them and do what they do, and if you do not match the example there must be something wrong with you.

It is difficult to fathom the full destructiveness of this rule. You might think that I am overestimating the importance of the issue when I say that the pendulum rule is the worst and most harmful thing humanity has ever invented. And yet not at all. I express myself quite modestly.

The number of broken marriages is enormous and the number of happy families that never were is perhaps even greater. The main reason for separation is ultimately lack of fulfilment in the sexual relationship. Everything else is either a consequence of the lack of fulfilment or an excuse when people do not want to acknowledge the true cause of their problems.

Lack of fulfilment occurs as a consequence of the fact that the couple follow the pendulum rule. They both know that in accordance with the model they must do it like this and like that. The pendulum rule sounds: "Do as I do!" which means *change your-*

self and betray yourself. People try and adjust to the established standard and as a result they experience inner discomfort and dissatisfaction.

The mistake people usually make when they have a problem with sex is that they are trying *to play a role.* It is very simple. Of numerous models the individual chooses the one that suits them the most and another for their partner. As the relationship continues the individual adopts their particular role and projects their corresponding expectations on their partner. The amazing thing is that the role is usually played according to the principle of Transurfing – dispassionately, in the style of the participating member of the audience because they are constantly comparing themselves and their partner to the standard model wondering whether everything is working out right.

As a result, things go pear-shaped because the nature of sex is that it requires being relaxed, free and devoted. Sex is the only instance when you have to become totally immersed and forget about roles totally. *When sex is natural and normal it is a game played according to rules that you make up yourselves without giving a moment's thought to how others do it or how it is supposed to be done.*

Things become even more complex when the notions of love and sex are confused. It is sickening to hear the often sanctimonious use of the expression "let's make love". Would not it be simpler to call a spade a spade? Sex is not love and love is not sex. Are they compatible? Indeed they are but that does not change the fact that *love is not sex and sex is not love.*

They can be combined and they can exist independently of one another. But the pendulum rule stops this from happening *naturally.* I would say that the nature of all problems experienced in sexual relationships is linked with the fact that in following the pendulum rule people try to artificially combine love and sex. The result is a kind of awkward hybrid.

If you forget about the rules and standard models it is actually all very straightforward. Imagine a scale with zero at the centre of the baseline. The values to the left indicate affection and to the right – aggression. If the arrow shifts to the left then it is love. If it shifts to the right then it is sex. Whether you like it or not sex is more about aggression than affection.

Many people are shy or fearful when their 'devilish' instincts are awakened thinking that it is somehow unnatural. In reality what happens is that two people meet and at first their behaviour shows no signs of anything unusual. But then they get a predatory glint in their eyes and start doing things that do not fit with…. with what exactly?

Here the pendulum rule comes into play. On the one hand accepted notions of decency do exist which it would be inappropriate to defy. On the other hand within these boundaries of decency it is impossible to take full pleasure from sex. We want both.

In order to fit with the standard model of things people start playing certain roles. Fearing their animal instincts they water sex down with what they consider to be necessary ritual. This in turn evokes a certain amount of inhibition. When two people should be letting go the reigns, the pendulum rule will not allow them to. And the opposite is true, when the arrow moves far to the side of aggression the need for reassurance arises: "Do you love me?"

So there are always two participating members of the audience on the stage. They are like puppets hanging on the strings on control they have attached themselves to. What are they really doing? *They are desperately trying to pull the arrow to one side or the other.* All they would have to do, would be to ditch the pendulum rule and let go of the arrow letting it move freely in correlation with the feelings of the heart and not the ideas of the mind.

Some may protest that in this way we would be reduced to the level of animals. But once again, this is the pendulum rule at work. Who set the boundaries for where humanity ends and the level of animals begins? It is not even so much a matter of where this level actually is so much as that each individual has to make their own rules rather than following rules set by others. As a human being you have the right to establish your own criteria for humanity and decency.

I hope you understand that I am writing this for the benefit of those who have certain issues around sex, especially for those who love each other. All that is required to eliminate the problem is to let go of the arrow as consciously as you maintain control over observing the pendulum rule.

There is also a certain type of person who experiences no problems at all in their sexual life. Many issues cease to have weight if you can just be direct and speak things the way they are without confusing different notions and being consciously aware of what you wish to get out of a relationship and being able to communicate it to your partner. Life becomes instantly easier the moment you behave openly. You can be certain that your partner also has their own hidden desires. What should you do if a situation arises where one person desires something their partner finds unacceptable?

Firstly, it is important to remember the first principle of Frailing: *let go of the intention to receive and replace it with the intention to give and you will receive the very thing you let go of.* This wonderful principle works every time even if you do not always understand how.

Secondly, you have to reject the pendulum rule totally and replace it with the rule of Transurfing which sound: *be yourself and allow other to be themselves also.*

As you know, in order to feel fulfilled by a sexual relationship you have to feel free and uninhibited. You cannot feel free if you are carrying excess potential in the form of complexes such as an inferiority complex. However much you try to relax balanced forces will not allow you to.

But the majority of tension arises not so much as a result of balanced forces but as a result of dependent relationships. Inner intention is predominantly aimed at receiving rather than giving. In addition, people usually hang projections on their partner in accordance with their expectation of a given role. We just do not seem to want to let other people be themselves.

As you know, dependent relationships generate polarisation, which evokes the winds of balanced forces which ruin everything.

The Transurfing rule instantly neutralises the polarisation created by the dependent relationship. And so, even if you cannot get rid of your complexes you can follow the Transurfing rule which will noticeably reduce the tension.

To be yourself means accepting yourself as you are in all your imperfection. Allowing another to be themselves, means taking back the projection of your own expectations of them. As a result, any situation in which one person wants something another would find unacceptable is automatically resolved.

I repeat that all you need to do is *reject the pendulum rule, replace it with the Transurfing rule and then direct your intention in accordance with the first principle of Frailing.* If both partners in a couple can do this they should not experience any further problems in the relationship. I will leave more detailed explanations for why this works to the psychologists but it works. That is all.

In a more general sense, why should the pendulum need its rule? You can see that in the case of flash-pendulums they feed on resonance energy and so they require synchronised action, but what keeps more long-lasting pendulums going who do not require their adherents to act as one?

Above all, the pendulum rule establishes behavioural norms and types of thinking, i.e. standard models of what is considered 'normal'. People do not understand that they are being offered an ersatz product, a surrogate success. Someone else's success can never serve as an example in the sense of a model to be replicated. True success is only achieved by those who have the courage to breaks the rules and go their own way.

When you follow in someone else's footsteps you are sentenced to the eternal task of trying to catch the setting sun. Standards of success are a mirage but people do not know or perhaps do not want to know that the pendulum rule traps them in a web of illusion. Illusions are often sweeter, more convenient and clearer than reality and the unknown.

When a person comes face to face with the fact that they do not fit with the established standards they experience inner discomfort. They are filled with the fear of failure, feel inadequate and all alone in a hostile world.

What can they do? Rejection is one option. A person often surrounds themselves with a wall of their rejection of unattainable models of success. Or, they continue chasing after the model following the pendulum rule, trying to change themselves and forcing their soul into a box of social conditioning. This approach leads only to dissatisfaction and a lack of fulfilment and once again the person tries to change.

When people chase after standard models they radiate the energy of dissatisfaction and disappointment. It is inevitable. It is the same as a donkey going round in circles after a carrot. This is the energy that destructive pendulums feed on.

The wall of rejection in turn requires no less energy. It is very hard to maintain a defence field around you all the time when everywhere and at every step you are being bombarded with rules you are unable to observe.

There is a way out of the labyrinth though. The way out lies in *refusing to follow the pendulum rule and walking your own path.* Those who manage it acquire a unique quality that takes your breath away, *inner freedom.* There are people who have this quality and the lady who wrote the letter below is standing just a step or two way from this freedom.

> *"I am nearly thirty years old and I have never been with a man. The sexologists say that this is a serious abnormality but I do not see why. It is not written anywhere that you have to sleep with someone before you hit twenty-five or that virginity should be punished on moral grounds. I am an attractive woman and there have been plenty of opportunities for an intimate relationship but the truth is, I have not wanted to. The problem is not physiological. Everything is ok on that front too. I just have not yet met a man I have felt I wanted to go to bed with. Recently though, the issue has been weighing on me more heavily because everyone is indulging in carnal love except me. It is natural and I am an exception to the rule...I have never felt enslaved to social stereotypes but this part*

of social conditioning is evidently really beginning to get to me. Sometimes I feel like I am some kind of moralistic freak. The fact of my solitude does not affect my self-esteem because not sleeping with someone I do not feel particularly drawn to is a conscious decision. Am I really an exception, abnormal in some way?"

I said "a step or two away" because you still have a fear of being different. Nonetheless, you clearly have inner strength and are independent. Obviously you are not abnormal. You just must not be afraid that you are not like everyone else. Be happy about it although of course, there is no need to go over the top. Perhaps you could lower the bar of your expectations and approach things more simply.

If we judged by the information we are constantly being bombarded with, you would think that having sex is all people ever do. But this is an illusion. Far from everyone leads an active way of life in this context and many people do not have a partner at all. But fear of loneliness and being different cause people to buy into the illusion.

Take Paris for example, with its air of freedom and relaxed atmosphere. Paris has won the reputation of being 'the city of lonely hearts'. Every day early in the morning people rush out and tour the many cafes. Why? After all, they could have their coffee at home. Loneliness drives them out of their houses.

It might seem as if pendulums deliberately enslave society to its rules. They do enslave people, but they do not set the rules. *They exist because of the rule!* The rule creates the pendulum and only then does it start doing its dirty deed. The main feature of the pendulum that makes it so destructive is that it leads people away from the path that could make them truly happy.

Imagine a busy street where everyone is going about their own affairs when suddenly figures dressed in black appear and make everyone line up and start marching. One person tries to walk away but they are immediately and crudely forced to rejoin the line: "You! Stop! Where do you think you are going? Get back in line!

It is no coincidence that the film "The Matrix" was made. Science fiction has a tendency to become reality over time and this tendency is accelerating. If you observe carefully you will see that the gulf between science fiction and physical reality is becoming ever narrower. Of course people do not lie in containers with suction cups attached to their bodies but the analogy is pretty close.

People think that the line is reality. In fact it is the requirement to stand in line that is the illusion. True reality lies in the fact that you can break the line and go your own path. It just is not that easy to have this awareness. People are so used to living with their illusions that they need a really good shake or as Carlos Castanaeda would have it to "shift the assemblage point" before they can discern the difference between reality and illusion.

People who are handicapped are genuinely in a position of having no choice. They either suffer their entire lives, tortured by their deficiency or neglect the pendulum rule. If a person understands that they have nothing to lose they give up chasing after standard models and begin living for their own pleasure.

Invalids who play basketball in their wheelchairs are infinitely happier than able-bodied teenagers trying to copy Michael Jordan. These teenagers even come across as being less natural because they march in line. None of them will actually become anything like Michael Jordan until they realise that they need to break out of the line.

Those who break the pendulum rule either become leaders or renegades. Some make their way to stardom whilst others end up social outcasts. The difference between them is that the former know they have the right to break the pendulum rule whilst the latter still have doubts.

Stars are born but pendulums light them up. Those that dare to break out of line become new models of success. Pendulums will not put up with individuality. They see a rising star and have no choice other than to make it their favourite. Then a new rule is made. The line turns round and marches after a new star. Can you see what is happening?

In order to break out of the line you have to know how. If you fight against the figures in black you will lose. In the battle against pendulums you will always be defeated.

The secret lies in leaving the line without a fight. You can walk away calmly, smiling and waving goodbye to the figures in black and then go your own way. They will do everything they can to force you back in line but ultimately there is not anything they can do if you do not enter into conflict with them.

In order to fully understand this simple truth you have to first reconsider your current worldview. In the world we live in today many things have to been turned on their head. In this sense Transurfing puts everything in its place and assists in resisting the pendulum rule.

It is true that many people will be adverse to the idea that they are caught up in a matrix. Transurfing will not be of any interest to those who prefer for their ego to stay sleeping. We all receive the things we choose. An illusion is also a choice, and anyone who prefers to stay with the illusion has every right to do so.

It is not my intention to force information on anyone neither do I feel obliged to prove my ideas. Anyone can put the principles shared here into practice and prove or discredit them as they see fit. I am simply the person walking past who says: "Hey! Did you know that there is something called Transurfing Reality? "Really?" "Yup! That is where I am headed but you can go where you like." That is all.

Stabilising the Structure

In accordance with its law the pendulum does all it can to augment the energy of an existing conflict. The battles from which pendulums draw their energy are constantly going on around us and they usually involve two or more opposing structures. There are many examples of this: war, revolution, competition and other forms of confrontation.

However, besides demonstrating aggression towards its enemies, another distinguishing feature of any pendulum is its drive to maintain and strengthen the structure that makes its very existence possible.

Information-energy entities are formed and grow simultaneously with the emergence of an ordered structure created by living representatives of the natural world. The existence of any pendulum is wholly dependent on the stability levels of the newly created structure. So, the pendulum *will do anything necessary to stabilise its structure*. This is the second law of the pendulum.

As an illustration of this law let us take the very simple example of a school of baby fish. The school behaves as if it were a single organism. If you frighten it from one side all the fish turn and swim in the opposite direction synchronously. How is this phenomenon of synchronism explained?

If we assume that every individual fish is reacting to the movements of the next fish swimming beside it then the response to the disturbance would take on a chain-like effect. However, however fast the signal was passed on to the other fish in the school there would still be some kind of delay between the response times of different fish. The point here is that there is no delay. The school can grow to quite large proportions and yet the same synchronism is observed.

Birds demonstrate the same behaviour. If you have ever seen a large flock of small but fast moving birds you will have noticed what incredible coordination is expressed in their movements back and forth.

Perhaps what we are seeing is the workings of a different kind of mechanism, for example, some kind of telepathic contact. This is unlikely though. In water, where there are no schools of fish if you frighten one fish another situated just one meter away will not respond at all. So, it is not a matter of telepathic connection. The signal is transferred only when the fish are together in a school, which in essence represents an extremely simple structure. Or could it be that no signal is being transferred at all?

Let us take the example of a higher-level structure such as an anthill. Science has not yet been able to provide a persuasive explanation to how to colony is run. In an anthill there is an absence of social hierarchy and yet incredibly there is precise allocation of duty enabling all the insects to work in a coordinated manner as in any other organisation run by centralised management.

Ants communicate with each other by excreting odorous substances called pheromones. Trails of odour enable them to find their way home and locate food. However, this does not explain how information is simultaneously passed to all colony members. There is no question of any higher form of information exchange existing between the ants, otherwise, why would they be using such a primitive data source as odours?

So what does unite individual members into an organised colony? The answer is *the pendulum.* At the same time that the structure is created and developed an informational-energy entity is formed which adopts the function of managing and stabilising that structure. Direct and feedback links exists between the pendulum and structural elements. The pendulum exists on account of the energy of its adherents and it synchronises their activity uniting them in one organised community.

It may seem from the outside that the structure is self-organising but this is not the case. Self-organisation is only applicable to inanimate nature where the laws of physics serve as the organising principle. For example, during the process of crystallisation water molecules are arranged into a lattice structure which is determined by the shape of the molecules and the forces of interaction.

Uniting living organisms into a structure requires the presence of an outer organising factor. That factor is the pendulum. How exactly the pendulum carries out its organising function no-one can yet say. Evidently a certain type of informational-energy exchange takes place between the entity and the living organism.

Any structure that unites living organisms has a pendulum as a controlling super-structure. However, one cannot say that the pendulum controls the structure via the quality of reason because it is not capable of conscious intention. The consciousness of an informational-energy entity is similar to an algorithm. Rather than implementing a design in the way that an intelligent being does, it manages the structure roughly as a programme directs the working of an automatic device.

The extent to which the elements of the structure act 'automatically' depends on their level of awareness. The more primitive the living organism is, the less idea it will have of its motives and actions. When a being lives in isolation its actions are determined by the internal programme of its own set of instincts. However, when living beings come together in a group, an outer programme of the pendulum begins to take effect, directing the behaviour of the community as a whole.

The aggressive world in which all beings eat each other developed as a consequence of the first law of the pendulum. Given that aggression is a product of the pendulum is does not have to be a necessary feature of the natural world. Confirmation of this can be found in various corners of the planet, for example, as in New Zealand, a country with hardly any predators.

Many inhabitants of the Earth have to unite in groups in order to secure their survival in a hazardous environment. Pendulums force living beings to become elements of a given structure according to the principle: "OK, squit, if you want to survive do as I do".

People also have a tendency to gather in groups according to their interests. This can be explained by the fact that it is easier for them to communicate with others who are like-minded. It might seem strange but many people experience difficulties communicating. However effortless interpersonal relationships might seem on the surface, they are incredibly strained for a variety of reasons, inner and outer. In order to establish a closer contact with one another, people instinctively look for something they have in common that could potentially unite them. This is where the stabilising function of the pendulum comes in. When two people in conversation are swaying to the same pendulum they are 'on the same wave length' and easily find a common language. This enables the relationship to acquire a quality of ease making it possible to have a smoke or a drink, sit and have a special meal together, go camping, play a game etc.

Indeed the most impressive illustration of the second law of the pendulum must be the birth of human civilisation. Have you ever wondered how cities came into being? Why did people who had lived for thousands of years in nomadic camps and villages and then suddenly start building civilised settlements? What were they based on, craft, trade, war perhaps?

The most ancient cities in the world date to the same period as the pyramids. Caral for example was discovered quite recently in Peru. This lost city stood unnoticed by archaeologists for almost five thousand years. It was finally discovered when it turned out that raised hills in the desert were once pyramids, one of which equalled in size to the Egyptian pyramids. Archaeologists were surprised to find that excavations yielded no evidence of ceramic ware or weaponry. The people of that time used primitive tools made from wood, stone and bone.

It was later established that the inhabitants of the city grew cotton and made fishing nets which they exchanged for fish with the inhabitants of shoreline areas. And yet the inhabitants of a village could have easily engaged in the same livelihood. There were no defence structures surrounding Caral which rules out the question of a military prehistory to the city. So what caused the emergence of this city?

From ancient times human beings had lived in villages engaging in primitive forms of craftsmanship, either trading or busy waging wars with other factors inhabiting the same region. And yet they did all this without needing to construct stone towns or erect pyramids. In all likelihood the pendulum served as the organising factor, or more precisely, the stabilising factor for these settlements.

It is impossible to say exactly why this happens. The truth is never to be found far away. Likely as not at a certain point in time a pendulum structure is spontaneously formed which carries the capacity for further development. For a city is in essence a complex pendulum hierarchy of production, consumption and exchange. If the construction of the self-organising system is stable at the outset then it will expand and strengthen. The structure may even evolve into the formation of a complex civilisation. This process will continue until such time as a defect in the architecture brings the gigantic construction tumbling down. Of course, there is a long way to go before that happens to us, although, it all depends....

Let us get back to life as it is now. The Human beings are 'more awake' in comparison to other representatives of the animate world and yet are we always consciously aware of our actions? The human mind is capable of creating complex structures and mechanisms, building whole cities and researching the world we live in and yet in the context of awareness man has not developed much further than the animal kingdom.

All of society is organised in a complex structure consisting of separate formations from the family to large corporations and whole nations. Like in nature, if a person lives in relatively isolated conditions they are consciously responsible for their actions. As we know, enlightenment was reached by those who isolated themselves from society. However, once a person becomes an element of a structure to a large degree they are asleep which does not appear to hinder the mind from engaging in advanced technological production.

A modern day factory is a lot more complex than an anthill and yet in essence both structures are controlled by pendulums. All achievements of scientific and technological progress if considered all together are the products of a structure rather than a specific individual. The television as a piece of apparatus is the invention of one man but television in the wider sense of television broadcasting is the product of an entire system which is controlled by a pendulum.

When a person becomes an element of a larger structure they are obliged to follow the pendulum rule. As a result, an unavoidable contradiction arises between the individual's personal interests and the conditions imposed by the structure. The worst thing is when a person is not aware of this and obediently toils and sweats away for the system unable to take the time to lift their head up, look around and become conscious of what they are doing.

You may think this is all nonsense! "Why do you think that I am not aware? Quite the opposite; I am perfectly aware of what I am doing, why and wherefore I am doing it." Unlikely.

Children's summer camps are a good example. The vulnerable psyche of teenagers, relatively free from lessons serves as fertile soil from which pendulums can sprout. Due to their aggressive essence pendulums create an environment in which the spirit of competition can blossom. In this environment if you are in some way different to all the others, i.e. you do not meet the parameters of the structure you can be made a mockery, "driven out of the herd" or simply beaten up.

In these conditions the teenager falls into a deadly waking sleep. They live as if they were in a dream unable to take full account of their actions either as part of the crowd or in opposition to it. The sedative is the heavy residue competitive relationships leave them with, and the strong suspicion of their own inadequacy and inability to keep up with the "standards". The teenager is never for a minute free of the feelings of oppression and wariness even if to all other intent and purposes they appear calm, confident and buoyant.

It is the same feeling of oppression bordering on hopelessness that a person experiences in non-lucid dreaming when they are at the total mercy of what is happening in the dream. Life in an aggressive environment "happens" to the individual like in dreaming. A rapid flow of circumstances "carries" the individual along forcing all their awareness to be focused on just staying afloat and keeping an anxious eye open in anticipation of the next thing.

Unless a teenager has a strong sense of self which gives them an inner strength to hold to they begin instinctively, even subconsciously looking for another source of strength to strengthen their position. The pendulum is there to offer this support, but not freely, only in exchange for submitting to the rules of the structure.

In an environment like a summer camp there always seem to be a few raucous boisterous kids who appear to be extremely confident and feel quite at home. Their false confidence relies on the strength offered by the pendulum.

Imagine two kids like this, one a "slacker" and the other a "prankster": "Hey you! Look at me! Do as I do! Do as I do!"; "Hey you! What are you waiting for? Stop picking your nose, chill, have some fun man!"

No-one else realises that these two kids are dangling on the pendulum's hook like a puppet on a string. The source of strength although ephemeral creates the illusion. The others see how confident the puppets are and act in a similar manner. They too gain a source of strength in exchange for following the rule: "Do as I do". Eventually, they all end up dangling together as one, the 'slackers' and the 'pranksters'. This is how the structure is made.

The important thing to realise is that the pendulum's adherents comply with the rule unconsciously. They are totally under the illusion that this is the right thing to do. In following the rule the adherents can get away with doing whatever they want to, as long as they all follow suit. For example, people do not just swear when they are arguing anymore; they swear as part of their ordinary speech. It does not occur to anyone anymore that swearing is vulgar. Vulgarity is a sign of poor taste and low social class. It is the same as not washing or wearing dirty clothes. People might not be wearing their dirty clothing at the moment but they surely will as soon as someone makes it a rule to do so.

For example, at the court of the French King Louis IV no-one ever washed because the King had a pathological aversion to hygiene and reduced it to rinsing his hands in cognac. The court members were obliged to follow his example and to conceal the unpleasant odour coming from their bodies they doused themselves in perfume as a result of which a heavy stench reigned throughout the palace grounds. And because they all inevitably suffered from lice the dames and cavaliers introduced the 'sophisticated' habit of carrying fine sticks around enabling them to scratch themselves in a delicate manner.

As you can see, the rule is capable of rehabilitating any nonsense at all. The main point is that those who observe the rule act absolutely the same, on mass, like a flock of sheep. For example, the first person who ever said "wicked" should consider themselves a true shepherd. But everyone else after who repeat this and other convenient words like parrots in chorus act just exactly like sheep.

Do you recall the school of baby fish? Has humanity really progressed very far in terms of consciousness?

It is not only teenagers who are subject to the influence of pendulums. It is also the adults, especially when they come together in a crowd. For example, at a meeting when someone or something is being discussed by a group a person may find that they can suddenly stand up and start a huge spiel, taking themselves quite by surprise. In hindsight they will wonder how on earth they got through it and convince themselves for ages that everything they said was right. The crowd forces its members to behave in a way that is often uncharacteristic. This is how the pendulum influences those who seek a source of strength and security.

So if someone thinks they have found security within a structure what of it? This is one solution to the problem. But you should bear in mind that if you observe the structure's rules you can forget about your individuality. You will be like 'everyone else' and find peace and security. At the same time, you relinquish your divine gift, the uniqueness of your soul on which the genius part of yourself depends, to say nothing of the fact that unity of heart and mind becomes impossible. When a person is entirely under the power of the structure they are almost entirely unconscious and unable to perceive the voice of the heart which means they will never search for their true path and will spend their life in back-breaking service to the structure.

I am not saying that everyone's personal path can only be found beyond the limits of a given structure. Of course, you can disappear into the mountains and cut yourself off from the world of pendulums but if life continues to be a subconscious waking dream in the mountains as well, then you will not change a thing.

The challenge is to remain the captain of your fate whilst you are within the structure. Is it possible for example to acquire the self-confidence a child so needs without submitting to the pendulum's rule or becoming a social outcast? Easily. All you have to do is wake up and observe the scene through the eyes of an observer whilst you are still on the stage. Then it immediately becomes evident who are the pendulums favourites, the slackers and the pranksters and adherents who follow the rule.

You must not judge or disdain people for following the rule. If as a result of your awareness of the way of things you start comparing yourself to those who are 'asleep' dependent relationship arise, polarisation occurs and the "awakened" one inevitably becomes an outcast. It is very important to remember that it is not enough to simply reject the pendulum's rule. You have to replace it with the Transurfing rule: "Be yourself and allow others to do the same."

Then you will be able to find your source of strength and security within. Once you understand what is happening around you, you are already half way home. This knowledge alone brings a reliable, calm belief in oneself because lack of self-confidence comes from fear of the unknown. When a person is unfamiliar with the rules of the game the world seems scary and hostile. Then feelings of loneliness and depression take over sending you to sleep and making you submit to the pendulum's rule.

Knowing all this you are now capable of turning life into a conscious waking dream which means having control over a situation. Either you become a shepherd or at the very least you stop being a sheep.

As far as strengthening your position goes, we have talked about this in quite a lot of detail in the theory of Transurfing. Firstly you have to be rid of feelings of guilt which means you have to stop justifying yourself and explaining your actions to others who have the outright audacity to judge you. Secondly, stop protecting or proving your worth. If you follow the Transurfing rule at the same time then these two things will be more than enough to acquire a sense of strength and security within i.e. to begin living in accordance with your own beliefs.

Bear in mind that you cannot simply thoughtlessly oppose a given structure desperately trying to be rid of its influence. I should repeat that we are not talking about freeing yourself from pendulums entirely but about how to avoid being a puppet on a string.

Once you are awake you will feel and see how the structure weighs on you (do you want to live?) when it tries to impose its own rules. Then you will be able to decide for yourself whether you want to refuse to follow their rules or whether you want to observe them. The important thing is to make a conscious decision whilst others are asleep. This is the strategy of the person who is master of the situation. As an example, I cite a letter which is quite characteristic.

> *"Why is it sometimes the case that when you do your work to a high standard or do even more than is expected, suggesting new ideas that are very well received no-one notices it and someone else gets to take the credit? Even if there is a raise in salary available I am quickly forgotten as if I had not even been in the running and if I am initially offered a small promotion in the process of formalising it someone else takes the position before me or it is postponed. It is as if I am invisible. Why does this happen?"*
>
> *It would appear that the reader who asked this question works in the administrative system. Any system is a pendulum. The informational-energy structure first arises in the form of a set of ideas and principles and then it is materialised materially, i.e. into a system. The system then starts to develop independently submitting its adherents to its laws.*

Pendulums place their adherents in key positions not based on merit and high service but based on how fully they fit into the system. It would be naïve to think that on the career ladder or in the power hierarchy people are arranged according to their distinguishing qualities and achievements. Perhaps this is the case to some degree but nonetheless, distinguishing qualities and achievements are not the main thing.

The most important criteria is not how well a person carries out their work so much as how correctly they do it from the point of view of the system. The pendulum is most concerned with stability. And so first and foremost you should direct your actions towards supporting the system's stability.

If you want to climb up the career ladder you have to understand the difference between "well" and "correctly". Here everything depends on the team. Pendulums are different too.

In the majority of teams, creativity, initiative, enthusiasm and independence are welcomed but in the case of a management apparatus or large enterprise the laws and ethic are totally different, i.e. corporative.

Corporate ethics entail more stringent regulations, discipline and diligence. Taking the initiative can be punished, independence met with caution, and creativity far from playing the most important role. In this type of system you have to be 'more correct' not 'better'.

So you have to be able to behave in a conscious and flexible manner in line with the reality of the pendulum world. It is not as difficult as it might seem. The important thing is to wake up sooner rather than later.

The Indigo Arrivals

One of the clearest manifestations of the onset of a new reality is the phenomenon known as the "Indigo Children" described in detail in the book of the same name by Lee Carroll and Jan Tober. The term was coined by the clairvoyant Nancy Ann Tappe who researched the connections between a person's personality and the colour of their aura.

At the beginning of the nineteen seventies Nancy Tappe discovered an unusual phenomenon: children of a new kind were entering the world with a previously unseen colour in their aura: indigo (blue-violet).

The Indigo children were shown to be different in personality to other people. They are often diagnosed with hyperactive disorder and attention deficit disorder. The have difficulty sitting still unless they are doing something they find interesting. Not all children who display these disorders are necessarily indigo and vice versa. Every child is different.

What all Indigo children have in common is an inherent sense of status and dignity and a strong independent spirit. The indigo child does not doubt their worth for a moment as if they were confident that they deserve a place here in this life. That is just how they are!

These children surprise adults displaying a wisdom and awareness that is beyond their years. Indigo children will not conform in order to fit into society and have low tolerance of authority figures.

The Indigo child is an independent thinker. To them it seems quite obvious that certain things should be done differently whilst other people follow widely accepted norms and rules.

You certainly would not call the Indigo child pliant or accommodating. Indigo children can be very difficult to bring up and fail to respond to usual forms of discipline. They are also very intelligent. To some degree these qualities are typical of every new generation but the Indigo children are particularly different to other children.

For thousands of years the generation shift has been fairly uniform and measured. Recently however, a quickening in the process of generational renewal has been observed. Each new generation is even more radically different from the previous generation. The first generation Indigo children now have their own children who in their development have already gone beyond the characteristic qualities of their parents.

So what is happening here? The process of the revolutionary renewal of human consciousness does not occur without cause. As we know, in nature and in society everything strives towards balance. Consciousness renewal therefore develops in counterbalance to some other process. It is not difficult to guess what this process is. Over recent decades at the same time as information and telecommunications systems a powerful network of pendulums has developed ensnaring the entire planet.

Scientific and technological progress is not as scary as its informational component which creates fertile soil for the birth and existence of pendulums. The larger the group of adherents who think in the same way the more powerful the pendulum and the power it can exert.

To gain control over a large number of people you do not have to place them in containers with suction caps attached to their bodies like in the film "The Matrix". It is enough to create an all-encompassing information network because then people will automatically take their places in its cells.

So what does a person in an information cell look like? It is the so-called social *element* whose level of consciousness is conditioned by their place in the *structure* which in reality is similar to the matrix.

The structure imperceptibly but persistently envelopes each member with a set of conditioned thought and behaviour patterns. People think they are acting according to their own free will but in reality they have no conception of true freedom because the "configuration" is created by the structure. Each individual plays their role with the will they have been designated in a play that has been imposed upon them.

It would appear that everyone is free to do what they *want*. We are declared to have this freedom. The only thing is that we can only want things that coincide with the interests of the structure. *The structure teaches us to want what it needs us to want.*

This process of *enslaving individual will (intention)* is what we are going to look at next. By nature this process is synergetic, that is, it is self-organising because pendulums do not have the capacity of conscious intention. Everything happens of its own accord as ice crystals form in the process of freezing. The pendulum network is like a colony of parasitic plants that covers the Earth's entire biosphere.

This is potentially a frightening thought. Some might be amused by it. How we respond to this type of information is a very personal thing. If you like you can attribute all this to the realms of science-fiction. And yet, when everyday reality adopts an unfamiliar form its tough realism goes beyond even the boldest examples of science fiction.

But let us get back to the kids. The tendency to enslave the will has generated a response in the form of a type of child that strives for independence. Their appearance is the result of a natural process and the action of balanced forces in response to the pendulum network.

On the one hand, pendulums try to organise the world driving people into structures similar to the Matrix. On the other hand, the Indigos even out the pendulum's domination as if thereby fulfilling a predetermined mission. The children's behaviour is aimed at challenging established systems. Whenever they find themselves squeezed in to fit the boundaries of conditioned stereotypes they strive to break free.

All children but Indigo children especially are very sensitive to excess potential. For example they recognise falsity immediately. When an adult tries to ingratiate themselves they answer back and if you praise them too much they start playing up.

Any type of order or discipline creates polarisation which the children try to challenge. "I do not want to go to sleep! I do not want porridge! I can do it myself!" The tendency these children display for disobedience and naughtiness is not a result of nastiness so much as a natural desire to be free from external control. Sometimes it might seem that these children do things to annoy us on purpose but in fact their behaviour is unintentional and subconscious. Their provocative behaviour is neither planned nor thought through. It is a natural form of expression. It is a manifestation of the action of balanced forces in response to the discipline adults try to force upon their children.

The Indigo's striving for independence is very evident in their attitude to religion. "The new type of children may find it difficult to accept the contemporary church" write Lee Carroll and Jan Tober. "Indigo children come into the world with a heightened sense of dignity and unshakeable faith that they are children of God". If this is the case, do they really need mediators to communicate with God? Hardly.

Indigo children are governed mainly by the voice of the heart then the mind. Adults think that they are doing well when they behave correctly. Children are of the opinion that the most important thing is to do everything with soul, with love and not necessarily in the way that is considered correct.

What if in some past life your current children were you parents and now you have changed place? What if now these old souls have come to continue to teach you, giving many wise lessons.

The wisdom of the Indigo children results from their heightened awareness. They are very aware of what is happening around them and who is who. Awareness is heightened when the focus of attention is directed inwards and not outwards. When a person is totally immersed in the cares imposed on them by the outside world their mind dives into the game subconsciously. The Indigo awareness counters the tendency of the "sedated mind" within the pendulum networks.

All children are marked by strong individuality from birth. In their early childhood they are very beautiful and charming. The secret to the child's charm is unity of heart and mind. They accept themselves the way they are and so their essential inner beauty is not distorted by the false masks of the mind.

Why is it then, that as these wonderful creations mature they show certain unpleasant traits and weak sides to their character? For these are the children of God and so beautiful and powerful like God himself despite the vulnerability of their early years. Initially they are imbued with the power of the Creator capable of creating a new reality. But the talents and abilities of the children of God do not have time to blossom and find practical realisation before the pendulums deprive them of their divine power – unity of heart and mind.

Children come into the world and look around them with large, trusting, shining bead-like eyes. Life seems instantly full of promise and hope. But the world is ruled by pendulums according to the principle of "Divide and rule".

Pendulums unify people's motivations and desires at the same time destroying their uniqueness and the integrity of their individuality. *The separation and alienation of the heart from the mind leads to the loss of divine beauty and strength.*

With time small and big hopes are dashed. For some this process takes place slowly and painlessly. In others who are less lucky it happens quickly and harshly. If you look in the eyes of children at orphanages you see two seemingly incompatible things – hope and despair. It is as if an unfinished question has gone cold in their eyes: "Is this really how it is?"

The world of pendulums is always proving to children how imperfect and vulnerable they really are. At first suspicion takes hold in their consciousness and then fear takes hold so firmly that it becomes habitual. You cannot run away just because you are frightened. You have to somehow survive in this aggressive environment. Finding themselves under the powerful influence of the structure the children of God are forced to become elements of it.

With age children become wary of not being like everyone else because those who are "like everyone else" might "get them" which is what often happens. It is safer in the crowd. If you stand apart from the crowd you risk becoming an outcast. Gradually, children lose the gifts they have been given at birth: independence, awareness, intuition and individuality.

These qualities are most characteristic of the Indigo children but such characteristics mean certain death to the structure and so the process of enslaving human will continues. Who will win this battle, no-one can say.

The only truly important thing is that until such time as the structure has declared outright victory we try here in this life to return if just a small portion of the strength gifted to us by God. Transurfing can help us with this task.

Could you, dear listener, be an Indigo? It does not matter either way. We are all in essence the same, either grown-up children or the grown-ups' children.

Energy Lords

It is a strange thing, quite normal and yet strange at the same time. Cultural plants and pets were once wild and existed independently in a natural environment. But then man "woke up" and realised that he could establish control over them. It is the quality of conscious awareness that enabled man to rise above the plants and animals and exploit them for his own needs whilst they continued to exist in a state of unconscious dreaming. Then structures had to be created that would determine where and how the enslaved species would live.

Whatever goals the plants and animals have, and undoubtedly they do have them, the discipline and order of the structure reduces them to nothing. From man's point of view the life purpose of his little brothers could be reduced to the primitive need for food and reproduction. However, if this is what the 'higher' being really thinks then it proves the truly primitive level of his supposedly perfect mind.

In reality, every living creature has its own goal. But why? What for? *The process of striving to fulfil purpose is the driver for evolution.*

We will return to this question later. For now, we will simply state the following fact: the true goal of any living being, whatever its nature, can only be achieved in its natural habitat. Any structure subjects the goals of its elements exclusively to its own interests. The development of tamed or "disciplined" plants follows the direction man chooses for them. As a result, the elements of the structure sleep even more deeply and finally, completely loose touch with their true goals.

The life of wild animals and plants is a lot more intelligent and rich than we would otherwise think. Take for example a herd of wild deer. They have more than enough to deal with: the problem of defending themselves from predators, bringing up the offspring, foraging for food, dealing with family relationships, the group hierarchy as well as simply enjoying life.

The life of a herd of cows in the structure of a farm could hardly be more wretched. By providing them with food and shelter man solved all sorts of problems for these animals, but in exchange they had to sacrifice their goals to their master who determines how, for what purpose and how long they will live. It is similar to man "selling his soul to the devil" is it not?

So what of man? The reality is that in creating these structures man becomes a slave himself. *He loses himself and ceases to understand who he is and what he really wants,* the range of his activities being finally reduced to the production, buying and selling of various products. At the head of any structure there is a superstructure pendulum which has no interest in the products at all and focuses purely on actively developing the structure that produces them. Why is this?

Energy is the prime product. People buy things for their pleasure and comfort, right? Aside from products that give us pleasure other products exist that are designed to cause problems for others. In both cases energy is radiated, positive or negative because this is what the pendulums need.

As you can see, it does not all stop at the production and trading of material objects. The greatest commodity is *energy* and the energy market is of course controlled by pendulums. A small portion goes to the individual, but the larger piece of the cheese always goes to the pendulums. One person gets the hay; someone else gets the milk.

There are even operations conducted on the energy market that mirror operations that take place in the financial market. For example, alcohol is pure energy. When you drink alcohol you get energy on credit. Alcoholic induced euphoria is like an energy advance and the subsequent hangover the return with interest. You always have to give back more than you borrowed. Pendulums never give away energy for free without profiting somehow from the transaction.

Drinks with a low alcohol content make you feel relaxed. The pendulum sucks the energy in little bits. Stronger drinks on the other hand evoke a rush of energy: "Let the vodka be drunk! Let the music flow!" However, the pendulum lends the energy at high rates of interest. Soon enough things tilt the other way: "Let the vodka flow! Get drunk on the music!" After the euphoric high comes the lowest of lows. The more intense the excitement, the more tangible the depression that follows.

The hangover comes not so much because of the physiological blow to the organs so much as because whilst you are hung over the pendulum desperately pumps out the person's free energy. The sufferer then has to either accept it and suffer or take the hair of the dog. Then the pendulum can lend you energy again. The pendulum is in no rush. Sooner or later it will be paid off. If it were the barman you could make a run for it out of the bar without paying but you cannot run from a pendulum. The further a person gets into "debt" the crueller the payback will be!

In this condition the free energy of the debtor is at the pendulum's full disposal. The person quite literally feels as if ticks had dug their claws into his energy body in the area of the heart chakra. The pendulum declares the ultimatum: "either have something to drink or the torture will continue". Given that a person's will depends on their free energy they become weak and lacking in will when that energy is taken from them. This is the main reason for alcoholism. When a person drinks he is again credited energy with a portion of energy but what inevitably follows is an even heavier payback. A person's heart can stop beating, as is often the case. The pendulum will leave a person in peace only when there is nothing more than can be taken from them and whether they survive it is a matter of luck.

The first credit is always the most generous and joyful, like at a presentation. As you know, the first glass of wine you ever taste in your life has a very impressive effect but with every glass after that the sensation is not the same and it is not just that the sensations become duller, they are all the more unpleasant. Pendulums 'fork out' only with the objective of drawing people into their net. Payback is always carried out strictly without question of any concessions being made. So if you take out a loan of this kind you must maintain a high level of awareness be realistic with regard to your overall "creditworthiness".

The drunks we see living on the street are not people who have fallen into moral degradation as we tend to think. These poor souls are people who were unable to calculate their resources properly and pay off their credit in time and to this day remain in debt. They take out loan after loan which becomes increasingly difficult to pay off. And it all started so well with holiday cheer! The process of the fall is not noticed in its initial stages but then it gathers force and speed creating an inevitable and irreversible snowball effect. The nature of an *induced shift* is quite treacherous and anyone can be drawn towards the centre of its vortex.

In general, all intense, energy-consuming experiences tend to be related to harmful habits and these are the credits given out by pendulums. Why are they harmful? Because pendulums are by their very nature aggressive and inclined to exacerbate the energy surrounding conflict. Everything that is tantalising but bad for you ultimately ends badly. The greater the harm the more negative energy is emitted. Positive energy is never emitted in such large quantities.

The greatest 'yield' is 'harvested' from individuals who take drugs. The short-lived increased state of euphoria the substance gives the user is nothing compared to the depression that follows. And if the next dose does not kick in soon enough the awful withdrawal experience will suck every last drop of the sorry user's energy.

There are also other types of credit with lower interest rates such as tobacco, coffee, tea, non-alcoholic drinks and chewing gum. You may wonder what on earth chewing has to do with anything.

As I have already said when any need, material or spiritual is fulfilled energy is emitted. It could be the energy of pleasure, comfort or something else. In any case, when you want something, you experience a build up of energy. When you receive the thing you desire you radiate that energy. In the process of chewing a person experiences a certain feeling of comfort which has very ancient roots. The nature of this feeling is quite evident: when you eat everything is ok. When you are the one being eaten things do not look quite as rosy.

The same thing goes for any habit. Once you are a "regular client" you become part of the "herd". There is no need for a pen because whilst the client's attention is caught in the pendulum's noose they are not going anywhere. When a person thinks about the object of their habit they radiate energy at the pendulum's resonance frequency. All the "debtor's" thoughts are focused on receiving the next portion of energy – credit. They are not capable of thinking about anything else because the pendulum will not release their attention.

This type of capture is possible due to a specific feature of the mind. Our attention can become fixated on one thing and when this happens it is like the arrow on a weather vane with the pendulum driving the wind in one and the same direction. The capture of the arrow of intention can be observed in the simple example of when you cannot get a particular song out of you head.

You should not assume that a dependence develops solely due to physiological factors. These are part of it but they do not play the key role. For example, when the most inveterate smokers set out on a submarine mission the fact that they are unable to smoke does not distress them at all. Once the hatch is battened down and the command to dive has been given any thought of being able to smoke vanishes completely because objectively speaking there can be no opportunity to smoke. The smoker totally accepts the objective condition and does not even think about having a cigarette. It is as if the arrow of intention has switched and is now pointing in a different direction. So what of the physiological dependency? The submarine returns from its mission and if the smoker has not decided to give up they remember that they might just fancy a cigarette and the insistent creditor catches the arrow of intention in its noose.

The capture of the arrow of intention can also be observed in the phenomena of game or internet addiction (dependency). A huge number of people have become so addicted that they are only able to feel comfortable when they are sitting in front of a computer screen. Should someone who has succumbed to this kind of addiction actually tear themselves away from the screen for an hour or two they will go into remission and begin to experience all the symptoms of withdrawal. They may experience headaches, muscles pain and an unbearable feeling of discomfort. Yet as soon as the client returns to the screen the symptoms subside instantly. Obviously, in this case there can be no question of physiological dependency.

All dependency arises because the arrow of attention has been caught in the pendulum's noose. *In order to "come off the needle" you have to switch your attention to something else.*

Will power is rarely enough to free yourself from the noose in the same way that you can only get a song out of your head when you switch to a different tune. A harmful habit is as a rule accompanied by a specific script and set of scenery. Together they create a characteristic scenario such as a smoke break at work which facilitates the capture of your attention. There is only one way to pay off all your debts and walk away from the grievous bank: *change the script and scenery.* It is not difficult to do, you just have to want to do it and then apply a little imagination.

In any case, even if you do not have a "credit debt" but use the products of civilisation irrespective of your own will you give away a portion of your energy to the pendulums. People are literally "herded" if not "cultivated". The entire life of civilised society represents one continual process of consuming and giving away energy and the entire exchange is controlled by pendulums.

Of itself, the fact that human energy is harvested is not such a bad thing. The greatest peril the structure imposes is that it reduces the individual paths of its elements to nothing. The members of the structure forget the very notion that an individual path may exist for them. People not only carry out whatever the structure orders, they begin wanting the very things that are of sole benefit to the structure. Do not delude yourself with the idea that man is a rational being and would never permit themselves to become enslaved in such a way.

We have already shown that human awareness functions at a low level. The structure is slowly but surely causing the last remains of awareness to be reduced even further. In order to secure total victory the structure must unite all its elements into a single informational field and this process is already being facilitated, rapidly and very successfully. Man may only have a few bricks left before he finally walls himself in completely.

What can be done? It turns out that if you consume the products of civilisation you are being shepherded (now without inverted commas). There have been occasions where people have tried to escape civilisation and settle in communities somewhere in the wilds of nature. It is not for me to judge how successful they were. Even so, contemporary man is no longer capable of separating themselves from civilisation entirely. They can no longer adapt to that extent. It does make sense however to reduce the harmful products you use to a minimum and replace them with the natural gifts of nature.

For example, you can set up an area of family owned land with a garden and vegetable plot. The greatest advantage of having an oasis of nature in the desert of civilisation is that the norms and standards there are established by the owner and not the structure. And you do not have to start digging the ground if it is not your thing. Everyone should have the opportunity to establish the rules of everyday life independently. If you want to cover everything in concrete you can and if you want to keep the garden wild in all its diversity, that is up to you too.

Another approach for someone living in the city may be shifting to a diet of exclusively organic and natural foods. But first you would have to wake up and become aware of the fact that a beautiful apple cultivated within the structure and bought in a supermarket will only be suitable in quality for a "fully-fledged" element of the structure with the corresponding set of illnesses that result from living off this kind of food.

There are many different paths and ways of living but each individual must choose the one which is right for them. A role model for me will always be one particular feral cat with whom I had the "honour to be acquainted".

My friend and I loved to escape to the forest and have a "delicious campfire" to get a break from the benefits of civilisation. On one occasion a huge cat approached our little camp attracted by the interesting smells we were making. The cat had clearly once been someone's pet but for some reason had ended up in the forest and turned wild again. Judging by his size the ragged animal was very successfully hunting birds and mice and could probably have taken down a hare. The cat did not refuse our offering of titbits but neither did he stand around on tiptoe. He grabbed it and ran.

After that meeting we had the pleasure of seeing the cat again on quite a few of our trips to the forest. The whiskered fellow loved to help himself to our offerings but he would not allow either of us to get too close. The cat was a true transurfer. He had learned the taste of true freedom and although he sometimes dipped into civilisation he would never have exchanged his independence not for any creature comforts.

There is nothing wrong with making the most of the benefits of civilisation as long as you do not become addicted or dependent. You can tell a free individual from the herd because of their awareness. All you have to do is wake up and become aware of what is really happening. I have learned these things and am sharing them with you now for the simple reason that…well, actually it is a secret. But I will share it with you dear listener. I have returned to the wild. I have run away from the farm.

Declaration of Intention

Until now we have only focused on how to free yourself from pendulums and escape their influence. But is it possible to benefit in some way from a pendulum? Any dream is essentially brought about with the help of pendulums. There is no getting away from the fact that we all live and work in some structure or another. It is simply a question of whether the structure deprives you of your dream or helps you to realise them.

Are there methods by which one can impact a pendulum directly? This is unlikely. You cannot tame a pendulum, let alone control it. However, it is possible to use the qualities of a pendulum to your own interests.

Have you ever wondered why people make toasts when they are having a meal with friends? Does this tradition have a practical purpose or is it purely symbolic ritual? It turns out that toasts are not just spoken for the sake of it. At times folk wisdom produces customs that appear to be no more than meaningless superstition. People follow these established rules without suspecting that they actually represent a kind of method for shaping reality.

The thing is that alcoholic drinks as we described above represent a kind of energy credit. Free energy receives an additional source of support and is raised one rung higher. Given that this is really the energy of one's will, the result it brings will depend on where you direct it.

For example, if you drink to drown your sorrow reality will descend into an even darker hole. When people drink from happiness they will mind find more reasons to make merry. If drinking is mixed with a feeling of anxiety and fear life will give you something worth fearing. The same principle works in each case.

Thought energy strengthened with a spark of energy shifts the individual on to a life line of a corresponding quality. When a pendulum gives a credit it serves to strengthen the energy of intention. No matter how hard it sways the pendulum itself has no access to outer intention and so it is incapable of materialising a sector of the alternatives space. Yet reality can be controlled by living beings, so when a person makes a toast they focus the direction of their intention. Do you see what is happening when they do this?

The qualities of the energy belonging to the pendulum creditor are as a rule quite negative. However, when a person attributes goodwill to this energy they change its polarity. Hence a toast is not just an empty ritual. It is a *declaration of intention.*

However, despite the beneficial action of toasts they all inherently contain the same unfortunate mistake: the good wishes are usually expressed for the future. Because of this, the energy made available by the pendulum is only transformed into positive energy. It does not have any impact on reality. The desire expressed in the toast remains out there somewhere as an unattainable promise of something better. This is quite natural. After all, the mirror is not capable of producing the future. It only ever reflects the present.

So what can we conclude from this? All toasts should be uttered in the present tense. They might sound a little weird as a result but they will be effective. For example, instead of saying “We will be”, say “We are”; or “We have good health”, “we won!”, “Those who are not with us – are always with us!”, “Lucky are those at sea”, “Our wishes come true!”, “Good fortune is always with us!” etc.

This type of declaration of intention will immediately start pulling your wishes into the reality of today rather than putting them off until a tomorrow that never comes.

Do not assume that you can easily turn your desires into reality with the help of alcohol. As you know, this is a double-edged sword. The larger the credit, the higher the rate of interest; to say nothing of the fact that as the credit debt increases consciousness, which means a person’s intention shifts into an area of the alternatives space that does not correspond to reality. And there can be no question of carrying out such manipulations with the help of drugs. It is not always possible to transform a pendulum’s negative energy into positive energy and not everyone is capable of doing so.

Black magic works in accordance with the same principle. An evil magician calls on dark powers in order to exploit their energy and strengthen their hostile intention.

It is never lucrative in any respect to get credit from a pendulum. However, if you do end up doing so it is essential that you stick to the following rule: *When you are dangling on a pendulum’s hook think only of the positive.*

You can even take the example of the Transurfing pendulum. It will not harm you and the declaration of intention may significantly increase its efficacy. Every time you come across any information related to Transurfing remind yourself that it can assist you in the realisation of your goals. Attuning your intention in this way will position the vector of the alternatives flow in the right direction.

You should take the same approach with regard to any other pendulum even if it bears no relation to your life. For example, whilst you are watching a television series or show, in one way or another you are exchanging energy with a pendulum. Whilst observing the action, keep your *target slide ready* i.e. the picture of what you wish to receive. You will always be able to spot some kind of connection with your goal in the flow of information, however small. For example, when the heroes of the series set off in a fabulously flash car express the fact that you intend to buy something similar for yourself.

Never ever think of anything negative in the moment that you receive a credit. Worrying thoughts, pressing problems, despair, fear, as all these emotions will be amplified by the boost of energy you are receiving. Here are some examples.

When you are having a smoke break think about your forthcoming success as if it were already a done deal; or, an advert encourages you to sit and enjoy the aroma of a nice cup of coffee. It would be better in this moment to enjoy the good fortune you already have, whatever happens in the future. Do you recall the *principle of coordination?* For example in the moment that you are having a smoke or drinking coffee instead of letting your thoughts go to run their own lazy course declare your intention: Everything is going wonderfully because I shape my reality with my intention. I know how it is done."

Tea ceremonies are organised according to this same principle. Saying prayer before the onset of a meal and dedicating the food to God has become custom among many different peoples. However, once you have acknowledged God do not forget about yourself.

If you "make offerings" to yourself with the same love and care saying something like "eat, eat my dear one, get well!" the effect will be completely unexpected and unbelievable. It is even possible that certain illnesses will disappear. Your body will be surprised at first and will be then be glad and blossom like a flower that has been tenderly cared for. The most important thing is to serve yourself with sincerity, love and words like: "If you do not feed yourself, no-one else is going to do it for you".

This type of declaration carries enormous power. If previously you treated yourself with indifference or even aversion then similar rituals will bring about amazing change. Do not just take it from me, try it.

Judging from the above it might seem that the declaration of intention can be used in the games of cunning pendulums like the stock market, casino or betting on the races. In principle, why not? The chances of success will be increased if in the moment of placing your money and likewise during the game you visualise a slide of inevitable winnings. It is not easy to do but it is possible. As a rule the player's thoughts run along the lines of: "If only I could win!"; "What if I lose? But no, I have to win!"; "This time I will be lucky!"

This is no good for in these thoughts there is everything from desire, considering how to win and fear of losing to hopes of success. You have to put all thoughts and emotions including hope for success to one side. You must eliminate all this until all you have left is the unconditional and dispassionate *will to win.* Your declaration of intent should be: "I am a winner!" and your declaration should sound without need for explanation, conditions or exclamation marks. If you manage to achieve this state of dispassionate and unconditional will to have your chances of success will be rapidly increased.

Yet that is not all. Over the course of a single game session you may be successful once, twice or even three times. But winning cannot go on forever because everyone is human and no-one can keep *importance* to a minimum level forever. Any form of gambling is basically a type of energy credit which is capable of imperceptibly transforming into an *induced transition* with a tragic finale. These issues are covered in detail in the first part of the Transurfing materials so we will not go into them again here.

You could say that there is only one way of avoiding having to pay interest on credit: know when to leave the game. Do not just leave the game but free yourself entirely from the slightest connection with the pendulum and extinguish any thoughts that resonate at the pendulum's frequency. In other words, for a certain period of time you have to switch your attention to something else so that the game does not even enter your head for a moment. This is the only way you can save yourself from being drawn into the vortex of the induced transition. Stop swaying with the pendulum. Once the tie has been totally cut you can begin a new game session.

It should be said though, that playing with a pendulum is a dangerous and unpredictable adventure because not one individual can possibly be endowed with a superhuman dispassionate will to have. Essentially, it is not a game. It is a *dance with a shadow*.

A pendulum is an invisible, cold, merciless shadow. It is not endowed with conscious awareness, nor does it have the power of intention. It does not have a heart or a mind, the opposition of which generates feelings, impulses and weaknesses. You can never get the better of a pendulum just as you can never outrun your own shadow. The pendulum observes your movements knowing you have no escape. The shadow can never be defeated and playing with it is meaningless. So what can do you?

Either abandon the dangerous game or create your own venture and become a pendulum's favourite. Now that would be meaningful.

In trying to beat a pendulum you are just chasing your own shadow. Any effort you make to win and all the emotional concerns that go with those aspirations are the subject of inner intention and inner intention always leads blindly to what is right in front of your nose failing to see anything else at all. To put an end to the mindless chasing you have to stop, look around you and begin moving in your own direction independently. Then the roles are swopped. The pendulum will have to keep up with the individual rather than the individual struggling to keep up with the pendulum. Anyone who abandons narrow inner intention becomes the master of the game, the producer in the dances with shadows.

In order to initiate your own game you have to be yourself. Your personal game is the shaping of your own reality at your own discretion. You can do it. You just have to claim the privilege. Only you can give away of deprive yourself of your own privileges. This has to be understood.

However, it does not all come down to giving yourself permission to be the producer. Stars are born but they are lit up by pendulums. You could be as wise as King Solomon himself or create a stunning masterpiece but no-one will ever learn of it unless a powerful pendulum sweeps you up. However incredible your masterpiece is, this is the only reason it will not have been successful. In culture, science and art outstanding creations only become an object of great interest if a new pendulum emerges or it is for some reason beneficial to an existing pendulum.

In order to become a star in your field you have to know how to exploit the features of a pendulum. Have you never wondered why certain works that were immensely successful at some point in the past lose their popularity despite the fact that they retain their unique features?

There are a vast number of cultural achievements whose amazing qualities would more than fulfil any contemporary standards. And yet today there is no market for these achievements because their pendulums that shone in the past have faded or been extinguished. When it comes down to it popularity and fashion are always created by pendulums. Why else would people simultaneously desire the same item en mass?

You can see the phenomenon of fashion in the example of the two massively popular groups "Beatles" and "Abba". Both groups achieved worldwide recognition not because they created something fundamentally new or particularly outstanding. Nothing they did was totally new. On the contrary, the musical genres of disco and rock were created by other musicians much less well known. So how do you explain the phenomenal success of these two groups in particular?

The Beatles career began with a run of mishaps and failures. Initially the quartet represented a fairly ordinary band not unlike many others at the time. They were not even particularly skilled musically. The level of their professionalism never went beyond local pubs where they did in fact perform. Yes the Beatles were talented but that is not enough to make it in show business. The old pendulums will always try their best to keep the new up and coming young at bay.

By 1962 the group had carved its own style and would soon produce the songs that rocked the entire world. But that was only later. Although the group had a few loyal fans at this time no-one had really noticed the "Beatles". That year the band unsuccessfully hammered on the doors of various recording studios but were everywhere flatly turned down. It was beginning to look as if the group had no chance of ever reaching any higher than club level.

In the authorised biography of the "Beatles" Hunter Davies writes: "And yet we still believed that we would make it and become number one", said George. "When things were really bad and there were no opportunities at all for us we used to do a kind of special ritual. John would shout: "Where are we headed boys?" We would yell back: "Upwards Johnny, to the very top!" "To the top of what?", he would ask. "To the top of the very top Johnny!"

Yet it was not their determination that secured their ticket to success. In 1963 they managed to finally release their first record, a single. Unexpectedly, the song made number one in the charts. This was their first significant achievement and yet no-one considered the event to be any big thing. The press presented the single as a moment of success for a short-lived star and missed the soon to be sensation. The success of the first single was followed by another period of quiet anonymity which turned out to be the clam before the storm.

Six months later Beatlemania was taking England by storm and soon afterwards it spread throughout the world. "Every country in the world" writes Hunter Davies, "witnessed the mass psychosis that just a short time ago had been unimaginable and which is unlikely ever to be repeated. Today no-one believes in this kind of thing any more and yet just yesterday it was all real".

A similar phenomenon was repeated in the "Abba" story. In 1972 this brilliant quartet failed to qualify in the semi-finals in order to perform at the Eurovision Song Contest. Finally in 1974 they managed to get through the competition and unexpectedly for everyone secured a stunning victory leaving the other contestants way behind. At that time though no-one expected anything more of the group. Everyone thought that a band labelled as "Eurovision" winners could only be a short-term wonder and would never make more than one hit. After winning the contest everything went quiet again, just as it did with the Beatles. Hardly a year had passed before the world was gripped by another powerful wave this time "Abbamania".

Two clear patterns can be traced in both stories. Firstly, popularity develops in a wave-like trajectory. Initially there is a fairly lengthy period of anonymity during which a small but stable fanbase is formed. Then a moment of sudden flight follows after which there is another period of quiet as if the wave has pulled back from the shoreline to gain power. Finally, after a period of relative inactivity comes a sudden and powerful wave of astounding success. Popularity remains high for a certain period of time but with time the wave inevitably fades as new pendulums emerge and squeeze the previous pendulums out of the spotlight and into the background.

The most interesting pattern in these stories consists in the fact that the works that consequently become a huge hit are not acknowledge during the initial period of anonymity. People listen to the songs but they do not draw any attention. And then there is a sudden moment when the songs begin to create a different, unusual impression on people of something innovative and original. The sound acquires a hint of something very stylish and fashionable. And for some inexplicable reason everyone simultaneously agrees that it is brilliant.

So where does this common sense of novelty and style come from for the "Beatles" sound was already characteristically "Beatles" back in 1962. Why did not it capture anyone's imagination? Why was no-one mad about "Abba" in 1972? They were singing the same songs then so what happened; why did people suddenly find them so electric in 1975?

This phenomenon can be explained by the fact that every epoch has a characteristic quality, sound or hue, in other words, its own charisma. *However, a new epoch is not just initiated of its own accord. It is drawn into being by the intention of the people, like a cloud in the alternatives space. Then the pendulum stabilises the collective intention.*

At first a small group of fans forms. Each fan radiates thought energy to the tune of "I like that". A pendulum is then created which unites and synchronises the thoughts of the admirers into "we like that". In the alternative space where as we know everything exists there is an area of sectors with one quality in common: "Everyone likes that". The collective intention of the first group of fans drives the movement of material realisation towards this area. As a result, after a certain time reality takes on the hue of the new era. The number of fans continues to increase and the pendulum acquires strength. Eventually collective intention reaches and exceeds critical mass and the cloud with the charisma of the new era encompasses material reality in its entirety. This cloud drawn towards the united intention of the pendulum's adherents creates the charisma specific to the new time.

Now you know how new trends are born you can boldly make the most of your lawful privilege to be yourself without looking back at the rest of the world. This is the only way to realise the opportunity to communicate to the world your unique individuality. Pendulums will not put up with unique individuals. They will be forced to make you a star. Stop chasing your shadow and set out on your path independently. Then the pendulums will have no other choice than to follow you. You are quite capable of becoming a trendsetter by virtue of the fact that the qualities of your soul are totally unique. A luxury individual cloud has already been prepared in the alternatives space and awaits your arrival. Announce your declaration of intention!

SUMMARY

The life goal and purpose of all living beings is to shape reality.

Boredom as such does not exist. Boredom is simply a constant and insatiable thirst to shape reality.

Appraisals based on comparison generate polarisation.

Balanced forces eliminate polarisation by means of clashing opposites.

An object or quality which is attributed special significance attracts objects with the opposite qualities.

The pendulum rule is "Do as I do!"

The Transurfing rule is: give yourself permission to be yourself and allow others to do the same.

The Transurfing rule eliminates polarisation.

Awareness: in this moment I am awake and am clearly aware of what I am doing, why and why in this manner specifically.

The first law of the pendulum: it tries to exacerbate the energy of conflict.

The second law of the pendulum: it does everything possible to stabilise the structure.

Pendulums coordinate the existence of organised structures.

The enslavement of will (intention): the structure teaches people what they should want.

In order to free yourself of the zombifying effect of the structure you must adopt the role of the participating spectator.

The process of achieving the goal is what drives evolution.

The individual loses themselves in the structure ceasing to understand who they are and what they really want.

Dependence arises due to the fact that the arrow of attention falls into the pendulum's noose.

To "come off the needle" you have to switch your attention and occupy it your mind with something else, changing the scripts and scenery.

The charisma of a particular epoch is drawn in by the intention of a group of people, like a cloud from the alternatives space.

Whenever you receive any energy credit announce your declaration of intention.

It is impossible to beat a pendulum. You have to either abandon the dangerous game altogether or create your own venture and become one of its favourites.

In order to create your own game you have to give yourself permission to be yourself.

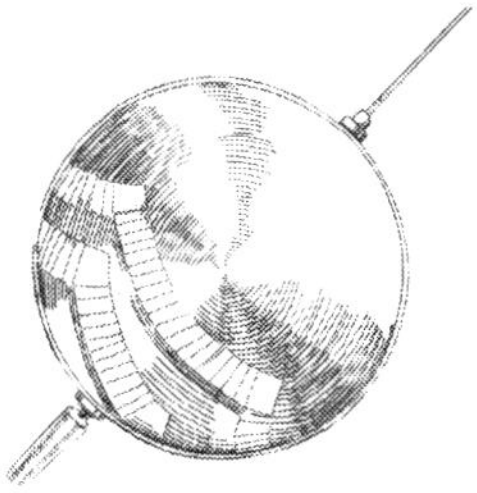

Chapter XVII. THE DREAMS OF THE GODS

I take care of my world.

The Two Sides to Reality

From time immemorial people have understood that the world has a dual nature. On the one hand everything that happens on the material level can more or less be understood and explained from the point of view of the natural sciences. On the other hand when we encounter phenomena from the subtle planes the laws cease to be applicable. Why is it that we are unable to unite different aspects of reality in a single knowledge system?

It is a strange picture. It is as if the world plays hide and seek with humanity not wishing to reveal its true essence. Hardly have scientists discovered a law to explain one phenomenon than a new phenomenon is observed that seems to contradict it. The search for the slippery truth is like a shadow so long it goes on forever. The interesting thing is that the world is not only hiding its true identity. It also readily takes on the image assigned to it.

This is the case with all fields of the natural sciences. For example, if you imagine that an object of the microworld is a particle then there will undoubtedly be experiments to prove it. If you imagine that it is not a particle but an electromagnetic wave the world will not protest but willingly reveal itself in the corresponding manner.

You can ask the world what it is made of with equal success. If you ask whether the substance it is made up of is matter that has mass it will reply "yes". If you ask whether it is not in fact made up of energy it will again answer in the affirmative. As you know, in a vacuum there is a continual process taking place of the birth and annihilation of micro-particles as energy is transformed into matter and vice versa.

There is no point in asking the world what is primary: matter or consciousness. It will cunningly change its masks turning towards us with the side we wish to see. Representatives of different teachings will argue amongst themselves trying to prove conflicting points of view, but reality always comes up with its dispassionate verdict: essentially they are all right.

So it turns out that the world does not just slip away from us, it agrees with us, in other words, it behaves like a *mirror* in which literally all our ideas surrounding the nature of reality are reflected. So what are we left with? The world always agrees with our observations of it and yet avoids giving us a direct answer. Are all out attempts to explain the nature of reality to be in vain?

It is all actually much simpler than it seems. There is no point in searching for the absolute truth in individual manifestations of a reality that is multi-faceted. We just have to accept the fact that reality is like a *dual mirror* that has two sides, one that is physical that can be touched and the other metaphysical that lies beyond perception but which is no less objective. At the present time science deals with what is reflected in the mirror whilst esotericism tries to peek at the other side. This is what the argument about the nature of reality comes down to. So what is hidden on the reverse side of the dual mirror?

The *alternatives space* is what is to be found on the other side of the mirror, that information structure in which the scripts of all possible events are contained. The number of alternative realities is infinite just as the number of possible coordinate points on a graph is infinite. The alternatives space records everything that ever was, is or will be. The event that actually takes place in the physical world represents the material realisation of one of those many alternatives.

This might be difficult to believe. Where exactly is the alternatives space? How can this be possible? From the perspective of the three dimensions the alternatives space is everywhere and at the same time, nowhere at all. It could lie beyond the limits of the visible universe or it could be in your coffee cup. Either way, it is not to be found in the third dimension.

The paradox lies in the fact that we all go to the alternatives space every night. Dreams are not illusions in the normal sense of the word. We carelessly attribute our dreams to the realm of fantasy without suspecting that they reflect real events which could have their place in the past or the future.

We know that in dreams people see pictures that do not seem to be of this world. Sometimes people see things in dreams that they quite obviously could never have seen anywhere before. If a dream is like the brain's imitation of reality, then where does it get these incredible pictures and stories?

If we conventionally attribute the conscious aspect of the human psyche to the mind and the subconscious aspect of the human psyche to the soul then you could say that dreaming is the flight of the soul into the alternatives space. The mind does not imagine its dreams, it genuinely sees them. The soul has direct access to the information field where all scripts and sceneries are permanently stored like frames on a film roll. The phenomenon of time, i.e. the development of events appears only in the process of the 'film roll' moving. The mind plays the role of observer and 'ideas generator'.

Memory has the same direct relationship to the alternatives space. It has already been proved that the mind is not physically capable of retaining all the information it accumulates over a lifetime. So how does the mind memorise? Rather than retaining the information itself it keeps a kind of address for the data in the alternatives space.

The mind is not capable of creating anything fundamentally new. It can only compile a new version of a house from old bricks. All scientific discoveries and masterpieces are received by the mind from the alternatives space via the soul. Clairvoyance and intuitive knowledge are received in the same way and from the same place.

"No scientific discovery" wrote Einstein" "is made by means of the logical mind. It only acquires logical form later when you describe it. Every discovery, even very small ones are always an insight. The solution always comes from the outside and unexpectedly as if someone had hinted it".

The alternatives space should not be confused with the popular concept of the common information field in which data can be shifted from one object to another. The alternatives space is a stationary matrix, a structure which defines everything that is or that could possibly take place in the physical world.

As yet, mainstream science is unable to explain or confirm the existence of the alternatives space. Quite the opposite in fact, science will try to discredit the Transurfing model which is not surprising because official science is a typical pendulum. Generally speaking, science, for all its indubitable merits and achievements is prone to brush to one side anything that does not fit into its framework. When it encounters anything that defies explanation it wriggle every which way accusing its opponents of being charlatans, of juggling the facts or of simply ignoring the obvious, anything to remain on its pedestal of granite. There was one person however, academic Vyacheslav Bronnikov who managed to completely snooker science by combining the totally incredible with the more than obvious.

Children taught at the International Academy of Human Development created by Bronnikov demonstrate extraordinary abilities. These individuals are capable of seeing with their eyes closed just as well as when they are open. They can memorise huge volumes of information. They have the gift of clairvoyance and can perceive distant objects as clearly as through a telescope. It is difficult to believe but a fact is a fact. They see through walls as if there were no obstacle there at all. How do they do it?

Neurophysiologists who carry out research into the effect of direct vision describe their observations in the following way: "in normal sight the apparatus registers the area where the signal enters, its movement in the brain and how it is processed. In the case of direct vision the point of entry is not registered and there is no apparent movement of the signal in the brain and yet the equipment very precisely register that the signal is processed. All attempts to block signal entry to the brain gave a negative result. We are discovering something that displays features totally unrelated to electromagnetic processes."

It appears that the brain is capable of seeing without the means of the apparatus of sight and that the way the information is received remains unknown. How should this be interpreted? Bronnikov describes this phenomenon in terms of a connection between the conscious mind and something he calls higher consciousness. "Higher consciousness " he writes, " lies outside of the human mind as a kind of environment". You have probably guessed already that in the context of Transurfing this environment is understood to be the alternatives space. It does not really matter how one refers to it. The essence remains the same.

The mind or, if you prefer, the brain "sees" what is in the alternatives space by means of the soul whereas the eyes observe physical reality. In the case of direct vision the brain attunes to the metaphysical information field where quite literally the entire mould of physical reality is stored. Once you have access to this bank of data you can perceive objects irrespective of where they are physically located, behind a wall, under the ground or many miles away.

The alternatives space consists both of areas that have been manifest as material reality and areas that have not been realised. In order to develop direct vision you have to learn to perceive the current realised sector. From a physiological point of view this could be interpreted as a certain synchronisation between both hemispheres of the brain. Bronnikov developed an entire system of special (and at the same time very straight forward) exercises enabling ordinary individuals to develop these abilities. If you want to you can find relevant information on the internet and try it yourself. It is all very possible.

The alternatives space stores information about all possible alternatives of the past and future which means that access to this field also develops the ability for clairvoyance. The only problem with clairvoyance is that an infinite number of alternatives exist and so one can also see events that will never be realised in the physical world. This is why clairvoyants sometimes make mistakes in their prognoses for they can also see things that have never been and things that will never happen.

In this sense you can rest assured that no-one can know your future because no-one can determine which alternative will eventually be realised. Likewise there is no guarantee that in a dream you see the sector of the field which will become streamed into physical reality.

This is great because it means that the future is not fatally predetermined and we can continue to hope for the best. The task of Transurfing is not to look at the past with regret or the future with uncertainty but to intentionally create your own reality.

Under certain conditions human thought energy is capable of materialising a given sector of the alternatives space. Under the condition that in Transurfing is referred to as *unity of heart and mind* the magical power of outer intention is born which is what turns a possible future into reality. Everything that is usually associated with magic has a direct relationship to outer intention. It is with the help of this magical power that the ancients constructed the Egyptian pyramids and created other similar miracles.

This type of intention is called outer intention because it is located outside of the human being and is not subject to the human mind. True, in a certain condition human consciousness is capable of gaining access to it. If you subject your own will to this mighty force you can create unbelievable things. However, modern man has long lost the type of abilities possessed by the inhabitants of ancient civilisations such as Atlantis. Fragments of ancient knowledge have survived to the present day in the form of scattered esoteric teachings and practices. Applying this knowledge to everyday life is relatively difficult.

And yet it is not impossible. In Transurfing there are indirect methods which can help you to get outer intention to work in other ways. People are capable of shaping their own reality but you have to observe certain rules. Your ordinary state of mind tries unsuccessfully to manipulate the reflection in the mirror whereas what you must do is change the actual image. The image is the focus and nature of your thoughts. In order to transform what is desired into reality desire of itself is not enough. You need to know how to work with a dual mirror and then you will learn how to create your own reality.

You will have to fundamentally undermine the monolith of so-called "common sense" which in actual fact is not very common sensical at all. If you can accept that two sides to reality exist simultaneously, the physical and the metaphysical old stereotypes will crumble and the picture of the world will become clearer. Dualism is an integral part of our reality. For example the soul relates to the alternatives space and the mind to the material world. Inner intention relates to material reality and outer intention to the virtual sectors of the alternatives space.

When these two aspects of reality connect on the surface of the mirror, phenomena arise that are referred to as paranormal or unexplained. An obvious example of the connection between the two sides to reality is the wave-particle dualism that occurs when a micro-object behaves either as a wave or as a particle. The birth and annihilation of micro-particles in a vacuum is another example of a borderline condition in which reality fluctuates between physical and metaphysical form.

However, the most surprising example is human beings who simultaneously combine in ourselves the material and the spiritual. In one sense you could say that we are living on the surface of a gigantic mirror, which has our material universe on one side and the black eternity of the alternatives space on the other.

In such a unique position it would be at best short-sighted to live within the limits of the conventional worldview and use only one side of reality, the physical side. You will learn how to work with the dual mirror of the world and how to accomplish things that would previously have seemed impossible. You will be convinced yet, that your potential is limited only by your intention.

The Waking Dream

When a potential possibility is manifested as reality the surface of the dual mirror shows a symmetrical image. The sector of the metaphysical alternatives space lies on one side of the mirror and its material manifestation lies on the other. All living beings are balanced on the edge of the mirror because their body and mind relate to the material world while their soul remains inseparably connected to the alternatives space.

We all came into this life from the alternatives space and we will all return to the alternatives space as if to the wings of a stage for a costume change to then reappear on the surface of the mirror in a new guise. In this theatre of masks the actors return to a never ending cycle of parts. Having played in one role the actor runs backstage for a minute, puts on a different mask and once again re-enters the game having completely forgotten anything that happened prior to his latest appearance on stage. The actor is so immersed in the image of the character they are playing that they lose all sense of who they are as an individual. Sometimes the wool falls away from the actor's eyes and they suddenly become aware that this is not their first life here on the stage.

Ian Stevenson, American professor of psychiatry gathered more than two and a half thousand registered cases of remembered past lives, in which the majority of respondents were children. Without the medium of hypnosis the children gave accounts of their lives in the distant past and other countries.

In his books Ian Stevenson quotes extremely interesting facts. There was one particularly characteristic story of two twin brothers who spoke to each other in an unintelligible language. At first everyone thought that its was just childish sounds until when they were three years old their parents finally realised that something was not right. They brothers were shown to linguists who were surprised to find that the children were speaking to each other in Old Aramaic, a language widely spoken during the time of Christ but which is today no longer spoken.

Another example is of a Yugoslavian girl who became ill and was unconscious for a period of time. When she came round she could no longer recognise the people around her and spoke in a foreign language. Specialists established that the language she was speaking was a Bengali dialect. The child asked to be taken home to India. When the girl was taken to the town she had named she recognised her house. However, it turned out that the parents and the little girl had passed away long ago.

There are numerous stories about children similar to these but the same thing also happens to adults. A twenty seven year old woman, travelling with her husband through Germany was surprised to find that she recognised the places they were visiting although she was there for the first time. She even saw her own home and could remember the names of her parents and brothers. At the local pub the woman recognised an old man who had known her family and told her of the tragic accident in which a horse had kicked up one of its hooves and killed the family's little daughter. The woman expanded on his story in minute detail.

In his book "Do We Only Live Once" Andjhei Donimirski describes the experiments of an English psychiatrist Arnold Blacksman who used hypnosis to help patients return to past lives. One of his patients recounted in detail six past incarnations. In the first she was the wife of tutor to a Roman older man in England, then the wife of a Jewish usurer, then a servant girl in the house of a merchant in Paris. She was also a dame at the court of the Spanish Infante at Castile, a London seamstress, and a nun living in one of the states of America. And all these lives were lived over the course of two millennia. Historians carefully checked the dates and events she described and confirmed everything.

If you consider all these facts there can hardly be any doubt in the existence of reincarnation. There is just one thing that leaves me undecided. Why are cases of remembered past lives so rare and occur in such a small number of people? People mainly remember past lives in their early childhood but with time they are erased from memory.

To be more specific, it is not that memories are erased so much as that awareness is blocked. Everyone can remember their past incarnations if they wake up from the daydream of life. We know that up until the age of four a child is incapable of distinguishing a dream from reality. It may be that children can also recall their past lives but the 'rational' worldview is strongly imposed upon them before they become aware of it.

Also, very few people have any memories before the age of four. Why is this do you think? Is it because the child is "irrational" not yet self-aware? No. This is a great common delusion, for in reality, awareness in children is much higher than it is in adults. It is the adults who become immersed in the subconscious daydream and are as a result unable to recall their past lives or their early childhood. Let us look at how this happens.

When the soul is reborn into a new body it sits in the background whilst the mind takes the leading position. So what is the mind? From the moment of birth the mind is a clean sheet of paper on which anything can be written. From the very beginning, a template is placed onto the sheet in accordance with which the individual perceives themselves and the reality of their day to day life. The more detailed the template is the greater the chasm between the heart and the mind. An *individual's awareness of reality will be exactly what they have been taught it should be.*

Awareness can be divided into two levels: the first is attention and the second is perception. In the initial period after birth perception has not been clouded by anything external and so the child's ability for intuition and clairvoyance are wide open. In other words, the child has direct access to information from the alternatives space and perceives the world just as it is.

However, "dream-seeing" adults take the newborn in hand and immediately squeeze it into the narrow dream-framework they take to be conscious existence. This is achieved by limiting the child's freedom and holding its attention on certain things. The child is forced to concentrate its attention on the attributes of reality: "Look here! Listen to me! Do not do that! Do this!" Once the attention span is captured the child's perspective is sharply narrowed; awareness is lost and the individual sinks into a condition differing little from unconscious dreaming.

In reality, when your attention is focused on a narrow range of objects you walk as if your gaze was glued to your shoes and so naturally, you do not look around you. The worldview template in turn places you in the Procrustean bed of false stereotypes which define "how everything should be". In subconscious dreaming the programming of attention and perception reaches its maximum level. The dreamer accepts the situation for what it is suspecting that they are impotent to affect the course of events. As a result, the dreamer finds themselves utterly in the hands of circumstance. The dream "happens" to them and there is nothing they can do about it. The script develops spontaneously in accordance with one's fears and expectations which continue with one's thoughts in an uncontrollable flow.

In lucid dreaming the dreamer has a higher level of awareness and can affect the course of events with their will power. As soon as the individual grasps the idea that it is all just a dream they develop incredible capacities. In conscious dreaming there is nothing that cannot be accomplished. The dreamer can direct events and do inconceivable things such as fly and all because their attention and perception are freed. It is as if the individual has lifted their head up, looked around and become aware of their position.

In waking, however strange it might seem one's level of awareness drops again. In the majority of cases a person's thoughts fly spontaneously jumping from one theme to another; the things that concern, worry or irritate us are usually the things that control our consciousness, gnawing away at us to one degree or another. It can be difficult to control the flow of thoughts such as these. Our worst expectations and negative, knee-jerk reactions shape a person's reality irrespective of their will. Perception and attention are held by problems, oppressive thoughts and circumstances. As a result a person becomes engrossed in their cares like in a daydream. This is how we become "grown-ups".

A mature person considers a child irrational in as far as they fail to fit with the dream. Naturally, the child has to learn how to survive in new conditions. Yet inevitably the paradox arises: the more efficiently the child assimilates the rules of behaviour within the narrow limits of the material world, the lower their level of awareness falls which leads to a loss of capacity to influence the course of events and perceive the metaphysical side of reality.

Grown-ups become prisoners of their own games and consequently, of circumstances from the moment they begin to take them seriously allowing their mind to become engrossed. The child however is the sole master of their game. They have a higher level of awareness because in every moment they know that it is all just a game. Likewise, the child keeps importance at a low level because they understand that it is just a game. The child acts dispassionately at the same time observing like a spectator because again, they are aware that it is all just a game.

There are no more games for adults though, for life is a very serious matter. On the one hand this is true. On the other hand this attitude changes human existence into an unconscious waking dream. Of course the adult person is aware of the fact that in any given moment they are awake rather than asleep. Yet does that really change anything, for desires are not fulfilled, dreams do not come true and our worst expectations are confirmed as if to spite us. Life unfolds randomly and not in the way we want it to. It turns out that the individual is master of their reality in lucid dreaming and yet is impotent in waking. It is all relative.

The ability to control your dreams comes from being aware of your self inside a dream relative to physical reality. At this level of awareness the individual has the support and reference point of reality to which they can return after they have woken. Reality in turn is like an unconscious waking dream in that life just "happens". The individual does not remember their past lives and they do not have a point of reference relative to which they can step up to the next level of awareness.

In lucid dreaming you remember who you really are. You are the person seeing the dream. You understand that the moment you wake up the dreams will disappear but that you can also remain in the dream and direct it with the power of your intention. Until such time as you become aware that you are seeing a dream and remember your point of reference you are completely under the power of the dream. You are dependent on circumstances and closed in the box of conditioning.

Reality differs from a dream in that you always return to it. In order to determine whether it is a dream or reality you have to determine your point of reference because both the dream and reality are relative. Dreams are not real relative to reality. Relative to what then is reality itself unreal? Where is the reference point for reality?

When a person dies they return to this initial reference point. But every time they are reborn they forget their starting point and become engrossed in the new dream, the next life. If you could remember who you really are you would become conscious of the fact that you are capable of directing this dream, the dream that is life.

This is incredibly difficult to do and the difficulty lies in the fact that you have to change the template of your worldview. It is like a kind of stencil that has been rubber stamped into your mind making it impossible to correct or erase. All you can do is create an additional one and this requires tearing your mind away from the former. The mind can be torn away from its previous template when it is in an altered state of consciousness occurring during sleep or the impact of psychotropic agents.

In a normal state of consciousness the heart and the mind are synchronously attuned to a realised sector of the alternatives space. The mind observes material reality as if it were looking through a window. In a state of alcoholic or drug-related intoxication the mind releases its grip of control, disturbing the synchronicity and allowing the soul to deviate to an unrealised area of the alternatives space. As a result, a person is physically present in the real world but perceives it quite differently depending on the degree to which there is deviation from the former synchronicity.

Simply put, a person under the influence of alcohol will find that their old familiar house or street has a weird look to it like it is in dreams. This is because the person's mind observes the picture from close but unrealised sectors of the alternatives space where the scenery is somewhat different. The content of these sectors can be anything. For example, a person simply cannot find the door because they cannot find it where it was before. The place might appear a total mess as if it was being totally redecorated making it almost unrecognisable. People you know can also look entirely different. In reality nothing has changed it is just that the person sees unreal scenery because they are "watching" from a different area of the alternatives space.

In non-lucid dreaming the mind relaxes its control even further which is why the soul flies into very distant sectors where the script and scenery are quite unimaginable. In these sectors anything is possible starting with cloud nine in heaven and ending in the kind of hell that would make demons and cauldrons a day out at a health spa. The dreamer may end up in a technological world filled with huge clanking machinery or they may find themselves in a world reminiscent of a slaughterhouse with nothing but dirt and piles of raw meat. You may end up lost in an unfamiliar city where all you can do is desperately walk the streets with no idea how you got there and where to go. People in such areas may be ugly and weird and the animals wild and rabid.

When you wake up from a dream like that you experience a huge sense of relief: Thank God it was only a dream! And yes, it was a dream but not an illusion in the normal sense of the word, an unrealised metaphysical reality. The scariest thing about it is that the dreamer sees all these virtual characters and can do whatever they want with them in accordance with their fears and expectations. God protect us from ever ending up in such a physical reality.

When cosmonauts are in orbit they apparently see quite unearthly dreams. For example, in his published diaries Gennady Strekalov writes: "I have strange dreams. Sometimes I am filled with wonder and I have no motivation or will to communicate. Clearly the brain like a highly complex computer malfunctions from exhaustion or receives external information from the planetary information field where everything is written and recorded for eternity". After experiencing dreams like this that could never have originated from ordinary human consciousness the Transurfing postulate on the existence of the alternatives space would not have surprised this cosmonaut at all.

A model of human perception is well described in the books of Carlos Castaneda and Theun Mares. Their model reflects the ideas of the Toltec, the last people to originate from Atlantis. According to their teachings the human being is surrounded by a shining cocoon of energy consisting of numerous threads. Somewhere in the area of the shoulder blades the threads join in a single focus called an 'assemblage point'. The position of the assemblage point determines the nature of your perception.

If you combine the Toltec model with the concept of Transurfing you could say that when the assemblage points are in their customary position a person perceives physical reality in its usual form. In this position physical reality coincides with the corresponding sector of the alternatives space. If the point shifts to one side the synchronicity is disturbed and a person is capable of perceiving unrealised area of the field. In most people the position of the points is firmly fixed. However, when for various reasons the focus is disturbed and the points start to "wander" a person develops clairvoyant skills. Naturally, our dreams are determined by shifts in the assemblage points. It is important that the focus of our perception not only shift to one side but also return to its former position, otherwise, if it gets stuck in an unnatural position the mind undergoes changes that are ordinarily referred to as insanity.

People who are capable of intentionally shifting their assemblage point can shape reality and are lucid dreamers. This ability appears of itself if you return to the point of reference relative to reality, i.e. if you are conscious of how you really are. This is not an easy task. You can count the people who have been known to reach enlightenment on the fingers of one hand. Reaching enlightenment is like being in a strange city desperately wandering along narrow winding streets and then soaring high up into the sky where you suddenly have a birds-eye-view of everything below you. Like a line on the palm of your hand the path to your goal becomes instantly obvious.

Transurfing will not lift you up to the height of a bird but it will show you a path you can walk along with your eyes closed. To wake up in a dream you have to have a reference point. You understand that it is a dream when you remember that there is another reality, true reality. Your reference point can be the knowledge that in life you can raise your consciousness up a rung or at the very least half a rung, and that this of itself is quite something.

Imagine that you are walking along a street, talking to someone or going about your day to day chores. Wake up! Look around and with a sober mind observe what is happening. You are capable of setting your world in the right direction with the power of intention. The result will not be like a dream in which the storyline changes fluidly submitting to the slightest movement of your will. Material realisation is inert like tar but it can be manipulated nonetheless through the principles of Transurfing. The first thing you have to do is wake up.

Be aware that reality is like a dream. Only in lucid dreaming can you fully control the situation. When you are daydreaming you are not in control of the situation, you are battling with pendulums.

Come down into the auditorium and observe. *Behave dispassionately, rent yourself out and remain the observer.*

In order to retain your level of awareness it is essential to keep consistent control of the flow of your thoughts. When this becomes a habit it is automatic and requires no effort. For once you have woken up in your dream you no longer have to make any effort to maintain the awareness that it is all a dream. You can learn to control the flow of your thoughts in the same way. At first though you have to systematically call yourself to "wake up" before it becomes a habit.

When in waking you remember that you are supposed to be acting dispassionately you become conscious, i.e. you come down from the stage into the auditorium or you remain on stage as a participating spectator. This is the half rung of awareness that is enough to carry out the other Transuurfing principles the most important of which are: *to reduce your importance level, to go with the alternatives flow and coordination.* These principles enable you to move confidently through the labyrinth of life avoiding all sorts of problems even with your eyes closed. Further on in the text you will learn more about the next powerful instrument you can use to shape your reality which is the dual mirror.

We round up this topic with one more question: if somewhere in the alternatives space there is a point of reference prior to your current life relative to which reality seems a dream, then what would mark the origin of this initial reference point? Obviously, God Almighty himself. *The soul of every living being is a part of God. Every life is a dream.* You could continue to ask: is there an initial reference point for God himself?

Let those who like to be nourished by hope struggle with this question. It is the same as asking whether anything exists beyond the visible Universe. We can never know, just as butterflies collecting nectar in Africa cannot know that there is such a place as America and that flowers grow there too. Is not our world wonderful enough? Why should we constantly demand an explanation to everything from it when we could simply enjoy the nectar of the flowers we can reach.

The Children of God

From the dim and distant past people have had the habit of ascribing exclusively positive traits to god-fearing citizens and accusing the godless of all kinds of sin. The devout citizens created the stereotype for themselves and for everyone else as a sort of presumption of their innocence. And the habit existed at the same time as horrendous atrocities were committed and continue to be committed based on the goal that would supposedly please God – to persecute dissidents. But in reality, faith of itself does not make a person righteous.

So how is it then that the followers of religion are so confident in their own infallibility or rather their own righteousness that even the atheists are prone to respectfully agree? They say: "We are the believers; we go to church, pray and are the quintessence of everything spiritual and light. You are the atheists and so you wallow in your sins. We are right and you are wrong."

The source of this confidence serves as a support point which a person acquires within the pendulum of religion. There is nothing it cannot give you: confidence in God's mercy, forgiveness for one's sins, the absolution of guilt via repentance, belief in the kingdom of God as well as hope that God will assist you and a feeling of oneness with your fellow followers of the faith. Things are much more difficult for the atheists in this regard. They have to rely on their own strength and there is nowhere they can be rid of their guilt.

But why would a person strive towards God if they already consider themselves righteous? In many cases it is not love for the All-Highest that draws people to Him, but feelings of fear and insecurity. There are people who believe that they are striving towards God with all their soul, but this is an illusion. What they are really doing is trying to escape their own ego. There is nothing wrong with having an ego and generally it does not bother you unless it is offended. The ego is generated by dependent relationships in which a person compares themselves to others and discovers that they are far from perfect.

The ego's only goal is to assert its own significance. If it does not receive this confirmation it is insulted. When this happens a person begins to experience a sense of inner discomfort which they try to be rid of. How can this be done? If increasing your sense of importance does not work out then there are only two things you can do: either let go of the reigns and let the ego gallop off or suffocate it entirely. Those who choose the first method become egoists whilst those who choose the second method become altruists.

Often, in an attempt to avoid the discomfort of being alone the ego takes the desperate step of negating itself. The ego proclaims that to love yourself is bad, that you have to love others instead. A person then abandons care for their own soul and turns to face God and others dedicating their lives to anything that will provide them with support. Sometimes the opposite happens; the ego is devoured in aggression and people become criminals, villains and cynics. Both the religiously spiritual and the fallen are a product of the ego, they just represent opposite polarities of the same process.

You might believe that if you turn to God you will manage to rid yourself of the ego. The paradox however lies in the fact that the ego is the very thing that is pushing you to search for God in the first place. God is inside you, not somewhere outside of you! There is a particle of God in every living being which is how he governs the world. The ego worships some kind of abstract symbol turning away from the true God, from their soul. Jesus, Mohammed, Buddha and Krishna are all higher manifestations of the Lord. Ordinary people may not be higher manifestations but they are manifestations of the same lord nonetheless. So it works out that one manifestation worships another manifestation? What good is that?

Striving towards God with the purpose of ridding oneself of the ego is the path of inner importance. Inner importance is always present when you give yourself up to be judged by others. Returning to self without looking round at others is the true path to God. If I eliminate the necessity to check the opinion of others around me then I am self-sufficient and my ego will cease to exist leaving nothing but my integral personality. Do not listen to others who call you to change and sculpt of yourself something that will match a certain set of standards. They pressure you to change, to turn away from your soul and to follow the pendulum rule: "Do as I do!" Turn to face yourself, accept yourself the way you are, be yourself. Assert your right to be right. To dedicate yourself to serving an abstract God means to abandon your soul. And this is nothing more than adherence to the pendulum of religion.

Such is the theosophy of Transurfing that is not forced on anyone. I am not proclaiming absolute truths. I am simply trying to uncover certain lawful patterns. Everyone is free to draw their own conclusions.

Naturally, religious figures do not like arguments of this kind although you can come across people with all sorts of different beliefs and convictions even among religious institutions. Zealous adherents of the pendulum of religion can be distinguished from genuine priests in the hostile manner in which they oppose all other dogmas. The aggressive pressure they exert gives adherents of the pendulum away immediately. Fortunately gone are the days in which adherents could get away with burning dissidents at the stake. However, conflicts over religion remain and will continue because no-one has yet eradicated the pendulum's first law.

Essentially, religion is communication with God via a mediator. You cannot get away without having a priest at the rituals of baptism, wedding and burial. Surely God will not turn away his child just because they did not get baptised in time? If there is a particle of the Creator in all of us surely then we are all His children? Do you require a mediator in your relationship with your Mother or your Father? Everyone must answer this question for themselves.

The pendulum of religion is particularly harsh in relation to its adherents and calls them to give up all worldly pleasures. All spiritual paths tend to be linked with an ascetic way of life. It is commonly assumed that those who are "enlightened" achieve such heights on the path to spiritual perfection that they lose interest in anything remotely earthly. Do not get caught on this hook. Everyone can and must continue to take care of their material wellbeing, comfort and general welfare. If that is not the case then it indicates that a person is completely in the power of some kind of idea. Most probably the idea belongs to one of the pendulums be it of religion, philosophy or some other "spiritual" area.

In accordance with their second law the pendulums force their adherents to dedicate themselves entirely to the interests of the structure. If a person gets firmly caught on this hook then they genuinely lose interest in anything except the pendulum. A person can even find themselves under the power of the illusion that they are totally devoted to their own soul or that they are having "a conversation with God". In fact the soul of this kind of "enlightened" being is immured in a heavy box unable to make their true needs known.

Why does the soul come into the material world–to prepare you for life ever after? That is total rubbish! If your soul comes into the world regardless why would it need to prepare itself for life back in heaven? And is it even possible to prepare for that life here on the ground? Life in the physical dimension is a unique chance for the soul which comes here from the spiritual world to experience all the joys of the material world. It will always have time to get back to the spiritual world later. What would be the point of depriving the soul of all the amazing temptations this wonderful, miraculous, magnificent world has to offer?

By dedicating yourself totally to the worship of God you actually distance yourself from Him. The Creator has made many realities through living beings as its living embodiment. God's intention is to experience all the facets of the reality he has created. This is the reason why he sends his children into the material world. God has given you the freedom of action, so enjoy your freedom! You do not have to lock yourself away in a monastic cell and spend long hours in prayer. This is not serving God. It is depriving Him of the joy that one can experience from a full life. It is like refusing to let a child go and play outside forcing them to spend all their time cramming.

Adherents of the pendulum of religion will instil in you that you are incapable whilst God is all-powerful. The structure has nothing to gain from your freedom or your power. All it requires is hard-working, serviceable cogs for the bigger machine. The pendulums have already gone a long way towards enslaving the will of human beings. You can only imagine how great their influence must be for the very children of God to lose the memory of their own power and magnificence.

Man was originally given the power to create the layer of his world by streaming potential alternatives from metaphysical space into physical reality. Pendulums have succeeded not only in eroding our awareness of our true abilities, they have also distorted our understanding of the meaning of life substituting it with serving God via religious worship.

It is highly unlikely that God requires us to worship Him. Do you require your children to worship you? Or would you rather they became good friends? The *purpose of life* and *service to God lies in co-creation, creating together with Him.*

Many people believe that it is enough for them to believe in God. They believe in His existence and power. Ok, and so what? These people do not understand God. To them God is a kind of abstract, inaccessible and often frightening idol. They have been convinced that you have to worship God, follow the Commandments and lead a righteous life in order to prepare yourself for something, although no-one can say exactly what.

But belief is not the same as understanding. Prayer does not automatically facilitate communication with God. *The language of the Lord is creation.* You may accept this statement or not but certainly there is no point in arguing or discussing it. It is not a philosophical issue, but a question of choice and so there can be nothing more to say on the matter.

You communicate with God by shaping the layer of your world, your reality. When you take joy in your creation God takes joy with you. This is what true service to God means. Belief in God is above all belief in yourself and in your own strength as a creator. There is part of the Creator in each and every one of us. Make the Father happy. As far as you believe in your own potential you will believe in God and carry out the words he spoke: “According to your faith be it unto you”.

The Dream Theatre

As we said already at the beginning of the book, the primordial motive that underpins the behaviour of all living beings is the need to somehow independently manage one’s life. Any purposeful activity or process can be largely described as an attempt to control individual reality. Anything that happens in life can always be reduced to one and the same task: to establish control over one’s immediate environment.

So, what does God do? The answer to this question is obvious and requires no proof. Creating and shaping reality is the goal and purpose of all life. No-one would doubt God’s leading function. The only question is how He does it.

From the moment that the pendulums of religion began distorting the very notion of God everything related to God became surrounded in a strange and paradoxical mystery. God does exist apparently, but no-one has ever seen Him. On the one hand, God rules the world and on the other hand, His activity is not directly evident. So we conclude that He is, but He is not. He is not and yet He is. The paradox of this situation enables the pendulums to interpret and exploit the notion of God in any way they see fit.

Without going into too much detail the main reason for the distortion of God’s true essence is a series of substitutes that have been brought about by religion. Serving God has been replaced with worship and the obvious nature of His existence has been replaced with blind faith. Pendulums have declared man powerless in contradistinction to God’s omnipotence. Man’s primordial divine essence has been reduced to nothing thereby annihilating his former connection with the Creator.

In this sense man is like a kidnapped child that has been separated from its Parents and forced to forget its true origin and purpose. As a result man has lost all understanding of his ability and power to behave as a creator together with the Highest Creator of all. The Son of God has been told that he is incapable of deciding his own fate and that it is his duty to honour the Father from a distance worshipping Him as an idol. It is said that the children of God are incapable of anything and have no rights. Their life is totally in the hands of a despotic parent who will be merciful only if you obey him unconditionally with head bowed low.

Once subject to the influence of pendulums man was divorced from a worthy role of service and simply made to serve. This does not only apply to pendulums of religion. Atheism is also a kind of religion only with atheism everything works the other way around. Here faith has become ignorance, ignorance negation and negation outright denial. Yet whatever worldview a person chooses their position is essentially the same: the pendulum of religion places fate in the hands of God and the atheist in the hands of Providence or the power of circumstances which it is customary to fight against.

In both cases man is attributed the unenviable role of the puppet: either pray and await the mercy of God or jump into the battle and fight the obstacles because nothing happens just like that without a struggle. Whatever you do, however hard you struggle you remain under the power of the pendulum and circumstances until such time as your actions go beyond the limits of inner intention. We always receive the things we choose. If you believe that your lot on life is to wander through a thick forest then you will have to stumble through the fallen trees. But if you can permit yourself the boldness to believe that you ran reach up into the sky you will soar about the forest and fly freely. No-one is holding you down except you.

You will not believe that you are capable of receiving everything just like that, no conditions attached with the help of outer intention unless you can accept the fact of your divine essence. This is very difficult to do because the essence of God has been distorted beyond recognition: from Creator God had been turned into a Ruler demanding worship. And what does a ruler do? The ruler assumes the role of judge, dishing out justice, punishment, reward according to just deserts, issuing commands and finally helping and looking after his subjects.

Yet in the real world we see none of this. Instead we see abuse of power and lawlessness. The righteous suffer whilst the sinners go about their dirty deeds unpunished. Justice "triumphs" at a stretch. Appeals and prayers fail to bring results you want. And yet why would not God fulfil your request and ensure that justice is done given that he is all-powerful?

In order to explain the obvious discrepancy the pendulum adherents interpret events to adjust the scenario to fit the specific role they have ascribed to God. They use all kinds of fabrications and inventions like: "Such is the will of God", or "Each will receive what is due us when we finally stand before Him". You would think that people were naughty children who had run away from their teacher and could get up to all sorts of mischief before being finally caught and harshly punished.

If you put all speculation to one side what is God's real Intention? To answer this question we will not guess or philosophize but simply state the fact that the intention of every living being one way or another is to control their reality; not judging, dealing out justice, fulfilling wishes and requests, not rewarding according to merit or punishing, not ruling over people or looking after them. The control of reality is what it is all really about.

No-one can do anything that God does not want them to do. Everything really is under His control it is just that He does not rule in centralised fashion sitting high up on a throne but through all living beings. Could God really rule the world if He existed somewhere outside of it? Every living being carries a particle of God and so the intention of an individual being cannot fail to coincide with His intention.

By placing a soul as a part of himself in every living creature God gave them the ability to control reality according to their consciousness. All things have the quality of consciousness beginning with man and ending with minerals. Naturally, man stands at the upper rung of consciousness, but this does not mean that stones are not living their own kind of life; they just exist in a different temporal dimension. Everything that exists in reality contributes to how it is shaped. Rivers make the path for the river bed, mountains rise up amidst plains; deserts and forests, land and sea are constantly competing for territory for each is endowed with a portion of consciousness and so strives to control its reality. The higher the level of consciousness, the greater the capacity for control.

Take plants for example. Plants are a commonplace part of our lives and yet they are also quite mysterious. No-one would deny that plants are living but few would consider them alive in the full sense of the word. People see plants as soulless biological material incapable of feeling and awareness of self and others. This however, is a huge misconception. Plants have their own type of nervous system. Their cells exchange electric potentials. These incredible beings can in their own way see, hear, feel, taste and perceive smell. Moreover, they can communicate with each other; they have the capacity for memory, analysis and even concern.

Cleve Bakster the American researcher once carried out an experiment in which he connected a plant to a lie detector. Two people took part in the experiment: one broke the stem and tore off leaves. The other was caring and spoke to the plant affectionately. The plant learned to distinguish between the two individuals. When the "bad" person entered the room the plant "screamed" and the polygraph registered a sharp rise and when the "kind" person approached the plant calmed down. As a result of his experiments Bakster came to the conclusion that plants are capable of perceiving electromagnetic fluctuations and even thoughts! The participant only had to think about pulling off a leaf and the plant reacted vigorously. Bakster's research was tested by other academics several times each time producing the same result.

In one laboratory where similar experiments were being carried out a house plant gave clear signs of the feeling we call love. A female lab assistant who used to remove the plant from the encephalogram noticed that it "purred" when she watered it and spoke to it in a soft voice. As soon as she entered the room the flower would display great delight and yet it would show no reaction to any other of the lab personnel. And imagine how surprised the researchers were to discover that the plant had started displaying signs of jealousy! If the object of the plant's love even began flirting with a member of the opposite sex the flower would fall into a state which can only be described as depression.

And it is not just plants! Researchers have shown that even DNA displays the beginnings of primitive responses. The energy transmitted from a DNA molecule placed in a spectrometer carries information not only relating to its structure, but also, and this is the most amazing part, relating to its "mood". When the molecules feel comfortable their radiation is calm. When the spectrometer cell is heated up they begin to "scream" responding to the excess heat. Once the heat reaches a certain temperature the molecules are destroyed and die. The most incredible thing is that even in an empty cell where DNA molecules have been destroyed their "death screams" can still be heard for *forty days* subsequently. The spectrometer registers the phantom radiation of dying particles that are no longer physically present. These results were first obtained in the mid nineteen eighties by the Russian scientist Peter Gariaev, who worked at the Institute of Applied Physics USSR Academy of Science. The official line of science, as one would expect, takes a very sceptical approach to these experiments.

Plants cannot cry out loud nor can they assert their rights, communicate their feelings or concerns. But they do have a soul and they too are capable of suffering and of experiencing delight. It is just that plants, in comparison to man, are in a deep sleep. They are like a person who is sleeping who smiles in their sleep when they recognise an affectionate voice or frowns when they hear a hostile shout. These wonderful dreamers serve as a source of life, they beautify our world and give us everything from a cup of healing drink to shade on a scorching day. And with all that they make neither demand not complaint.

Although perhaps less clearly, plants are capable of feeling all the things we do as humans. They love us when we take care of them and try to thank us with their fruits. It is embarrassing to think what they must feel when we insult them. What must a tree feel when a more developed but heartless two-legged creature comes past and breaks off its branches–fear, pain, insult? Is it possible to convey the horror that grips this defenceless being when a two-legged creature approaches it with an axe? It is difficult to imagine the suffering a tree goes through when the axe sinks its blade into its body causing life to slowly fade away.

We will never know what plants feel, these silent witnesses of human cruelty that treats them as if they were mere biological material. We can only hope that they sleeping deeply enough not to experience suffering as acutely as other creatures that are further up the consciousness ladder. There is nothing that can be done. The world is a cruel place in which one life exists on account of another. Yet this does not give anyone the moral right to consider that in this world of dreamers only they are endowed with a soul and with awareness and so have the right to treat all others with neglect or disdain.

There is a reason why in cultures that have not yet been spoiled by pendulum civilisations the people ask for forgiveness before killing an animal or felling a tree. Followers of Buddhism for example always look where they are walking to avoid unintentionally squashing an insect or will avoid treading on the grass if there is a path they can walk on. All living things deserve respect and in this world everything has equal rights. And if a person does not agree with this opinion what is their worth?

In comparison with all other inhabitants of this planet human beings are only relatively "awake" but no more than that. For life is a kind of dream. We are surrounded by an incredible world inhabited by dreaming beings. Every one of them lives out their own dream and always wants something, is striving towards something and has its rights and its goal. Every living being has its own purpose. "But why does it? What for?", asks the person who considers themselves to stand at the pinnacle of perfection. *The process of striving towards one's goal is the driver for evolution.* Evolution is the manner of creation, shaping reality chosen by God himself.

The notion of evolution arose comparatively recently. Previously it was thought that the world is not subject to fundamental change and exists in the form that God originally created it. The essence of evolution can briefly be characterised as a consistent process of quantitative change gradually transforming into qualitative change. Charles Darwin was the first to clearly demonstrate this idea in a biological context. According to Darwin the driving forces of evolution are *genetic variation* and *natural selection.* Variation is what generates new traits in the structure and function of a given organism whilst genetics consolidate these traits. The battle for survival results in the preferential survival of the fittest.

Darwin's theory works and yet it overlooks one major question: what determines variation? Natural selection and genetics eliminate or consolidate various traits as accomplished facts. But where do these traits come from? What causes them to appear in the first place? Why does a species grow fins, claws, fur, horns etc when they did not have them previously?

In evolution one can observe jumps, lapses, backward movement and the appearance of fundamentally new forms which from the point of view of an ordered picture of evolution defy explanation. For example, it has proved impossible to establish a chain of development for the emergence of organs of sight. How did we end up with the capacity for sight? Sight represents a jump in evolution, a fundamental change that must have been more than a mere random development. And what of the origins of life: should we conclude that one day the genetic code for life just happened to appear as pure coincidence?

From within the context of the Transurfing model one draws the obvious conclusion that *variation is shaped by intention.* Every living being creates the layer of their world including itself.

The striving to control reality includes the goal of achieving this in the best way possible and this requires changing and adapting to one's environment. The intention of all living beings from unicellular organisms to man himself can be expressed in the following manner: *In my being and my behaviour I strive to act in such a way that allows me to effectively control reality*. This intention materialises corresponding sectors of the alternatives space as a result of which new traits appear in the physical.

For example, it is a known fact that the earliest species of bird had claws on the ends of their wings which enabled them to climb trees. It is likely that before these birds learned to fly they had to climb up a tree to gain height, take off and then soar. Controlling reality in the form of: "I climb trees" is not very effective. It would not be a bad thing to add another function: "I can soar and glide towards the ground". And it would be even better to add: "I fly freely". The intention to fly freely gradually materialises ever new alternatives into reality, each one an improvement on the last. Consequently, over a long period of time covering many generations sectors are materialised in which wings take on ever more perfect form.

There are destructive as well as creative processes in evolution. Both the first and the second pendulum law apply here. In the process of evolution pendulums fulfil a destructive as well as a stabilising function. Their never-ending battle leads to one species being squeezed out by another or to their complete extinction. On the other hand pendulums also synchronise the intention of individual living beings. How else would the same traits develop in the population of a single species across an extensive geographical habitat?

All development in the material world takes place as a result of the combination of internal and external factors such as in this case the striving of individual beings and the activity of pendulums. This is how *God creates reality and rules it through the intention of all living beings.*

Our world is a theatre of dreams in which God is audience, writer, director and actor all at the same time. As a member of the audience He observes the play which is unfolding on the stage of the world. As an actor He feels and experiences everything the beings whose role he is playing experiences. This seems to be God's objective, to experience everything one possibly can in this kaleidoscope of dreams. So why is it that there is so much injustice and tragedy in the play? Why does He let this happen? Pendulums are a worldwide source of evil. Does He really endorse their existence?

There are no answers to these questions. God's motives are known only to Him. We can only state the fact that as writer and director He gives the play the opportunity to unfold freely in accordance with the intention of the participants. Each player makes their contribution to the shaping of reality as a result of which the overall picture is compiled, God's dream, woven from a variety of dreams, his individual manifestations in the form of all living beings.

The questions to which we cannot provide the answers do not actually matter that much. There is just one significant conclusion we can draw from all that has been said above: *God has given every living being the freedom and power to shape their own reality in accordance with their consciousness*. Depending on the level of consciousness life either turns into an unconscious dream in which the dreamer is powerless and at the mercy of circumstance or into a conscious dream which can be controlled and shaped with the power of intention.

Every one is given the freedom of choice, but very few people make use of the privilege. Why else would the process of evolution extend over such a long period of time if intention is capable of realising necessary sectors of the alternatives space? Hardly any living beings make use of the power of intention consciously and constructively. In unconscious dreaming it is as if they vaguely desire something but are not aware of what exactly. Intention becomes blurred, indefinite and unaccountable.

In this sense man has not progressed any further than the animal kingdom. As we have said previously, pendulums have not only eroded man's ability to control reality with the power of thought but have deprived him of the knowledge that such a thing is even possible. Drawn into destructive pendulum games man can only enjoy the backlash effect of outer intention realising their negative relationship to life and their worst expectations. In all other things the individual is limited to the narrow realm of inner intention and forced to achieve their goals only by investing massive effort.

A person with a relatively high level of awareness is capable of escaping the circle and transforming their life into a lucid dream in which reality is subject not only to direct influence but to their will also. If there is a particle of God in each and every one of us it means that our intention is also the intention of God. By shaping our reality with the power of intention we fulfil the Will of God. *When you express an intention consider it to be God's intention. How then could you have any doubt that it will be fulfilled?* And all you have to do for this to be is simply claim your right to it.

Do not ask, do not demand, do not struggle, just create. Shape your own reality with the help of conscious intention. Would God really ask himself for something to be given him. Is there anyone alive from whom God would demand something for himself? God just takes whatever he wants.

When you pray to God it is exactly the same as if God were praying to himself. When you ask God for something it is the same as if you were asking yourself for it. You can look at it the other way around too: you are praying to yourself and asking of yourself.

If your intention is the intention of God then who do your fears and doubts belong to? Also to Him. He gave you the freedom of choice. It is within the power of your will to choose whatever you want. When you choose a tough path you struggle to achieve your goals having to overcome all sorts of obstacles and this is inevitable, for you are convinced that nothing is given just like that and so you receive according to your belief.

Is God so powerless that he would have to struggle? He does not have to waste his efforts on the battle with an unyielding reality. He is capable of shaping a new reality in whatever way He desires. People can do just the same if only they can accept the idea that it is possible. So what is to stop you from waking up into the dream and exploiting your former privilege? If you are ready the rest is just a matter of technique. The next part of this book will teach you how.

SUMMARY

The world is like a dual mirror. Material reality is on one side and the metaphysical alternatives space is on the other.

The individual perceives reality in the way they have been taught to.

Life is like a waking non-lucid dream in which the individual has no reference point for reality.

Come down into the auditorium and observe. Act dispassionately, rent yourself out and remain the observer.

Reducing importance levels, going with the alternatives flow and coordination will enable you to navigate the waking dream with your eyes closed.

The life of every living being is one of God's dreams.

The purpose of life and likewise service to God lies in co-creation together with Him.

The process of striving towards a goal is the driver for evolution.

Species variation in the process of evolution is conditioned by intention.

God creates reality and controls it through the intention of everything in existence.

The gift of God to every living being is freedom and the power to shape reality according to consciousness.

If you express an intention, consider it the intention of God. How then could you doubt that it could be fulfilled?

Do not ask, do not demand, do not struggle, just create.

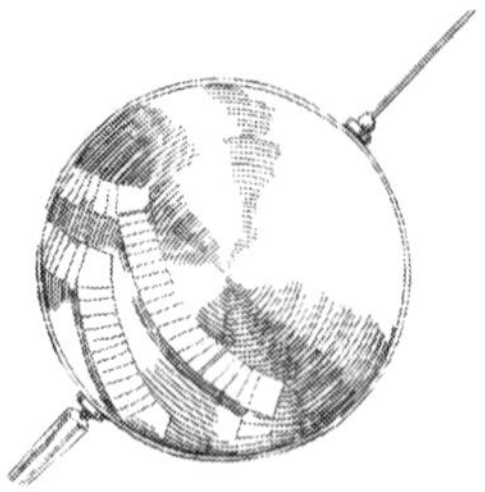

Chapter XVIII. THE MIRROR WORLD

My world takes care of me.

The Dual Mirror

The manifestations of reality take two forms: the physical, that which can be touched, and the metaphysical, that lies beyond the realms of perception. Both types of manifestation exist simultaneously, each form penetrating and complimenting the other. Dualism is an integral part of our world and many things are comprised of opposites.

When you stand in front of a mirror you represent a real, living physical object. Your reflection on the other hand has no material substance. It is metaphysical, imaginary and yet just as real as the object reflected.

The whole world can be seen as a gigantic *dual mirror*. On one side of the mirror lies the physical Universe and on the other side of the mirror lies the metaphysical alternatives space. In the dual mirror, unlike in an ordinary mirror, the material world serves as a reflection of the intention and thoughts of God, as well as all the living beings that are an embodiment of Him.

The alternatives space is like a matrix or template which is used for the "cut", the "stitching" and the "fashion show", for the movement of all matter. The alternatives space contains information relating to what can happen in the material world and how. The number of possible realities it contains is infinite. Each alternative represents a sector of the field that is made up of scripts and scenery, i.e. a trajectory for the movement of matter. In other words, the sector determines what will happen in each specific case and what that will look like.

The mirror therefore separates the world into two halves, the actual and the imaginary. Everything that has acquired material form lies in the real half and develops in accordance with the laws of natural science. Science as well as the conventional worldview is only applicable to what happens in "reality". Reality is usually understood to mean everything that is subject to observation or direct impact.

If you take away the metaphysical side of reality and only take into account the material world the activity of all living beings, including man, is reduced to primitive movement within the limits of inner intention. As we know, using inner intention a goal can be reached by means of direct impact on the environment. In order to achieve a goal in this way you have to take certain steps, push and shove, elbow your way forward and do a specific job.

Material reality is physically tangible. It responds instantly to direct impact which creates the illusion that this is the only way in which results can be achieved. However, in the realms of the material world the range of realistically achievable goals is significantly narrowed. You can only count on things that are present. Everything depends on finances which are usually lacking and opportunities that are severely limited.

Absolutely everything in this world is seeped in the spirit of competition. Too many people want to achieve the same thing and there is not enough for everyone, at least within the realms of inner intention. So where do we get the conditions and circumstances that are essential to achieving our goals? This is where they come from–the alternatives space.

On that side of the mirror there is an abundance of everything and there is no competition. The goods are not physically present but the great thing is, your can choose anything as if from a catalogue and then place an order. Sooner or later the order will be fulfilled and you will not even have to pay for it. You have to observe certain manageable conditions, but that is all. Sounds like a fairytale?

It is far from it. It is more than realistic. Thought energy does not ever disappear without trace. It is capable of materialising a sector of the alternative space that corresponds in quality to the thought energy being radiated. It only appears that everything in life is the result of the interaction between material objects. Processes that take place in the subtle planes actually play no less an important role in the physical incarnation of alternatives that exist in the virtual dimensions. We rarely notice the element of cause and affect in subtle processes. Nonetheless they form the greater half of our reality.

As a rule the materialisation of sectors in the alternative space takes place independently of one's will because as human beings we do not use thought energy in a deliberate, focused manner, and this is even more the case with less developed beings. As we showed in the first part of Transurfing the effect of mental images on reality mostly manifests in the form of our worst expectations.

Being grounded in "real life" people make their way along the empty shop shelves rushing to reach their hand out for a product that already has a "sold" sign hanging on it. Only goods of a poorer quality are left but even these are expensive. Rather than simply flicking through a catalogue and making an order people rush off in random search for what they want, waiting in long queues and trying to somehow squeeze their way through the crowd only to get into arguments with the sales staff and other buyers. The approach still does not give you what you want and you end up with more problems than you started with.

This bleak picture of reality usually originates in the mind of the individual and gradually materialises transforming into physical reality. Every living being creates the layer of their world with their thoughts on the one hand and their direct actions on the other. All the layers arrange themselves one on top of the other as each living being contributes to the formation of reality.

A layer is characterised by a specific set of conditions and circumstances which make up the way of life of an individual being (from now on we refer to human beings specifically). Habitat conditions vary from favourable to scanty, comfortable to harsh, friendly to aggressive. Naturally, the environment in which a person is born plays an important role, but how their life will develop later largely depends on their attitude towards themselves and the world around them. Subsequent changes in lifestyle are largely determined by that person's mental outlook. The sector of the alternatives space that becomes embodied, will correspond in script and scenery to the nature and direction of that person's thoughts.

So two factors take part in the creation of a individual layer of reality: inner intention on one side of the mirror and outer intention on the other. A person affects objects within the material world via direct action whereas with their thoughts they embody in physical reality things that are not yet present.

If a person is convinced that all the best things in this world have already sold out then in reality, the shelves for them will remain empty. If they think that they will have to wait in a huge queue for hours and then pay a large sum of money that is what will happen. If your expectations are pessimistic and filled with doubt they will instantly be confirmed. If you expect to encounter a hostile environment your premonition will be realised. However, if a person allows the innocent thought to permeate their being that the world has saved the cream for them this too is what will become manifest.

The eccentric who does not realise that nothing is meant to come easy turns up one day at a counter where they have literally just had a delivery of goods as if they had been brought in especially for him. It turns out that the first customer gets everything for free whilst behind him a long queue is already forming of people who are convinced that the reality of life is much darker and eccentric fools are just lucky.

Life is a game in which the world is constantly setting its inhabitants the same riddle: "Go on guess what I am like". Everyone replies in accordance with their own perception of the world: "You are aggressive" or "you are cosy", or "cheerful, sorrowful, friendly, hostile, happy, ill-fated".

The interesting thing is that everyone wins the quiz. The world agrees and stands before each participant in the image they ordered. If the lucky eccentric decides to change their attitude once they come up against the "realities of life" their world will change accordingly throwing the "enlightened" fool to the very back of the queue.

This is how the individual creates the layer of their world with their thoughts. The process can be explained using just a few simple principles. The first mirror principle is this: *the world is like a mirror that reflects your relationship to it.*

The world literally consents to your thoughts about it. So why it is that our worst expectations are generally confirmed whilst our hopes and dreams do not come true? There are reasons for this and they are expressed in the second mirror principle: *reflection is formed in the unity of heart and mind.*

As long as the mind does not contradict the wishes of the heart and vice versa an unfathomable power emerges – outer intention, which materialises the sector of the alternatives space that corresponds to the image of one's thoughts. In the unity of heart and mind this image acquires clear contours and as a result is immediately embodied in physical reality.

However, what usually happens in life is that the soul strives for something but the mind is filled with doubt and will not allow the soul to follow the urge or the other way around, the intellect provides convincing arguments for something but the heart remains indifferent. When unity is broken the image becomes blurred. It is as if the image splits because the heart desires one thing and the intellect insists on another. There are only two things that bring the heart and mind together unconditionally, aversion and fear.

For when a person hates they do so with all their heart and when they feel fear it fills their whole being. In the unity of aversion a clear image is generated depicting the thing you want to avoid. As two manifestations of reality, material and metaphysical, the heart and mind come together at the same point and the thought form is embodied in physical reality. As a result, you get whatever it is you cannot stand.

Unlike fear, desires are not as easily fulfilled because in this case of our desires unity is rarely achieved. The heart resists the mind because, having succumbed to the influence of pendulums it strives towards other peoples' goals. The mind in turn either fails to have any awareness of its innermost desires, or it does not believe in the possibility of their fulfilment.

Some people believe that to achieve your goal you have to clearly formulate your order and then release the corresponding thought form into the universe and then do nothing to avoid hindering its realisation. If only it were all that simple…

This technique works only on the condition that the second mirror principle has been fulfilled. However, unity of heart and mind is only achieved in rare cases because it is almost impossible to be fully rid of treacherous doubts. So what should you do?

This leads us to the third mirror principle: *there is a delay in the reaction of the dual mirror.* If you cannot fulfil the second principle the fortress must be taken by lengthy siege.

Try to imagine this rather unusual scenario. You stand in front of a mirror but here is nothing there except emptiness. Only after a little time does the image of your reflection begin to appear, like in a photograph. At a certain point you smile but the reflection still shows the same serious expression. You lift up your arms but the mirror image remains the same. You put your arms down straight away and again, nothing in the mirror has changed. In order to see your reflection with raised arms you have to hold them up for a longer period of time.

The dual mirror works in exactly the same way except that the time delay is much longer and so the changes taking place in the mirror are practically imperceptible. Material realisation is inert like tar. Nonetheless, a thought form, or slide as it is referred to in Transurfing can be materialised. All it requires is one basic condition: *you have to run the slide in your mind systematically for a significant period of time.*

As you can see the secret is simple and this really is all it takes. It is hard to believe that it could all be so trivial. No magic, just ordinary, every day effort, and it really works; it is just that most people do not have the patience to follow it through. They are lit up and inspired by some idea but quickly lose their enthusiasm and file the idea for later. In order to materialise a thought form you have to take specific steps to work with a slide. If you do not do the work you cannot expect a miracle.

How much time is needed to realise the slide depends on the complexity of the goal you set. Whilst the mind is in doubt that the goal can be realistically embodied the image will remain hazy but sooner or later some kind of representation will begin to appear in the mirror. Then you will begin to see for yourself how outer intention opens the necessary doors and provides the necessary opportunities for you to reach the goal. This will assure the mind that the technique is bearing fruit and that the goal is in fact realistically achievable. Gradually heart and mind will come to a position of unity focusing the radiation of thought energy into a sharper image. As a result a reflection will be formed creating what is normally considered a miracle: the dream that seemed impossible is transformed into reality.

The Reality Amalgam

With the help of the slide technique described earlier on in Transurfing you can successfully create an image which the world mirror will stream into physical reality. Aside from any concrete image though, it would not be at all bad to maintain an unchanging background to the layer of your world that would consistently create a favourable atmosphere.

You may have noticed in the past that your reflection is different when you look in one mirror than it does when you look in another. It is the same face but every mirror brings out different nuances in the reflection. Very slight yet tangible differences are revealed such as the emotional colouring, mood or even psychological type. Depending on the mirror, the reflection will be kind or angry, healthy or sickly, attractive or less so, and warm or cold.

You might wonder what could account for the disparity, for the reflective surface of each mirror should objectively convey an exact copy of the same image. However, there are a range of factors that can have a tangible effect on the transmission of an image. Like in a photograph, a lot depends on lighting, background colour and the mirror itself.

Venetian mirrors were noted for their particular charm as early as in the Middle Ages. Venetian glass was renowned throughout the world for its fabulous quality. But it was not the glass that gave the mirror its special quality. People noticed that for some unknown reason it was much more pleasant to admire their reflection in a Venetian mirror than in an ordinary mirror as it gave the reflection of the face a noticeably more attractive look.

It turned out that the Venetian masters had their own special secret. They would add gold to the amalgam, the composition of the mirror backing which had the effect of making warm tones dominate in the reflective spectrum.

You can perfect a small part of the dual mirror for yourself. To make the layer of your world more cosy, you can try mixing your own amalgam. The layer of your world consists of a multitude of different reactions relating to your relationship to yourself and to various manifestations in the world around you. It is essential to pick out one particular line within the spectrum of these relationships to determine the prevailing background.

You could for example choose the following formula as a dominant: *"My world takes care of me"*. People will readily express their attitude to life when they are dissatisfied with something whereas when anything good happens they take it for granted, almost indifferently. We do it unconsciously, reacting like oysters by force of habit.

Now you can go beyond the level of the oyster, wake up and use the advantage that you can express your attitudes to life consciously. Deliberately attune your outlook to align with the dominant idea and then you will see how the mirror will react. It will be your first step on the path to shaping reality.

Remember when you were a child, the world really did look after you but you did not truly value it then taking it for granted. Look into the past. Perhaps you experienced this feeling when you were visiting your grandmother in the country. Cast your mind's eye back to those days in the distant past when you felt secure and serene. Fragments of memories can be very clear. It is as if a divine aroma is coming from the kitchen where your grandmother is still baking cakes. Or perhaps you are sitting on a river bank with a fishing rod or sledging down a hill. What was it like then? Do you recall that feeling of serenity?

It was like that then because the world did take care of you and although you may have vaguely suspected it to be true you would not have attributed it any particular meaning. That said, you would not then have had any particular complaints to make either. Everything was just fine. Even when a child is playing up they do not put their heart and soul into their dissatisfaction. They will scream and stamp their little feet, waving their hands about but the world still carries the child carefully and caringly, affectionately repeating: "What is the matter little one? Did you make a mess and get yourself all dirty? Let's go and clean it all up then shall we?"

As the person grows and develops the world saves the best for them, making them gifts of exciting, new toys and caring for them lovingly. The world takes care of its little charge, its favourite, its pet. The lucky child discovers all sorts of new pleasures whilst everything is new and fresh, unaware of the fact that they are enjoying life in the moment. The person understands this only many years later when they remember how good everything was in comparison to how it is now.

So why is it then that with time all life's colours fade and light serenity is replaced with anxious concern? Perhaps it is because as we grow older the number of problems we have to deal with increases? No, it is because as we grow up we adopt the tendency to express a negative attitude. Dissatisfaction is a more powerful feeling than the satisfaction that comes from comfort and being at peace.

Failing to understand that we are in fact happy now despite everything, we demand more and more from the world. The charge's requests become bigger and the charge itself more spoiled and unthankful. Naturally, the world cannot keep up with the charge's quickly growing needs and the pet starts to make complaints changing their attitude to the world: "You are bad! You do not give me everything I want! You do not take care of me". At this point the negative relationship is charged with all the power of the unfulfilled soul and the capricious mind.

The world is a mirror and so it can do nothing except throw up its hands in dismay and reply: "As you wish, my sweet. Let it be your way". As a result, reality as a reflection of human thought changes for the worse. When things get to this stage, a person has more reason to feel dissatisfied as a result of which their relationship to life breaks down even more. And so the former favourite and pet is transformed into a grump, short-changed by fate and constantly complaining that the world owes him something.

It is a sorry picture. People do not remember that they were the ones to ruin it all. Spotting certain less pleasant features in the mirror's reflection they focus their attention on them until expressing their negative response becomes an automatic response. As a result everything gets worse than it was before. In the reflection reality gradually becomes dimmer as does the image. This is why the layer of an individual's world loses its former brightness and becomes more and more dull and uncomfortable.

However, you can bring it all back very simply; the feeling of calm serenity, the taste of ice-cream as it was in your childhood, the feeling of newness, hope for something better and the joy of life. You will not believe how easy it is. But you do not have to believe it. Try it! It does not occur to anyone that they can renew the layer of their world by taking control of their relationship to reality. Whatever you make of your perception of the world is what your world will become. This should not be interpreted as some wishy-washy challenge to look at life more optimistically but as genuine steps to shaping your own reality.

From this moment onwards, whatever happens, make it a rule to consciously control your outlook on life. It does not matter that right at this very moment things are not as good as you would like them to be. Things are not actually that bad and they certainly could be a lot worse. There are no stones dropping from the sky; the earth is not in flames under your feet, and there are no wild animals chasing you. Indeed the world has changed considerably since you cooled your relationship to it. Do you remember how it used to cradle you in its arms, feed you with grandma's cakes and tell you stories? Then you grew up and a wall of estrangement appeared between you and the outside world. Warm spontaneity grew into estrangement; trust was replaced with fear and friendship turned into cold calculation. Yet the world did not get angry and turn its back on you. It simply went quiet and walked beside you deep in thought like an old friend offended by a cold welcome.

Look around you. Your world is still taking care of you. He planted these flowers and these trees for you. You do not pay any attention to the sun, sky or clouds but imagine what life would be like if they were not there. In the evenings after a hard day's work you can enjoy a moment of relaxation and comfort whilst outside it pours down with rain and a cold wind blows. The world still feeds you and puts you to bed. The world looks at you and sighs in longing for those happier times. Yet you turn away and fall asleep thoroughly convinced that world is not what it used to be and that the past can never be retrieved.

The world has not changed, just as a mirror never changes. It is your relationship to the world that has changed and with it reality as a reflection of your thoughts.

Now rouse yourself, open your eyes, sit up in the bed and look about you: It is the same world as it was before that took care of you and with whom you once so enjoyed spending time. Imagine how delighted the world will be when you finally come round from the illusion.

Now you are together again and everything will be as it used to. Never again must you offend this old faithful servant with your thankless attitude. Most importantly, do not hurry. For according to the third mirror principle he needs time to get back to his former self. Initially you will need to show patience and self-control. You have to understand that this is part of your specific work on shaping your reality.

The work you are going to do consists in the following: In any circumstances, even the most minor confirm you amalgam formula. It does not matter what is happening, whether it is something good or bad. When something fortunate happens do not forget to tell yourself that the world really is taking care of you. Cite this confirmation at every minor detail of life. When you come up against something that might disappoint you make sure that even so you tell yourself that everything is unfolding as it should according to the principle of the coordination of intention.

However circumstances unfold your reaction must be unwavering. The world is always looking after you, no matter what. If something happens and you are lucky pay particular attention to what is happening, and if you are not lucky observe the principle of the coordination of intention and that way you will always remain on a successful life line. You do not have to know what dangers the world is protecting you from or by what means it does so. Place your trust in the world.

It is essential that you learn to trust. When a person finds themselves in a difficult position they are more inclined to rely on themselves than hope things will turn out for the best. An adult will always insist "I can do it myself!" So the world places them down on the ground and gives the opportunity to manage on their own: "Ok, Ok, my darling. Run along without my help then".

Break the ice of mistrust. Every time you face a problem, even if it is relatively minor, say to yourself: "I let my world take care of me". This does not mean that you should do absolutely nothing and sit there with your arms folded. It is a matter of adopting the thought that everything will turn out well of its own accord by default. The mirror will reflect your perception flawlessly: "If that is how you perceive it to be, then let it be so".

Make a habit of allowing the world to take care of you, from the tiny details of everyday life to the most important issues in your life. If you have walked out of the door without an umbrella and it looks as if it might rain, do not head back inside. Tell yourself: "My world and I are going for a walk". Tell your world: "You will look after me won't you?" Your world will of course answer you: "Of course my darling". You can boldly rely on your world. It will not rain and if it does, the world will provide you with somewhere to shelter just in time.

If things do not turn out so successfully do not be offended or doubt bitterly whether the world takes care of you. Remember that you are standing in from of a mirror. All the mirror does is reflect your mental outlook, no more and no less. There is no point in getting upset and even less so on battling with your doubts. It is useless. Leave room for mistakes and setbacks. The most important thing is to hold to your overall course.

You can rely on the world for all sorts of things if you allow it to take care of you. People are not capable of solving all their own problems. Give them to the world to deal with for the world has immeasurably greater capacity to solve them than you do. For example, you cannot avoid all threats with the help of inner intention because the layer of your world intersects with numerous other layers. Rather than directing your intention towards your own safety direct it towards creating a world that takes care of you and protects you. Then your world's intention will start working for you.

Depending on what concerns you most you can choose your own special amalgam. For example, you could choose one of the following: "My world chooses the best for me. When I go with the alternatives flow the world meets me halfway. I create the layer of my world with intention. My world protects me. My world eliminates my problems. My world takes care of things so that my life is easy and comfortable. I place an order and my world fulfils it. I might not know how to take care of myself for the best but my world does know. Everything that happens contributes towards the realisation of my intention and everything happens as it should".

You can even create a new, unique amalgam or several for that matter. I should emphasize though that the most important thing is to be patient and not tire of stating the amalgam formula at every convenient instance. Persistent effort is only required initially until it becomes habit. From there onwards it is all plain sailing.

This simple technique is the key to a force more powerful than you would ever expect. *You control reality by controlling your relationship to the world.* The dual mirror will embody into physical reality areas of the alternatives space in which the world takes care of your welfare. With time you will create a very cosy reality.

Prepare yourself for a magnificent cascade of pleasant events. I am not over exaggerating for a moment. The layer of your world will literally become transformed in front of your very eyes. You will be surprised at how quickly things start to change and in this moment you will realise that you will never look at the mirror of the world in the same way again. You will have experienced the rising wind of change. The wind will take care of you. You can be sure of that.

Chasing Your Reflection

Each person creates the individual layer of their world, their own reality, with their mental outlook. Their reality acquires a certain tone depending on their attitude. Figuratively speaking, certain "weather conditions" are set: there may be morning freshness in the sunshine, cloudy skies and heavy rain or even a raging hurricane and natural disaster.

To some extent reality is created, as is commonly thought, as a result of a person's direct actions. Thought forms are no less powerful however, it is just that their impact is less evident. In either case the majority of problems are caused by a negative attitude to life. The mess that is created on the metaphysical layer then has to be sorted through on the physical level, which complicates the issue.

Overall, the picture of a person's separate reality depends on how they position themselves in relationship to everything that surrounds them. At the same time, a person's frame of mind is conditioned by what is happening around them. So what we have is a closed feedback loop: reality is created as a reflection of an individual's thought forms, and those forms in turn are greatly determined by the reflection itself.

When a person stands in front of a mirror they focus all their attention on the mirror without trying to look inside themselves. It turns out then that the ruling role in the feedback chain is played not by the image but by the reflection. The person finds themselves under the mirror's power because they are mesmerised by their own copy. It does not occur to them that they can change the original. It is specifically due to this obsessive focus on the reflection that we actively get what we do not want.

Usually, our negative feelings have a total grip on our attention. We are absorbed with the thoughts of the things we would prefer to be different. We think about the things we do not want and we do not want the things we think about. That is the paradox. The mirror does not take into account a person's willingness or reluctance. It simply conveys an exact reproduction of the content of the image, no less and no more. It is quite absurd. People voluntarily lug around with them the things they cannot stand. The saying should be not "my tongue is my enemy" but "my thoughts are my enemy". Despite its absurdity, this is how things are.

What happens when a person feels hate? They pour their entire heart and mind into the feeling. The sharp image is perfectly reflected in the mirror filling the layer of that person's world. Whatever you hate you will encounter in your life in abundance. This causes one to be even more irritable which in turn embellishes the intensity of the feeling. Mentally, a person reaches a point where they are ready to tell everyone to get lost: "Bugger off!" The mirror then returns the event like a boomerang. You told everyone to bugger off and they did the same to you. Does this cause the number of problems to escalate? You bet! If you stand in front of a mirror and shout: "Go to hell the lot of you!", the reflection you will see in the mirror is yourself going to hell along with the rest of your world.

In the same way the object being condemned penetrates the layer of the "prosecutor". Imagine this typical example: an angry elderly lady treats the whole world with bitter reproach. She of course is the perfect embodiment of strict and infallible justice "clear in conscience before others and her own soul". The rest of the world must answer to the fact that it has not been exactly to her liking. A clear, sharp picture is drawn with immense precision. Looking in the mirror with an attitude like this the lady creates the equivalent reality in the world around her i.e. total injustice. How else should the world respond? It does not judge her or justify itself. In its inherent quality the world becomes exactly as it is imagined to be.

Exactly the same thing happens when you are reluctant to accept something. For example, if a woman is sharply adverse to those who drink alcohol, she will be fated to encounter drinking at every turn. She will be constantly confronted with drunkenness in all its various manifestations as extreme as actually marrying an alcoholic. The greater the wife's aversion the more intensely the husband will turn to the bottle. The husband may try to give it up occasionally but his wife hates drunkenness with such vengeance that she actually savours it and insists: "You will never give it up!" Unless the husband has solid steel intent the wife's insistent aversion will end up instilling her thought form into the layer of his world.

The tendency for pessimism is a fairly unattractive quality. The mood of: "It will not work out anyway" is like a kind of sadomasochism. The pessimist gets a certain perverted pleasure from revelling in their sorry lot: "The world is so bad it could not get any worse. It is going to hell and taking me along with it". The pathological habit of getting a kick out of negativity develops alongside a tendency to bear grudges. "I am such a nice person. You just do not value me! It is so unfair! That is it. I am insulted. Do not try and talk me out of it. Soon I will be dead and then you will be sorry!" And where does this get you? The picture of fatal misery is not only reflected in the mirror, it is firmly consolidated. The bitter man orders a script for failure and then celebrates: "You see, I told you so!" All the mirror is doing is delivering the order: "As you wish!"

With the same mood of fatal doom the loser states their unenviable position: "Life is just darkness with no light at the end of the tunnel". They would not want to be stuck with this fate for anything and so they spend all their thought energy on whining and complaints. What else can the mirror reflect if the imagine is nothing but an expression of dissatisfaction? As the image: "I am unhappy", "I do not want to" such is the reflection: "It is true, you are unhappy and you do not want to". Again, the reflection is purely fact, no less and no more.

Dislike of self is just as paradoxical in nature. It is self-generating. There is one golden rule that can be included in the textbook for complete idiots: "If I do not like myself, I do not like myself". However strange it may seem, this tautology embodies a principle that is followed by the majority of the population.

Take external appearance as an example. You may have noticed that most small children are very sweet and attractive. So how is it that so many adults are dissatisfied with their appearance? It is all to do with the mirror that sends back all complaint. Those who grow up to be beautiful are those who admire themselves. That is the secret. These people are ruled by the principle: "If I like myself I will have all the more reason to like myself more".

It is quite another matter when an image tells its reflection: "I seem to have put on a little weight. I need to lose a few pounds". The mirror will dispassionately reply: "Yes, you are fat. You need to go one a diet". Or: "I have become a bit skinny, I should build up some muscle", to which the response will be: "Yes, you are puny, go and do some weights". Reality responds like an echo, confirming what it has heard.

This is how inferiority complexes are generated. Low self-esteem is followed by a corresponding verdict, which the mirror manifests as reality. "I do not think I have any particular talents". "It is true. You are mediocre". "I do not think I am worthy of upmost happiness". "Indeed, you have nothing to hope for".

If in addition to all this a person has an innate feeling of guilt their goose is cooked. "Am I to blame? Must I carry out my duty?" – "Yes, you deserve to be punished and you will be". How could it be otherwise? If a person feels guilty, even subconsciously, some form of retribution will be reflected in the mirror for certain!

Do I even need to say that stress and fear are realised just as instantly? People are afraid of so many things which do not occur because it would requite too much energy for them to be materially realised. Accidents and catastrophes always represent an anomaly in the alternatives flow when the balance has somewhere been disturbed. However, if an unfortunate event lies in the vicinity of the flow it will undoubtedly take place because people attract it with their thoughts.

Doubt however has the opposite effect. Unlike fear which focuses a person's attention on the possible realisation of a given event, doubt is more concerned with what does not happen. Obviously, in many cases as if to spite us, our doubts are confirmed. Yet why should it seem that things happen as if to spite us? In reality, the mirror is simply reflecting our thought content; nothing more.

In any case, the desire to avoid something greatly increases the likelihood of impact. Everything then seems to happen in defiance which usually causes the individual to be in a state of irritation most of the time. Irritation completes the overall picture of one's mental outlook. The result is an integrated image: "I feel uncomfortable". The individual's reality is organised accordingly and is created in such a way that the feeling of discomfort is maintained or exacerbated.

It is because of their own negative attitude that people paint the layers of their world black. Any attitude that is fuelled passionately by the heart and with the conviction of the mind will be reflected in reality. Moreover, the attitude will literally be replicated to perfection irrespective of what a person is actually trying to express: attraction or aversion. Here we can see the fourth mirror principle: *The mirror cites the content of the relationship but ignores its orientation.*

How do people react when they see that things they do not want are being realised? Rather than looking at the image they focus all their attention on the reflection of the image and try to change that. The reflection is physical reality and in physical reality your actions are limited to inner intention. This means that if the world is not listening to you and you cannot make it go the way you want it to you have to grip it by the throat and drag it with all your strength in the direction you want it to go; a difficult task to say the least and in some cases quite impossible. It is totally absurd to stand in front of a mirror trying to catch your own reflection in the hope of making something of it.

Inner intention attempts to change a reality that is ready and realised by means of direct action. The house has already been built but not as you would have liked. You have to take the house apart again and rebuild but the end result is not quite what you wanted either. Sometimes it can seem as if you are at the wheel of an uncontrollable car. The breaks do not work and the engine either stalls or roars in fifth gear. The driver tries to fit in with reality but the car is totally unpredictable.

It would seem logical that if you want to avoid an obstacle in your path you should turn to the side. However, quite the opposite is true. From the moment that the dangerous obstruction has captured your attention a collision becomes inevitable. You turn the wheel in one direction but you are carried in the opposite direction. The harder you press on the breaks the more quickly you slide into the skid.

It turns out that it is not man who rules reality but reality that rules man. It is like the feeling you might remember from your distant childhood when you are running and shouting with all your might. The world does not want to listen to you. It is so insulting!

I remember times when I did not want to hear or understand anything. I just ran and screamed and my shouts were intoned by the thud of my feet on the ground. Do you remember ever doing that? Why was I so stupid and obtuse? Grown-ups were trying to explain something to me but I have absolutely no desire to comprehend what they were trying to say. Everything has to be the way I wanted it, full stop!

Now I am a grown-up myself but nothing has really changed. I did not learn anything. I am still stamping my foot and demanding that the world listen to me. But the world does everything to spite me so I run and shout as I used to do. I run to meet reality but the wind of inner intention blows in my face and my efforts are in vain. Reality is controlling me and forcing me to react negatively, like an oyster, and this just makes everything that much worse.

So how do you control this crazy car? What should people do and where are people going wrong? The mistake we make is that we stare at our reflection. This is whole problem. This is what we should be doing: first of all we have to end the chase after our own reflection and stop for a moment. This means dragging our gaze away from the mirror and letting go of the inner intention to shift the world in the direction you want it to go. In this moment the crazy car will stop in its tracks and reality will also stop. Then something incredible will happen: the world will come to meet you.

The World Comes To You

The ordinary human mind tries unsuccessfully to impact the reflection in the mirror when what is required is for it to change the actual image reflected. The image is produced by the nature and focus of a person's thoughts. The problem is that people look first in the mirror and only afterwards express their relationship to what they have seen. By doing this, deliberately or not, they express an intention that exacerbates reality.

The tendency for negativity brings even more negative traits into the mirror. The individual layer is painted in gloomy tones and is filled with events that will be unpleasant for its owner. When a person falls into despair the dark clouds in the mirror gather even more. If you take an aggressive stance the world will instantly put its hackles up. You may notice that when you got into an argument with someone and sharply express your discontent something else equally as unpleasant will follow on just soon afterwards. The more irritated you get the more insolently new problems seem to cling to you. Everyone will annoy you with something.

People are attached to the mirror by the threads of importance, for everything that happens in the mirror represents our life and so has great personal significance. People either like what they see or they do not. Either way the content of their thoughts corresponds with the reflection which continues to strengthen the existing situation. A person will be dependent on their surrounding reality to the extent that the image is controlled by its reflection.

The greater the intensity of your feelings, the more powerful your attachment to the mirror. It does not matter *what* you are thinking about something; what is important is *what you are thinking about*. Whether you like the reflection or not, you are still focusing on it. Only the content of the thoughts has any meaning. Aversion is always focused outside of ourselves: "Leave me alone!" or "I am so sick of it all". Irrespective of its nature, your relationship is still focused on the object of your dissatisfaction. The passionate feeling which is born of unity of heart and mind gives the image sharp contours and as a result, the reflection begins to be dominated by everything that corresponds to the *content of the image.*

This is why the poor get poorer and the rich get richer. People admire themselves in the mirror of life and each subjectively states what their reality looks like. This reality pulls you in like a swamp. It is like the old woman in the queue waiting to pick up her pension, or a tired woman carrying heavy bags in a crowded bus, or a sick person being passed from one clinic to another. It is their thoughts that keep them tied to their gloomy reality. At the same time, someone else is enjoying life: the sea, yachts, travel, posh hotels, expensive restaurants, whatever their heart desires. In every case, whatever the nature of the circumstances, the same fact is stated: "This is how we live" whereas it should be, *"we live in the manner in which we think about our existence"*. The mirror confirms and continues to strengthen the content of our thought forms.

The standard objection to this explanation is that supposedly the starting conditions are different for everyone: one person is born in poverty while another person inherits a fortune. Of course, the starting point counts for a lot and determines how the image of one's life will initially be positioned and how it will develop later. But it does not mean that everyone totally depends on the start-up capital. There are loads of examples of how people who were born into the lowest levels of poverty ended up in the highest circles of society and vice versa. Perhaps these are just the rare examples that prove the rule? That may be true and yet if it is possible for there to be an exception the rule cannot be as immutable as you might think. Whatever dark hole you might find yourself in, know this: you can change everything and what is more, you can change it radically. It does not matter that you may have absolutely no idea of how to bring about that change. You do not have to be able to see a specific way out. The solution will present itself.

You think you are at the power of circumstances you are incapable of changing. Yet this is an illusion, a sham that you can easily destroy if you want to. The thing is that we are all subconsciously walking around in a closed circle: *we observe reality – we express our attitude towards it – the mirror consolidates the content of our attitude in reality*. In order to transform reality all we have to do is break the circle.

You look at the reality of your world and you feel as if change is impossible. And in some ways it is, because you try to influence your reflection with inner intention which does not have the power to significantly change anything. There are too few opportunities this side of this mirror. On the other hand you do have the capacity to control your relationship to reality and then outer intention can take things into its hands. There is nothing outer intention cannot do. There are alternatives to the development of events on the other side of the mirror of which the human mind could not even conceive.

In order to launch the mechanism of outer intention the fifth mirror principle has to be fulfilled: *switch your attention from the reflection to the image*. In other words, you have to take control of your thoughts. *Think about what you want and are striving to achieve rather than the things you do not want or try to avoid.*

Look once again at the closed circle formula. People literally move around the *mirror circle* like a donkey chasing a carrot on a stick. Attached to the mirror with its attitude, a primitive response to reality, the donkey tries just as unpretentiously to catch up the reflection in his striving to change something. Now let us see what happens if we reverse the mirror circle: *we express our attitude – the mirror consolidates the content of our attitude in reality – we observe reality*. So where does that get us?

The primitive and impotent statement concerning the reflection ends and is replaced by an intentional and goal-directed statement of the image. Rather than habitually expressing dissatisfaction at what I see in the mirror I tum and begin to create an image of what I would like to see. This is the way out of the mirror maze. The world stops and then comes out to meet me. I am not running anymore. I am standing still and watching reality come to me and a different wind is blowing in my face. Now it is the wind of outer intention.

This time I did everything the other way around: I ceased the futile chase after my own reflection, let go of the world and let it turn by itself in accordance with my thoughts. The mirror circle is still a closed circle only now I am not turning circles. The circle spins by itself driven by the power of outer intention. Outer intention substituted my inner intention because I abandoned the attempt to influence the reflection. I simply form a deliberate and desired image in my mind and the dual mirror realises the corresponding sector of the alternatives space into reality.

The only difficulty lies in the fact that the situation will appear strange. It is strange that the element "We observe reality" is placed at the very end of the circle. People are more accustomed to behaving according to the rule of: "What I see is what I bang on about". They send their attitude out into the world and the world returns a watered down version like an echo: "I really hope it is not going to rain" – "Rain, rain…"; "I do not want to study!" – "Study, study…"; "I do not want to work!" – "Work, work…" As a result the *purified content of an attitude* is what is materialised as physical reality.

You can imagine the kind of monologue the mirror would be having, tired of all the confusion.

"You do not feel well. Ok, so what do you need in order to feel better?"

You do not want to do what you are doing now. Perhaps then you could deign to explain to me what you do want? You do not like what you have now. Then tell me, dear, what do you want?"

It is very simple. *You have to change the negative attitude to a positive one.* Make an inventory of your thoughts and remove all the "not" particles. Dissatisfaction, reluctance, disapproval, hate, lack of belief in success etc all these emotions have to be shoved into a rubbish sack and disposed of at the dump. Your thoughts should be attuned to the things you do want and like. Then only pleasant things will be reflected in the mirror.

It needs to be understood that a favourable reality will not be created instantly. It requires patience and awareness. Nothing will be the same again: now *you no longer react to the reality of your life; you take command and deliberately send your chosen thought forms out into the world.* In contrast to the visible negative reflection you are expressing a positive attitude. It is a little *strange* but what is better: to be victim to the power of circumstances like *normal* people or determine your own fate as you see fit?

A person's mood is usually formed as a reaction to unfolding circumstances, be they favourable to your success or not. As a rule, the tendency for negativity keeps a person's spirits at a low point. You have to do the opposite and consciously create your mood. Even the knowledge that you are capable of shaping your own reality raises the spirits considerably. With my intention I choose the colours for my reality. Irrespective of the circumstances in my life I do what I need to do to feel upbeat. I do this consciously instead of reacting in a primitive manner to external irritants. This has to become a habit. Slides, visual or musical, whatever you prefer can help to create the right mood. Ideally, it should be a picture in which your goal is reached and you feel marvellous.

However, be prepared for there to be a period of time in which you do not notice any change in the layer of your world. Or the opposite might happen. There will be change but problems will creep out from under the floorboards just to spite you. Why? These are just temporary inconveniences related to the "move" to a new level of relationship with reality. You will recall that the mirror works with a delay factor. You just have to stick to your guns no matter what and quietly hold the pause whilst nothing is happening. It should literally be like in the fairytale: "If you look round you will turn to stone!" I let whatever is going on in the mirror in the meantime be, for I know that the mirror does not have any choice; sooner or later it will have to start reflecting the image I create in my thoughts. If I do not succumb to temptation of looking round and am resolute my reality will be created in the mirror. Everything will be the way I want it to be.

Your mental outlook should be as it would be if you already had what you want or are just about to receive it. Remember, the mirror materialises whatever is contained in your thoughts. For example, if you are dissatisfied with your external appearance you take no pleasure in admiring your reflection in the mirror. All your attention is focused on the less attractive traits that you dislike about yourself and which you state in your mind. You have to understand that what is reflected in the mirror of the world is your relationship to yourself.

Make it a new rule not to look into the mirror of the world but to glance or *peep* into it. *Ignore the negative stuff and search for the good* and let everything you perceive pass through this filter. Concentrate your attention on what you want. What did you do previously? You made a statement of fact: "I am fat and ugly".

"I do not like myself like this". The mirror consolidates this fact: "It is true, you are those things". Now you have a different task: to search only for the wanted traits in yourself and simultaneously create a picture in your thoughts of your desired image. From this moment this is all you do. You just look for constant confirmation of positive change: *things get better every day.* If you practice this technique regularly you will soon be left with your jaw dropping from surprise.

Basically, you have to create the relationship first and only then glance in the mirror and not the other way around. Naturally it takes a little time to get used to it but the game is worth the candle and a job worth doing is worth doing well. Now reality will not control you. You will control reality. Even taking account of the inert nature of material realisation very gradually the reflection will be transformed into a positive one. The layer of your world will become so filled with good things that you will not have to convince yourself to have fun. The mirror circle will spin easily and spontaneously. The important thing is to get it moving in the first place and then get it to pick up speed with your intention. It will all be downhill from there.

"Surely not! I do not believe it!" the boring listener will say. "If only it was all that simple". *Do not believe it if you do not want to.* Turn around if you so choose and a good journey to you around the mirror circle after your reflection. Who knows, maybe one day you will catch it up. However, *if you do not believe it but would like to believe it* then all I can say is that belief is not required here. You do not need to believe. Just practice the recommended technique and you will see the consequences for yourself. For the normal state of consciousness these things will always remain inaccessible because the workings of outer intention are discreet and inconspicuous. The mind will never understand how a dream it considers unattainable can come true. It will never believe it to be possible until it is right up against a realised fact. Let the mind be. It is ok for the mind to be pottering about in a room of doubt whilst you get on with what you have to do.

"Yeah right! It is not working!" the lazy listener will say. Indeed the mirror technique is too simple for us to believe in its efficacy. We are used to having to find complex solutions to difficult problems. People find it hard to believe that their thoughts really do affect the shape of reality and so these things are rarely taken seriously and as a result they do not try. This is the first reason for the absence of visible results. The second reason is the usual lack of methodical action. Usually people are instantly inspired by some idea but then lose the feeling of enthusiasm just as quickly as it appeared. There are no miracles here! It requires doing a certain amount of work, only this time the work has to be done with the head and not your hands. Does the mirror which works with a delay factor really have a chance to shape your reflection if all you do is stand in front of it for a fleeting moment and then run away?

Now that you are acquainted with the main mirror principles all that remains is to put them into practice. It really is very straight forward. *In order for a thought form to become established as physical reality you have to produce it methodically.* In other words you have to regularly run the target slide round in your mind. Unlike impractical dreaming that enters your mind randomly, this is a specific task.

By taking control of the feelings that tie you to your reflection you are freed from the mirror. It is not about suppressing your emotions for these are just a consequence of the relationship. You have to change the essence of the relationship, the manner in which you perceive and respond to reality. Once you have your freedom you acquire the ability to create the type of reflection you wish to see. In other words, *by managing your thought process you manage your reality*. If you cannot manage your thought process reality controls you.

The process of taking control of reality can be approached with varying degrees of intensity and application. Using an amalgam is the simplest and easiest method. It enables you to create a general background of comfort and well-being which in the majority of cases is quite sufficient. Realising a dream demands more patience and focus. Anyone can use the mirror technique to the extent to which their needs require it.

There is nothing new about the idea that our world is a reflection of our thoughts. It is as if everyone understands the idea implicitly but at the same time it remains vague and ambiguous and so there is not much practical benefit from such knowledge. What should you do and how should you do it? Few people have the time to work towards spiritual enlightenment, comprehend the secrets of the forces of nature or develop their own.

Now though, you have a specific technique at you disposal. You understand how it works and how to use it. Stop running round the mirror circle and you will see that the world will come to you.

The Maker's Intention

So, in order to see the reality you desire in the mirror of the world you have to take certain elementary steps: intentionally shape the corresponding image in your mind's eye paying no attention to the delayed reflection and peeking at it only in search of any new manifestation of the emerging reality.

The thing is that even when you are aware of the delay it can be quite difficult to get used to this quirky mirror. The idea is deeply rooted in our consciousness that reality is either instantly obedient as if we holding a stick to it or cannot be controlled at all. We think that if a desire is not fulfilled right this moment it is not possible for it to be realised at all. You cannot do what cannot be done. People are then resigned to the idea that all they can do is dream and that magic is something inaccessible or transcendental.

We are all accustomed to the idea that magic must be something set apart from reality. Мы все The world of fantasy is somewhere out there in the beyond or in our imagination whilst real life is here. There is no getting away from it and you cannot change it. Magicians and people with extrasensory abilities also live in a special separate world whilst we ordinary people with our ordinary problems are left to trudge through this grey reality.

In truth there is no such thing as magic. There is just knowledge of the principles of the dual mirror. This knowledge is not hard to access. In fact it is so transparent and unsophisticated that it could never fit with the cannons of the "magical". And yet Alladin's lamp looked like an old can and the Holy Grail was not made of gold. Everything that has greatness is inconceivably simple. It has no need of decoration or secrecy. In contrast, it is always the things that are empty and useless, that are hidden under a veil of magnitude and mystery.

Once magic has been integrated into the mundane and relieved of its fairytale attributes, it ceases to be associated with the realms of the mystical and the secret. When magic takes its place here in everyday life it loses its fascinating element of mystery. The wonderful thing about the transformation is that everyday reality in turn ceases to be everyday and is transformed into an unknown reality which can be controlled a waking dream as long as the mirror principles are observed.

You may already be acquainted with the Transurfing method and know how to work with a target slide. Time is passing but nothing is happening. It is the same feeling as when you send a letter and wait ages for a reply. The mind becomes restless with impatience. You begin to wonder whether you might not be doing it right or whether it is all in fact a load of rubbish.

But the world does not stop and the process of reflection being materialised in the mirror continues. It is just that the process is subtle and imperceptible and so it appears as if nothing were happening. At this stage the scales in the mind shift between the knowledge that the mirror reacts with a delay and the old habit of observing an almost instant correlation between direct action and the consequent result.

What does the mind think when it perceives no visible result? It thinks that the action taken is ineffective or wrong. So what then does the mirror reflect? Exactly, *it reflects the same.* The process ends up being slowed or taking a different direction. You can imagine the mind having this kind of dialogue with the world.

– I want a toy!

– Of course you do darling.

– But you promised!

– Well, yes. You asked and I said that you would have your toy. You seemed quite satisfied that you would have it.

– You misunderstood me! I want a toy right now, this minute!

– No, I understand perfectly: you want it now.

– So where is it then?

– Exactly, where is it?

– One of us must be an idiot.

– Undoubtedly.

– Damn it! I totally forgot that you are nothing more than a stupid mirror. How can I talk to you? Then I remembered: you are giving me a toy.

– ok, ok, my sweet.

– So, shall we go and get it then?

– Of course, dear, come to me and I will carry you.

And then they set off to get the present that was so desired. Now all that remains is to have a little patience and devote your time to happily preparing for the occasion. The heart sings and the mind rubs its hands in glee. Why should not they be satisfied for they are going with the world to buy a toy! The Transurfer will understand that the choices a person makes are transformed into an indisputable law that will inevitably be fulfilled. All it takes is to focus your attention on the end goal. Yet people are never satisfied.

– Do you think we are going the right way? I do not see any toy shops here?

– Do not worry dear, we will be there soon.

– But when? I think we have taken a wrong turn and ended up in some back streets.

– Do you think?

– Yes, of course, we are lost!

– Whatever you say pumpkin, you know I always agree with you.

– Stupid mirror! I knew I should never have relied on you! Where have you brought me?

– I wanted to pop into the park on the way and push you on the merry-go-round whilst we are out.

People feel unsure of themselves when they are lead blindfolded. The mind just cannot come to terms with the fact that nothing is happening or that events are not unfolding as they had expected. The mind is like a cybernetic machine. When the work algorithm is disturbed a red light comes on. The only difference between them is that the mind creates its own program or scripts, naively assuming that it can account for all future variables in advance. The primitivism of so-called common sense lies in the fact that it not only chooses a stereotypical program of action, it also insists on it.

In the moment that the choice is made and the final goal-image is set, the mirror of the world receives the order and sets about realising it according to a specific plan. Only the mirror can know how the image's reflection will be formed, as the means is inaccessible to the mind. Yet when the mind sees that events are unfolding according to some strange scenario it sounds the alarm and the individual then takes the world by the throat. For surely something must be done about it! The person thinks that nothing is working out which begins to distort the target slide. On top of all this the person then takes action to support the scenario they consider more fitting and again ends up hindering the realisation of the other plan they cannot fathom and yet would lead them to certain success. It is as if you snooker yourself with your own ball, or as the Russian proverb has it, "It won't fit in the box, it won't come out of the box and it won't give the box up"

By taking a deadly grip on their own version of the script, which they feel sure must represent the path to their goal, the person prevents the goal from ever being realised. But that is not all. The irrepressible desire to have the toy as soon as possible pumps up so much excess potential that the mirror is literally distorted and what good is a distorted mirror?

Desire of itself is essential because without desire there would be no striving. And if you add to this the resolve to act you have the will to achieve your goal. But if you add doubt plus fear of failure to the mix you end up with *longing*. This is the *importance* that has to be consciously reduced. Of itself desire does not create tangible excess potential. It is only a problem when your doubts and fear make you take the world by the scruff of the neck.

People usually think more or less along the lines of: *I want to but I am afraid it won't work*. Carrying the self-imposed responsibility of success or failure is a heavy yoke and causes people to place harsh conditions for themselves and the world around them. They make excessive demands of themselves and have high expectations of life. As a result the mirror is distorted three-fold: *I want, I fear, I can't let go*. It is a distorted three-way mirror.

If you think that intention means firmly *demanding* what you think the world owes you the results you want to see will elude you. If you *request* that the world give you what you want you will still end up with nothing. It is important to understand that all you have to do is make an order and *allow* the world to carry it out for you. You just will not permit the world to do so because of your *demands, requests, fears and doubts*. In response the world also demands, requests, fears and doubts perfectly reflecting your condition, for the world is just a mirror.

You have to get a sense of this feeling. Let the world go, allow it to be a comfortable place for you to be right now. It is a subtle, fleeting feeling that passes quickly but it must be caught hold of. Imagine for a second something incredible. Imagine that the hostile, problematic, difficult and inconvenient world has become joyful and comfortable. *You can allow the world to be so*; whether you do so or not is up to you.

It is not a matter or being happy by default. It is about allowing happiness to enter your life. We are only as happy as we allow ourselves to conceive of the possibility of unbelievable luck. You do not have to force yourself to be happy you just have to allow yourself the luxury of being so. Trust the world. It knows best how to reach the goal and will take care of everything. You do not usually concern yourself with the question of how a normal mirror can produce such a perfect reflection, do you? When you stand in front of a mirror you only think about what you would like to see in the reflection. The mirror of the world works just at precisely just with a delay.

Just in case you do not yet feel confident that you really can rely on the world there are two more mirror principles. It may be that some people find it easier to act following a set of instructions. However, before we move into the sixth and seventh principles let us quickly recall the *fifth*.

Let us suppose that you have determined what your goal is and began working systematically with the target slide. You understand that the results will not be instantaneous. And yet your mind is fidgety. Time is passing and nothing seems to be happening or things are happening that you did not expect. In these moments when your mind is full of doubt activate your conscious awareness. You have forgotten the rule: "turn around and you will turn to stone".

Your attention must be focused on the end goal as if it had already been reached. The world comes to you whilst you are focused on the image. As soon as you turn to the reflection in the mirror where God knows what (or nothing at all) is happening the world stops and you resume the exhausting and fruitless run around the mirror circle.

You have to constantly remind yourself that the mirror works with a delay and requires a certain pause whilst it puts the reflection together, that is whilst the image is materialised into physical reality. For the time the pause lasts you have to stick to your guns and believe in the conditions and in success when it seems as if everything is going down the pan. What you eventually receive will depend on how courages you are in not giving in to despondency. This is true magic, stripped of magical attributes but having real power.

You should only turn round to look in the mirror, i.e. express your attitude towards what is happening to note positive shifts and to allow yourself to experience a pleasant feeling of surprise. In other words, your eyes must be wide open to anything that gives evidence of the world moving towards your goal and firmly shut to accompanying (and inevitable) negative phenomena. If you have the tenacity "not to look back" then as a rule the results will exceed your highest expectations. You will not only be given a toy; they will spin you on the merry-go-round and treat you to an ice-cream.

In a general sense the rule for how to use the mirror can be expressed in the following way: *When looking in the mirror do not try to move the reflection; instead, try to move the image–your relationship to it and focus of your thoughts.* In other words *"move yourself"*. Do not try and catch your own reflection as a kitten does when it plays with its "double" not understanding that the double is its own reflection. A song by the famous musician and philosopher Boris Grebenshikov contains the lyrics: "She knows how to move herself…to her full height".

Spinning around your own axis you observe that with some delay the world begins to slowly turn after you but you do not rush to grab hold of it and make it spin. This is the difference between *inner* and *outer intention*. Inner intention forces you to try and have an impact on the reflection. Outer intention is about leaving the mirror alone and concentrating your attention on your thought forms thereby having a true power at your disposal, a power capable of moving the world. "What will we do Mama when she moves herself!"

The secret to this power lies in letting you go of your grip. The human mind meets any circumstance it had not foreseen разум and the slightest deviation from its script with hostility. A reaction promptly follows that is just as natural as it is primitive – to try and correct the situation, to object, refuse, insist on one's own way, to argue, make sudden movements, to be proactive etc. Basically, the mind grabs at the reflection and insists in having its way.

Of course, when your attention is glued to the mirror you succumb to the illusion that you only have to reach out your hand and reality, which is so close you could touch it, will instantly submit to your will. No such luck. The silly little kitten is deceived into playing with an ordinary mirror and yet man who stands one rung higher in consciousness falls into exactly the same trap. The only difference is that the illusion of the dual mirror is more sophisticated. That is all.

It is essential that you keep your hands away from the mirror and allow the world *to move*. In the majority of cases no proactive action is necessary. It is enough to be mild and flexible and go with what is happening. As you may recall, the alternatives flow will direct events along an optimal course if it is not hindered. The primitive mind is inclined to slap its hands about in the water and row against the current insisting on upholding its own ideas. Now, in order to free yourself from the illusion you have to turn round the short-sighted intention of the mind, making it dynamically correct its scripts to include the unpredictable. The task will be new and unfamiliar to the mind but it is the only way out of the kitten role.

The *sixth* mirror principle sounds: *release your grip and allow the world to move with the alternatives flow.* Inner intention will then turn round and move in the opposite direction which brings us to the following paradox: by abandoning the position of control you acquire real control over a situation.

Try to observe all that surrounds you with the eyes of the observer. You represent part of a play and at the same time you act in a detached manner noting any movement in the set. If someone offers you something do not be quick to refuse it. If someone gives you a piece of advice, think it over. When you hear a different point of view, do not be too quick to enter into debate. If it appears to you that something is doing something wrong, let it go. If circumstances have changes rather than sounding the alarm try and embrace the change. Whatever you are involved in take the simplest course of action. If you have to make a decision or choice give preference to the option that comes most naturally.

This does not mean that you should agree with everything wholeheartedly. It is one thing to close your eyes and let yourself be taken by the power of the current and quite another to consciously and intentionally move with the flow. You will sense when you need to tighten the reigns and where you should consciously give somc slack. Let the world go and then observe how it moves. Watch the world as if you were a wise mentor allowing the young pupil freedom of choice only occasionally giving them a push in the right direction. You will see how the world begins to spin around you.

Now has come the time to introduce you to the last, most important and powerful of the mirror principles. Aside from the capacity for impeccable reflection the mirror has one more quality: in a mirror right becomes left and space that stretches far into the distance seems to move in the opposite direction. People have long become used to this quality and have learned in their mind to transform illusion into reality. However, the mind still has not managed to overcome the challenge of the illusion of the dual mirror.

The problem lies in our tendency to see the bad in the good and to turn the positive into the negative and to perceive one's good fortune as an evil lot. In reality the world is not intent of machinating against its inhabitants. Problems are not the norm because they require a greater expenditure of energy and nature never wastes energy. The alternatives flow always takes the path of least resistance. You could say that it follows *the path of fortuitous circumstances*. The majority of problems are caused by thc individual slapping their hands about in the water and rowing against the still current. The main thing however is the tendency for negativism that generates a corresponding image which the mirror streams into physical reality.

Remember: all the world does is reflect your relationship to reality with total precision. However gloomy the reflection appears it will only become darker if you treat it as something negative. Likewise, the negative can be transformed into the positive if you declare it as such. Any circumstance or event carries an inherent unfavourable as well as beneficial potential. By expressing your attitude at this crossroads you determine how events will unfold further, successfully or not.

In the long run, you will always end up winning even in the most unfavourable of circumstances if you observe the *seventh* mirror principle: *embrace any reflection as positive.* Whatever you see in the mirror you can never know for certain whether it is for your good or to your detriment but you can decide to choose the best for yourself!

Moreover, when things do turn out well, do not take it for granted or remain indifferent. Be glad, express your pleasure and sharpen your awareness of the fact that everything is going so well. *Whatever happens, everything is unfolding as it should.* This is none other than the *principle of coordinating intention* which was described in detail earlier in Transurfing.

For example, imagine that you face some kind of problem. When you first encounter the problem it is as if you are standing at a crossroads where only you can decide whether to declare the problem complex or straightforward. The tendency for negativism and weariness from the burden of life force people to bow under the yoke of their problems and sorrowfully state: "Oh how difficult! What a complex issue." The world instantly agrees: "As you wish, my love".

The world always complies, so, given that this is the case it makes sense to do the opposite and tell yourself: *everything is being sorted out very easily*. Even if you do not really feel it, declare the problem straightforward. Let this be your postulate. For in essence the problem is only made complex by one small detail, its accompanying circumstances. This small detail is determined by your relationship to the issue. *Whatever happens*, the world will again agree to everything.

"Is everything going to pot?" "No, not at all. Everything's going great!"

And although you may appear a complete idiot to any "sane" and sober individual, rub your hands in satisfaction (It's all fine!), clap your hands or make a little jump of pleasure. Then you will soon discover that circumstances that previously seemed detrimental are actually ace cards in your hand. This mirror quality always has such a sudden and unexpected impact that you never get used to it. Every time a failure turns to victory in your eyes you will experience a feeling of incomparable delight making you want to cry out: "No, you do not say! It is magic!"

Previously, from the point of view of "common sense" you would have reasoned quite differently which would have accounted for all the full range of hardships and privations you previously had to experience. From this moment onwards, every time you come across any kind of problem or unpleasant situation remember that whatever the circumstances the world will comply with the nature of your relationship to what is happening: "Whatever you wish, my dear."

Do you see what you now have at your disposal? You no longer have to sit and wait for the bluebird of happiness to deign to visit you or for the wheel of fortune to turn in the right direction. *You are the master of your success.* You use your will to declare any event or circumstance beneficial and to your favour.

This approach goes beyond just relying on the good will of the world to take care of you because it loves you. The entire world is one dispassionate mirror and if it takes care of something it is only because you are looking at it in that way. Neither is it a case of confidence which circumstances could shake at any moment. Nor is it self-assuredness that comes from blind faith in success. It is not even a matter of being optimistic by nature. It is the *intention of the Maker.* You create the layer of your world; you are the maker of your own reality.

You are the Maker of your reality as long as you know how to "move yourself" without denying the world its own freedom to move. To move yourself means to follow the last three mirror principles. The maker is not so much an active agent as an observer. The will of the maker is different in that it does not *subordinate*, it *allows.*

Now you know how to work with the amazing dual mirror. You need no longer fear the things of the world that others would consider hostile, problematic or intractable. The world is yours! Take it by the hand and say to yourself: *"My world and I are going for a walk."*

The League of Mirror Makers

It would seem that the question of fate in the context of Transurfing is covered. People have free choice of their future by virtue of the existence of the alternatives space which can be controlled by applying the principles of the dual mirror. Nonetheless, it is worth elucidating on the theme a little more.

Opinions differ. Some people think that fate lies in the hands of its owner. Others believe that fate is predetermined. Yet others go even further and view fate as a personal lot we are doomed to, delivered from above and determined according to our deeds in past lives. So which point of view is closest to the truth?

They all are. All these views are correct and equally well-founded. Could is really be any other way in a world which represents a mirror? Everyone that stands in front of the mirror receive confirmation of the image in their thoughts. There is no point in asking the mirror whether the reflection of your face is destined to be is less trivial than On the one hand the mirror reflects what is and on the other hand I will become however I wish to see myself. Therefore, the issue of fate is a question of choice: to choose a predestined fate or to prefer your fate to be free. It is all a matter of conviction. Whatever you choose is what you will receive.

If a person is convinced that their fate is predetermined and that there is no escaping it then indeed, a foregone scenario will indeed be realised. In the alternatives space there undoubtedly exists a separate stream along which the little boat of life will travel if you set it adrift to the will of the waves. The one so doomed gives in to infantile wallowing and reverently raise their head to face the skies from where arrows of misfortune rain upon them like cones fall from a pine: "O power of providence! Oh right hand of fate!" In reality, it is not so much written in the stars as stamped on their forehead that they are a fool, simply caught up in a subconscious and pointless dream to which they have condemned themselves.

When a person takes hold of the reigns their life ceases to be dependent on circumstances. The little boat can be taken in any direction away from the allegedly predetermined "fate". It is all very simple: life is like a river. If you take the paddles and row you can choose your direction but if you simply give yourself to the current you will be forced to drift within the stream you find yourself carried by. If karma is what you want, karma is what you will get. Believing that your lot in life hangs on inexorable circumstances or the mistakes committed in a past life this is the alternative you stream into reality. It is your will, for you are the son of God. And yet if you desire to become the maker then this is also within your power. The dual mirror will agree to anything. It all comes down to whether you know how to work with it.

This all makes good sense within the context of the Transurfing model. The only unsolved mystery concerns the alternatives space. Who "placed" all that it contains into the alternatives space? Where does the alternatives space come from and why? And what existed prior to the alternatives space?

To be honest, *I do not know.* I can merely put forth the following hypothesis: no-one "created" the alternatives space. It had always existed. It is the nature of the human mind to assume that *everything* in this world was created by someone or something and has a beginning and an end. And yet it would appear that is *not true of everything.* I am afraid that even if human awareness was raised enough to surpass that of an oyster it still would not be sufficient to philosophise on such matters. There are things in this world that lay far beyond the capacity of the mind. For the mind, despite being capable of abstract thought is really just an apparatus of logic.

The level of my abstract thinking allows me only to construct a primitive, mathematical model. If you were to take a person's conventional level of awareness to the level of infinity by which our correct level of awareness but represents a dot the question we have posed would be reduced to the following: "Why is it that I, a dot, can occupy any position at all on the coordinates plane? Who created the coordinated grid? What is it for and who existed before the coordinates grid? ...It is all quite incomprehensible." And if you were then to tell the little dot that aside from the second dimension there is also a third dimension and an *n*-dimensional space you would quite *simply "blow its mind"*.

It is easier to believe that fate is preordained by a higher power and that it can be "calculated" or "foretold" than to believe in the existence of some unfathomable alternatives space that contains absolutely everything. Either way, no-one likes to live with uncertainty and so people try to get some kind of hint about the future turning to astrologists, fortune tellers and hierophants. This is also a question of choice. What is my intention, to know what to expect or to co-create what I want?

If you choose a passive position then of course, all you can do is turn to another who has the audacity to claim that they can read the "Book of Destinies". Yet is that even possible? Is anyone really capable of foretelling or "calculating" the future? Undoubtedly they are. Moreover, this is possible due to the existence of the alternatives space. Where else can clairvoyants source fragments of our past and future?

There is no doubt that events cannot develop randomly. The sectors of the alternatives space are linked in chains of cause and effect, life lines, which are subject to given laws. How can these laws be evaluated? Evidently by certain external phenomena such as the position of the heavenly bodies, dreams, a card layout and even coffee grounds. There is no such thing as coincidence. The notion of coincidence is merely a special way of perceiving an effect in the absence of detailed information relating to the cause.

Yet, once again, it is by the very virtue of the existence of the alternatives space, this archive of film on the past and the future, that the prognoses are often far from accurate. There are an infinite number of alternatives and so there is no guarantee that "the film reel taken from the shelf" is destined to "end up in the projector". Any prognosis can only ever rest on a portion of probability.

One of the most "accurate" was the Bulgarian clairvoyant Vangelia Dimitrova, known throughout the world as "Vanga". Losing her sight in her early years Vanga acquired the gift of "seeing" the alternatives space. Yet even with her unique abilities the number of accurate "hits" relating to the past as well as the future varied in the range of seventy to eighty percent.

Prophecies can also be distorted by the perception of the individual psychic and their subsequent interpretations. "The Centuries" by Nostradamus is to this day given wildly different interpretations. People try to see in prognoses things that are not really there and the opposite, they fail to notice the obvious. When Vanga foretold that "Kursk would sink" no-one could understand what was meant for Kursk is located a long way from the ocean. Yet when the submarine of the same name sank those who knew of the prophecy must have come out in goose pimples.

So if we can only talk about the chances of a psychic seeing the "right" sector in the alternatives space in terms of probability then how do we explain the fact that the level of accuracy turns out to be relatively high? This has to do with the fact that once a prediction has been imprinted into a person's memory whether they desire it or not, that prediction becomes their intention.

An individual's relationship to various interpretations and horoscopes is a very personal thing as it is made up of a balance between belief and mistrust. On the one hand people are not generally inclined to rely wholly on such things and on the other hand somewhere in the depths of their subconscious there is a thought that asks: "What if...?" Importance in one's attitude towards predictions is minimal as we tend to think that it may come true or it may not. It is like a game that is played simultaneously for fun and in all seriousness. As a result, a kind of underlying unity of heart and mind emerges providing the conditions for a sharp if fleeting image to be created which the mirror of the world willingly transforms into reality. Unbeknown to themselves the individual also begins to manifest what they have been foretold which explains why the level of probability in such cases is higher than average.

Vanga's biography creates the impression that she intentionally programmed her future fate early on in her childhood. Her favourite pastime was to "heal" her neighbours children, her "patients". She was good at telling various imagined stories which her audience listened to as if under a spell. Aside from that Vanga used to enjoy another curious little game. She would hide something in an obscure place and then begin to search for it blindfolded feeling her way towards it. As you can see, the pictures of the images she created were so precise that the mirror of the world recreated them in physical reality. Vanga became a healer and clairvoyant after she lost her ordinary power of sight in an accident. When she was just twelve years old she was carried away in a hurricane and found later in a field covered in sand.

It should be noted that Vanga was convinced that you could not escape your own fate and that no effort could change what was preordained. When she received visions of accidents that were going to take place in the future she tried to avert the tragedy but she was never successful in doing so. There were times when Vanga, knowing that death awaited someone tried to persuade them not to set out on their journey or to leave a certain place but it did not help. People did not believe her. This would seem to contradict the model of Transurfing. Might fate be predetermined after all?

In actual fact there is no true contradiction here. No one person is capable of influencing the life of another with their own intention. People are endowed with the power to create the layer only of their own world. Even when from the outside it seems as if an influential politician has the fate of whole nations at their disposal in reality they are merely carrying out the will of the structure that created them.

Everyone is capable of managing their own fate but only under the condition that they take the wheel in their own hands. It all depends what position you take, active or passive. You can live as each day comes, reading the horoscopes and accepting your fate as if it was granted from above. On the other hand if you can really get down to business with all the diligence of foolish and end up creating such a fate that heaven forbid should be bestowed upon you! Therefore, by active position we take to mean the ability not to splash your hands about in the water or row against the current and *the intention to control your thoughts in accordance with the mirror principles.*

This position gives you genuine power over your fate at which point the services of a seer become irrelevant. I am not saying that all predictions are false. Individual predictions are indeed often confirmed. The point however, is that these services are only needed by people who decide to choose life as subconscious dreaming, and these will always be the overwhelming majority. Yet if you intend to transform your life into lucid dreaming that you can control then you will undoubtedly no longer require the services of *mirror makers.*

And who are the astrologists, hierophants and prophesiers if not mirror makers? The predictions they give you are not just a harmless prognosis but a surrogate part of your own fate, a small part of the mirror in which you will have to look. How could it be any different? It makes no difference whether you take the prediction seriously or not. Once you have heard it, the image will continue to occupy a place in your subconscious programming your fate. Even if you place the issue of money to one side did you really think that you could have a piece of your future just like that? There are consequences for taking a peek at the Book of Fate. The payment for these goods is always the same. *You must take them with you and make them a part of your life, whether you want to or not.*

Such a payment could prove fatal. The blame or shall we say, responsibility lies not with those who sell fate as a product but with those who make the purchase. When you show interest in a prediction you acquire a mirror and you ask the mirror maker whether it would be ok for you so smile in it that day. You already have a mirror, the layer of your world, from which you can create anything at all. In relation to my own mirror I am free. If I wish I can with the will of the Maker turn any defeat into a victory and that is how it will be and I could not care less about psychic predictions.

If however, you have no desire to become the Maker of your own reality you can successfully make use of the services of the mirror makers. This also represents a choice and is one way of living, or rather, a safe way of moving along the stream of fate. Predictions can serve as signs that give warnings of possible unfortunate events and they can instil you with hope of success. In this sense the mirror makers fulfil a helpful role, although perhaps not all of them. The most harmful among them are those who foretell events of a global scale. By predicting forthcoming catastrophe and "the end of the world" they attune large groups of people to destructive thinking, or in other words, they programme the collective consciousness. This will inevitably leave its mark.

What is interesting is that scientists are also part of the league of mirror makers although they do not necessarily have a direct impact on the fate of others. Over the course of human history scientists have worked on the one task of trying to explain how the world works. Once the Earth was flat and rested on the hump of three whales, an elephant and a turtle or something like that. In former times the stars rotates around the Earth. Many centuries have past since then and some things have become clearer but the process of trying to find a model that fits continues as before. Classical physics has been replaced by quantum physics. Objects of the micro-world were first declared particles and then turned out to be waves who had no objection to being particles from time to time. Then came another theory telling us that these obscure objects are neither waves nor particles but strings in tenth-dimensional space-time. The world stands in the fitting room and agrees with this model too. Even then, something did not quite fit; something was not quite right. Scientists were forced to add one more dimension the eleventh dimension as a result of which a supernova M-theory is born according to which the string is transformed into a membrane. It is amusing is it not? What will they think of next?

No doubt this process will continue for infinity. Ever new models will be found to replace the previous one. If you stand in front of one mirror and hold a second mirror in your hand you will understand why the world has an infinite number of models. In the mirror in front of you, you see yourself holding a mirror in which there is a reflection of you in a mirror holding a mirror, in which…you see?

Perhaps there is no answer to the question of how the world works. Within the context of the human mind if one were to climb to the top of the most abstract peak in our range of definitions we would see that the world *does not actually look like anything.* It is simply a mirror of our ideas. We get what we think about the world. The most we can confirm with any confidence is that reality is multi-faceted and then state a few of its laws.

The process of scientific research into how the world works is similar to the example of the mirrors given above. When you take one natural phenomenon as a starting point you get a specific version of a model which is like having one section of the mirror. Standing with that section in front of the main mirror you see a new aspect of reality reflected. If you take one of the manifestations of that aspect we once again get another version of reality. And again out of yet another tiny mirror a new one will appear having been reflected in the image of the mirror before that.

So what is the world really like? You can try and imagine what the world is really like using the example of two identical mirrors placed opposite each other. Each mirror reflects the mirror that is placed in front of it. Both mirrors give the reflection of nothing, reflected an infinite number of times. It is a black infinity of images in which nothing is reflected from nothing. Does this picture fit any description provided by the concepts the mind has at its disposal? Hardly.

To conclude it should be understood that the pendulums of the mirror makers have no concern for your fate. They follow their own interests, which is to receive a constant source of energy from their "clients". People would like to know every day what tomorrow has in store for them and so they constantly turn to the "well-informed" making a contribution with their energy and in exchange receiving a surrogate, a piece of fabricated fate. If a person's attention has been caught in a pendulum's noose that is trading in fate then they will not feel confident until they have read the next horoscope or had their next dream interpreted. They become addicted as if to drugs. They have to keep getting their dose to support their illusory confidence in tomorrow whilst the pendulums sway and blossom.

Transurfing does not require the same source of energy supply. Learn about the principles and then do whatever you want with them. Knowledge in itself is not a pendulum. A pendulum is only created when the corresponding structure emerges. Neither does Transurfing explain how the world works. It simply offers a utilitarian model which enables you to understand why it is possible that reality can be controlled and how. It is the same as being perfectly capable of driving a car without having the slightest idea of how the engine was put together. Transurfing's mission lies in issuing the "driving license".

The mirror makers try to convince the dot that it must move along a strictly defined line in the graph and that any other form of movement just is not meant to be. This will in fact be true but only if the dot accepts these conditions. Reality exists independently of you whilst you agree to this condition. You can never change the entire world but the individual layer of your world is fully at your disposal. You do not have to change yourself. It is enough simply to exercise your right as the Maker.

Now you have a dual mirror a bit like a genie that makes your wishes come true except that it is not a fairytale any more; it is an aspect of reality that had perhaps remained hidden from you until now under the cover of routine. Unlike the genie in the fairytale you cannot command the mirror genie. There is no point in making appeals to the mirror genie or seeking his compassion. Yet as soon as you declare your intention the magic mirror will willingly comply: "Ok, ok my dear". *You are the true Maker of your fate if you intend to be so*. Do not give your fate away to the mirror makers!

SUMMARY

The mirror principles:

The world like a mirror reflects your relationship to it.

The reflection is formed in the unity of heart and mind.

There is a delay in the reaction of the dual mirror.

The mirror states the content of the relationship and ignores the nature of the relationship.

Do not think about what you do not want; think about what you are striving to attain.

Release your grip and allow the world to move with the alternatives flow.

Any reflection should be perceived as positive.

You control reality by controlling your chain of thought.

Cite the amalgam formula at every convenient opportunity.

You have to move the image, not the reflection, i.e. change your mental outlook and the nature of your thoughts.

Your attention should be focused on the end goal as if it were already achieved.

To materialise a slide you must turn it methodically in your mind's eye for a sufficient period of time.

Do not suppress your emotions – change your relationship to the problem.

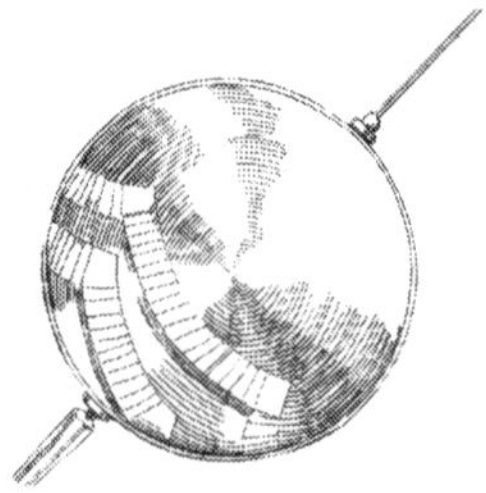

Chapter XIX. THE GATEKEEPER TO ETERNITY

My world and I are off to buy a toy

The Energy of Intention

In the previous chapter you were introduced to the principles of controlling reality. Now we are going to look at specific methods. The first essential condition without which Transurfing is totally impossible is that you must have good energy levels.

There are two kinds of energy, *physiological* energy and *free* energy. You feel the former as warmth and physical strength and it is released as a result of metabolism. To support your levels of physiological energy it is sufficient to eat well, rest, exercise and get fresh air.

Free energy originates in the cosmos flowing along energy channels and it manifests itself as vigour or vitality. This energy is the *energy of intention* which enables a person to feel capable of decisive action. If you slog every day when you only have enough strength to carry out routine activities and most importantly, if you are apathetic about life then this indicates that you have extremely low energy levels.

You could say that free energy is the same as life force. In youth the energy of intention is overflowing. Imagine an old lady with a sickly guise. She dodders and groans and you can tell that every movement is hard for her. Imagine then that she unexpectedly breaks into a run, take a skip and a jump and leaps into the air with a victorious shout of "Yes!" swiping the air with a sharp movement of the hand. It seems inconceivable and yet this is exactly what the old lady would want to do if her energy levels were increased sufficiently.

Why is it that a person produces their best creations in the first or second third of their life? It all comes down to the energy of intention. Yet if you maintain your energy at the right level you can create masterpieces at any age.

Life force and creative energy atrophies when a person ceases to strive. There are people who look upon the world with indifference. They know everything already; they have experienced everything and the feeling of satiety it gives them would seem to be to their liking. They see the world as a well-trodden path in an oft-visited park where nothing could ever surprise them any more. You can hear them in their indifferently-lazy voice lecturing others, and proving that they know it all. People like this age early. Never tire of looking at the world with wide open eyes and you will have more energy – such is its quality.

When a person no longer allows themselves to wonder at the world or to strive for new ideas, it is not only that their development comes to a halt, but a process of degradation sets in and they age. Life is a process. There can be forward and backward movement but there can be no stops along the way. In nature stops and total lack of movement just do not exist. Even a cliff transforms its appearance. In order to activate the energy of intention you have to "hitch" it with a goal.

Energy is ignited when you create dynamic action. It is like a feedback loop: dynamic action generates intention, intention ignites life force. If you remain apathetic and sit with your arms folded doing nothing try to set about doing something, anything and then energy will come to you. Sometimes all it takes is some kind of initial push to get you going.

You might think that you are low on energy and that you need to get some from somewhere. However, this is not the case. In reality you have mountains of energy because it comes from the cosmos and you can take as much as you can carry. The fact of the matter is that you have probably already taken as much as you could. Energy does not disappear so it is probably already being put to use. All its titanic power is spent on maintaining two kinds of burden.

First and foremost the burden is the limitations and obligations you have taken upon yourself. You agree to some kind of obligation and it is as if a heavy plummet is hung on you. Then you place certain conditions upon yourself and you carry another plummet. Then you promise yourself or someone else something and there comes the next one. How many plummets do you have round your neck? Whilst they are relatively few in number a person can go on. But one day there will come a time when the burden can no longer be lifted. Then there is a crisis. Pushed into a corner the person becomes ill, falls into depression or something tragic happens. They become tense and look at the world with fear and mistrust. As a result reality as a reflection of their thoughts begins to genuinely taken on ever gloomier shades. A difficult patch in one's life begins that can go on for a very long time.

The second type of burden consists of the load of excess potential. Ascribing excessive significance to various objects you encumber yourself with an immense burden. It becomes an unmanageable mountain of baggage. These are: the feeling of inferiority. I must be "cool", protect and consolidate my importance; the feeling of guilt and responsibility: I must work my service and fulfil my duty; exaggerating the complexity of problems: I have a huge amount of work to do as well as other doubts and concerns that constantly weigh you down.

A lot of people live like this, weighed down on all sides by all sorts of obligations, unfinished business, harsh conditions, plans and numerous goals. The goal will activate the energy of intention but only on the condition that it is realised and does not just hang at the project stage. There is nothing easier than planning a job, placing conditions on it and making promises. Take into account though that by pinning even the smallest obligation to yourself you hang a weight around your neck which draws on part of the energy of intention and you will have to go forward carrying this weight.

In addition, one of the main causes of low energy levels is the basic accumulation of toxins in the body. It is very simple. The energy channels narrow like an old pipe with a build up of scale as a result of which the energy flow is reduced to a small trickle.

This creates a deficit of free energy which causes various other problems including a poor physical condition, low levels of creativity, illness and everything associated with it.

What happens is that the greater portion of energy that squeezes through the narrow energy channels goes towards maintaining an entire garland of useless weights. The pitiful portion of energy that remains is your total reserve for vitality which gives you alertness, proactiveness, cheerfulness, optimism, the desire to have everything you want right now and the feeling that you can move mountains. Judging from their condition everyone can roughly make out what reserve of vitality they have left. You will not find many individuals who are "wealthy" in this regard.

So all your free energy is employed in a whole range of unrealised, potential intentions (plans), which only weigh you down. *In order to free up resources you have to either get rid of a portion of the potential intentions or bring them into being.*

Ask yourself, what is oppressing you? If you give it some thought you should be able to drop many weights without regret. You may feel that you really need many of these weighty trinkets and could not possibly get rid of them. Yet what is the point if you are continually carrying them around with you but cannot ever realise them? For example: I have to be better than everyone else; I must always be at my best; I will prove to others and myself what I am worth; I do not have any other choice than to continue walking the path I have chosen; only winning is an option otherwise I will not be able to respect myself any more; I cannot make a mistake, and so on and so forth, like giving up smoking, learning a foreign language and generally beginning a new life as of this Monday.

It is true, that everything that is endlessly put off until later is a useless load to carry. These things should either be eliminated from your list or brought into being, because they take up energy which it is just stupid to waste. For example, when a person is in the process of giving up a bad habit of some kind a double portion of energy is spent; on the one hand you still have to pay the pendulum interest on the loan and on the other hand you still have to carry the heavy burden of the obligation to drop the habit.

This kind of rigmarole can end up being drawn out for years. Forcing yourself to do something should be replaced with conviction. If you are going to give something up then do so with conviction and not because you feel that for some reason you have to. If you force yourself into a corner by volition you pump up the tension even more and this inevitably leads to a crisis. Therefore, it is more sensible to choose one means of the other: either decidedly realise your intention, or relieve yourself of the burden of the weight of obligation and channel the habit into a more manageable flow.

For example, rather than scrounging cigarettes or collecting cigarette butts it would be better to get yourself a decent pipe and purchase good-quality tobacco. Rather than doing a pub crawl or drinking in secret hiding round a corner it would be better to carry a presentable hip flask. Basically, this means building a partnership relationship with your creditor. As a result, the harmful vice will become more measured and manageable. The bank is more likely to give a respectable client preferential terms; to say nothing of the fact that the habit once set free is much less harmful than a habit you hate but cannot do anything about. Declaring your intention at this point will only make matters worse and of course, this is not an ideal solution. Before you turn a harmful habit into a civilised manner you need to have a good look at yourself and be honest with yourself about what you are doing.

Another type of burdensome weight would be studying, or rather cramming. When your intention is to fill your head with information you end up creating huge tension. In this case intention is not realised, it is simply pumped up with tension. And so even if I am repeating a truism it is worth repeating. There is no point in memorising information. It just ends up becoming more lifeless baggage that takes a disproportionate amount of energy to "load". Knowledge unlike data is only properly assimilated in action, through concrete examples of when an intention is realised. For example, if you are used to helping children with their lessons try the opposite approach. Let them explain the lesson to you and you will feel the difference straight away. It all comes down to the focus of intention: intention has to be redirected, so that *passive intent is transformed into active intent.* When this happens useless weights that require memorising will fall away instantly.

You might have one huge weight that you have secretly been thinking off dropping for a long time but have not yet been able to finally do it. Imagine how light and relieved you will feel if you drop it. Let yourself go. Give yourself more freedom. Compile a list of things that oppress you and take the weight from your shoulders. You will immediately free up reserves of the energy of intention which will enable you to go forward.

As we said before, a goal activates the energy of intention in the process of its realisation. It is best of course to find your own innermost goal. If you find it the problem of having a deficit of energy will no doubt no longer be an issue for the heart and mind will perk up and rush with enthusiasm towards their cherished dream. However, if at the present time you do not feel able to take action and conquer new heights there is no point in trying to determine your goal. In this case it is very probable that the pendulums will exploit your weakness and force their own goals upon you. In order to find your own goal you have to have a certain level of freedom above all from obligations to others and yourself. And to be successful you have to be able to free yourself from one final weight. *You have to allow yourself not to have a personal goal for the time being.* The search requires a certain amount of free energy and so achieving it should be your first priority.

There are three methods you can use to increase your energy levels: free up resources, exercise your energy channels and widen your meridians.

When you free up resources you get a tangible influx of strength. Whereas previously you gave energy to pendulums related for example to alcohol or tobacco, this energy will now be at your disposal. Previously you spent energy on stress and anxiety. Now this energy can be transformed into the resolve to act. Previously you spent energy on doubt and hesitation, tortured by the question of whether what you were doing was right or not. Now you decide what 'right' means for you. Previously energy went on worry and obligations related to a sense of guilt. Now this energy is free. Previously you were tormented by the need to confirm your significance. Now you allow yourself to live according to your own beliefs and you feel more at ease. Your previous outgoings have been transformed into income, into the energy of intention which will help you to create your own reality.

Earlier in Transurfing we talked about the fact that the energy of intention can be improved with exercise. Just as physical exercise develops the muscles achieving new goals increases your energy levels. However, when the main peaks are taken and life takes on a calm flow the energy of intention atrophies. This fall in energy level can be compensated for by doing *energy exercises*. As you may recall the principle lies in focusing the attention on the rising and descending currents whilst doing any physical exercise. If to this exercise you add *visualising the process* in which you play a slide in your mind's eye in which you see your reserve of the energy of intention increasing with every day the exercises will be even more effective. Once induced the energy of intention will increase of its own accord.

If you have exercised your energy levels intensely on one day, you can expect there to be consequences on the next. Do you think you will already have more energy? If only that were the case! On the contrary, you will be broken. If you restart physical exercise after a long break from training all your muscles ache the following day. It is the same when you exercise the energy of intention except that the next day it is not pain you feel but tiredness and a feeling of being downcast. This is nothing to worry about. It will soon pass and things will return to normal again. The important thing is to take a methodical approach. Tell yourself every day: My intention energy increases with every passing day". After a few sessions you will feel such a boost that you literally want to jump up and down and fly.

Finally, the most direct route to increasing your energy levels is to cleanse the body and shift to a diet of natural foods that have not been treated with heat. Why? This is a separate and far from superficial theme and we will come to it later. For the time being, for the sake of brevity I will introduce the following analogy. Energy flows through the body like water flows through a pipe. When the body is cleansed it is like when a pipe is clean and the water pressure is strong. It is quite natural and straightforward to cleanse the body and maintain it in that condition. You can also take another approach. You can clean the pipe with the aid of a high-pressured water source. This approach requires the practice of meditation. This approach is long and complex and so I suggest the simplest and most direct approach which involves physiological cleansing.

High energy levels bring a person to a state that is called inspiration. When you are inspired you are capable of generating ideas, coming up with innovative solutions and creating master pieces. A muse like a moth is always drawn towards the light. Scepticism and apathy are evidence of low energy levels. When you experience a deficit of energy you always look pessimistically at the world and this will instantly be streamed into physical reality. When you have high levels of vitality you transmit into the mirror of the world the image of a successful person and then success comes towards you without you having to chase it.

There is one more thing to add about inspiration. You may have noticed that inspiration sometimes behaves strangely. Sometimes there are peak moments when the impossible seems possible, but for some reason the enthusiasm quickly fades and is replaced with pragmatism. The fire of optimism burns out quickly and the former gloom of the grey world reigns in which ideas about to take flight begin once again to appear hopeless. What is the point of inspiration if all it does is build castles in the sky?

The answer is that what we have just described is not so much inspiration as euphoria. This condition is experienced when there is a sharp shift from low energy levels to high energy levels. Such a shift happens when strong stimulants are used or simply when some unusual piece of information excites the imagination. An anomalous burst of energy opens the conscious mind to sectors of the alternatives space that lie at a great distance from those that are currently realised materially. Theoretically, these alternatives can also become realised except that they are situated further from the stream of the alternatives flow and so their physical materialisation requites greater energy expenditure. It is for this same reason that ideas that seem brilliant in a dream fade upon waking. In dreaming the soul mostly flies into areas of the field that have very little in common with physical reality.

Genuinely real ideas are only born of the stable energy of intention. Equally they lie relatively close to the alternatives flow. In order for the conscious mind to go beyond the limits of the material world and touch on these ideas one either has to be endowed with a special gift or have consistently high energy levels. Hence one can easily compensate for a lack of talent in this area.

The benefit of the energy of intention is not limited to providing a person with high levels of vitality which enable them to act effectively in the material world. What is much more interesting than this is that the higher your energy level the faster your desires are manifest in physical reality. When the energy of the cosmos passes through the human body it is programmed by their thoughts and acquires ordered form. It is in exactly this way that a radio transmitter transforms electricity into a signal carrying specific information. Once it has received an informational structure, a person's energy can "illuminate" the corresponding sector in the alternatives space. As a result, the metaphysical potential reality is made manifest on the physical side of the dual mirror and the thought is realised materially.

Obviously, the greater the power of the emission, the more effective the process of materialisation. As you know from previous chapters the realisation of a thought does not take place instantaneously otherwise our life would be like a computer game in a world of total chaos. In order to form a reflection it is essential that there be a sharp image born of the unity of heart and mind or a relatively lengthy period of deliberately concentrating one's attention. Perhaps one day someone will invent a "materialiser" for the alternatives space, if of course God allows it. After all, artificial intelligence is still unattainable to us and so it should be for who knows how it would all end if it were not. The most important thing here is that *we* are capable of transforming our dreams into reality.

Having high energy levels do not necessarily mean using force. In order to effectively create the layer of your world you have to feel a sense of oneness with it and even identify yourself with it. You have to take a fresh look at your surrounding reality: *I am master of my reality just as I am master of my body.* You have to enter into the same time patterns as reality and not expect instant change. You need to be calm, patient and focused on your goals.

It is easy for you to control your body for that is something you see as a matter of course. However some people lose this capacity as a result of certain illnesses. The body may make controlled movements or enter into a paralysed state becoming deaf to intention. When we are embarrassed it is also difficult for us to have total control over our bodies. For example, the hands of a person who is inhibited and shy often make uncontrolled movements. In this state there is no unity of heart and mind.

The relationship between a person and the layer of their world is much more difficult. People feel isolated from their surrounding reality. They feel as if the layer is somewhere outside of them, as if it too makes uncontrolled movements and the person can do nothing about it. Once a person begins to feel a sense of oneness with their world they acquire the ability to control it, just as they control their body.

This ability has totally atrophied but it can be restored. To do so you have to constantly pay attention to the circumstances that surround you, feel yourself to be part of this world, to be in context with it and look for what connects you with it. In other words, *to be a separate particle of the world at the same time as dissolved within it.*

I will not try and hide it. This is not an easy task. It is not something that can be taught. A person can only acquire a sense of oneness with the world by means of their everyday experience of life. And this path may turn out to be as long as life itself. So for those who do not find the idea of the painstaking practice of spiritual perfection attractive there are simple, accessible instructions.

The thing is that you do not always get what you want immediately. But whatever happens you get that which you have focused your intention on. For example, if you need to increase your muscle mass your attention should be focused on a slide which depicts your muscles growing. If you need to lose some weight all your thoughts should be about how your body is becoming leaner. If you goal is to increase your levels of the energy of intention then you must focus on your energy channels and energy body. And finally, if your intention is not directed towards anything, you will not get anything.

Doing exercise without a specific purpose is a waste of time and effort. When your attention is focused not on the goal but on the effort physiological energy is expended but that is all; for effort is a path to the goal, a means to an end. You will find yourself constantly on the path because the mirror simply reflects the content of the image.

Children are overflowing with energy but this energy is uncontrollable and is usually uselessly scattered into the atmosphere. In the same way, if a person develops their vitality to a high level but fails to give it a specific direction the energy will be equally as useless. A simple lamp can only light up the area immediately surrounding it whereas a narrowly focused laser beam will shine on a point many kilometres away. Therefore, *if you want your energy to work for you it is essential that you focus it in the specific direction of a goal.*

Purposefulness directs the energy of intention in a strictly determined direction. Concentration is essential and *concentration means focus, not tension.* The thought-mixer works automatically. Ideas are born and fade uncontrollably. Thoughts jump from one theme to another. The mind will restlessly "swing its legs" like a little child. In order to control reality you have to strive to keep your thoughts under control. It might feel a little awkward at first but with time it becomes a habit.

In order to develop this as a habit it is sufficient to follow one simple rule: *teach yourself to think about the thing you are doing in the moment.* Do not do anything just for the hell of it, swimming in an amorphous juice of uncontrollable thoughts. *Proclaim a declaration of intention.* This does not mean that you always have to be on your toes. You can let your mind drift as much as you want to but make it intentional, by principle: *if my mind wanders it is only because I allow it to do so.* In this way you can deliberately return to a state of concentration when it is required.

Essentially, the point is to make the image in your thoughts mostly contain the picture you would like to see reflected in the dual mirror. It is not necessary to remain in an ideal state of organic unity of heart and mind all the time to achieve your goal. It is enough to *systematically* focus your attention on the target slide. *By controlling your train of thought you subject reality to your will.*

It does not matter that your thoughts keep going out of control. The important thing is to acquire the habit of returning them to the stream of the target slide. When you have the habit of returning your thoughts again and again to the goal, the slide becomes a constant companion and its image will always be in the background in the context of all that happens to you. Have no doubt, the image will be formed and the mirror of the world will inevitably reflect it in reality.

Every individual has their own layer of the world. You could say that the reflective surface of the dual mirror is many-layered. Every living being has a mirror plate at their disposal from the moment they are born. The individual's thoughts and intentions construct an image which is reflected as a separate reality. The entirety of all realities are arranged in layers creating what we observe as physical reality.

In the case of man the layer is his habitat i.e. everything that surrounds him. Individual reality is created in two ways: physical and metaphysical. In other words, the individual creates the layer of his world by thought and action. It is difficult to judge which of these two aspects influences reality more. It is probable that thought forms play the leading role because they create a significant portion of the material problems a person spends a great deal of their time battling with. As you will now understand Transurfing deals exclusively with the metaphysical aspect of reality.

Every individual lives in a specific environment in which they are surrounded by a multitude of people and material objects. So how does one delineate a separate sphere of existence within this motley environment? It is very simple. If you out the material aspect of the environment to one side for a moment you are left with an essential quality that interests us above all: *how are things going, well or badly?* A person's surroundings may be abundant or poor, friendly or aggressive, comfortable or less so, but this is not important. What does have meaning is the extent to which that person is happy in these conditions, whether they receive what they strive for, and whether circumstances seem to unfold fortuitously. This quality of the layer, its hue, has the deciding influence on everything that happens in material reality.

A layer can have light and dim hues. It all depends how a person organises their forms of thought. The more negative their thinking the gloomier their particular reality will be. The worse things go the more resentment builds up, which due to the feedback chain causes the layer to darken even more. From this we conclude that your individual reality must be kept clean just like the body.

All negative thoughts must be decisively and sharply driven out so that they do not have time to ruin your world. Away with them! It is just the same as having to take the rubbish out or do the cleaning. You have to get rid of old junk, otherwise, however hard you try things will always go badly.

However, there is a certain kind of junk that is not that easy to eliminate from your world. This junk is *feelings of guilt, inferiority complex, doubt, stress, fear, dissatisfaction, hostility and negative expectations.* These are like our aches and pains that we would only be too glad to be rid of but we do not know how to. So you have to treat them. A remedy is available.

Image this scene: a person and their world set off in a magic bus to a place where dreams are transformed into reality. "So, my dear, here we are then, off to get you a toy". "That is great world!"

The happy journey seems most promising. Everything is going brilliantly. What else could you ask for? Yet the anxious mind is not used to it. The mind is always glancing to one side hoping to spot a problem. It is not possible for everything to be ok! "Hey! Stop the bus! Over there, the righteous that judge me, we should give them a lift so that I can make amends." "No, my sweet. That is nonsense!" "Please, we must, otherwise I will not have any peace". The bus stops, and a group of dubious looking types climb aboard and start complaining and making demands. "We are your judges!" they say.

Nothing can be done about them and so the bus drives onwards. Overall, the situation is not too bad but the person keeps fidgeting. "Look!", he tells the world, "look at those lovely people. Let us take them with us. They will set a good example for us". "I ask you, what would we want of extra passengers?"

The world makes weak attempts to protest but is forced to agree and the bus is filled with haughty individuals who make it quite plain in their manner that everyone else is below them. "We are your ideal!" Along the way Fear, Stress, Doubt and Negative expectations are all hitching a ride and of course, the person tries to rationalise the situation wisely: "Perhaps these are wise travellers who will give us direction and save us from getting lost?" "As you wish, my dear!" The world agrees and welcomes the clamouring public aboard. "We are your common sense!" they claim and continue with their common sense moaning to turn the journey into hell.

In addition to everything else the road is blocked by Displeasure, Blame and Aversion. The person really does not want to meet with them but the world is so accustomed to taking with it everything the mind gives it attention to. "We are your nightmare!" scream the unsavoury types as they burst through the doors.

By now the person would only be too pleased to get rid of his annoying companions but it is too late. The bus is overloaded and can drive no further. The manipulators, cardboard idols, hysterics, advisors and other vermin have ruined everything. But who is to blame? Why did they have to come along in the first place?

The most destructive type of all this junk is the feeling of guilt, whether the individual is conscious of the feeling or not. If you have noticed that the world punishes you and behaves as if it is mocking you or trying to undermine you then you have all the symptoms of the disease. Drive this infection out. Give it a good kick. The feeling of guilt is an unwanted and cocky guest who sinks into your armchair, puts their feet up on the table and starts to dictate their conditions. You are quite capable of throwing them out if you are conscious of the fact that this is within your power. Even if you are genuinely guilty of something you have the right only to have to ask for forgiveness once.

The feeling of guilt generates punishment in the most varied form, from tiny inconveniences to huge problems. You might just cut your finger or you might end up in some kind of accident. Outer intention will undoubtedly include some kind of punishment in the script. This is how the template worldview works: a misdeed is followed by retribution and the heart and mind are quite unanimous.

In addition, the feeling of guilt puts serious strain on polarisation. As a result, balanced forces bring all kinds of misfortune onto the head of the one who has recanted. The worst of these misfortunes is the manipulator, who will stick to you like a persistent fly. Manipulators have made of a fine art of inducing a feeling of guilt in their "clients". If a person has a tendency to absorb guilt and take it readily upon themselves, the manipulator will do everything it can to dump even more guilt on them.

Guilt complexes are seeded within us as early as childhood. Adults often use forbidden methods to force their charges to obey them. If a child spends a long time in the care of a typical manipulator a kind of microchip is firmly inserted into their vulnerable psyche in the form of an unconscious feeling of duty and obligation to make amends for some misdeed.

Having been successfully "programmed" the child is forced to bear a heavy cross and is a puppet in the hands of the manipulators all the time that the microchip remains in their subconscious. So, how can it be removed? You cannot suppress guilt, neither can it be got rid of just like that because it is too deeply instilled. The heart and mind have lived like this for a long time, eternally obliged to someone. Only a concrete course of action can draw a person out of this condition.

Specifically, they have to stop *justifying* themselves. This is a case where treating the illness eliminates the cause. You do not have to try and convince yourself that you do not owe anyone anything. Simply be mindful of your actions. This requires awareness. If previously you had the habit of apologising for the slightest reason now try to adopt a different habit: *only explain your actions when it is absolutely necessary.*

There really is no need to tell yourself that you are not beholden. It is ok for the feeling of guilt to be inside you but do not reveal it externally. Once the manipulators realise that they will not get the same output from you anymore they will leave you alone. Meanwhile the heart and mind will gradually get used to the new feeling: you do not justify yourself which means that must be right and consequently, your guilt simply does not exist anymore. As a result, there will be fewer and fewer reasons for your "atonement". So, thanks to the feedback chain external form tidies up inner content. The feeling of guilt disappears and with it various associated problems.

The inferiority complex is another illness from which practically everyone suffers to some degree. This baggage makes a person feel unworthy and incapable and this is then reflected in physical reality. Earlier on in the Transurfing materials we talked in detail about *inner importance* and the various kinds of problems that arise when a person actively strives to elevate their significance as a result of feeling flawed in some way. The paradox lies in the fact that a law applies here which is very similar to the principle of uncertainty in quantum physics: importance decreases equal to the extent that it is emphasised. The opposite is also true. A person who has no concern for their significance has it automatically.

The attempt to strengthen your position and emphasise your positive qualities is an illusion and a chase after the reflection around the mirror circle. But how do you prove to yourself that you are special and have no need to prove it? There is one more feedback chain by which the cause eliminates the effect. You have to consciously redirect your intention: rather than trying to prove yourself or show off you have to *give up all attempts to increase your own significance*. When a person manages to stop (and we all know that practically everyone in does this in their own way) the people around you intuitively sense that your significance does not need to be confirmed. And as this is so, people are more drawn to them and begin treating them with more respect. As a result the heart and mind are gradually penetrated with the conviction that "I am in fact worth something". There comes a moment when the mirror circle grinds to a halt, turns in the opposite direction and starts moving towards you. Self-esteem improves and it is as if there never was an inferiority complex at all.

Doubts, stress and fear also substantially ruin the picture of a person's individual world. Do not forget, that once these thoughts have been reflected in the mirror something will enter the layer of their world that is really worth fearing. But the greatest damage caused by anxiety is suffered by the goals one has set because as you may recall from the previous chapter anxiety transforms desire into longing.

The stronger desire flames like the fear before defeat, the more intense outer importance will be and the fewer the chances of success. Abandon any form of waiting that feels like longing otherwise you will not get anywhere. Intention is essential to the achievement of your goals and intention is free of doubt and emerges when simple "wanting" transitions to doing.

In order to dull the itch of impatience you need to have a safety net, a backup plan in case of failure as well as accept the idea of defeat at the onset. The question might arise as to how can you accept defeat beforehand if you are tormented by a desperate thirst to have what is yours? But you will see that when things do not work out, despair or perhaps anger will make you wave your hand at the result you had expected.

Despair can also help you eliminate *inner importance* i.e. painful feelings of self importance. If something is not working out for you and hits yours ambitions hard the feeling of hopelessness make you give it all up and ditch your self importance like a dead weight. You will immediately feel better, free and light. Things will pick up at once.

Doubts in the successful completion of a project usually arise when the mind tries to work out the path and means to achieving the goal. In "Transurfing Reality" we have talked a lot about why there is no point in thinking about these things. You cannot know exactly how things will work out for the best. Your task is to concentrate your attention on the goal as if it had already been achieved and then outer intention will open the right doors at the right time.

Now that you know the rules relating to the use of the dual mirror you have nothing to worry about. The mirror principles constitute the most effective remedy for doubt and fear. Firstly, direct your intention towards maintaining the amalgam "my world takes care of me". Secondly, you must follow the last three of the mirror principles very precisely.

For example, you are planning to go to university and want to pass the selection procedure successfully. Prior to the examination you say to yourself: if I do fail the exam maybe that would be the best thing for me? Then you will be able to go into the exam feeling cheerful and relaxed. This is called accepting the possibility of failure and moving with the alternatives flow. You are doing what is required of you at the same time as being indifferent to the end result, or rather, *being prepared to think of any outcome as successful.*

There is no point in "pretending" you do not want to achieve the goal. Self-deception will not work. You have to not think about how the goal will be reached and not get caught up in the script. Your task is to do the work of visualising the slide and placing one foot in front of the other in the direction of your goal. The mind's control should be focused on following the mirror principles and not on the script.

What is the point in worrying if success awaits you in any case? It is for you to decide how you determine your relationship to the outcome, positively or negatively. We are all accustomed to relating to our setbacks negatively which is why we are all forced to submit to the rules of the game in which success in difficult to achieve by default. Instead, when you take an inappropriate step, name your failure a success. Then you will stand out from the crowd and your victory will be secured.

The feedback chain works here just as it does in the case of feelings of guilt and self-importance. By switching your attention from the mirror to the image and ceasing the chase after the reflection you stop the mirror circle. Then you do not have to believe in success or persuade yourself of anything. *All that is needed is to refocus your intention on the observation of the mirror principles.* Once their effect begins to kick in you will notice that reality is changing substantially. Your mind is convinced that the mirror really does work. Then you finally understand that the road to success is entirely different to how you had previously imagined. As a result the heart and mind are calmed; fear and doubt disappear and the mirror circle comes towards you.

The rest of the junk that has to be cleared from your world includes condemnation, dissatisfaction, aversion and negative expectations. As far as the first is concerned, you have to be clear about the fact that any form of criticism even if it is justified is extremely disadvantageous. Criticism is an extremely thankless task. In their attempt to restore the balance between good and bad balanced forces will do everything in their power to make sure that the accuser be the one to sit in the dock. There will never be a shortage of cause or reason. It is advisable to make any form of criticism on your part taboo.

As far as all other negative responses are concerned there is just one thing to say. By playing in the performance "my world does not suit me and I do not like my life" you shape and maintain specifically that kind of reality". Remind yourself again and again that you are standing in front of a mirror and that the amalgam and final three mirror principles can transform the layer of your world into a cosy little corner. Aside from this there is nothing more to be said.

Finally, if you feel bad at the moment, so bad that you have no strength to follow some set of principles, what should you start with? *How can you straighten things out and get your reality back on track?*

Sometimes life does become unbearable. It is like when an alcoholic sobers up and discovers that their life is bleak and harsh. We will take as a typical example how gloomy morning arrives after a great party the night before and you have to drag yourself to work. There are all sorts of problems after work parties. The fact that people find it difficult to get back into the rhythm of work is obvious but strangely, a similar thing happens to technical equipment too. Statistics show that more cars, computers and other appliances break down on a Monday than any other day in the week. So what is happening to reality?

This aspect of reality is created by people when their layers lie one on top of the other. During the hangover period people have to pay back the pendulum the "interest on the loan". When there is a deficit of free energy the thought form contains a large portion of negativity. This creates a collective tension at the workplace and nothing comes together. The mirror responds accordingly and reality is warped. If at home electrical appliances get out of sink it is not so tangible but in companies the combined warp effect leads to more noticeable consequences: accidents happen, machinery breaks down and complex and particularly precise technology works irregularly.

The thing is that if a person is suffering from depression or is in an altered state of awareness, the layer of their world is drawn into *muddy areas* of the alternatives space. Reality appears to be veiled in a haze. Everything about the surrounding environment remains in place; the conditions are the same as they were previously; the weather may even be fine and yet something oppressive hangs in the air. If you have not paid attention to the hues of reality on days like this before observe them in the future. You will feel as if the material world is staring at you with cold hostility. The quality of its layer has changed: "everything is going badly today". This quality is the cloudy haze and it has a very tangible impact on everything including technical equipment.

The onset of a bad patch in life comes either with physical ailments brought about by a deficit of free energy or from negative emotions that are experienced when our expectations are not fulfilled. To avoid letting cloudy areas into your reality it is essential that you increase your energy levels. When your vitality reaches the necessary level you no longer feel irritated. You must also do everything mentioned above about keeping the layer of your world clean.

But for now, if you are depressed you have to first straighten out your reality and lead the layer of your world out of the cloudy haze into a clear area of the alternatives space. How is this done?

There is one recipe for this and like all things of genius, it is very simple. What do you do when a child is crying? How do you comfort it? Words do not have any effect. You have to walk with it, show some care and attention. When you feel down it is the child in you crying. Take care of it. Despite the fact that many of you appear to be serious, respectable, imposing or cool etc we all essentially remain the child. "Push yourself on the merry go round" meaning, do a little of what you like doing most. Take some special time out to relax without thinking about problems that distress you. "My world and I am going for a walk". It will be time well spent because it is essential to clean your layer out. Much depends on this. Buy your favourite treat: "Eat, eat my love, get better". Devote the entire day to yourself and to your pleasures. Look after yourself and put yourself carefully to bed: "Go to sleep now, my dear. Your world will take care of everything".

There you have it. The next day if you are diligent and observe the mirror principles you will feel that the reality that surrounds you has begun to acquire warmer, softer hues. Your layer is coming out of the haze.

If you are observant you will be amazed at how *real* it all is. The material world that previously seemed stationary will begin to literally transform before your very eyes. The oppressive atmosphere will lighten, stopped clocks will start ticking again and people will be more drawn towards you. The way the gigantic dual mirror works is simply stunning. Reality moves unnoticeably in the alternatives space like the minute hand on a watch, but that does not mean it is not moving!

That is how you can "decorate" your reality. But that is not all. Would you like to do a full-blown renovation? Think back to what it was like in your childhood. All the colours were bright and vivid and life was wonderful and full of promise. You were happy, happy because the layer of your world like your body was fresh and clean. The world took care of you. True, you might not have valued it immensely but you did not have any particular complaints either. With time complaints and negativity in the image of your thoughts increased. As a result, the hues in your layer faded and life entered into a period where people started to say: "Those were the days…!"

This effect is described in the early materials of Transurfing as the *generation shift*. Time flies by. The past feels as if it were only yesterday and yet it was all such a long time ago. Age tenaciously and inevitably takes its toll. Hopes fade and the world begins to deteriorate. Surely the party is not coming to an end already?

No. There is still time to bring it all back, the former colours, the newness of feeling and the delights of hope. If you adhere to the mirror principles you will encounter an amazing phenomenon. *The former freshness of the layer of your world will be restored.* When you manage to straighten out the generation shift for yourself then you will feel fully what it really means to *control your own reality*.

Correcting the Mirror

Throughout history man has created all kinds of models for controlled reality from rock art to complex instruments and mechanisms. All these models share one feature in common. They are all subject to the inner intention of man. Being a product of pure reason, inner intention acts in a linear fashion according to the principle of "where I make a turn that is where I will go".

Man can only wilfully control the parts of reality he has made an attribute of the game. For example, you can control part of a river as a way of generating energy but as a whole the river will remain an independent component of uncontrolled reality.

You can make a donkey move with inner intention by applying force but it is impossible to make a donkey do anything it does not want to. Independent reality is subject only to outer intention which is born of the unity of heart and mind.

A person has two means of controlling reality. The first is to make attributes of objects in the surrounding world. These objects are then subject to inner intention. The second means is to work with outer intention and live in harmony with nature. These means represent two fundamentally opposed paths for the development of human civilization.

Contemporary society is developing along the lines of the first and least effective model. It is a path that will prove disastrous for the planet and mankind. Man can never totally tame nature and so we find ourselves in constant battle with the natural environment. One day we are polluting the environment, the next day we are trying to conserve it. In short, everything is done according to the same principle: transform everything into an attribute in order to subject it to the will of inner intention.

Untamed reality exists independently and acts like a mirror in that it reflects the human relationship to physical reality. But this is no ordinary mirror.

Let us suppose that a person wants the reflection in the mirror to turn to the right. Acting within the limits of inner intention the person tries to turn the reflection itself. Excess potential is created as a result and balanced forces turn the reflection in the opposite direction. The world does not respond because the mirror has become distorted.

The mirror of the world is distorted by the phenomenon of polarisation. As you may recall polarisation takes place for two reasons. The first is dependent relationships based on comparison, juxtaposition or stipulated conditions. For example: "I am good so you must be bad", or "You will be good if you acknowledge my superiority".

The second reason for polarisation to take place can be defined as "turning the screws". When a person tries to put pressure on the reflection with inner intention nothing happens. This makes the person think that they need to apply even more pressure and so with brute force they continue to push for what they want. Balanced forces eliminate polarisation through the collision of opposites. Consequently, the result turns out to be the exact opposite of the person's inner intention.

The mirror can be straightened out if polarisation is eliminated. This is quite simple just like straightening a bicycle wheel. The wheel bends in areas where the spokes are too tight. If the world will not obey and seems to act as if to spite you it is essential to determine what has caused polarisation to occur and then to relax the corresponding potential.

The Indigo children will help us understand these processes as they are extremely sensitive to excess potential. The Indigo child is characteristically independent and intuitive with a strong sense of their own individuality and high levels of awareness. These qualities develop as a reaction to the attempts of others to force them to conform and fit in to rigid social *structures.*

Every cell within the greater structure including the family unit strives to control children's behaviour making it as orderly as possible. To some extent this is necessary. But not to the extent that a child is made into an attribute of a game in which the main rule is: "You will do what I tell you to".

Obviously, this primitive type of approach can only create polarisation and it makes children uncontrollable like leaves swept up by the winds of balanced forces. The adults who are foolish and dissatisfied usually do whatever is within their power to turn the screws of discipline. In response the children either become even more wildly or become broken in spirit allowing themselves to be transformed into attributes – elements of the structure for whom "everything in life is correct but not ok".

Naturally no parent would want their child to become a social outcast. Yet the fate of the common screw is not to be envied either. Many adults will confess that in their life they "did everything right but nothing good came of it" or "did many things wrong and nothing was right". Every parent wants things to be different for their own children and so in their efforts they ever more strongly cause polarisation, unyielding in their ignorance of what they are actually creating.

All inner intention of any tutor-ignoramus can be reduced to one idiotic formula: "I want the best for you with all my heart (with all my ill-conceived might) and so you will do what I tell you to".

Any problems associated with the upbringing of a child can be resolved by abandoning short-sighted inner intention and contemplating what might have caused the mirror to be warped.

Firstly, one has to determine where the opposite poles of polarisation are manifest. If the spokes on one side of the wheel are too tight then they should be released a little on the other side. The striving of the Indigo child to independence and refusal to accept discipline can be seen as the "loose spokes". What is making the spokes on the other side too tight? The tension comes from the pressure placed on Indigo children to submit to the will of the adults around them.

It turns out that orderliness can give rise to huge chaos. What happens if you keep turning the screws? The spokes elsewhere will become even looser and eventually something will break.

Obviously, *in order to reduce the effect of polarisation the over-tightened spokes have to be loosened.* How? *Orderliness needs to be mixed with a dose of reasonable disorder.* There are many ways of doing this. You can jump on the bed, thwack each other with pillows, howl or make strange sounds, push and shove, crawl around on all fours or think of other ways of getting up to mischief.

You could also lie in wait for someone in the family and jump on them. At the table it helps to smear jam on each other if there are no cakes to hand. Or in the summer if you are playing near water and find a muddy puddle then that is a treasure and you know what has to be done.

Generally speaking the more of this kind of "sensible" foolishness, the more obedient the child will be. The reason behind the paradox should be clear to you by now.

Orderliness can equally as successfully be broken with British humour in which seriousness is taken to the absurd. Cheerfulness like boredom is a reflection of the state of the soul. We have already mentioned that boredom of itself does not exist but just an eternal need to control reality. This need represents an inherent quality of the soul.

Why does the soul need to have fun? Probably because when you are having fun you feel good. Why do you feel good? Because humour and cheerfulness reduce importance. It is impossible to shape reality when excess potential is present that blocks the energy of intention and warps the mirror of the world.

If you make someone bend over backwards and tie them up will not their body feel discomfort? The soul feels exactly the same kind of discomfort when it is held squeezed into a vice of excess potential which is always there to some extent. The restless mind is always twisting the arm of the soul.

When fun reduces tension the soul is set free. That is why it is *good* when we are cheerful. We experience a feeling of inner comfort which is just as real as any physical sensation.

In principle the mirror can be corrected without the use of humour. If you are not inclined to fun and mischievous tricks by nature you can simply contemplate on where you can relax the wheel a little.

Any form of inevitable coercion should be diluted with freedom of choice. For example: "Do you want to wash the dishes or pop to the shops?" Even discipline can be transformed into a free display of will if it is based on conscious necessity.

When an adult dictates by the rule "you can't and do not answer back" backing it up with the argument "because..." then they are not an adult at all but a fool endowed with power. Would not it be better to discuss things as equals and model the situation according to the principle of "what will happen if...?"

Coercion distorts the mirror and so generates the opposite result. To reduce the effect of polarisation you have to reconsider your stance and shift from a demonstration of power to an attempt to win respect, and replace authoritarianism with trusting relationships.

Instead of using coercion it is better that a child desire to do whatever is being required of them. The necessary approach here is to think of a way of turning what is a burdensome duty for the child into something that increases their importance. Affirmation and consolidation of personal significance is a fundamental motivating factor for all people but children especially. The most appropriate method of interacting with children is described in the principles of Frailing set out earlier in *Transurfing Reality*.

Intuition is another quality that should be developed as a priority. In Indigo children the right hemisphere of the brain dominates. The education system however utilises the left hemisphere approach, the goal of which is far from developing skills and abilities. The system forces children *learn* the content of the lessons and then regularly *report back.*

In this approach it is predominantly the left hemisphere of the brain that works although the state is a passive one. The desire to fill up the mind with information generates an unambiguous response: "I do not want to!" Knowledge acquired in this way is useless. It is simply held by the memory in passive form like goods stored in a warehouse and very quickly loses its worth and is forgotten.

The established state of the education system could be easily corrected. All it would require is to focus the students' intention differently.

Firstly, the very roots of the teaching methodology would have to be changed from *learning by heart to learning in practice.* The brain would then work as it is supposed in its capacity as creator rather than as storage warehouse.

Secondly, the objective of teaching would have to be changed from *reporting to teaching others.* Yes, exactly. There are special schools set up in which the children literally teach each other, that is they alternately play the role of teacher and student. Children that attend schools of this kind brilliantly assimilate complex curriculums in record time and it is all down to the fact that intention has been set to be active. In passing school such as these are very few and far between and difficult to get into. You would think this innovative method could be implemented across the board since it has been proven to be one hundred percent effective. But no, not for anything!

The reason for this is that it is not in the interests of the *structure.* The structure does not need talent, great individuals or eccentric personalities. What it needs are reliably functioning components. That is why everything is fine and the education system is perfection itself! The system produces serviceable components and does it in the manner demanded by the structure – the world of pendulums.

Yet as we know, trees also grow on rocks and a genius will sometimes grow from the vice of common order. If you do not want your child to become an outstanding exception pressure them in the spirit of all the canons of the system. But if you genuinely desire your children the best when you are interacting with them constantly observe the level of polarisation taking place that warps the mirror and makes the child uncontrollable.

The Indigo children (now the majority of the younger generation) display many wonderful qualities, the most important of which is individuality. In the world of pendulums it is very difficult for children to preserve this quality. For this reason it is extremely important to always bear in mind the main rule of Transurfing: "Be yourself and allow others to be themselves".

The spokes should not be loosened too much either; all things in good measure. So where is the golden mean to be found? It is a matter of observing, figuring things out and applying the principle of correcting the mirror rather than blindly following your typical approach. It is within your power to assist children in becoming outstanding personalities. They will be capable of working out for themselves how to fit into the structure.

The Reality Maker

Up until now we have talked about how to transform your life into a conscious dream and the layer of your world into a cosy corner. The mirror principles have a tangible and yet a subtle impact on reality. Now you will be introduced to more powerful approaches.

The target slide is the central instrument of Transurfing, visualising a picture in which the goal has already been achieved. I will not repeat here all the ideas that were described in detail earlier on in the book. I will just remind you of a few key elements.

The slide should not be seen as an external moving picture. You have to be inside the events of your imagination: what you are doing, when the goal was achieved, what you are feeling, your immediate environment and anything else that is happening. When you place yourself at the centre of the slide you can imagine yourself with everything you strive for. This is not a technique. There are no strict rules that must be followed. Practice the slide approach in your own way. There is just one principle to keep in mind: *you are standing in front of the mirror of the world and you are shaping an image in your thoughts of what you would like to have streamed into physical reality.*

The target slide determines the vector of the alternatives flow. It you methodically turn the slide in your thoughts the flow of events and circumstances you encounter will be aimed towards the goal. You do not need to have a precise plan or know how it might be realised. There is no need to think about the means. The right doors will open at the right time – concrete paths and opportunities, and you will sot them. *You must not place strict conditions on how the goal should be reached. Your task is to concentrate on the final result.*

Aside from the target slide there is also the *visualisation of the process* also described in the early chapters. Once you are on the path towards your goal, have fathomed how it will be realised and are doing everything that is necessary in the material world, the process can be accelerated through visualisation. The principle here is the following: *everything is going extremely well and today I am doing everything better than yesterday and tomorrow will be better than today.* You could say that this is like working with the oar in harmony with the alternatives flow. As long as you hold the target slide in your thoughts you can be sure that circumstances are working towards achieving the goal even if it does not seem that way.

You can play the slide in your mind's eye as much and as often as you like but make sure you do it for at least half and hour each day if you genuinely intend to achieve the goal. There are several methods that can consolidate the effect of visualisation.

The first is the *energy currents.* The sector of the alternatives space is materialised via energy which passing through the human body is programmed by thought and transformed into the energy of intention. The more powerful the transmission of energy, the more powerful the effect. The force can be increased by concentrating one's attention on the energy currents. This involves imagining that from the centre of the body, somewhere in the area of the stomach or the solar plexus, two opposite arrows exit to the length of about one metre. Mentally turn the arrows simultaneously so that the front arrow points upwards and the rear arrow points downwards. "Turning the key" in this way activates the descending and rising currents. Imagine without putting too much effort into it that they flow along the spine in two opposite directions and reach out one into the sky and the other into the ground. Focusing your attention partly on the currents of energy launch the slide and play it to your heart's content. This exercise is best practiced when you are on a walk in a quiet place when few people are around.

The next technique is called the *frame*. Think about what you would like to be doing when your goal is achieved and what would represent an integral part of the target slide, its indispensible attribute. You might be sitting by a fireplace in a rocking chair, standing at the helm of your personal yacht, planting roses in your garden or shaking hands with a business partner having sealed a successful deal. Imagine any characteristic fragment of the slide. Turn the picture in your thoughts several times. It should create a kind of integral impression, an instant mold of the slide, containing a flash image and accompanying feeling. This is the frame. For the sake of convenience you could give it a short heading. From time to time turn it on in your memory for an instant as you would turn on a light. Do this whenever it naturally occurs to you to do so, again, without applying too much effort. The frame represents another thread that connects you with the target sector of the alternatives space. The effectiveness of the frame can be embellished with the help of the so-called *explosion wave*.

Shape a frame or simply a picture in your thoughts that you would like to translate into reality. Immediately follow it by imagining that a sphere is expanding outwards from your body in all directions as if your energy field had suddenly exploded. The explosion wave can extend as far as you are able to imagine it. You can repeat this exercise several times until you are tired of it. So what is happening here? You create a mental image and send it out into the universe. You can be certain that your thought will not be lost without trace. You just have to bear in mind that the mirror works with a delay.

Another technique is the *outer sphere*. You may never have experienced your energy membrane or felt it expanding as it becomes subject to your imagination. This will be because your actions are motivated by inner intention. Now imagine a sphere surrounds you that does not belong to you. Imagine that the sphere draws you. You can feel that something outside of you is trying to stretch out your body. Somewhere within a radius of five to seven metres lies an invisible front. If you try and stretch it or squash it slightly it will show a springy resistance.

Now you will have felt the sphere more clearly. This is the borderline that connects you with the outside world. What is inside the sphere is yours and what is outside, the external, is not yours. At the same time you could say that the sphere belongs to you to the extent that you can feel it pulling you. Intention has been redirected. The proactive essence now lies on the outside rather than inside of you.

By way of analogy if you try and control an object with the power of inner intention such as by moving a pencil with your willpower it will not work. Instead try and imagine that the pencil draws you with invisible threads. It is by means of this connecting link that you can move the pencil. Likewise if you try and rise up into the air you will not take off and fly. Instead imagine the opposite happening as if the world itself is lifting you up into the air. You might have some success, if you manage to transform inner intention into outer intention. The point is to try and go beyond the point where "your will tries to make the world obey it" to "allowing the world to do it itself".

This is all quite complex, and yet for our purposes it does not have to be. It is enough to feel the presence of the outer membrane. Once you sense it do not lose that feeling. Partly focus your attention on it and then begin to play the target slide in your mind. The sphere will serve as a kind of antennae for the transmission of thought energy and this will substantially strengthen the efficiency of the slide.

Another technique is *scenery reduction.* Try and reduce all the thoughts that come into your mind to the common denominator of your goal. Ordinarily, even arbitrary thoughts arrange themselves in a logical order each one connected to the last. Complete the logical chain with a fragment of your target slide. Just remind yourself from time to time what you are striving towards. Whatever you find yourself thinking about, whatever you are doing, return your attention to the goal. Make a background image of your slide. Every event, every chunk of information should be perceived within the general context set by that image. Then you will shape the layer of your world more effectively and your intention will b e manifest in reality.

Your surrounding environment can also be brought into alignment with your expectations of the goal. You may be walking in the park and turning the target slide over in your mind in which you are working in the garden in front of your house. Look at the trees and the grass through the prism of your slide. You will feel the scene transforming, acquiring new hues. You might have the feeling that in a virtual sense you are already in that garden. This effect arises as a result of the slide being projected over the scene. Your attention is partly focused on the sector of the alternatives space where your future garden exists whilst your eyes perceive material reality of the present moment. What happens is a kind of transformation of current reality in the manner of the sector representing your goal. In these moments the process which involves the materialisation of your mental image acquires greater intensity.

You may recall how you felt in your childhood when things were relaxed and comfortable and the world took care of you. You were not conscious of it then. Things were just ok, and that was that. Yet with time you became increasingly demanding and likely to express your dissatisfaction and this caused the world to lose interest in you. What do you associate with this feeling of calm and cosiness you experienced as a child? You can make this association your key to scenery reduction around which you feel safe and secure. From time to time recall that carefree, happy setting and your world will again gradually become friendly and comfortable.

The final technique, one especially for the lazy, is the *goal amalgam*. The most important condition for visualisation to be successful is that you do not force yourself to practice it. If you find yourself putting pressure on yourself to turn the target slide in your mind because you are not getting any enjoyment out of it you will generate excess potential. Balanced forces will reduce your work to nil as a result. It is better in this case to abandon the burdensome task and pass it off onto the shoulders of your world. Ask you world to "carry you". Let your world take care of realising your choice.

Tell yourself: *although the 'how' may be unbeknownst to me, everything will work its way through.* In declaring this intention you program your world to let events spontaneously unfold in such a way that they will bring you closer to your goal. As a result you let go your grip and allow outer intention to realise the goal. Now you can relax and give yourself permission to simply enjoy the target slide. You are no longer obliged to work on it. The world is doing that for you. Whilst relaxing in the world's embrace do not forget to remind the world from time to time what you expect to receive from it. And of course, do not float in the clouds. Carry out whatever is required of you on the physical plane for the goal to be achieved.

Whatever technique you use always remember that you are not expressing a wish, you are expressing a firm intention and see the goal as an inevitable finale. If you cannot bring yourself to say, "I have", at the very least say, "I plan to have". In order to genuinely intend to receive your order you must take some concrete action that will confirm the seriousness of your intention. For example, if you want to get up in the morning at a certain time you might risk oversleeping. But if you set your alarm clock you are likely to wake up a few minutes before it goes off.

The point is to *give focus to your intention*. This is what you are doing every time you "touch wood" or "through salt over your left shoulder". Any folk custom that presupposes carrying out some kind of ritual will be based on this principle. For example, in ancient times, in order to hold on to the timid bird of happiness people used clover to help them. In a moment of good fortune a person would hold an object decorated with a clover leaf and in a moment of danger, the same. The triple-leafed clover was also considered a means of protection from evil forces.

The point here is not that a certain object is endowed with exceptional qualities which enable it to serve as a talisman. The magical power of any given object lies in one's relationship to it. When a person is filled with the belief that a talisman or ritual is capable of producing some kind of magic effect they will be *giving focus to their intention*. You can make up similar kinds of 'hooks' on which you can comfortably hang your intention. This approach however is as they say, "an acquired taste". You do not necessarily have to make up magic rituals but you do need to take concrete steps that demonstrate that you are serious. For example, if you want to have your own house act as if you are about to move in any day: look through the advertisements and catalogues and choose furniture and household equipment in the shops. Right now, investigate everything associated with moving in. Giving focus to your intention is a very powerful thing.

The fact that there is a wide variety of techniques that can be used to strengthen the slide does not mean that one is necessarily more effective and another less so. You can choose to try out more than one technique at the same time or stick with just one. The criteria for your choice: *the preferred technique for you personally should be the one you like the most and that you think works the best.*

When you are applying these techniques in practice avoid going to extremes either being excessively diligent or sloppy. Some visualisation methods recommend carrying out the visualisation with enthusiasm and passion whereas others suggest shaping a thought and then letting it go into free flight or even forgetting about it there and then thereby not getting in the way of the realisation of the order. As you know the optimal approach is always the golden mean. Instead of racking your brains over where to find it adopt the following principle as a rule: *however it works out is how it should be.*

You are perfectly capable of developing the right methodology for you and practicing is successfully. The most important thing is that the heart and mind agree that you are taking appropriate action. You create your own reality like a reflection in a mirror. How you will stand in front of the mirror only you can decide. Create the layer of your world in a way that *suits you*. What do I mean by this?

You must not feel any inner discomfort when you are practising the visualisation technique. Outer intention appears only when there is unity of heart and mind. This unity cannot be achieved if you are forcing yourself to carry out a compulsory task. This will not get you anywhere and it will simply be a waste of time.

Visualisation of the target slide should be carried out in a way that most suits you, that you find comfortable and pleasant with the only limitation being that you must not look at the slide from the outside as if it were a static image; live inside of it, at least in a virtual sense. Imagine yourself living inside the slide, not external to it. Everything else should be done in the manner that most appeals to you.

The one thing you must not do is try too hard. Regularly, take pleasure from thoughts of your goal as if it had already been achieved. Surely you will enjoy thinking about the various consequences of your success? So do something nice for yourself. Do not turn it into a chore. When you think about something that gives you pleasure you are moving directly towards your goal and the knowledge that you are moving closer to it also gives you pleasure. You can be quite certain that if you manage to set up this vicious circle of pleasure the goal will inevitably be reached.

Success loves *regularity* the most. It might seem unlikely to you that you are capable of shaping your own reality that easily with the power of your thoughts. Yet have you ever tried even over the course of one month to systematically and consciously focus your thoughts on a goal? Probably not. You are used to letting your thoughts free flow. They become diffused into a formless mass in the atmosphere and so they produce no visible result. Only our worst expectations, the things that worry us and therefore occupy all our thoughts really come true.

Imagine this absurd scene that you had planted an apple tree and were seriously hoping that the tree would give fruit this instant. Because apples do not appear as you hoped you lose patience and leave waving your hand in despair while the apple tree wants to shout: "wait a bit longer, for goodness sake!" The same thing happens with the goals we set. Reality cannot be shaped with a single wish.

These are the main techniques for actively influencing reality. If you practice them you will come across a very curious phenomenon. Let us say that today you are inspired and practising visualisation with intense enthusiasm. The next day you notice that something unusual is happening to your reality. For example, throughout the day you meet several individuals with a very unusual appearance. They are either too tall, strangely dressed or ugly. You might notice that people are inexplicably irritable and that conflict are arising where there is no need, or that there is something strange about the day as if you were in dream.

This phenomenon can be explained in the following way. In the ordinary state of consciousness the layer of your world moves with the alternatives flow that is, in the stream of least energy expenditure. Intense visualisation causes the stream to be straightened so that it takes the most direct route to your goal. Narrowly-focused thought energy carries your individual reality into intermediate areas of the alternatives space which lie to the side of the normal flow and where everything functions at an optimal level. These are *transit zones* which we usually come across in dreams but which are rarely realised in reality because they involve unnatural scripts and scenery and require heightened energy expenditure.

The energy of your thoughts has amore forceful influence on your reality causing it to become deformed like the surface of water when the stillness is disturbed. You are no longer surprised by ripples in the water. Now you can expect to see something amazing – *ripples in reality*. This does not mean that the anomaly you observe is pure coincidence and that the fact that people are more irritable on these days is connected to magnetic storms or that sometimes you do just so happen to see characters with a strange appearance. An unusual reality bursts into the layer of your world when it passes transit zones. Ripples appear specifically after an intense visualisation practice. When you observe it you will understand. It makes quite an impression.

So, you can influence your reality with varying degrees of force depending on which technique you use. In principle the amalgam is sufficient to transform the layer of your world into a cosy corner. But you can achieve much more by initiating the intention of the Maker in unison with the other techniques described above.

For the sake of comparison image a scene in which two toddlers meet up: the world pushes one in a pushchair while the other takes its world by the hand. As children are given to doing the first proudly announces: "My world takes care of me!" The other retorts: "Well, my world and I are going for a walk!" Do you see the difference?

Finally, the last thing I would like to share is that I once received a letter from a listeren in which she inadvertently expressed the main idea of the practice: "I do not really understand the Transurfing techniques but as I started to change my relationship to life I began to get the clear impression that everything was wonderful and would get even better; that everything was simply unfolding as it should".

If you are able to maintain this kind of *integral feeling* then you might as well forget about all kinds of techniques because this will be sufficient. *Integrating intention* expressed as *"everything is wonderful and unfolding as it should"* creates a general image of success which is then reflected in reality.

So, your potential is only limited by your intention. Make your own reality!

Coordinating the dream

Everyone begins their life in a certain set of circumstances. I was born into poverty and I cannot climb out of it; I have to make the best of what I can get; I have to do what is expected of me. The situation hypnotises, grips the person so that they fall under the influence of the daydream that *happens* to them. All the while that the person is seeing the situation from within the dream it is all the more firmly consolidated in the world's mirror. A person who is caught by the power of their reality simultaneously maintains it. The poor get poorer and rich get richer.

You may recall that in the previous chapter we talked about the illusion of the dual mirror. It is focusing attention on the reflection that turns life into a subconscious daydream in which you are at the full mercy of circumstance. Reality will dominate you all the while that you spellbound and anxiously watch what is happening in the mirror. In exactly the same way your attention is immersed when you watch a film on a screen only in life the immersion is considerably deeper. You are hypnotised by the reflection which literally pulls you after it into the mirror circle. How can you transform your existence from a subconscious into a conscious dream that you can control?

You need to understand one simple thing. In this world there is *you* and there is *the mirror*. Whilst your attention is focused on the reflection *you are inside the mirror*. Everything that happens inside the mirror happens independently of you. Your life is like a computer game in which someone else makes up the rules. Of course, you are granted attempts to influence what is happening there but you are deprived of what is essential: you cannot leave the game.

There is only one thing keeping you locked up and that is your attention. *You are capable of quitting the mirror.* Inside the mirror there is non-lucid dreaming. Outside the mirror there is lucid dreaming. It is the same reality on both sides of the mirror, for it is a dual mirror. But there in Mirror land you do not control reality; it controls you. Inside the mirror you are in the hands of illusion that the reflection can be altered by touching it; but that is only possible from this side of the mirror where inner intention becomes outer intention. To escape from the inside of the mirror to the outside you have to switch your attention from the reflection to the image. Once you are conscious of the fact that you are standing in front of a mirror you acquire the ability to shape reality to a mental image.

Having freed yourself from the illusion you have to observe the fifth principle and redirect your chain of thoughts from "do not want" to "what you want"; from "do not like" to "what you like", from illness to health, from means to end goal. If you were to observe your life for a while you would soon notice that at almost every step you end up having to accept circumstances and obey things you assume to be inevitable. You are used to perceiving the dream passively, as it is. At best you try to resist events, insisting on your own scripts and battling with the alternatives flow. All you really have to do though is change your relationship i.e. the image in front of the mirror. At this point you will cease to be prisoner to the game. It will start unfolding outside of you and in accordance with your will. Instead of being a chip you will become the one throwing the dice.

Now however a new rule comes into play: if you face what you consider to be an unlucky combination you have to accept it and declare it successful. If you do not want to remain inside the mirror you have no choice other than to follow this rule. It is not enough just to redirect your train of thought. You have to *switch the mind's control from script development to dynamic, ongoing adjustment.* You are the master of your world whilst you observe the sixth and seventh principles.

Normally the mind objects if impending events do not fit with its ideas of what should be happening next. Now it has to be the other way around. Every time the mind expresses its dissatisfaction about a deviation from the script you have to quickly come to your senses and readily accept the change: *everything is going as it should.*

The mind really struggles with the idea that at the beginning of the road, when everything remains unclear, there is still no need to worry about the means. The mind will constantly catch itself thinking about how the journey will possibly happen and picks over all sorts of negative scenarios. How one would like to tell the mind: "Just get it, idiot! It is none of your business! Your task is to focus your attention on the end goal!"

People prevent their own plans from being realised. When you make a wish the mind always makes a rough plan beforehand of how events will develop. This is the nature of the mind. When events do not fit with the scenario we feel that things are not working out whereas in fact everything is going as it should! Because the mind is accustomed to thinking in clichés and adopted thoughts patterns and does not want to make changes to its script, the person carries on according to the original plan and spoils everything.

The paradox is that no-one can ever know how events should develop in order to realise their order. If a person nonetheless insists that they do know, nothing will work out. Your dreams seem difficult to achieve because you are held in the grip of certain standards and simply will not let these dreams be realised. Your door is locked shut with stereotype locks.

Create the desired image – goal in your mind and then just place one foot in front of the other in the direction of your goal. Everything that happens to you is all for the sake of reaching the goal. Adopt the intention of the Maker: *everything is going as it should because that is what I have decided.* I manage my world in the way I see fit. I am no longer at the mercy of circumstance but neither do I try and control everything. By playing the target slide in my mind's eye it is not the circumstances I am shaping but an ultimate picture of the world I intend to live in. Attempts to influence events are the work of the mind's inner intention which tries to push for its own scenario. The mind has no way of knowing what awaits it on the path to the goal. Circumstances are created by outer intention and the alternatives flow. My task is to determine the vector of the flow, but what channel it takes does not concern me.

Imagine that you are woken up from your mirror daydream because something is happening. The events and scenery are all as they should be but you are seeing things differently as if you had escaped the flow of events and come to your senses in the middle of a huge spherical mirror. A gigantic kaleidoscope spins around you sparkling with the many facets of reality. You are a part of this reality and at the same time you exist separately and independently of it. It is the same kind of realisation of one's "separateness" that a person experiences when they wake up in a dream and understand that the dream now depends on them and not the other way around. In the mirror daydream everything is just the same, the only minor difference being that reality reacts more slowly. Once you get used to its slower gear you discover something quite wonderful. Reality is quite pliable and changes adapting to the image in your thoughts. What does this mean? Where are you?

You are now outside of this world. *You have exited the mirror.*

The Maker's Verdict

Now dear Listener you know everything you need to know to create your own reality. You cannot change the whole world but your individual reality is at your disposal. When you escape the illusion of the dual reflection and stand external to the world's mirror Eternity lies before with its limitless possibilities. There is not meant to be a single drop of artificial pathos in these words. The alternative space holds three truly invaluable gifts: your future which you are capable of materialising, sacred Knowledge which can transform you into a genius and something else that takes your breath away.

What this last thing is you will learn a little later. First we will talk about Knowledge. You might think that only certain outstanding minds have the answers to your questions and so you search for information in various sources and try to learn from someone else. This process can go on forever. You can spend your entire life interacting with enlightened individuals who supposedly know what you should do and how. But how do they know such things? Perhaps they became so knowledgeable by reading a huge number of books or perhaps, unlike you, they have a special talent? Neither is true.

Imagine that you have flown to Earth from a distant planet. Everything is different, unfamiliar, confusing. The people in your group have split up setting off in different directions. Each makes their own discovery. It turns out that you can gather mushrooms in the forest, you can swim in the sea and fish and in the mountains you can ski. All sorts of creatures inhabit the Earth, some of which are harmless and other will quite happily devour you.

In the same way, humanity is constantly discovering something new. The flow of knowledge is inexhaustible. However, those who do the inventing and the creating are very few; the rest watch with surprise. What made them think of it? They must be one of the chosen ones. So what makes a person "chosen"?

Their goals and doors are unique inherent to their unique *path*. When you walk your own path the treasures of the world are revealed to you. Then others look at you with amazement wondering how you did it. It is that simple.

The paradox lies in the fact that although this principle is superficially quite obvious the awareness of it remains obscure. Everyone can see that in order to reach new, previously unknown heights of success you have to step out of the rat race and set out on your own path and yet they continue to walk in the footsteps of others trying to repeat their experience.

I remember when I was little my parents took me to the forest for the first time. My mother and father found some wild mushrooms and joyfully announced their find to the entire forest. I on the other hand could not find a single one and wandered between them in despair naively thinking that if I just followed behind a grown-up good fortune would smile upon me, for they were finding the mushrooms so they obviously knew where to look. But my efforts were in vain. It was only when I set off independently in a different direction that I at last found a massive mushroom. My parents were green with envy and I swelled with pride, the great explorer.

In that moment I understood something but did not fully integrate it into my awareness. Later there were many occasions when the world showed me that if I turned off the beaten path and went my own way I would discover the treasure but again and again I would be drawn back into the general flow giving in to the herd instinct.

This is the difference between *conscious knowledge* and *integrated awareness*. You might suspect something to be true but that will not help. A huge abyss stands between suspecting something to be true and having articulate knowledge. The first unlike the second cannot serve as a guide for action and so has no practical value. In this regard Transurfing crosses all the t's and transforms a hunch into an articulate expression of knowledge describing what to do and how to do it.

Specifically, at some point you have to stop studying the old and start creating the new or rather, not even create but *take* from where all discoveries and masterpieces are found – from Eternity. In order to gain access to information stored in the alternatives space you have to lay a foundation of elementary knowledge concerning the area that interests you. Without a certain initial foundation you will not be able to attune to the corresponding sector of the alternatives space. In other words, *tune into the data base.* As soon as you have assimilated the initial stages you can forget what you have been taught. At that point you will be ready to make your own discoveries and create a new masterpiece.

Any book, picture or melody is "pulled out" of the alternatives space. You just have to "hook into" the sector. The hook for a melody might be two or three essential chords. For a picture it may be a mood; for a book, a situation. You do not necessarily have to think of a plot in order to write a book. It will come to you later. The entire plot will emerge from the situation if you can pacify the presumptuous mind and allow the characters to extricate themselves from the scene. There is no need to make things up. It is all already *there*. You just have to calmly follow the alternatives flow. All genius is surprisingly simple. The alternatives flow follows the same unexpectedly simple path which people generally would not be capable of guessing at.

Even computer programmes and technical equipment can be designed in this way without a particular plan working from a certain starting point. Of course, in some instances a project plan is essential but where this is not the case at least in separate areas you should go with the alternatives flow and allow the concept to grow independently. In its attempt to plan everything beforehand the mind complicates things with an elaborate construct. The alternatives flow will always come up with the most elegant and optimal solution which will leave you amazed. How could things have worked out so well without a meticulously designed blueprint?

Overall it is better not to try and dream things up but simply to carry out the task methodically moving from the beginning to the end. In any project the idea serves as the starting point. This is the most important thing. The alternatives flow will complete everything else. You do not have to come up with an idea either. So where does the idea come from? It all comes from the same place. All brilliant conjectures exist in Eternity and come to the mind via the route of the soul. The mind's task is not to come up with an idea but to *recognize* it when it hits you. And it definitely will if you *step away from the crowd and walk your own path obeying the dictates of the heart.*

The heart has direct access to the alternatives space whereas the mind detects subtle notions and insights and works on interpreting them. Reason does not know – the heart knows. All you have to do is listen to it. You can totally rely on this seemingly superficial statement. The problem here once again is that people have a vague understanding of this rather than a clear awareness of the principle. Everyone seems to agree that the heart basically knows everything but nobody takes it seriously. People pass it by assuming it to be a metaphor and attribute it no meaning. Common sense reasons: "Of course there is insight, the inner voice and intuition but these are all shaky, intangible and unreliable. Now iron logic is a different matter entirely based on indisputable facts".

So if you have basic information of a given field the heart can attune to the corresponding area of the alternatives space and source new Knowledge from there that cannot be read in any book. Ask yourself a question. Express it clearly and then forget about it for a while. Within a few days the answer will come to you. If it does not, ask the question again from time to time. The answer may come to you over the next few months but it will definitely come to you.

It is all just a matter of whether you have enough resolve to break the established stereotypes, free yourself from the hold of conventional norms and *break the pendulum rule*. It requires having the audacity to exercise your own right to Knowledge so that you stop seeking answers in books written by others. You just have to change the focus of intention from *being given* to *creating*. How are you different from the authors of the books you are reading? Only in that they changed their intention focus, stopped searching and started creating. They escaped being tied to the opinions of acknowledged authorities and had the courage to set out on their own path. *You too can claim your right to be the one who knows.*

That brings us to what I meant by the third gift that awaits you in the alternatives space.

Try and imagine how a person feels when they are in the role of the superstar. Their fans see only what lies on the surface, their shining talent, the gloss of fame and wealth. It all creates the impression that this person is no mere mortal but endowed with exceptional qualities. Is it even possible for the average person to rise to the very peaks of success and hold themselves with sufficient confidence that no-one would ever dare doubt their exclusivity?

However, for the chosen one all their attributes of fame seem quite ordinary, even mundane. These individuals hardly see themselves as an inhabitant of Mount Olympus because at the end of the day they know that they are one of many other like them. So what is the difference? What separates a country girl from a star of show business, a shaky student from a luminary in the world of science and the average person from the chosen one?

It is a matter of just a single step. One type claims their right and the other type cannot bring themselves to or does not believe they are capable or worthy of it. In the minds of the timid their sits a firmly rooted notion that in this world the chosen ones exist because they have been chosen by all the others by virtue of their exceptional qualities. In reality this idea is a false stereotype. *The chosen ones chose themselves.* Only later because of this did anyone else pay them any attention.

Assert your right to be a chosen one. From this moment onwards *I have chosen myself.* You do not have this right because you are worthy or capable. You have this right, because it is your birthright. The alternatives space contains everything including the most important thing intended for you personally – *the verdict that you have this right.* This is your ticket to Eternity and sanction for your privilege to be Maker of your own reality.

Your entire life you have been taught how you are expected to be, how you should behave, what you should revere and strive for. Now claim your lawful right to establish your own cannons. It is for you to decide what is right for you and what is not because only you can shape the layer of your world. You are quite justified in considering something to be correct that others consider false if it does not harm anyone else. *When you use your privilege in life to deliver your own verdict, you can remain true to your own credo.*

There are as many opinions in life as there are people. Some insist that something is "black" and others will claim "white!" Who should you believe? As you may recall, the world is a mirror that agrees with anyone who dares deliver their own verdict. You however are no mirror! You are either the one who accepts other people's verdicts or you are the Maker who delivers their own verdicts. When you realise this the question of which truth you should consider the only one truth, and whose side you should be on, the "blacks" or the "whites" ceases to be relevant. Now you can determine your own truth: *I have decided this to be true because I am the Maker of my own reality.* And it will work because you have the alternatives space and the dual mirror at your disposal, everything you need to stream your plans into physical reality.

It is really that's simple, is not it? The only condition is that you absolutely must have the temerity to assert your right. If you experience doubt or pangs of conscience your verdict loses its power and you go from being the lawmaker to the accused. When you doubt you do the wrong thing regardless. *It is not a mater of how appropriate your thinking and actions are, but the extent to which you are confident you are right.* This needs to be integrated fully into your awareness so that the heart and mind merge into one. You already have the explanation. All that remains is to turn familiarity into true knowledge. How? Through experience; act and become convinced of it.

You must not let the will of the Maker become the dictate of the mind. The verdict only has any power when the heart and mind are one. Anyone who fails to listen to the voice of the heart is not '*making*', they are '*making mistakes*'. Everywhere you go you see people doing things badly. For example there are people who have no voice, no ear for music and yet love to sing. Sometimes you come across blatant ineptitude and yet the individual is convinced they are a star even though success eludes them. Why does not their verdict work? Because in their heart they know that they are no good at what they are doing. The mind cannot accept the truth and so tries as hard as it can to prove the opposite. There are no totally incompetent people as such. These are just people who have not found their true talent and are walking someone else's path.

The third gift offers many advantages. The right to declare your own verdict represents freedom from oppressive circumstances and everything that places a shadow over your life or creates obstacles on your path. It will help you acquire a quiet confidence. *My world takes care of me and I am strong enough to allow myself the weakness of accepting the attention.*

From the moment you claim the right to declare your own verdict on what is good and bad, or right and wrong for your world you can eliminate any judgement imposed on you from the outside including anything connected with Transurfing itself, as long as you do not give in to guilt, indecision or pangs of conscience, and as long as your verdict does not cause anyone any harm.

That brings me to my final point. The alternatives space contains everything and everything that you wish for with heart and mind is yours. You should be aware however, that a Gatekeeper stands at the threshold to Eternity, an absolute law that guards access to everything to be found there. This implacable guard only permits access to those who have the boldness to assert their right as Maker. Your verdict is your entrance pass: I am capable and worthy because I have decided it is so. *I do not want or hope, I intend.* Claim your right and the Gatekeeper will open the gates of Eternity before you.

SUMMARY

Accumulation of toxins in the body, excess potential and unrealised intention reduces your energy levels.

In order to free up energy reserves you have to either let go of some of your potential intentions or stream them into reality.

In order for the energy to work you have to concentrate on the end goal.

Concentration is not tension, it is focus.

Teach yourself to think about what you are actually doing in the moment.

Systematically focusing your attention on the target slide is essential.

Stop justifying yourself.

Stop trying to prove how important you are.

Maintain the amalgam and follow the mirror principles.

To reduce the effect of polarisation you have to release the over-tightened spokes.

Techniques for shaping your own reality include: the target slide, visualising the process, energy channels, the frame, the explosion wave, outer sphere, scenery reduction, target amalgam, focusing intention and integration.

The preferred approach for you personally should be the one you find works the best.

Do everything in the way that feels most comfortable.

Regular practice is the most important condition for success.

You have to escape from the mirror.

Once you have a foundation of knowledge you can change the focus of your intention from "receive" to "create".

You do not have to come up with ideas; just recognise them when they hit you.

Departing from your starting point go with the alternatives flow.

Claim your right to be right.

Leave the crowd and deliver your verdict; assert the right of the Maker.

I have taken this decision because I am the Maker of my own reality.

Afterword. A STRANGE REALITY

To conclude I would like to go a little further in strengthening the ground under the mind's feet. There is so much in Transurfing that seems incredible that alas, one has to keep explaining to the mind that it is all indeed real.

Whatever model had been chosen to serve as a foundation for Transurfing, its principles would still be valid. In other words, *all the principles included here are invariant in relationship to the model.* The key principle expresses the idea that the energy of our thoughts not only has an indirect influence on our physical reality but a direct impact too. The formal line of science still refuses to acknowledge this phenomenon because so far experimental testing has yielded ambiguous results. Regardless, you and I need to solve our problems now and cannot wait for the scientists to give their word of approval.

We are all aware that the world is subject to the laws of causality in which every effect has its cause. Cause it usually understood to mean some kind of action. The problem is that thoughts are usually perceived as an instruction to a subsequent action and not as the transmission of a physical energy capable of influencing the world around us. Nonetheless, the facts are stubborn and will eventually have their way.

The unexplained phenomenon of outer intention has not been totally ignored by science. Carl Jung the great Swiss psychiatrist carried out research into phenomena linked to the interaction between thought and material reality. Jung analyzed hundreds of curious instances which appeared to be unaccountable coincidences with no visible cause. Jung defined this kind of coincidence "synchronicity". In his lecture "On Synchronicity" he provides a classical example from his personal practice.

"On April 1, 1949, I made a note in the morning of an inscription containing a figure that was half man and half fish. There was fish for lunch. In conversation someone mentioned the custom of making an "April fish" of someone. In the afternoon a former patient of mine whom I had not seen for several months showed me some impressive pictures of fish. In the evening I was shown a piece of embroidery with sea monsters and fish in it. The following morning I saw a former patient who was visiting me for the first time in ten years. She had dreamed of a large fish the night before. A few months later when I was using this series in a larger work and had just finished writing it down I walked to a spot by the lake in front of the house where I had already been several times that morning. This time a fish about a foot long lay on the sea wall. I had no idea how it could have got there."

I cannot resist citing another extract from Jung's lecture about a principle you will learn more about later. Jung writes: "I could tell you a great many such stories which are in principle no more surprising or incredible than the irrefutable results arrived at by Rhine (with reference to the experiments involving extrasensory perception, for example, card guessing. – *Author's note*), and you would soon see that almost every case calls for its own explanation. But the causal explanation, the only possible one from the standpoint of natural science, breaks down to the psychic relativization of space and time, which together form the indispensable premises for cause-and-effect relationships.

My example concerns a young woman patient who, in spite of efforts made on both sides, proved to be psychologically inaccessible. The difficulty lay in the fact that she always knew better about everything. Her excellent education had provided her with a weapon ideally suited to this purpose, namely a highly polished Cartesian rationalism with an impeccably "geometrical" idea of reality. After several fruitless attempts to sweeten her rationalism with a somewhat more human understanding, I had to confine myself to the hope that something unexpected and irrational would turn up, something that would burst the intellectual retort into which she had sealed herself.

Well, I was sitting opposite her one day, with my back to the window listening to her flow of rhetoric. She had had an impressive dream the night before, in which someone had given her a golden scarab – a costly piece of jewellery. While she was still telling me this dream I heard something behind me gently tapping on the window. I turned round and saw that it was a fairly large flying insect that was knocking against the window-pane from outside in an obvious effort to get into the dark room. This seemed to me very strange. I opened the window immediately and caught the creature in the air as it flew in. It was a scarabaeid beetle, or common rose-chafer (Cetonia aurata), whose gold-green colour most nearly represents that of a golden scarab. I handed the beetle to my patient with the words, "Here is your golden scarab." This experience punctured the desired hole in her rationalism and broke the ice of her intellectual resistance. The treatment could now be continued with satisfactory results".

About half an hour after I had been considering whether to include Jung's beetle in the text as an example, a Wanderer of quite impressive appearance flew in through the window. It was a beetle similar to the one described above. You may or may not believe me, but I have to confess that I was not at all surprised by the rare visit. It is not that I am so used to the phenomena of synchronicity that they no longer catch my attention. On the contrary, absorbed in my own thoughts I did not attribute any meaning to it at all. I automatically let the beetle out of the window so that it would not have to look for its way out. It was not until a little time had passed that it suddenly struck me: I am such an idiot! Every time outer intention announces its presence I am still wide-eyed with amazement. They were tugging at me with all their might trying to show me a sign whilst I was in a deep, deep waking sleep. If I was at all superstitious I would have taken it to be a sign from above. You can imagine how other people are also living life asleep and fail to notice the manifestations of outer intention.

There are many more examples like this. From the point of view of Transurfing the situation is quite clear. In isolated cases visualisation generates a strong gust of the wind of outer intention. However, Jung did not rush to make any final conclusions concerning the reason for such coincidences; whether thoughts caused the event or thoughts arose as a result of a subconscious premonition of the event. On the one hand Jung states that "thoughts create the foundation for a series of chance events" and on the other hand "I sometimes cannot get away from the idea that there is a certain premonition of the onset of a series of specific events".

In his work "Synchronicity: An Acausal Connecting Principle" (1960) Jung defines synchronicity as "the simultaneous occurrence of a certain psychic state with one or more external events which appear as meaningful parallels to the momentary subjective state". Jung hesitated for a long time about whether to publish his work because the phenomenon of synchronicity was inconceivable to traditional scientific thinking.

Jung makes a vague and yet, according to the standards of traditional science, relatively bold conclusion. "Synchronistic phenomena prove the simultaneous occurrence of meaningful equivalences in heterogeneous, causally unrelated processes; in other words, they prove that a content perceived by an observer can, at the same time, be represented by an outside event, without any causal connection. From this it follows either that the psyche cannot be localized in space, or that space is relative to the psyche".

There is no contradiction of the law of causality in the phenomena Jung is describing. There is always a cause, it is just that the interaction dynamics between thought and environment remain elusive to our current understanding. Which is the *cause* in synchronistic coincidences? Are events shaped by thoughts or do thoughts arise as the premonition of an event? From the point of view of Transurfing both explanations are acceptable. The heart has access to data held in the information field which can then be interpreted by the mind. The mind in turn shapes thoughts which, under the condition of unity of heart and mind, can be manifest as physical reality. These tenets lie at the very core of the Transurfing model. However, I should emphasize once again that the alternatives model does not claim to serve as a detailed description of the world. Instead it represents a benchmark, an aid for the comprehension of certain principles. We still know very little about the world we live in, but this need not prevent us from applying the Transurfing principles. The fact that the principles work is for you to discover.

All phenomena related to the impact thought energy has on the surrounding world can be substantiated by the well-known theorem put forth by the quantum physicist John Bell. The theorem sounds: "There are no isolated systems; every particle in the universe is in "instantaneous" (exceeding the speed of light) connection with every other particle. The entire System, even if its parts are separated by huge distances, works as a Unified System". This theorem has been theoretically proven and is already substantiated on a practical level. Despite the fact that "instantaneous" connection contradicts the special theory of relativity which claims that energy cannot move faster than light, the theorem has its place.

It would seem then that outer intention fails to conform to the theory of relativity. In general, quantum physics is all based on unproven postulates, which means that it too represents a specific kind of model. And there is not just one inexplicable contradiction in the world of quantum physics but many, which once again confirms, that undue significance should not be attached to any one particular model. It should be noted that Jung's ideas have found support among the very founders of modern physics, such as Wolfgang Pauli and Albert Einstein. In addition, it is quite probable that the process of information exchange does not have anything to do with energy at all, which is why it can take place faster than the speed of light.

The alternatives model is not without its own contradictions, but nonetheless, it succeeds in explaining many aspects of reality. The alternatives model may not totally resolve certain known paradoxes of time and space but it does at least "iron out a few of the creases". Until now we have been looking at the transitions from one life line to another in synchronicity with time. Life lines have always existed in parallel to the temporal axis. In other words, the transition is always made from one point in time to the exact same point.

Imagine if two life lines existed that were not parallel to the time axis. A projection of the same point from the two lines onto the time axis would show the points in different places. The transition between them would indicate a shift in time into the past or the future depending on the direction of the obliquity. The relative steepness of the declination would define the extent of the time difference between the two points.

By analogy, if two life lines were not parallel relative to the space axis the transition through space from one point to the other would happen instantly (or at least at an unbelievable speed). The steepness and direction of the gradient would determine the distance and direction involved in the shift. This is obviously a very rough explanation but sufficiently acceptable to the relevant context.

The painstaking Listener will no doubt object: but what about the paradox, the contradiction of cause-and-effect relationships in time travel? Suppose I went back in time before my birth and... brutally murdered my parents. How then did I come into the world? Within the framework of the alternatives model this is only a seeming paradox. I cannot be born into that same life line but so what? I can be born into a different life line. You may recall that there are an infinite number of life lines – alternatives where I both exist and where I do not exist. The most bloodthirsty paradox lover could even return to their childhood, meet with themselves and do away with the innocent creature. In this scenario the listener would not be meeting with their actual self but with a separate realised alternative which exists along with endless others.

The past cannot be changed because it has already happened. It happened not only because a past section of a life line was realised but because the alternatives of those past events already existed. In this sense you could say the same thing about the future; that it has already happened. And so cause-and-effect relationships are not contradicted in the phenomenon of the shift from one life line to another. You could cross out one of the frames in a film roll but it would not damage any of the others frames. Time is static. It is only the realisation of potential life line alternatives that has the quality of dynamic change. The force for realisation moves across life line alternatives in the same way as the circle of light from a torch moves across forest trees in the dark.

It is however possible to travel into the past or the future on one and the same life line and here we do come across a paradox. Is this not why the predictions made by clairvoyants are only approximate and often quite simply inaccurate? Clairvoyants are somehow capable of scanning fragments of the future. If these scanned fragments are part of other life lines then it is easy to explain the element of error in their predictions. The alternatives model has it, that the greater the distance between one line and another, the greater the difference in the scenery.

Scientists are also baffled by the movement dynamics of UFOs. They accelerate instantly, then stop or make sudden changes in direction at right angles. Given the quality of inertness this type of movement pattern is impossible to say nothing of the huge stress it would cause to the inhabitants of these devices. From the point of view of Transurfing there is nothing supernatural about these phenomena. Aliens do not experience physical stress because UFOs do not fly like an aeroplane or space shuttle. It is probable that what we are observing is not so much the movement of the object, as its realisation at different points in the alternatives space.

Much remains unclear to us in questions relating to the heart and mind. Materialistic science presents the world as if it were a mechanical system. In other words, matter is primary and determines consciousness. However, in the light of recent achievements made by the same area of science this model is increasingly losing its position of authority. The substitution and review of scientific models will be an ongoing process all the while that man erroneously believes himself to be capable of penetrating to the very essence of the laws of nature. A simple hen could equally well express its preferred concept of the creation, construction and development of a poultry farm. Man stands a rung higher than a hen in his intellectual evolution but that does not bring the infinite complexity of the world any closer. Man is not meant to know and understand everything.

The pendulums of science and religion that claim to represent the last instance of truth have won their dominance not so much on account of a correct interpretation of the truth as on account of the fact that they have successfully persecuted their dissidents. The constant conflict exists not only between the pendulums of science and religion but also between individual branches within the same pendulums. The battle is ongoing and it is a battle not for the truth but for adherents.

When I was substantiating the mind's inability to store all information I based my argument on the model of imagining information in the form of computer bytes. However, this particular model could turn out to be incompatible with the neural activity of the brain. Who knows how information is really stored? Imagine, how would a scientist have researched a television or radio if they were born in an age prior to the invention of these devices? They would have tried pushing buttons, removing various parts and watching for changes on the screen. Not having any idea how a TV works and basing their findings on the results of "scientific" observation the scientist would have come to various conclusions at the root of which would stand one seemingly undeniable fact: a television generates all these different programmes by itself. They are born right there in the transistors and micro circuitries.

This is roughly how adherents of the mechanistic model explore the human brain. It is true that damage to individual areas of the brain can have a predictable impact on a person's perception and cognitive ability. The functional principle of the human intellect however remains a mystery and yet these adherents conclude that matter and nothing else determines consciousness. Conservative followers of the mechanistic model proudly refer to themselves as scientists and declare haughtily that their science is the true science based on factual information and not the speculations of amateurs. Anything that fails to fit the theory is declared anti-scientific and is not only rejected byt made the object of persecution. Fortunately, the number of scientists of this nature is dwindling.

You may agree or disagree with the information shared in this text; either way, remember that is it just a model. No-one can say exactly how things really happen. The mind tends to negate anything that does not fit into its context of sensible explanations. Until the mind is convinced of the rational nature of knowledge it will never allow it to be integrated into the worldview template. Transurfing works. Of that there is no doubt, but to apply it the mind must have its explanation.

The alternatives model gives us the benefit of some solid ground beneath our feet but no more than that. It remains nothing more than a diagram that could be transformed into a more sophisticated model. For example, you could get rid of the assumption that so-called life lines exist which would make the early part of the book easier to understand. This would transform the alternatives space from discrete to continuous. There would no longer be any paths through the forest. Only the forest would remain. Yet this would not change the essence of Transurfing. No matter what the model is, it can only ever provide an approximate, more or less adequate reflection of reality. The path of studying reality is as eternal as the diversity of natural phenomena is infinite.

You may have noticed that the Transurfing principles overlap with the principles of similar teachings. There is nothing strange about that. Any teaching is relatively insular and represents an autonomous model. However, given that we are all people with roughly the same quality to our worldviews different models will have certain aspects in common. To ask which of these many models provides a more adequate description of the world is pointless. The only thing of any significance is the practical results one can achieve from any given model.

You could take mathematics for instance. Different branches of mathematics represent separate models which describe material realisation. A physics problem can be solved in different ways depending on the mathematical apparatus applied. There is no point in arguing whether analytical geometry or differential calculus is better in either case. You can only choose which particular approach you prefer. You too must make your choice.

The Intention of the Ancient Magicians

In conclusion I would like to align myself with the intention of the ancient magicians. By this I mean the Knowledge keepers who lived in our reality until the break-up of the civilization that existed before this one. Fragments of this Knowledge have been preserved to this day in the form of isolated esoteric teachings and practices.

There is information to suggest, although not yet proven, that certain ancient magicians shifted into a different reality and at this time are trying to pass their Knowledge to humanity by transcendental means.

Until recently I would have treated claims like these with more than a healthy level of scepticism. Yet over the past few decades there have been an increasing number of cases where people in different parts of the world have independently put forward similar interpretations of the same Knowledge. Now I too have come into intimate contact with this same type of knowledge, which, as I said, I could never have made up myself.

I cannot say with confidence whether the Guardian (the meeting with whom I described in the first chapter) exists, at least in our reality. Having said that, I do have plenty of reason to suppose that he does in fact exist.

I have come across many different characters in dreams but they had absolutely no effect on my highly conservative worldview. My meeting with the Guardian not only turned my worldview upside down, it turned my life around.

Suddenly, for no particular reason a former physicist showing no previous signs of aptitude started to write books. It would be too incredible and extravagant to accept that the motivation for all this was a run of the mill dream.

The Guardian never appeared to me again after that first meeting although sometimes it seems to me that I can feel his presence. Either way, I have never considered Transurfing *my own* Knowledge.

I am just a repeater tuned into the corresponding area of the alternatives space. I do not consider the work to be my own merit although I must confess I found it extremely difficult to express and systematise the Knowledge of Transurfing. It is one thing to learn something but quite another to be able to talk about it.

You too will not only learn about this Knowledge, you will assimilate it, for having devoured the book in one go you will not have received Knowledge so much as an awareness and adeptness. These are different things!

Transurfing offers quite concrete methods for turning your dreams into reality. This might not be enough for some people. If you are looking for tricks that can be spelt out like the procedure for tying a tie you could spend your life searching in vain. Creating your own fate cannot be reduced to a simple rule that goes: "step one, two, three".

Transurfing cannot be reduced to a technique of executing certain moves. *It is not about technique but about becoming aware of your inner freedom and the feeling that you are master of the layer of your world.* Once you experience that feeling everything will unfold of its own accord without the need for any particular technique.

In order to achieve this level of awareness you have to make Transurfing a way of life. There is no other way. It is not at all laborious or burdensome. It is actually quite entertaining like playing with a mirror.

The world is a mirror of your relationship to it only with a delayed reaction. By comparing your relationship to the world with the subsequent reaction of the mirror you teach your mind a simple truth and yet one that is difficult for one's consciousness to truly assimilate: *You shape the layer of your world with intention.*

It is also essential to become comfortable with the simple but strange truth that you do not need to be concerned with the means and ways of achieving the goal. One fundamental principle lies at the foundation of this statement: *the focus of intention determines the vector of the alternatives flow.*

All you have to do is maintain the focus and let the alternatives flow takes its course. The means of achieving the goal will present itself. You cannot and need not know exactly how the goal will be realised. *Whatever happens, if you keep your target slide in mind and observe the principle of coordination the alternatives flow will carry you to your goal.* Such is the law.

GLOSSARY

Importance

The energy of importance becomes present when disproportionate meaning is ascribed to something. Importance is pure excess potential and is eliminated by balanced forces creating problems for the person generating the potential. There are two kinds of importance: *inner* and *outer*.

Inner or personal importance manifests when a person over-estimates their own virtues or shortcomings. The form of expression for inner importance sounds: "I am an important person", or "I do important work". When the arrow on the importance measure goes off the scales balanced forces come in and take things into their own hands. The "hot shot" then receives a good slap. Once balanced forces come into play disappointment also awaits the person whose work is so phenomenally important. Either there will turn out to be no demand for their work or the quality of the work will be shoddy. The other side of the coin is when a person self-deprecatingly downplays their own virtues playing smaller than they really are. In both cases the magnitude of excess potential produced is the same. The difference is only in the polarity expressed.

Outer importance is also artificially created when a person attributes excessive meaning to an object or event in the outside world. The form of expression for outer importance might sound: "Such and such is extremely important to me" or "it is extremely important to me to do such and such…" This generates excess potential which ruins everything. Imagine having to walk along a log lying on the ground. Nothing could be simpler. But what if you had to walk along the same log placed across the roofs of two high-rise buildings? The short stroll would become extremely important to you and there would be nothing you could do to convince yourself otherwise.

Wave of fortune

The wave of fortune is created by a cluster of life lines that are particularly favourable to a specific individual. There is nothing the alternatives space does not contain including such golden veins. If you arrive at an outer line of this form of irregularity and experience some form of good luck you can slide onto other lines within the same cluster by inertia and consequently other fortuitous circumstances will follow on from the first. However, if you experience a bit of a bad patch after the first stroke of luck it means that a destructive pendulum has latched onto you and lead you away from the wave of good fortune.

Choice

Transurfing proposes a fundamentally different approach to achieving one's goals. According to this approach a person makes an order as they would in a restaurant without any consideration for the means of achieving the goal. As a result the goal is realised to a large part of its own accord independently of the direct actions of the customer. Desires are not fulfilled; dreams do not come true. Yet your choice is an immutable law and will inevitably be realised. It would be impossible to explain the essence of choice in just a couple of words. Transurfing is basically all about what choice is and how to actually make choices.

Unity of heart and mind

Will is inherent to the mind and yet despite this fact the mind cannot control outer intention. The heart on the other hand is capable of identifying with outer intention and yet it is not endowed with the power of the will. The heart flies around the alternatives space like an uncontrolled kite. In order to bring outer intention in line with your will you have to achieve *unity of heart and mind.* In this state the feelings of the heart and the thoughts of the mind are as one. For example, when a person is filled with joyful inspiration the heart "sings" and the mind "rubs its hands in glee". In this state a person is capable of being highly creative. It can also be the case that the heart and mind find agreement in emotions such as anxiety, fear and non-acceptance. This is when our worst expectations are realised. Finally, when common sense insists on one thing and the heart resists there is discord between the heart and mind.

Guardian's Riddle

"Everyone can have the freedom to choose whatever they want. How can such freedom be obtained?" People do not realise that they do not have to struggle for what they want and can simply *have* it. It sounds very unlikely but nonetheless it is true. The key to the riddle can be found by reading *Transurfing Reality* in its entirety. You will not understand the solution to the riddle fully if you peek at the last chapter without reading the previous chapters.

Signs

Guiding signs are signs that indicate a forthcoming turn in the alternatives flow. If something is approaching that could have a substantial impact on the future course of events then a sign appears to signal it. When the alternatives flow takes a new turn a person shifts onto a different life line. Each line is more or less uniform in quality. The stream of the alternatives flow can transect various lines which differ from one another in the parameters of their conditions. Change may be fairly insignificant but the difference can be felt nonetheless. This type of qualitative change is experienced either consciously or subconsciously as a sense that something is not quite right.

Guiding signs only appear at the onset of a shift to new life lines. Not all individual phenomena catch our attention. For example, a crow caws. If you do not notice any qualitative difference in this event it means that you are still on the former life line. If however, there is something about it that alerts you for some reason then it should be taken to represent a sign. A sign can be distinguished from more ordinary phenomena in that it signals the start of a transition to a very new type of life line.

Excess potential

Excess potential represents tension, a localised disturbance in an otherwise stable energy field. The irregularity is created by thought energy when an object is attributed excessive and disproportionate meaning. Desire represents an example of excess potential because it strives to draw the object of attraction to a place where it is not naturally present. The desperate desire to have something you lack creates an energetic "differential in pressure" which drums up the winds of balanced forces. Other examples of excess potential include: dissatisfaction, blame, admiration, worship, idealisation, over-evaluation, contempt, vanity, and likewise feelings of superiority, inferiority and guilt.

Induced shift

Catastrophes, natural disasters, armed conflicts and economic crises all develop in spiral fashion. First there is the germ of the event, then its development. Tension rises until things reach a culmination with emotions spilling all over the place. Finally the accumulated energy is released into the atmosphere before a temporary ensuing calm. A whirlpool functions in relatively the same manner.

A pendulum catches the attention of a whole group of people in its *noose* and begins to sway with increasing force drawing people after it onto calamitous life lines. The individual responds to the pendulum's first push by for example reacting to the negative event, taking part in the confusion and thereby entering the spiral's impact zone which turns and pulls like a vortex.

The phenomenon of the pull into the vortex is defines as an induced transition onto a life line in which the individual takes on the role of victim. The individual's response to the pendulum's push and the consequent mutual exchange of energy induces a transition into a life line similar in frequency to the oscillations of the pendulum. As a result the negative event becomes a part of the layer of that individual's world.

Coordination of importance

Do not attribute excessive meaning to *anything*. Your importance energy is beneficial to the pendulum but not to you. Pendulums control people like puppets with the *strings of importance*. People are afraid to let go of the strings of importance because they are under the power of dependence which creates an illusion of support and confidence.

Confidence represents the same kind of excess potential as insecurity; it is just the opposite polarity. Awareness and intention equip you to stay out of the pendulum's game and get what you want with having to battle for it. When you are free from the battle you do not need confidence. If I am free from importance I have nothing to defend and nothing to conquer. I just go ahead and calmly make my choices.

To become free of pendulums you have to abandon inner and outer intention. Problems and obstacles appear on the path towards the goal because of the excess potential of importance. Obstacles are built on the foundation of importance. If importance is reduced the obstacles will crumble and cease to pose a problem.

Coordination of intention

The fact that people who have a tendency towards negativity see their worst expectations realised proves that people are capable of influencing the course of events in their life. Every event on a specific life line has two *branches* extending from it; one favourable, the other unfavourable. Every time you encounter an event you make a choice about your relationship to it. If you choose to see an event as positive you find yourself on the favourable branch of the life line. However, a tendency for negativity makes you express dissatisfaction and choose the unfavourable branch.

As soon as something disappoints you something else equally as disappointing follows soon after. This is why we say that "misfortune never comes alone". However, the chain of misfortunate events does not follow on from the first event but from your relationship to it. The pattern is created by the choice you make when you stand at the fork in the life line. If you analyse how inclined you are to think negatively you will have a good idea of where a series of negative branches on the life line has led through over the course of your life.

The principle of the coordination of intention can be expressed in the following manner: *If you decide to perceive seemingly negative changes in the scenario as positive then that is how things will be.* By following this principle you can achieve the same success in the positive as the negativists achieve in realising their worst expectations.

Life line

A person's life just like any other example of matter in motion represents a chain of cause and effect. In the alternatives space effect is always located close to the cause. Just as one effect follows another sectors that are in close proximity in the alternatives space are organised into life lines. The scripts and sets of scenery on one life line are more or less uniform in quality. A person's life unfolds fairly stably along a given life line until an event occurs that substantially changes the script and scenery. At that point fate takes a turn and shifts into a different life line. You are always on a life line that corresponds in its parameters to your thought energy. By adjusting your relationship to the world, i.e. your mental image, you shift onto a different life line in which potential events can unfold in different ways.

Material realisation

Under certain conditions the information structure of the alternatives space can materialise. Any thought like any sector in the field has certain parameters. When thought energy is transmitted it "illuminates" the corresponding sector of the field and realises that specific alternatives of possible physical realities. Therefore, thoughts have a direct impact on the course of events.

The alternatives space serves as a template. It determines the form and trajectory of the movement dynamics of matter. The potential for material realisation moves in time and space whilst the alternatives themselves remain in a specific space for eternity. Every living being creates the layer of their individual world via the transmission of thought energy. Numerous living organisms inhabit our world and every single one of them contributes to the shaping of reality.

Pendulum

Thought energy is material and does not totally disappear without trace. When a group of people begin to think in a similar way their "thought waves" accumulate in layers and invisible but real energy-information structures – pendulums are created in the greater ocean of energy. The structures begin to evolve independently until they reach a stage at which they are able to subject people to their own laws. When a person comes under the influence of a destructive pendulum they lose their freedom and are forced to become a small cog in a large machine.

The more people – adherents – feed the pendulum with their energy, the more forceful its "sway". Every pendulum has its characteristic oscillation frequency. For example, a swing will gain height only if you apply effort to pushing it with a certain frequency. This is what is meant by the resonant frequency. If the number of a pendulum's adherents decreases its sway becomes weaker. If the number of adherents declines to zero the pendulum dies and ceases to exist as a separate entity.

In order to pump energy from people a pendulum hooks into their emotions and reactions: indignation, dissatisfaction, hate, irritation, anxiety, worry, depression, confusion, despair, fear, pity, attachment, admiration, tenderness, idealisation, adulation, delight, disappointment, pride, arrogance, contempt, aversion, insult, duty, guilt etc.

The greatest threat of the pendulum's suppressive influence is that it leads its victim away from life lines in which that person would have been truly happy. It is essential to free oneself from imposed goals after which one battles straying ever further from one's own true path in life.

In essence the pendulum is an "egregore" and yet it is much more than this. The notion of the "egregore" does not reflect the entire range of subtle interaction between the individual and the energy-information structures referred to here as pendulums.

Intention

Intention can be roughly defined as the *resolve to have and act*. Intention is realised. Desire is not. You may desire to put your hand up. The desire is shaped in your thoughts and you become aware that you wish to put your hand up. Is it the desire that actually raises the arm in the end? No. Of itself desire does not generate any physical action. The arm is only finally raised when the thought has been processed leaving just the resolve to take action. So it is the resolve to act that lifts the arm? Once again, no. You may have decided that you will lift up your arm but it will not yet be moved. So what exactly is it then that causes you to put up your hand? How do you define what lies beyond resolve?

Here the mind is powerless to provide an intelligible explanation for what intention really is. Our definition of intention as the resolve to have and act demonstrates the prelude to the force that actually manifests the action. All we can do is state the fact that the arm is lifted neither by desire nor by decision but by something we are referring to as intention.

Intention is divided into two kinds: *inner* and *outer*. Inner intention presupposes active impact on the world around us. This is the *resolve the act*. Outer intention is the *resolve to have* which causes the world to fulfil the individual's will. Inner intention is the concentration of one's attention on the process of moving towards one's goal. Outer intention is the concentration of attention on the process of how the goal realises itself. Inner intention causes the goal to be *achieved*, whereas outer intention allows it to be *chosen*. Everything that is associated with magic and paranormal phenomena relates to the areas of outer intention. Everything that can be reached within the context of the ordinary worldview is achieved by the power of inner intention.

Dependent relationships

Dependent relationships are defined by a statement of conditions such as: "If you do this then I will do this". "If you love me you would drop everything and come to the edge of the world with me. If you do not want to marry me you obviously do not love me. If you praise me I will be friends with you. If you do not give me your spade I will drive you out of the sandpit."

When love is transformed into a dependent relationship *polarisation* occurs and balance is destroyed. Unconditional love is love with the right to possess and admiration without adulation. In other words, this feeling does not create dependent relationships between the one who loves and the object of their love.

Balance is destroyed when one thing is compared or juxtaposed to another. "We are like this and they are different!" For example, national pride: in comparison to which nations? A feeling of inferiority or pride in oneself: in comparison to whom?

Where there is contradistinction balanced forces will inevitably get involved. The action of balanced forces is either aimed at dragging the subjects of contradiction apart or at bringing them together in mutual agreement or in collision. If you are the one who created the polarisation then in the majority of cases the impact of balanced forces will work against you.

Polarisation

Excess potential arises when certain qualities are attributed excess meaning. Dependent relationships are formed between people when they begin to compare themselves and place conditions upon each other, such as "If you do this then I will do this." Of itself excess potential is not necessarily a problem while the distorted evaluation exists irrelatively, on its own. However, the moment that the artificially inflated evaluation of one object in placed into a relative relationship with another object *polarisation* occurs, which calls forth the *wind of balanced forces*. Balanced forces strive to eliminate polarisation and their action is usually aimed against the person responsible for creating the polarisation in the first place.

Alternatives space

The alternatives space represents an *information structure*. It is an infinite information field containing all the alternatives of all possible events. You could say that the alternatives space contains everything that ever was and everything that ever will be. The alternatives space serves as a template and coordinates grid for the movement of matter through space and time. Both the future and the past are held in a constant position as if on a film roll. The effect of time is only created as a result of the movement of a single frame in which the present is lit up.

The world simultaneously exists in two forms: physical reality that can be touched and the metaphysical alternatives space which lies beyond the realms of perception and yet whose existence is no less objective. In principle the information field can be accessed. Intuitive knowledge and clairvoyance are sourced in the alternative space. The mind is not capable of creating anything fundamentally new. It can only create a new version of a house from old bricks. The mind does not store information so much as a kind of address to the information which is contained in the alternatives space. All scientific discoveries and masterpieces are sourced by the mind from the alternatives space via the heart.

Dreams are not illusions in the normal sense of the word. The mind does not imagine its dreams it genuinely sees them. Everything we see in physical reality represents a realised alternative. In dreams we are capable of seeing things that have not been realised, that is plays with virtual scenarios and sets of scenery. Dreams show us what could have taken place in the past and what could potentially take place in the future. Dreaming is the journeying of the soul through the alternatives space.

Balanced forces

Wherever excess potential is present balanced forces appear aimed to eliminate it. Potential is created by human thought energy when excess meaning is ascribed to a particular object.

Compare these two situations: you are standing on the floor in your house or you are standing at the edge of a precipice. In the first case there is nothing to worry about. In the second the situation has great meaning: if you make one careless movement the situation would be fatal. On an energetic level that fact of standing has the same meaning in the first situation as it does in the second. But when you are standing above a precipice your fear pumps up the tension creating an irregularity in the energy field. Balanced forces arise as a result aimed at eliminating the heterogeneity. You can actually feel their impact. On the one hand an inexplicable force pulls you downwards and on the other hand it draws you to take a step backwards away from the edge. In order to eliminate the excess potential of your fear the balanced forces will either have to drag you away from the edge or throw you downwards and be done with it. It is their influence that you sense.

The action of balanced forces in eliminating excess potential generates the majority of the problems people face. The intrigue is that a person often gets a result directly opposite to what they originally intended. At the same time there is no clear reason why this should be. This is what makes us feel that some inexplicable dark force is at play, similar to "sod's law".

Sector of the alternatives space

A specific *alternative* of any given event exists at every point of the alternatives space. For the sake of clarity we will assume that the alternative consists of *scripts* and *scenery*. Scenery represents the external view of form of a phenomenon whereas the script is the path along which matter moves. For convenience sake the alternatives space can be divided into sectors, every sector endowed with scripts and scenery. The greater the distance between sectors the greater the difference in scripts and scenery. Each person's fate is also represented by a multitude of alternatives. Theoretically, there are no limits to the number of possible turns of fate in a person's life because the alternatives space is infinite.

Slide

Our perceptions of ourselves and our environment are often far from the truth. The distortion is caused by *slides*. For example, you are worried about certain personal shortcomings that cause you to experience a feeling of inferiority because you think that others dislike and disapprove of them too. When you are interacting with people you insert an inferiority complex slide into your "projector" which causes you to see things in a distorted light.

The slide is a distorted picture of reality that exists in your mind. As a rule a negative slide is generated by *unity of heart and mind* which is why it is manifested into physical reality. Our worst expectations tend to come true. Negative slides can be transformed into positive slides and forced to work for you. If you intentionally create a positive slide it is capable of miraculously transforming the layer of your world. A target slide is a mental picture of the goal as if it had already been reached. The systematic visualisation of the slide leads to the materialisation of the corresponding sector in the alternatives space.

World layer

Every living being materialises a given sector of the alternatives space with their thought energy and thereby creates the layer of their world. All these layers lie one on top of the other and in this way every living being contributes to the shaping of reality.

The individual creates the layer of their personal world, their separate reality with their mental outlook. This reality acquires a certain hue depending on that person's attitudes. Metaphorically speaking, certain "weather conditions" are set: morning freshness in the sunshine or cloudy and raining. Sometimes a hurricane whips wildly or there might even be a natural catastrophe.

Individual reality is created by two means: physical and metaphysical. In other words, a person builds their world with their thoughts and actions. Here thought forms play the leading role because they are responsible for creating a significant portion of the material problems a person has to battle with for a lot of the time. Transurfing deals exclusively with the metaphysical aspect.

Alternatives flow

In the alternatives space information is static, like in a matrix. The information structure is organised in interconnected chains. The *alternatives flow* is generated by causal relationships.

The restless mind constantly experiences the tremors of pendulums and decides to solve all its problems in an attempt to keep the situation under control. In the majority of cases the mind's wilful decisions are no more useful than pointlessly slapping your hands about in the water. Most problems, particularly minor ones, resolve themselves if you do not hinder the alternatives flow.

The main reason one should not actively resist the flow is because doing so a huge amount of energy is wasted either in vain or to one's detriment. The flow takes the path of least resistance and so it contains the most rational and efficient solution to a problem. Resisting the flow on the contrary generates a mass of new problems.

A powerful intellect is of no purpose if the solution already exists in the alternatives space. If you do not get involved in the refinements and let the alternatives flow take its course the solution and what is more an optimal solution will present itself. Optimality is an inherent part of the structure of the information field. The alternatives space contains everything but it is most likely that the least energy-consuming alternative is the one that will ultimately be materialised. Nature never wastes energy.

Transurfing

I did not invent the word *Transurfing*. It just came to me from out of nowhere just like all the other terms and content of this book. It was a while until I came to understand its meaning. It is not even entirely clear how to explain the associations linked with it. The meaning of Transurfing can be interpreted as "gliding through the alternatives space", or "transforming potential alternatives into reality" or "shifting across life lines". Generally speaking though, if you practice Transurfing you are balancing on a wave of fortune. The word is pronounced Trans*e*rfing in the same way as it is spelled. If the reader prefers to pronounce it in the English manner – be my guest, but bear in mind that the sound "yo" does not exist in the English language.

Frailing

Frailing is an effective technique that can be applied to interpersonal relationships and it represents an integral part of Transurfing. The most important principle of Frailing can be expressed in the following manner. *Abandon the intention to get and replace it with the intention to give and you will receive the very thing you let go of.*

The action of this principle is based on the fact that your inner intention uses the inner intention of your partner without compromising their interests. As a result you receive from that person the very thing you were unsuccessful in achieving by the ordinary methods of inner intention. If you follow this principle you will achieve impressive results in personal and professional forms of communication.

Goals and doors

Everyone has their own true path in life that will bring them true happiness. Pendulums impose false goals on people that tempt them with the prospects of prestige and their seeming inaccessibility. By chasing after false goals you will either achieve nothing or you will achieve the goal only to discover that you did not really want it after all.

Your goal will transform your life into a celebration. The process of achieving your innermost goal will bring about the fulfilment of all your other wishes and the results will exceed all expectation. A person's door represents the particular path that will lead them to their innermost goal.

If you head towards your own goal through your own door no-one and nothing can stop you because the key of your soul fits the lock to your path. No-one can take from you what is truly yours. There should not be any problem therefore in achieving your innermost goal. The only potential problem lies in finding your goal and your door. Transurfing will give you the tools to do this.

Made in the USA
Middletown, DE
26 October 2022

13586365R00422